HARDSHIPS AND DOWNFALL OF BUDDHISM IN INDIA

HARDSHIPS AND DOWNFALL OF BUDDHISM IN INDIA

GIOVANNI VERARDI

Appendices by

FEDERICA BARBA

MANOHAR
2011

First published 2011

ISBN 978-81-7304-928-6

Published by
Ajay Kumar Jain *for*
Manohar Publishers & Distributors
4753/23 Ansari Road, Daryaganj
New Delhi 110 002

Typeset at
Digigrafics
New Delhi 110 049

Printed at
Salasar Imaging Systems
Delhi 110 035

Contents

Maps and Figures

MAPS

FIGURES

Acknowledgments

I had completed the first draft of this book before joining the Institute for Research in Humanities of Kyoto University for a semester. In Kyoto, I could avail myself of the critical comments and suggestions of colleagues and friends, to which the final version of this work owes much. I thank Minoru Inaba, who made my sojourn in Kyoto possible and assisted me in every way. He is one of the colleagues who read the whole text or parts of it, and in this respect, my sincerest thanks also go to Claudine Bautze-Picron, Toru Funayama and Giuliana Martini. I am also indebted to Christoph Cüppers and to Silvio Vita, Director of the Italian School of Eastern Asian Studies in Kyoto. Tiziana Lorenzetti provided me with photographs that allowed me to analyse monuments and icons and that are at the basis of some of the drawings accompanying the text. Daniela De Simone found reference material otherwise unavailable to me in Delhi. Thanks are also due to Jason Hawkes, Peter Skilling and Chiara Visconti. Special thanks go to Geraint Evans, who corrected my English to the extent that it was possible for him because of the *paperoles* I was continuously adding. Finally yet importantly, my heartfelt thanks go to D.N. Jha and Ramesh Jain of Manohar, who made the publication of this book possible, as well as to Manohar's production team, whose very attentive proof-reading saved me from many mistakes.

GIOVANNI VERARDI

Introduction

This book is not so much about Buddhism, as about Indian history, a general knowledge of which is taken for granted. It is a kind of advanced history of India aimed at discussing the mechanisms that started to set in motion the events that, with increasing force, characterised the Indian middle age until the thirteenth century, and at examining the often elusive or disregarded evidence that document the weakening and collapse of Buddhism. I do not share the inclusive paradigm that assumes that in ancient India, for all the recognised differences, there was – we speak here of the structured systems – a single development model, broadly shared by all the forces in the field. I see India as the only civilisation of the ancient world that generated two opposing models of social and economic relations that coexisted for a long time in conflict, whatever the attempts to reduce or mask the incompatibilities. Far from being a history with a low level of conflict, it was highly confrontational. Despite the widespread tendency to underestimate historical discontinuities and create inclusive paradigms, it is possible to deconstruct Indian history entering it through the visible fractures that mark its surface. These fractures are comparable to those encountered in volcanic soils, where fumaroles and sulphurous deposits make one understand that an explosive magma is lying beneath. In many cases, fissures have unexpectedly widened, allowing a vision that, if not unprecedented, is nevertheless noteworthy.

The issues raised in this book are numerous, but two emerge, I think, with particular clarity. The first is that whereas the idea of state and society the Buddhists had in mind was compatible with the extremely varied peoples inhabiting the subcontinent, the Brahmanical model implied their forced incorporation into the well-guarded perimeter of an agrarian society. It was not just a state society that, especially from the Gupta period onwards, started being established in vast portions of India but a *varṇa* state society, and this made the difference. Its establishment caused the arising of an extremely strong opposition, generally underestimated by historians. The *varṇa* state was opposed not only by the natives who, against their will, saw themselves downgraded to the lower peasantry ranks, but also by the Buddhist brāhmaṇas who were in favour of a trading society less dependent on agricultural resources, and consequently less bound to the strict rules of *varṇa* and *jāti*. The second point is that the imposition of the rules of the *varṇa* state implied much violence. This appears most clearly in the non-brahmanised regions of central and north-eastern India where, from the eighth century onwards, the followers of the Vajrayāna decided to play the card of social revolt, but is already clear from the very beginning of the process: hence the central position that Gupta policy is given in this book. Intimidation and violence also caused a number of transformations in the religion of Dharma, where, rather early, a section of the *śramaṇa*-s started organising themselves according to a community model paralleling the Brahmanical priesthood and lifestyle.

The historical domain covered by this book is thus one where an antinomial model takes the shape of a religious system, Buddhism, which is bound, by ideology and violence, from within and without, to renegotiate continuously and dramatically its own antinomial position. In the course of the historical process, this resulted either in being suppressed or else in being cornered into subaltern positions. The antinomial stance of early Buddhist thought and early Buddhist communities condemned them to the impossibility of emerging out of their subaltern positioning throughout the whole of ancient and medieval history.

The large gaps that still exist in Indian history favour the persistence of a positivist approach. Positive data are in demand not just for filling these gaps, however, but because they have the unparalleled force of always being there, whatever the theoretical construct. The extraordinary force of philological research work, for example, derives from this. Nevertheless, data do change their position on the chessboard according to constructs, and while some of them come fully into focus, others end up in an indistinct periphery. My aim has been not so much to accumulate data, although a number of new facts are provided, but, rather, to reconsider them and rearrange them in the puzzle that the early historical and medieval history of India still is. Much though there is to explore within the inclusive historiographic model we have received, I think that new, decisive data are the product of new perspectives, and not the other way round. I hope this book can serve this purpose.

The great progress of Buddhist studies worldwide, aimed at constituting the 'literary corpus' of Indian Buddhism (Cristina Scherrer-Schaub) and largely focused on the recovery of texts lost in India but preserved in other traditions, has led to a perceptible decline in interest towards Buddhism in modern Indian scholarship and society. Western and East Asian scholars working on the corpus often have – there are naturally many remarkable exceptions – an episodic, incomplete knowledge of Indian history, and, in addition, they do not interact with Indian scholars as happened in the past. For their part, scholars in India have pulled out of the venture, their interests, and those of their country, lying elsewhere. In a sense, India is reverting to a pre-nineteenth century situation, when Buddhism was forgotten when not remembered with hostility. Yet it was precisely the great Indian intellectuals of the past, especially Bengali intellectuals, who, at least with regard to the facts discussed in this book, had a clear perception of how things had gone, and who preserved the memory of events that, in some parts of the country, belonged to a not too distant past.

As regards the 'data archive' of Indian Buddhism, the situation is partly reversed, but to nobody's advantage. Archaeology has long since become the exclusive concern of Indian scholars, and this has created an asymmetry that contributes to deepen the gap between the parties and risks undermining the validity of the new evidence, allocating it to the exclusive domain of nationalistic self-congratulation and tourist use. For all the criticism that today we reserve for the idea of Indian Buddhism created in the second half of the nineteenth and early twentieth century, its force lay in the close interrelationship which then existed between the literary corpus and the data archive. The restoration of the Pāli Canon and of a certain number of Mahāyāna texts remains closely related in everybody's mind to the stūpas of Sanchi and the monasteries of Taxila. It was an extraordinarily powerful model, regardless of whether those associations were right or wrong. This unity is now broken. The data archive is broken in turn, because Indian scholars monopolise fieldwork but show little interest for the iconographic section. Here non-Indian scholars are again more active, although often disinclined to come face to face with the darker aspects of Indian history.

An important limitation to the understanding of both early and medieval Buddhism is the scarce attention paid by students of the religion of Dharma to the Brahmanical world – a traditional attitude that has now become more widespread because of the shifting north- and eastwards of philological studies. Yet we might provocatively argue that while it is possible to write a history of India that ignores Buddhism, the more limited task of writing a history of Indian Buddhism that ignores Brahmanical India seems hardly possible. Nevertheless, this is frequently done, and the result is a partial if not mistaken view of the matter that risks affecting also the work of the most self-confident, specialised fields of the research. Brahmanical sources, be they prescriptive texts, literary works or religious-mythical compilations like the Purāṇas, contain a surprising amount of information on Buddhism. Students of Brahmanical literature have taught us to read literary texts paying attention to the multiplicity of meanings and references particular to *sandhyābhāṣā*, and recently the idea has come to the fore that iconographies respond to the same subtle, complex network of allusions and overtones. Nothing new under the sun, some will say, except that the teachings and methodology of the Warburg school have so far failed to establish themselves in Indian studies, where the barrier interposed by the constant resorting to a symbolism nurtured by the ideas of the 1930s seems unbreakable. Though it is not only a question of *sandhyābhāṣā*, if the breach is now open by acknowledging the existence of instruments specific to India for understanding texts and images, we can only rejoice. The task is intimidating, because historians of religions should also contribute to this effort by offering us a more realistic view of the Brahmanical world.

The reference made above to the Warburg school suggests some considerations. Students of classical antiquities and of the Renaissance, whatever their specialisation may be, know that colleagues are up to in bordering sectors of their own field of research, and the wealth of such studies comes from a continuous dialogue between all the sectors, and many a scholar can competently address different sets of data. Some may say that in the case of ancient and medieval India data archives and literary corpora have too many empty boxes to allow us to proceed in this direction, desirable as it may be. I believe this is only partly true. When Aby Warburg began his investigations on the Italian Renaissance, things were not much different from at least some periods of Indian history, given the strong discontinuity in the history of Italy that we can symbolically fix to the year 1527. The Catholic Reform had strongly reshaped, and in part deleted, the past, and it was now necessary to retrieve it using a methodology that broke the boundaries between disciplines. There are no cheap shortcuts here: for those who use the tools of the Warburg school, it would be unthinkable to make easy escapes into the region of ill-defined or consolatory symbolisms, either fuelled by texts or iconographies, and, above all, to adhere to any form of reassuring (and authoritarian) inclusiveness. Historical modelling goes together with extremely careful distinctions.

The idea of writing this book has its distant origin in the unexpected results of an excavation carried out in Kathmandu in the 1980s, which the reader will find briefly summarised in a section of Chapter IV. There was indisputable evidence of a Buddhist sanctuary dismantled and interfaced to make way for a Vishnuite temple, the operation being sanctioned by an inscription containing a *damnatio memoriae* of the Saugatas. My career as a student of things Indian had begun in the 1970s, when the long debate on the end of Indian Buddhism held in the past had gone out of fashion. My explanation of the facts proved correct but rudimentary, and as to the papers I wrote on this subject from different angles in the following years, they turned out to be mere attempts, only partly successful, to fill a gap in the knowledge. During the sabbatical year 1997-98, I spent a few months at the Ecole Française d'Extrême-Orient in Pondicherry and at the Asiatic Society in Kolkata, where I could go through much of what had been written on the matter in the nineteenth and early twentieth century. In Kolkata, I met a young *paṇḍita* with whom, for a few years, I exchanged an extensive correspondence regarding known and less known texts containing material relevant for the work I felt an increasingly urgent need to do. At the time, the idea of re-examining known textual sources and making new sources known – some in Bengali – seemed feasible. It became increasingly clear, however, that this would have meant preparing a set of preliminary works each implying a considerable effort. Moreover, for the book to be written, several other sources were needed, and they were written in a number of Indian languages, from Tamil to Kannada, let alone the Tibetan, Chinese and Islamic sources. All the relevant passages, it appeared, would have required, for one reason or another, a very careful re-examination. In the end, the only viable solution has been for me to give the texts in the available translations. Regarding the Brahmanical texts, I have limited myself, when confronted with some passages glossed by learned insiders, to indicate to the reader how challenging their interpretation may happen to be. The subtle implications of these texts can hardly be understood without opening a dialogue with learned *paṇḍita*-s.

Iconographies are often better dated than texts, and cannot be easily altered. Moreover, they are part of specific, recognisable contexts, to which they can be referred, at least to an extent, even when they have been moved away from their original place. Since patronage is necessary for iconographies to come into existence, they often provide us with precise references to the historical reality of a given place. Far from providing a mere illustration of a text, they often make explicit what in the texts is left out or only ambiguously alluded to. Here we are in the domain of iconology, which, as already said, is still struggling to make its way into Indian studies, where the mechanical juxtaposition of text and image continues to be proposed almost unchallenged. The recovery of meaning in the sense indicated by Erwin Panofsky still seems, with notable exceptions, a distant objective. For all the information gaps that characterise the contexts discussed in this book, I have tried to give a contextualised interpretation of images or suggest for them a credible scenario, deliberately ignoring the metaphysical and theological level. I have aimed neither too low (a mere description of little significance for my argument) nor too high (a discussion of overburdening priestly symbols, of equally little significance), and if some conclusions sound disturbing, this interpretive level provides us, I think, with the maximum historical information. The enormous weight of violence expressed by a large proportion of Brahmanical images and, later on, by the images of Vajrayāna Buddhism, cannot be ascribed, *sic et simpliciter*, to the world of symbols but require a more specific, historically motivated explanation. Limitations and constraints have affected this part of the work, too. With few exceptions, I have utilised material published in art history studies. During the writing of this book, I could visit only some major museums and a few sites, and it has been impossible for me to organise extensive and repeated surveys in central and north-eastern India, where I especially wanted to go. The iconographic output of Indian regions other than those mentioned in the book is ignored, and inevitable though this is, it is not less regrettable. Finally, I regret that only a part of the drawings could be provided that *in votis* should have accompanied the text.

The third class of sources I have utilised are archaeological, but although this is my particular area of investigation, there is, regrettably, not much to say. *Per se*, the archaeological evidence is the only one definable as objective. The facts underlying both the setting in of the process of stratification and the production of artefacts are of course due to players comparable to those who produced texts and iconographies, but the slow formation of the archaeological deposit escapes the control of political players and ideologues. When diggings begin, a mound is really the objective whole of what has taken place. Unfortunately, even the best excavation is a compromise, because of its complexity and the technicalities involved. As regards the majority of the sites mentioned in this book, we face, in addition, inadequate excavations, where the loss of evidence has been enormous. The situation cannot be remedied because, unlike literary texts, which can be re-examined now and again, the archaeological text is difficult to reassess in that it is destroyed on reading. What we have is thus scattered evidence, partly handed over to us, if ever, by incomplete reports, and partly forgotten in inaccessible storehouses. Nevertheless, the reader will find information based on this kind of data throughout the book, and will also find a reassessment of the sites of Bodhgayā and Sarnath by Federica Barba in the Appendices.

The book is divided into six chapters. In the first, the issues I have raised are seen in perspective. Although the scholars of the past generations had access to a smaller amount of information and paid little attention to the social implications of the issues at stake, many of them had a more realistic vision of Indian past than the historians of the period of Independence and even modern historians. I fully distance myself from the current trend that sees a colonial construct in any position taken by nineteenth- and early twentieth-century scholars. Many of the ideas that nurtured foreign students were those of the learned babus they worked with, and by the end of the nineteenth century Indian scholars mastered the new methodologies very well, influencing the debate.

The second chapter explains why Buddhism belongs to a cultural horizon than is vaster than India, something that has marked its destiny, in India, in the first place. For all the paramount contributions of Indian historians to the understanding of early Buddhism, it has not been fully realised how unprecedented was the attempt at building an antinomial society. The role of Aśoka as a Buddhist *cakravartin* must be clearly asserted, while the early attacks on the religion of Dharma ought to be seen within the framework of a deeply revised chronology provided by the archaeological evidence. This revision ends up with assigning to the Śuṅgas the role of pioneer supporters of a new Brahmanical orthodoxy based on the encounter of Vedic ritualists and new theistic movements, without compromising with the world of the *śramaṇa*-s. If we pay due attention to chronology, we also realise that the Guptas – we go now to the third chapter – have nothing to do with Buddhism, which succeeded in re-establishing itself in some regions only around the mid-fifth century to coincide with the loosening of the powerful political and administrative network created by a dynasty that was supported by the new orthodox powers. The Kali Age literature is an unequivocal sign of Brahmanical hostility towards the *śramaṇa*-s and the social sectors they represented. While the difficult times experienced by Buddhism in the middle Ganges valley in the early fifth century is documented by Faxian and other sources, in the new kingdoms of the Deccan this hostility turned into a cleansing policy. The idea of a large Buddhist oecumene, fuelled by new trading perspectives, came to the fore at the time of Harṣavardhana and of an expanding Tang China, but Xuanzang's enthusiasm and involvement in the project did not prevent the great Chinese intellectual bearing witness to the ground lost by Buddhism in many Indian regions, starting from the North-West.

In the fourth chapter, after addressing a few methodological issues, I have discussed the poorly understood question of the doctrinal debates characteristic of the Indian scene. The stakes were the loss of political power and, therefore, of patronage, and the presence of militant, theistic groups transformed the debates into ordeals where the Buddhists were doomed to be the losers. All this should be seen as part of the slow but unrelenting occupation of the agricultural lands by the brāhmaṇas, who dislodged the former owners or put under cultivation the lands of the natives, clashing with non-agricultural peoples. Intimidation and violence became frequent. Militias were created which brought destruction to the Śramaṇic establishments and social network, pushing for the construction of temples of the gods and the imposition of *varṇāśramadharma*. In border regions like Orissa (the Pālas were ruling in the neighbouring territories), minority groups like the Kāpālikas were tolerated in that they took upon themselves the great sin of selectively getting rid of high-caste Buddhists.

The fifth chapter addresses at some length the question of the long, multi-faceted fight against the heretics as allegorised in Brahmanical texts and iconographies. A distinction is made between the battlefield, a ground where official war was waged, and the suppression of those who opposed not just the state but the *varṇa* state. The latter was a qualitatively different war. At the representational level, goddesses like Cāmuṇḍā and the *yoginī*-s are shown to have been performing this task on the fault-line along the Vindhyas beyond which the Buddhist strongholds of Bihar and Bengal were located. As to the Buddhists, they probably started reacting to violence rather early, but developed a coherent system of defence at the theoretical and factual level with the Vajrayāna.

The last chapter opens with the attempt at providing a picture of the Indian scene at the eve of the Muslim invasion. A section of Buddhist *śramaṇa*-s was a priesthood composed of married monks, and the others were increasingly radicalised exponents of the Vajrayāna, either *siddha*-s or monks, pitted against the attempt at normalisation and integration into the *varṇa* state of the Buddhist strongholds of Magadha, Bengal and upper Orissa. When the Brahmanical powers understood that striking an agreement with the Muslims – that which had not happened in Sind – could better serve their interests than continually lost battles, they bargained for the establishment of tributary but strict *varṇa* states (the best example is Mithilā) against the final suppression of Buddhism.

The implosion of Magadha has thrown a long shade on northern India, conditioning its history to the present day, and awaits proper investigation. It would be high time for Indian historians, the only ones who are in a position to access and discuss the large amount of existing documentation, to abandon every form of reticence and give us the true story.

Kyoto, September 2010

CHAPTER I

Historical Paradigms

THE PARADIGM OF DISCOVERY

Very little was known on Indian Buddhism when scholarly research began at the end of the eighteenth century. Today we are inclined to believe that, though neglected for a long time, the monuments characterising the landscape of South Asia, from the monasteries of Taxila in north-western Panjab to the stūpas of Sanchi in the Vindhyas, from the holy place of Sarnath near Benares to the caves of Ajanta in western Deccan, have always been there as the visible, concrete witness of a complex but shared history. But it is hardly so. Two centuries ago none of these places was known, their ancient names having also been forgotten. The physical traces of Buddhism had vanished but for some abandoned and unaccountable ruins in remote estates and jungles. The Indian landscape looked rather different from what it is now. Similarly, nowhere were the Buddhist texts we are familiar with available, and nobody retained any memory of them. What today, after two centuries of research, is for us a crucial part of the history of India and Asia, had disappeared from the horizon of Indian history. The little that was known was based on the living tradition of South-Eastern Asia, China (of which few had direct experience) and Sri Lanka, a country that only later was to play a central role in the recovery of the religion of Dharma. And yet, in 1788, it was well known that '[t]he *Brahmans* universally sp[oke] of the *Bauddhas* with all the malignity of an intolerant spirit':[1] Sir William Jones, unable to understand why, despite this, they considered the Buddha an incarnation of Viṣṇu, imagined the existence of two Buddhas, and it is interesting for us to know that 'another Buddha, one perhaps of his followers in a later age, assuming his name and character, attempted to overset the whole system of the *Brahmans*, and was the cause of that persecution, from which the *Bauddhas* are known to have fled into very distant regions'.[2]

It was in 1794 that at Sarnath the workmen of Jagat Singh, *dīvān* of the *rājā* of Benares, discovered the inscribed pedestal of a Buddha image and two stone reliquaries.[3] When in 1798 Jonathan Duncan, British Resident of Benares, broke the news of the discovery,[4] a great interest developed for the antiquity of the site. Several British officers started digging 'in many places around' and unearthed a great number of 'flat tiles, having representations of Buddha modelled upon them in wax [...]. Many were deposited in the Museums and collections of private individuals', any trace of them being soon lost.[5] Only later, in 1815, it was possible for the members of the Asiatic Society in Kolkata to admire the sculptures found by Colonel Colin Mackenzie during the excavation he had carried out at the site.[6] In 1788, Charles Wilkins, the translator of the *Bhagavad Gītā*, had published an inscription found at Bodhgayā in the first issue of the *Asiatick Researches*. The Buddha there appeared as a manifestation of Viṣṇu, and was recognised as the deity of the place ('the province of Keekătă'), where he had erected his 'house'.[7] The inscription drew attention to the place of the Awakening.[8] Bodhgayā was the only Buddhist site that had never been completely forgotten, and in 1811 Francis Buchanan, the indefatigable surveyor and intelligencer we are indebted to for a number of works,[9] gathered a still living tradition regarding the mechanisms by which the brāhmaṇas had appropriated the place.

According to '[t]he only person of the sect of the Buddhas' found in the district,

> Gautama [...] lived some years in that vicinity, under a large tree which is therefore considered holy by his followers, and is called the Gautama Bat. The orthodox call the same tree Akshay Bat, and it is one of the chief places of worship at Gayā. A sacred pool near this tree is called Gautama kunda by the Buddhists, and Rukmini kunda by the orthodox.[10]

Buchanan's informant stated that 'all the other places of worship at Gaya are the invention of Vyas, a person who lived long after Gautama, who introduced the doctrine of caste, and the worship of Vishnu, and who, having fabricated the legend of Gayasur, pointed out places to correspond'.[11] The site had been spoilt of many Buddha images, which had been carried to Gayā, where there was 'no trace of any considerable building of the least antiquity'.[12]

Buddhism remained almost unknown until the 1840s,[13] but it was commonly believed that the relationship between Buddhism and Brahmanism had been marked by deep conflict. In the sixth part of his long essay devoted to the origin and decline of Christianity in India published in the *Asiatick Researches*, Lieutenant Francis Wilford reported that the brāhmaṇas 'unanimously acknowledge[d]' the former practise of holding 'conferences' (i.e., doctrinal debates) between them and the Buddhists, and that towns appointed for the purpose, called *Charchita nagari*, were selected. 'One of them is mentioned in the *Cumáricá-c'handa*, according to which "[i]n the year 3291 of the *Caliyuga* (or 191 after Christ) *King* Sudraca will reign in the town of Charchita-nagari, and destroy the *workers of iniquity*." This points out a persecution in religious matters, at a very early period.' Wilford further noted that

> [t]hese conferences ended in bloodshed, and the most cruel and rancorous persecution of the followers of Budd'ha, even from the confession of the Bráhmens themselves. They were tied hand and foot, and thus thrown into rivers, lakes, ponds, and sometimes whole strings of them. Be this as it may, the followers of Budd'ha did not fail to retaliate whenever it was in their power; for Dr. F. Buchanan informs me, that in the *Dekhin* the *Jainas* make their boast of the cruelties that they exercised at different times upon the Bráhmens, and that there are even inscriptions still extant in which they are recorded.[14]

Wilford largely depended, for his works, on the misleading information provided to him by the *paṇḍita*-s of Benares,[15] and was prone to 'hasty generalizations'[16] and groundless theories, but the information given in the quote above reflects ancient and widespread beliefs handed down by the brāhmaṇas themselves.[17] To make just an example, one century later T. A. Gopinatha Rao, the founder of modern research on Indian iconography, was to report that as late as the mid-nineteenth century the belief among the teachers of history in the schools and colleges of Travancore was that 'Buddhism died in the land of its birth not long after its birth, and that the Brahmans killed it and drove away all of its followers'.[18]

Horace Hayman Wilson, who was appointed Secretary to the Asiatic Society in 1811 and was to become the most distinguished student of Sanskrit of his times,[19] shared these opinions for a long time. In the preface to the first edition (1819) of his *Sanskrit Dictionary*,[20] he devoted several pages to the question of anti-Buddhist persecutions, gathering the evidence on the role played by Kumārila Bhaṭṭa and

Śaṅkara.[21] His knowledge of Sanskrit texts and, for what was known at the time, of Indian history, as well as his familiarity with Indian *paṇḍita*-s, allowed him to sketch a tentative chronology of the events concerning the relationships of Buddhism and Brahmanism:

[...] we know that the utter extermination of the Bauddha sect in India did not take place till some time between the twelfth and fifteenth centuries, and we must conclude, consequently, that the contending parties were for a long period too equally matched for any permanent and vigorous persecution of either by the other to have taken place, and especially for some time after the beginning of the conflict. If therefore the contest began in the third century, and the temporary ascendancy of the Brahmans was established some time before the eighth, we may conjecture, with every appearance of conjecturing happily, that the fifth and sixth centuries form the season, in which the Bauddhas were most actively and triumphantly assailed by the interested professors of the orthodox creed.[22]

Today we would suggest a different chronology, but it is interesting to note that Wilson dated the first serious crisis of Buddhism to the time of the collapse of the Kuṣāṇa empire and of the establishment of the Gupta dynasty, of which he had no knowledge.[23]

Even more interesting is the fact that Wilson had collected enough evidence to be convinced that 'the persecution of the followers of Buddha by the Brahmanical order' was 'a subject on which both sects are agreed'.[24] Wilson wrote that

[t]he concurring traditions of the Brahmanical, Bauddha, and Jaina sects report a two-fold persecution of the second, by each of the others severally, although they are not agreed about the order of their occurrence. If I have conjectured rightly, the priority seems due to that instigated by the members of the orthodox faith, and they effected a partial suppression of the Bauddha heresy about the fifth and sixth centuries [...][25]

further observing that

[...] it does appear that an utter extirpation of the Bauddha religion in India was effected between the twelfth and sixteenth centuries. By whom then was this important revolution brought about? I cannot answer this question with confidence, but think it highly probable that the Jainas performed an important part in the event, especially as there is reason to suppose that the period assigned for the overthrow of the Bauddhas was that in which the Jainas had attained in many parts of India their highest pitch of power and prosperity.[26]

By the early nineteenth century the religion and customs of the Jains were already well known: much information had been collected by Buchanan in *A Journey from Madras through the Countries of Mysore, Canara, and Malabar*, published in 1807, and the manuscripts that Colonel Mackenzie was gathering in south India had begun to circulate.[27] In 1828 Wilson wrote that 'the papers related to the *Jains* were the most novel and important, and first brought to notice the existence of a Sect which is very extensively dispersed throughout India [...]'.[28] The often violent confrontation between Buddhists and Jains, the Brahmanical repression of Jainism and the final transformation of the latter into a bastion of caste orthodoxy, were facts better known in the nineteenth century than they are today.

Wilson, who became professor of Sanskrit at Oxford in 1832, was to change his opinions radically, but the idea that Indian history had many skeletons in the cupboard spread, and several scholars remained convinced that much violence had been exercised. Some of them, belonging to different fields of research and deriving their evidence from separate sets of sources, can be counted among the sharpest minds ever engaged in the study of Indian history.

ALLEGORIES

An insightful scholar was Reverend William Taylor, entrusted by the Asiatic Society with the task of examining the manuscripts collected by Mackenzie after Wilson abandoned their classification after publishing a volume in 1828.[29] Taylor was a resident of Madras and a member of the Madras Literary Society, auxiliary of the Asiatic Society,[30] and from 1838 to 1850 (although the bulk of the work was already concluded in 1839), published an accurate and often detailed summary of the manuscripts, first in the *Journal of the Asiatic Society*, and then in the *Madras Journal of Literature and Science*.[31] Left without sufficient support, he suspended his work in 1850, leaving only the Kannada documents unexamined.[32] Taylor realised that the accounts reported in the Mackenzie papers, often available in different versions and languages, framed a disquieting history of south India.

In these manuscripts, Jains and Buddhists appear as the earliest rulers of south India,[33] subsequently suppressed by the brāhmaṇas who put pressure on local kings with the purpose of getting rid of them. During the doctrinal disputations attended by the conflicting parties, Taylor observed, the Buddhists were always the losers and were killed, martyred, or forced to leave the country. To make an example, when king Cēramā̠n Perumāḷ[34] intimated to the brāhmaṇas that they must unite with the Buddhists and follow their system,

> [...] the brahmans went to the king and remonstrated with him, calling for a public disputation, when if they, the brahmans were vanquished, their tongues should be cut out, and the like done to the bauddhas if these should be overcome. The dispute was held, terminating favourably to the brahmans in consequence of a magical influence emanating from the head brahman at *Tri-Cárúr*: the tongues of the bauddhas were cut out and they were banished the country. The king who had adopted their system was dethroned, and some lands were set apart for his support.[35]

The Jains were crushed with equal violence, as was reported in relation to the well-known story of the eight thousand Jains put to death in Madurai on instigation of Campantar.[36] In the manuscripts collected by Mackenzie there were several other stories set in small villages that made the hypothesis that a thorough elimination of the heretics had taken place more credible: the village of Patuvur, for instance, 'was formerly in possession of the Jainas, as is visible from the remains of their *Bastis*, or fanes. They were destroyed by the Brahmans in the time of Adondai; and some embraced the Brahmanical system';[37] in the Cota village, 'a dispute arose between the Brahmans and the Jainas; and many of the Jainas were killed. The remains of their class emigrated towards the south'.[38]

In other contexts, the Jains appeared to share the brāhmaṇas' hatred against the Buddhists. The story of Akaḷaṅka is repeatedly reported, according to which the Digambara *ācārya* overcame the Buddhists in a public disputation. 'Some of the *Bauddhas* were intended to be put to death in large stone-oil-mills; but instead of that were embarked on board ships, or vessels, and sent to Ceylon.'[39] Elsewhere, at the end of the same dispute, which lasted eight days, 'the conquered sect he bruised to death in oil-mills of stone'.[40]

Taylor observed that '[t]he punishment by grinding to death in oil-mills, is one well known to Indian History; and in the progress of development of these papers it will be seen that *Bauddhas* and *Jainas* were subjected to it, at a later period, by Hindu kings, under Brahmanical influence'.[41] The India which disclosed its past to William Taylor was marked by a continually resurgent violence. The Jains were crushed, later on, by the Vīraśaivas: in the *Cennabasava Purāṇam*, both Basava and Cenna Basava were fit agents for the work of exterminating a *Jaina* king, and *Jaina* people; which they accomplished. [...] the development of the whole *Jangama* system *ab oro usque ad nauseam,* certainly is an object of some interest in itself, and connected with the historical details of the N.W. of the Peninsula: where the destruction of the *Jainas*, and the establishment of a champion system of extermination, are distinguished features.[42]

Taylor can be easily accused of having believed in the facts as reported in the sources without keeping any critical distance from them,[43] but it must be admitted that the evidence was impressive. Taylor, pushing his convictions farther, sensed that the epics and the Purāṇas had to be deconstructed in order to understand what lies at the core of a literature—produced by the brāhmaṇas in late ancient and medieval India—which is at the same time outspoken and reticent. In his *Sixth Report*, after examining a Telugu version of the *Varāha Purāṇa*, he remarked that

[t]he use of this *Purána* in illustrating mythology is considerable. In so far as historical enquiries are concerned the most remarkable sections are 10 and 11. The latter, in particular, very clearly relates to the great exterminating war made against the votaries of *Buddha*. The combat of *Durga* against *Mahéshásura* has been, by some, ridiculously termed the combat of personified virtue, against personified vice. No doubt there is personification, and mystic allegory; but not precisely to that said effect. There are several great wars indicated in *Hindu* stories; some of them under a similar mystic veil; as:

1st. That of *Subrahmanya* against the *Asuras*.
2nd. That of *Parasu Ráma* against the *Cshetriyas*.
3rd. That of *Ráma* against *Rávana*, and other *Rácshasas*.
4th. That of *Durga* against *Mahéshásura.*

And *Mahéshásura*, in my opinion, is very probably only another name for the mysterious personage more usually in the south denominated Sáliváhana.

The clue of symbolical writing which I have been enabled to get hold of in the course of these enquiries, will, I am persuaded, if patiently, and perseveringly followed out, by individuals more capable in the earlier languages than myself, ultimately tend to solve much of the marvellous, and paradoxical, contained in *Hindu* writings [...].[44]

With reference to a Kannada manuscript book on Satyendra-Colaraja [Sātyēndra Cōḷa Rāja], a devotee of the Vīraśaiva sect, and on the basis of other Vīraśaiva sources, Taylor further observed that the destruction of the *asura* whose skull Śiva used for the head of his *vīṇā* had 'an enigmatic meaning', and was led 'to conjecture that the aforesaid *asura* [wa]s a personification of the *Jaina* system; exterminated by the two *Vasavas*, and their followers'.[45]

Another case in point was the myth of Paraśurāma, exterminator of the kṣatriyas and founder of a well-ordered Brahmanical society.[46] Taylor believed that Paraśurāma was at the centre of a recent foundation myth, and had no doubts

> that all the alleged *avatáras* of Vishnu shadow forth, each one, some great historical event; not always possible to be rescued from the obscurity of fable. [...] from Parasu Ráma downwards, all clearly appear to have occurred within the boundaries of this country. Hence I think the incarnation of Parasu Ráma points to the first acquisition of power by the brahmans, after their coming to India from the northward of *Himálaya*.[47]

Taylor was persuaded that in Hindu texts there was 'much enigmatical, or symbolical, writing and when such a veil is studiously employed, as seems to be the case in all early Hindu writings, it may be inferred, that the earliest colonists of India wished to conceal their true descent, or to falsify something concerning themselves'.[48]

There are several reasons for the facts narrated or alluded to in the Mackenzie Manuscripts to have sunk into oblivion. The gradual vanishing of the early interpretive paradigm of Indian history was joined by the views later historians had on these types of sources. Their task was to discover and discuss positive facts, dates and names; they did not take late and tainted texts into any consideration. It is more difficult to understand why the Mackenzie material is ignored today, when modern historiographic currents favouring history written out of the most disparate materials have also made their way, and for quite a long time now, into the circle of Indian historians.[49]

Taylor's insightful views were not immediately lost. In his monumental *History of India*, the first to be written on an ambitious scale, James Talboys Wheeler re-discussed some of the issues raised by Taylor. The *rākṣasa*-s of the *Rāmāyaṇa*, he observed, are 'the especial enemy of the Bráhmans', and 'are not to be simply confounded with the original population', nor are they to be regarded

> as mere creations of the imaginations, like the cannibal Asuras who were conquered by Bhíma. They are described as forming an empire, more or less civilised, having its capital in Lanká, in the island of Ceylon; but having military outposts in different quarters of the Dekhan, and extending their operations as far to the

northward as the right bank of the Ganges. [...] the Rákshasas are described as being violently opposed to the sacrifices of the Bráhmans, and as being utterly wanting in faith in sacred things; circumstances which seem to identify them with the Buddhists [...].[50]

Wheeler also realised that six of the *avatāra*-s of Viṣṇu

possess a substantive historical value, namely, the avatáras as a lion and dwarf, and those of Parasuráma, Ráma, Krishna, and Buddha. One idea runs through them all, namely, that Vishnu became incarnate in order to destroy the giants or demons who sought to dethrone the gods. [...] But the myths of the incarnations or avátaras of Vishnu [...] belong to the age of Brahmanical revival, when the persistent efforts of Buddhist teachers to deny the authority of the Vedas, and to dethrone or ignore the gods in general, had created an antagonism which culminated in a persecuting war.[51]

Wheeler and Taylor ended up considering the epics and the Purāṇas as allegorical texts provided with historical meaning, but later historians have addressed them (the Purāṇas in particular) mainly to reconstruct past lineages and dynasties.[52] Wheeler also made available to a large audience the often forgotten evidence on the destruction of Buddhist Sarnath carried out by the brāhmaṇas:

The ashes and charred remains sufficiently indicate that the whole was destroyed in some sudden conflagration; and as Buddhist pagodas have been converted into Brahmanical temples, suspicion points to a sudden outbreak instigated by the Bráhmans. Possibly some bitter disputation had been brought to a violent close; and a nest of infuriated fanatics had poured out of Benares to destroy the heretics and atheists of Sárnáth as enemies of the gods. [...] At present, however, the story lies beneath the mounds; Sárnáth was sacked and burned at the instigation of the Bráhmans.[53]

Taylor found an heir in Rajendralala Mitra, one of the most brilliant scholars of the second half of the century and a representative of the first generation of those extraordinary Bengali intellectuals who have marked the history of India until half a century ago. Born in 1824, in 1846 he was appointed librarian to the Asiatic Society, and became the first Indian president of the association in 1885.[54] Two of his major works, *Buddha Gayá, the Hermitage of Śákya Muni* and *The Antiquities of Orissa*[55] deserve special attention.

When Mitra started his work, important contributions had already been made on Gayā and Bodhgayā, the most important by Alexander Cunningham.[56] Mitra's book on Bodhgayā was the object of an anonymous, severe review in *The Indian Antiquary*,[57] where Mitra's blunders in iconographic matters were especially deplored. The majority of the British residents of Kolkata disliked Mitra,[58] who was, in particular, on extremely bad terms with James Fergusson:[59] there was nothing better than showing Mitra's amateurishness in the field of archaeology and art history. Yet the *babu*, who enjoyed Max Müller's admiration,[60] was a gifted intellectual embodying tradition and an innovator who understood both the pettiness of the colonisers and the mental attitude and ideological manipulations of Hindu intellectuals, including past manipulations.

Referring back to Buchanan's account on the 'monstrous legend' of Gayā, a powerful *asura*,[61] Mitra maintained that the story, narrated in the *Gayā Māhātmya* attached to the *Vāyu Purāṇa*, was yet another foundation myth based on violence. The *asura* 'practiced the most rigorous austerities for many thousand years on the noble hill of Koláhala. The Devas were oppressed by his austerities, and dreaded serious misfortune.'[62] The *asura* agreed to have his enormous body purified by a sacrifice performed by Brahmā, but, to the latter's surprise, at the end of the ritual 'the demon was still moving on the sacrificial ground',[63] continuing to move even when all the gods sat on the *dharmaśilā* or sacred stone placed on his head. Not even a 'fierce form' drawn forth from Viṣṇu's person and placed on the stone could stop the demon, and only 'by plying his mace, Hari rendered the demon motionless', being therefore called 'the first or sovereign wielder of the mace (*ádigadádhara*)'.[64]

The allegory is transparent, and Mitra observed that Gayāsura

> revels not in crime, he injures none, and offends neither the gods nor religion by woes or deed. [...] The most serious charge brought against him was that he made salvation too simple and summary. The epithet in his case can, therefore, only mean that he did not profess the faith of the Bráhmans, nor follow their ways: in short, he was a heretic. This character has always been assigned to the chief among the Buddhists. They were pious, they were self-mortifying, they devoted themselves greatly to penance and meditation; but they did away with the sacrifices and ceremonies of the Bráhmans, and Gayá therefore may safely be taken to be a personification of Buddhism. [...] The attempts of the gods to put down the head of the monster typifies the attempts of the Hindus to assail Buddhism at its inspiring centre, the head-quarters; and the thwack of Vishṇu's mace indicates the resort which had been made to force when religious preaching had failed to attain the end. The rock of religion was placed on the head of the infidel, and the force of the gods kept it fixed and immovable. It was the blessing of the gods,

too, which sanctified the seat of Buddhism into a principal sanctuary of the Hindu faith.[65]

Hard to say it better: the brāhmaṇas, who displaced to Gayā a number of stūpas from Bodhgayā transforming them into *liṅga*-s,[66] built their hegemony on the control of *śrāddha* rituals. Mitra observed that no mention is generally made of Buddhism or any other heterodox system in Brahmanical texts.[67] Discussing ancient Puri, Mitra maintained that '[i]t is impossible to suppose that they [the brāhmaṇas] knew nothing of the ascendancy of Buddhism, and the omission, therefore, can be attributed solely to religious hatred. They would do anything to avoid naming the Jains and the Buddhists […].[68]

Gayāsura's enormous size (576 × 268 miles) was for Mitra an allegory of the large territory, from Kaliṅga to the Himalaya and from central India to Bengal, where Buddhism had spread and held out.[69] Gayā represented the head of Buddhism, Puri its navel, or an equally vital part, and Yājapur (Jajpur) its chest:[70] 'Viṣṇu, to mark his success over the demon, left his foot-mark at Gayā, his lotus at Koṇārak, his club at Yājapur, his discus at Bhuvaneśvara, and his conch-shell at Puri'. In the latter place, the revivalists were few in number, and could not forcibly subdue the Buddhists, and the plan of action was that of gradual appropriation and assimilation:

> It was not the Moslem sword that was brought into play, not the *Qoran* in one hand and the scymetar in the other, but the policy of conciliation and compromise […] The Buddhist belief of the sanctity of the Bo tree [was] made a part of the Hindu religion; the Buddhist repugnance to animal sacrifices [were] taken up by the Vaisnavas and Buddhist emblems, Buddhist temples, Buddhist sacred places, and Buddhist practices [were] appropriated to Hindu usages.[71]

Even when there was no open violence, the brāhmaṇas' appropriation of Buddhist sites was not exactly pacific:

> [w]here it was impossible to appropriate a Buddhist temple to Hindu worship, rival temples were erected in close neighbourhood, and services and ceremonials were so moulded and adapted as to leave nothing to the former to maintain its pre-eminence in the estimation of the people.[72]

We wonder how would the history of India have been written in the past century if William Taylor's insights and Rajendralala Mitra's interpretations had been given due credit. But Taylor was a marginal scholar who soon lost all support, and Mitra was an unwanted member of the academic establishment. After his death, little was made to keep alive his memory and scientific contributions. Right on the pages of the *Journal of the Asiatic Society of Bengal* – a deplorable perfidy – Louis S.S. O'Malley criticised Mitra's theory on the assumption that Buddhism had never been prominent at Gayā and that the *Gayāśrāddha*-s were connected to popular demonolatry.[73] In the 1930s Benidhab Barua, one of the most distinguished pre-Independence scholars, refuted it with weak, unproblematic arguments.[74] Only in recent times the question of the identity of the *asura*-s with actual political and religious opponents has started being discussed again.[75]

FIELDWORK

The work of philologists and linguists was accompanied from the beginning by that of sociologists, such as Buchanan, as well as by that of antiquarians. To the former goes the merit of having gathered still living traditions (generally ignored by later positivist historians); to the latter, that of having laid the foundations for the development of archaeological and art-historical research. Alexander Cunningham was a distinguished epigraphist and historian,[76] but he was, above all, the founder of Indian archaeology: in 1871 he was appointed Director General of the Archaeological Survey of India and initiated the publication of the *Archaeological Survey of India Reports*. When he started excavating at Sarnath in winter 1835-36 he was only twenty-one years old, and one wonders what his work was like—not just because of his age, but because archaeology as an autonomous discipline was not yet born.[77] However, when some thirty years later he published the results of his juvenile work (further excavations at Sarnath had been carried out by Major Markham Kittoe) and started writing the reports on his other tours and excavations in northern India, he had accumulated remarkable experience and knew very well what he was talking about. He was seldom mistaken at the level of macro-analysis: he could easily distinguish between the collapse and the wanton destruction of a structure, its complete abandonment and partial reuse, its having been slowly robbed through time or voluntarily sacked. His tireless, extensive travelling from site to site for decades, his analysis of thousands of monuments made him fit for observing patterns and creating models.[78] His observations were often crucial because, whereas the relationship between facts and the narrations made known by the philologists was uncertain, the material remains objectified facts, or pretended to. During his visit to Nālandā in 1861, he examined the north-eastern corner of the terrace of Temple Site 3, where he found the dismantled remains of several small, carved stūpas:

The solid hemispherical domes are from 1 foot to 4 feet in diameter. The basement and body of each stupa were built of separate stones, which were numbered for the guidance of the builders, and cramped together with iron to secure greater durability. No amount of time, and not even an earthquake, could have destroyed these small buildings. Their solid walls of iron-bound stones could only have yielded to the destructive fury of malignant Brahmans.[79]

In Mathurā, he fixed the downfall of Buddhism to the period between Xuanzang's visit in AD 634, when there were only five *deva* temples, and the raid of Maḥmūd of Ghazni in AD 1017. It is worth noting that he did not attribute *all* destructions to the Muslims, as the majority of historians had started doing. He was able to unfold various levels of complexity:

Of the circumstances which attended the downfall of Buddhism we know almost nothing; but as in the present case we find the remains of a magnificent Brahmanical temple occupying the very site of what must once have been a large Buddhist establishment, we may infer with tolerable certainty that the votaries of *Sakya Muni* were expelled by force, and that their buildings were overthrown to furnish materials for those of their Brahmanical rivals; and now these in their turn have been thrown down by the Musalmāns.[80]

At Bodhgayā, a site to which Cunningham devoted particular attention, the pilgrims who in the fourteenth century still continued to visit the place found that the brāhmaṇas had appropriated the site:

It seems probable also that their claim to the holy site was disputed by the Brahmans, as there still exists a round stone which formerly stood in front of the Temple with the feet of Vishnu sculptured on its face, and the date of Saka 1230, or A.D. 1308, carved on its side. This stone was originally the hemispherical dome of a Stūpa. The square socket hole still exists on the rounded face for the reception of the pinnacle.

From this time I believe that both the holy Pipal Tree and the Temple were appropriated by the Brahmans, although the place must still have been visited by occasional pilgrims from Nepāl and Burma. At present there is a large Brahmanical monastery, with a Mahant and upwards of 200 followers.[81]

Cunningham thought that '[f]rom the fifth to the seventh century the decline of Buddhism was gradual and gentle', but that 'from the eighth century the fall was rapid and violent'. In the eleventh or the twelfth century 'the last votaries of Buddha were expelled from the continent of India. Numbers of images, concealed by the departing monks, are found buried near Sárnáth; and heaps of ashes still lie scattered amidst the ruins to show that the monasteries were destroyed by fire.'[82] In the notes he wrote during the fieldwork, published in 1863 with only marginal additions, Cunningham had written that

[i]t will have been observed that every excavation made near Sârnâth has revealed traces of fire. I myself found charred timber and half burnt grain. The same things were also found by Major Kittoe, besides the evident traces of fire on the stone pillars, umbrellas, and statues. [. . .] he [Major Kittoe] summed up his conclusions to me in a few words: "*All has been sacked and burnt*, priests, temples, idols, all together. In some places bones, iron, timber, idols, &c., are all fused into huge heaps; *and this has happened more than once*." Major Kittoe repeated this opinion in almost the same words when I saw him at Gwalior in September, 1852.[83]

Cunningham also reported a passage from Edward Thomas's paper about the great conflagration which destroyed the monastery,[84] but what is worth noting is that he emphasised the fact that Sarnath had been the object of repeated destructions: the message was, once again, that the Muslims, held responsible for the end of the sanctuary, could not conceivably be the authors of earlier attacks. Towards the end of his career, Cunningham was more than ever convinced that three conflicting forces had been at work in medieval India, and rejected the binary system according to which a culturally unified India had been subdued by the Muslim fury. In the twentieth volume of his *Annual Reports*, Cunningham noted that

it is the fashion now to attribute the ruin of all temples to the iconoclastic Muhammadans, and certainly the followers of Islâm have plenty to answer for in India. But it must be remembered that Buddhism had disappeared in Northern India long before the Muhammadan conquest, although it still lingered in Bihār, or Magadha, where it first originated.[85]

The evidence on Buddhism having been suppressed by the brāhmaṇas was provided by the brāhmaṇas themselves, as for instance by Mādhavācārya and Kṛṣṇa Miśra, the author of the *Prabodha Candrodaya*. Cunningham gave the essential details of the morality play, which, as we shall better see in Chapter V, bears witness to the forced Buddhist diaspora.

The Jains suffered the same fate, and all their wealth and influence have not been able to save them from the persecution of Brâhmans. Everywhere, even at the present day, at Delhi, at Agra, and at other places, the Brâhmans had succeeded in preventing the Jains from holding processions. The persecution has not proceeded from the bigotry of the Musalmâns, but from the more rampant intolerance of the Brâhmans.[86]

A contemporary of Cunningham's was James Fergusson, who founded the study of Indian architecture. Many a difference separated the two men, even without considering the long controversy on the reconstruction of the Mahābodhi temple at Bodhgayā,[87] though their views did not differ on the subject we are dealing with. Fergusson made a statement that is perhaps the most lucid among those made in the nineteenth century. In his most celebrated work, the *History of Indian and Eastern Architecture*, published in 1876, he wrote:

[...] the curtain drops on the drama of Indian History about the year 650, or a little later, and for three centuries we have only the faintest glimmerings of what took place within her boundaries. Civil wars seem to have raged everywhere, and religious persecution of the most relentless kind. When the curtain again rises we have an entirely new scene and new dramatis personae presented to us. Buddhism had entirely disappeared, except in one corner of Bengal, and Jainism had taken its place throughout the west, and Vishnuism had usurped its inheritance in the east. On the south the religion of Siva had been adopted by the mass of the people [...]. My impression is that it was during these three centuries of misrule that the later temples and viharas of the Buddhists disappeared, and the earlier temples of the Jains; and there is a gap consequently in our history which may be filled up by new discoveries in remote places but which at present separates this chapter from the last in a manner it is by no means pleasant to contemplate.[88]

Indian chronology was still tentative, but Fergusson saw clearly that the deep Indian crisis began with the death of Harṣavardhana (AD 657), and that three centuries were necessary for neo-Brahmanism to win the battle against its opponents and remain unchallenged. The above passage remained unchanged in the various editions of the book, but in *The Caves Temples of India*, published in 1880, Fergusson's statement was so mitigated that nothing remained of its original force, perhaps because of young James Burgess's co-authorship, and certainly because of the quickly changing intellectual climate. It is surprising to read that

[i]n the seventh century of our era it [= Buddhism] had begun to decline in some parts of India; in the eighth apparently it was rapidly disappearing: and shortly

after that it had vanished from the greater part of India, though it still lingered about Banāras and in Bengal where the Pāla dynasty, if not Buddhists themselves, at least tolerated it extensively in their dominions. It existed also at some points on the West coast, perhaps till the eleventh century or even later. It has been thought that it was extinguished by Brahmanical persecution; but the evidence does not seem sufficient to prove that force was generally resorted to. Probably its decline and final extinction was to a large extent owing to the ignorance of its priests, the corruptions of its early doctrines, especially after the rise of the Mahāyāna sect, the multiplicity of its schisms, and its followers becoming mixed up with the Jains, whose teachings and ritual are very similar, or from its followers falling into the surrounding Hinduism of the masses.[89]

THE WORM WITHIN

Between 1824 and 1838, Brian Houghton Hodgson, Assistant Resident and then Acting Resident and Resident to the Nepal Darbar, started collecting Buddhist manuscripts and sending reports to the Asiatic Society.[90] As is known, the manuscripts he sent to Paris allowed Eugène Burnouf to write the first comprehensive study of Buddhist doctrines ever presented to the intellectual elite of the West.[91] Hodgson shared the idea that Buddhism had been persecuted,[92] and he had, in addition, the clear perception that it had been pushed by force from the plains towards the mountains:

> Nor, though furious bigots dispersed the sect, and attempted to destroy its records, did they succeed in the latter attempt. The refugees found, not only safety, but protection and honour, in the immediately adjacent countries, whither they safely conveyed most of their books, and where those books still exist, either in the original Sanskrit, or in most carefully made translations from it.[93]

Despite his visible annoyance at 'Brahmanical ignorance',[94] it was difficult for Hodgson to understand and accept Mahāyāna and Vajrayāna Buddhism as they were slowly disclosing themselves in texts and living practices. The doctrine to which they bore witness was such that 'few Bauddhas can be called wise'; the principle according to which '*man is capable of extending his moral and intellectual faculties to infinity*' was brought to 'its most extravagant consequences', becoming the corner-stone of their faith and practice.[95] Hodgson was keen to defend Buddhism against the ill-informed, but took his distance from it ('I had no purpose, nor have I, to meddle with the interminable sheer absurdities of the Bauddha philosophy or religion'), nor did he intend to defend '*details as absurd as interminable*'.[96] It was not a question of considering Newār Buddhism a 'modern corrupt Buddhism'[97] because this would have implied the existence of an earlier acceptable form of Buddhism, which had never existed. It was, rather, a structural problem.

The information on Newār Buddhism supplied by Hodgson was a shock to many, and was responsible for a change of perspective. As early as 1828, H.H. Wilson, after illustrating the contents of the texts sent from Kathmandu to Kolkata, remarked:

> Such is the nonsensical extravagance with which this and the Tantrika ceremonies generally abound; and we might be disposed to laugh at such absurdities, if the temporary frenzy, which the words excite in the minds of those who hear and repeat them with agitated awe, did not offer a subject worthy of serious contemplation in the study of human nature.[98]

Not only did some scholars begin to consider Buddhism extravagant – to say the least – but became persuaded that, if it had been violently uprooted by the brāhmaṇas, it had deserved its fate. The evidence of violence against the Buddhists started being played down, as Wilson did in 1854 in his précis of Buddhist history,[99] where he abandoned his former views. The brāhmaṇas, once 'aroused from their apathy', had set to work

> to arrest the progress of the schism. The success that attended their efforts could have been, for a long time, but partial; but that they were ultimately successful, and that Buddhism in India gave way before Brahmanism, is a historical fact: to what cause this was owing is by no means established, but it was more probably the result of internal decay, than of external violence.[100]

Wilson could not get out of recalling the 'traditions of persecutions', and reported a passage of the *Lotus Sūtra* translated by Burnouf to that effect.[101] He claimed, however, that only 'local and occasional acts of aggression were perpetrated by the Brahmanical party'.[102] There were no record of persecution having been universal,

> and its having been of any great extent may be reasonably doubted: it seems more likely that Buddhism died a natural death. With the discontinuance of the activity of its professors, who, yielding to the indolence which prosperity is apt to engender, ceased to traverse towns and villages in seeking to make proselytes, the Buddhist priest in India sunk into the sloth and ignorance which now characterise the bulk of the priests of the same religion in other countries, especially China, and seem there to be productive of the same result, working the decay and dissolution of the Buddhist religion.[103]

Thus it was not only Newār Buddhism that was inherently corrupt. In China, '[t]he people in general do not seem to take much interest in the worship of the temples, nor to entertain any particular veneration for their priests',[104] and as regards Sri Lanka, Wilson made his own the words of Robert Spence Hardy, 'in no part of the island that I have visited, do the priests as a body appear to be respected by the people'.[105] Things went even worse 'in the most northern provinces of Russia', where

> Buddhism, degraded to Shamanism, is nothing more than a miserable display of juggling tricks and deceptions, and even in the Lamaserais of Tibet, exhibitions of the same kind are permitted, whatever may be the belief and practice of those of the community who are better instructed, and take no part in them themselves. Ignorance is at the root of the whole system, and it must fall to pieces with the extension of knowledge and civilisation.[106]

The Buddhist population – this was the advice of Christian missionaries – needed to be educated:

> The process is unavoidably slow, especially in Central Asia, which is almost beyond the reach of European activity and zeal, but there is no occasion to despair of ultimate success. Various agencies are at work, both in the north and the south, before whose salutary influence civilisation is extending; and the ignorance and superstition, which are the main props of Buddhism, must be overturned by its advance.[107]

It would be easy to accuse Wilson of religious zeal and colonial conceitedness, if his target had not been so univocal. Wilson's distancing from his earlier positions went along with a growing admiration for the world and life of the brāhmaṇas, due to his familiarity with the learned *paṇḍita*-s he had been in contact with and to his own work as translator of Brahmanical texts. He maintained that, if the greatness of Brahmanical literature had not been recognised before modern times, it was because of the Muslims and 'their disdainful intolerance with which they regard the languages and literature of all nations that profess a different religious faith'.[108]

THE PARADIGM OF EXOTICISM

The generation of scholars that came to the forefront in the 1870s-80s and exerted their influence well into the twentieth century had at their disposal an impressive amount of evidence, which they contributed to enlarge further. This allowed for the drafting of ambitious, comprehensive works in several fields of Indian history. Buddhism was no longer an unknown religion, as it had been at the beginning of the century. The interest towards the living Buddhist tradition of Sri Lanka, where, after the pioneer work of George Turnour, Robert C. Childers had started collecting Pāli texts, replaced that towards Tantrism shown by Hodgson a few decades earlier. Sri Lankan Buddhism had been made known by Robert Spence Hardy in his *Manual*,[109] and the first Pāli dictionary, edited by Childers, started being published in 1872. Thomas William Rhys Davids, who had arrived in the island in 1871 and was at first involved in the excavations of Anuradhapura, would establish the Pali Text Society in 1881. Between 1881 and 1885, Rhys Davids and Hermann Oldenberg would publish the translation of the *Vinaya*.[110]

In 1880, John Ware Edgar, author of a *Report on a Visit to Sikhim and the Thibetan Frontier in October-December 1873*,[111] wrote an article on later Buddhism containing a particularly virulent condemnation of Tantric Buddhism and criticised the scholars who, at least in part, defended it in the name of a theism which 'seem[ed] to have obscured their moral sense'. Edgar concluded his presentation as follows:

> It seems an accepted notion among people who get their ideas from the worthless books which have long passed current as Buddhist history, that the religion was driven out by Brahminist persecutions somewhere about the end of the seventh or the beginning of the eighth century after Christ; but I believe this to be an almost groundless fiction. These two centuries seem to have been pre-eminently a time of public controversy, when Brahmins challenged Buddhists, and men of one sect of Buddhism challenged those of other sects, to support their opinion in public. [...] the Buddhists were sometimes defeated, and had to pay the penalty. It is also quite possible that local disputes may have led to local persecutions. But it is a matter of absolute certainty to me that the Brahminists and Buddhists lived on fairly good terms till Buddhism in India was destroyed by the Mussulmans in the eleventh and twelfth centuries [...].[112]

Similar statements were to be uncritically repeated for more than a century. The publication, ten years later, of Monier Monier-Williams's comprehensive volume on *Buddhism in its Connections with Brāhmanism and Hindūism, and in its Contrast with Christianity* made a particular impact.[113] Monier-Williams was Wilson's successor as professor of Sanskrit at Oxford, the founder of the Indian Institute, and the author of a Sanskrit-English dictionary in use to this day. His prestige as a scholar was enhanced by his being an Evangelist of the Church of England,[114] whose missionary zeal was, at the time, ambitiously addressed to the conversion of India to Christianity. Besides identifying the 'truest and earliest form of Buddhism' with Pāli Buddhism,[115] he introduced a construct destined to become commonplace: Buddhism, originated within Brahmanism, reverted peacefully to it. Buddhism becomes an episode of Brahmanism:

It may, I think, be confidently affirmed that what ultimately happened in most parts of India was, that Vaishṇavas and Śaivas crept up softly to their rival and drew the vitality out of its body by close and friendly embraces, and that instead of the Buddhists being expelled from India, Buddhism gradually and quietly lost itself in Vaishṇavism and Śaivism. [...]

Its ruined temples, monasteries, monuments, and idols are scattered everywhere, while some of these have been perpetuated and adopted by those later phases of Hindūism which its own toleration helped to bring into existence.

At all events it may be safely affirmed that the passing away of the Buddhistic system in India was on the whole like the peaceful passing away of a moribund man surrounded by his relatives, and was at least unattended with any agonizing pangs.[116]

It was thanks to Vishnuism and Sivaism if Buddhism 'dropped its unnaturally pessimistic theory of life and its unpopular atheistic character, and accommodated itself to those systems'.[117] For Monier-Williams, even the establishment of a celibate monastic order had in it 'something altogether agreeable to the spirit and usages of Brāhmanism',[118] although he certainly knew that the celibacy of monks was one of the targets of the orthodox, who considered it a major threat for social order. The difference between Buddhism and Brahmanism is admitted, but is minimised also from the social point of view – a construct that continues to enjoy much credit. The core of the Brahmanical system, i.e. the preservation at any cost, for all the necessary adaptations, of caste privileges, largely escaped Monier-Williams, for whom caste division was just one of the innumerable Indian oddities:

It has been usual to blame the Brāhmans for their arrogant exclusiveness, but their arrogance has been rather shown in magnifying their caste-privileges and carrying them to an extravagant pitch, than in preventing any discussion of their own dogmas, or in resenting any dissent from them.

The very essence of Brāhmanism was tolerance. Every form of opinion was admissible [...]. The only delicate ground, on which it was dangerous for any reformer to tread, was caste. The only unpardonable sin was the infringement of caste-rules. Nor was anyone tempted to adopt the rôle of a violent agitator, when all were free to express any opinion they liked without hindrance, provided they took care to abstain from any act of interference with caste-privileges.[119]

India as depicted by Monier-Williams is entirely unreal, an exotic dream: we can easily imagine him, once the Mutiny was put down, seated in his bungalow attended by well-trained and silent servants:

The peculiar calm of an Indian atmosphere, though occasionally disturbed by political storms sweeping from distant regions, has rarely been stirred by violent religious antagonisms. The various currents of Hindū religious life have flowed peacefully side by side, and reformers have generally done their work quietly. As for Gautama, there can be little doubt that [...] he imbibed his tolerant ideas from the Brāhmanism in which he had been trained.[120]

At Ellora, brāhmaṇas, Buddhists and Jains 'lived on terms of fairly friendly tolerance, much as the members of the Anglican, Roman Catholic, and Wesleyan communions live in Europe at the present day', and even in modern Benares, he said, in 'the stronghold of Brahmanism, I witnessed similar proofs of amicable mutual intercourse'.[121] Even well documented conflicts are denied or played down, the only exceptions being those in south India, for which the evidence was too strong to be ignored:

It must nevertheless be admitted, that in the extreme South of India, and perhaps eventually at Benares and a few other strongholds of Brāhmanism, the difference between the systems became so accentuated as to lead to grievous conflicts. Whether blood was shed it is impossible to prove; but it is alleged, with some degree of probability, that violent crusades against Buddhism were instituted by Kumārila and Śaṅkara – two well-known Southern Brāhmans noted for their bigotry – in the seventh and eighth centuries of our era. It does not appear, however, that they were successful either in the conversion or extermination of Buddhists.

Thomas William Rhys Davids, the then highest authority in the field of Buddhist studies, put a seal on Monier-Williams's assessment with a paper at the Paris Conference of 1897 addressed to the parterre of orientalists to whom he devolved the *interpretatio autentica* of Indian history. He made a distinction between war massacres and persecutions, and questioned the existence of the latter, from those of Puṣyamitra and Śaśāṅka to that promoted by Kumārila Bhaṭṭa. Conversely, he gave full credit to the sources that documented, or seemed to document, Muslim violence. At Nālandā, 'they not only destroyed the buildings – without any military necessity – but burnt the books and murdered the unoffending students. It is impossible to deny in this case that religious rancor was as much to blame as mere ignorant savagery. And the signs of murder and arson at Sarnath are probably due to the same gentle hands'.[122]

The logic of war could be invoked also in the case of Nālandā,[123] but the principles appealed to by the author in relation to the conflicts between Indian-born religions did not seem to apply in that case. In India, with a few negligible exceptions,

> [...] the adherents of faith logically so diametrically opposed lived side by side for a thousand year in profound peace. It is a phenomenon most striking to the Western historian, who will not refuse to recognise, as one continuing factor, the memory of the marvellous tolerance of the great Buddhist emperor Asoka. But this tolerance itself rests on anterior causes. It must be reckoned to the credit of the Indian people as a whole; and it is evidence of the wide spread, in the valley of the Ganges, during the centuries before Asoka, of a higher level of enlightenment and culture than has, I venture to think, been hitherto sufficiently recognised in the West.[124]

The statements contained in texts such as those divulged by Reverend Taylor, 'written centuries after the events they refer to, and unsupported by details sufficient to form any judgement as to what is really meant, are not evidence of persecution at all. They are only proof the belief of the persons making the statements.'[125] Rhys Davids did not seem to realise that his words could easily backfire on him, since Indian texts written much later than the described events were very numerous indeed, and included Pāli texts. But the construct had already been introduced that in the crucial field of religious tolerance and freedom India was, from time immemorial, a different place, and a model to draw inspiration from. A decade before, the movement for universal peace had been launched, and the first Universal Peace Congress had been held in Paris in 1889 (the last being held in Zurich in 1939). The question of religious intolerance was one of the debated issues, and the scene was dominated by the Indian model. The need for interreligious dialogue was underlined by Max Müller:

> If the members of the principal religions of the world wish to understand one another, to bear with one another, and possibly to recognise certain great truth which, without being aware of it, they share in common with one another, the

only solid and sound foundation for such a religious peace-movement will be supplied by a study of the Sacred Books of each religion.

One such religious Peace-Congress has been held already in America. Preparations for another are now being made; and it is certainly a sign of the times when we see Cardinal Gibbons, after conferring with Pope Leo XIII at Rome, assuring those who are organising this new congress: 'The Pope will be with you, I know it. Write, agitate, and do not be timid'.[126]

Here is at work the bourgeois secularism of the nineteenth century: religions have the right to exist, but cannot go beyond certain limits and pretend to represent the whole reality. Modern society can work only if each religion takes a step back, leaving the state as final arbiter. The principle of religious neutrality, reinforced after the Mutiny, introduced in India one of the cornerstones of the bourgeois state: it would work only in part.

Rhys Davids reintroduced a binary interpretive model: the incompatibility between brāhmaṇas and Buddhists was replaced by that between the Muslims and a unified, non-Muslim India. Just around the mid-1890s, the separation between Hindus and Muslims was becoming a political issue,[127] and it is hard to determine whether the political events weighed on the interpretation of the past, or else the new paradigm legitimised them.

Exoticism marred fundamental political questions, and an exotic 'elsewhere' was created. It was the equivalent, as far as religion was concerned, of the exoticist views of China, dreamt of by the Enlightenment as a country ruled by a tolerant and wise hierarchy, an example for obscurantist Europe. Exoticism applied to the world of religion goes probably back to Edgar Quinet's magniloquent *Du génie des religions*, published in 1842. Son of the Enlightenment and of the French Revolution, Quinet did not commit himself to any religion, but, in accord with the spirit of the *Romantik* – he translated Johann Gottfried Herder into French – expressed sympathy for them all.[128] In his book, Quinet devoted a remarkable space to Indian religions and lavished praise on them, although he concluded stating that the common denominator of Indian religions was inaction – a construct that, as we shall see in the next chapter, will nourish Max Weber. He also introduced the idea of the incalculable antiquity of the Vedas and of the extraordinary wisdom of Indian thought: 'les orientalistes publièrent qu'une antiquité plus profonde, plus philosophique, plus poétique tout ensemble que celle de la Grèce et de Rome, surgissait du fond le l'Asie. Orphée cédera-t-il à Vyasa, Sophocle à Calidasa, Platon à Sancara?'[129] We find in embryo much of the bad literature that was to follow, marked by pseudo-history, exoticism and spiritualism.[130]

When, at the close of the century, Rhys Davids attributed religious tolerance to the 'Indian people as a whole' – a statement that had to sound rather absurd even in the cultural context of the period – we are before an extremist form of exoticism. It is the beginning of that process which, in the following century, thanks to the unwanted complicity of Leninist theories, will see many Westerners overburden themselves with a sense of guilt for being the heirs of a historical past deemed to be, when compared to that of other cultures, not only extraordinarily aggressive towards the exterior, but terrible in itself.

THE YEARS OF INDEPENDENCE

Indian upper caste elites were quick to take advantage of the unexpected bonus granted to them by Western scholars. Before and after Independence, a conscious revision of ancient Indian history was firmly pursued. It was pursued to such a degree that nowadays early nineteenth century constructs and the facts discovered at that time are very little known. Hindu revivalists were very active on the political scene from the 1870s, when the history of Indian religions started being rewritten, in Max Müller's footsteps, in the exclusive light of the Vedas, as was done, in particular, by Dayananda Saraswati, who in 1873 founded the Ārya Samāj.[131] The positions of Monier-Williams and T.W. Rhys Davids became *idées reçues* accepted by all but a few European scholars and a few Indian intellectuals who were staunch nationalists but not conformists, as for instance K.P. Jayaswal. The religious and social tolerance attributed to Hinduism (an increasingly popular term), was turned into an identity trait and into a card which was played at the political level until very recent times. The Mahātmā would place tolerance side by side with *ahiṃsā* so as to cause a complete merging of the two concepts.

The conceptualisation of the positions matured between the end of the nineteenth and the early decades of the twentieth century was due to Ananda K. Coomaraswamy. He was in line with what was being written on Indian cultural identity, and made his own even the exhortation to awakening made by Pierre Loti to young Egyptians, as we read in the preface to the *Essays in National Idealism*.[132] He also made his own the concept of swadeshi [*svadeśī*], criticising no less than the capitalist ownership of the means of production typical of the West.[133] Coomaraswamy shared the opinion that 'India is the land of religious tolerance',[134] but his intellectual refinement put him in the position of discussing the relationship between Brahmanism and Buddhism in a much more original and complex way than scholars like Monier-Williams would have ever been able to do. 'All writers upon Buddhism – he wrote in 1916 – are faced with the difficulty to explain in what respect the teaching of Gautama differs from the higher phases of Brāhman thought', given that the polemics of the Buddhists 'was after all merely the popular aspect of Brāhmanism'.[135] Such polemics was addressed towards a wrong target, however: probably the Buddha had never 'encountered a capable exponent of the highest Vedāntic idealism', and the Buddhists had never 'really understood the pure doctrine of the Ātman'.[136]

Two points raised by Coomaraswamy are worth mentioning. The first is that the teaching of Gautama, emphasised by the 'exponents of Buddhism' (namely, the Western advocates of Pāli Buddhism) was too limited an ideal to stand comparison with Brahmanism. Only Buddhism as a whole, inclusive of Mahāyāna and Vajrayāna, stood comparison with Brahmanism. This allowed Coomaraswamy to state that '[t]here is no true opposition of Buddhism and Brāhmanism, but from the beginning one general movement, or many closely related movements. The integrity of Indian thought [...] would not be broken if every specifically Buddhist element were omitted.'[137] He did not understand, or did not want to see, that Mahāyāna and Vajrayāna aimed at preserving the core of Buddhist identity in a situation where Brahmanical pressure had become so great as to put the religion of Dharma with its back to the wall. The second point is that Coomaraswamy, radicalising earlier views, considered 'unhistorical' the assumption 'that Gautama was a successful reformer who broke the chains of caste [...]'.[138] The real reformers were the brāhmaṇas

> who have seen a profound significance in the maintenance of the order of the world, considering it a school where ignorance may be gradually dispelled. It is they who occupied themselves with the development of an ideal society, which they anticipated in the Utopias of Vālmīki, Vyāsa, and Manu.[139]

At the time of the Buddha, 'the so-called chains' of caste system did not even exist, and in any case the existing system 'is a sort of 'Guild Socialism' within which each caste is 'self-governing, internally democratic'.[140] This extraordinary reversal of facts delegitimised Buddhism as an autonomous system also from the point of view of its social impact: nothing remained of it after its doctrine had already been denigrated. India never gave birth to opposing, incompatible systems: there was one India that, in the past as in the present, mediated internal conflicts having as her guides the great founders of neo-Brahmanism: Manu, Vālmīki, Vyāsa.

Coomaraswamy discussed again the relationship between the two systems forty years later, when the influence of René Guénon had been manifest in his writings for a long time: it is now the champion of *philosophia perennis*, the esoteric Coomaraswamy who speaks, as distant as possible from the concerns of history, which is entirely reabsorbed within a principial reality.[141] We are in the 1940s, and Coomaraswamy's position appears unchanged: 'The more superficially one studies Buddhism, the more it seems to differ from the Brahmanism in which it originated; the more profound our study, the more difficult it becomes to distinguish Buddhism from Brahmanism, or to say in what respect, if any.'[142] Coomaraswamy repeats that the Buddha was not a social reformer: if he ever was a reformer at all, it 'is not to establish a new order but to restore an older form' that he descended from heaven.[143] The Buddha was not even a man, but Man, whatever 'a majority of modern scholars, euhemerist by temperament and training' may say.[144] Buddhist myth and doctrine are de-historicised in a sea of learned quotations where the reader, though lost in admiration, cannot but get drowned – from Plato to St. Bernard, from Meistér Eckhart to Descartes back to antiquity to Plutarch, let alone those borrowed from Indian texts.[145] Although little read and not always well understood in India, Coomaraswamy's positions *vis-à-vis* its cultural and religious history were perfectly clear. They were much more conservative than those professed by the majority of Indian intellectuals, from which he was separated by a personal history that had made him an Indian nationalist but also, and even more deeply, a European Indologist who paid a high price to his own intelligence.[146]

If we turn from Coomaraswamy's a-historical level – legitimate in itself but invalidated by a strong ideological bias – to the level of historical research, mention should be made of one of the most important works written and edited around that time by Ramesh Chandra Majumdar, the historian of Independent India. The first volume of *The History of Bengal*, was published in 1943, but was composed in the 1930s. It contains a thorough acquittal of brāhmaṇas'responsibilities; there we read with interest the pages exculpating Śaśāṅka from the accusations of both Xuanzang, 'whose writings betray a deep personal prejudice, amounting to hatred, against him',[147] and Bāṇabhaṭṭa. With reference to the murder of Rājyavardhana in AD 606, Majumdar, distancing himself from other historians who, underlining the agreement between contemporary sources, were inclined to give credit to the story, maintained that

> [...] Hiuen Tsang made no secret of his wrath against Śaśāṅka for his anti-Buddhist activities. That Hiuen Tsang was ready, nay almost glad, to believe anything discreditable to Śaśāṅka, is abundantly clear from the various stories he has recorded of Śaśāṅka's persecution of Buddhism, and his ignoble death. The attitude of Bāṇa is also quite clear from the contemptuous epithets like *Gauḍādhama* and *Gauḍabhujaṅga* by which he refers to Śaśāṅka.
>
> Such witnesses would be suspect even if their stories were complete, rational, and consistent. But unfortunately both the stories are so vague and involve such an abnormal element as would not be believed except on the strongest evidence.[148]

Had Majumdar really required 'the strongest evidence' for other events of Bengal history, he would have hardly been able to start writing his book. The task of a historian is not just to produce incontrovertible documents, but generate hypotheses based on whatever traces may be available – traces which, though difficult to assess for many periods of Indian history, are nevertheless extremely important. It is hardly fair to use a double standard when dealing with them. Although Majumdar raised doubts on the 'numerous acts of oppression perpetrated by Śaśāṅka against the Buddhists', he could not discard a piece of information of a typically historical nature, that Harṣavardhana's mission, as explained by Xuanzang, was to 'raise Buddhism from the ruin into which it had been brought by the king of Karṇasuvarṇa', and that Śaśāṅka, a fervent Sivaite, waged war against him to hasten the decline of Buddhism. Majumdar's comment was that the truth about Śaśāṅka's 'acts of oppression' rested upon 'the sole evidence of the Buddhists writers who cannot, by any means, be regarded as unbiased or unprejudiced, at least in any matter which either concerned Śaśāṅka or adversely affected Buddhism.[149]

With his authority, Majumdar eclipsed Indian intellectuals who had not entirely fallen into line. Radhagovinda Basak, for instance, had maintained that Śaśāṅka could not be exculpated from his cruel actions.[150] K.P. Jayaswal, who died in 1937,[151] had not denied the facts reported in the last chapter of the *Mañjuśrīmūlakalpa*, even when anti-Buddhist persecutions were mentioned,[152] but for Majumdar even this evidence was 'somewhat vague and uncertain', and it would have been, therefore, 'extremely unsafe to accept the statements recorded in this book as historical'.[153] The point is that he denounced *all* the sources providing evidence on what he was not willing to admit. Instead, quite unproblematic is Majumdar's treatment of the collapse of the Pālas and the normalisation of north-eastern India carried out by the Senas. He considers it as a normal political rotation, the only real break in the history of the region being, predictably, the Muslim conquest. The idea that Sena policy substantially contributed to the final collapse of Buddhism does not seem to have ever come to his mind. We see here at work one of the most unfortunate, inclusive construct of Indian historiography, that of the existence of a unified 'Pāla-Sena period'.

If we have lingered over *The History of Bengal*, it is partly because it would be impossible to analyse in detail Majumdar's major work, the planning and editing of the monumental *History and Culture of the Indian People*, the first volume of which was published in 1951, and the last in 1977. Majumdar's presence as editor is constant. He makes himself heard through brief introductions and *mises au point*, unifying the message he wanted Indian students and the outside world to receive. The *History and Culture*, reprinted many times and considered the best achievement of Independent India in the field of historical research, is the product of a century-long debate. The idea that India was the guardian and guide to universal peace and tolerance is central and even more effective in that the tone of the work is seldom over the top.

Three points deserve our attention: the insistence on the 'catholicism' of Brahmanism, the responsibility of Buddhism for its own crisis and that of Islam for its final destruction. Regarding the first point, almost universally accepted and already discussed, the role of the brāhmaṇas in actively fighting Buddhism is ignored because conflict in Indian history is seen as exclusively imported from the outside. Even in later times, Hindus 'did not show any lack of the spirit of toleration which marked the religious evolution in India through the ages. This spirit was displayed even towards the Muslims in the face of the greatest provocation caused by their iconoclastic fury'.[154]

Regarding the second point, Majumdar maintained that the degradation of religious life became a widespread phenomenon with the introduction of Tantric practices. Tantrism, which affected both Buddhism and Brahmanism, was responsible for

> [...] the degradation in ideas of decency and sexual morality brought about by the religious practices. How far this evil corroded the whole society would be plain from a study of contemporary literature. [...] It is impossible to describe in a modern book some of the worst features of Tāntrik theories and practices which have been described by an eminent Indian scholar to be "at once the most revolting and horrible that human depravity could think of". Fortunately the esoteric character of Tāntrik religion limited its field of operation, and it may be conceded that such debased forms of religious practices were exceptional and not normal.[155]

It was the 'universal appeal' of Buddhism that 'wrought its own ruin'. In order to satisfy the masses, it 'had to come down from its high pedestal to their level and present itself in a popular garb', and by an 'inevitable process it also incorporated to a large extent the crude ideas, beliefs and religious practices held by them'.[156] Here Majumdar hits the point: late Buddhism had advocated the cause of the outcastes, rousing a real social war. And yet, instead of laying his cards on the tables, he prefers to avoid a difficult discussion, maintaining that whereas 'the growth of Tāntrik ideas was sapping the vitality of Buddhism, Brahmanical religion was enthroned on a high pedestal by philosophers like Śaṅkarācārya, whose 'triumphant career' did not simply assure the success of Sivaism, but of Brahmanism as a whole.[157]

The real destroyers – this is the third point – were the Muslims, who were not only foreign conquerors, but had deeply wounded the religious susceptibilities of the Hindus 'by indiscriminate demolition of temples and destruction of images of gods on a large scale'.[158] The disappearance of Buddhism 'from the land of its birth' seems to have as its principal reason 'the destruction by foreign invaders of the numerous monasteries in Bihār and Bengal which formed the stronghold of that religion',[159] a commonplace view that we shall discuss in Chapter VI.

An example of reasoning where facts are provocatively turned upside down is contained in a passage by K.A. Nilakantha Sastri, the distinguished historian of south India:

In view of the fact that religious persecution in ancient India was an exception rather than the rule, and keeping in mind the tendency of the Buddhist writers to distort facts and invent imaginary accounts of the evil deeds of non Buddhists – even Aśoka has not been spared – we cannot give the same credence to these accounts as has been accorded by some writers. While it may be conceded that some Buddhists, particularly the monks, may have suffered from certain disabilities, the story of a general persecution of all and sundry is evidently the invention of frustrated minds which found that the state patronage was rapidly being shifted to Brahmins, and were aghast at the revival of the ancient Vedic ritual of the *aśvamedha*. It is not even unlikely that the hardships of the Buddhists were in many cases due to political reasons and were of their own inviting.[160]

That certain facts never happened, and could never have happened in India, here becomes axiomatic. What Nilakantha Sastri noted a few years later in relation to the well-known episode of the execution of the Jains by Kūṇ Pāṇṭya ('This, however, is little more than an unpleasant legend and cannot be treated as history. There is no reason to believe that, even in those days of intense religious strife, intolerance descended to such cruel barbarities') may reassure us on his good faith, but warns us against his blindness as a historian.[161]

To conclude with *The History and Culture of the Indian People*, the assessment on Aśoka's personality and deeds is of particular interest because it is part of a broader debate on Indian culture and policy. Radha Kumud Mookerji, who wrote the chapter on the Mauryan emperor, was persuaded that Aśoka became a Buddhist convert. A few years earlier, B.M. Barua, had shown that Aśoka's *dhamma* derived directly from the Buddhist scriptures.[162] For Mookerji, however, what Aśoka really stood for was the religion of *ahiṃsā*: 'His was a total pursuit of non-violence in every sphere', and if he was unable to abolish capital punishment, it probably was because 'man who can distinguish between right and wrong' is less innocent than animals. The India that had just attained independence had little to offer to the world emerging from the Second World War besides the ideology of non-violence, which was made partly credible by Gandhi's political action and partly ludicrous by the bullet that killed him and the disasters of Partition. Making *ahiṃsā* the body bolster of Indian history from so remote a time, meant adding further authority to the model and providing it not only with political, but also with historical dignity.

Political use of an idealised Aśoka was made by Jawaharlal Nehru when he decided that the *cakra* surmounting the Aśokan capital at Sarnath should be reproduced on the central, white band of the Indian flag. It was 'a symbol of India's ancient culture', a symbol 'of the many things that India had stood for through the ages'. Aśoka for Nehru was 'one of the most magnificent names not only in India's history but in world history', especially in a 'moment of strife, conflict and intolerance'.[163] When a few years later, in 1950, the whole Sarnath capital – accompanied by a motto taken from the *Muṇḍaka Upaniṣad* – was chosen as the emblem of the country, and reproduced on banknotes and passports, the appropriation of a past rewritten to serve the official ideology was completed. Since then, the Sarnath capital, brought to light in 1905, speaks with a voice that is not its own: it also shows that excess of polishing typical of the chemical treatment that had become common in Britain at the end of the eighteenth century, when the original lustre of stones and marbles was revived according a practice that continued for a long time.

In actual reality, Aśoka had been cast into oblivion for two millennia, and modern Indians had first heard of him by James Prinsep in 1837:[164] his *ahiṃsā*, though based on historical facts, was not authoritative for the orthodox, who could not but consider it as milk originally pure, put into a dog-skin bag.[165] Now Aśoka had been transformed into the inimitable model of Indian history. Contemporary divided India could not be said to have a unified history, but ancient India could. Vasudeva S. Agrawala ratified the brahmanisation of the *cakradhvaja* overloading the Sarnath capital with a heavy symbolism where the Buddhist pertinence of the artefact gets entirely lost.[166] The historians of Independence transformed beliefs nourished by exoticism into the tools that made up the image of their country. This image lasted for decades to come, even when the ideology of non-violence turned into pro-Soviet pacifism. The emergence of *hindutva* and the modernisation of the country have eventually outdated it.

ANOTHER INDIA

A few nationalist scholars followed an entirely different approach to the Indian past in the effort to shape Hindu identity, directly or indirectly recognising that India had not a unified history but many histories. For Kashi Prasad Jayaswal, Buddhism was an alien system and an anti-national movement, fought against not only by the Śuṅgas but also by many other dynasties. The Indian 'nation' is identified with the 'nation' of the brāhmaṇas, and is not an all-inclusive concept. Jayaswal's influential book of 1933, *History of India, 150 A.D. to 350 A.D.*, may sound outdated today, but comes as an exception to historiographic conformism and raises non secondary questions. Jayaswal's nationalism may be regarded as naïve concerning certain aspects, but is not overflowing with sentiment and is closer to the actual facts. The 'legitimate' dynasties that emerged in several parts of India from the second century AD onwards voiced a deep-rooted identity that would emerge fully in Gupta time. They tried to put an end to the unbearable abuses of the Buddhists and the Kuṣāṇas such as that carried out by Vanaspara, who was first the Kuṣāṇa governor and then Viceroy in the territory of Benares:[167]

> He made the population practically Brahmin-less (*prajāś ch-ā-brahma-bhūyishṭhāḥ*). He depressed the high-class Hindus and raised low-caste men and foreigners to high positions. He abolished the Kshatriyas and created a new ruling caste. He made his subjects un-Brahmanical. The same policy was followed by the later Kushans [...] – a policy of social tyranny, and religious fanaticism – both actuated by political motives. Vanaspara created a new ruling or official class out of the Kaivartas (a low caste of aboriginal agriculturists, now called *Kewaṭ*) and out of the *Pañchakas*, i.e. castes lower than the Śūdras—the untouchables.[168]

Jayaswal was aware of the existence of a structural, identitarian question and captured the link between the fortunes of Buddhism and foreign domination and influence. Orthodox dynasties performed rituals exclusively intended for brāhmaṇas, such as the *bṛhaspatisava*,[169] not to speak of the *aśvamedha*, which was a symbol of political revival in strict connection with military campaigns.[170] Jayaswal clearly saw that when no foreign kings were left, it was against the Buddhist kings that the *aśvamedha* was performed. He understood the reasons of the otherwise unaccountable revival of the horse ritual by Puṣyamitra Śuṅga and Śātakarṇi Sātavāhana, and understood as well the role played by the Guptas after AD 344 and the reasons of their Bhāgavata commitment. The identification, made possible by *bhakti*, between king and God made the former 'the missionary and agent of the Lord', and the Guptas 'felt and believed that they were Vishṇu's servants and agents, that they had a mission from Vishṇu, that like Vishṇu they should conquer the unrighteous and rightless sovereigns, and that like Vishṇu they should rule in full sovereignty [...].'[171] We are far from the conformist glorification of the Guptas as tolerant rulers and patrons of the arts popularised by Independence scholars – a groundless vision, as we shall see. Jayaswal confers to the Guptas the importance they have for the right reason, that of embodying a political model that was both profoundly rethought with respect to Vedic tenets and alternative to the thought of the *śramaṇa*-s.

The nub of neo-Brahmanical and Hindu identity and, conversely, the anti-Brahmanical, *mleccha* nature of Buddhism were perfectly caught by Babasaheb R. Ambedkar, the neglected *pater patriae*, advocate of a political project that aimed to overturn Indian society from its very foundations. He was as distant as possible from a man like Jayaswal, but he shared the same opinion on the incompatibility of the two systems. Both Jayaswal and Ambedkar, from the opposite poles of the social hierarchy (or, better to say, from two separate worlds inhabiting the same territory), had in common very deep roots in traditional India and were indifferent to good manners.

Ambedkar shared the opinion that Buddhism had been overthrown by the Muslims, but made unusual observations. The first was that at the time of the Muslim invasion the Indian states were entirely under Brahmanical control and Brahmanism had the support of the state, whereas Buddhism did not enjoy such support. The second, very perspicacious (although not entirely true), was that Buddhism was handicapped by the creation of its priesthood, which was neither so organised nor so pervasive within society as in Brahmanism, where *gṛhastha*-s are not less entitled as priests than *bhikṣuka*-s. The difference between the two systems was so great that 'it contain[ed] the whole reason why Brahmanism survived the attack of Islam and why Buddhism did not'.[172] Buddhist priests could not be easily replaced, while '[e]very Brahmin alive became priest and took the place of every Brahmin priest who died'.[173]

Ambedkar's third consideration stemmed from the question, posed by Surendra Nath Sen, of the distribution of Muslim population in India. Sen had observed that it was no accident that 'the Punjab, Kashmir, the district around Behar Sharif, North-East Bengal where Muslims now predominate, were all strong Buddhist centres in the pre-Muslim days'. As had happened in Sind, this was ascribable to the prospect of improvement that the Buddhists expected regarding their political status.[174] Ambedkar observed that 'the causes that have forced the Buddhist population of India to abandon Buddhism in favour of Islam have not been investigated', but was inclined to believe that the persecution of the Brahmanic kings was responsible for the result. He concluded by saying that 'the fall of Buddhism was due to the Buddhist becoming converts to Islam as a way of escaping the tyranny of Brahmanism'.[175] Ambedkar would have certainly developed this intuition if he had had at his disposal a more reliable chronology and a less reticent literature.

PARADIGMS OF OBLIVION

In the 1950s and 1960s, a new class of historians emerged which, in the light of Marxist theories and of the increasingly successful analyses provided by the methods of the social sciences, started replacing the concerns typical of the previous generation with investigations aimed to retrieve an Indian past freed from both narrow nationalism and official Indology. The founder of this new group of historians was Damodar Dharmananda Kosambi, followed by Ram Sharan Sharma, Irfan Habib, Dwijendra Narayan Jha, Romila Thapar, Radha Champakalakshmi, and a few others. Despite their different attitudes towards Marxist orthodoxy, their contributions have several points in common, including the capacity to exploit the known sources with new insights and the new ones with unusual attention.[176]

Despite his approach to Indian history, Kosambi accepted without discussion the vulgate on the end of the Buddhist monasteries of north-eastern India, making his own the idea of India as 'a land that could tolerate many incompatible systems at the same time', even though 'they [the Indians] would not bother to make a permanent record of their traditions and doctrine'. The latter was a surprising statement for a scholar so attentive to micro-history and well aware that brāhmaṇas have recorded absolutely everything with regard to their own institutions and customs: what they did not want to perpetuate was the history that was not their own. For Kosambi, '[t]he question of the "restoration of Hinduism" or of some king being Buddhist or Hindu [wa]s meaningless': the donations made at Sarnath about AD 1150 was due to a 'Buddhist' (in inverted commas) queen of a Hindu king, Govindracandra Gāhaḍavāla.[177] Paradoxically, Kosambi seems to go beyond nationalist historians. R.C. Majumdar denied facts, but tried to explain; Kosambi seems to have been persuaded that the problem did not even exist, refusing, against his own convictions, to understand that a sovereign embracing one religious system rather than another is likely to indicate radical changes in the social and political set-up of a given territory.[178]

Economic activity is crucial, but may be seen – not considering deep, *longue durée* processes – as just one of the several activities to which man is committed; many other activities, inextricably intertwined with it, are carried on at the same time. Historians take the task of arranging a huge and confused mass of material and, in the impossibility of analysing the phenomena in all their aspects, hierarchising them, but we do not *know* if man's activities and perceptions, as well as social phenomena, are ordered, *per se*, according to some objective hierarchy. For Marxist and post-Marxist historians, who often forget how important is the 'superstructure' in Marx's construct, religious and ethnic identities, ideological factors and even the role of the élites (despite the importance of vanguards in Marxist theory and praxis) are generally subordinated to what is taken to be the economic 'base' of society, or are at best thought to be enacted by social 'forces' often escaping analysis. The scattered knowledge we have of this economic 'base' for many periods of ancient India makes the constructs all the more fragile.

With regard to the questions examined here, Romila Thapar's positions as they have developed through time are worth mentioning. She is the only modern historian who has paid some attention to the matter. In a conference held in 1987, she observed – and it was a criticism long due from official historians – that

> [t]he insistence on the tradition of religious tolerance and non-violence as characteristic of Hinduism, which is built on a selection of normative values emphasising *ahiṃsā*, is not borne out by the historical evidence. The theory is so deeply ingrained among most Indians that there is a failure to see the reverse of it even when it stares them in the face. The extremity of intolerance implicit in the notion of untouchability was glossed over by regarding it as a function of society and caste. The fact of this intolerance is now conceded so casually, that the concession is almost beginning to lose meaning. Apart from this, we also need to look at more direct examples of religious persecution. Curiously, even when historians have referred to such activities as indications of intolerance and persecution, there has been a firm refusal on the part of popular opinion to concede that Hindu sects did indulge in religious persecution.[179]

Thapar recalled the anti-Buddhist persecutions in Kashmir and the manifest hatred against Buddhists and Jains transpiring in literary works and iconographic sources.[180] After mentioning the anti-Jain persecutions in south India by the Sivaites, she rightly observed that '[w]e have here a major historical problem which requires detailed investigation': if the question had not been tackled by historians, it was because of the desire 'to portray tolerance and non-violence as the eternal values of the Hindu tradition'.[181] For the first time a modern historian recognised the existence of a serious historiographic problem. 'A related question – Thapar further noted – is whether the Hindus as a community were aware of or perpetrated this hostility, or whether it was perpetrated only by a segment of the Hindu community, substantially the Śaivas.'[182] Thapar supported the latter interpretation, even though it was not 'to suggest that the Vaiṣṇavas were altogether partial to Buddhists and Jainas. But there seem to be fewer examples of persecution perpetrated by the Vaiṣṇavas.'[183] This conviction, probably conditioned by the later developments of Vishnuism, has prevented Thapar from evaluating the events in their complexity and extent, as also did her opinion that religious violence originated only about the middle of the first millennium AD, gaining force 'through the centuries until Buddhism eventually fled the country and Jainism was effectively limited to a few pockets'.[184] That, at a certain point, the process accelerated, is true, but a careful analysis shows that violence played an important role since a much earlier time, since when the *śramaṇa*-s showed their capacity to build an actual, theoretically autonomous political power. But Thapar has never subscribed to the idea that Aśoka's policy was strictly dependent on his having embraced Buddhism,[185] and it has thus been impossible for her to identify a real, dramatic fracture in ancient Indian society. She admits that the Mauryas supported heterodox sects, but maintains that they 'were not hostile to Brahmanism', the principles of Aśoka's *dhamma* being such 'that they would have been acceptable to people belonging to any religious sect'.[186] In Thapar's construct Aśoka embodies, to a certain extent, the principles of secularism.

Postponing the discussion on this point to the next chapter, it matters here to underline that in a lecture delivered in 1999, Thapar partly retracted her statements. She observed that even though conflicts are to be expected in a complex society, in India

> the conflict was limited to specific areas and groups, and was not pan-Indian. There was no sense of holy war – a *jehad* or a crusade. Religious intolerance was

less severe when compared to Europe or west Asia, but acute intolerance took a social form, with untouchability constituting the worst form of degradation known to human society.[187]

Thus while it is reaffirmed that untouchability is a form of violence, the other 'major historical problem' requiring detailed investigation identified in 1987 – that of religious violence – reverts to a minor question. The two issues, as we shall see, may be said to be one and the same, and if Buddhism was eventually defeated, it was because the revolt of the natives and of the untouchables ended in failure. Thapar, forgetting the nature and role of the elites (the brāhmaṇas in India), believes that Hindus had no consciousness of belonging to a religious community, and that, therefore, their stand against other sects was segmented and episodic.[188] Eventually, in the revised edition of *Early India, from the Origins to* AD *1300*, published in 2002, a book destined to a large audience, the issues raised in 1987 are ignored.[189]

Moving to the opposite side of the historiographic debate, mention should be made of the consequences of *hindutva* theorisation. The extent to which Vinayak Damodar Savarkar, the founder of the *hindutva* movement,[190] was indebted to the interpretive paradigm of Indian history created at the end of the nineteenth century is all too obvious, but contemporary *hindutva* intervenes with devastating violence at the social and political level.[191] Such is its ideological furore that we would be tempted to drop the question. However, *hindutva* ideology is so pervasive that it affects the works of scholars who would never subscribe to its political programme.

Hindutva preaches that being Hindu means having one's own birthplace and sacred sites in India, unlike foreigners and unlike those Indians – Muslims and Christians – who have their main places of worship, and thereby frames of reference elsewhere. The Buddhists are, therefore, Hindus (an old if crudely expressed construct), something that rules out the possibility that anti-Buddhist persecutions ever existed. In the words of a heated supporter of Hindu fundamentalism,

[i]n the case of their purely concocted grand theory of pre-Muslim persecution of Buddhism by Hindus, we see our leftist historians throw all standards of source criticism to the wind. Such is their eagerness to uphold this convenient hypothesis, and their care not to endanger what little supportive testimony there is. After all,

from the millennia of pre-Muslim religious pluralism in India there are not even five testimonies of such persecution, so these few should be scrupulously kept away from criticism.[192]

It is not clear who the secularist historians mentioned by Elst may be, since no Indian scholar has ever tackled the problem of the formation of neo-Brahmanical identity in relation to the other Indian systems. The critics of *hindutva* have been unable or unwilling to discuss the fundamentals of Indian history, and have thus ended in subscribing to at least some of its positions. From the one hand, they have forgotten the contributions of historians such as Jayaswal, driven back by his outspoken nationalism,[193] and on the other, have ignored Ambedkar's insights. However, history weighs, and especially when it is denied, it ends up presenting the bill. In addition to this, scholars with a command of ancient and medieval India history are fewer and fewer,[194] and questioning the fundamentals has become a very difficult task.

Oblivion also comes as the result of a more general trend in modern historiography, which is largely the work of secular, globalised scholars who prefer to smooth edges and tend to ignore hot issues such as the role of religion in both ancient and modern societies. Religion is reduced to an unfortunate component of human behaviour, and there is a propensity to deconstruct it into a number of less controversial issues. The role played by conflicts tends to be equally overshadowed. This attitude is a function of academic interests: to access funds that are increasingly managed by supranational organisations, for all borders to be open, and a quick relocation of activities to take place, conflicts must be kept to a minimum or ignored. A common way to minimise them in writing history is to overlook the role played by strongly motivated elites and the devastating effects that their theories and actions have caused. An analysis of historical issues at the level of the common people is often preferred, because questions of political power are not posed at the base of the social pyramid.

Last but not least, most scholars seem to be culturally and ideologically conditioned by a middle class, as it were, frame of mind – which does not necessarily reflect individual background and upbringing but rather results from an increasing levelling of education and formation in terms of unquestioned bourgeois assumptions. International scholarly exchange is no longer limited to the elite level but, with the development of mobility, information networks and facilities, becomes part of intellectual practice and identity. An awareness of larger issues, however, does not generally foster critical, let alone antagonistic, reorientation of one's methodologies and approaches to the past. The predisposition to turn one's head away from the tragedy and violence of history, inherent to bourgeois ideology and world-view, finds thus new expression within the context of a post-modern middle-class homogenisation, unless issues are involved that can be capitalised to create a distinct profile as scholars of a globalised world.

To a greater or lesser degree, we are all affected by the paradigm of globalisation, and only our successors will be able to clarify the deep reasons of our beliefs and our choices.

NOTES

1. *AsRes* 2 (1790): 123 (W. Jones in his essay 'On the Chronology of the Hindus. Written in January, 1788', pp. 111-46).
2. Ibid.: 124.
3. *ASIR* 1 (1871, A. Cunningham): 114-15, 118-19.
4. *AsRes* 5 (1797): 131-33. For Duncan, 'the worshippers of Buddha [were] a set of Indian heretics', a piece of information that only *paṇḍita*-s could have provided him.
5. Cunningham (1863: cix) quoted Emma Roberts (R. Elliot & E. Roberts, *Views of India, China, and on the Shores of the Red Sea*, 2 vols., London 1835; vol. 2, p. 8). The 'flat tiles', of which 'there were cart loads', were, clearly, votive tablets.
6. Sahni (1923: 7).
7. *AsRes* 1 (1788): 284-87; cf. pp. 286-87; R. Mitra (1878: 202-03). The inscription, dated vs 1005, had been copied from a stone found in Bodhgayā in 1785. For Kīkaṭa, see below, Chapter V.
8. According to some, the inscription was a forgery (R. Mitra 1878: 203-06), but Horace H. Wilson thought that there was no reason to question its authenticity (Wilson 1865*a*: 180); cf. also Fergusson (1884: 80, n. 1).
9. On Buchanan, see Allen (2003: 10 ff. and passim).
10. Buchanan (1936, I: 100).
11. Ibid.: 100-01. An abridged version of Buchanan's report on Patna and Gayā was published by Montgomery Martin in the first volume of *The History, Antiquities, Topography, and Statistics of Eastern India [. . .]*, published in London in 1838. Vyāsa (Vyas) is the *ṛṣi* variously considered to be the arranger of the Vedas, the *Mahābhārata* and the Purāṇas. On the Brahmanical appropriation of Bodhgayā, see below in this chapter, in Chapters V and VI, and especially Appendix 1.

12. Buchanan (1936, I: 101).
13. In his essay on the history of Kashmir based on the *Rājataraṅgiṇī* (*AsRes* 15, 1825: 1-119), Horace H. Wilson wrote, '[. . .] it is equally inexplicable also how a prince of central India, should have borne so prominent a share, in the introduction of a religious innovation, the earliest vestiges of which are so clearly referable to the North West of India, to Bactria or even to Tartary' (p. 112).
14. *AsRes* 10 (1808): 91-92. This issue of the *Asiatick Researches* contains the fifth part, dealing with the 'Origin and Decline of the Christian Religion in India' (pp. 27-157) of Wilford's 'Essay on the Sacred Isles in the West, with Other Essays Connected with that Work'. No mention is made of Carcitā Nagara in the *Kumārikā khaṇḍa* translated by G.V. Tagare (AITMS). On doctrinal debates, see discussion below in Chapter IV.
15. 'Poor Wilford was the laughing stock of the Benares Brahmins for a whole decade' (Keay 1988: 46; cf. also Kejariwal 1988: 43).
16. Kejariwal (1988: 52).
17. Wilford also mentioned the anti-Buddhist persecution 'begun by "Cumarilla Bhattacharya" and carried on afterwards by Sancaracharya, who nearly extirpated the whole race', a topical issue in the nineteenth century. Wilford's main concern was not Buddhism, although he was struck by the fact that '[i]n many parts of the Peninsula, Christians are called, and considered, as followers of Buddha', something that was confirmed by Paolinus a S. Bartholomaeo in his *Systema brahmanicum* (1791: 161).
18. Rao, T.A. Gopinatha (1920, II: 123). Gopinatha Rao, however, accepted the opinion, which had become commonplace, that 'the downfall of Buddhism [wa]s due to Muhammadans' (ibid. 124).
19. R. Mitra (1885: 78-79). On Wilson see also Kejariwal (1988: 118 ff.).
20. Cf. Wilson (1865*a*).
21. Wilson (ibid. 191) distrusted the accuracy of the tradition which attributes to Śaṅkara the annihilation of the Buddhists. See discussion in Chapter IV.
22. Ibid. 197-98.
23. As late as 1838, on the evidence of the Purāṇas, Guptas was for Wilson 'a term indicating a Śúdra Family' (cf. Wilson 1864: 136). It was, in 1837, James Prinsep's translation of the Allahabad Fort inscription, first brought to notice in 1834, which opened a new field of study (Chhabra & Gai 1981: 203).
24. Cf. Wilson (1865*a*: 187).
25. Ibid.: 224-25.
26. Ibid.: 226.
27. The three parts into which the manuscripts were divided ended up in Kolkata, Chennai and London, respectively. Those deposited in the library of the Asiatic Society in Kolkata were eventually moved to Chennai. On Colonel Mackenzie's life, see Mackenzie (1952) and *Mackenzie Manuscripts* (*Mahalingam*): i-xxii.

28. Wilson (1828: xiii).
29. Id. (1828).
30. On the branches of the Royal Asiatic Society and their libraries, cf. Otness (1998).
31. *Mackenzie Manuscripts* 1-6 & Suppl. Summaries of the Mackenzie manuscripts kept in Chennai have been provided in more recent times by T.V. Mahalingam, thanks to whose efforts a catalogue is now available; see *Mackenzie Manuscripts* (*Mahalingam*). We will usually refer to Taylor's work, which provides more expanded summaries than Mahalingam's.
32. *Mackenzie Manuscripts* 7: 100-01.
33. Ibid. 1: 109-10, 121; 3: 6, 32; 5: 14, 18, 25; 6: 430; etc.
34. On Cērumāṉ Perumāḷ, who ruled at the end of the eighth and early ninth century (Sastri, K.A. Nilakantha 1966: 162), see below in Chapter IV.
35. *Mackenzie Manuscripts* 1: 183. See also Logan (1887, I: 228); Menon (1937, III: 124-25); Alexander (1949: 50-51). *Tri-Cárúr* is Trikkariyur (Thrikkariyoor) in Ernakulam district; the Nampūtiri brāhmaṇas had moved there to escape the hardships of the new Buddhist rule.
36. *Mackenzie Manuscripts* 1: 123; 4: 295-96; 5: 328.
37. Ibid. 3: 32. The deeds of Atontai *cakravartin* is often recorded in the manuscripts (e.g. ibid. 1: 110, 120): he is told to have been the son of King Kulottuṅka Cōḷa (ibid. 2: 399).
38. Ibid. 3: 61.
39. Ibid. 4: 284.; cf. also ibid. 1: 121-23; 3: 423, 436.
40. Ibid. 4: 260-61. On this ordeal, see below in Chapter IV.
41. Ibid. 1: 123.
42. Ibid. Suppl.: 83.
43. There is little doubt that Taylor was a stern rationalist: he even took on John Milton because of 'his absurd pauranical description of war in heaven' (ibid. 2: 384).
44. Ibid. 6: 401 (misprints corrected). Sāḷivāhana was a king of Kāñcīpuram protector of the *śramaṇa*-s against which the orthodox waged war. He is mentioned several times in the Mackenzie manuscripts, the most comprehensive text dealing with him being the *Chola púrva Patayam* [*Cōḷa pūrva patayam*], examined by Taylor in his Second Report (ibid. 2: 371-84).
45. Ibid. Suppl.: 81.
46. Ibid. 1: 183; cf. also ibid. 2: 490, 493-94; 6: 418; in a Marathi manuscript with an account of the Kadambas, Paraśurāma's founding exploit is transferred in the Kannada country (ibid. Suppl.: 66).
47. Ibid. 2: 501.
48. Ibid. 4: 11. Here Taylor hit again the mark; see note 51.
49. Recently Kesavan Veluthat has struck a blow for the *Kēralōtpatti* as a reliable historical source (in its own terms), observing that it is expressed in the forms that were found more suitable in the given situation (Veluthat 2006). I hope that Veluthat's observations will encourage a thorough exploration in

terms of actual history of the large amount of un-Rankean material awaiting investigation. We will deal these types of sources throughout this work, and will discuss them in Chapter IV.

50. Wheeler (1869: 232-33).
51. Id. (1874: 369-70).
52. A notable exception has been, for all his reticence on the subject, Vasudeva S. Agrawala (below, Chapter III). For K.P. Jayaswal, cf. below in this chapter. As to Pargiter (1913), the founder of modern Purāṇic studies, he believed some passages of the Purāṇas to be fabrications of the brāhmaṇas and later readers (cf. p. XIX), but considered them as direct sources of history. It should be clear that the construction of the lineage (and thereby of lineages) is in itself part and plan of the Brahmanical ideology of historical, as it were, traceability of the (pure) lineage as an agenda for legitimation.
53. Wheeler (1874: 359-60).
54. Information on Rajendralala Mitra's life can be found in D.K. Mitra (1978).
55. R. Mitra (1878; 1875-80).
56. Cunningham (1863: iii-xii); *ASIR* 1 (1871, id. 79-105; 107-39).
57. *IA* 9 (1880), pp. 113-16, 142-44.
58. D.K. Mitra (1978: 61-62).
59. Fergusson replied to Mitra's criticism in a violent pamphlet with partly racist and partly heavily patronising attitudes of a real scholar who had to mingle with a native *babu* (Fergusson 1884; cf. also U. Singh (2004: xiv-xv).
60. B.N. Mukherji in D.K. Mitra (1978: 53).
61. Buchanan (1936, I: 98-99).
62. R. Mitra (1878: 10); cf. *Gayā Māhātmya*: II.5-6 (pp. 28-29). Kolāhala corresponds to the Brahmayoni hill at Gayā.
63. R. Mitra (1878: 12).
64. Ibid.: 13. For this part of the myth, cf. *Gayā Māhātmya*: II.47-52 (pp. 50-53).
65. R. Mitra (1878: 16-17).
66. Ibid.: 121. Cf. *ASIR* 3 (1874, A. Cunningham): 87, note: 'I suppose they [= the stūpas] have been carried off to Gaya, and are now doing duty as lingams, or symbols of Mahādeva. No conversion is required, as the people accept one of these votive *stūpas* of the Buddhists as a ready-made lingam'. As we shall see in Chapter IV, votive stūpas transformed into *liṅga*-s are also known from Kathmandu.
67. As we shall see, this would have meant admitting the existence of other histories that do not originate from and are not controlled by orthodoxy.
68. R. Mitra (1875-80, II: 175).
69. Id. (1878: 17).
70. Id. (1875-80, II: 180). The author maintains elsewhere that Gayā's navel 'was located at Yājapur, and its memory is preserved in the name of the place Nābhī Kṣetra' (ibid. II: 257).
71. Ibid. (II: 180). The *babu* was far from accepting the apocalyptic vulgate on

the Muslim conquest of India introduced by H.M. Elliot's edition of *The History of India as Told by its Own Historians* in 1849.

72. R. Mitra (1875-80, II: 111). A similar occurrence is recorded by Faxian at Śrāvastī (Chapter III).
73. O'Malley (1903).
74. He based his discussion on the assumption that '[i]t is difficult to associate the demon Gaya with Buddhism for the simple reason that he figures nowhere in its long tradition', and that '[w]e have every reason to doubt if Gaya proper or Benares proper was at any time a site for Buddhist sanctuaries' (Barua 1931-34, I: 40, 45).
75. See, e.g. Granoff (1984). We shall discuss the matter at length, especially in Chapters III and V.
76. In *The Ancient Geography of India*, published in 1871 (see Cunningham 1963). Cunningham restored a number of place names of a rewritten past. Wilson spoke ironically of his linguistic and philological competence defining him 'a courageous etymologist' (Wilson 1862*a*: 313), but, as observed by Chakrabarti (1999: 9) the criticism by some of his contemporaries in retrospect sounds generally 'malicious and invariably trivial'. See Cunningham (1963).
77. We cannot consider the work carried out by Cunningham of the same quality as that of the philologists of his times, who came from a centuries-old tradition. Strata started being recorded in the second half of the nineteenth century, and even then methods and techniques were still too poorly developed for the stratigraphic method to give satisfactory results. An example of primitive stratigraphic reasoning is the following observation regarding the Mahābodhi temple: '[...] five successive layers of flooring were also discovered indicating well-marked and distinct epochs in the history of the temple' (*ASIR* 16, 1883, A. Cunningham & H.B.W. Garrick: 135).
78. Cf. his model of India as a country swinging between political unity and fragmentation (Chakrabarti 1999: 8).
79. *ASIR* 1 (1871, A. Cunningham: 32-3). Temple Site 3 is now numbered Temple F. The first volume of the *Archaeological Reports*, which includes the report on Nālandā, reproduces Cunningham (1863) without any modification.
80. Ibid. 237.
81. Cunningham (1892: 56-57). The last contacts between Bodhgayā and the outside world before modern times seem to have taken place in AD 1472 when King Dhammazedi sent a mission from Burma to take plans of the Bodhi Tree and of the temple as a model for buildings of Pegu (Harvey 1925: 119).
82. Cunningham (1854: 106). It is unlikely that the images were concealed, however (see Appendix 2).
83. Id. (1863: cxv-cxvi); *ASIR* 1 (1871, id.: 126). Major Markham Kittoe, who, as Archaeological Enquirer to the North-Western Provinces, had excavated at Sarnath in 1851-52, died before publishing his notes and drawings (ibid. xxiv-xxvii).

84. Cunningham (1863: cxvii-cxviii); cf. E. Thomas (1854: 472).
85. *ASIR* 20 (1885, A. Cunningham: 103).
86. Ibid.: 104-5.
87. See the controversy on the restoration of the temple summarised in U. Singh (2004: 218-30).
88. Fergusson (1876: 209). Fergusson's early text on Indian architecture was published in 1867 as the second volume of *A History of Architecture in All Countries*, London 1865-67 (cf. vol. 2, pp. 445 ff.).
89. Fergusson & Burgess (1880: 19).
90. Hunter (1896: 35). Hodgson's life and activity in Kathmandu have been recently examined by a group of scholars whose contributions have been edited by Waterhouse (2004).
91. Burnouf (1844). The attention paid to Hodgson's manuscripts in France (they had been largely ignored in Kolkata and London) was to mark the distance separating, until recently, French and Francophone Buddhist studies from those carried out by Anglo-Saxon scholars: by the end of the nineteenth century, the latter steered *en masse* for Pāli Buddhism. Burnouf never doubted the existence of anti-Buddhist persecutions. With regard to preaching, something unheard of in India before the Buddha, he insightfully observed that 'elle donne le secret des modifications capitales que la propagation du Buddhisme devait apporter à la constitution brahmanique, et des persécutions que la crainte d'un changement ne pouvait manquer d'attirer sur les Buddhistes, du jour où ils seraient devenus assez forts pour mettre en péril un système politique principalement fondé sur l'existence et la perpétuité des castes. Ces faits sont si intimement liés entre eux, qu'il suffit que le premier se soit produit, pour que les autres se soient, avec le temps, développés d'une manière presque nécessaire' (it explains the secret of the capital changes that the spread of Buddhism was to bring to the Brahmanical organisation, and of the persecutions that the fear of a change could not but draw on the Buddhists from the day when they would become strong enough to jeopardise a political system largely based on the existence and perpetuation of caste. These facts are so closely interrelated that it is sufficient that the first occurred for the others to have developed in time in an almost necessary way). Ibid.: 194-95.
92. Hunter (1896: 66).
93. Hodgson (1874: 99).
94. Hunter (1896: 135).
95. The point raised by Hodgson is crucial, because it shows that the Buddhist conception of the position of man, which we shall discuss in Chapter II, remained unchanged over time even in the most changed circumstances. Hodgson also realised that 'the Bauddhas of Nepaul have not *properly* any diversity of castes' (ibid. 63), and that Buddhism was born as a heresy within the Brahmanical system (ibid.: 68, 121).
96. Hunter (1896: 99).

97. Ibid.: 63.
98. Wilson (1862*a*: 39).
99. 'On Buddha and Buddhism' was the title of the lecture that Wilson published two years later. Cf. Wilson (1862*b*).
100. Wilson (1862*b*: 364-65).
101. The reader will find it below in Chapter III. Burnouf had published his translation of the *Saddharmapuṇḍarīka* and the accompanying essays two years before (Burnouf 1852).
102. Wilson (1862*b*: 365).
103. Ibid.: 367.
104. Ibid.: 368.
105. Ibid.: 369. Hardy's famous *Manual of Buddhism* was published in 1853.
106. Ibid.: 377-78.
107. Ibid.: 378.
108. Wilson (1865*b*: 256). Only Akbar was spared general condemnation.
109. Hardy (1853).
110. T.W. Rhys Davids & Hermann Oldenberg, *Vinaya Texts*, 3 vols. (The Sacred Books of the East 13, 17, 20). Oxford 1881-85.
111. It was published the following year in Kolkata.
112. Edgar (1880: 820-21).
113. Monier-Williams (1889). Some key constructs were already present in *Hinduism* (id. 1877: 81, 137).
114. On Monier-Williams, especially with reference to his contribution to the history of religions, see Thomas (2000: 84-89).
115. Monier-Williams (1889: 12, 14).
116. Ibid.: 170-71.
117. Ibid.: 165.
118. Ibid.: 163.
119. Ibid.: 164-65.
120. Ibid.: 163.
121. Ibid.: 169-70.
122. Rhys Davids (1896*a*: 91). We shall see that the Muslims had nothing to do with the fire that destroyed the Ratnodadhi Library of Nālandā (Chapter VI).
123. I refer the reader to Chapter VI for the reconstruction of the events that took place in Nālandā in the late twelfth and early thirteenth century.
124. Rhys Davids (1896*a*: 92).
125. Id. (1896*b*: 108).
126. Müller (1895: xi).
127. M. Misra (2007: 81).
128. With the typical exception of Roman Catholicism – in the wake of Voltaire and in keeping with a tendency that persists to this day.
129. Quinet (1842: 62).
130. With regards to Buddhism, Quinet shared the 'paradigm of discovery'. The

Buddha 'devait rejeter comme une profanation la lettre trop grossière des livres canoniques, et par là provoquer contre lui la haine réunie des peuples et des brahmanes. [...] Dans cette lutte, la doctrine qui cessait de s'appuyer sur la foi populaire devait nécessairement être vaincue par l'autre' ([The Buddha] had to reject as a profanation the rudimentary letter of the canonical books, and thus cause the hate of both the people and the Brahmins to rise against him. [. . .] In this struggle, the doctrine that no longer relied on popular faith had to be inevitably defeated by the other). See Quinet (1842: 268).

131. M. Misra (2007: 70). On early Hindu revivalism, cf. also Bandyopadhyay (2004: 234-47).
132. Coomaraswamy (1909: viii).
133. Ibid.: 162.
134. Ibid.: 149.
135. Ibid.: 197.
136. Ibid.: 197-98.
137. Ibid.: 218.
138. Coomaraswamy (1916: 214).
139. Ibid.
140. Ibid.: 215.
141. It was, however, the Coomaraswamy of the 1930s and 1940s who wrote some of the best essays on symbolism in Indian art, which influenced a generation of scholars, from Stella Kramrisch to Vasudeva S. Agrawala. See them collected in Lipsey (1977-78, I-II).
142. Coomaraswamy (1943: 45).
143. Ibid.
144. Ibid.: 50. Here the author draws on Hendrik Kern and his *Manual of Indian Buddhism* (Kern 1896). Coomaraswamy's polemic against the supporters of Pāli Buddhism continues, not without reasons, as for instance when he maintains that if it is true that the means employed by Buddhism are partly ethical, *nirvāṇa* is not an ethical state (Coomaraswamy 1943: 66).
145. Ibid.: 57 ff.
146. Coomaraswamy's father, Sir Mutu, was a Sri Lankan Tamil. The infant Ananda was brought to England by his mother who, left a widow, remained in her home country. The boy was educated in England, and made his first journey to South Asia in his twenties. On Coomaraswamy's life and works see Lipsey (1977-78, III).
147. Majumdar (1943: 62).
148. Ibid.: 73-74.
149. Ibid.: 67.
150. Basak (1967: 134). The first edition of the book goes back to 1934.
151. For a short biography of Jayaswal, see Ram (1981).
152. Jayaswal calls Śaśāṅka, accused in the text to have tried to destroy the religion of *dharma*, 'an orthodox revivalist' (Jayaswal 1937: 51).

153. Majumdar (1943: 64).
154. Id. (1957: 404).
155. Ibid.: 400-01.
156. Ibid.: 400.
157. Ibid.: 258.
158. Ibid.: 399.
159. Ibid.: 401.
160. Sastri, K.A. Nilakantha in HCIP 2: 99.
161. Id. (1966: 424). The book was first published in 1955.
162. Barua (1946); see below in Chapter II.
163. The resolution moved by Nehru and passed by the Constituent Assembly in July 1947 is reproduced in V.S. Agrawala (1964: 94-96).
164. Prinsep's successful reading of the early Aśokan inscriptions which had been brought to notice and the final identification of Piyadassi with Aśoka Maurya have been told by Allen (2003: esp. 186-88).
165. Cf. Kane (1930-62, III: 843).
166. V.S. Agrawala (1964).
167. Vanaspara, cited in the Kaṇiṣka inscription of the year 3 (*EI* 8, 1905-6, J. Ph. Vogel: 173-79, l. 8), has been identified with the Viśvaphani, Viṃśapaṭika and Viśvapurja of the Purāṇas. Cf. *IA* 47 (1918, K.P. Jayaswal: 298-99). The inscription of Rabatak has shown the extent of Kuṣāṇa rule in the middle and eastern Ganges Valley (Sims-Williams & Cribb (1995-96: 78, lines 5-6).
168. Jayaswal (1933: 43).
169. Ibid.: 65-66. This ritual is an *aṅga* of the *vājapeya* ritual (Kane 1930-62, II: 1211, note).
170. In relation to Pravarasena I, cf. Jayaswal (1933: 90 and passim).
171. Ibid.: 121.
172. Ambedkar (1987: 233).
173. Ibid.: 235.
174. Ibid.: 236-37.
175. Ibid.: 238.
176. R.S. Sharma, in particular, has exploited the archaeological evidence without being discouraged in the face of often incomplete and elusive excavation reports (see for instance R.S. Sharma 1996).
177. Kosambi (1965: 181). The queen whom Kosambi does not think worth mentioning was Kumāradevī. See also what Kosambi says in relation to Harṣavardhana (id. 1975: 314).
178. In fact, Kosambi had also written: '[...] historical periods must be demarcated according to the means and relations of production, not by fortuitous changes of dynasty or battles. Even here, it can be recognised that major wars, great changes in rulers, significant religious upheavals do often signalise fundamental changes in the productive relations of the people. That such critical changes manifest themselves through wars or reformation in religion

is due to the undeveloped stage of society with its attendant concealment of the true social forces guiding or forcing historical development [...] (Kosambi 1950: 358).

179. Thapar (1994: 15-16).
180. Among the first, Mahendravarman's *Mattavilāsa*, Viśākhadatta's *Mudrārākṣasa* and the *Prabodha Candrodaya* by Kṛṣṇa Misra; she also mentioned the offensive representations of *śramaṇa*-s at Khajuraho. We will discuss some of this evidence in the following chapters.
181. Ibid.: 18.
182. Ibid.: 18-19.
183. Ibid.: 20.
184. Ibid.: 19.
185. Thapar devoted a volume to Aśoka in 1961, and has not changed her views in the revised edition of 1997. Already Wilson (1850: 236; cf. also p. 250) had doubted that the inscriptions of Aśoka were made public with the design of propagating Buddhism, and had wondered if they had 'any connection with Buddhism at all'.
186. Thapar (2002: 201-02).
187. Id. (1999: 17).
188. Id. (1992: 74-75).
189. Only one of the examples brought up in previous works, that of Puṣyamitra Śuṅga, is cited, and here Thapar gives credit to Puṣyamitra's anti-Buddhist policy, distancing herself from the opinion expressed in the first edition of the book (id. 1997: 200).
190. Savarkar's *Hindutva: Who is a Hindu?* was published in 1921.
191. There was still much of Mazzini in Savarkar, but the Italian patriot would be horrified before many a theory and the practice of present-day *hindutva*.
192. Elst (1991: 87).
193. S.P. Gupta, a scholar indebted to K.P. Jayaswal, distancing himself from the official positions of *hindutva*, has maintained that no doubt is possible on Aśoka having been a Buddhist and on Aśokan sites being Buddhist sites (S.P. Gupta 1980: 47), further asserting Puṣyamitra Śuṅga's hostility against the Mauryas and all *śramaṇa*-s (ibid.: 215).
194. Among the exceptions, mention must be made of the *People's History of India*, ed. Irfan Habib, the first volume of which was published in 2001.

CHAPTER II

The Open Society

BUDDHISM *VERSUS* UPANIṢAD-*S*: THE GNOSTIC PERSPECTIVE

Many misconceptions formed over time on Buddhism and its position towards Brahmanism depend on the assessments made on the relationship between early Buddhism and the world of the Upaniṣad-*s*. The phenomenological aspects common to the two systems conceal the profound difference that separates them. Buddhist speculation has significant points in common with the systems that implicitly affirmed that the sensible world is evil and set liberation as their goal,[1] and the earliest, very influential Upaniṣad-*s* share this vision. Many authoritative scholars have seen here a dualism that is anthropological and cosmic together: on one side there would be being and eternity, on the other becoming and temporal succession, soul and body, *ātman* and things.[2] Between *ātman* and cosmos there would be an irreducible antinomy. Geo Widengren accepted this interpretation when he drew a parallel between the anti-cosmic dualism of the Upaniṣad-*s*, of which he underlined the concept of *māyā*, the illusion or error that this world is and that of the Gnostics.[3]

Is it really so? The *māyā* doctrine is only just mentioned in the *Bṛhadāraṇyaka* and *Śvetāśvatara Upaniṣad*-s;[4] in the *ātman/brahman* relationship, perceived and insistently indicated as identical, empirical diversity comes from the *brahman*, to which it returns,[5] so that the cosmos cannot be absolutely 'other' from the absolute. The stated *ātman/brahman* identity is, rather, an example of monistic idealism,[6] and Upaniṣadic speculation on asceticism is not without significant limitations. It would seem that the Upaniṣad-*s* hesitate to proclaim complete detachment from the world: the phenomenal aspects possess a part of truth as reflection of the *brahman*, and thus are all justified. Renunciation is recommended, but life comes first, and the idea is present that the apparent reality must come before the intuition of the

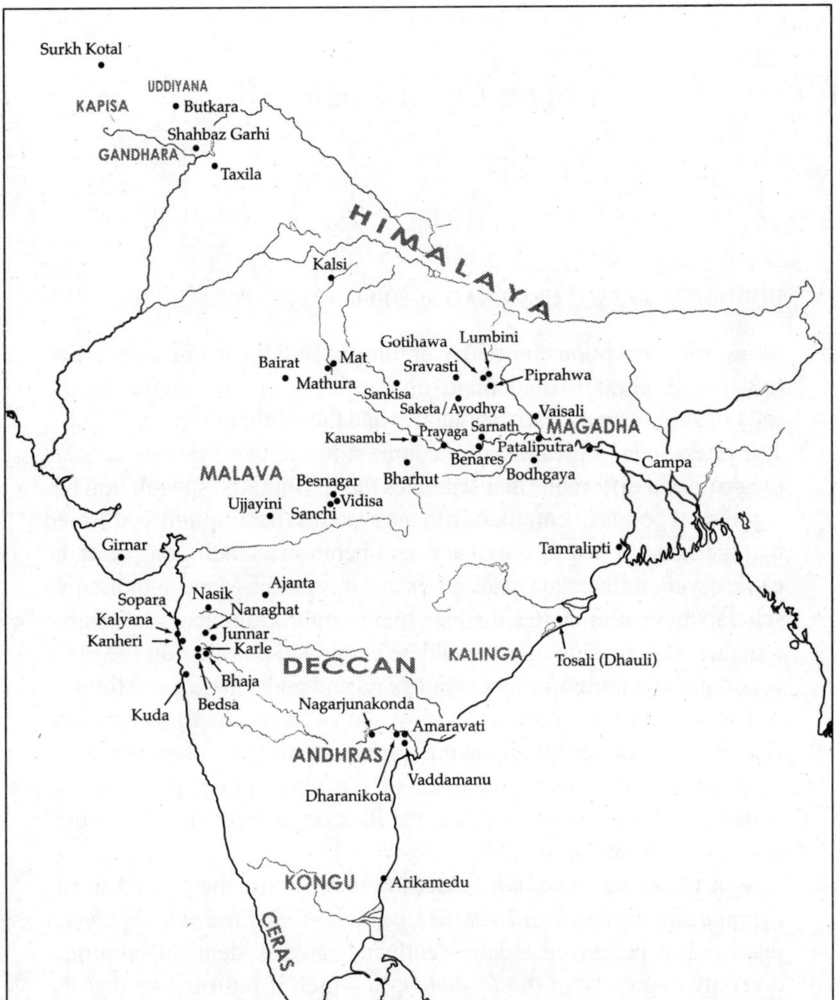

Map 1: Early historical India.

ultimate reality, which without the former is mutilated. Man, therefore, anchored to earth, cannot abstract from the experiences of his condition.[7] All the Upaniṣad-*s* proclaim their bond with the Veda and Brahmanical authority, thus stopping not only before any speculation that is effectively dualistic, but also before too explicitly anti-cosmic, antinomial and anti-sacerdotal positions.

Even allowing for more radical positions of Upaniṣadic thought before neo-Brahmanical normalisation, it can be maintained that in the early centuries BC/AD two distinct models of ascetic life developed in India. The first, for all the differences within it, did not break with Brahmanical authority and let itself be controlled by it; the second, just as differentiated (besides the various Buddhist schools there were the other Śramaṇic systems), rejected Brahmanical authority.[8] They catalysed anti-system movements and institutions having their political-social propellant in a part of the kṣatriyas, in the vaiśyas – the 'free commoners'[9] – and even in a part of the brāhmaṇas.

It is precisely early Buddhism that shares many features with the Gnostic systems.[10] At the phenomenological level,[11] we observe anti-cosmism (the phenomenal world is sorrow, and the causal chain keeps men bound to it) and dualism (*saṃsāra* is in sharp contrast with *nirvāṇa*, however, the dynamics between the two came to be represented). The subordination of the divine is another typical feature of early Buddhism and of the Gnostic systems, different as the two perspectives may be: god is evil for the Gnostics, an obstacle for the achievement of *sophia*; for the Buddhists the gods are not relevant with respect to either the teaching, revelation and attainement of *prajñā*.[12] Antinomism is expressed by the refusal to recognise that caste division is sanctioned from above; it has, if ever, only a *de facto* validity. Destructuring the self, Buddhism tends to destructure society.[13] Here then is an anti-clerical position: the brāhmaṇas, from whose ranks the priestly class comes (they are both priests and *gṛhastha*-s) have no rights deriving from birth. The true brāhmaṇa is whoever enters the spiritual élite founded by the Buddha. The opposition to rituals, especially bloody ones, has the aim of emptying the sacerdotal functions. Another shared feature is individualism: while *jñāna* or gnosis is a means of individual salvation valid for the *ārya*-s, corresponding to the pneumatics or spirituals of the Gnostics and to the Manichaean *electi*, an individualist ethic informs as well the *upāsaka*-s, which are the equivalents of the Gnostic psychics and the *auditores* or hearers of the Manichaeans. The individual moral action guarantees their well-being on earth and a favourable rebirth.[14] We also note the typical hierarchy of human beings: the Buddha of the Pāli Canon maintains that humans fall into three categories, of lower, medium or higher quality, like lotuses in a pond. Some do not emerge; others surface on the water; and still others 'stand thrusting themselves above the water', unwetted by it.[15] As for universalism, a feature common to all Gnostic systems, the Buddha's preaching is freed from social, ethnic, national and even religious ties. Lastly, Buddhism soon developed a saviour figure, the bodhisattva. The Gnostic saviour was similarly conceived as an enlightener (*phōstḗr*) whose teaching saves.[16]

In a subordinate position,[17] two other features characteristic of the Gnostic systems should be mentioned: docetism, favoured especially by the Mahāsāṃghikas, and adopted by the movements forming the Mahāyāna: the Buddhas have nothing in common with the world,[18] and as in Gnostic docetism, the idea is implicit that what belongs to this inferior world cannot possess and grasp that which is luminous and divine.[19] Docetism is connected to the negative judgement of the body, 'privileged place of the action of the demons' for the Gnostics.[20] For the Buddhists the body is foul, transient, and seat of desires: hence the meditation on its impurities, which takes place in cemeteries, where the body is found in varying states of decay and decomposition.[21] If the common feature of the Gnostic systems is a dualist anthroposophy at the basis of which there is an anti-cosmic and anti-demiurgic polemics,[22] the Gnostic perspective clarifies better than any other the historical-religious position of the religion of Dharma.

The two models of ascetic life in ancient India mentioned above, whose common phenomenological aspects risk obscuring the differences separating them at the historical level,[23] recalls the distinction between the models of asceticism in the eastern Mediterranean. Christian ascetics believed in the goodness of creation, which includes matter *and* the body: the possibility of regaining the original purity was its proof.[24] For the Gnostics, as for the Buddhists, asceticism meant rather to put all possible distance between oneself and the world – not, however, as maintained by Max Weber, the world *tout court*[25] – but that submitted to the *nómos*. The fundamental point of the dissent[26] was that Christian ascetics always recognised the authority of the Great Church, while Gnostic ascetics did not, preferring, if anything, to create alternative churches. For both Gnosticism and Buddhism, the breaking point with orthodoxy passes very clearly through antinomial and anti-sacerdotal positions, something that caused similar sanctions.

THE FREEDOM OF THE INDIAN OCEAN

Buddhism has long been judged as belonging to an urban and mercantile environment, of which it represents the religious and ideological referent. Early Buddhist establishments were located just outside the cities and, in the vast non-urbanised regions of the sub-continent, along the communication routes that joined distant and different areas. Overseas trade was already well developed from the second half of the second century BC, in the times of Republican Rome,[27] but intensified enormously from the age of Augustus and Tiberius onwards. The new large ships that made the direct route between Aden and the Deccan possible attest to the extraordinary boom of maritime traffic in the Arabian Sea.[28] The Buddhist monasteries were often able to supply merchants and caravans with the capital they needed;[29] loans and sales to cultivators and merchants are documented, especially by the Mahāsāṃghika communities,[30] which we have mentioned for their docetist orientation. To give some examples, at Nāsik the local *saṃgha* received a money grant from the wives and daughters of some merchants thanks to the investments of the corporations of potters, plumbers, and the owners of oil presses.[31] At Junnar, the *saṃgha* invested with the corporations of the bamboo workers and of the coppersmiths.[32] The monasteries were not only stopping places but also centres with functions of supplying and banking.[33] The models are, clearly, the banking functions of the Greek and Hellenistic temples, which in Roman times prospered especially in the eastern Mediterranean area.[34]

Taking, in this, our cue from Max Weber, we can say that between merchants and monasteries a relationship was created deriving from the need for warehousing and roads.[35] By using a particular road and storing the goods in a particular port or at a certain crossroads, the earnings from the commercial activity were maximised, and it became possible to create the infrastructure of trade and to bear the costs of the building of roads and other services. At the same time – the example comes from Junnar, a major terminus on the Western Ghats for the ports of Kalyāṇa (the Kalliena of the *Periplus*) and Sopara/Sūrpāraka – the monasteries were subdivided into small groups widely spaced to permit separate rapports and patronage between different schools and different classes of merchants.[36]

Giving a quick look at the inscriptions from the first century BC to the second century AD, we get a vivid picture of the social sectors supporting Buddhism: at Kanheri, due north of Mumbai, we find among the donors merchants, jewellers, treasurers, blacksmiths,[37] some of whom lived in Kalyāṇa and Sopara. At Kuda, on the Ghats, at the beginning of the second century AD, the lay donors included traders, bankers, scribes, doctors;[38] in the same period we find bankers, perfumers and carpenters at Karle[39] and bankers at Bedsa.[40] At Junnar, the *yavana* Irila, arguably a merchant, pays for two cisterns;[41] and donations of the corporation of the grain merchants and from a goldsmith are recorded.[42] The picture does not change if we move to one of the greatest Buddhist foundations of eastern Deccan, Amaravati, which stood near the river port of Dharaṇīkoṭa.[43] Here too we find merchants, perfumers, bankers,[44] and still other artisans.[45] Further north, on the Vindhyas, Sanchi and the nearby Buddhist monasteries channelled the commercial traffic along the valley of the Betwa towards the western part of the Gangetic plain and Mathurā, while Bharhut channelled it along the Son, towards Pāṭaliputra and the south-eastern part of the great plain. At Sanchi, the majority of donors were from Mālavā (Malwa), and included a chief artisan, a tailor, weavers, masons, the corporation of the ivory artisans of Vidiśā and some corporations of Ujjayinī.[46] The Buddha would have preferred that the young kṣatriyas should enter the *saṃgha*, which instead was largely formed of monks from the social background we have just described[47] and supported by merchants and bankers.[48] The monastic order, centre of gravity of the economic system, thus linked the urban and mercantile circles to the circle of the upper-caste administrative officials,[49] to the higher ranks of the army,[50] and to the petty kings and princes, who also appear in the inscriptions,[51] whose importance was crucial for the political fortunes of Buddhism. The female presence deserves at least a mention: they are the wives, the daughters, the mothers, the sisters of merchants, bankers and princes who appear in the foreground: many joined the *saṃgha* as nuns.[52] The link between Buddhism and the mercantile world is genetic: suffice it to recall that the Bactrian merchants Trapuṣa and Bhallika were the first to whom a *deva*, astonished witness to the Awakening, ordered to run and pay homage to Śākyamuni.[53]

Similarly, the variables from which Mediterranean Gnostics developed have been identified in the city-country conflict and in the opening of trade.[54] They originated in the most Hellenised Jewish milieus of Alexandria, but were rejected by orthodox Judaism and were not accepted, although they sought assimilation, by the Greek élite, being denied access to Greek institutions. Born from the transformation of the Ptolemaic mode of production into the privatisation of land favoured by the Romans, they felt a profound personal and social alienation.[55] The response mechanism they set in motion may be compared to that started by a part of the kṣatriyas and their allies, to whom the Brahmanical elite denied equal social status.

Among the Alexandrian Jews there were, in addition to small owners, tenants, soldiers, officials, farm workers, shepherds, petty bureaucrats, artisans organised in professional groups.[56] The demonopolisation of key industries had placed in private hands, quite often those of the Hellenised Jews, the production of and trade in papyrus, glass, perfumes and unguents.[57] Even the shipping industry was in good part in their hands.[58] Everything indicates their involvement in the trading enterprises, which proliferated not only in relation to the traffic between Alexandria and Jerusalem or Rome, but also to that of the Red Sea[59] and therefore with India. Dio Chrysostom, addressing the inhabitants of the Egyptian metropolis (we are in the second half of the first century AD), states that 'not only have you a monopoly of the shipping of the entire Mediterranean [...], but also the outer waters that lie beyond are in your grasp, both the Red Sea and the Indian Ocean, whose name was rarely heard in former days'.[60]

Under Vespasian (AD 69-79) the value of the goods imported by sea amounted to 55 million sesterces a year – not only an impressive figure in itself, but, as has been written, 'the largest that could ever have been realised in the ancient world with free private trade, without controls and state subventions of any sort'.[61] It is especially in maritime trade, which partially escaped the sanctions of the anti-chrematist ethics,[62] that the Gnostic communities, composed of men from the middle class and characterised by individualist and antinomial positions, prospered. Marcion, who was from Sinope on the Black

Sea, was a shipowner.[63] In the *Acts of Thomas*, the Indian merchant Ḥabbān buys Thomas, a carpenter and mason by profession, from Jesus to take him to King Gondophares, who ruled at Taxila: we would expect a trip by land. Instead, 'Judah [Thomas] went and found Ḥabbān the merchant carrying his goods on board the ship, and began to carry (them) on board with him'.[64] The activity of merchants on the sea trade was private, and the area involved in the mercantile operations – the Arabian Sea – was free from government controls. We are, as in the deserts of Xinjiang that also started being crossed by Buddhist merchants,[65] in a geographic context where the existence of strong landed powers cannot even be imagined, in an open society where the very diversifications of the Gnostic groups can be considered functional, according to the Buddhist model,[66] to economic development.

Mercantile activity in Alexandria resumed after the crisis caused by the policy of the Ptolemies, and especially by that of Ptolemy Euergetes and his successors.[67] After Actium (31 BC), Alexandria boomed again thanks to the Roman policy of privatisation and the enormous volume of trade with the countries on the Arabian Sea, and in particular with the west coast of the Deccan.[68] Dio Chrysostom, in the above-mentioned oration addressed to the inhabitants of Alexandria, remarks that among his addressees in the theatre, besides Ethiopians and Arabs, Bactrians, Scythians and Persians, there were 'some of the Indians'.[69] The recent discovery on the Egyptian coast of the Red Sea of *óstraka* inscribed with the names of Indian merchants in Prakrit and Tamil[70] and the documented presence of Indians on the island of Socotra off the Horn of Africa[71] point to the same conclusion.[72] It is very unlikely that merchants of south India could be, in the first and second centuries AD, other than lay supporters of the *śramaṇa*-s. The maximum expansion of the heterodox movements in the Deccan coincided with the epoch of the overseas trade with Rome and South-East Asia.[73] A Tamil-Brāhmī inscription records the donation of a cave to a Jain monk probably made by a merchant from Laṅkā, and in the Buddhist sites of Āndhra there were Siṃhala merchants along with monks and nuns.[74] Gifts to the Buddhist and/or Jain ascetics by the Cēra ruling family and by merchants are recorded in inscriptions from the Koṅgu region of Karnataka.[75] It seems that there was a division of tasks between the *śramaṇa*-s, and thus also boundaries to be observed: Buddhist monks mostly lived in coastal areas and were actively involved in maritime trade, whereas the Jains were mostly involved in internal trade.[76] Except for brief periods, Brahmanical dynasties had not yet succeeded in controlling the Deccan,[77] and a market mechanism had probably been developed by the Tamil kings.[78]

The Gnostics, like the Buddhists, define an urban and mercantile phenomenon: besides Alexandria, we find them at Seleucia, Antioch, Ephesus, and Rome.[79] In the capital of the empire, Valentinus and Marcion, and before them Cerdon and other groups, had opened schools,[80] probably with the aim to protect and extend the network already created in the eastern Mediterranean and on the south-eastern borders of the Roman territories, to seek political patrons and open a breach in the élites. Here enter the women, 'who come from good families and who have fine clothes and are very rich'; their contributions made Marcus the Magian wealthy.[81] In the Gnostic communities, women were offered possibility of self-fulfilment unthinkable elsewhere.[82]

The social position of the merchants was superior to that of the artisans, workmen, and peasants, but inferior, in the West, to that of the landed aristocracy,[83] and, in India, to that of the brāhmaṇas and kṣatriya landowners. Despite this, a substantial part of the goods and the money from and to India passed through their hands, whether they belonged to Gnostic or Buddhist communities. The reason why late ancient sources continue to know, in relation to India, only the world of the brāhmaṇas—familiar to them since the early classical period—and to ignore Buddhism[84] is because it was not 'Greeks' and 'Romans' who were in direct contact with India but Roman Jews and Gnostics. The fact that the first Western writer to mention the Buddhists and Jains is Clement of Alexandria (*c.* AD 150-215)[85] is significant: his informants had certainly plied the maritime trade routes and frequented the ports of the Deccan.[86]

Moses Finley contended that mercantile society was always marginal in the ancient world, even in the periods of greatest commercial growth, but we cannot follow him,[87] as we cannot accept the belief that the Gnostics were none other than marginal intellectuals, as maintained by Max Weber, who is behind the poor understanding of the Gnostic phenomenon to these days. Significantly, Weber also gave an erroneous interpretation of Buddhism. Weber was the first to define the Gnostics as a stratum of de-politicised, frustrated intellectuals, lacking an ethics of responsibility and incapable of political action.[88] He removed Gnosticism from the ambit of the classical world, placing it on the side of the 'Asiatic religions'.[89] He was on the right track when he considered the two systems as structurally related, but drawing Brahmanism together with Gnosticism and Buddhism was a serious, misleading mistake.[90] Western asceticism represented for Weber the intramundane model; the various types of Asiatic asceticism, the model of the rejection of the world and contemplative withdrawal from it.[91] In his distinction between ethical and exemplary prophet, the Buddha represents the latter, indeed capable of indicating a path of personal salvation but not of founding a universal ethics.[92] Buddhism, the Asiatic religion to which, as has been observed, Weber did least justice,[93] would have been a religion of ascetic mendicants, apolitical and anti-political. This interpretation has been dismantled and abandoned for decades:[94] in early Buddhism not only a great capacity to organise the world of the laymen has been recognised, but also one that promoted in them the principle of individual moral responsibility centred on the puritan ethics of saving and investment.[95] Early Buddhism is now placed in a perspective practically the opposite of what Weber maintained.

As for the Gnostics, it is in the wake of Max Weber that scholars continue to maintain that the Gnostics' response to their social and psychological alienation was mystic, and not political. The institutional forms they worked out would have developed in isolation from the dominant culture, and gnosis – an individual liberation – would have exempted them from the necessity of reforming the world.[96] They would have been only an intellectual class placed at the margins of the Roman Empire, prisoners of an a-historical perspective.[97] It is difficult, however, to believe that the Gnostics were satisfied with a simple role of intellectual opposition: certainly not those who were able to organise themselves in the 'forest' mentioned by Tertullian.[98] Their geographic marginality in the empire was due, if indeed it was such – we think of the thousands of pages written against them by the Church Fathers – to their presence in the Indian Ocean and in those areas of the Mediterranean and Near East that were touched most directly by a proto-capitalist economy. We could rather agree with an observation of Ioan Couliano that Gnosticism represents an anthropological optimism without equal in the history of Western ideas.[99] The Gnostic communities, and with them the Buddhists, were the optimistic bearers of a model of an open economy and society freed from the impositions of *nómos*.[100] The withdrawal of the Gnostics from the urban centres after the second century – a fact probably triggered by the great epidemic of the third century[101] – did not mark, like the similar withdrawal of the Manichaeans after the fourth century,[102] their rescue from the shipwreck of ancient culture,[103] but rather the collapse of an economic and political model.

Buddhism and the Gnostic systems remain linked from a systemic point of view, and it would be high time to resume discussion on the relationship between *sophía* and *prajñā*,[104] and on that between the Mahāyāna concept of *bodhicitta* and the divine Gnostic spark in relation to their identification with sperm.[105] The relationship between the Gnostic identification of the self with the divine and the Mahāyāna doctrine of the original presence of the Buddha nature within the individual[106] is another point awaiting clarification. For the early centuries of our era, it is possible to identify not only how the loans between the Gnostics and the Buddhists took place, something that was still unclear to Edward Conze,[107] but also the reasons why they had doctrinal points in common.[108] Both systems had the need to adopt similar strategies to represent similar social situations, and were both interested in a response to the great organised powers.

As to the Manichaeans, who according to some embody the essence of the 'Gnostic religion', we know that its fortunes east of Iran were linked to the merchants of Chorasmia and, after the fall of the Sasanian state, to those from beyond the Amu Darya[109] – from Sogdia, and Samarkand in particular.[110] In the West, the Manichaeans were present especially in the cities,[111] and when, with the decline of the mercantile economy, the merchants settled down as local landowners,[112] they lost their most typical supporters. In the Mediterranean, Manichaean groups came into strong conflict with the society where they lived[113] and were regarded with horror[114] because the economic-social model proposed by the *electi* was disruptive to the secure world of conservative Romans, and then of the Christians of the victorious Church. The characteristic prohibition for them of any act against the life of animals and plants[115] says a great deal about the Manichaeans' hostility towards and extraneousness to the world of farming, namely, to large landownership and closed society. The position of the *electi* recalls the *ahiṃsā* of the Buddhists and Jains (whose teachings and practices were known to Mani and his followers).[116] Lay Jain followers were not allowed to farm, and restrictions were imposed on the very ownership of land.[117]

The Gnostics were suppressed by the Church, and Manichaeism did not succeed in taking hold even marginally in Mani's homeland, where it was cut-off at birth. Instead, Buddhism realised in India, at least in part, an alternative model to the world as it was structured socially and mentally. The success obtained is remarkable in historical terms, and is something that finds no comparison in any other society of the ancient world. As for the ascetics of the Upaniṣad-*s*, they have very little to do with all this, since they were one of the polarities of the closed society.

AŚOKA OR THE CHANCES OF DESPOTISM

Unable to get the support of the traditional powers, it became essential for the Buddhists to seek the support of the monarch, the only figure capable, under favourable circumstances, to oppose the establishment. The function of the ruler for an antinomial system to take hold and checkmate the anti-urban aristocracies justified by sacerdotal classes, is very clearly observable.[118] Putting the question into focus is difficult because the nature of the Buddhist kingdoms of India and the role played by Buddhism in elaborating a specific political vision and specific institutional mechanisms have not attracted sufficient attention.[119] The breaking point was the Kaliṅga war: Aśoka was certainly crowned king according to tradition, but he probably distanced himself from traditional kingship introducing new rules regarding the enthronement rituals. In the *rājasūya*, animal sacrifices played an important part, especially in connection with the relationship between the king-sacrificer and the people,[120] and it is unlikely that Aśoka would leave a similar legacy to his successors.

Aśoka's Buddhist kingdom was perhaps not far in time from the preaching of the Awakened One,[121] and the policy of the emperor was aimed at creating a Buddhist model of kingship and society. Mainland India was far from both the Arabian Sea and the deserts, where commoners were not subject to any hierarchical control, and with Aśoka, who made himself *upāsaka*,[122] the economic initiative of the new urban classes that erupted after the expedition of Alexander, Buddhist political ideology and *imperium* consolidated. For the first time an antinomial, antisacerdotal, anti-*varṇa* state founded on the axis formed by the monarch, kṣatriyas broken off from Brahmanical tutelage, apostate brāhmaṇas, monasteries and commoners was established. If its nature is not always recognised, it is because it was established in the conditions possible, that is, in relation to a society where the weight of Brahmanical power remained crucial. The problem remains that of evaluating the extent to which it differed from the Brahmanical model.

It is generally recognised that *jāti* differentiation within the four traditional *varṇa*-s gained importance in Mauryan times, and the phenomenon may be understood as the inability of the landed aristocracies to propose a theory of the state both capable of protecting their interests and starting up, at the same time, an innovative process. When faced with the growing disparity between the agrarian horizon and the new moneyed urban classes, they preferred to close ranks tightening the caste system and squaring up against a revolutionary attempt that threatened to reduce them to insignificance.[123] In the alternation of kings and dynasties that followed the downfall of the Mauryas – an issue to which modern historians have attached little importance – we can discern the attempts to translate into terms of political power the antinomial model of society or, from the Brahmanical point of view, the rising and setting up, in successive waves, of the Kali Age. The memory of Aśoka, always kept alive in Buddhist countries, was to disappear from the horizon of Indian history not because of an inexplicable refusal or inability of the Brahmanical élites to keep the record of past and present events in chronicles and histories, but because of a targeted hostility to handing down whatever history was not their own. They would have been obliged to acknowledge that what they cared for most of all, intellectual supremacy and political power, had escaped their control for quite a long period.

Two antithetic positions on Aśoka's rule still oppose one another in the historiographic debate. The first is upheld by the majority of Indian scholars, disinclined to acknowledge the central role played by the heretical movements in the first territorial unification of the country and recognise a catalysing function and an autonomous role of historical causality to religious factors. Aśoka, as already observed in the preceding chapter, is often considered the founder of a secular genealogy that continues up to the present day: hence their assessment of Aśoka's edicts – in particular of the major edicts – that exhort to the diffusion of *dhamma*/*dharma* without apparently mentioning

Buddhism, its value system and precepts. They inevitably recognise the Buddhist content of the *Aśokavacana* only in relation to the pillar and minor edicts, which are too explicit to allow for a secular interpretation. We are thus facing an Aśoka alienated in the modern manner, in some cases manifesting his personal religious choice,[124] and in others declaring himself promoter of a policy borrowed from the Brahmanical tradition supported by the *Arthaśāstra* and/or founded by himself.[125]

The *Arthaśāstra*, discovered in 1905 and published in 1909, was attributed, not without oppositions, to the Mauryan period by identifying its author, Kauṭilya, with Cāṇakya, the minister of Candragupta Maurya.[126] The treatise appeared unencumbered by the religious and ritualistic burden of Vedic and post-Vedic texts – a 'secular' text and an early testimonial of an autonomous conception of politics.[127] However, the *Arthaśāstra* is not only a stratified text, but is not earlier than the second century AD, and probably written in its present form in the mid-fourth century AD.[128] It is a Brahmanical treatise on *artha*, the science of government based on the concepts of *daṇḍanīti*, or politics exercised through coercion, and of *rājadharma*, the king's duty to preserve, as a first thing, the order of the four *varṇa*-s. It is not surprising that fines (100 *paṇa*-s) would be applied for 'one feeding Śākya, Ājivaka and other heretical monks at rites in honour of gods and manes',[129] the venues where getting food was easiest. Significantly, the *Arthaśāstra* sanctions the killing of calves, bulls and milk cows,[130] keeping silent on the killing of animals destined for sacrifices.

Historians often belittle the historical value of early Buddhist texts, denying their authority as sources endowed with a sufficient level of objectivity to integrate the epigraphic evidence.[131] It is yet another way of reaffirming Aśoka's extraneousness to Buddhism. The Indian scholars who have not hesitated to recognise the Buddhist nature of Aśokan *dharma* are not many.[132] Benimadhav Barua, for all his judging of the inscriptions of Aśoka as 'not altogether inconsistent with those of other systems',[133] following the observations of preceding authors provided a list of the correspondences between them and the *Buddhavacana*, the Buddha's sayings. Technical terms drawn from the scriptures are numerous in the major rock edicts,[134] and direct loans or indirect inspirations from Buddhist scriptures on a number of issues are present.[135] The Bairat edict mentions several texts,[136] and loans from the *Buddhavacana* are frequent even in often apparently anodyne words of the emperor. We detect for instance traces of the *Dhammapada* and of the debate on the *cakkavartin/cakravartin.*[137]

Few things are more distant from Brahmanical orthodoxy and praxis than the texts and monuments left by Aśoka, the use of writing being by itself a dramatic break with tradition. The Sarnath capital was crowned by the symbol of Buddhist *dharma*, the *cakra*, the wheel that the *cakravartin* sets in motion instead of holding the *daṇḍa*, the coercive staff of command. The *dharmacakra* is more effective than force even in the work of conquest. The three hierarchical levels of Brahmanical political thought – *dharma*, or the principle securing the correspondence between cosmic order and worldly order on the basis of caste order; *artha*, the policy that guarantees the pre-eminence of the brāhmaṇas in society; and *kāma*, all what brings pleasure – are replaced in Buddhism by a *dharma* at two levels, the absolute level that can be experienced by the renouncers, and that of the rightful sovereign. The conqueror and ruler of the world, Aśoka, and the *saṃgha* are strictly complementary. The Buddhist theorisation of *dharma* opens to the *cakravartin* a grandiose imperial conception,[138] unknown to Brahmanism, where the ambitions of the kṣatriyas must be continuously watched over: the brāhmaṇas are co-indispensable to whatever form of political government and prevent kṣatriyas from taking autonomous decisions, potentially detrimental to Brahmanical power.

Despotic consequences are inherent in the Buddhist model, as was the case of many Buddhist rulers, not only in India.[139] Aśoka's absolutism sought and found support in the social groups that considered caste organisation repressive, and saw in the *cakravartin* the guarantor of their freedom. It was not the individual freedom of the moderns, but the freedom that merchants and artisans experienced in the guilds, not recognising traditional affiliations, and that of non-brahmanised peasants. The emperor's despotic drift found a strong deterrent exactly in the vaiśyas: the guilds were even allowed to issue coins, which circulated after receiving the royal marks.[140] Imperial order had the advantage of keeping at bay the intrusiveness of the *póleis* and the serious limits they would interpose, if left completely autonomous, to the freedoms of the organised social groups.[141]

In an attempt at modelling, and at clarifying the mechanisms of Aśoka's policy, the European absolutism of the seventeenth and eighteenth century, which hinged upon a monarchical power that was, or tended to be, unrestrained by other institutions, be they churches or social elites, can be a useful reference to an extent. It was associated with the unification and reinforcement of the state and the strengthening of royal power to the detriment of well-established interests, as well as with the rise of professional armies and bureaucracies, the codification of state laws, and the rise of ideologies that justified absolute monarchy. The monarch bound himself to supporting the economic development of the state with reforms that favoured progress and assured better conditions of life to his subjects, rescuing them from the conditioning of a closed culture. The relationship between the state and the trading classes was based on policies that protected business interests. In exchange, taxes were paid to support the military-bureaucratic structure of the nation state. The merchants and allied classes freed their behaviour from the current morals and operated in the world according to principles of economic rationality, performing their functions as traders, undertakers and bankers. The despotic state remained largely based on agriculture, but merchants were encouraged to operate in order to increase the wealth and prestige of the state and their own: the state guaranteed stability, public order and the enlargement of the market through territorial conquests. In the area of agriculture, canalisations and specialised cultivation (works and activities theorised by the physiocrats) were aimed at increasing agricultural productivity and modernising agriculture.

From the standpoint of historical modelling, the points in common with Aśoka's policy are significant. The absolute monarch even bound himself to the task of providing for the 'happiness of the people' in the same way that Aśoka reigned on the basis of a new – Buddhist – ethic with the aim of securing 'the welfare and happiness of the people'.[142] Here ends, in fact, every possible parallel with modern despotism. The latter could do without being backed by a religious perspective, but ancient despotism, like ancient democracies, could not.

The anti-Brahmanical character of the *Aśokadharma* is very clear. In his first major edict, Aśoka maintains that no living being must be killed and sacrificed,[143] and in the rock edict IV observes that '[i]n times past, for many hundreds of years, there had ever been promoted the killing of animals', and warns that now this is not to be done.[144] *Avihiṃsā/ahiṃsā* implies the delegitimation of the functions of the brāhmaṇas-priests, who drew authority and earnings from the enormous number of blood rituals. The past centuries mentioned by Aśoka are those – the *Buddhavacana* not heard yet – of Vedic rituals. In the pillar edict V, the emperor orders that living animals must not be fed with other living animals, tries to regulate the castration of bulls, he-goats, rams, boars and whatever other animals are subjected to castration, and forbids the killing of a number of animals, including all the quadrupeds which are neither useful nor edible.[145] Here the target are the activities of the agrarian horizon, largely controlled by the *gṛhastha*-s.[146] The request to abstain oneself from killing animals is insistently repeated in other edicts, such as the rock edicts I, IV and XI, as well as in the pillar edict II, where Aśoka recalls having conferred various benefits, including the boon of life, on bipeds and quadrupeds, on birds and aquatic animals.[147]

In the rock edict IX Aśoka takes note of the most widespread rituals, including the crucial rites of passage, but maintains that they bear little fruit. To consider useless the rituals performed 'at the marriage of a son or a daughter' and 'at the birth of a child', so strongly identifying and requesting the presence of the brāhmaṇa-priest, is an extraordinary polemic initiative, inconceivable outside a Buddhist vision of society. Though aware that few people will renounce them, Aśoka makes fun of all the other rites, particularly those performed 'by mothers and wives', that he unhesitatingly defines 'vulgar and useless'.[148] The brāhmaṇas, settled in a considerable number of villages, prospered thanks to a myriad of minor rituals. However, it is not Aśoka who is against them but, in the first place, Buddhism, which makes of them one of its principal polemic targets. Aśoka's explicit attack against family life is addressed to the priestly coercion exercised upon it; brāhmaṇas made profits from this fundamental institution. Once again, Buddhist tenets are behind Aśoka's convictions and political measures. Because of his hostility to household life, orthodox ascetics such as Māgaṇḍiya/Mārkaṇḍeya called the Buddha *bhūnahā*, *bhūnahū*, foetus killer.[149] It would take a long time for the Buddhists to reconsider the matter.

The liberality and courtesy towards *śramaṇa*-s and brāhmaṇas recommended by Aśoka in the rock edicts III and IV, and the famous passage of the edict XII where he declares to honour 'all sects: both ascetics and householders', warning that 'all sects should be both full of learning and pure in doctrine', and that wronging other sects means injuring one's own sect, has been interpreted as a call to religious tolerance. It is not, however, tolerance as understood in a modern secular state; the admonition must be seen within a Buddhist perspective. The Buddhists tried hard to convert and proselytise, but did not interfere with the non-Buddhists, once the freedom and prosperity of the *saṃgha*-s were safeguarded. Thus Aśoka's sayings reflect a twofold concern. The first is about intellectual proselytism: it was from the ranks of Brahmanical intelligentsia that the most influential disciples of the Buddha, such as Mogallāna and the Kassapa brothers, had come, and the Buddha's attempt at bringing the brāhmaṇas to his side or not antagonising them is all too apparent in the *sutta*-s.[150] Several among the Buddhist thinkers would be brāhmaṇas by birth,[151] nor could it be otherwise. This fracture in the Indian elite that the Buddhists were able to produce would grow deeper and deeper and overshadow the rift between kṣatriyas and brāhmaṇas of earlier times. Aśoka, who already enjoyed kṣatriya support – his well-organised army proves it – tries to split the orthodox front addressing the modernising brāhmaṇas and encouraging them to become part of the new monastic elite. To avoid the intermediation of non-cooperative brāhmaṇas, he sends his trusty officers, the *mahāmāta*-s/*mahāmātra*-s, to spread *dharma*.[152] In any case, it is significant that in half of his edicts, he places the *śramaṇa*-s before the brāhmaṇas.[153]

The second concern is keeping the *śramaṇa* front united, the various groups being often in open conflict one with the other.[154] Aśoka tries to channel all the *śramaṇa*-s towards his autocratic project of building an alternative society. Before his conversion to Buddhism, he had the rock-cut caves in the Barabar hills, the earliest in India, hewn for the Ājīvikas,[155] and as for the Jains, their association with the Mauryas went back to the time of the founder of the dynasty, Candragupta.[156] The apparent oddness of that passage of the already mentioned pillar edict V, where the killing of the most unexpected species of animals is prohibited, from bats to porcupines, and the prohibition of burning the husks containing living creatures[157] tended to reassure the followers of systems even more radical than Buddhism. At the time, Jainism was mainly urban and very rigid in its anti-agrarian stand, and polemically attentive to not sacrificing any living being, however infinitesimal.

If so much ambiguity hovers about Aśoka's *dharma*, it is because when the emperor addresses his people – mainly the *jāti*-s of third *varṇa* – he does not overlap with the *saṃgha*: it is not his task to predicate the religion.[158] What he intends to teach them is a conception of benevolent kingship and an exertion of political authority inspired by Buddhist ideas and values[159] and the Buddhist optimistic ethics of work and social relationships. For this reason, a technical term like *nibbāna/nirvāṇa* is not mentioned in any of his edicts, where the term *svaga/svarga*, heaven, is mentioned. *Nirvāṇa* is the concern of monks, not of merchants and householders, who know very well that it is only for those who, having crossed an almost infinite number of rebirths, have attained the condition of awakened beings – a very rare occurrence, and an objective alien to the urban trading middle class. The attainment of *nirvāṇa* is foreign to Aśoka, a layman.[160] His message to the vaiśyas is condensed in these words, 'And whatever effort I am making, is made in order that I may discharge the debt which I owe to living beings, that I may make them happy in this world, and that they may attain heaven in the other world.'[161] This statement is in line with the optimism of doing, the virtuous enrichment, and a reasonable reward after death: Buddhism, precisely, such as we know it today in the countries where it is professed. In his major edicts, Aśoka addresses the layman with the Buddhist language for layman. They complement the edicts addressed to the monastic community and the *upāsaka*-s, and represent the other end of a policy that is as simple as it is coherent, by no means divided between personal religious choices and the general needs of the state.

In the pillar edict VII, Aśoka states to have had banyan-trees planted along the roads in order that they might afford shade to cattle and men and have also had mangroves planted; to have caused stepped wells dug at intervals of 8 *kos*, and numerous drinking-places to be established, here and there, for the enjoyment of cattle and men, with the aim of following the practice of *dharma*.[162] The passage may sound bizarre and marginal, and at first we do not understand what *dharma* has to do with planting trees: but is not so in the perspective of the Buddhist *cakravartin*, who supports specific social groups. Caravans led by merchants, whose journey must be protected and whose animals must be saved from harm, pass along the roads connecting one town to the other; hence the need for halting places and water supply. The wealth of the empire and a more effective protection against Brahmanical revanchism depend on the economic multiplier constituted by trade. In this perspective, we can explain a passage from the rock edict XIII (where Aśoka declares his repentance for the Kaliṅga massacres) regarding the tribal populations. It would sound surprising if we did not know that punishment by death would not be inflicted:[163]

> [...] even the inhabitants of the forests which are included in the dominions of Dēvānāṁpriya, even those he pacifies and converts. And they are told of the power to punish them which Dēvānāṁpriya possesses in spite of his repentance, in order that they may be ashamed (of their crimes) and may not be killed.[164]

Which were the crimes they, the natives inhabiting the regions not controlled by Pāṭaliputra, soiled themselves with? Aśoka could not permit them to be a menace to the safety of the roads, which penetrated into their territories for hundreds kilometres, and endanger trade.[165] At the same time, the emperor blandishes these populations trying to attract them into the orbit of his project. To appraise the fruit of this policy is not possible, but less than one and a half century after Aśoka, we see tattooed demi-gods, arguably modelled on local princes and princesses politically emerged thanks to the instruments offered by Buddhism, on the *vedikā* of the stūpa at Bharhut.[166] Later Buddhist rulers, and Buddhists in general, will adopt the same policy, as we shall better see in the following chapters.

Archaeology is the weak point in the debate on the Mauryas and Aśoka. No Mauryan settlement has ever been excavated, nor have the relationship been examined between *dharma* pillars and stūpas and the territorial contexts where they were erected. While the debate on the nature of Aśokan policy continues,[167] no monumental area has been re-examined through fieldwork,[168] and our knowledge on the Aśokan pillars and the nearby stūpas is only slightly better than it was after the inaccurate excavations carried out in the nineteenth century.[169] No significant excavations have been carried out at Patna/Pāṭaliputra in the last decades, and no useful information is available on Aśoka's capital town, which is impossible to coherently describe. Its plan remains the object of speculation.[170] What we know a little better today, thanks to extensive surveys and modelling, is the territory of ancient Magadha and nearby regions and their settlement history, especially the area of the plain that stretches up to the Tarai.[171] The network of roads and junctions, checking points, river crossings and monumentalised areas show a complexity which goes far beyond the traditional notion of an *uttarāpatha* that, dotted with *dharma* pillars, runs along the left bank of the Gandak River. The network of roads and sites is much more complex than previously believed, pointing to the fact that economic transformation touched rather vast territories.

Regarding the *saṃgha*, or, rather, the *saṃgha*-s,[172] Aśoka proceeds in three directions. As a first thing, he breaks with the tradition and invests in monumental sanctuaries, causing stūpas to be erected along with high pillars symbolising the preaching of the Buddha and his role as model of the earthly *cakravartin*. The impact of Aśoka's monuments, the earliest in India, must have been extraordinary, granting the Buddhists an absolute prominence with respect to the competing systems. The social groups involved in his project had to step much ahead, in terms of prestige, of the most titled Brahmanical aristocracies. Interpreting Aśoka's *dharma* as an improvised ethics means to underestimate the complexity of artistic patronage and its motivations, which are never restricted, in antiquity, to the realm of policy. For its scale and the investment required – and we know only a limited number of Aśokan sites – Aśoka's patronage is unthinkable outside a religious perspective, peculiar and non-conformist as it may have been.[173] His monuments, in particular the *dharma* pillars, represent an extraordinary novelty, and the breaking off with the past a radical move. In the middle Ganges plain, where the conflict between Buddhism and Brahmanism was, and would remain, more acute, they characterised the whole territory, rising at the centre of sanctuaries: their meaning and importance were underlined by the pilgrimages Aśoka personally made. In the rock edict VIII, the emperor emphasises the clean break he has made with the past: he, the Buddhist *cakravartin*, goes on pilgrimage and not, as the sovereigns of yore used to do, on 'pleasure-tours' during which 'hunting and other such pleasures were enjoyed'.[174]

As a second thing, Aśoka intervenes directly to ensure the integrity of the *saṃgha* through infiltration that might undermine its stability and efficiency. Aśoka's choice in favour of Buddhism aroused resentment and led to attempts from the excluded religious groups, which tried to influence it from within. These attempts were suppressed, like that carried out at the Aśokārāma in Pāṭaliputra.[175] Aśoka took care that copies of this edict be available in the places reserved for the *upāsaka*-s, who were thus informed that the *saṃgha*-s had the right to carry out expulsions should infiltration take place elsewhere.[176] Every form of disorder in the *saṃgha*-s imperilled the double level of the Buddhist *dharma* and the political action of the *cakravartin*. Fostering cohesion in the local *saṃgha*-s and avoiding conflicts was also a means for not interrupting the smooth flow of trade along the long-distance routes.[177]

Finally – we have already recalled the Bairat edict – the emperor does not hesitate to point out to the local *saṃgha*, by mentioning them one by one, those discourses of the Buddha that in his opinion are best suited at assuring a long life to his political project.[178] Monks and *upāsaka*-s were the recipients of both the edicts copied on the pillars raised in the proximity of stūpas and of the minor rock edicts expressly written for the Buddhist community.[179] The *mahāmāta*-s had the task of making the *Aśokavacana* known to as many people as possible. The political challenge consisted in the urban transformation of the agrarian horizon, in the promotion of individual merit that is worth acquiring for this and the next life, and in the wealth-producing activities governed by a personal ethics borrowed from the *Buddhavacana.*

The state established by Aśoka and the policy he pursued are a unique phenomenon. No other Gnostic system succeeded, even approximately, in achieving a similar result. The Mediterranean Gnostics were suppressed before they could develop a large-scale, politically significant project. As regards Manichaeism, Mani long sought political support in Iran: only the court would have been able, from above, to oppose the Magi and the establishment. Mani was the scion of a princely family and obtained the protection of Šāpur's brothers, Mehršāh and Piruz, managing to draw to his side also a few petty princes.[180] The political-religious orientation of Šāpur's successors was decisive for Mani's personal fate and for that of Manichaeism in the Sasanian state. Where the Manichaeans did not obtain the support of the prince, or whenever he was overthrown, it was impossible for them to bring together the social sectors supportive of an antinomial society. In the West, the attempts at occupying social spaces and seeking political protection must have been unrelenting, though unavailing. In the fourth century, the *dux* Sebastianus, a Manichaean hearer, was on the point of becoming emperor.[181]

The disparity between Buddhism, on the one hand, and the Gnostic groups and Manichaeism on the other is accentuated at the historical level by the fact that in the centuries that followed Aśoka's reign, the Buddhists held power in a considerable part of Indian territory.

Numerous inscriptions dated to the second century BC/AD are both due to petty sovereigns and their immediate entourage and to major rulers. When, towards the end of second century BC, the orthodox wave raised by Puṣyamitra Śuṅga's *coup* calmed down, the *saṃgha*-s managed to take advantage of the social and geographic spaces left empty by the multi-faceted Brahmanical power and of the favourable international conditions. At Kanheri we find a minister and the daughter of a *mahārāja*,[182] at Kuda, the daughter of a royal minister and that of a *mahābhoja*, another word for 'king',[183] at Mahad there is a prince.[184] At Karle mention is made of the son-in-law of the Kṣatrapa king Nahapāna,[185] among the donors at Sanchi there is a queen, and at Bharhut there are no fewer than seven princes and princesses and a local chief;[186] and so on. Buddhist kingdoms, whatever their nature in terms of state organisation and social complexity, mushroomed with extraordinary rapidity and force.

KANIṢKA AND HARṢAVARDHANA

The foreign dynasties that from the first century BC to the second century AD ruled over a considerable part of India could not make themselves into 'national' dynasties, and allowed Buddhism, but also neo-Brahmanical movements, to grow. The case of Kaniṣka I is particularly interesting. Under his reign (second quarter of the second century AD),[187] Indian Buddhism reached, as documented by the imposing building activity and the iconographic output, its greatest economic power and territorial expansion. Unlike Aśoka, Kaniṣka was not Buddhist. The inscriptions of Surkh Kotal[188] and Rabatak[189] document his personal relationship and that of the dynasty with the Iranian gods, something that characterises also his coinage. In the complicated Indian universe, where traditional Brahmanical power drew new nourishment from the Sivaite movements from the one side and from Bhāgavatism from the other, Kaniṣka, like other Kuṣāṇa rulers, addressed the circles of theistic brāhmaṇas for acceptance. Nothing is more explicit than his image in the Māṭ *devakula*, where the Kuṣāṇa rulers appear as seeking legitimisation appealing to Sarva and Caṇḍavīra, two forms of Śiva.[190] The standing emperor holds a sword, which suggests his self-promoted status of *digvijayin*, and a *daṇḍa*, the symbol of political coercion. Neither attribute is compatible with the idea of a Buddhist *cakravartin*, rather suggesting a tentative

Sivaite theorisation of kingship. In the Rabatak inscription, Kaniṣka says of the Iranian god Srōš that 'in India [he] is called Mahāsena and is called Viśākha-Narasa, (and) Mihir'.[191] Mahāsena is a name of Kārttikeya, the warlike Sivaite god, and the same is true for Viśākha.[192] The attempt at building a bridge between the dynasty's power-conferring gods of Iranian stock and the gods of Sivaism is clear, and may shed further light on the experiment being carried on at Māṭ.

For all the attempts of the Kuṣāṇas to compromise with the theistic movements, it was the growing economic power of the Buddhist *saṃgha* and its supporters that ensured the stability of both the dynasty and the king, who left them free to operate. In the North-West, which was the hinge of the empire, the Buddhists were hegemonic, and Kaniṣka stood there as their great patron, gaining the everlasting gratitude of the Buddhists of later ages, who transformed him into a second Aśoka. Kaniṣka is credited as having convened a great Buddhist council in Kashmir (a tradition that also Xuanzang made his own),[193] although it is probably a pious fabrication.[194] As foreigners, the Kuṣā. nas did not – could not – close the society within an agrarian horizon, because this policy would have quickly swallowed them up. Thanks to unparalleled international conditions, they opened the society as had never happened before. This did not take place in the paradigmatic, dramatic way Aśoka had done by generating an alternative model of state from within Indian society: with Kaniṣka we do not have a founding axis with Buddhism, but rather a *de facto* axis. If an example of religious tolerance (hardly a convenient expression, since it was rather a question of maintaining the balance between the various factions) is ever to be found in Indian history, it is to Kaniṣka and the Kuṣāṇas that we should look.

Aśoka's equal, albeit in an entirely different context, was Harṣa-vardhana of Kānyakubja/Kanauj, a vaiśya by caste and, like Aśoka, a convert after six years of bloody military campaigns and a number of family misfortunes.[195] Political motivations may have played an important role in Harṣa's conversion: his worst enemies, Śaśāṅka of Gauḍa and Pulakeśin II were staunch Sivaites. His actual role as Buddhist *cakravartin* is often ignored,[196] yet the testimony of Xuanzang is certainly reliable in this respect: 'Once in five years he held the great assembly called *Môksha*. He emptied his treasuries to give all away in charity, only reserving the soldiers' arms, which were unfit to give as alms.'[197] Here Xuanzang describes the *pañcavārṣika*, a ritual the origins of which are perhaps traceable to the tours made every five years in the provinces of the empire by the *mahāmātra*-s appointed by Aśoka,[198] and to Brahmanical rituals.[199] The ceremony, which is not mentioned in the early Buddhist literature, took shape and acquired momentum in the Indian versions of the Aśoka legends and in their Chinese translations, where it was understood as deriving its legitimacy from the Mauryan emperor.[200] This literature was popular not only in India, but throughout the Buddhist world, in Central Asia and China: Faxian describes the *pañcavārṣika* as performed by the king of Kashgar,[201] and Xuanzang explains its mechanism in full with reference to the king of Bamiyan:

The king of this (*country*) every time he assembles the great congregation of the Wu-che (*Môksha*), having sacrificed all his possessions, from his wife and children down to his country's treasures, gives in addition his own body; then his ministers and the lower order of officers prevail on the priests to barter back these possessions; and in these matters most of their time is taken up.[202]

In his account, Xuanzang also describes a religious assembly that took place at his presence in Kanauj with the active participation of Bhāskaravarman, king of Kāmarūpa, an ally and a friend of Harṣa's.[203] A detail of the ceremony is worth quoting:

The king, on leaving the resting-hall, made them bring forth on a gorgeously caparisoned great elephant a golden statue of Buddha about three feet high, and raised aloft. On the left went the king, Śîlâditya, dressed as Śakra, holding a precious canopy, whilst Kumâra-râja, dressed as Brahmâ-râja, holding a white *châmara*, went on the right [...]. The king, Śîlâditya, as he went, scattered on every side pearls and various precious substances, with gold and silver flowers, in honour of the three precious objects of worship. Having first washed the image in scented water at the altar, the king then himself bore it on his shoulder to the western tower, where he offered to it tens, hundreds, and thousands of silken garments, decorated with precious gems. At this time there were but about twenty Śramaṇas following in the procession, the kings of the various countries forming the escort.[204]

Buddhism makes Indra and Brahmā, the highest gods of Brahmanism, the conscious subordinates of the Buddha, whom they entreat to preach the Law, and it is interesting for us to note that in the ceremony described by Xuanzang, Harṣa, the great monarch, incarnates Indra, the king of the gods, and Bhāskaravarman, a Sivaite kṣatriya representing a subordinate power,[205] Brahmā. This apparently curious ritual probably has its roots in the *avadāna* literature, where the

Tathāgata accepts by his silence Śakra's proposal to perform a ceremony that is also called *pañcavārṣika*,[206] but we must consider it, in the first place, one of the rituals that were part of the attempts at establishing an autonomous model of kingship, free from Brahmanical conditioning and interference.

If we turn to China, we note that Liang Wudi had performed the *wuzhe hui* several times, the first in AD 519, and the last in AD 547.[207] In the second half of the sixth century, the emperors of the southern Chen dynasty had also performed it.[208] Particularly significant are the *wuzhe hui* ceremonies performed by Wendi, the first emperor of the Sui Dynasty, in AD 601 and 606. He had attained power ruthlessly, and claimed legitimation by repenting the deeds of the past and directly referring to Aśoka.[209] Even Gaozu, the founder of the Tang dynasty (AD 618), felt the need to perform a *wuzhe dahui*, or great *pañcavārṣika*, although he was inclined towards Taoism:[210] in that period Buddhism was growing inordinately in China, and could hardly be ignored.

Harṣa's policy should be weighed up in the context of the Buddhist kingdoms of Central Asia and early Tang China, all strongly shaped by Buddhism. He must have perceived as real the possibility of building an empire destined to be the most important part of a Buddhist oecumene: the holy places were all in northern India. Powerful but minor states such as the Brahmanical kingdoms of eastern India and upper Deccan would not prevail against an Asian block. Harṣa assumed the title of 'King of Magadha' in AD 641,[211] when steps were finally taken to send an embassy to Tang China. This is not without significance: to be the king of Magadha, the land of the Buddha, was an added value to his stature as a sovereign.[212] For all his successes, Harṣa's position was more difficult than Aśoka's. Brahmanical power had already re-organised itself, and brāhmaṇas were a constant presence in his court. If we have to give credit to Xuanzang, who dwells at length on the episode, they even tried to murder him through a hired killer because of the resentment they felt for being ill-treated.[213]

Harṣa's was not only 'the last, great, personally administered, centralised empire'[214] of India, nor simply an example of 'feudalism from above' before 'real' feudalism set in.[215] He embodies the last attempt at establishing a Buddhist kingdom based on an open society and open borders, where trade would continue to play a crucial role. Xuanzang mentions the 'valuable merchandise' collected at Kanauj 'in great quantities',[216] a piece of information implying the still flourishing conditions of the commoners. Harṣa, a vaiśya, may be considered an expression of the social sectors that had been able to reaffirm their position after the end of the Guptas and that neo-Brahmanism was still unable to represent or suppress. The interest towards Tang China, which was booming thanks to the economic revolution introduced by the Buddhists in the urban areas, may be taken as an indication of what was being foreshadowed at the political level.

Towards the end of the sixth century, as we shall better see in the next chapter, the Karakorum route between India and Central Asia, and hence with China, had shifted westwards through the passes of the Hindukush (Xuanzang came to India through the new variant); yet a more direct route, shorter but difficult, was opened through Nepal and Tibet. The Tibetans, then in good terms with Tang China, established the Buddhist king Narendradeva on the throne of Nepal in the early 640s[217] to coincide with the beginning of the official relationship between China and Kanauj. His kingdom represented an important pawn in the game that the Buddhists intended to play. Harṣavardhana sent an embassy to Chang'an in AD 641, reciprocated by the Tang Emperor Taizong who sent Liang Huaijing to Kanauj. At the end of AD 643, a second Chinese embassy reached India, sent on behalf of the Chinese Buddhist clergy. It was led by Li Yibiao and Wang Xuance; the latter, who was a lay Buddhist,[218] was again sent to India in AD 646, but by that time Harṣa was dead, and the situation was rapidly evolving in a direction entirely different from the project on which the powerful Buddhist lobby at the Tang court was working.[219] It is worth noting that among the gifts that Harṣa sent to China with Li Yibiao when the latter left India there was a sapling of the Bodhi tree.[220]

The multiplication of embassies to and from Chang'an in the 640s shows that the design of an alliance of the Buddhist kingdoms and Tang China was becoming an actual political project. Scholars have shown that the Sino-Indian missions were inspired by political, commercial, and religious motives,[221] but they should be more precisely seen in the frame of an ambitious project that included also Central Asia and had Buddhism as its engine.[222] This explains, *a latere*, the otherwise incomprehensible episode of Xuanzang's invitation to the court of Bhāskaravarman, which caused a crisis in the relationship between the king of Kāmarūpa and Harṣa. Bhāskaravarman claimed that he expected 'the opening of the germ of religion' within himself: Xuanzang's refusal would have caused the world 'to be for ever plunged in the dark night (of ignorance)' and would have been detrimental to his 'invincible longing to think kindly of and show respect to (the Master) [...]'.[223] That two close allies had come at loggerheads for a monk in search of Buddhist *sūtra*-s is hardly believable. Xuanzang had to play an important political role, making proposals to which both Indian kings were deeply interested. The pilgrim had left China without formal authorisation, and his activism aimed, among other things, at avoiding repercussions on his return.[224] Bhāskaravarman eventually gave in, leaving Harṣa as the only interlocutor of the Tang, but after the death of his ally, he had further contacts with the Chinese.[225]

It is hardly the case of resorting to counterfactual history, but hypotheses allow us to give a better assessment of the situation. The death of Harṣa put an end to a project that might have changed Asian history. A large Buddhist oecumene economically strong, thanks to the engine of early Tang China (nearly a substitute of the Rome and Alexandria of a few centuries before) and strongly motivated from a religious point of view, might have stopped the Muslim advance and would not have easily sold cheap to Islam the social sectors involved in trade and industry. To make use again of Kosambi's categories, northern India might not have shifted from 'feudalism from above' to 'feudalism from below'.

CLOSING THE SOCIETY: VIOLENCE AND NEW STRATEGIES

The main reason why even unbiased scholars have embraced and perpetuated the idea of the religious tolerance of the Śuṅgas despite much contrary evidence, is the chronology once assigned to famous monuments. Coomaraswamy dated the stūpa of Bharhut to *c.* 150 BC, Stūpa 2 at Sanchi to the second century BC, and the railing of Bodhgayā to *c.* 100 BC.[226] Percy Brown, in the third revised edition of his widely read *Indian Architecture (Buddhist and Hindu Periods)*, published in 1956, still maintained that the gateway of the stūpa at Bharhut was built at a slightly later date than the palace of Aśoka in Pāṭaliputra.[227]

In 1958, in an epoch-making article published in *The Art Bullettin*,

Walter Spink radically revised the chronology of the so-called 'Śuṅga' and 'Śuṅga-Sātavāhana' monuments, none of which can be attributed to the second century BC, i.e. to the epoch when it would be possible to speak of a Śuṅga dynasty in full power and capable of promoting the construction of important monuments. Spink dated Bharhut to *c.* 90 BC, the gateways of Stūpa 1 at Sāñcī to the years AD 1-30, and as for the rock-cut caves of Deccan, he dated Bhaja (just to mention one) to 100-50 BC, that is, one century later than the date suggested by Coomaraswamy[228] and several other scholars after him. This change of perspective was quickly registered. In 1971, Jeannine Auboyer and Herbert Härtel dated Sanchi 2 to *c.* 100 BC, Bharhut to 100-75 BC, and Bhaja to the first century BC,[229] and similar dates were proposed by Susan Huntington in 1985.[230]

Another good reason for believing that the Śuṅgas were patrons of Brahmanism and Buddhism alike depended on John Marshall's chronology of the building phases of Stūpa 1 at Sanchi. The monument was first erected about 255 BC by order of Aśoka,[231] and its original structure of burnt bricks suffered great damage before an outer casing was added to it. Such damage was 'wantonly inflicted', and was arguably done by order of Puṣyamitra, 'who was notorious for his hostility to the Buddhists and his vindictive acts of vandalism in destroying their sacred monuments'.[232] Marshall maintained that the subsequent additions to Stūpa 1

> were effected under one of the Śuṅga kings about the middle of the second century B.C. They comprised the existing envelope of stone [...]; the lofty stone terrace and two flights of stairs at its base; the stone flagging of the procession path; the three stone balustrades [...]; and, lastly, the *harmikā* and umbrellas [...]. Under which particular king this transformation took place, we do not know [...]. It seems probable [...] that it took place during the reign of Pushyamitra's son Agnimitra, or of the latter's immediate successor, Vasujyestha.[233]

Marshall's relative chronology of Stūpa 1 has Aśoka at one end and the four *toraṇa*-s, dated by him to the latter part of the first century BC, at the other. But since the *toraṇa*-s go back to the early decades of the first century AD, the chronology of the monument should be correspondingly revised. It is reasonable to assign the reconstruction of Stūpa 1 to the years when the yard reopened on the Sanchi hill and Stūpa 2 was also erected, that is, around 100 BC. The investment was made possible thanks to the profits made after the real beginning of overseas trade, and especially after 127 BC, and was operated by the

Buddhist masters grouped in the Hemavata school who, under the guide of Gotiputra, had established themselves in the region some time before. The relics of these masters were deposited in Stūpa 2 at Sanchi and in the nearby stūpas of Andher and Sonari.[234] The weakening Śuṅga rule and the divided Brahmanical front could not make a stand against the positive results of the quickly expanding trade benefitting the Buddhist communities. Around the same time, in the periphery of the Śuṅga state, local kings were quick in supporting the resurfacing Buddhists: the *vedikā* and *toraṇa* at Bharhut were built by Dhanabhūti Vātsīputra, grandson of the local king Viśvadeva Gārgīputra, during the reign of a late Śuṅga ruler.[235] It took the brāhmaṇas about thirty years to react.

There is a complete halt in the patronage of Buddhist monuments between Puṣyamitra's coup and *c.* 100 BC. A second halt is observable between 75 BC and the early first century AD, after that Devabhūti's minister Vāsudeva, a brāhmaṇa, murdered the Śuṅga king in *c.* 73 BC, starting the orthodox Kāṇva rule. During the first halt, there is no trace of Buddhist monuments having been built anywhere in the Śuṅga territories. Whenever the situation allowed it, the orthodox wing intervened to re-establish proper rule,[236] but for all the conflicts between the brāhmaṇas of different persuasions, the Vidiśā court appears to have been no less extraneous to Buddhism than the northern Śuṅga territories. It was described from within by Kālidāsa, a dramatist and poet whose very existence shows how talented were the minds which contributed to the re-organisation of Brahmanical power.[237]

Regarding the second halt, we can indirectly form an opinion on the religious policy of the Kāṇvas by observing that there is no trace of what – with the Besnagar temple – had made Vidiśā one of the capitals of theistic Brahmanism, and that the building activity at Sanchi was resumed only after they left the stage. The Kāṇvas thus seem to have followed a strict Vedic path operating against the religion of the *śramaṇa*-s and providing only limited support to neo-Brahmanical strategies. The impressive *nāga* images from the Sanchi area date to the mid-first century BC,[238] and we do not know if they are part of a Bhāgavata or a Buddhist attempt at controlling 'lower' agricultural cults.

The corresponding halt in patronage that we observe in the Deccan in the same period may help to throw some light on what was happening in the north. The building activity on the Western Ghats was resumed only in the early decades of the first century AD after the long break[239] caused by the taking over of power by the Sātavāhanas. The founder of the dynasty, Śātakarṇi I, was an *aśvamedhin* king, as we know from the *praśasti* at Nanaghat.[240] As to the most famous monument ascribed to Sātavāhana patronage, the first and second phases of the stūpa railing at Amaravati are pre-Sātavāhana, and the third is ascribable to the declining years of the dynasty and to the early Ikṣvāku period.[241] The very existence of a 'Śuṅga art', if by this term we mean a set of monuments and iconographies datable to the second century BC or to the Śuṅga-Kāṇva phase, is questionable.

The fallout of Mauryan policy, which opened India to the outside world, and the emergence of an urban society in a proper sense[242] caused an unprecedented acceleration of social dynamics and the partial setback of Brahmanical power. Social mobility, controlled by the heterodox movements, neutralised Brahmanical opposition, which needed time to reorganise and react. When this happened, we witness both an outburst of violence and an extraordinary intellectual effort in the production of new religious models. These often were in strong contrast with each other, but all were adequate in the opposition to the state and society – disruptive of Brahmanical order – that the heterodox tried to realise.

Puṣyamitra Śuṅga, a Bhāradvāja brāhmaṇa,[243] either a general (*senāpati*) of the Mauryan army[244] or simply a leader of an army division,[245] taking responsibility for the needs of the first *varṇa*, carried out a *coup d'état* against Bṛhadratha Maurya in 186 BC, performed *aśvamedha*, and started a campaign aimed at dismantling the Buddhist monasteries, that were the nerve centres of the open society. The most extraordinary events in Puṣyamitra's career were certainly the two performances of the *aśvamedha* ritual, revived thanks to the pressure of the most revanchist wing of Brahmanical lineages. It was something unheard of since ancient times.[246] The ritual implied a great number of animal sacrifices[247] – an overt challenge to the *Aśokavacana*. The *aśvamedha* had extremely archaic traits, hardly compatible with the new era India had entered with the Mauryas, and marked a step back of centuries, yet it was performed not only by Puṣyamitra but, for many centuries to come, by a considerable number of kings. Some adjustments were introduced, and *aśvamedha*-s were performed not only with the aim of reaffirming orthodox kingship, but to complement the rituals introduced by the theistic groups which, fiercely opposed to the *śramaṇa*-s, were exploring new paths. During the main rite, the dead horse, a solar animal with which the king was equated, was made to lie with the first queen representing earth, and the rite took place during the month of *Phālguna*, to coincide with the public festivals connected to the bestowal of fertility upon earth.[248] The whole ritual appeared functional to the needs of an agrarian society, acknowledging the role of the king as guarantor of the regular sequence of the agrarian cycles.

The distance from the model of kingship propounded by Aśoka could not be greater, and behind the revival of the ritual we detect, besides the reference to the Veda, the world of the *brahmadeyya* lands and of the *brāhmaṇāgama*-s. The economic fallout of the *aśvamedha* amounted to the *dakṣiṇā*-s bestowed upon brāhmaṇas. These were usually cattle, whose great number[249] implies the gifting of lands, and gold,[250] which the brāhmaṇas traditionally hoarded up in contrast to the economic and monetary mechanisms of the open society. More *dakṣiṇā*-s were distributed for the performance of other rituals, the multiplication and segmentation of which was meant to satisfy as many brāhmaṇas as possible. The most vivid description of these donations is contained in the *praśasti* at Nanaghat, referring to a context not too different from that of Puṣyamitra. A *dakṣiṇā* of 1,101 cows, to be arguably divided among the officiating priests, recurs frequently, and larger figures occur in relation to certain other rituals, as for instance the *ṛika yajña*, which involved the donation of 11,000 cows and 1,000 horses, and the *bhagala daśarātra yajña*, for which a sacrificial fee was given consisting of 10,001 cows. Donations of money were also made, such as the 24,400 and 6,001 *kārṣāpaṇa*-s given for a ritual that remains unknown due to a gap in the text.[251] For the second *aśvamedha* performed by Śātakarṇi, a village was donated along with 14,000 *kārṣāpaṇa*-s; golden objects and an elephant, as well as '1 excellent village', in addition to other donations, were given for the unknown ritual mentioned above.[252]

We ignore which policy Aśoka had followed regarding the economic expectations of the brāhmaṇas – whether his request to respect them was accompanied by concrete measures making up for the consequences of *ahiṃsā*: probably not. Landowners had to feel discriminated when they compared their condition to the treatment reserved for commoners and urban bourgeoisie. However, it would be difficult to believe that the representatives of agrarian interests organised the anti-Buddhist reaction for economic reasons only. The question of power – an issue at the centre of classical historiography that is often neglected by modern historians – must have played a crucial role. The urban revolution could have hardly been prejudicial, in itself, to agrarian interests, but the new society in the making was an unprecedented challenge at the level of political power.

When placed in this framework, the sources, all well known, that accuse Puṣyamitra of having persecuted Buddhism, appear less questionable, although they are not such to make us take them literally. According to a famous passage of the *Aśokāvadāna*, Puṣyamitra, 'intending to destroy the Buddhist religion' equipped a fourfold army and proceeded to attack the Kukkuṭārāma monastery in Pāṭaliputra,[253] from which he was repelled by the roar of a lion that was heard at the gate. The Kukkuṭārāma, or Aśokārāma, was the central royal monastery founded, according to a tradition, by Aśoka himself.[254] Eventually Puṣyamitra destroyed the monastery, but the town stūpas escaped destruction. Puṣyamitra is said to have gone forth destroying stūpas and monasteries and slaughtering the monks throughout northern India. When he reached Śākala (Sialkot), he 'proclaimed that he would give a hundred dināra reward to whomever brought him the head of a Buddhist monk'.[255] As reported by the *Mañjuśrīmūlakalpa*, '[h]aving seized the East and the Gate of Kashmir, he the fool, the wicked, will destroy monasteries with relics, and kill monks of good conduct'.[256] Puṣyamitra did not succeed in his plan and was killed in battle by Kṛmiśa, a king whose identification is problematic, whom the *yakṣa* Daṃṣṭrānivāsin, arguably a Buddhist king of north-western India, called for help.[257] Literary sources are, in one way or another, almost always partial, but with all due caution it must be said that, like many other Buddhist sources, the *Aśokāvadāna* (absorbed into the *Divyāvadāna*), and more so the *Mañjuśrīmūlakalpa* (a later text), have not been given the credit they deserve. The story under discussion has been handed down unchanged from an earlier source or an earlier version of the *Divyāvadāna*. A Chinese translation of *c.* AD 300 is in accord with the present version of the chronicle.[258]

Puṣyamitra's attacks were particularly violent in Magadha – the centre of Mauryan power and heartland of Buddhism – and caused the weakening of eastern Buddhism, marking an era of decentralisation, and the monks' diaspora towards the mountain regions,[259] the first of a long series.[260] The destruction of the Kukkuṭārāma had a strong symbolic meaning, and showed the extent to which destructions were effective: Buddhism was structured in such a way that the devastation or forced abandonment of a monastery meant the beheading of the Buddhist community at a local level. Lay followers were left without interlocutors and could not but fall under the control of one of the numerous neo-Brahmanical groups.

An assessment of the religious and social repression attempted in the early years of Śuṅga rule is particularly difficult because the anti-Buddhist reaction was closely connected with the wars waged against the Yavanas of north-western India, in turn actuated for reasons to which religious considerations were not extraneous.[261] The Buddhists, as was to happen in later history, sided with the invaders, whose presence was considered as an opportunity to react against the Brahmanical attempt at shaking the fundamentals of the open society. The 'anti-national' nature of Buddhism ought to be understood as an attempt at giving Indian society an entirely different course, finding allies wherever possible, be they apostate brāhmaṇas, representatives of lower castes or tribal and foreign populations extraneous to the logic of *varṇa*-s and *jāti*-s.

Puṣyamitra had to perform *aśvamedha* as soon as he reached power to formally inaugurate his patronage of the Vedic religion,[262] but the Ayodhyā inscription records the performance of two horse sacrifices. The inscription was engraved by order of Dhanadeva, a descendant of Puṣyamitra's,[263] whose sixth ancestor, Sarvatāta, had also performed the horse sacrifice.[264] The decision to record Puṣyamitra's great ritual shows the extent to which the memory of epoch-making events was preserved, and shows the growing role of Ayodhyā (where Dhanadeva was arguably ruling) as a centre of orthodox power. We do not know to which event the second *aśvamedha* refers,[265] but the emergence of an orthodox Ayodhyā is significant in relation to the Vālmīki *Rāmāyaṇa* and to the message this work conveys. Ayodhyā corresponds to the Sāketa of the Buddhist records,[266] and the fact that Brahmanical tradition calls it with a different name is an early example of the parallel geography that in the course of time would cancel all undesired identities.

The hero of *kaṇḍa*-s II-VI of the *Rāmāyaṇa* is an antagonist of the Buddha, since his duty is to protect the four *varṇa*-s and rule the kingdom as a householder. Whatever the distant origin of the narration, Rāma appears as an alternative to the Buddhist *cakravartin*, his righteous kingdom being challengingly located at a short distance from the territories that marked the history of Buddhism. In the poem, Ayodhyā appears as a pole of orthodox rule, opposed to unorthodox Pāṭaliputra. Situated at a short distance from Śrāvastī, it is a response to the Buddha's claim for supremacy towards the brāhmaṇas, whom the Buddha had confounded appearing to them in the form of Agni.[267] The date of the poem is a much debated question, but the bulk of the work goes back to the third-first century BC:[268] the poem in the Vālmīki version is thus part of the effort at re-establishing Brahmanical power after the dramatic setback endured in Mauryan times. The poem is all the more remarkable in that, while accepting old rules and rituals, narrates a story that is in itself a new and sophisticated operative model.

In the kingdom of Rāma, the virtual model of the Śuṅgas, other strategies started being experimented, which incurred the condemnation of the strictest Brahmanical circles. The complex phenomenon of Bhāgavatism[269] acquires an extraordinary visibility in Vidiśā, the capital of Agnimitra. The early phase of the temple at Besnagar may go back to the first half of the second century BC.[270] It was reconstructed in the years 120-100 BC, when in its proximity were erected six *stambha*-s, the capitals of which bore the emblems of the *pañcavīra*-s, the 'five heroes' of the Bhāgavata religion.[271] The seventh *stambha*, rising just in front of the temple, bears an inscription in honour of Vāsudeva made by Heliodorus, the Indo-Greek ambassador to king Bhāgabhadra.[272] The autonomy of the regions forming the Śuṅga state favoured the development of different strategies to reassert Brahmanical rule. According to the *Yuga Purāṇa*, a work from the end of the first century BC, Agnimitra had 'a terrible quarrel with the Brahmins', causing a 'very dreadful and very terrible conflict'.[273] That it was caused by 'a girl of exceedingly beautiful form' may be doubted (although Cleopatra's nose has its weight in history), and it can be conjectured that the reason for the confrontation was the implementation, at the court of Vidiśā, of a different strategy for opposing the Buddhists. There is evidence of frictions between the brāhmaṇas of Udayagiri and the low-caste *śramaṇa*-s of Satdhara in the second century BC, as appears from the *Mātaṅga Jātaka*, a story set in Vidiśā where the Buddha, born as a low-caste *cāṇḍāla*, is abused by the brāhmaṇa Jātimanta.[274]

The enlarged Bhāgavata temple of Besnagar, where new rites could be performed in consonance with the physical and symbolic reality of a monumental structure, is something unheard of and clearly antagonistic to the Buddhist sanctuaries of Sanchi, Satdhara and Sonari lying to the south-west of the town. The temple implied image-worship and *bhakti* worship, which required a re-orientation of the priestly functions. The opponents of the Bhāgavatas pretended image-worshippers not to be brāhmaṇas and be non-Vedic,[275] and the conflict between the two parties was to be a long one.[276] To the *vaidika*-s, the idea that the divine could be expressed anthropomorphically was a Greek, *mleccha* idea. However, Bhāgavata monotheism and iconism were to prove a successful strategy against Buddhist hegemony: the *Yuga Purāṇa* attests that as early as the end of the first century BC the four-armed Keśava, i.e. Viṣṇu, 'bearing the conch, disk and mace [will be] called Vāsudeva'.[277] A consistent, complex Bhāgavata system of thought and practice existed from the beginning, favouring the integration of social sectors with low or no ritual status through appropriate rituals.[278] The challenge to Buddhism was thus open. Etienne Lamotte observed that it was the first time that 'Buddhism was confronted with a living theist doctrine positing in precise terms the problems of God, the soul and their interrelationship'.[279]

The breakthrough caused by lower, modernising brāhmaṇas in Vidiśā can be further appreciated if we give the place it deserves to the colossal statue of Kubera, the largest in a group of standing images found at Baba Dana Ghat on the river Betwa at Besnagar, not far from the Heliodorus pillar.[280] It was the main object of worship in a *yakṣa* precinct, to which pertains at least another image, that of a life-size *yakṣī*, and a *kalpavṛkṣa* from which Kubera's *nidhi*-s hang.[281] These sculptures, now dated to the second half of the first century BC and later,[282] are the result of a determined, conscious patronage. Towards the end of the first century BC, Balarāma images replaced former *nāga* sculptures on the edge of ancient irrigation systems, pointing to the involvement of Brahmanical institutions in landownership and agrarian production, suggesting competition with Buddhism.[283] This early Brahmanical pantheon spread into the surrounding rural areas from Vidiśā, a town at the centre of a large geographical area invested by Bhāgavata innovation that in promoting theistic doctrines played a role equivalent to that of Mathurā.

It is more difficult to suggest a pattern for early Sivaism. Patañjali, a contemporary of the early Śuṅgas and an advocate of theirs (he mentions one of Puṣyamitra's *aśvamedha*-s),[284] speaks of Śivabhāgavatas bearing iron spears,[285] and it is reasonable to assume that the movement had been in existence for a certain time, being possibly identifiable with that of the Pāśupatas.[286] The point, however, is when it became so relevant as to stimulate the interest of a part of the Brahmanical élite. The beginning of the iconographic output may be taken as the litmus test for evaluating the social relevance of the Sivaites, because it implies a complex theological system, the acquired capacity to conceive icons and to have them realised. The earliest images and *liṅga*-s go back to the second-first century BC and are mostly found in the upper and middle Ganges Valley.[287] Icons such as the *pañcamukhaliṅga* from Bhita and the *ūrdhvaretra* Śiva from Rishikesh[288] show that the fundamentals of Sivaite speculation were already developed, and that, in the case of the Śiva image from Rishikesh, the patrons could count on skilled sculptors.

The Pāśupatas, or some of the groups which bore this name, were ostracised by the *vaidika* brāhmaṇas to an even greater extent than the Bhāgavatas, but their hostility to Buddhism was such that no organised opposition to the latter could do without them. Their social radicalism found its limit in the theistic perspective,[289] but they had the extraordinary capacity of organising the vast Indian countryside. They modernised it ideologically by offering it, for the first time, a unified reference model and arming it, metaphorically and in actual facts, against the urban modernity of the Buddhists. Pāśupata opposition to Buddhism can be best appreciated from the daring creation of a new model of ascetic, Śiva, who is not a Gnostic creation – a prince, a *guru* and a saviour in the way of the Buddha, but a God, and an immensely powerful one for that. The uncritical endorsement of the majority of scholars of the alleged continuity of Śiva with Vedic Rudra, searched for and built up to obtain credit in orthodox circles, is an obstacle to understanding the upsetting rise of the God-ascetic, who would soon acquire the physical attributes of a violent, fighting divinity.

The Buddhists felt the impact of the new Brahmanical theistic movements, of both Bhāgavata and Sivaite orientation: they offered ontologies, something that the Buddhists could not do. The emergence of docetist positions in Buddhism, aiming at conferring on the Buddha an extra-mundane status,[290] may be traced back to the need to present a viable alternative to the faithful. Indian Buddhism should not be studied *per se*, but in counterpoint with Brahmanical theorisations.

There is little doubt that the closing down of the open society of the Buddhists and the resulting weakening of the religion of Dharma coincides with the fall in international trading activities, and in particular with the much decreased demand for Indian goods from Rome. Kuṣāṇa currency, circulating over a vast territory, had been linked to the Roman currency system. The collapse of the Han dynasty in China (AD 221) contributed to changing the picture in Central Asia. By that time, we observe a change in the Indian landscape, namely, a rapid process of de-urbanisation.[291] It is every archaeologist's experience that even in the case of continuous human occupation, post-Kuṣāṇa levels display much poorer building techniques and reuse of earlier building material. A great number of small and large towns were abandoned in the third century, and in certain areas, as is shown by territorial surveys, the collapse of a whole network of roads and small settlements, which had been kept functioning by Buddhist monasteries, is observable.[292] This process was probably aggravated by the collapse of the trading activity with the West that followed St Cyprian's plague of the years AD 251-66, which is an important component of the 'crisis of the third century' in the Roman Empire.[293]

It was imperative for the Buddhists to enact new strategies. They had sufficient intellectual resources and supporters to survive and grow even stronger, as happened in the North-East and in the regions bordering India to the north-west. If Buddhism disappeared from many areas as early as the third century, the reason cannot only be the change in the economic horizon. The active, de-legitimising hostility of the Brahmanical élites is to be taken into account because their strategies were not aimed at weighing more in the construction of an open, affluent society, up to taking control of it, but at introducing a different economic model.

If we unburden of the nationalistic load, ideological obsessions and occasional mistakes the depiction of the political-institutional situation of the third century AD given by K.P. Jayaswal,[294] we see that in many Indian regions the rulers followed the same policy of the Śuṅgas and Kaṇvas, opposing both Buddhism and Kuṣāṇa rule, only occasionally supporting the theistic brāhmaṇas. The number of kings who performed the great Vedic rituals, including the horse sacrifice, is astonishing. The Bhāraśivas performed ten *aśvamedha*-s,[295] Harītīputra Pravarasena I, in the Deccan, performed four, assuming the title of *samrāj*,[296] and an *aśvamedha* was also performed in the third century by Cāṃṭamūla I of the Ikṣvāku dynasty,[297] who claimed descent from the mythical Ikṣvākus of Ayodhyā. The lack of artistic patronage at the élite level with regard to the theistic movements in the territories controlled by these dynasties (an exception is Cāṃṭamūla I) indicates the strength of orthodox brāhmaṇas, who exercised control over the personal faith of the rulers[298] and drained all royal resources. Once the conditions created by Kuṣāṇa rule dissolved, and the imposing building activity and impressive amount of artistic output in key-cities like Mathurā and in Buddhist sanctuaries came to a halt, India, besides being de-urbanised, appeared as an iconic desert.

PĀṢAṆḌA-S AND *NĀSTIKA*-S

The *pāṣaṇḍa*-s are the impious, the impostors, the supporters of false doctrines. The epithet very often denotes the Buddhists in the literature, as we shall see: but why did the Buddhists continue to be branded as *pāṣaṇḍa*-s until the end, while the Bhāgavatas and Pāśupatas did not? The doctrines propounded by the theistic movements were as distant from Vedic orthodoxy as Buddhist doctrines. Could there be anything more extraneous to Vedic doctrine and praxis than the worship of the *liṅga*? Yet the Pāśupatas found their place in the Brahmanical system, ultimately governed by the *vaidika* brāhmaṇas, reserving sectarian rivalry (often very serious) for the other great theistic religion of the Bhāgavatas-Pāñcarātras. The divide between strongly dissenting voices and actual anti-system heretics may seem at first difficult to trace.

A scholarly tradition that emphasises inclusiveness rather than differentiation does not favour investigation on an issue such as orthodoxy/heterodoxy, and a comprehensive study on the question is lacking. However, several scholars – especially in the past – had very clear ideas on the matter. Rajendra Candra Hazra summed up the position of the religious movements that rose in ancient India before AD 200, classifying them, according to their position *vis-à-vis* Vedic orthodoxy, as anti-Vedic (Jainism, Ājīvakism and Buddhism) and semi-Vedic, in particular Vishnuism and Sivaism. These movements, besides looking upon the worship of their gods as the means of attaining salvation, were imbued with non-Brahmanical ideas and practices and violated the rules of caste and *āśrama*-s, but within them soon emerged a class of 'Smārta-Vaiṣṇavas' and 'Smārta-Śaivas' (as Hazra proposed to call them). They looked upon the Vedas as authorities, attached great importance to *varṇāśramadharma* and *smṛti* rules, and did not want to give them up.[299] The call for Vedic orthodoxy goes back to a very early age in Bhāgavatism,[300] and neo-Brahmanical orthodoxy was the result of the conciliation of the Vedic rules and the need inherent to the theistic systems to open their ranks to converts of different social stands. In this regard, it is interesting for us to note that the revived *aśvamedha* ritual appears to have been performed by King Gājāyana, the Bhāgavata ally of Puṣyamitra.[301] Despite the caveats, we have here an early example of Vedic and theistic compromise.

Buddhism, despite numerous, and sometimes substantial adjustments to Brahmanical diktats (we will discuss the point in the coming chapters), resisted submitting to the principle of the existence of either a divine, preordained social order[302] or an omniscient and omnipotent being. The latter point explains why the Buddhists were always called *nāstika*-s, atheists. In the medieval literature, the term applies almost exclusively to them, since the other atheist schools had long since disappeared from the Indian religious horizon and the Jains, as we shall see in Chapter VI, had conformed to Brahmanical order to an even greater extent than the Buddhists.

A parallel with the religious situation of early Christianity, especially of the second century AD, would help clarify concepts and would serve the scope of modelling. The canon of the Great Church based on the four gospels and a few other texts was established in that period to coincide with the creation of an orthodox theology and praxis and in opposition to the Gnostic interpretations of the scriptures,[303] and in the two following centuries heresiological categories and classifications were established.[304] We are forced to limit the scope of our investigation, limiting ourselves to making our own the methodological considerations made by Tadeusz Manteuffel in relation to the heretical movements of medieval Europe. The relationship between orthodoxy and heterodoxy/heresy was not defined once for all, but was the consequence of the establishment of the medieval Church. The papacy judged some opinions orthodox, and other, almost identical ones, heterodox. The decisive factor was the obedience towards the Church authorities: this and not the substance of the professed ideas decided the attitude towards the innovators. An unconditioned submission to Rome usually allowed the innovators to remain faithful to the professed ideology without opening up a conflict. Conversely, any refusal to obey, determined the condemnation of the ideas propounded by the rebels, as heretical.[305]

Likewise, the theistic movements of ancient India could propound the most eccentric doctrines and rituals inasmuch as they accepted the Vedas and what the Vedas meant in terms of social order: *varṇāśramadharma* and, within it, the superiority of the *brāhmaṇa-varṇa*. Instead of opposing the brāhmaṇas, the theistic innovators made themselves acceptable to the highest *varṇa*, if they were not already part of it. On the contrary, the Buddhists refused to recognise the superiority of the brāhmaṇas, disobeying and opposing them. Buddhist heresy is definable in relation to the progressive formation of neo-Brahmanical orthodoxy and to the obedience that any orthodox system requires. Here comes another important point discussed by Manteuffel, that is, the question of heretical tenacity and obstinacy, and of heretical doctrines reaching a point when no compromise with the orthodox is possible and a final break occurs. This is what, despite the numerous attempts at establishing conditions of non-belligerence and coexistence, happened in mediaeval India.

The use of the expression 'inter-sectarian rivalries', so common in the literature, should be avoided when discussing the relationships between Buddhism and orthodoxy. The differences and clashes between Bhāgavatas and Pāśupatas or between the *vaidika*-s and the theistic groups can be rightly described as 'sectarian', but those between the *vaidika*-s and the neo-orthodox from the one side and the Buddhists from the other are not:[306] in this case, differences and clashes are systemic.

NOTES

1. Tucci (1977, II: 30).
2. Ibid.: 52.
3. Widengren (1952; 1967). Cf. also id. (1964: 78).
4. S. Dasgupta (1932-55, I: 50).
5. Ibid.: 48.

6. Della Casa (1976: 20).
7. Ibid.: 23-24.
8. Johann Bronkhorst has observed that it is a mistake to reinterpret the distinctive features of early Buddhism so as to agree better with what we know of the other Indian religions of its day, and that (as maintained here) it has no links with Vedic asceticism, being distinct as well from the other forms of non-Vedic asceticism (Bronkhorst 1998: 95-96).
9. The definition is Max Weber's (1958: 58).
10. The very existence of 'Gnosticism' as a usable historical category has been questioned. The better knowledge we have of the formation of Christianity after the discovery of the Nag Hammadi library would advise us not to use it, even not considering the cheap intrusions of alien subjects and concepts into the construct (M.A. Williams 1996: 3-5 and passim). However, 'biblical demiurgy' is hardly an expression that can replace the term 'Gnosticism', especially for the discussants who, trying not to be cheap, seek a relationship between the Gnostic groups of the Mediterranean and other religious movements of antiquity.
11. Edward Conze, who devoted an important paper to the correspondences between Gnosticism and Mahāyāna in the early centuries of our era, warned that not all the Buddhist doctrines that were close to gnosis were 'exclusively Mahayanistic' (Conze 1967: 651). He did not think, however, that a systemic relationship could exist between Buddhism and Gnosticism.
12. The devotional practices of the laymen were admitted and encouraged, although, as observed by Lamotte (1958: 477), even in the Mahāyāna the devotion is depersonalised and focuses on the original aspiration that consists in the reawakening of the thought of *bodhi*. However, orthodox brāhmaṇas always remained convinced that the Buddhists were atheist.
13. In the countries where no pre-existing Brahmanical control over society existed and where Buddhism put down roots, there is no trace of a caste system. According to Thapar (1978: 53), the Buddha distinguished between caste system understood as a frame of the socio-economic structures, which he accepted, and the notion of caste purity inherent in the upper castes, which he rejected. Buddhism thus succeeded only partially, and only in certain periods, to hegemonise Indian society, against which it could more often set up only that sort of counter-society represented by the *saṃgha* (ibid.: 87). On the Buddhist position on caste, the reader is referred to Eltschinger (2009), which we shall often recall.
14. Thapar (1978: 52-53, 78, and passim; 1992: 49-50 and passim). In a study on Ajanta, Bautze-Picron (2002), subtracting a large number of images to the class of 'decorative motifs', has shown that besides having a protective function, they are owners of wealth, their attendants pouring money from a bag or holding a cornucopia full of flowers or coins. For all their possible 'higher' symbolic meaning, they indicate that material wealth matters, functional though it is to the well-being of the *saṃgha* (cf. p. 234).

15. *Saṃyutta Nikāya*: VI. I.1 (vol. 1, p. 174).
16. Puech (1985: 286-87).
17. See in any case Conze (1967) for important observations.
18. Lamotte (1958: 690-91); for a brief précis on the Mahāsāṃghikas and Lokottaravādins, see P. Williams (2008: 18-20).
19. Bianchi (1967: 13).
20. Filoramo (1993: 135); cf. Puech (1985: 222-24).
21. See for instance *Dīgha Nikāya*, *Mahā Satipaṭṭhāna Sutta* 8-10 (pp. 338-39). The meditation on impurity is known as *aśubhabhāvanā*.
22. Bianchi (1967: 13).
23. Eliade (1982) is as illuminating in examining and comparing complex phenomena as he is misleading in considering them expressions of a unified historical tradition, and as to historians, Thapar (1978), for all her penetrating vision, does not distinguish clearly between the phenomenical and the historical-social level.
24. Drijvers (1984: 115); Brown (1992: 304).
25. For instance, Weber (1995, II: 193, 230-31, 233). See discussion below.
26. At times violent, as in Syria (Drijvers 1984: 109; Brown 1992: 302-3).
27. The demand among Mediterranean élites for goods from India was already high (De Romanis 1996: 169), and during the Republic Greek and Roman merchants were aware that the Indian goods demanded on the market could be obtained more directly and probably at lower prices by sea (Lyding Will 1991: 154). After 127 BC, the merchants began to crowd the ports of Syria and Alexandria (De Romanis 1996: 165).
28. Ibid.: 170.
29. Kosambi (1965: 182).
30. Ibid.: 183.
31. *Lüders List*: no. 1137.
32. Ibid.: no. 1165.
33. Kosambi (1965: 185). On the lending on interest by Buddhist monasteries, see Schopen (2004), with relation to the *Vinaya* of the Mūlasarvāstivādins. Lending on interest, a crucial activity for economic development, was forbidden in a number of religious traditions, and the ban had somehow to be circumvented (see the role played by the Jewish communities in the middle age, both in Europe and in the Islamic world).
34. Liu (1988: 121).
35. Weber (1993: 200).
36. Kosambi (1965: 185).
37. *Lüders List*: nos. 987, 995, 998, 1000-01; no. 1005; nos. 993, 996, 1033; no. 1082 respectively.
38. Ibid.: nos. 1055, 1062, 1065-66; nos. 1063-64, 1073; nos. 1037, 1045; no. 1048 respectively.
39. Ibid.: nos. 1087, 1090, 1092.
40. Ibid.: no. 1109.

41. Ibid.: no. 1154.
42. Ibid.: no. 1180.
43. At Vaddamanu, a few kilometres from Amaravati, located immediately outside ancient Dharaṇīkoṭa, there was a Jain sanctuary, one of the few that have been excavated. Only a few fragments of inscriptions have come to light, but the presence of lay donors is attested (Sastri, Kasturibai & Veerender 1992: 267).
44. *Lüders List*: nos. 1213-14, 1229, 1281-82, 1285; nos. 1210, 1230; no. 1261 respectively.
45. Ibid.: no. 1298.
46. Lamotte (1958: 455-56). For the inscriptions of Sanchi, edited by N.G. Majumdar, see Marshall & Foucher (1940: 264 ff.); cf. also *Lüders List*: nos. 162-668.
47. Cf. also Thapar (1978: 71). This was made easy by the fact that for merchants, artisans and small owners it was possible to embrace the monastic state only for a limited time after which they would return to lay life (Lamotte 1958: 61).
48. Ibid.
49. See, for example, for Amaravati, inscription nos. 1250 and 1279 of *Lüders List*; for Nāsik, cf. ibid.: nos. 1141, 1144, etc.
50. See at Nāsik the dedication put up by the wife of a general (ibid.: no. 1146).
51. Lamotte (1958: 455; for Bharhut, cf. *Lüders List*: nos. 687 ff.). The documentation is plentiful for almost all the monasteries of the Deccan and the Vindhyas that have left epigraphic material.
52. B.C. Law (*IA* 57, 1928: 49-54, 65-68, 86-89) has provided an account of the most prominent women in early Buddhism.
53. Bareau (1963: 106 ff., with discussion of the different versions of the episode). Bactria never became part of the westernmost provinces of the Mauryan Empire annexed by Aśoka, but circulation of men and merchandises with the regions south of the Hindukush and India had been continuous since the remotest times.
54. This is the historiographic perspective opened by Rudolph (1977*a*; 1977*b*). Green (1985: 3-4), who judged it not sufficiently motivated, has given it a more analytical basis.
55. Ibid.: 262.
56. Ibid.: 94-95; cf. also Rudolph (1977*a*: 38), who observes that the Gnostics recruited followers in almost all social strata where the communities of the great Church had their roots, a serious reason for the Church Fathers to react.
57. Green (1985: 66).
58. Ibid.: 136.
59. Ibid.: 136, 97. For the trade in the Red Sea and in the Arabian Sea, see details in Casson (1989: 11 ff.) and, especially in relation to the information gathered from Pliny, in De Romanis (1996: 157 ff., 167 ff.).

60. *Lógoi*: XXXII.36 (vol. 3: 207). The Indian Ocean was already known as *'Indikḗ thálassa* to Dio.
61. Weber (1993: 7-8).The information come from Pliny, *Naturalis Historia*: VI.101; according to another version of the passage, the sesterces would have been 50 million (De Romanis 1996: 202; Conte in *Naturalis Historia* I:710-11). Weber relied upon Karl Julius Beloch's studies of economic history, and recent studies (Miller 1974, Casson 1989 and De Romanis 1996) amply confirm the estimates made at the end of the nineteenth century and up to Warmington (1974 [1928]). The figures given by Pliny (also in *Naturalis Historia*: XII.84, *minimaque computatione*) are considered exact and reliable (Miller 1974: 225-26).
62. Weber (1993: 38-39).
63. Harnack (1921: 1 ff., 21 ff.).
64. *Acts of Thomas*: I.3 (p. 61).
65. It is generally believed that Buddhism was introduced into China during the reign of Emperor Mingdi (AD 58-76), the first monastery to be established being that of the White Horse (*Baimasi*) in Luoyang in AD 65. By that time, Buddhism had already been introduced into the country, however (Ch'en 1964: 31), and the Xinjiang trade routes must have been already used by Buddhist merchants. According to an apocryphal tradition, eighteen Buddhist monks brought *sūtra*-s to Xianyang in Shaanxi as early as 242 BC (cf. Zürcher 2007: 19-20).
66. What has been said above for Junnar, could also be said for Bhaja and Karle, located almost opposite one another in the same small valley.
67. I follow Lamotte (1953: 100); however, 'at least from 62 BC and perhaps as early as 74/3 BC' in the Ptolemaic bureaucracy there was a superintendency on the Eritrean and the Indian Sea (De Romanis 1996: 165).
68. Casson (1989: 22).
69. *Lógoi*: XXXII.40. Cohoon (cf. vol. 3, p. 111) translates 'a few Indians', but *'Indṓn tivas* is rather 'some of the Indians'; Dio was aware that India was inhabited by different kinds of people.
70. Salomon (1991); I. Mahadevan in Begley (1996: 291). Inscribed sherds in Tamil-Brāhmī script with the names Kaṇaṉ and Cātaṉ dated to the first century BC, have been found at Quseir al-Qadim (Myos Hormos; on this toponym, see De Romanis 1996: 147 ff.). The fact that the name Kaṇaṉ was also found on the rim of a thick jar at Arikamedu on the Coromandel coast (Begley 1996: 309) may not be a coincidence (ibid. 23-24). An inscription reading 'Koṟṟaṉ, the chieftain' comes from Berenike (ibid. 291).
71. Didri (2002: 581-83) and esp. Strauch & Bukharin (2004).
72. The old question whether there was a Buddhist settlement at Alexandria, answered in the negative (de Lubac 1987: 20 ff.) should now be reopened.
73. Thapar (1978: 72).
74. Champakalakshmi (1996: 105, 114).
75. Ibid.: 119.
76. K. Rajan (2008: 57-58, 67).

77. In the second half of the first century BC the Sātavāhanas (an orthodox dynasty) took possession of the region of Junnar and of other parts of upper Deccan. I limit myself to referring the reader to Sircar (1965*b*: 190-97) for the inscriptional evidence and to id. (HCIP 2: 191 ff.), for the historical picture, as well as to Cribb (1998) for a reappraisal of the whole question. Around the mid-second century AD, Gautamīputra defeated the pro-Buddhist Kṣatrapa Nahapāna and took possession of Nāsik, where, at least initially, he confirmed the privileges granted to the monasteries (Sircar in HCIP 2: 201; cf. Cribb's revised chronology). We will see below that a famous monument ascribed to Sātavāhana patronage such as the stūpa of Amaravati has little to do with this dynasty.
78. Whittaker (2009: 11).
79. Rudolph (1977*a*: 41); Kippenberg (1984: 121).
80. Cancik (1984: 175).
81. *Adversus haereses*: I.13.
82. Rudolph (1977*a*: 39).
83. Green (1985: 71).
84. This aspect of the classical sources has been underlined by some authors; cf. e.g. Filliozat (1949: 27-28); Daffinà (1977: 32-33).
85. *Stromata*: I.76.6; II.60.2-4.
86. Daffinà (1995: 36).
87. Finley revised his own theories, which have been again questioned on the basis of the archaeological evidence (Cameron 1993: 123). This new perspective is clear to Thapar (1992*b*: 4). Finley's ideas were accepted by Henry Green (1985: 67).
88. See, e.g. Weber (1995, II: esp. 196-200); see also Kippenberg (1981).
89. Drijvers (1984: 110).
90. We have already noted Max Weber's dependence on positions such as those of Edgar Quinet. Here the influence on his thought of the paradigm of a socially and culturally unified India must be also underlined.
91. Weber (1995, II: esp. 230-31, 233).
92. Ibid.: esp. 147, but passim. Weber (1958: 193 ff., 203 ff.) marvels that Buddhism became one of the world's greatest religions given that 'Buddhistic monastic ethic simply does not represent a rational, ethical endeavor' (p. 218). For the discussion on Weber's constructs, the reader is referred to Schluchter (1984), Bechert (1986) and, for a critique as dispassionate as it is acute, to Thapar (1992*b*: 41-58).
93. Ibid.: 56.
94. See especially Kosambi (1952; 1965) and Thapar (1978; 1992*b*).
95. Thapar (1978: 52-53, 93; 1992*b*: 56).
96. Green (1985: 176; 263); Rudolph (1977*a*) rejects these positions.
97. Kippenberg (1970: 225). Odo Marquard stated, from his particular view point, that 'gnosis is de-politicised Platonism' (cf. ibid.: 134).
98. *Adversus Valentinianos*: 39.2 (p. 940).

99. Couliano (1989: 189). This author does not include Marcion in the picture.
100. Although it is difficult for me to accept Kippenberg's interpretation of the Gnostic phenomenon, he is certainly right in considering central their passion for liberty (Kippenberg 1970: 225), which can be experienced, however, not only through gnosis (characteristic of the pneumatics), but (for the psychics) through operating in a social and economic context that eludes *nómos*. For the 'vocation for liberty' of the Gnostics, cf. also Rudolph (1977*a*: 43).
101. A devastating plague started spreading in AD 251, and ravaged the Roman world for fifteen years. If it affected Alexandria, as is extremely likely, the blow to an economical model based on urban growth, trade, and production of non-primary goods must have been serious. The symptoms of the plague, not exactly identified, have been imprecisely described by St Cyprian, bishop of Carthage (in present-day Tunisia), who was interested in transforming it into an opportunity for the triumph of Christianity. See the description of the 'horrible and deadly plague', causing a high number of deaths in *De mortalitate*: esp. 14-15.
102. Brown (1975: 97).
103. Kippenberg (1984: 121 ff.).
104. It was first suggested by Conze (1967: 656-57).
105. For the Gnostic side, we can recall the Valentinian Marcus (*Adversus haereses*: I.13.3), and for the Phibionites, I refer the reader to Eliade (1982, with bibliography). According to St Augustine, the Manichaeans and dependent groups believed that the divine substance was imprisoned in food and drink and should be purified; the *electi* would 'consume a sort of eucharist sprinkled with human seed in order that the divine substance may be freed even from that' (*De haeresibus*: 46. 25-100; pp. 86-91).
106. See the discussion on the theory propounded in the *Tathāgatagarbha Sūtra*, a third-century work, by Zimmerman (2002: esp. 50 ff., 62 ff.).
107. Conze (1967: 665-66). For Kennedy, who had not read Weber, it was instead very clear that 'Indian merchants, as a rule, have always been Buddhists or Jains. Buddhism was a merchant religion par excellence' (Kennedy (1902: 386-87): it was their monopoly of the Indo-Alexandrian trade that made possible the meeting between Buddhism and the Gnosticism of Basilides (the object of Kennedy's investigation).
108. A further question Conze (1955: 162) would have been pleased to see clarified.
109. H.-Ch. Puech in Doresse, Rudolph & Puech (1988: 180).
110. Widengren (1964: 153).
111. Brown (1969).
112. I follow Brown (1975: 98-99).
113. Ibid.: 94.
114. Ibid.: 92.

115. Widengren (1964: 114).
116. It is in relation to this that also Gardner (2005) and Deeg & Gardner (2009) have shown that the contacts between Indians and the people of the eastern Mediterranean were direct. It is not always the case to call in question Iran as an intermediary, as is often done.
117. Thapar (1978: 44). The Manichaeans have in common with the *śramaṇa*-s also the practice of fasting (see Henning 1954 and Doresse, Rudolph & Puech (1988: 238 ff.) for the former and Deo (1954-55) for the Jains. Although the Buddha had rejected extreme asceticism, several groups of monks, in the light of a docetist interpretation, considered the life of the Buddha as a model worthy of imitation, including his severe fasting. We have Gandharan iconographies of the first century AD attesting the monks' worship for Siddhārtha fasting (Verardi 1994: 38-39), and in the third century AD Dharmarakṣa translated into Chinese a text on the 'three months of prolonged fasting' (Forte 1971), which developed out of the *uposatha/poṣadha* days. Forte & May (1979: 396-98) have pointed out the passages of the Pāli Canon documenting the periods of fasting of the *upāsaka*-s. On the *uposatha*-day observance, see also Norman (1994: 208 ff.).
118. See, for example, Conze (1955: 80 ff.).
119. Gokhale (1969) has underlined the special relationship between early Buddhism and the monarch, and has analysed the relation between *dhamma* and *āṇā*, the state, emphasising as well the impasse Buddhism reached when a vicious king was ruling. Ruegg (1995) discusses later developments.
120. Heesterman (1957: 201). We do not know the degree to which the ritual described in the texts correspond to the practice of the third century BC. The inclusion of both a barren and two pregnant cows among the sacrificed animals (ibid. 168, 201) would indicate an early practice.
121. See Bechert (1991-92) for a discussion on the long and short chronology of the Buddha, and in particular his own contribution (vol. 1, pp. 222-36).
122. MRE I [Sahasram, Bairat and Siddhapura versions] (Hultzsch 1925: 166-69; cf. note 18 on p. 167); MRE II (ibid. 169-72); *Dīpavaṃsa* 6. 55 (cf. p. 151). Here and below, the quotations from Aśoka's edicts are taken from Hultszch's translation (integrations not reported). Occasional reference is made to Ulrich Schneider's critical edition of the rock edicts.
123. I prefer this explanation to that provided by Baechler (1988), who has contended that the caste system developed as a response to the check of Mauryan imperialism and to the political inconsistency that followed the end of the dynasty. The caste system was reinforced under Śuṅga rule as a response to the anti-*varṇa* policy of the Mauryas.
124. See Tambiah's criticism of Thapar (Tambiah 1976: 59).
125. Thapar's statement that '*Dhamma* was Asoka's own invention' (Thapar 1997: 149) can be accepted only within a modelling of political categories and behaviours. See below.

126. On the difficulty of this identification, endorsed by Kangle (1965, III: 101 ff.), see Burrow (1968).
127. Hence, also the parallels with Machiavelli (Max Weber again!), entirely out of place: the *Arthaśāstra* is an orthodox text created within and for the maintenance of Brahmanical power, while Machiavelli radically breaks off with the establishment and the current conceptions of his time.
128. Willis (2009: 62); after Trautmann's book (1971), Scharfe (1993: 293) has proposed a second-century AD date. Trautmann attracted a barrage of criticism in India, and still does (Mital 2000). Thapar (1997: 292-96) still maintains that the core of the treaty goes back to the Mauryan epoch, an opinion shared by Habib & Jha (2004: 46-50). In an earlier contribution, Irfan Habib had contended that it is not easy to assume the existence of a Mauryan core in *Arthaśāstra*'s Book II, and did not make use of the evidence in 'Mapping the Mauryan Empire' (Habib & Habib 1989-90: 57). For the range of early opinions on the date of the treatise, see Mishra (1989). The belief that the *Arthaśāstra* is a Gupta work is gaining momentum, however (see, e.g. D. Ali (2007: 9) and shall be accepted when both the nature of the Gupta state and policy and, conversely, the nature of the Mauryan state are understood.
129. *Arthaśāstra*: 3. 20.16.
130. Ibid.: 2.26.10. It also sanctions the killing of animals kept in reserved park enclosures (ibid.: 2.26.1-3), arguably destined for royal hunting.
131. Cf. Ananda W.P. Guruge in Seneviratna (1994: 145 ff.).
132. An example is Basak (1959: XXV).
133. Barua (1946, I: 225).
134. Ibid.: II: esp. 62 ff.
135. Ibid.: II: esp. 38 ff.
136. See on this K.R. Norman's observations in *Sutta Nipāta*: Introduction, pp. xxix-xxx.
137. Tambiah (1956: 40). I make my own Tambiah's arguments also for the statements that follow.
138. Ibid.: 52.
139. The most sensational case was that of Empress Wu Zhao (AD 690-705), on which see Forte (2005: 204-42).
140. Kosambi (1975: 178-80).
141. This statement should be toned down if the thesis of Vigasin is accepted, according to which not only was the structure of the Mauryan state neither bureaucratic nor centralised, but the cities were governed by a council of *mahāmāta*-s constituting a *pariṣad* (Vigasin 1993-94: 20-21).
142. PE VI (Hultzsch 1925: 128-30). See also RE VI, Kalsi (ibid. 34-36): 'For I consider it my duty to promote the welfare of all men' (p. 35). Schneider (1978: 109) has '[...] werde ich selbst die Angelegenheiten der Leute behandeln'.
143. RE I, Girnar (Hultzsch 1925: 1-2).

144. RE IV (ibid.: 30-31).
145. PE V (ibid.: 125-28).
146. Gokhale (1980: 69-71) has shown that *brāhmaṇagāma*-s designated in a proprietary way for the residence and maintenance of learned brāhmaṇas and *brahmadeyya* lands given as royal gifts to brāhmaṇas, of which they became an absolute property, existed from early times. The relevant epigraphic evidence is naturally later than the third century BC, and chronological questions exist for the villages owned by brāhmaṇas mentioned in the Canon (below, Chapter III).
147. PE II (Hultzsch 1925: 120-21).
148. RE IX, Kalsi (ibid.: 37-39); 'primitive und unnütze' in Schneider (1978: 111).
149. Barua (1946, I: 242) explains why the word *bhūna*/*bhrūṇa*, which may occasionally stand for learned brāhmaṇa, normally means fetus, as in the case discussed here. In a recent translation of the *Māgaṇḍiya Sutta* ('Indeed, Master Bhāradvāja, it is an ill sight we see when we see the bed of that destroyer of growth, Master Gotama'; *Majjhima Nikāya*: 75.5 [502]; p. 607), an explanation at the symbolical level is suggested (cf. note 740 on p. 1281).
150. Gokhale (1980) has calculated that 40 per cent of the early Buddhist élite was formed by brāhmaṇas, some of *mahāsāla* families. Cf. also below, Chapter III.
151. For example, Nāgārjuna and Aśvaghoṣa, Asaṅga and his brother Vasubandhu, Buddhaghoṣa, Diṅnāga and Dharmakīrti, and several others (see the question discussed in Chapter IV). Others were kṣatriyas, often recognisable as bearing a *-varman* (armour) name (I thank Toru Funayama for this information).
152. RE V, Kalsi (Hultzsch 1925: 32-34). Vigasin (1993-94) maintains that the term *mahāmāta* does not denote a professional bureaucrat, but either an important person sent by the emperor on tours of inspection or a member of the local bodies of self-government.
153. Habib & Jha (2004: 66).
154. See for insance the Buddhist and Jain charges against the Ājīvikas (Basham 1951: 121-25, 134-41).
155. *ASIR* 2 (1871, A. Cunningham): 40-53, pls. 18-20; S.P. Gupta (1980: 189-221).
156. Unanimous Jain tradition claims that Candragupta abdicated and followed Bhadrabāhu as his teacher to Sravana Belgola, where he died. Cf. Mookerji (1966: 39-42).
157. PE V (Hultzsch 1925: 125-28). A substantial step forward in the identification of the animals mentioned by Aśoka in his edicts has been made by Norman (1990*b*) with reference to PE V. In this case, the apparent random list of animals cited includes talking birds, a series of aquatic birds, aquatic animals, a series of reptiles and three birds of the pigeon/dove family.
158. Tambiah (1976: 54).

159. Ibid.: 60.
160. Even Habib & Jha (2004: 70), who raise this point and get close to an explanation in terms of social history, hesitate in recognising the nature of Aśoka's *dharma*. Some of Weber's undervaluations of Buddhism still linger about.
161. RE VI, Girnar (Hultzsch 1925: 11-13, cf. p. 13).
162. Cf. ibid.: 130-37; cf. pp. 134-35; see also RE II, Girnar. ('On the roads wells were caused to be dug, and trees were caused to be planted for the use of cattle and men'; Hultsch 1925: pp. 2-4).
163. Cf. Norman (1990*a*).
164. Cf. Hultzsch (1925: 69).
165. The urbanised regions of the empire under direct Mauryan administration were situated at a great distance from one another, connected by long corridors crossing territories inhabited by tribals (Allchin 1995: 133-51, 207-09). The opinion that the whole subcontinent was controlled by a centralised and many-eyed administration – an idea derived from the *Arthaśāstra* – is almost completely abandoned today. According to Fussman (1988), the Mauryan empire had a strong central administration but regional governments were looser and looser proceeding towards the periphery. We may update this interpretation, in part, considering that the local *saṃgha*-s had an active role in the transmission of the emperor's edicts (Tieken 2000: 27) and, therefore, an active political role at a local level.
166. Coomaraswamy (1956: pls. XXI, XXXVIII.114); Cunningham (1979: pl. LII).
167. See the lively debate among scholars in Seneviratna (1994).
168. An exception is the site of Gotihawa (Verardi 2007*b*: 104 ff., 131 ff.), on which see more in the next chapter.
169. I refer the reader to Falk (2006) for a thorough re-examination of all the Aśokan sites. Maps, photographs and drawings, as well as an exhaustive bibliography, makes this book an indispensable companion to Aśokan studies. The author has checked the texts of the edicts, accounting for the discrepancies between the present state of the inscriptions and their earliest documentation.
170. Patil (1963: 371-421) has collected all the relevant information on Patna, and S.P. Gupta (1980: 227-46) has tried his best to deduce a *forma urbis* from the scattered and insufficiently checked evidence. De Simone (forth.) has recently questioned S. P. Gupta's conclusions and has proposed a mapping of the Mauryan town that includes the Kumrahar hall.
171. Chakrabarti (2001: 160 ff., 191 ff., 209 ff.).
172. The discussion on this important point was raised by Bechert (1961) in relation to the Sarnath edict, and has been joined by several scholars.
173. We should not need to remember that in antiquity, even the realities perceived by us as near to modern mentality, were deeply set in a religious perspective. Explaining Pericles's Parthenon with the ascendancy of the democrats, the

response to the Persian wars and Pericles's own political objectives is patently insufficient: there would have been no Parthenon, and even no Pericles without Athena to be installed in the sanctum.

174. RE VIII, Shahbazgarhi (Hultzsch 1925: 59-60). See discussion on this point in Schneider (1978: 135-36).
175. For the so-called schism edicts, see the Sarnath Pillar inscription (Hultzsch 1925: 161-64). I follow K.R. Norman's interpretation of the events alluded to (Norman 1992).
176. Cf. ibid.: 90.
177. Tieken (2000: 27).
178. Calcutta-Bairat inscription (Hultzsch 1925: 172-74). For the texts cited, see A. Sen (1956: 132-33); see also Barua (1946, II: 32-37).
179. A copy of the Sarnath pillar edict was expressly ordered to be deposited with the *upāsaka*-s (cf. Hultzsch 1925: 163; for an updated translation of the Sarnath text, see Tieken 2000: 9-10 and discussion).
180. Widengren (1964: esp. 42-43; 51). See the existing texts on the life of Mani collected in *Manichaean Texts*: 5 ff., 141 ff., 185 ff.
181. Brown (1975: 94). It is not by chance that the political fortunes of Manichaeism coincided with the reign of the Uighurs in Mongolia once the Manichaeans of Central Asia and China obtained the support of the third *qaġan* Bögü. The Uighurs, after defeating the Chinese, found in Manichaeism the ideological tools to support their new state (Hambly 1970: 63-64), which was modern in comparison to their previous semi-tribal organisation, and at the same time free from the influence of bureaucracies and landed aristocracies. On the conversion of Bögü and the presence of the Manichaeans in the eastern part of Central Asia, see also Golden (1992: 159-60, 174 ff., 172-73). For the trilingual inscription of Karabalgasun, see *Manichaean Texts*: 235 ff.
182. *Lüders List*: nos. 994, 1021.
183. Ibid.: no. 1053.
184. Ibid.: no. 1072.
185. Ibid.: no. 1099.
186. Lamotte (1958: 455-56; see also nn. 55, 60).
187. Falk (2001).
188. This famous inscription has been published and commented upon several times; I refer the reader to Göbl (1965) and Gershevitch (1979). For the archaeological evidence, see Schlumberger, Le Berre & Fussman (1983: 70, 136-37).
189. Sims-Williams & Cribb (1995-96); Sims-Williams (2004).
190. Lüders (1961: 143-45).
191. Sims-Williams (2004: 56).
192. For a thorough examination of Kārttikeya's names in the literature, some of which documented at a very early age, cf. A.K. Chatterjee (1970: 2 ff., 7 ff.). In the Purāṇas, Viśākha is also one of Skanda's brothers (Dikshitar, V.R. Ramachandra (1951: *s.v.*).

193. *Xiyuji* a: III (vol. 1, pp. 151-56).
194. Rosenfield (1967: 31-32).
195. Thaplyal (1985: 71).
196. See, however, Tripathi (1964: 163-64).
197. *Xiyuji* a: V (vol. 1, p. 214).
198. RE III (Hultzsch 1925: 4-5 [Girnar], 29-30 [Kalsi], 52-53 [Shahbhazgarhi], etc.); see the discussion in Deeg (1995-97, I: 69-71).
199. The corresponding Buddhist ritual, as shown by V.S. Agrawala, was called *nirargaḍa* (cf. Deeg 1995-97, II: 66 ff.).
200. Deeg (1995-97, I: 71 ff.). Aśoka's performance of the ceremony was recorded, according to Xuanzang, in 'a mutilated inscription' on a pillar at Pāṭaliputra: 'Aśôka-rāja with a firm principle of faith has thrice bestowed Jambudvîpa as a religious offering on Buddha, the Dharma and the assembly, and thrice he has redeemed it with his jewels and treasure; and this is the record thereof' (*Xiyuji* a, VIII; vol. 2: 91). In the seventh century the Aśokan script could not be read, however.
201. *Faxian b*: 7-8; see discussion in Deeg (1995-97, I: 83-84).
202. *Xiyuji* a: I (vol. 1, pp. 51-52). *Wuzhe hui* is the Chinese term supposedly corresponding to an undocumented *mokṣa pariṣad* which came to indicate the ritual (Deeg 1995-97: esp. II, 63 ff.).
203. On Bhāskaravarman or Kumāra and his relationship with Harṣavardhana the reader is referred to Basak (1967: 189 ff.). His kingdom may be considered one of the numerous kingdoms that Kanauj protected and controlled.
204. *Xiyuji* a: V (vol. 1, p. 218).
205. Bāṇa maintains that from childhood Bhāskaravarman's resolution was 'never to do homage to any being except the lotus feet of Çiva' (*Harṣacarita*: 246; p. 217). For his interest in Buddhism, see below.
206. Deeg (1995-97, I: 74).
207. There is evidence for an even earlier performance than that of AD 519 not recorded in the official histories (ibid. II: 76 ff.).
208. Ibid.: 80-81.
209. Ibid.: 81.
210. Ibid.: 82.
211. For the exchange of embassies with China, see below.
212. Devahuti (1983: 249) maintains that Harṣa counted on the fact that Magadha had a reputation as the seat of imperial power from pre-Mauryan days, but I do not think this to be the real point.
213. *Xiyuji* a: V (vol.1, pp. 220-21).
214. Kosambi (1975: 310).
215. Ibid.: 295; 308 ff.
216. *Xiyuji* a: V (vol. 1, p. 206).
217. On Narendradeva discontinuing the previous royal lineage, see Verardi (1992: 33).
218. Sen Tansen (2003: 40).

219. Devahuti (1983: 238 ff.) has collected all the available documentation, again discussed by Sen Tansen (2003: 16-25).
220. Ibid.: 45.
221. Devahuti (1983: 249, 253-54). Sen Tansen (2003: 38-40) recalls the transmission of the sugar-making technology from India to China.
222. Ibid. 37 ff. has emphasised the role of Buddhism in Tang-India diplomacy.
223. *Life*: 170-71.
224. Sen Tansen (2003: 17).
225. Ibid.: 45-46.
226. Coomaraswamy (1927: 32, 34-35, 231).
227. Brown (1956: 10).
228. Spink (1958).
229. Auboyer & Härtel (1971: 161-62).
230. Huntington (1985: 62, 65).
231. Marshall & Foucher (1940, I: 28-29).
232. Ibid.: 23-24.
233. Ibid.: 29.
234. See Willis (2001), who has underlined the presence at Vidiśā of the Hemavata masters and their importance.
235. Sircar (1965*b*: 87, n. 4) observed that '[t]he absence of the Śuṅga king's name in the inscription may suggest that the Śuṅga power was then on the decline'.
236. Vasudeva's political murder was not the first by which the brāhmaṇas had ruthlessly called the ruling family to order. According to Bāṇa (*Harṣacarita*: VI.222; cf. p. 192), Agnimitra's son Sumitra had also been killed by a brāhmaṇa, Mitradeva (or Mūladeva), possibly a scion of the same brāhmaṇa ministerial family to which Vāsudeva belonged (HCIP 2: 97-98). Sumitra is identifiable with the fourth Śuṅga king Vasumitra.
237. Kālidāsa's chronology, discussed in a number of papers and in practically every edition and translation of his works (cf. e.g. Rajan 2006), is not well established. He has been often associated with the Guptas, more in the attempt at shaping the Gupta period as the golden age of Indian history than on a factual basis. Several scholars consider him a contemporary of the Śuṅgas or the Kaṇvas (see, for instance, B.C. Sinha (1977: 143-44).
238. J. Shaw (2004: 22-23; figs. 2-3).
239. Spink (1958) dated Kondane to AD 1-10, the *caityagṛha* at Nāsik to AD 10-30; etc. The new chronology of the Deccan caves has been generally accepted, an exception being Nagaraju (1981).
240. Georg Bühler in Burgess (1883: 59-64).
241. Shimada (2006: 133-34). The role played by the Sadas of the Aira family, ruling locally, would be worth investigating. Their rule in the Krishna-Guntur region came as a consequence of Khāravela's expeditions, and lasted until the time of the Kṣatrapas and later (cf. D.C. Sircar in *EI* 32, 1957-58: 85-

86). Śivamakasada, known from an Amaravati inscription, is still wrongly identified with Śivaskanda Śātakarṇi (Knox 1992: 13). The names of other Sada rulers have emerged from the excavations at Vaddamanu (above, n. 43), where their coins appear only in around AD 200.

242. Scholars have usually accepted the opinion propounded by Ghosh (1973), according to which the second urbanisation of India started in the sixth century BC in the Ganges Valley, being part of the same process which led to the formation of Buddhism. Horizontal excavations are still wanting, but in any case the recent archaeological evidence no longer supports a similar view (Barba 2004). The real urbanisation is to be seen in the frame of the building up of the Mauryan state, which in turn was the result of the establishment of new powers in the former Achaemenian territories.

243. B.C. Sinha (1977: 59 ff.).

244. *Harṣacarita*: 222 (p. 193).

245. Bagchi (1946: 82, n. 3). As such, Puṣyamitra could count on his armed men, perhaps the *puṣyamanava*-s mentioned in some sources (see Alahakoon 1980: 119). To this author I refer the reader for a narration of Bṛhadratha's murder (ibid.).

246. It is 'a disused sacrifice' in the *Śatapatha Brāhmaṇa* (XIII. 3.3.6; vol. 5, p. 334), where it is revived.

247. See for instance the twenty-one animals sacrificed to Agni and Soma on the twelfth day of the ritual (Dumont (1927: 96-97), those sacrificed with the horse (ibid. 175), the twenty-one sterile cows sacrificed at the end of the *soma* ritual (ibid.: 228-29); etc.

248. Dange (1967); on the sacrificed horse and the *mahiṣī*, see Dumont (1927: 178-79). The fertility aspects of the *aśvamedha* have been emphasised, in particular, by J.J. Meyer, after reporting the dialogue between the *mahiṣī* and the *hotṛ* priest (Meyer 1937, 3, Anhang: 246 ff.), and the identification horse/sun by Bhawe (1939: 68) in his search for the meaning of the *aśvamedha*. The conceptualisation of a sacred king as a solar deity periodically re-enacting fertility rites goes back to James Frazer. On the methodology followed, in particular, by Meyer, who, for all his erudition and insight, made a completely de-historicised use of the sources, some reasonable doubts could be raised today.

249. In relation to the *soma* ritual the *Śatapatha Brāhmaṇa* (IV.3.4.3; vol. 2, p. 340) states that no priest should officiate for a fee less than 100 cows; other sources give much larger figures. Cf. Kane (1930-62, II: 1188-90).

250. *Mālavikāgnimitra*: V. 1 ('Ever since the Queen heard that Prince Vasumitra was appointed the guardian of the sacrificial horse by the General, she has been bestowing on worthy (Brāhmaṇas) *Dakshiṇā* amounting to eighteen *suvarṇas* of gold'; cf. p. 163); *Mahābhārata, Aśvamedha Parvan*, section 4 ('Desirous of celebrating a sacrifice, that virtuous monarch [...] caused thousands of shining golden vessels to be forged'; ibid, section 10 ('Then that monarch, the slayer of his enemies, with a delighted heart, placed heaps

of gold on diverse spots, and distributing the immense wealth to the Brahmanas, he looked glorious like Kuvera, the god of wealth'; vol. 12, pp. 5, 16).

251. Sircar (1968: 2-3) wondered why only few gold *kārṣāpaṇa*-s, frequently referred to in early literature, had been discovered, and assumed that they had a very limited circulation, being used, in addition, as ornaments. If the *kārṣāpaṇa*-s distributed to brāhmaṇas in the circumstances examined here were of gold, as is probable, they were probably melted to make jewellery, etc.
252. Georg Bühler in Burgess (1883: 59-64). See the inscription re-edited by Sircar (1965*b*: 192-97).
253. *Aśokāvadāna*: 133 (p. 293).
254. John S. Strong's introduction to *Aśokāvadāna*: p. 86.
255. *Aśokāvadāna*: 134 (p. 293).
256. *Mañjuśrīmūlakalpa*: [53], 532-33 (cf. §10 , p. 18).
257. I follow, in part, Bagchi (1946), according to whom Puṣyamitra's defeat took place at Barikot, in Uḍḍiyāna, and Kṛmiśa is identifiable with Demetrios of Bactria. It is difficult, however, to establish which Demetrios he may have been, the chronology of the Indo-Greek kings being still much debated. According to Cribb (2005), Demetrios I would have ruled between 200 and 190 BC (too early for Puṣyamitra), and Demetrios II between 175 and 170 (but his figure remains elusive: ibid.: 2009; Mac Dowall 2005: 203). As for the *yakṣa* Daṃṣṭrānivāsin, Bagchi identified him with Menander, whose accession to the throne is now generally dated to *c.* 150 BC.
258. Bagchi (1946: 83).
259. Przyluski (1967: 101).
260. The statement of Tāranātha that the majority of the monks who had not been killed 'fled to other countries' (*Tāranātha*: 42B; p. 121) may refer to later events, which we will discuss in the following chapters.
261. Bagchi (1946: 90). See Chapter III for a discussion of the Kali Age literature, which equates (with the due exceptions) *nāstika*-s, *yavana*-s and *mleccha*-s.
262. I follow Bagchi (1946: 89-91).
263. Chanda (1929: 604-7). This author dated the inscription to the mid-first century BC, but Sircar (1965*b*: 95, note 1) maintains that it 'cannot be much earlier than the first century AD.'
264. Sircar (1965*a*: 42).
265. Most scholars, on the basis of the *Mālavikāgnimitra*, relate it to a victory over the Yavanas, but for the Indo-Greeks Sāketa/Ayodhyā was only a stage towards Pāṭaliputra, from where the Greeks withdrew for internal reasons (Bagchi 1946: 88). The *Yuga Purāṇa* (56-57, p. 105) seems to confirm this.
266. Bareau (1979: 77); for the history of Sāketa/Ayodhyā during the period discussed in this section, see Bakker (1986: esp. 19 ff.).
267. The Buddha, represented as a pillar of fire at Amaravati (Coomaraswamy

(1935: 9-10), in Gandharan art is depicted as emanating flames from his shoulders or with the head in the form of flame, while water flows from below his feet: Agni, as is known, originates from water. See a few Gandharan examples in Kurita (1988: pls. 381-84, 388). The 'great miracle' of Śrāvastī is known from the post-canonical literature; see the twelfth chapter of the *Divyāvadāna* (*Divyāvadāna* b: esp. 270-281).

268. Brockington (1985: 329); Baley & Brockington (2000: 353). It is a largely accepted opinion that the first and seventh *kāṇḍa*-s are later additions to the poem (Brockington, 1984: 13-14; Thapar 2000: 655-56), but scholars are not lacking who have considered the Vālmīki *Rāmāyaṇa* a unitary work (Renou & Filliozat (1947-53, I: 404). The very early date suggested by Robert P. Goldman (1984: 14 ff.), ultimately depending on his accepting an early chronology of the towns of the Ganges Valley, is debatable.
269. The early authors who studied Bhāvagatism did not doubt that it was to be understood in the light of 'the struggle for life and death between Brahmanism and Buddhism' (see George Grierson in *IA* 37, 1908: 251-62, 373-86; cf. p. 257).
270. Khare (1967: 24) dated the early temple to the end of the third century BC, but the relevant ^{14}C date (295± 110 BC) hardly supports a similar chronology. The date suggested by M.D. Khare in Ghosh (1989, II: 62), the fourth-third century BC, is even less acceptable. The foundations and the base of the early temple were of backed bricks, and there is definite evidence of baked bricks used in Aśokan monuments (Verardi 2007*b*: 115 ff.), though this is not enough for attributing the temple to as early an age as this.
271. Härtel (1987).
272. Sircar (1965*b*: 88-89).
273. *Yuga Purāṇa*: 78-79; the date of the work is discussed by Mitchiner (2002: 92-94).
274. The merit to have contextualised this *jātaka* goes to Dass & Willis (2002: 31-32).
275. S. Dasgupta (1932-55, III: 17).
276. The reader is referred to von Stietencron (1977) for a vivid description of the conflict and the relevant sources. In strictly orthodox circles the Bhāgavatas were considered outcastes (S. Dasgupta 1932-55, I: 546-47).
277. *Yuga Purāṇa*: 29-30 (p. 102).
278. Hudson (2002).
279. Lamotte (1958: 434). The quotation is from the English translation.
280. R.C. Agrawala (1969: 47); Dass & Willis (2002: 30).
281. Ibid.
282. J. Shaw (2004: 23). Julia Shaw's study of the Vidiśā-Sanchi region, is an example of the results that can be obtained combining the methods of landscape archaeology with art-historical analysis.
283. Ibid.: 20. For the early involvement of Buddhist monks in agricultural activities, see Shaw & Sutcliff (2001: 71-73; 2005: 18-19).
284. Raychauduri (1938: 315-16); B.C. Sinha (1997: 97).

285. Bhandarkar (1913: 165); Kreisel (1986: 19 [*Mahābhāṣya* on Pāṇini V.2. 76]).
286. Banerjea (1974: 449-50). David N. Lorenzen is very cautious about this identification, and prefers to consider the Pāśupatas as an order founded, and not only systematised, by Lakulīśa (Lorenzen 1972: 175). D.C. Sircar warned long ago that the authority of the *Mahābhāṣya* is not beyond doubt when chronological questions are involved, given the uncertain date of the present text (Sircar 1939*a*). However, different groups of Pāśupatas existed, and not only the better-known Lakulīśa Pāśupatas (Dyczkowski 1988: 20 ff.).
287. Srinivasan (1984). Including the Gudimallam *liṅga* among the early Sivaite icons (cf. also Kreisel 1986: 45) seems wrong to me, and I rather follow Sarcar (1986). The excavations carried out in the Paraśurāmeśvara Temple of Gudimallam (I.K. Sarma 1994) has provided much new information but has not clarified the question of the date of the *liṅga*.
288. These early, monumental images are still waiting for a comprehensive study. See them in Srinivasan (1984: 35 and pls. 22, 23). On the *liṅga* from Bhita, see Kramrisch (1981: 179 ff.); the faces carved on the *liṅga* would point to the Sadāśiva form (B.N. Sharma 1976: 1 ff.).
289. van Troy (1990) has underlined that for the Pāśupatas the decisive cause of man's distress was the tight grip of *varṇāśramadharma*; at the same time, they sought liberty in the union with Śiva. It is in this contradiction that the different Pāśupata traditions (on which see Dyczkowski 1988: esp. 24-25) grew.
290. See above in this chapter. This is a difficult question to tackle, but from a relatively early period, many if not all the Buddhist sects started, to give an example, to conceive the Buddha symbolically as a white elephant, and make his birth from Queen Māyā's side a miraculous one, thus considering him a super-human being.
291. R.C. Sharma (1987). B.D. Chattopadhyaya's thesis, according to which the growth of new urban centres compensated for the collapse of the early historical towns has been endorsed by Deyell (1990: 11-12), but we may object that the new settlements either were *tīrtha*-s or small, short-lived dynastic capitals. The similarities with the early historical towns, characterised by a proto-capitalist economy (and transformed, in turn, into *tīrtha*-s), are superficial. It should be underlined that Chattopadhyaya's vision is much articulated (Chattopadhyaya 1994: 130 ff., 155 ff.).
292. Cf. the territory of Taulihawa, in the Nepalese Tarai, where the Aśokan sites of Gotihawa and (questionably) Nigali Sagar are located. The early abandonment of Gotihawa and, on the other side of the border, of the Piprahwa monastery, is in relation with the abandonment or decrease in size of a number of settlements. See Verardi (2007*b*: 20, 23 ff.).
293. Above, n. 101, and McNeill (1998: 131, 135-37). The plague is likely to have especially affected urban centres and port towns (we know of its effects

in Rome and Carthage), and even though it was not as deadly as the pandemic of the sixth century, it caused a shortage of human resources, affecting communications and trade. We must imagine a well-working machine suddenly coming to a halt for lack of fuel.

294. Jayaswal (1933).
295. Ibid. 8.
296. Ibid. 65, 94. This king seems to have died about the end of the first quarter of the fourth century (HCIP 2: 221).
297. Jayaswal (1933: 175). On the Ikṣvākus, see Chapter III.
298. The Vākāṭakas were strict Sivaites (ibid. 94).
299. Hazra (1940: 193, 203). On the definition of heresy in the Brahmanical world, see also O'Flaherty (1971: 272-73; 275 ff.).
300. Matsubara (1994: 136-37).
301. Joshi & Sharma (1991-93: 58-59), reexamining the Ghosundi inscription.
302. See the penetrating analysis of the Buddhist positions *vis-à-vis varṇa* and *jāti* made by Eltschinger (2000), a question we shall touch again in our discussion.
303. Pagel (2005) has recently re-ignited an ever-lasting debate setting the Gnostic gospel of St Thomas, according to which each of us can individually come into contact with God, in opposition to St. John's fourth canonical gospel, some passages of which imply priestly mediation (on the fourth gospel and Irenaeus's role in creating an orthodox system, see esp. pp. 96 ff.).
304. Humfress (2007: 217 ff.).
305. Manteuffel (1982: 125-26).
306. Cf. O'Flaherty's argumentation on the two levels of heresy (O'Flaherty 1971: 273-74).

CHAPTER III

The Gupta Sphinx

QUESTIONING THE SPHINX

The India of the third century and of the early Guptas, notably so that of Candragupta I and Samudragupta, almost appears as an iconic desert, an age of strictly orthodox rule. The Guptas ignored artistic patronage as the Śuṅgas had done. It is possible to speak of 'Gupta art' only with Candragupta II, and to a limited extent: the reference is to the Brahmanical caves at Udayagiri near Vidiśā, which go back to the early years of the fifth century, to Padmāvatī (Pawaya),[1] and to the patronage granted to a Sivaite (probably Pāśupata) temple in Mathurā.[2] Even less possible is to speak of a patronage dispensed with equal generosity to brāhmaṇas and *śramaṇa*-s – a still current opinion which is not only contrary to historical truth, but to every historical likelihood[3] – the exceptions being the inscribed images of Candraprabha that 'the illustrious Mahārājādhirāja Rāmagupta' caused to be made in Vidiśā 'under instruction from the mendicant Chēlla [Cella]'.[4] Rāmagupta's turning to a Jain *guru*, whose *paramparā* is also reported in the inscription, may find an explanation in his distancing from his father Samudragupta and his younger brother Candragupta II, who murdered him.[5] As is known, he underwent a *damnatio memoriae*.

Buddhist texts preserved in Chinese translations convey the sense that in the late third century and when the Gupta power was established Buddhism was tested very hard. The *Mahāpārinirvāṇa Mahāsūtra*, composed after the end of Kuṣāṇa rule, at the time of the *aśvamedhin* kings and of Gupta rule,[6] predicts that it will not be long before the teaching of the Buddha disappears. When the *sūtra* reports the Buddha saying that '700 years after my death, the devil Māra Pāpīyas will gradually destroy my True Dharma', it indicates that the end of Buddhism 'was in process in AD 317'.[7] In the fifth century, Buddhaghoṣa, in his five-stage scheme for the disappearance of Buddhism,

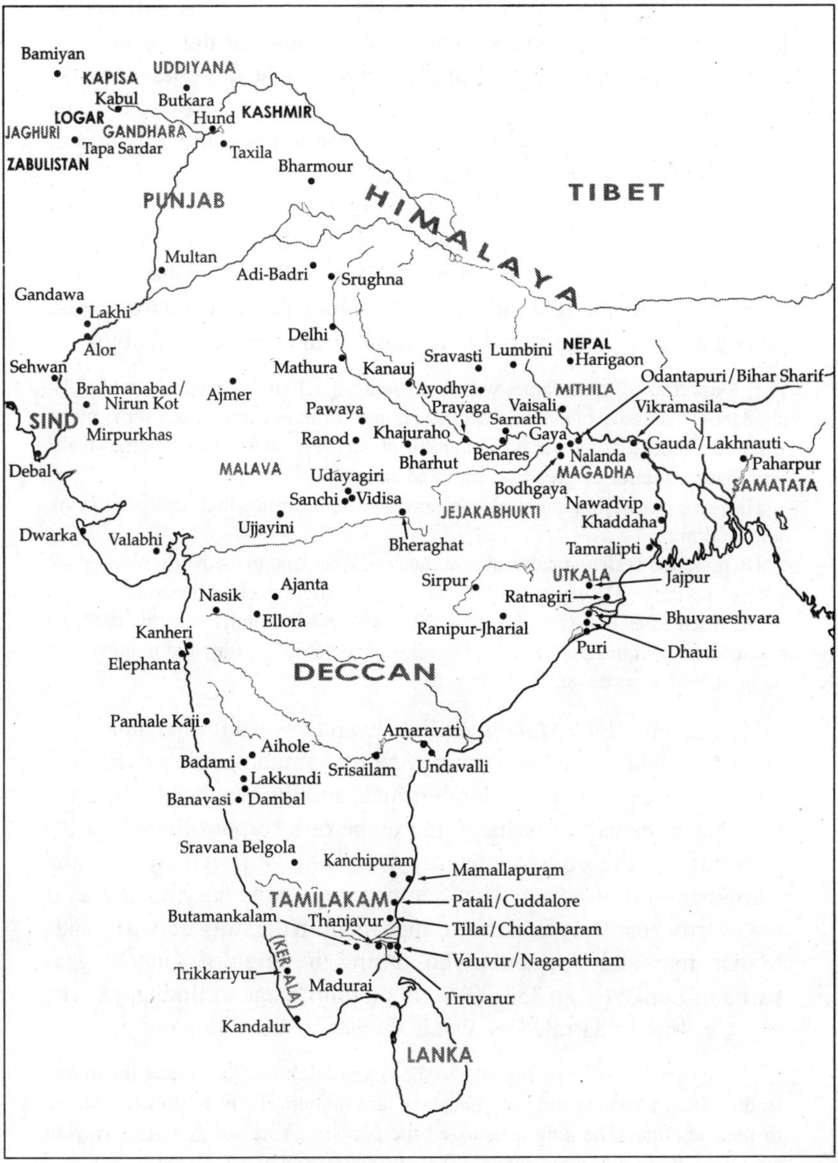

Map 2: Late Ancient and Medieval India.

argues that the *saṃgha* will not be supported, novices will not be taught, and the scriptures will gradually be lost for the world.[8] The passage implies not only lack of patronage, but the diaspora of monks (who, in fact, are not in the position to teach new novices) and of the scriptures. The latter detail grabs our attention because it is a rare, early mention of the dispersal of texts.

An interesting testimony on Samudragupta's conduct is provided by the *Mañjuśrīmūlakalpa*, which, though a later text,[9] is a vigilant sensor of whatever negative occurred to the religion of Dharma. This work is one of the few independent sources on the Gupta emperor, whose deeds we otherwise know from his inscriptions and coins:

> [...] Samudra, of good fame, will be *nṛipatiḥ*. [...] He (Samudra) was lordly, shedder of excessive blood, of great powers and dominion, heartless, ever vigilant, (mindful) about his own person, unmindful about the hereafter, sacrificing animals; with bad councilor he greatly committed sin.
>
> His government [or kingdom] was inundated with carping logicians (*tārkikaiḥ*), vile Brahmins.
>
> He marched systematically and reached the West, and in the North reached the gate of Kashmir. He was victorious on the battle-field even in the North.
>
> He ruled after that (conquest) for 22 years and 5 months. On this earth on account of a fell disease he fainted several times (at his death), and in great pain he died, and went down.[10]

The author of the *Mañjuśrīmūlakalpa* relies on a former, unknown chronicler who was clearly impressed by Samudragupta's deeds and who, while deploring the bloody rituals and the free hand left to the brāhmaṇas tends to discharge the emperor's responsibilities to his entourage – the consequence of a well-known technique in the administration of power. That Samudragupta was unsympathetic, if not overtly hostile, to Buddhism, appears from the story of two monks, Mahānāman and Upa[sena] who, during the reign of King Megha-varṇa of Laṅkā (*c*. AD 352-79) went on pilgrimage to Bodhgayā. The story, as briefly narrated by Wang Xuance, is the following:

> [...] The two *bhikṣus* paid homage to the Diamond throne [...] under the tree of Bodhi. The monastery did not offer them any shelter. The two *bhikṣus* returned to their country. The king questioned the *bhikṣus* 'You had gone to pay your compliments to the sacred spots. What suspicious omen was found o *bhikṣus*'? They replied 'In the large country of Jambudvīpa there is no place where we could live'. The king having heard them sent them with precious stones for offering to the king *San-meou-to-le-kin-to* (Samudragupta). And it is for that

reason, uptil now, the *bhikṣus* of the kingdom of Ceylon are residing in that monastery.[11]

The gems were given to Samudragupta in addition to the usual gifts,[12] which was the same as paying a tribute of subjection. For Meghavarṇa, as for any other Buddhist king, the construction of a monastery near the Bodhi tree had crucial political implications; Samudragupta was well aware of this fact, and made them pay dearly for the privilege. In the Allahabad inscription, the Siṃhalas would be enlisted among his vassals.[13] What is most striking in the story is that there was no place for the Siṃhala monks to live in the whole of India: there were no patrons who would protect and benefit them.[14]

Buddhist icons of the end of the fourth century or datable to *c.* AD 400 are known from Bodhgayā, Sarnath and Mathurā, and are very few.[15] The early standing Buddha images in what we consider the typical Gupta style were produced in Mathurā in the decade of the 430s,[16] and a real artistic output, in both Mathurā and Sarnath, is documented only from around the mid-fifth century.[17] None of these images has any relation with the Gupta ruling class. An exception whose circumstances are difficult to evaluate is the donation that a high officer of Candragupta II, Āmrakārdava, together with three local rulers, made to the monks of the monastery of Sanchi presiding over the main stūpa.[18] The donation was made towards the end of Candragupta's life, arguably in a climate of political difficulties and change, both at central and local level. What is usually labelled as 'Gupta art' is a set of monuments and iconographies that are either ascribable to the fifth century or, in their majority, to the complex period that followed the death of Skandagupta in AD 467 and to a much later age. Gupta art has been made too comprehensive a container since the times of A.K. Coomaraswamy and V.S. Agrawala, whose great talent were at the service of the nationalist cause.[19] They distorted the questions involved and injected into them a poison from which even liberal historians have not since been immune. V.S. Agrawala, in particular, tackling cultural problems at large and ignoring the contradictions and discontinuities that distinguish Indian history between the fourth and the mid-seventh century, postulated the existence of a unified golden age with Kālidāsa at its beginning and Bāṇa at its end.[20]

During Skandagupta's reign the game restarted, and in places the

Buddhists even succeeded in re-establishing themselves as rulers, as happened at the time of the Vākāṭaka King Hariṣeṇa (AD 460-77) in western Deccan. Whether it was this ruler, 'long thought to be only one of a number of different (presumably Hindu) sovereigns from a number of different generations and houses of kings' who made of Ajanta 'a royal Vākāṭaka site'[21] – a hypothesis that is ill-suited to our interpretive model, which questions the 'catholicism' of Indian orthodox rulers, and the Vākāṭakas were such, or a local ruler,[22] we witness that kind of sudden, hectic building activity that characterises the rise of many a Buddhist site, and to an equally typical, sudden collapse of the patronage. In any case, the rather long period during which everything seemed to be once again at stake, at least in central and northern India, came to an end with the death of Harṣavardhana.

A picture of Gupta India towards the end of the reign of Candragupta II (who died in AD 414) is provided by the travelogue of Faxian. The North-West, including Panjab, was firmly controlled by Buddhist rulers.[23] In the region of Mathurā there was a Buddhist revival, and Dharma was in full blossom.[24] The situation starts changing when the pilgrim enters Madhyadeśa. Here Faxian, usually exclusively concerned in retracing the steps of the Awakened One and his disciples and in collecting pious stories, observed the extent to which the burden of taxation fell upon the peasants working on the king's lands, and was struck by the social phenomenon of the *cāṇḍāla*-s. He was also a witness of the popularity of the vegetarian diet among high-casters,[25] and of the mushrooming of apparently Brahmanical schools (ninety-six, according to him), believing in the real existence of this and the next world.[26] Only proceeding further east, Faxian found other flourishing Buddhist communities, and it was in a monastery of Tāmralipti (Tamluk) in coastal Bengal that he eventually decided to reside for two years 'copying out sūtras and drawing pictures of images'.[27] Neither the two monasteries at Sarnath nor those in Pāṭaliputra, despite their close connection with the Buddha and Aśoka, respectively, had offered him the conditions he was looking for. Only in Bengal he felt at ease, living in what we may call a Buddhist society that satisfied him, comparable to the society still existing in the North-West, and to that which he would experience in Sri Lanka after his departure from India.

This picture matches other known facts. It was in Mathurā, in the first half of the fourth century, that the Saṃmitīya School propounded, arguably in response to the Brahmanical theory of the *ātman*, the audacious idea of the *pudgala*.[28] In an inscription dated AD 332, the Buddha is given the attributive of Pitāmaha, which pertains to Brahmā as creator, thus suggesting – to the opposite field, at least – that the Buddha might be a sort of god and creator of the universe.[29] Buddhist casuistry, developed out of theistic pressure, would succeed in keeping this and similar theories distinct from those of the orthodox, and it is, indeed, typical of mature and later Buddhists, though not of Vajrayāna, to yield, or pretend to yield, to the arguments and constrictions of their adversaries in order to preserve an identity in peril. The theories of the Saṃmitīyas were probably helpful in limiting the losses to neo-Brahmanical movements, very powerful in Mathurā, as were the other numerous attempts at adjusting the doctrine to Brahmanical tenets, as for instance the idea, variously presented and discussed, of the eternalness of the Buddha.[30] The variety of positions and adjustments took a doctrinal form because Brahmanical pressure, as we shall see in the next chapter, resorted to public debates, which, became hot political issues, crucial for the survival of Buddhism.

The most effective Gupta rule was exercised, apart from the central Vindhyan region and Bengal, in the Doāb.[31] Candragupta II's coins are in plenty here, while only a few have been found in Bihar, particularly so gold coins.[32] They are usually believed to have circulated in relation to trade in luxury articles,[33] but the difference between their number and that of the other circulating coins (Gupta copper coins are few) points to the absence of a real monetary economy. This strongly suggests that the gold coins were almost exclusively minted to serve as gifts to brāhmaṇas and for propaganda.[34] Gold is scanty in India,[35] and hunting for gold and hoarding it up has been a constant behavioural pattern of the Indian well-off and politically influential milieus up to the present. If this assumption is correct, the spatial distribution of the Gupta gold coins indicates that the majority of royal rituals were performed in the lower Doāb. In Magadha, orthodox Gupta rule was less incisive, and the Brahmanical model of society more difficult to introduce and implement.

In relation to allegations of slaughter against some rulers of his time, Voltaire maintains that there is nothing more likely than crimes, but that it is at least necessary that they are ascertained.[36] Lack of patronage, hostility towards the *śramaṇa*-s, strengthening of caste rules do not necessarily imply violence. They may simply point to a strategy based on the assertion of hegemony over society. Even though a better chronology of sites and iconographies allows us to reject well-established opinions regarding the purported 'catholicity' of the religious and social attitudes of the Guptas and the Brahmanical élite of their time, we are not authorised to conclude, on the basis of the unyielding silence of contemporary Indian sources, that rulers and brāhmaṇas resorted to physical violence against the Buddhists. However, Faxian provides us with some valuable information, encouraging deeper investigation.

In the region of Sāketa-Śrāvastī, the centre of Gupta power at the symbolic level,[37] the situation was marked by conflict. In Sāketa, says the pilgrim,

[o]utside the south gate of the city, on the eastern side of the road, is the place where Buddha formerly stuck in the ground a piece of his willow chewing-stick (for cleansing the teeth), which forthwith grew up to the height of seven feet, never increasing nor diminishing. Heretics and Brahmans, in their jealousy, at one time cut it down, at another pulled it up and threw it to a distance; but it always came up again as before on the same spot.[38]

As for Śrāvastī, half of the town was abandoned, including the house thought to have been Anāthapiṇḍika's. Here, on the site of the monastery of Mahāprajāpati (Queen Māyā's sister), as well as on the site of Aṅgulimālya's conversion, stūpas had been erected by 'men of after ages', and '[t]he heretic Brahmans, growing jealous, wished to destroy them; whereupon the heavens thundered and flashed lightning with splitting crash, so that they were not able to succeed'.[39]

At some distance from the Jetavana, in the place where Devadatta had fallen into hell, a shrine had been built, over 60 ft in height, which contained an image of the seated Buddha:

On the east side of the road there is a heretical Brahman temple, called 'Shadow-covered'. It stands opposite the above-mentioned shrine, on the other side of the avenue of trees, and is also over sixty feet in height. It was called 'Shadow-covered' because when the sun is in the west, the shadow of the shrine of the World-Honoured-One darkens the temple of the heretical Brahmans; whereas, when the sun is in the east, the shadow of the temple darkens the north, and never falls upon the shrine of Buddha.[40]

In this case, the quarrel between the Buddhists and the brāhmaṇas ended up with the conversion of the latter, which 'at once gave up their family ties and entered His [the Buddha's] priesthood'.[41]

The unsuccessful attempt at destroying the stūpas in the city implies the fact that in other cases it had been successful, at either Śrāvastī or elsewhere. The construction of a Brahmanical rival temple just opposite a Buddhist temple provided with a particular symbolic meaning (Devadatta's final defeat), is an early testimony of the encircling technique brāhmaṇas resorted to, along with the harassing techniques observed at Ayodhyā, when getting rid of their adversaries was either impossible or untimely. These techniques, which, in Chapter I, we have already seen explained by Rajendralala Mitra, have been in use to these days.

According to the *Waiguo shi* or *Matters of the Outside Countries* of Zhi Sengzai, a Chinese monk active towards the end of the Jin dynasty (AD 265-420)[42] and therefore a contemporary of Faxian, Śrāvastī was ruled by a Gupta prince acting as viceroy, and the people of the kingdom did not follow the law of the Buddha:[43] the cleansing policy must have started some time in the fourth century. The *Waiguo shi*, an independent source, probably records the situation of the Buddhists in India as it was known in China before Faxian's journey.

The most instructive story reported by Faxian is set in Pāṭaliputra:

> There was living inside this city and belonging to the Greater Vehicle, a Brahman (by caste) whose name was Raivata. He was a strikingly enlightened man of much wisdom, there being nothing which he did not understand. He led a pure and solitary life; and the king of the country revered him as his teacher, so that whenever he went to visit the Brahman, he did not venture to sit beside him. If the king, from a feeling of love and veneration, grasped his hand, when he let go, the Brahman would immediately wash it. He was perhaps over fifty years of age, and all the country looked upon this one man to diffuse widely the Faith in Buddha, so that the heretics were unable to persecute the priesthood.[44]

We are struck by the behaviour of a Buddhist master, a brāhmaṇa by birth, who considers the contact with a stranger (arguably a petty king of lower birth) polluting. Yet it was this very behaviour that induced the orthodox to consider him as one of their folk, and leave the monastic community in peace. The elimination of high-caste adversaries was a painful and difficult task for the orthodox, since caste identity was the real bonding agent of orthodoxy. As for the Buddhists, or a part of them, adaptation to caste rules, despite the radical criticism of Brahmanical essentialism in this regard,[45] and the creation of an elitist priesthood, were a fait accompli.

The persecution of the Buddhist monks is only hinted at by Faxian, but this should not be dismissively interpreted as referring to sporadic occurrences that do not deserve to be reported. The tone of Faxian's statement implies that in the given case (and certainly in many others) persecution could not be put into effect but that it was something that could be expected. The pilgrim's homeland, China, was as different a country from India as can be imagined, but Buddhism found a staunch opposition there, too. To agree with Paul Demiéville, Buddhism in China had introduced private capitalism, which jeopardised state capitalism and the privileges of the bureaucrats, and from the fourth century at least, the state took various measures to put the Buddhists under control.[46] As early as AD 335, Wang Du, minister of Emperor Shi Hu of the Later Zhao Dynasty presented a memorial calling upon the ruler to forbid the worship of the Buddha, who was 'a foreign deity', and to return to the laity those who had become monks,[47] a measure that was repeatedly taken in the following centuries. In AD 340, at the court of the Eastern Jin, the question arose as to whether or not the monks should show respect like just any other subject, and that if the *saṃgha* should occupy a position equal to and independent of the state, there would be confusion within the land.[48] This burning issue was destined to provoke serious clashes. In south China, the literate Cai Mo (AD 312-85) upheld that Buddhism was 'the custom of the barbarians',[49] which became a frequently utilised polemical tool, similar to that utilised in India, with even less reasons, by the brāhmaṇas, who equalled the Buddhist folk to the *mleccha*-s. In fourth-century China, there was also an acrimonious debate between the Buddhists and the Taoists over the problem of historical priority of one system over the other.[50] Naturally, Faxian could not foresee the first anti-Buddhist measures that were taken in China in AD 444-46 under Tai Wudi (AD 424-52) of the Northern Wei dynasty,[51] but could not ignore that in both China and India Buddhism did not enjoy the support of the establishment. What he saw in Madhyadeśa and Pāṭaliputra could not surprise him, but he preferred to proceed to Tāmralipti and Sri Lanka to carry out his work. In some respects, the choice of Faxian is ahead by almost two centuries of that of Yijing and the other Chinese pilgrims of the second half of the seventh century (Chapter IV), and is due to reasons of the same order.

The excavations carried out at Maheth in the latter half of the nineteenth century and at the beginning of the last century[52] are rather confusing; yet there is some ground to believe that an anti-Buddhist revolt, implicit in Faxian's narrative, was actually kindled. A temple decorated with panels depicting scenes from the *Rāmāyaṇa* was apparently erected in Gupta times on the remains of a Kuṣāṇa monument of uncertain nature and, as reported by Jean Philippe Vogel, of two stūpas.[53] We are unable to be more detailed in terms of both archaeological analysis and chronology, but the evidence is made credible, *ex-post*, by the description of the town of Śrāvastī made by Xuanzang two centuries later. He states that the majority of Buddhist monasteries were in ruins, and that the brethren, followers of the Saṃmitīya School, were very few. The only great stūpa was that of Anāthapiṇḍika, already mentioned by Faxian, the others being small structures standing at the top of the ruins. This detail indicates that the destruction and/or de-functionalisation of earlier buildings had been followed by a period of abandonment, after which a minor building activity had taken place. This is a very common occurrence, and only a careful analysis of the interface(s) could allow us a re-construction of the facts. Xuanzang maintains that in Śrāvastī there were one hundred *deva* temples 'with very many heretics'.[54] A similar change cannot take place according to the theory of the 'slow decline' of Buddhism and its 'natural death', unless one intends to offend not only the intelligence of the historian but also common sense. Xuanzang may have amplified the situation at Śrāvastī (even though the pilgrim's interest was rather that of depicting a flourishing Buddhist India), but it would be difficult not to see that it was the coherent consequence of the tense state of affairs described by Faxian two centuries earlier. Despite the effort of the Buddhists to describe Śrāvastī as a place of their own, Brahmanical opposition had been obstinate, as is shown by the 'miracle' performed there by the Buddha and if, as reported in the *Divyāvadāna*, a banker had to apply for the help of the royal army in erecting a stūpa.[55] The latter story is told as having occurred at the time of the ancient kingdom of Kośala, but is likely to reflect more recent events.

Regarding the town of Vaiśālī, Faxian limits himself to mentioning the existence of the stūpa erected by the courtesan Amradārikā, and for the rest he speaks of his visit to a few stūpas outside town,[56] soon leaving the region. The above-mentioned *Waiguo shi*, which, as we have seen, depicts a situation preceding that observed by Faxian, reports that the house of Vimalakīrti, where the *Vimalakīrtinirdeśa*, or teaching of Vimalakīrti, was imparted,[57] was destroyed and that only the site where it once was standing and its foundations were visible. In this case, too, the people of the kingdom did not honour the Buddha, and were heterodox in everything.[58]

Archaeologists have paid little or no attention to late Kuṣāṇa and Gupta sites but for a few Buddhist sanctuaries the remains of which have often been wrongly dated.[59] Yet the study of the phases of abandonment of once flourishing settlements and a careful study of non-monumental sites would be of the utmost interest. Even a limited number of excavations, if carried out under a strict stratigraphic control, would provide a great amount of evidence regarding the present matter. A case in point is the Aśokan site of Gotihawa in the Nepalese Tarai, for whose abandonment a *terminus post quem* in the third century has been established. When the stūpa was deserted, the nearby sandstone pillar was deliberately pulled down, probably at the level of the footing, as can be inferred from the find of one of its fragments in the first layer of obliteration of the *pradakṣiṇāpatha* and of two more fragments clearly infiltrated from an overlying layer, also related to the abandonment of the sanctuary. The other finds point to the emergence of a new cultic use of the site associated, in all likelihood, with the still visible stump of the Aśokan pillar, interpreted as a *liṅga*,[60] a usual occurrence. The reasons why the pillar was pulled down would appear a matter of mere speculation, but the archaeological context suggests that it was demolished when other important Buddhist sites west of the Gandak River such as Piprahwa were also abandoned.[61] They are to be looked for in the determination to demolish a symbol. The removal of the marble columns from Greek and Roman buildings in late classical antiquity was carried out for re-using them in churches, or for producing lime, but re-use can be excluded in the case of Gotihawa, because only a few domestic utensils were worked out of its fragments,[62] and all the dwellings were of wattle and daub.

In Gupta times, Benares, the most famous and least known of ancient Indian towns,[63] had become the spearhead of the religious movements of the Pāśupatas and Bhāgavatas. The latter, in particular, carried out a complete reorganisation of the Brahmanical institutions between the fourth and fifth century. The seals found at Rajghat [64] attest to the existence of centres devoted to the study of the Vedas, and Benares took the leading part in the Bhāgavata movement for the resuscitation of the *sanātana dharma*. The early-fifth century image of Kṛṣṇa Govardhana from Bakaria Kund attests, by its imposing size, to the existence of a large Bhāgavata shrine, as well as a polemical intent against strict orthodox circles.[65] It has been shown that the story of Sūrya as Lolārka narrated in the *Vāmana Purāṇa* delineates the conflict between the Buddhists, represented in Benares by Yogācāra monks residing in a monastery situated near the present-day Lolārka Kuṇḍa, and the theistic groups. The conflict erupted 'in its most severe form', and 'the struggle was ultimately settled in favour of the Brahmanical way of life'. V.S. Agrawala, to whom a brilliant if reticent reconstruction of Gupta and post-Gupta Benares is due,[66] did not go into those details that his erudition and insight would have allowed him to disclose, but his analysis of this passage of the *Vāmana Purāṇa*[67] is an example of the difficulties we have in grasping the subtleties, as well as the historical information, contained in the stories narrated in the Purāṇas. How to understand, outside the more authentic Brahmanical tradition, that the earthly Sun oscillating between the river Varaṇā/Varuṇā, flowing near Sarnath and binding the ancient town of Benares to the north and the river Asi flowing to the south[68] alludes to Buddhism (the Buddha's lineage is *sūryavaṃśī*) and that the Vijñāna Sūrya of the Buddhists is seen in opposition to the Sūrya firmly replaced in the sky by Śiva, a symbol of the stability of the Vedas? Yet the story is consistent with the other evidence at our disposal for believing that Sarnath, the stronghold of Buddhism in the region, was temporarily appropriated by the brāhmaṇas. A fourth-fifth century structure in the so-called Hospital area and Court 36, as well as the Gupta Brahmanical sculptures found on the site point to the life of the Buddhist sanctuary having been discontinued.[69]

THE FULFILMENT OF A DUTY

The Guptas fulfilled the political answer that the authors of the early Kali Age literature were overtly expecting and pressing for.[70] The picture becomes even clearer if we look at the Guptas as a dynasty of brāhmaṇas.[71] The targets of this literature are typical: merchants and artisans (and in the Kali Age *all* had turned into traders)[72] were responsible for the social disorder,[73] and the vaiśyas refused to pay taxes and offer sacrifice[74] in a context where the possession of wealth was the only source of acquiring high family status.[75] A few excerpts from a passage of the *Vāyu Purāṇa*, which is perhaps the oldest of the major Purāṇas,[76] exemplify all the relevant points:

In Kali Yuga, people do not accept the authority of Smṛtis. [...] There is danger and fear to people owing to wrong performance of sacrifices, neglect of (Vedic) studies, evil conduct, misleading religious scriptures and faults in the performance of holy rites of Brāhmaṇas. [...] There is much of agitation and turbulence at the advent of Kali Yuga. There is no regular study of the Vedas. The Brāhmaṇas do not perform Yajñas. All men inclusive of Kṣatriyas and Vaiśyas gradually decay. Low-born and insignificant persons have contact with Brāhmaṇas in sharing beds, seats and food in Kali Age. Kings are mainly Śūdras propagating heretic ideas. People never hesitate to kill a child in the womb. They behave in such way. [...] When the end of the Yuga approaches, thieves and robbers administer kingdoms like kings; kings adopt the methods of thieves and robbers. [...] Women become unchaste and disinterested in holy rites. They become fond of wine and meat. When Kali Age sets in, they resort to deceptive means.[...] Then, when the end of the age approaches, even the great goddess like the earth will yield but little fruit. Śūdras will begin to perform penance. [...] The kings do not belong to the Kṣatriya clan. Vaiśyas maintain themselves with the help of Śūdras. The noble Brāhmaṇas perform obeisance to Śūdras at the end of the Kali Age. [...] In this base Yuga, people will have trading propensity. By false measures, the buyers will be deceived of their due share in the commodities. The whole society abounds in heretics of foul conduct and activity with their false appearance. Men will be in a minority and women will be many, when the end of the Kali Yuga is imminent. [...] When the close of the Yuga is imminent, Śūdras exhibiting their white teeth, with clean shaven heads and wearing ochre-coloured robes will perform sacred rites, proclaiming that they have conquered the sense-organs. [...] The maximum life expectations of the people afflicted by misery will be a hundred years. In Kali Yuga, the Vedas will be seen in some places and not seen in some places. Yajñas are forsaken when Dharma receives a setback. There will be many types of heretics like wearers of ochre-coloured robes (Buddhists), Jainas and Kāpālikas. There will be sellers of the Vedas and of the sacred places. Heretics antagonistic to the discipline and arrangement of different castes and stages of life will be born. When Kali Yuga sets in, the Vedas will not be studied. Śūdras will be experts and authorities in the affairs of Dharma. [...] People will kill and destroy children in wombs. [...] The Vedas will be seen somewhere and not seen in some places. When Dharma is harassed Yajñas are forsaken.[77]

Whole regions were thus under the control of the *pāṣaṇḍa*-s, protected by non-orthodox kings. A part of the population had turned to religious practices extraneous to the teaching of the Vedas and performed by priests who often belonged to low castes; many brāhmaṇas had apostatised; women had reached a certain degree of independence from male control. The main people responsible for the changed situation were śūdras and merchants. The detail on foetuses being killed is particularly interesting, because it takes us back to the allegations made to the Buddha in the *Māgaṇḍiya Sutta* (Chapter II), further clarifying that the Kali Age is the actual age of the Buddha and of Buddhist hegemony.

Similar concepts are found in the *Viṣṇudharma Upapurāṇa*, a work of the Bhāgavatas, dating from the same period as the *Vāyu Purāṇa.*[78] Referring the reader to the quotations provided by R.C. Hazra,[79] we confine ourselves to quote a passage on mendicant monks showing that the target were, in particular, the Buddhists:

> At the time, the vile Śūdras, bearing the signs of mendicancy, will not serve the twice-born people, nor will they practice their own *dharma.* Some will become Utcokas, Saugatas, Mahāyānists, and the heretical Kāpilas and Bhikṣus, while other wicked Śūdras will turn Śākyas, Śravakas, Nirgranthas and Siddhaputras in the Kali age. Turning wandering mendicants the villainous Śūdras will undergo no (physical) purification, have crooked nature, and habitually live on food prepared by others.[80]

Going through the copious evidence at our disposal, the 'general commotion amounting to a revolt and agitation' on the part of the subject castes and the 'general tenor of intense hostility between the brahmanas and the sudras' identified by R.C. Sharma[81] are one and the same thing with the Buddhist hegemony over urban society and the reaction against Buddhism. Not that Buddhism was the only dissident voice in the third and fourth century, but it exercised hegemony over change and was identified with it. Missing this point, and failing to understand that Buddhism, in deconstructing the notion itself of identity, deconstructs society, has perpetuated inclusive paradigms. Even when the target is multiple, we must make the convenient distinctions. A passage from the *Ṣaṭtriṃśanmata* maintains that

> [a] man should bathe with all his clothes on if he chances to touch the Bauddhas, the Pāśupatas, the Jainas, the Lokāyatikas, the Kāpilas, and those Brāhmans who have taken up the duties not meant for them. But if he touches the Kāpālikas, he should perform Prāṇāyāma in addition.[82]

The Pāśupatas, or at least some of the groups known by this name, became part of the neo-Brahmanical synthesis in early Gupta time, and perhaps even before, after Lakulīśa's reform (Lakulīśa was a brāhmaṇa), and the social impact of the Lokāyatas, for all their criticism towards the theists, was not relevant.[83] As for the gruesome Kāpālikas, not only were they never a threat to the Brahmanical order, but found their place very early in the political system[84] and were utilised by it, to be got rid of when they were no longer needed. Their unpardonable, if necessary sin, as we shall see, was apparently that of physically eliminating apostate brāhmaṇas, whom the passage quoted above includes in the lot. For the orthodox, the need of (re)establishing *varṇāśramadharma* and the role of brāhmaṇas in society was made urgent not so much by the emergence of śūdras (a process that could be handled) but by the drift of many brāhmaṇas towards the value system of the heretics. The *Vāyu Purāṇa*, after observing that brāhmaṇas had turned heretics like the other castes, says that 'A Brāhmaṇa who keeps matted hair without any specific aim, who shaves off his hair for nothing, and goes about naked purposelessly' is called *nagnādaya*, namely, an apostate brāhmaṇa who has joined the Buddhists and Jains. These heretics are naked because they are not protected by the three Vedas.[85]

The above discussion is briefly but effectively summed up in a passage of the Jābāli episode in the Ayodhyā Kaṇḍa of the *Rāmāyaṇa*. Here the Buddha is reviled as a thief and an atheist.[86] The accusation of being a thief is not easily understandable at first, but the *Harivaṃśa* gives us a clue when it states that in the Kali Age thieves and robbers would become rulers and rulers would behave like thieves and robbers, and that oppressed by kings and thieves, people would be driven to destruction.[87] In the Bhāgavata perspective of the Ayodhyā Kaṇḍa, Rāma, guarantor of *varṇāśramadharma* and punisher of śūdra ascetics,[88] considers the Buddha a thief because he sees him in his function of *cakravartin*: the Buddha robs him of the royal function that is due by right only to a kṣatriya who has remained faithful to the Brahmanical order. The Buddhist *cakravartin* is the usurper presiding over an alternative society: Aśoka and the *mleccha* kings, not considering the petty *rājā*-s ruling locally are clearly alluded to. A further clue on the real stakes is contained in Rāma's speech when he says that his father Daśaratha had tolerated the presence of *nāstika*-s but that from now on no such people will be tolerated. Thus the revised poem becomes a literary companion to the *Manusmṛti*, a turning point in the attitude of the orthodox: they must now do away with the Buddhists.

A crucial corollary of the disastrous depiction of Indian society in the early centuries AD made by the Brahmanical sources is the request for mechanisms of coercion aimed at radically redressing the situation. The exercise of *daṇḍa* acquires a previously unknown importance, and the role of the king as suppressor is emphasised.[89] R.C. Sharma would have been able to bring a sharper focus on the responses developed against the Kali Age if he had accepted a more convincing date for the *Arthaśāstra*, a text that shows the complete, full reorganisation of Brahmanical power. When there is a king (to be understood as a king-*daṇḍa*), states the *Rāmāyaṇa*, even the atheists, who have unhesitatingly broken all norms, can revert to a better behaviour.[90] The *dharmamahārāja*-s of the Pallavas, Viṣṇukuṇḍins, Vākāṭakas and other dynasties of the Deccan claimed to have established *dharma*,[91] which, in that context, meant the *varṇa* system. But the attempt at restoring Brahmanical *dharma* had already been the concern of the early *aśvamedhin* kings, whose pioneer work was brought to completion in northern and central India by the Guptas: this point should not be missed. The question is: up to what extent was the work of suppression exercised, and upon whom? If the *cāṇḍāla*-s had to be physically punished and suppressed according to the Śānti Parvan, and if this measure was extended to the śūdras in general,[92] was physical punishment extended to the ones responsible for the śūdra revolution, the *pāṣaṇḍa*-s? Was it possible to impose *varṇāśramadharma* without disconnecting the middle and lower ranks of society from their intellectual élites? What could physical punishment be in this case? Faxian's mentioning Buddhist monks being persecuted points to the fact that they were not simply the metaphoric target of literary compositions, but the real object of actual discrimination and violence.

A passage from the Sanskrit version of the *Saddharmapuṇḍarīka Sūtra* should convince us of the actual situation. This famous Mahāyāna text is generally thought to be a very early one, because it was translated into Chinese by the *yuezhi* monk Dharmarakṣa in AD 285.[93] However, there is strong evidence that this translation was based, like the translations of the other Buddhist texts circulating in China until the third century, on a version written in a Prakrit vernacular.[94] The Sanskrit text we have is therefore a post-third century redaction, and can arguably be dated to the fourth or fifth century, although later interpolations are possible. The passage, which is given here in the vintage, condensed translation from the French of Eugène Burnouf made by Horace H. Wilson is the following:

When you have entered into Nirváńa, and the end of time has arrived, we shall expound this excellent Sútra, in doing which we will endure, we will suffer patiently, injuries, violence, menaces of beating us with sticks, and the spitting upon us, with which ignorant men will assail us. The Tírthakas, composing Sútras of their own, will speak in the assembly to insult us. In the presence of kings, of the sons of kings, of the Brahmans, of Householders, and other religious persons, they will censure us in their discourses, and will cause the language of the Tírthakas to be heard; but we will endure all this through respect for the great Ŕishis. We must endure threatening looks, and repeated instances of contumely, and suffer expulsion from our Viháras, and submit to be imprisoned and punished in a variety of ways; but recalling at the end of this period the commands of the chief of the world, we will preach courageously this Sutra in the midst of the assembly, and we will traverse towns, villages, the whole world, to give to those who will ask for it, the deposit which thou hast entrusted to us.[95]

The passage seems free from propagandistic aim, and has the accent of truth. Injuries and menaces, punishment and imprisonment, as well as expulsion from the monasteries, though not detailed, are precisely reported facts. The most interesting detail is the mention of public debates in the presence of the king, of which we have a good documentation from the first half of the seventh century onwards and of the bullying behaviour of the brāhmaṇas, which were to become increasingly common in the course of time, as we shall see in the next chapter.

When it comes down to facts, who attacked the monks and carried out the destruction of the Buddhist institutions? In some cases, we can think of operations directly organised by the Gupta leadership under pressure of *vaidika* brāhmaṇas and, later on, of Bhāgavatas and Sivaite groups. Although not detailed, the references to Samudragupta as a great sinner and to the responsibilities of his entourage contained in the *Mañjuśrīmūlakalpa* lead to this conclusion. Army units were probably responsible for operations of the kind carried out by Puṣyamitra Śuṅga against the Kukkuṭārāma and by Śaśāṅka's attack on Bodhgayā. The anti-Buddhist violence of the king of Gauḍa is too well known to be recalled in detail, and the reader is referred to Xuanzang's *Xiyuji* and to the last chapter of the *Mañjuśrīmūlakalpa*.[96] In his case, there is no distorted chronological and cultural perspective to rectify, but, at most, a biased negationism. D.D. Kosambi, usually insensitive to historical explanations at the religious level, observed that the remarkable feature of Śaśāṅka's invasion of Magadha was 'its novel religious guise': the destruction of Buddhist monasteries and the burning down of the Bodhi tree would show 'some conflict at the basis which, for the first time, was fought out on the level of theological consciousness. [...] This was an entirely new development, not to be compared to the earlier differences between Vedic Brahmin and early Buddhist'.[97] Our point is that the *post quem* for these 'developments' is probably the third-fourth century.

It is possible that, on occasions, armed groups were organised by the leaders of the theistic movements. A set of archaeological finds from all over northern India, notably from the middle Ganges plains, which, in spite of their diffusion, have not attracted due attention, may help us to clarify the religious landscape once we set foot outside the deputed places of the dynasty. They are the fragments of small or middle-size terracotta images, especially heads, which are unmistakably those of ascetics, as is shown by their hair arranged in a *jaṭā* (Fig. 1). A number of heads display a circlet on the forehead, further pointing to the Sivaite affiliation of a production spread with impressive uniformity over a very large territory and dated to the second-third centuries AD and later.[98] These fragmented materials have never been found *in situ*, and archaeologists have only seldom tried to place them in context on the basis of their spatial distribution and associated finds, nor have these images attracted the attention of art historians, usually concerned with works related to higher forms of patronage. Their pertinence to places of worship is beyond doubt, however – small shrines with wattle-and-daub walls. They cannot be dismissed as belonging to 'folk cults' because of their iconographic traits, uniformity and territorial distribution, which imply conceptualisation and organisation from above. At Pipri, a site near Gotihawa in the Nepalese Tarai, these images are associated with figurines of animals, and in particular with a large terracotta bull.[99] Those groups of Pāśupatas who identified with Śiva's bull,[100] are the best candidates to whom the creation of models, the territorial diffusion of images (all locally executed) and the related cults can be attributed. This may explain, at one and the same time, the great impact of the proselytising activity of the Pāśupatas and their invisibility in the sources, in which they emerge only when they were granted high patronage. In the case of Pipri, less than 1 km from Gotihawa, these finds are contemporary to

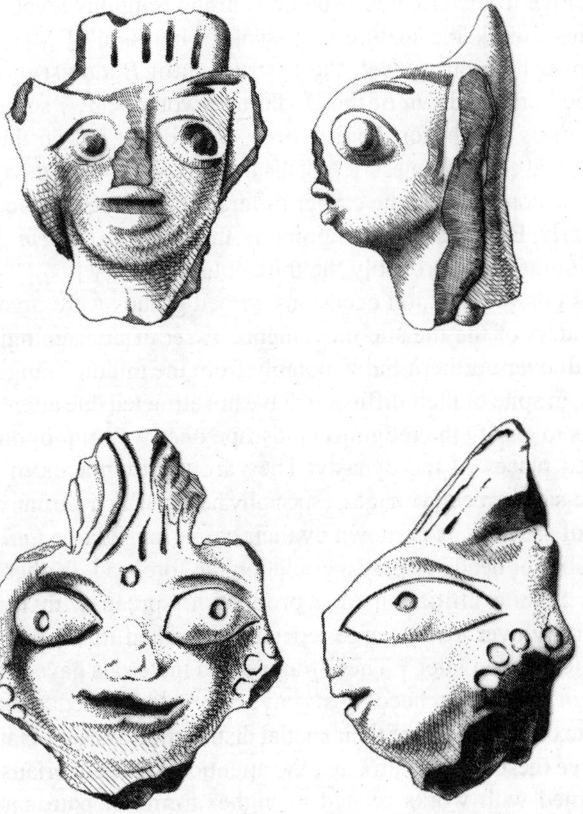

Figure 1: Heads of Sivaite ascetics, second-third century AD. Pipri, Kapilbastu district (Nepal).

the late phases of the Buddhist sanctuary or to its end, and tell a history of extraneousness and opposition.

Conversely, there is no evidence of the involvement of *bhaṭṭa*-s and *caṭṭa*-s, as has been surmised.[101] Early mention of the official status held by *bhaṭṭa*-s and *caṭṭa*-s is found in the Mota Machiala grant of Dhruvasena I of Valabhī dated AD 525[102] and in Harṣa's Madhuban and Banskhera copper-plate inscriptions, where they are listed after the rulers of districts (*viṣayapati*-s) and before the servants in a long list of authorities addressed by the emperor.[103] If their role was that of keepers of the custom houses (*ghaṭikā[sthāna]*-s), we can suppose, at most, that they could put pressure on the king, but we have no other information on their activitics for this period.[104] Their being mentioned at the end of the list make us doubt that in Gupta times they were in possession of the royal seal as they did later, when their bargaining power, as we shall see in the next chapter, increased dramatically.

VILIFICATION, RESPONSES, AND THE RIFT IN THE NEW *YĀNA*

The extent to which the brāhmaṇas disliked *śramaṇa*-s in general and Buddhist monks in particular is well-documented in the Pāli Canon, where the distance between the two sides is often enormous, despite the imperative need of the Buddhists to proselytise.[105] From the Aggañña Sutta of the *Dīgha Nikāya* (where the Buddha's argument against Brahmanical social order is strongest), we learn what the brāhmaṇas thought of the *śramaṇa*-s. The Buddha requests Vaṣettha, a young brāhmaṇa who has apostatised, to report to him the criticism to which he and his companion are exposed, and Vaṣettha replies that the blame thrown upon them is absolute because, whereas the brāhmaṇas are born from Brahmā's forehead and are consubstantial with him, the shaven petty ascetics are unclean, born of Brahmā's foot like servants and dark-skinned individuals:[106] they are, in a word, śūdras. In the Vasala Sutta of the *Sutta Nipāta*, the Buddha, who had gone to Śrāvastī for alms, approaches the house of Aggika, and a Bhāradvāja brāhmaṇa who was performing a fire ritual in his house, greets him at first with these words: 'Stop there, shaveling; stop there, wretched ascetic [*samaṇaka*]; stop there, outcaste [*vasalaka*]'.[107] Buddhist texts attest to the discrimination against the *śramaṇa*-s, despite their interest to focus on the successes of Buddhist predication. Proselytising among the brāhmaṇas collided with the strict social control to which the latter, however, well-disposed, were submitted, precluding them the possibility to make choices that were at odds with *āśrama* life, as is shown by the story of Soṇadaṇḍa narrated in the *Dīgha Nikāya*. Soṇadaṇḍa, a learned brāhmaṇa well versed in the Three Vedas,[108] was convinced of the greatness of the Buddha but even after inviting the Buddha and his monks to his house and sharing food with him felt uneasy at the idea of having to rise from his seat to bow down before Gautama in public because the upper caste citizens of Campā would criticise him. The Buddha was to understand that his taking off his turban on entering the assembly was equivalent to having bowed at his feet, something that he could not publicly do. Soṇadaṇḍa's company would despise him if, when riding in his carriage, he were to alight to salute the Lord, who must be satisfied that he merely raise the goad in greeting.[109] What is striking in this story is that the Buddha (or the learned monks who were responsible for the drafting of the text) seems to accept this as inevitable. The usual behaviour of the proud brāhmaṇas towards the *bhikṣu*-s is that disrespectfully shown by the young brāhmaṇa Ambaṭṭha on meeting Gotama for the first time. The Lord was seated, but Ambaṭṭha 'walked up and down' uttering 'some vague words of politeness' because 'as for those shaven little ascetics, menials, black scourings from Brahmā's foot', it was fitting to speak as he did.[110]

In the Piṇḍolya Sutta of the *Saṃyutta Nikāya*, the Buddha goes for alms to Pañcasālā, a village inhabited by brāhmaṇas where a festival is being held and where, consequently, there is abundance of food to beg for. Inspired by Māra, the brāhmaṇas refused to give him anything, and 'even as with washen bowl he entered Pañcasālā for alms, so with washen bowl came he back again'.[111] The story reflects behaviour that had to be fairly common: by attributing the unpleasant episode to the Buddha, the monks were encouraged to persevere. The brāhmaṇa householders of the Māratajjanīya Sutta, possessed by Māra,

> abused, reviled, scolded, and harassed the virtuous bhikkus of good character thus: 'These bald-pated recluses, these swarthy menial offspring of the Kinsman's feet, claim: "We are meditators, we are meditators!" and with shoulders drooping, heads down and all limp, they meditate, premeditate, outmeditate, and mis-meditate.'[112]

As regards the post-Canonical literature, the *Divyāvadāna* remains, like the Jātakas, a mine of information. It reports the story of a young brāhmaṇa, Panthaka, who is unable to receive an education appropriate to his status. Thus he decides to become a monk, and he is quick to learn the Buddhist tenets. However, he is careful not to wear the monk's robe in his own town, where he is known by everybody, and asks permission to live aloof, devoting his life to meditating and to the scriptures.[113] There were brāhmaṇas who, without renouncing their status and duties, honoured the Buddha as a holy man, but many were openly hostile to him and his followers. In another story narrated in the *Divyāvadāna*, that of the householder Meṇḍhaka, it appears that at Śrāvastī the *nirgrantha*-s had made an alliance with the *ṛṣi*-s (an early testimony of the Jains' positioning)[114] and had now settled in the town of Bhadraṅkara, from where they feared to be dislodged after being again defeated in a doctrinal debate. They announced the visit of the Buddha as of one 'hurling his razor-like thunderbolt, making many women childless widows', and suggested the following strategy:

Drive all the people away from the areas around Bhadraṅkara', they said, 'and force them to live in the city of Bhadraṅkara.' Plough under the grassy meadows, break down the altars, cut down any trees with fruits or flowers, and pollute the water sources with poison.[115]

The 'influential men' whose services had been requested adopted a scorched earth strategy, and only the intervention of Śakra as *deus ex machina* saved the situation. In the tales of the *Divyāvadāna*, as in the Canon, the brāhmaṇas are in many cases convinced and converted by the Buddha, whose deeds are extolled, but a story like that of Meṇḍhaka has, by contrast, a true ring about it. Its interest also lies in being another testimony of the early existence of public debates in which the losers, as we will better see in the following chapter, had to abandon the country where they lived.

The hostility to whatever form of religious and social movement that could jeopardise the *varṇa* system had found an early systematisation in the *Manusmṛti*, the founding text of the ideologised *dharmaśāstra*-s that in the early centuries AD became the standard source of authority in the orthodox tradition.[116] This text marked an important step in the belittlement and de-legitimisation of the Buddhists. The heretics, equalled to gamblers, bootleggers and the like, must be expelled from town because they are 'concealed thieves who, living in the king's kingdom constantly oppress his good subjects by their bad actions'.[117] A twice-born 'should not give honour, even with mere words, to heretics [*pāṣaṇḍin*-s], people who persist in wrong action, people who act like cats, hypocrites, rationalists, and people who live like herons'.[118] Women who have joined a heretical sect are equalled to those 'who live on lust, or have abortions, or harm their husbands, or drink liquor',[119] outcaste women in a word.

Derogatory references to members of both the *saṃgha* and the lay community are plentiful in Brahmanical texts, even taking into account the fact that the pattern of not referring directly to Buddhism is common to many of them:[120] here the totalitarian strategy of silence is generally adopted. The poor reputation enjoyed by monks and nuns is often explicit. Monks are probably referred to in the *Yājñavalkya Smṛti*, composed in Gupta times, where the sight of yellow-robed people is said to be an evil omen.[121] The accusation, often repeated in the Purāṇas, is serious, considering the context. Monks went out begging, and lived on alms in principle, and the charge is aimed at isolating them from the residents of a given place. The transformation of the *saṃgha* into either a landed, self-sufficient entity or into a set of family-based transmittable institutions has many causes, but it appears that from a certain period onwards monks would no longer been able to continue their door-to-door quest. Monks were becoming visible targets of social opprobrium. Sarcastic retaliations were not lacking. In the *Bodhisattva Womb Sūtra*, translated into Chinese at the end of the fourth or at the beginning of the fifth century,[122] there is a derisive description of *ṛṣi*-s, all, or almost all mainstream ascetics, practising twenty-six types of *tapas*:

Some detach their body parts at the joints searching for the location of their spirit [. . .]. (21.4.8)

Some say to themselves: I keep my own release back, and first release my father and mother. And after throwing their father and mother into their fire they sing for them to be reborn in Brahmā's heaven. (21.4.14)

Some eat cow dung. (21.4.15) [. . .]

Some make their food vessels out of bones. (21.4.21)[123]

If living in a monastic community was considered to be an unnatural life for men, nunneries were perceived as an explicit attack on social stability. Women were seen exclusively in the functions of marriage and procreation, and that a woman could make a choice, be it for the strictest monastic discipline, was inadmissible. The much-hated Buddhist nuns are the object of contempt in the texts, from the *Arthaśāstra*[124] to Vātsyāyana's *Kāma Sūtra*.[125] Here, a *viṭa* (a sort of gigolo) relies upon female mendicants, shaven-head female ascetics expert in the arts, women of loose morals and old whores as go-betweens.[126] The date of the *Kāma Sūtra* is debated: in an unspecified period,[127] the brāhmaṇa Vātsyāyana assembled a number of works that had become difficult to procure. Some details, such as Sāketa being depicted as the flourishing commercial town known from Buddhist literature, point to a relatively early context. The *Kāma Sūtra* has the merit, in its own way, of presenting the anti-Buddhist point of view rather clearly, like the *Arthaśāstra*: the only companions of Buddhist nuns are women of loose morals and whores, members of the seedy ambience typical of the low-caste sex workers. It does not contain a critique of individual cases; it rather implies that they *naturaliter* belong to a distasteful, if unavoidable, underworld. Blaming the Buddhist nuns of acting as go-betweens became commonplace, and accusations were made easier by the fact that nunneries were exclusively located in the towns.[128] We find examples of these charges in tales which still reflect a mercantile society. In a story of the *Daśakumāracarita* set in Ujjayinī, a loafer and member of the Mathurā demimonde, Kalahakaṇṭaka, finds an ally in Arhantikā, a *śramaṇikā*, to gain the favour of Nitambavatī, the wife of the merchant Anantakīrti.[129] In the story of Guhasena and his wife Devasmitā from the *Kathāsaritsāgara*, as soon as the merchant's false friends arrive in Tāmralipti, they get in touch with a Buddhist nun, Yogakaraṇḍikā, as an agent to try to subvert the fidelity of Guhasena's wife Devasmitā. In this case, the nun shows an intrinsically corrupt nature: she is already rich, and declines the reward that the four merchants are willing to pay for her services. Yogakaraṇḍikā's disciple, Siddhikarī, is worth her teaching, and is depicted as a tricky thief.[130]

Ostracism, in the form of imposition of customs and ferry and police stations dues, was exercised upon the merchants. The *Divyāvadāna* talks about the attempts of the latter to escape these impositions by various means.[131] From the orthodox side, the *Harivaṃśa* compares the markets, widespread in the countryside, to thorns.[132] The target of the orthodox is threefold: against the Buddhists, either monks and nuns or laymen, against the apostate brāhmaṇas, and against the economic sectors supporting the *saṃgha*.

The discussion carried out in recent years on the emergence of Mahāyāna and its nature allows for some considerations. The opposition between *araṇya* and *grāma* monks has been brought into focus by a number of scholars,[133] who have stressed the polemics of the *araṇya* bodhisattvas towards the monks roaming 'among upper-class patrons in town',[134] directly involved in agriculture and trade,[135] and settling in villages. The early bodhisattva path was for few: the bodhisattvas, who are at the centre of a value system centred on salvation, may be defined as the pneumatics of the new *yāna*, but it appears that a rift took place in the new doctrine in a relatively short time. An attempt to refer the different positions held within the

Buddhist community to the actual Indian reality may help to readdress the debate on the nature and functions of the bodhisattvas and the bodhisattvas-mahāsattvas.[136]

The early householder bodhisattva of the *Ugraparipṛcchā* (*The Inquiry of Ugra*) is ready to start his work as a saviour, not allowing even a single being to be born into any evil rebirth in the 'village, town, city, kingdom, or capital' where he happens to live.[137] He appears as a product of the urban revolution that between the first century BC and the second century AD created a dense network of large and minor settlements, too numerous in number to be controlled by the existing monastic institutions. Ugra is untouched by the enticements of urban life, and his critique of family life[138] conforms to the traditional Buddhist critique stemming from the example set by Siddhārtha the night he left his wife in disgust. We do not know exactly which people Ugra was addressing in his mission as saviour, but the evidence from the *Aṅgavijjā*, a Prakrit work on prognostication composed in the Kuṣāṇa period,[139] gives us an idea of the social context where the householder bodhisattva carried out his activity. There were people regarded as belonging to two *varṇa*-s at the same time, and in the most various combinations: *bambha-khatta* and *khatta-bambha*, *bambha-vessa* and *vessa-bambha*, *bambha-suddha* and *suddha-bambha*, *khatta-vessa* and *vessa-khatta*, *khatta-sudda* and *sudda-khatta*, *vessa-sudda* and *sudda-vessa*.[140] A further mélange derived by the intermarriage of the *anuloma* and *pratiloma* sons of the abovementioned misalliances had already been a serious concern for Manu.[141] The *Ugraparipṛcchā* bodhisattva is a brāhmaṇa who is not alarmed by social change and has given himself the task of introducing new means of hegemonic control. This is the reason why he is a brāhmaṇa, namely an intellectual who is given due reverence and is unassailable, from the crucial point of view of caste identity and of the authority deriving from it, by the enemies of the religion.

The *Mahāvastu* states that 'Bodhisattvas are born in one of two classes of families, either noble or brāhman'. The bodhisattva's family is 'distinguished, well-known, and dignified', and 'is of high birth and lineage [...].[142] Likewise, the *Abhisamayālaṅkāra* (*The Large Sūtra of Perfect Wisdom*), a text of uncertain date, in describing the varieties of bodhisattvas, says that those who are reborn in the families of men, 'are reborn in good families, i.e. among nobles, Brahmins and well-to-do householders'.[143] The new situation is enlightened by the emergence of Maitreya, the Buddha-Saviour who will be born in the *brāhmaṇavarṇa*. The emphasis on the social origin of the Buddhist élite shows that the new challenges were better coped with by educated, apostate brāhmaṇas.

Jan Nattier has observed that the bodhisattvas of the *Ugrapariprcchā* are typical family men, living at home and interacting with the organised monastic community on occasion. There is no evidence of a *guru*-disciple relationship,[144] and this raises the question of the legitimacy, within the Buddhist community, of their acts. Where did their authority come from? Nattier suggests that Ugra's position is not too different from that of a traditional *upāsaka*,[145] but his being named 'bodhisattva', a designation also used for ordained monks, prompts us to ask a number of questions. Nattier is probably right in maintaining that the *Ugra*'s authors were not trying to introduce a type of ordination different from the traditional one reserved for the monks.[146] However, the emergence of these new figures, subordinate as they may have been to monastic bodhisattvas, indicates new needs, new strategies and a shift of power within the world of the *śramaṇa*-s. Who in towns and villages did perform the rites of passage? Who celebrated, for instance, the marriage of a high-caste Buddhist, or, for that matter, of a Buddhist layman of the third *varṇa*? Since it is unthinkable that such rituals were celebrated in disagreement with the accepted rules, an enormous power was left in the hands of the orthodox brāhmaṇas. This resulted in a corresponding loss of power for the Buddhists, and this is the area where the lay bodhisattva acted. I have mentioned the rites of passages, but there were a number of other rites which common people could not renounce, either out of belief or for reasons of social constraint.[147] Ugra is a brāhmaṇa because his *varṇa* empowers him to perform rites and other operations of crucial social importance: to remain in the field of marriage, who made the horoscope of the couple, and who performed the rites for the new-born child? This was the way through which lay bodhisattvas became influential and, inevitably, compromised. This caused the reaction of the monks who, though willing to accept the novelties introduced by the Mahāyāna, were resolved not only to keep but potentiate the traditional monastic organisation.

The *Rāṣṭrapālapariprcchā Sūtra* depicts a situation where not only *grāma* bodhisattvas but also 'corrupt' monks have firmly established themselves on an independent or semi-independent basis. The autocephaly of the lay bodhisattvas is implied in the allegation that they '[do] not pay homage to the teachers and saints [*āryajana*]',[148] and as for their functions as independent rites performers, they are perhaps alluded to when the author of the text says: 'Taking up the banner of the Buddha, they perform services for people in the household.'[149] As regards the corrupt monks, '[t]hey keep cows, horses, asses, livestock, male and female slaves', and consider a single property '[w]hat belongs to the *stūpa*, to the *saṅgha*, and what is acquired for oneself'. Moreover, '[t]hey would have wives, sons, and daughters just like a householder'.[150] Here it would seem that family-based institutions run by Buddhist priests were already in existence, even though we read below that '[t]hey are not householders, and they are not monks', and that those who were always thinking to the village were all the same forest-dwellers of sort.[151] Moreover, real monasteries provided with cells are referred to.[152] It can perhaps be assumed that householder monks already existed who spent certain periods of the year in retirement.

We have other sources that hint at the existence of Buddhist priests. A passage from the *Xiyuji* seems to indicate the existence of householder monks in early seventh-century Sind. Xuanzang noted a group of adherents to the Little Vehicle who shaved their heads and wore the *kaṣāya* robes of the *bhikṣu*-s, 'whom they resemble[d] outwardly, whilst they engage[d] themselves in the ordinary affairs of lay life'. In the past, 'they had obediently walked according to the doctrine of religion', but 'the changed times have weakened their virtue', and now 'they live without any moral rules, and their sons and grandsons continue to live as wordly people, without any regard to their religious profession'.[153]

According to the *Rājataraṅgiṇī*, in early historical Kashmir, Yūkadevī, the second queen of king Meghavāhana of the Gonandīya dynasty, had a *vihāra* built in competition with the other queens, and

> [i]n one half of it she placed those Bhikṣus whose conduct conformed to the precepts, and in the [other] half those who being in possession of wives, children cattle and property, deserved blame for their life as householders.[154]

Here Kalhaṇa discusses a period of the history of Kashmir of which he knows little, and he may project a later reality into early Kashmir, but, from the other side, we must assume that his information were based on earlier sources. The above-quoted passage definitely indicates the existence of two separate classes of monks, or, better to say, of a priesthood and a monkhood which lived side by side. It also indicates that *vihāra*-s were open to monks and priests alike.

The hauteur towards the devious monks shown by both the author of the *Questions of Rāṣṭrapāla* and Xuanzang (an advocate of both Mahāyāna and Vinaya Buddhism), as well as by Kalhaṇa's source, should not lead us astray and make us consider the Buddhist priests a lot of unworthy, debased adepts, an accident in history. We are, rather, at the beginning of a process that led to the formation of two distinct Mahāyāna traditions. It appears that the tradition of the Indian Buddhist priesthood, which we will again briefly address in Chapter VI, is well rooted in history. Akira Hirakawa's view of the lay origins of the Mahāyāna is now discarded,[155] but some of his observations are worth recalling. He maintained that 'in the period of the *Yogācārabhūmi-śāstra* the renunciant bodhisattva received the upā-saṃpadā and became a *bhikṣu* like the *śravaka* by the vinayapiṭaka, but there also existed a bodhisattva śīkṣā with its own method of ordination and there were people who undertook it'.[156] Here I leave open the question of the possible relationship between the householder bodhisattvas and the *śākyabhikṣu*s, who in the fifth century formed a separate group of monks,[157] and which in Newār Buddhism we know as householder monks. The emerging awareness of the variety of relationships between *saṃgha*s and monks and of the different behaviours of the latter, in their own way legitimate, foreshadows a major breakthrough in our understanding of ancient Indian Buddhism.[158]

The frequent occurrence of the term *grāma* and the rare mention of towns, and the emergence of the *araṇya/grāma* polarity, point to a context of declining urbanisation, a process that started in the second half of the third century. We have seen how widespread the presence of the Pāśupatas in the villages was: they acted as priests, or at least as second or third-class pujaris (this depended on the degree of acceptance of the various Pāśupata groups). Their presence became increasingly important from the third century onwards, and village priests became a structured part of the religious and economic reality. Competing with them was no easy matter, especially when patronage towards Buddhist institutions sank as a result of the great economic crisis of the third century and when, in Gupta times, the monasteries came under attack. While the *araṇya* bodhisattvas probably started clustering in the regions where monastic life remained a viable possibility, in the rest of India the Buddhist communities had to organise themselves around a priesthood paralleling the Brahmanical priesthood. All the segments forming the Buddhist world were affected by the new situation to a degree: the Raivata mentioned by Faxian is seemingly a celibate *guru*, but has compromised on the caste issue.

Are there scriptures ascribable to the world of the *grāma* bodhisattvas? An early text that may be associated to the formation stage of a householder monkhood is the *Upāyakauśalya Sūtra* (*The Skill in Means Sūtra*), which justifies the behaviour condemned by the *araṇya* monks. This *sūtra* tells the story of a young brāhmaṇa lusted after by a female water-carrier whom at first he rejects so as not to break his *vrata*. Being not able to be with him, she prefers to die, and to save her life, he decides to break his vows. 'Taking the woman by the right hand, he said, "Sister, arise, I will do whatever you desire."' Thus he 'lived the home life for twelve years before leaving it again to generate the four stations of brahma'.[159] The Buddha sanctions this behaviour maintaining that in one of his former lives he was the young brāhmaṇa, the water-carrier being no other than Yaśodharā. Here, as in the *Ugraparipṛcchā*, family life is subordinate to celibate life, but the vows are broken: the young brāhmaṇa carries on the life of an orthodox *gṛhapati*, leaving his family to devote himself to spiritual practices only at a later stage in life.

The introduction of the concept of skill-in-means (*upāya*)[160] and the social ambiguity inherent in it opens an unexpected scenario, which we will better examine in a later chapter. In the *Upāyakauśalya Sūtra*, bodhisattvas 'attenuate even a great transgression with skill in means'.[161] As regards sense desires, the bodhisattva 'enters the great swamp of sense-desire but he will be reborn in the world of Brahmā'; he 'will take pleasure in the five kinds of sense-qualities; he will allow himself to be permeated by them', but 'will cut through all the sense-qualities whenever he so desires [...]'.[162] Thanks to *upāya*, he 'indulges in pleasure and play with the five kinds of sense-desire', so that some will say that if he cannot save himself, he cannot save others. However, whenever he so desires, the bodhisattva with skill in means 'slash all nets of defilement with his sword of wisdom and betake himself to a purified Buddha-field that is free from licentious women.[163] Sex is thus, predictably, the most important of the 'five kinds of sense-desire', and we must try to enter the reality of the time in order to understand these episodes and those reported above in the text. It is extremely unlikely that the lay bodhisattvas and the much maligned *grāma bhikṣu*-s could experience sex other than in a family context. Villages were too small to allow for casual sex (which, if ever, was easier for the *araṇya* monks), and that is why both the *Rāṣṭrapālaparipṛcchā* and the *Upāyakauśalya Sūtra*-s explicitly mention family life in connection with *bhikṣu*-s.

THE GODS IN ARMS

It has long been recognised that in the *Mahābhārata*, not only the Bhāgavatas, but also the Pāśupatas have become part of the new Brahmanical tradition born out from the compromise between the theistic movements and the orthodox.[164] The caves of Udayagiri near Vidiśā, owing to the fact that they date to about AD 400 (the inscription of AD 401 is outside Cave 6),[165] are even better evidence. They have been recently investigated in great detail and with great insight in relation to the Gupta ideology by Michael Willis, to whose book, which will remain for long the reference work for the students of early Hinduism, the reader is referred.[166] About the same time, an image of Hari-Hara, also from central India,[167] testifies to the compromise between the two great theistic systems. Thus the grafting of the theistic religions onto the Vedic tradition, besides producing works like the *Rāmāyaṇa*, a large part of the *Mahābhārata* and the early Purāṇas, was now able to create iconography of great emotional impact and the related rituals. The world of the gods was expressed with unprecedented potency and subtlety.

At Udayagiri, the Bhāgavata gods have a leading role but are flanked by Sivaite icons and by the goddesses. In Cave 3 there is an image of Kārttikeya, an avowedly warrior-god, and outside Cave 6 a four-armed Viṣṇu with his weapons and a twelve-armed Mahiṣamardinī who appears as a real war machine. Viṣṇu Anantaśayana, one of the polarities of the sacred layout of the site together with Viṣṇu-Varāha,[168] is obviously unarmed, but we know that he wakens to kill the two *asura*-s Madhu and Kaiṭabha. The disquieting Narasiṃha, Viṣṇu's *vāma* aspect, is also depicted: he marks the dawn of a new age[169] because he has killed the *asura* Hiraṇyakaśipu, thus being entitled to welcome the new initiates who abandon their asuric nature[170] to see the light of god. The *mātṛkā*-s, led by Skanda, are present outside Cave 4, and are in relation to the cremation ground and the rites performed by the Atharvavedic *purohita*, a Kāpālika:[171] we know that they play a non-secondary role in fighting the *asura*-s, whose blood they drink.[172] The Brahmanical pantheon, with his armed gods, is virtually complete.

In Brahmanical myth and iconography, we usually associate the concepts of violence and destruction to some aspects of Śiva and some forms of the goddess. Śiva is born as a destructive god, as is shown by the trident and the other weapons he is endowed with from the beginning.[173] He holds the trident on the third-century seals found at Sankisa, in the Ganges Valley,[174] as well as in a stele from the region of Kauśāmbī datable to the third-fourth century, which shows him four-armed and holding *ḍamaru*, a rosary and a pot.[175] His *aghora*, ferocious aspect on *caturmukhaliṅga*-s, well documented from Kuṣāṇa times onwards,[176] also betrays one of his main characteristics. Skanda is armed with a spear when he makes his first iconographic appearance in the North, and – as Subrahmaṇya – with a *vajra* in the South.[177] He is at the head of the mothers as early as the Kuṣāṇa period in Mathurā[178] and of the army of the *deva*-s, whom he victoriously leads in battle against the *asura*-s led by Tāraka, as stated in the *Vāyu Purāṇa*, where the god is called 'slayer of Asuras' and 'enemy of Daityas'.[179] The name of his spear is *aparājitā*, unvanquished.[180] Skanda's association with Śiva is sanctioned by a myth that makes him his son, and, at the same time, the son of Agni[181] in order to make him accepted in orthodox circles.

Vāsudeva, a deity on whose characteristics and worship the complex figure of Viṣṇu was largely to depend, is not less fierce a divinity. He is given, from the beginning, two deathly weapons, *gadā*, the club meant 'to strike the enemy at close quarters'[182] and *cakra*, 'resembling the modern quoit' which 'must have been used as a missile to be thrown against the enemy to cut him through and kill him'.[183] *Śaṅkha* is another tool used in war, its sound striking terror into the hearts of the enemies.[184] The Udayagiri Viṣṇu has Vāsudeva as his model, and he is in fact ready for the fight.

The ferocious nature of the gods of the Bhāgavatas, the *pañcavīra*-s, is exemplified in the third-fourth centuries by their association, in a famous relief from Piduguralla village in the Guntur district of Andhra Pradesh, with Narasiṃha, one of the most frightening Indian deities, who is two-armed and is endowed with *cakra* and *gadā*. As seen above, Narasiṃha kills the *asura*/*daitya* Hiraṇyakaśipu,[185] and is represented with increasing frequency from the Gupta period onwards:[186] after the Guptas, the god will be mostly shown as pulling out the *asura*'s entrails after having killed him.[187] The *Narasiṃha dīkṣā*, or Man-lion initiation, was the main rite of the *Pāñcarātra Āgama* through which *mleccha*-s could be cleaned up,[188] and the growing presence of the deity points to both proselytism and a call to arms against the enemies of Bhagavān.

As to the goddess, she makes an early appearance in the destructive form of Durgā slaying the *asura* Mahiṣa: the early images of Mahiṣamardinī were created in Kuṣāṇa Mathurā.[189] At Udayagiri the goddess is depicted thrice. In the first image, magnificently executed, the goddess has twelve arms holding the war attributes given her, according to the *Devī Māhātmya*, by the gods (the *śūla* by Śiva, the bow by Vāyu, the *vajra* by Indra, the sword and the 'spotless' shield by Kāla), as well as the lotus garland of the Ocean.[190] In the second, she has twelve arms, and is armed 'with sword and shield, bow and arrows, club, discus, and thunderbolt'.[191] The third, much worn out, is also multi-armed, and is sculpted on the northern wall of the courtyard of Cave 6.[192] The Udayagiri image suggests that the features and deeds of the goddess depicted in the *Devī Māhātmya* had already found a firm theorisation in the late fourth century. In this extraordinarily vibrant text, the goddess takes the place of Viṣṇu in fighting the *asura*-s Madhu and Kaiṭabha, who had assailed Brahmā,[193] and carries out a memorable battle against Mahiṣa and against the two other *asura*-s Śumba and Niśumba, whose myth is almost unknown in earlier literature. At Badoh-Pathari, in the Bina Valley (the Bina is a tributary of the Betwa), the mothers, some of whom are armed and led by Vīrabhadra, are sitting on thrones in a row, the set being dated to the first half of the fifth century.[194]

The alarming amount of destruction and violence that typify the new Brahmanical gods cannot find its reason buried in inexplicable myths. When we attribute the narrations of the epics, the Purāṇas and the Āgamas and their visual renderings to the realm of myth, we risk exempting us from giving an explanation at the historical level. Yet the more recent debate on the nature of myth has made the evolutionist hypothesis of the passage from *mýthos* to *lógos* obsolete.[195] Myth is reconciled with the demand for rationality to the point of not being considered inferior to science but in historical-factual terms,[196] and we should feel free to examine it from a historical and social perspective without prejudicing its autonomy.[197] In any case, myth has the inherent ability to continuously generate metaphors and allegories. These, taken one by one, have a shorter life than the myth's core (the symbol), their operational field being politics and ideology, but nonetheless remain a structural part of myth, and can outlive it for centuries, as is shown by the allegories nourished by the dead classical myths in Europe as late as the eighteenth and nineteenth century. Is it possible to anchor myths to history, without denying the atemporal and universal situations they embody.

Why are the Brahmanical gods born armed and manifestly hostile in aspect, looking increasingly destructive and terrifying? Which interpretation should we give of the *asura*-s, who appear to be so present and dangerous in an epoch so relatively near to modern times? Vedic gods were also struggling with the *asura*-s, and creation itself depends on Indra killing Vṛtrāsura.[198] The *devāsura* war may be described as the major scenario in which man's history is also set. Vedic *asura*-s, either human enemies or divine beings possessed of *māyā*, are not easily identifiable, as our knowledge of Vedic society remains very limited.[199] But whatever interpretation we may give of it, the demons who dispossessed the gods in late ancient and medieval times cannot be the same as those of pre-archaic India, just as the gods so familiar to us are not the same as the Vedic ones, despite the process of Vedicisation and the extraordinary effort to fuse them in a timeless perspective. This fusion made the transition from early to new Brahmanical order possible, but cannot persuade us that Śiva is really the same god as Rudra, and that his enemies are the same against whom the anger of the Vedic god was addressed.[200] As to Viṣṇu, some of his traits, like that of his Trivikrama form, are deliberately taken from the *Ṛgveda*,[201] and he is identified with late Vedic Nārāyaṇa,[202] but nonetheless he appears as a new, multi-faceted divinity with new functions to perform. As to the goddess, in spite of her pre-archaic connections, which are to be seen within the re-statement of the Vedas 'in the pattern of the Purāṇic style',[203] she hardly expresses the characteristics of Vedic female divinities.[204]

Only recently has it been recognised that the *asura*-s and *daitya*-s of the Indian myths are the practitioners of the heretical religions, and that the use of a mythological paradigm by saints and rulers has legitimised crusades and persecutions.[205] A thorough reinterpretation of the evidence still lies ahead of us, however. With the new Purāṇic myths (which, as all myths, mark the beginning of a world),[206] the brāhmaṇas tried to establish a new history, pushing historical events into a mythical past, that we should try to understand critically. The difficulty in writing history in India does not lie in the lamented lack of documentation (which is, on the contrary, imposing), but because of our inability to interpret the data in the right perspective. Ancient and medieval India is still understood as being not only different, but also exotically 'other'.

To limit ourselves to the myths mentioned above and to sources compatible with the period under study, we learn that Hiraṇyakaśipu, as soon as he was born out of the womb of Diti, 'narrated the verses of the four Vedas' and 'performed severe penances for a hundred thousand years without taking any food and standing topsy-turvy'. Through his yogic power and Brahmā's boon he attained the power of not being slain by any human being and obtained the lordship of all *deva*-s, whom he tried to make the equals of *dānava*-s and *asura*-s.[207]

> 'The Devas along with great sages made obeisance to that quarter which is resorted to by King Hiraṇyakaśipu.' O Brāhmaṇas, Hiraṇyakaśipu, the Lord of Daityas, had such prowess. In ancient times, Viṣṇu, in the form of Man-Lion, became death unto him [. . .]. He was torn by him by means of his claws. Hence the nails are remembered pure.[208]

The *asura* appears as a high-born, apostate *yogin* who, taking undue advantage of the boon bestowed upon him by Brahmā, tries to dispossess the *deva*-s, and is brutally punished by Narasiṃha. The *Viṣṇu Purāṇa*, also an early text,[209] specifies that Hiraṇyakaśipu 'had formerly brought the three worlds under his authority' and 'had usurped the sovereignty of Indra', appropriating to himself 'all that was offered in sacrifice to the gods'.[210] *Gandharva*-s, *siddha*-s and *nāga*-s 'all attended upon the mighty Hiraṇyakaśipu'.[211] The identity of the *asura* is transparent, once we rescale the time-span of the events (the one hundred thousand years of penance) and understand that the actors of the drama are all conceived as belonging to the sole existing reality, that created and controlled by the Brahmanical gods, the rest being nothing but *māyā*, delusion. Viṣṇu's role as deluder may be recalled, even if the story as is narrated in the *Viṣṇu Purāṇa* is not part of the early text.[212] The *deva*-s ask Viṣṇu to protect them, because the *daitya*-s 'have seized upon the three worlds, and [have] appropriated the offerings which [we]re [their] portion', and Viṣṇu, hearing their request, 'emitted from his body an illusory form, which he gave to the gods, and thus spoke: 'This deceptive vision shall wholly beguile the Daityas, so that, being led astray from the path of the Vedas, they may be put to death [...].'[213] Viṣṇu first approaches the ascetics identifiable as Jains, and then

> the same deluder, putting on garments of a red colour, assuming a benevolent aspect, and speaking in soft and agreeable tones, addressed others of the same family, and said to them, 'If, mighty demons, you cherish a desire either for heaven or for final repose, desist from the iniquitous massacre of animals [...], and hear from me what you should do. Know that all that exists is composed of discriminative knowledge. Understand my words, for they have been uttered by the wise. This word subsists without support, and engaged in the pursuit of error, which it mistakes for knowledge, as well as vitiated by passion and the rest, revolves in the straits of existence.' In this manner, exclaiming to them 'Know!' [...] and they replying, 'It is known' [...], these Daityas were induced by the arch deceiver to deviate from their religious duties [...], by his repeated arguments and variously urged persuasion. When they had abandoned their own faith, they persuaded others to do the same, and the heresy spread, and many deserted the practices enjoined by the Vedas and the laws.[214]

As we shall see in the next chapter, only one reality is admitted and, in history, only one player.

As to Vāmana and Bali, an apparently early version of the story is reported in the *Vāyu Purāṇa*:

> The noble-minded Bali who was a great Yogin was bound (by Vāmana). He took birth in the human womb, being desirous of children, as the family was nearing extinction due to absence of issues. He begot sons who established the disciplines of four castes on this earth. He procreated the sons Aṅga, Vaṅga, Sulha, Puṇḍra and Kaliṅga. These are called Bāleya Kṣatras [...]. That lord had Brāhmaṇa sons also called Bāleya Brāhmaṇas. They established the line (of Bali). Many boons were granted to the intelligent Bali by the delighted Brahmā. The boons granted were *Mahāyogitva* [...], longevity of life lasting for a Kalpa, invincibility in war, great inclination towards righteousness and piety, the vision of the three worlds, importance among his descendants, unrivalled state in strength as the ability to see the true principles of Dharma. 'You will establish the [...] four castes'—on being thus told by the lord, king Bali attained great peace (of mind).[215]

What had Bali done to become an *asura* king causing the wrath of Vāmana? The events we are familiar with are reported in another passage.[216] Vāmana addresses Bali while he is performing a *yajña*, but unlike Narasiṃha – the Dwarf does not represent the *vāma* aspect of the God – he does not kill the *asura*, but '[s]eizing the royal glory of Asuras from all the three worlds, he forced them to retreat to the bottom of the nether-world along with their sons and grandsons'.[217] The names of Bali's sons give us a clue,[218] because they correspond to as many countries of eastern India as where unorthodox rule prevailed. Bali and his sons are identified with the Kṣatriya rulers who have supported the heretics and have not played their role of righteous sovereigns and guarantors of *varṇāśramadharma*. This is why they have become *daitya*s, enemies of the gods/brāhmaṇas: hence Vāmana's punishment.

Iconographies may tell much more than the patrons who commissioned them meant to communicate. Moving to the second half of the sixth century, and to a region which played a major role in establishing a firm Brahmanical rule in the Deccan and all over India in continuity with Gupta policy, we see the story of Bali depicted twice in the rock-cut caves of Badami (Vātāpī), the Early Cāḷukya capital.[219] They were executed thanks to the patronage of Kīrtivarman I (AD 566-97). In Cave 2, the king of the *asura*-s is standing below the gigantic image of Trivikrama while he is offering the *arghya* water to the Dwarf, whom he has recognised as a venerable person (Fig. 2). Not only is Bali shown with clipped hair, long ears and a dress reminiscent of the monastic robe, but Vāmana, in order to trick him, has assumed the mocking features of the Buddha. Viṣṇu, coherently with the textual evidence, represents the whole reality, including heresy.[220] In the panel of Cave 3, the largest at Badami, the identification of the king of the *asura*-s with a Buddhist ruler is even more evident because he has an *uṣṇīṣa*. A crowned *asura* and his consort accompany him, and above him, there is another demon falling to the ground, defeated by Viṣṇu. Aschwin Lippe, to whom we owe a detailed analysis of the scene,[221] realised that the relief symbolises the triumph of Brahmanism over the Buddhists. However, he accepted R.D. Banerji's identification of Bali with the Buddha, which is proved wrong by the fact that the Dwarf, as a deluder, is ominously dressed up as the Awakened One. Bali is, rather, one of his followers and supporters, portrayed with the Buddha's features in order to be easily recognised as a king of an adharmic kingdom.[222]

Figure 2: Badami, Cave 2. Vāmana and Bali from Trivikrama panel.

In Cave 3, the inscription of Kīrtivarman's brother Maṅgaleśa, dated AD 578, helps us to circumscribe the events narrated in the reliefs. The recent conflict must have been considered very important for the iconographic programme of Caves 2 and 3 to be conceived by the brāhmaṇa advisors of either Kīrtivarman or Maṅgaleśa, because the latter, who was charged with completing the cave, expressly mentions Viṣṇu as destroyer of 'the army of the enemies of the gods with his discus'.[223] We know that Kīrtivarman fought successfully against a number of enemies, and Maṅgaleśa defines himself 'victorious in battle'.[224] The royal supporter of Buddhism alluded to in the reliefs is one of the defeated rulers. There is a Buddhist cave at Badami, and at Aihole (not far from Badami in the Malprabha Valley), there is a partly rock-cut and partly built, two-storeyed building identified as a Buddhist sanctuary.[225] The defeated king identified with Bali was probably ruling locally before the rise of the Cāḷukyas. The change of field of this king and a complete surrender of the Buddhists is implied in the iconographies. Another Badami inscription mentions the exploits of an unknown, important dignitary named Kappe Arabhaṭṭa, defined as 'an exceptional man in the Kaliyuga', to whose evils he can put an end. He is, in fact, a very Mādhava, an equal of Viṣṇu on earth. His enemies, 'saying "What is this to us?" came to injure and destroy the eminence that he had achieved, [but] they were worsted, and then they died […]'.[226]

We will examine in more detail in Chapter V the degree to which the identity of the *asura*-s with the *śramaṇa*-s and their royal supporters was carried out in the Purāṇic literature. Here we will conclude with V.S. Agrawala's remarks on the *Vāmana Purāṇa*, composed in the first half of the seventh century,[227] when Harṣavardhana was holding at bay the orthodox front. It contains a rich material on the *asura*-s, and the figure of Pulastya stands out as founder of the society organised according to the principles taught by the *asura*-s, as teacher of the doctrine, and Rāvaṇa's grandfather:

> […] the Asura is a pseudonim for the Buddhists in the mind of this Purāṇa-writer. The teachers of the moral code followed by the Asuras are said to be *Māgadha-munis*, i.e., the recluse-monks of Magadha, and the moral code which the latter preached is practically identical with the teachings of the Buddha. The Purāṇa-writer was a personal witness to the fact that the *Dharma* contained in those instructions was quite an exalted one and powerful enough to bring about a rejuvenation of society and naturally worthy of praise.[228]

A LANDSCAPE WITH RUINS

Albert Henry Longhurst's sharp mind can be appreciated both as a field archaeologist and as the author of essays such as *The Story of the Stūpa*,[229] one of the best on the subject. Between 1927 and 1931, he carried out excavations at Nagarjunakonda on the lower Krishna Valley, of which he published the results in 1938. Longhurst was not misguided by the unfavourable intellectual climate of the 1930s, and summing up the results of his investigations, stated that

> [t]he ruthless manner in which all the buildings at Nāgārjunakoṇḍa have been destroyed is simply appalling and cannot represent the work of treasure-seekers alone as so many of the pillars, statues and sculptures have been wantonly smashed to pieces. Had there been a town close at hand as at Amarāvatī, one can understand the site being used as a quarry by modern builders […]. But this never occurred at Nāgārjunakoṇḍa as there are no towns and no cart roads in or out of the valley.[230]

The considerations made on archaeological methods as being insufficiently developed to tackle the questions of the phases of abandonment in a given site are also valid for Nagarjunakonda, and doubts could be raised on Longhurst's conclusions. However, the destructions seem too radical to have been misinterpreted. In the absence of any positive or circumstantial evidence, Longhurst accepted a hasty explanation that many before him had given. It resorted to a local tradition – one among many all over India – according to which

> the great Hindu philosopher and teacher Śaṅkarācārya came to Nāgārjunakoṇḍa with a host of followers and destroyed the Buddhist monuments. Be this as it may, the fact remains that the cultivated lands in the valley on which the ruined buildings stand represent a religious grant made to Śaṅkara, and it was only with the sanction of the present Religious Head of the followers of this great teacher that I was able to conduct the excavations. The same Brahman Pontiff, who resides in the Nallamalais, which no doubt was acquired in the same manner, as it seems to have been a Buddhist site originally.[231]

Śaṅkarācārya lived in too late an epoch with respect to the reported destructions to be held responsible for them. The last artistic output at Nagarjunakonda goes back to the early decades of the fourth century,[232] and it would have been absurd for the followers of Śaṅkara to destroy monuments and images of a site long abandoned to the jungle. The monumental, iconographic, epigraphic and numismatic evidence, along with that of the material culture (they are all tightly woven at Nagarjunakonda) help to write a micro history of the short-lived kingdom of the Ikṣvākus, but the data on the declining town of the fourth century are scanty. Is it possible to find a more credible answer than that handed over to us by tradition?

The Ikṣvākus, stemming perhaps from the famous Ayodhyā lineage,[233] replaced locally the Sātavāhanas in the second quarter of the third century AD. Their capital town, Vijayapuri, which included a citadel built on the right bank of the Krishna, was at the centre of a complex settlement system, where some of the earliest extant Brahmanical temples[234] and numerous Buddhist sanctuaries rose. We know the names of the Ikṣvāku rulers, among which stand out Vāśiṣṭhiputra Cāṃṭamūla (AD 210-35), Māṭharīputra Vīrapuruṣadatta AD 236-60), Vāśiṣthiputra Ehuvula Cāṃṭamūla (Cāṃṭamūla II, AD 261-85) and Vāgiṣṭhiputra Rudrapuruṣadatta (AD 286-300),[235] all

Sivaites, to whose patronage the majority of the small Brahmanical temples on the river bank owed their existence. The presence of a shrine of Kārttikeya is notable, because it is a testimony of the early association of the god to Śiva, who, as Sarva (as in the Māṭ sanctuary), presided over the largest Brahmanical temple of the town.[236] The patronage of the Buddhist community was deputed to the female representatives of the dynasty, as for instance to Cāṃṭaśrī, sister of the first Cāṃṭamūla, who commissioned the *mahāstūpa* (site 1).[237] There is an embarrassing disparity, as far as we can determine from the artistic output (which is not the only standard for judging the actual situation), between the means that the Buddhists had at their disposal and the Sivaites' share. The Ikṣvākus, though unwilling to adhere to Buddhism as other rulers did, had clearly to come to terms with the Buddhists, whose economic activities probably ensured to the state a large part of its income. The presence in town of a small amphitheatre, which, although rectangular in plan, recalls Roman prototypes,[238] and the strict connection, observable in the artistic output, with north-western India,[239] show the degree to which, as late as the third century, the productive urban élites of the lower Krishna Valley were involved in the global economy or continued to share the spirit of that legacy.

A clue on the events that took place at Nagarjunakonda after the end of the balanced Ikṣvāku rule is the presence of a Viṣṇu temple, once housing an eight-armed image of the god, built by the Ābhīra king Vaṣuṣena between AD 332 and 348[240] downstream of the Nāgārjuna hill at a distance of about 2 km from the last in the row of the Sivaite temples built upstream by the Ikṣvākus. The Ābhīras in question were probably one of the small dynasties that arose to power after the decline of the Sātavāhanas[241] and which Samudragupta made his vassals: they are not, however, the Ābhīras mentioned in the Allahabad inscription,[242] but perhaps one of the unnamed ruling families of Dakṣiṇāpatha to which, after the conquest, the Gupta emperor showed his favour. The destruction of Buddhist Nagarjunakonda is arguably connected to the establishment of a stronger Brahmanical rule, and that it came as a consequence of Samudragupta's conquests is likely. It is impossible to say who precisely destroyed the Buddhist sanctuaries. This must have happened either with the strengthening of Bhāgavata power or in relation to the emergence of a strong anti-*śramaṇa* movement centred on nearby Śrīparvata (modern Srisailam in Kurnool district), presided over by Śiva Mallikārjuna.[243] V.S. Agrawala maintained that the account of the *Matsya Purāṇa* whereby one of the sites on which the burning city of Tripura fell was the Srisailam mountain may be of a historical character,[244] the myth being connected with the extirpation of the *asura*-s/heretics. The apparently silent fourth century AD again appears as a crucial turning point in the history of ancient India, and the Sphinx continues to give us answers less ambiguous than expected.

More clues on the real situation in Gupta times come from Kashmir, only apparently a peripheral area. Religious-political events show a trend not dissimilar from that of other parts of northern and central India, and, up to the fourth century, even comparable to the situation of the lower Krishna Valley. No archaeological evidence is available in Kashmir for the period under discussion, but the written sources allow a reasonable reconstruction of the events.

At the time of the Kuṣāṇas, Kashmir 'was, to a great extent, in the possession of the Bauddhas',[245] and even later, arguably under the protection of the Bodhisattva Nāgārjuna,[246] '[a]fter defeating in disputation all learned opponents, these enemies of tradition brought to an end the [observance of the rites] prescribed in the *Nīla[mata] purāṇa*'.[247] This happened in spite of the fact that the country was ruled by an orthodox king, Abhimanyu, who favoured the introduction of the *Mahābhāṣya* into Kashmir.[248] Orthodox observances were introduced, or reintroduced, by a brāhmaṇa named Candradeva who practised austerities to please Nīla, the Lord of those very *nāga*-s who had first opposed the introduction of Buddhism in the valley.[249] Nīla had caused heavy snowfalls that had endangered the land, but 'the Brahmans, who offered oblations and sacrifices, escaped destruction, while the Bauddhas perished'.[250] To Abhimanyu and Candradeva went the merit of having brought to an end 'the intolerable plague of the Bhikṣus',[251] although it was the concern of King Gonanda III to establish a righteous government,[252] and the concern of his great-grandson, Nara, to complete the work:

> A Buddhist ascetic (*śramaṇa*) who was living alone in a Vihāra, situated in *Kiṃnaragrāma*, seduced the [king's] wife through magic power. In his wrath over this the king burned thousands of Vihāras, and granted the villages which had belonged to them, to Brahmans residing in *Madhyamaṭha*.[253]

Thus two waves of anti-Buddhist persecutions seem to have taken place: the first, under Abhimanyu and his advisor Candradeva, who paved the way to Gonanda's orthodox rule; the second launched by Nara, arguably under Brahmanical pressure but under different circumstances. The relationship between his queen and the *śramaṇa*, maliciously interpreted by Kalhaṇa, makes us strongly suspect that the Kashmiri queens played a role similar to that of the wives and sisters of the Ikṣvākus, who guaranteed the balance of power between brāhmaṇas and *śramaṇa*-s by granting protection to the latter. With Nara, the balance was lost to the detriment of the Buddhists.

Gopāditya, who ruled after Nara, favoured the arrival of brāhmaṇas from Āryadeśa, 'removed those who ate garlic to Bhūkṣiravātikā, and transferred the Brahmans who had broken their rules of conduct to Khāsaṭā',[254] applying the rules established by Manu.[255] We see once again that measures were taken against apostatised brāhmaṇas, who must have formed the leadership of the Buddhist community of Kashmir. Gopāditya's son, Jaulaka, was a Sivaite like his father (they built the Tuṅgeśvara Temple in Srinagar),[256] and his instructor in the doctrines 'was the saint Avadhūta, the vanquisher of crowds of Bauddha controversialists, who at that time were powerful and flushed [with success]'.[257] Kalhaṇa adds that

> [h]e was endowed with mighty courage, expelled the *Mlecchas* who oppressed the land, and conquered in victorious expeditions the earth up to the encircling oceans. The place where the *Mlecchas* who occupied the land, were routed (*ujjhaṭitās*) by him, is called by the people even at the present day *Ujjhaṭaḍimba*. Having conquered the earth, including *Kanyakubja* and other [countries], he settled from that region people of all four castes in his own land, and [particularly] righteous men acquainted with legal procedures.[258]

Discounting Kalhaṇa's eulogistic exaggerations, the passage provides evidence of the fact that the brahmanisation of Kashmir was made stronger by the arrival of experts of *dharmaśāstra*-s and newcomers observing *varṇāśramadharma*. The fallout of Gupta policy is all too apparent, and we observe perhaps the effects of the *Arthaśāstra*. Orthodox brāhmaṇas replaced the *mleccha*-s supported by the apostates: their identity is unclear, but may be identified as late or post-Kuṣāṇa rulers and élite groups. The anti-Buddhist attitude of the court of Gupta and post-Gupta Kashmir is underlined by a passage of Śyāmilaka's *Pādatāḍitaka*, a play written in the second half of the fifth century.[259] Buddhism was restored some time between the fifth and sixth century by a foreign king whom Xuanzang knows by the name of Himatala, and flourished throughout the seventh and eighth century.[260]

The evidence provided so far makes us understand better the description of Buddhist India provided by Xuanzang's travelogue and by the *Life*. The *Da Tang Xiyuji* describes a severely wounded reality only partly softened by Xuanzang's political projects. A good, concise summary of the situation depicted by the Chinese monk with an eye focused on the approaching disintegration of the Buddhist world is found in *The Decline of Buddhism in India* by R.C. Mitra, the first edition of which goes back to 1954, being thus strongly affected by the nationalist ideology of the time.[261] We can make Mitra's words our own when he says that 'from the account of the Chinese pilgrim is the spirit of depression and despair which his narrative unmistakably conveys to the mind of his readers'.[262] The matter is worth discussing again because the *Xiyuji* is usually considered a source book useful to fill the many gaps in Indian history, from chronology to social history, and more rarely a source on the conditions of Indian Buddhism, and because it is possible to supplement Xuanzang's testimony with some other evidence.

Uḍḍiyāna and Gandhāra are a case in point. In Gandhāra the royal family had already become extinct and the deputies from Kapiśi governed a scarce population in deserted towns and villages. Most people followed the heretical schools and few believed in the True Law. There were one thousand *saṅgharāma*-s, which had been deserted, in ruins, filled with wild shrubs, and solitary to the last degree. The stūpas had mostly decayed, but the heretical temples, numbering about one hundred, were occupied pell-mell by heretics. Even the Buddha's alm-bowl, one of the relics that made the pilgrimage to the land worth undertaking, had disappeared.[263] In Uḍḍiyāna, of the fourteen hundred monasteries and eighteen thousand monks which were said to have once existed, only very few survived. The monks were followers of the Mahāyāna, but were unable to penetrate the deep meaning of the scriptures, being 'specially experts in magical exorcisms'.[264]

By the mid-sixth century, a major change had taken place in the North-West, crossed for centuries by the trade route for Khotan and

China. The Trans-Himalayan route remained under Buddhist control but had shifted to the west, which caused, among other things, the emergence of Bamiyan, whose monuments started being built around AD 600 thanks to the surplus accumulated by the trading activities.[265] The shift to the west was the consequence of the brahmanisation of Gandhāra and the neighbouring regions and of the hostility of the local kings towards Buddhism. Huisheng, who came to Uḍḍiyāna and Gandhāra through the old Karakorum route as a member of a small group of envoys in search of *sūtra*-s led by Song Yun in AD 519,[266] has left us a testimony on the cool reception, bordering on insult, which the king of Gandhāra had reserved to them:

> All the people in the kingdom are Brahmins and they like to read the *sūtra*s. But the king liked killing and was not a follower of the Law of the Buddha and had inflicted war on the territory of Jibin [...]. He received the imperial letter while seated, in a rude manner and without (keeping) the etiquette. He sent the envoys off to a monastery but offered very little.[267]

We have some clues about the events that took place in the region between Song Yun's mission and the years preceding Xuanzang's visit: the Buddha's bowl was still probably in its place in the 540s,[268] and it was probably before the eighth decade of the century that the Buddhist properties were devastated. The silence of the written sources has not been filled by archaeological research. In the fifth century, to coincide with the slackening off of Gupta hegemony, we observe a profound change in Gandharan art: stone sculpture is abandoned and figural art finds expression in clay and stucco images, whose shaping was cheaper and quick. There was an extraordinary rush to renovate sanctuaries and build new ones. It was this sudden output that came to an end in the sixth century.

What happened in Gandhāra and the surrounding regions between *c.* 550 and 580? The answer can only be indirect, but monks are likely to have departed *en masse*, and the merchant class as well. The impact, presumably heavy on the economy of Gandhāra, caused by Justinian's plague – the first large, well-documented epidemic of bubonic plague whose first, strongest wave affected the Mediterranean and the Red Sea from AD 540 to 594 causing the death of a considerable proportion of the population[269] – cannot be invoked as a reason for the shifting to the west of the economic axis of north-western India, because the distance from the former route is irrelevant from the point of view of a deadly plague of enormous proportion. If the change of the axis was the cause of the extraordinary flourishing of Buddhist Afghanistan and western Central Asia, for India proper it was another setback. Nor can we believe that the change of economic model in Gandhāra took place without any violence: a slow, peaceful transformation would have induced the Buddhists to get used to the new circumstances and transform their economy, as happened elsewhere.

The figure of Mihirakula (in power from *c.* AD 513 to 542) as depicted in both Chinese and Indian sources is the object of too great uncertainties to be fully discussed here,[270] but his favouring the import of Gandharan brāhmaṇas to Kashmir and establishing for them 1,000 *agrahāra*-s[271] in continuity with Gupta policy is an important clue to understanding what really took place. From his coins, he appears as a Sivaite,[272] and incessantly engaged in the worship of Paśupati in the Gwalior inscription.[273] The most likely thing is that Mihirakula, one of those rulers devoid of any recognisable social status – be they native of India or of foreign origin – was utilised by the Pāśupatas to strengthen their power and settle in those regions where they were still weak. His anti-Buddhist attitude was a consequence of this. Two Buddhist texts preserved in Chinese translation, the *Lianhuamian jing* (the *Lotus-face Sūtra*) and the *Da fangden daji jing* (*Sūtra of the Great Assembly of Great Doctrinal Universality*, translated in AD 566) reflect the hardships of Buddhism at the time of Mihirakula's rule,[274] or perhaps at a somewhat later period. It has been argued that Dao Chuo (AD 562-645), an early representative of Chinese Pure Land Buddhism, was influenced by the facts reported in these texts and by refugees who had probably entered China.[275] As for the years 550-80, for such a destructive climax to have set in Gandhāra, the local rulers must have turned from an unsympathetic and occasionally brutal attitude towards Buddhism into a systematic hostility.

The Turkic people who established themselves in south-eastern Afghanistan in the sixth-seventh century supported Buddhism, but the Turkī Ṣāhī dynasty that rose to power in AD 666 or slightly later was increasingly subject to Brahmanical pressure. We know the Turkī Ṣāhīs as patrons of Brahmanical temples in Logar and Kapiśi, characteristically, large, fertile valleys fit for agriculture.[276] The base of the family was in Zamin Dawar, but they had already migrated to or established their rule in Gandhāra before rising into prominence.[277] The Brahmanical temple atop the Barikot hill in Swat, erected in the seventh century,[278] is testimony of the transformation of Uḍḍiyāna, and the presence of a still another Brahmanical temple in the Kunar Valley,[279] just to the west of Swat, throws more light on the transformation of the region. The introduction of *varṇāśramadharma* and its strengthening must have been pursued with particular determination, if Uḍḍiyāna came to be identified with one of the four *pīṭha*-s.[280] The surviving Buddhist community was marginalised into the upper Swat Valley and the adjoining mountainous regions.[281] In Gandhāra, the still active monasteries remained probably confined to the edge of the plain and to the hilly regions.[282]

In the upper Ganges Valley, where Buddhism does not seem to have ever been particularly strong, the situation was near to a collapse but for a few strongholds such as Jalandhara and, to a lesser extent, Mathurā. In Sthāneśvara, the hometown of Harṣa,[283] there were three monasteries against some fifty temples. In Madhyadeśa, Xuanzang's list becomes even more stunted: in Śrughna,[284] there were five monasteries and one hundred forty temples, and only two monasteries survived in Prayāga. In a number of cases, we should probably interpret the word 'temples' (*tian ci*) as small shrines, but they testify to the Brahmanical control of the territory. Not everywhere were things so dramatic, but the pre-eminence of the Brahmanical faith was patent, the (presumably various) groups of Pāśupatas having a particular visibility. The exceptions were Ayodhyā, where the brāhmaṇas had only ten temples and the Buddhist monks numbered three thousand, Kanauj, where, for obvious reasons, there was a balance between the different parties, and Sarnath, where Xuanzang found thirty monasteries instead of the two noted by Faxian. We have seen the early symptoms of Buddhist revival at Sarnath around the mid-fifth century, and massive building activity is observable in the following two centuries.[285] Thanks to Harṣa's victory over Gauḍa, in Magadha and Bengal the situation was particularly favourable to Buddhism, but the unimaginable had occurred only a short time before Xuanzang's journey: Śaśāṅka's uprooting of the Bodhi tree gives the measure of the anti-Buddhist escalation wherever orthodox kings were ruling.

Xuanzang was more familiar with anti-Buddhist propaganda and persecutions than Faxian. In China, Confucian intelligentsia had continued to accuse Buddhism of undermining the imperial state. That foreign religion had brought three hundred years of confusion by denying the proper relations between father and son, prince and minister, etc.: the Confucian code of social relationships was seriously endangered.[286] In AD 574, the Emperor Zhou Wudi issued a decree proscribing Buddhism, calling for the destruction of Buddhist temples, images and scriptures; monks and nuns had to return to the laity, and the treasures of the monasteries were to be distributed to the Confucian aristocracy. Three years later, after the emperor's territorial conquests, the proscription was extended to the rest of northern China.[287] That the religion of Dharma was in constant danger was a matter of course. If Xuanzang narrates with unusually rich details Śaśāṅka's exploits, it is because their symbolic gravity could not be passed over in silence and because they had been counterbalanced by the victory of Harṣavardhana, who was his trump card at the Tang court.

Buddhism was virtually extinct in central and northern Rajasthan,[288] despite the fact that the king was a young courageous kṣatriya who believed in the law of the Buddha,[289] and at Ujjayinī only a few monasteries were still in existence, the king being a brāhmaṇa 'well versed in heretical books'.[290] The situation was better balanced in Mālavā, controlled by Valabhī.[291] The heretics, mostly Pāśupatas, were very numerous, and at only twenty *li* from the capital there was 'the town of the Brâhmaṇs'; however, there were one hundred monasteries and two thousand monks.[292] An interesting piece of narrative is about the public debate between a brāhmaṇa and the monk Bhadraruci, that the pilgrim projects into an undetermined past and supplements with fabled details. In this case, the proud brāhmaṇa had to confess himself conquered, and the king, reminding that '[h]e who is defeated in discussion ought to suffer death', 'prepared to have a heated plate of iron to make him sit thereon'. Bhadraruci interceded for the brāhmaṇa, who was let free. Such, however, was his hatred for the Buddhists, that he could not refrain himself from abusing the monk and the doctrines of Mahāyāna, so that the earth opened and swallowed him.[293]

Xuanzang's story reminds us that even in Valabhī and the dependent territories, where in the sixth and seventh century we witness a spectacular revival of Buddhism and where we are fortunate enough to have an inventory of the existing monasteries,[294] the presence of anti-Buddhist brāhmaṇas was paramount. The policy of kings was subject to sudden changes, and shifting of patronage and occasional crackdowns were a common occurrence. In the epigraphic record, mention of elephants being routed is plenty, and for us to understand whose elephants are meant, the records are to be put in context. In the copper-plate inscriptions of the Maitraka king Dharasena II we read that he was 'a great devotee of Śaṅkara' and that he '[h]ad even from his early age, his sword his only companion, shown marks of excessive valour by splitting open the temples of mad elephants/ belonging to his enemies',[295] and we wonder what the real target was. We are in Valabhī in AD 571-72, at the time of the strong Sivaite ascendancy that we have seen to take place, with dramatic destructions, in Gandhāra, and Dharasena II was one of those early Valabhī kings who greatly benefitted brāhmaṇas by granting them lands.[296] The reign of Harṣa was yet to come. Significantly, a few years after Harṣa's death, Dhruvasena III (AD 651-53) celebrated his ancestor Guhasena describing him as 'a devout worshipper of Maheśvara': 'ever sword in hand from his infancy, brightened the touchstone of his courage by splitting the temples of the rutting elephants of his foes', and made the word 'king' true to its meaning.[297] The implication here is that a rightful rule is based on *varṇāśramadharma* and that it is high time to establish it again. At the time of Xuanzang's journey, the king of Valabhī, Dhruvapaṭa, a relative of Harṣavardhana, had performed *pañcavārṣika* after being converted to Buddhism,[298] and this made a king not true to his function. Dhruvasena III's reign was brief and his armed repression of Buddhism perhaps only an episode, but we note that after him the donations of lands to Buddhist monasteries fall sharply, and then cease altogether.[299] We will see in the next chapter that the apparently rhetorical metaphors in the above-mentioned inscription (and in many others), like that of the king who, like the sun, destroys the dense darkness in all quarters, allude to the repression of the anti-Brahmanical forces.

From the history of Valabhī, we can appreciate the extent and effectiveness of Harṣa's control over the whole of northern India, where he succeeded in turning the situation to the advantage of the Buddhist cause. This also happened in Oḍra (northern Orissa), where he favoured the ascendance of the Bhauma kings, who assured Buddhist rule for quite a long time,[300] and in South Kosala. Here Buddhism, supported by a kṣatriya king (perhaps Mahāśivagupta Bālārjuna or one of his immediate predecessors)[301] was flourishing. The memory of Nāgārjuna was hovering about. There were, in any case, a great number of heretics who lived intermixed with the population, and *deva* temples.[302]

Proceeding southward, the identification of the places described by Xuanzang is not always easy,[303] and we cannot always relate his narrative with the events we know from other sources. The pilgrim spent much less time in Deccan than in northern India and in the other regions controlled by Kanauj. At Dhanyakaṭaka (in the Krishna delta, once crowded with Buddhist sites), the monasteries were 'mostly deserted and ruined', and of those preserved there were 'about twenty, with 1000 or so priests'.[304] The region had been conquered by the Cāḷukyas in AD 611, and a few years later the independent line of the Eastern Cāḷukyas had been established. The pilgrim lays the responsibility of the deserted state of the two monasteries of Pūrvaśilā and Avaraśilā, abandoned 'one hundred years' before, 'to the spirit of the mountain changing its shape, and appearing sometimes as a wolf, sometimes as a monkey, and frightening the disciples'.[305] This probably hints at the violent changes that had taken place in the region at about the same time that witnessed the transformation of Gandhāra. The variform spirit of the mountain seems to embody the various facets of the anti-Buddhist movements.[306] In the Cōḷa country, difficult to demarcate with accuracy since it is described as being 'deserted and wild, a succession of marshes and jungles', the monasteries were 'ruined and dirty as well as the priests' – a possible reference to householder monks – and the local population was attached 'to heretical teaching', the Nirgrantha heretics being particularly numerous.[307] They were equally numerous in Malakūṭa, which Xuanzang perhaps did not visit:[308] there were, in fact, 'the ruins of many old convents', of which only the walls were preserved, and 'few religious followers' were left.[309]

Lower Deccan, with the exception of Kāñcī where, despite the presence of many *nirgrantha*-s, there were 'some hundred of *saṅghârâmas* and 10,000 priests',[310] was lost for the faith. Xuanzang's journey after leaving South Kosala must have been a nightmare that convinced him to trace his steps back to upper Deccan and western India. The situation of Buddhism in the south was not only critical but had come near to collapse in places, as had happened in the North-West. The majority of the monks of Kāñcī, the most important centre of Tamil Buddhism, had become Mahāyānists in the fifth century,[311] clearly in the attempt at finding new means to counteract Brahmanical revivalism, and several of them had left the country.[312] The Pallavas, as is amply recognised, started claiming Bhāradvāja descent,[313] and their first known ruler, Śiva Skandavarman, performed *aśvamedha*.[314] The struggle for power against the Kaḷabhras, who supported the *śramaṇa*-s,[315] meant the strengthening of their religious identity. Hence the 'aura of menace' that south India was to assume in medieval Buddhist mythology: demonesses were ready to seize Buddhist monks and merchants, and blood-drinking kings were ready to sacrifice travellers to angry goddesses.[316] In the following chapters we shall see how the menace was brought to effect in central Deccan and in the Vindhyas, but the fact remains true that it was the south that embodied at best the policy of the Guptas and re-exported it.

In the first half of the seventh century, the survival of Buddhism as a religious and social system capable of upturning the fundamentals of Indian society was in the hands of Harṣavardhana. Huili, the author of the *Life*, attributes a prophetic dream to Xuanzang during his stay in Nālandā: the Bodhisattva Mañjuśrī appeared to him at night in the deserted monastery where he lived, and

> pointing to the outside of the convent, he said: 'Do you see that?' The Master of the Law looking in the direction indicated by his finger, saw a fierce fire burning without the convent, and consuming to ashes villages and towns. Then the golden figure said: 'You should return soon, for after ten years Śilâditya râja will be dead, and India be laid waste and in rebellion, wicked men will slaughter one another; remember these words of mine!'[317]

The chaos that followed Harṣavardhana's death, so critical that even China was affected by it to a degree,[318] had serious consequences on the fortunes of Buddhism. The enthusiastic rulers who had supported it were swept away by the orthodox powers. The 'impenetrable gloom' surrounding Kanauj,[319] Harṣavardhana's capital, until Yaśovarman occupied the throne some time about AD 725[320] bears out Huili's statement. According to the Korean pilgrim Hyecho (Hui Chao), who arrived in Bengal by sea in *c.* AD 724 and proceeded to Madhyadeśa, 'the country of Varanasi' was 'desolate' and there was no king.[321]

Buddhism remained strong in north-eastern India and, for a short period, in the Hindukush, but in the rest of the country it was marginalised in scattered pockets. The evidence points to an increasing religious hatred and the progressive setting up of a totalitarian vision of history. The situation became serious especially in those regions like Orissa that were on the fault line between the North-East and an almost entirely brahmanised south. A long period followed which, echoing James Fergusson, is not pleasant to contemplate.

NOTES

1. On Udayagiri, see discussion below; on Pawaya, cf. Gottfried Williams (1982: 52 ff. and pls. 49-54) and Willis (2009: 195-97) in relation to the famous lintel, a rather exceptional representation of a Vedic ritual.
2. Chhabra & Gai (1981: 234-42).
3. Scholars still rely upon assessments made when Indian archaeology was in its infancy and excavations were not carried out under strict stratigraphic control. The authors of the revised edition of the third volume of the *CII*, for instance, accepted Jean-Philippe Vogel's description, going back to 1914, of the flourishing conditions of Buddhism at Sarnath in Gupta times. This led them to overlook the absence of epigraphic material in the fourth and early fifth century and conclude that the sanctuary 'was in as flourishing a condition as ever before' (Chhabra & Gai 1981: 140). The association of the Gupta kings with Nālandā is equally groundless (cf. B.N. Misra 1987-89). The view that the Buddhists benefitted from Gupta patronage is shared by Davidson (2002: 75, 111) and Deeg (cf. *Faxian* a: 133), usually little inclined to trust received opinions. A notable exception is Nakamura (1987: 212, with statements made in previous works), followed by Chappell (1980: esp. 129, 139-40).
4. Chhabra & Gai (1981: 233-34); see the images in Gottfried Williams (1982: 25-26; pls. 12-15).
5. On Rāmagupta see Chhabra & Gai (1981: 46-52); P.L. Gupta (1974, I: 290-96); Mirashi (1975: 109-24).
6. It would be impossible for me to discuss the many issues raised by scholars on this famous work, a version of which was translated into Chinese by Faxian in AD 418 (two other translations are slightly later). An English translation of the work is available at http://www.nirvanasutra.org.uk. For the questions raised here, I follow Nakamura (1987: 211 ff.) and Chappell (1980: esp. 139-40).
7. Ibid.: 139.
8. Ibid.: 131. Buddhaghoṣa's scheme should be seen in the light of the complex reasons that in both India and China brought to the formulations of the predictions on the end of *dharma*, but this passage seems to adapt very well to Buddhaghoṣa's contemporary situation.
9. The date of this stratified text is discussed in Matsunaga (1985); see p. 893 for the last chapter of the work, translated and commented upon by K.P. Jayaswal.
10. *Mañjuśrīmūlakalpa*: [53], 699-718; cf. §31, p. 48.
11. *Wang Xuance*: 29, 97b, 2 (p. 15). Mahānāman has been considered the author of the long inscription of Bodhgayā (Fleet 1888: 274-78), for whose exegesis I refer the reader to Lévi (1996*b*) and Tournier (forth.). The Mahānāman of the inscription, which cannot be dated to the fourth century as suggested by Lévi, declares himself to be a native of Laṅkā, and to have inhabited Āmradvīpa, another name of the island (l. 9).

12. V. Smith (1967: 304).
13. Chhabra & Gai (1981): ll. 23-24, pp. 217-18. Lévi in *Wang Xuance* (38-39) recalls that Meghavarṇa was one of the titles preferred by the kings of Laṅkā, and correlates it with the part played by the traitor Meghavarṇa, the king of crows arrived from the island in the third book of the *Hitopadeśa*. The brāhmaṇa author of this work, modifying a story of the *Pañcatantra* to his ends, wantonly abuses the Laṅkan Buddhists, whose king bears a name that 'implies metaphorically a shameless person'. I report Lévi's argument to show how cryptic the derogatory allusions to the Buddhists in Indian texts may be. The *Hitopadeśa* is obviously a text composed much later than Gupta times.
14. The story, in a more extended but apparently more imprecise version, is also narrated by Xuanzang (*Xiyuji* a: VIII; vol. 2, pp. 133-35). The duress experienced on the continent by the one and only *śramaṇa* protagonist of the story appears equally serious, and the king of the island appears as a vassal king ('he gave in tribute to the king of India all the jewels of his country'), but in Xuanzang the narrative acquires a hagiographic tint intended to emphasise the final triumph of the religion.
15. Gottfried Williams (1982: 30-31 and pl. 19; 32 and pls. 21-22; 33-34 and pls. 25, 26).
16. Ibid.: 68-69 and pls. 61-63.
17. Gottfried Williams (ibid.: 76) observes, without attempting to explain the fact, that Sarnath 'burst into prominence in the 470s' after 'the limited artistic production of the fourth century'.
18. See the inscription in Chhabra & Gai (1981: 247-52); I follow, however, the interpretation of V.V. Mirashi (1982), who restores Fleet's translation.
19. Coomaraswamy (1927: 71 ff.); V.S. Agrawala (1977, a posthumous work). Monuments such as the Daśāvatāra Temple at Deogarh and the temple of Bhitargaon, which have become symbols of Gupta architecture, are better assigned, as Gottfried Williams has done, to 'Gupta art after the Guptas'. The difficulty in establishing a date for the end of the dynasty may explain the different attempts at defining a Gupta canon in terms of chronology, yet it is surprising to find the above-cited monuments included among the Gupta temples in Meister, Dhaky & Deva (1988), usually so fastidious regarding the questions of patronage. On the later Gupta history, see the observations made by Willis (2005).
20. See, for instance, V.S. Agrawala (1969: 2).
21. Spink (1992: 178). At the end of his long work on Ajanta, Spink has devoted a study in five volumes to the chronology of the site and to the historical setting that, according to him, made Hariṣena's patronage possible (Spink 2005).
22. Hans Bakker has questioned Spink's construction of Ajanta as a royal Vākāṭaka site (Bakker 1997: 37 ff.), and Cohen (1997: esp. 128 ff.), through a new reading of the relevant epigraphic material, has equally raised, among other things, the question of Hariṣeṇa's patronage.
23. *Faxian* a: 14-20 (pp. 524-28).

24. Ibid.: 20 (p. 528).
25. Ibid. (p. 529). Vegetarianism had found orthodox sanction in Manu. See Wendy Doniger's discussion in *Manu*: xxxiii ff.
26. *Faxian* a: 55 (p. 540); *Faxian* b: 34.
27. *Faxian* b: 65-66. Cf. *Faxian* a: 148 (p. 563).
28. The Saṃmitīya School was the most important among those of the Pudgalavādins, stemmed out from the Vātsīputrīyas. See Thích Thiên Châu (1999: 11-15 and 19 ff. for the literature and doctrine of the Pudgalavādins). In the Chakka Nipāta of the *Aṅguttara Nikāya*, the Buddha criticises a brāhmaṇa for excluding the self as an independent agent ('Pray, how can one step onwards, how can one step back, yet say: There is no self-agency; there is no other-agency?' (*Aṅguttara Nikāya* VI.iv.38; cf. vol. 3: 238).
29. Cf. Chhabra & Gai (1981: 140-42).
30. As is known, this idea is central to the *Mahāpārinirvāṇa Mahāsūtra*, to remain within the Gupta chronological horizon. The question of the Buddha's eternalness may have risen independently from the continuous debating with the orthodox because, after that the earthly *kāya* of the Buddha was no more, a solution for asserting the authority of Buddhist teaching had to be found. Yet the *Buddha*- or *Dharmakāya* doctrine lends itself very well, with the help of the iconographies, to build a paratheistic model of Buddhism.
31. Cf. the map showing the epigraphic and numismatic finds relative to the Guptas provided by Gérard Fussman for his 2006-07 course at the Collège de France (Fussman 2006-07: 704).
32. P.L. Gupta (1974, I: 293-94).
33. Kosambi (1965: 194).
34. There is no ratio between the amount of gold coins and that of silver and copper coins in circulation, and Kosambi (1965: 195) recognised that their total amount was not sufficient to support commodity production. The propagandistic aims of the gold issues have been underlined by B.N. Mukherji (1990: 16).
35. Gold deposits are mainly located in the Deccan, where there is evidence of ancient workings. See Nanda (1992: 7 ff.).
36. Preface to the 1748 edition of the *Histoire de Charles XII*.
37. Hans Bakker (1986: 26 ff.) has summed up the evidence on Ayodhyā in Gupta times. The disappointing lack of archaeological evidence (Bakker draws on B.B. Lal and his 'Rāmāyaṇa Project') arguably depends on the fact that the Gupta capital was rather an itinerant camp where the court resided as long as required by the circumstances, and not a permanent place with stone and/or brick structures, etc. A Gupta capital *sui generis* was certainly Udayagiri.
38. *Faxian* b: 29; cf. *Faxian* a: 37 (p. 536).
39. *Faxian* b: 30. Deeg has 'Verschiedene Häretiker *und* Brahmanen' (my emphasis); cf. *Faxian* a: 42 (p. 536).
40. *Faxian* b: 34-35; cf. *Faxian* a: 54 (pp. 539-40).

41. *Faxian* b: 35; cf. *Faxian* a: 55 (p. 540).
42. This monk never visited India, and his *Waiguo shi* is lost but for a few fragments. It probably dealt with the Buddhist sanctuaries of India and Sri Lanka (Petech 1974: 551).
43. Ibid.: 556.
44. *Faxian* b: 45-4. Deeg has: '[so daß] die Häretiker den buddhistischen *saṅgha* nicht übertreffen konnten'; cf. *Faxian* a: 97 (p. 548).
45. On the various Buddhist arguments against both *varṇa* and *jāti*, the reader is again referred to Eltshinger (2000).
46. Demiéville (1974: 18).
47. Ch'en (1964: 80).
48. Id. (1954: 261 ff.; 1964: 75-76).
49. Id. (1952: 169).
50. Id. (1964: 184). Taoist priesthood was organised, from the beginning, on the model of the Han Imperial bureaucracy and never rose as a challenge to state authority (Gregory & Ebrey 1993: 24).
51. Ch'en (1964: 147-51).
52. Hoey (1892); *ASIAR* 1907-8 (J. Ph. Vogel): 81-131; *ASIAR* 1910-11 (J.H. Marshall): 1-24.
53. *ASIAR* 1907-8 (J. Ph. Vogel): 94.
54. *Xiyuji a*: VI (vol. 2: 2-3).
55. Cf. Law (1935: 27 [*Divyāvadāna* a: XVIII, pp. 243-44]).
56. *Faxian* b: 41-44.
57. Vimalakīrti was a lay bodhisattva (although he followed the *śramaṇacarita*: cf. *Vimalakīrtinirdeśa*: II. 3, p. 127), and this *sūtra* has a place of honour in Mahāyāna; it was translated several times into Chinese.
58. Petech (1974: 557). Lamotte (introduction to *Vimalakīrtinirdeśa*: 81) rightly points out that the information provided by the local guides were not necessarily reliable. This point has not been critically discussed, but that the local guides took full advantage of the travellers' gullibility, often making up the information they were giving, is likely. In the case under discussion, what is important is the evidence provided by the last sentence.
59. An example is the Dhamekh Stūpa at Sarnath, attributed in the past to the Gupta period but datable to the time of Harṣavardhana, as is now maintained (see, e.g. Gottfried Williams 1982: 168-69).
60. Verardi (2007*b*: 131-32).
61. Cf. Chapter II, n. 292. The *Shuijingzhu*, mostly composed of material dating back to the third and fourth century, besides containing abridged passage from Faxian's travelogue (see Petech's introduction, p. 8), describes the situation of the kingdom of Kapilavastu as follows: 'The kingdom of Chia-wei-lo-yüeh has not got a king now. The city and the ponds are desert and dirty, and there is only the empty space. There are some *upāsaka*, about twenty households of the Śākya family; they are the posterity of King Śuddhodhana. […] In those days, when the stūpas were dilapidated, they

completely repaired them. [...] But now there are (only) twelve monks who dwell inside that (city)' (*Shuijingzhu*: 1, 9b-10a; p. 33). The description of Kapilavastu provided by this text is independent from those of both Faxian and Xuanzang. We still ignore the exact location of Śuddhodhana's town, located not far from Lumbini, either in Nepalese or Indian territory.

As for other evidence of destruction of Buddhist monuments during the Gupta period, a Brahmanical temple seems to have been raised on a stūpa base (the monument was thus interfaced) at Ahmedpur in the vicinity of Vidiśā in the fifth century (Dass & Willis 2002: 31) but no report has been published so far which can detail the evidence.

62. Grindstones, pestles, etc., were and are normally obtained from the large pebbles carried by the floods, easily available in the area, and the column was certainly not demolished for obtaining stone.
63. A brief excavation campaign was carried out by Krisna Deva at Rajghat in 1940 after that railway diggings had brought to light important materials. More extensive excavations followed in the late 1950s and early1960s (Narain & al. 1976-78). Despite the good work done (the chronology established at Rajghat has been a reliable reference for long in Gangetic archaeology), we still lack a convincing picture of the town history. The available evidence has been presented and discussed by B.P. Singh (1985: esp. 22-74). For a stratigraphic sequence in the territory of Benares (at Aktha), see now V. Jayaswal (2009).
64. V.S. Agrawala (1984*b*).
65. The people of Vṛndāvana had decided to become devotees of Kṛṣṇa, and Indra reacted stirring up a tempest to flood the country and kill the peasants and their cattle. Kṛṣṇa saved them by lifting mount Govardhana to shelter them. Indra, defeated, went back to heaven. Cf. *Viṣṇu Purāṇa*: X.16-49; XI (vol. 2, pp. 721-28). I follow Harle (1974: 46) for the date of the sculpture.
66. For the questions summarised here and below, see V.S. Agrawala (1983: 5-6; 48-52).
67. *Vāmana Purāṇa*: 16. 51-63 (pp. 90-91).
68. The two rivers give the name to the town (Vārāṇasī).
69. See Appendix 2. Today Sarnath is a jumble of badly excavated, poorly restored and little understood monuments where even targeted controls, desirable as they may be, would probably give scarce results.
70. There is agreement on assigning the epic and Purāṇic passages on the early Kali Age literature to the fourth century (R.S. Sharma 2001: 49).
71. Willis (2009: 200-01).
72. R.S. Sharma (2001: 56-57). Here and below I limit myself to refer to Sharma's paper, where the reader will find the references to the Kali Age texts (the Āraṇyaka and Śānti Parvan of the *Mahābhārata*, the *Harivaṃśa*, the *Vāyu* and *Viṣṇu Purāṇa*-s, etc.).
73. Ibid. Traders and artisans indulge in many tricks and sell enormous commodities by adopting fraudulent weights and measures (ibid.: 60-61).

74. Ibid.: 50.
75. Ibid.: 61.
76. Hazra (1940: 13). G.V. Tagare, in the introduction to his translation of the text suggests a date to the fifth century; see *Vāyu Purāṇa*: p. lxii.
77. *Vāyu Purāṇa*: I.58.34-70 (vol. 1, pp. 411-14; the transliteration fluctuates between Kali Yuga and Kaliyuga). The *Brahmāṇḍa Purāṇa* (I.2.31.34-70; vol. 1, pp. 305-8) makes these statements its own.
78. Hazra (1958, I: 137-43).
79. Ibid.: 147-49.
80. Ibid.: 149. It is not known who the Utcakas may have been. The presence of 'Mahāyānists' may lead us to think that this passage is a later interpolation, but Faxian mentions the 'Great Vehicle' (*Faxian* a: 97; p. 548). Schopen (1987) has shown that Mahāyāna was not perceived as an independent and organised set of beliefs and practices until a relatively late age, and it is difficult to say when the term started being used. Several other authors have questioned the inconsistencies of the term 'Mahāyāna' (see for instance Silk 2002), and the reader is referred to the considerations made below in this chapter for a possible explanation of some of these questions.
81. R.S. Sharma (2001: 54-55).
82. Quoted in the *Smṛti Candrikā* (II. 310; cf. Hazra 1940: 201, to whom the reader is referred for the Sanskrit text). See also Kane (1930-62, IV: 114-15; on the *Ṣaṭtriṃśanmata*, see ibid, I: 535-37). Hazra refers the passage to a pre-AD 200 context, which seems too early a date.
83. On their doctrine, see Tucci (1971). S. Dasgupta (1932-55, III: 512 ff.) identified the Lokāyatas with the Cārvākas, accused of resorting to tricky disputations. For other Purāṇic passages condemning Lokāyatas and Kāpālikas, see Choudhary (1956: 250 ff.).
84. Willis (2009: 172 ff.); see below.
85. *Vāyu Purāṇa*: II.16.31 (vol. 2, p. 613). This point was already clear to Abs (1926: 391).
86. *Rāmāyaṇa*, Ayodhyā Kāṇḍa: 109 (p. 376). Here we deal with a relatively late period.
87. Cf. R.S. Sharma (2001: 55).
88. Cf. the well-known episode of Śambūka in the last, added or interpolated *kāṇḍa* (*Rāmāyaṇa*, Uttara Kāṇḍa: 75-76; pp. 1381-84), an episode in keeping with the Kali Age literature.
89. Ibid.: 63.
90. *Rāmāyaṇa*, Ayodhyā Kāṇḍa: 67 (p. 298). Later evidence (Chapters IV and V) throws some light on the systems used by orthodox kings to reduce the nihilists to impotence.
91. R.S. Sharma (2001: 67).
92. Ibid.: 64.
93. Boucher (2006: 27).
94. Nattier (2007: 70 ff.). Nattier maintains that the *Lotus Sūtra*, so important

in East Asia, had a less important, and even marginal status in India. This, however, does not agree with the existence of one or more Prakrit versions of the text and of a version in Sanskrit.

95. Wilson (1862*b*: 365; cf. *Saddharmapuṇḍarīka Sūtra* a: 165-66). Although Indian chronology was far from established and Buddhism was little known, Burnouf scored an almost direct hit on the date of the text and the questions involved. The text was for him a testimony of the persecutions of the Buddhists monks before they left central India (that is, Madhyadeśa). The *sūtra* kept the memory of painful events, and can hardly have been written during the most flourishing period of Buddhism: either the text was written outside India or when the brāhmaṇas were the winners (ibid. 408). This said, Burnouf believed that Buddhism flourished in the fourth century, while we know that the Buddhist revival took place in the late fifth and early sixth century. For the quoted passage, cf. also *Saddharmapuṇḍarīka Sūtra* b (1884: 259-61).
96. *Xiyuji* a: esp. VIII (vol. 2, p. 118). In the *Mañjuśrīmūlakalpa*: [53]: 715-18 (§33, pp. 49-50), Śaśāṅka is accused of having destroyed the establishments of the Jains, too: 'Then Soma, an unparalleled hero, will become king up to the banks of the Ganges, up to Benares and beyond. He, of wicked intellect, will destroy the beautiful image of the Buddha. He, of wicked intellect, enamoured of the words of the Tirthikas, will burn that great bridge of religion (Dharma), (as) prophesied by the former Jinas (Buddhas). Then that angry and evil-doer of false notions and bad opinion will fell down all the monasteries, gardens, and chaityas; and rest-houses of the Jainas [Nirgranthas]'; cf. pp. 49-50.
97. Kosambi (1975: 305).
98. Discussion on these images in V. Jayaswal (1991) and B.B. Lal (1993: 109); cf. also Verardi (2007*b*: 196). The reader will find these terracotta fragments, heads in particular, published in practically all the excavation reports of historical sites. Heads, arms, legs and decorative parts were separately worked and joined to the main part of the body before the baking process. The heads, found in large number, were inserted into the body by means of a tenon.
99. Ibid.: 196; 206.
100. van Troy (1990: 7).
101. Veluthat (1975).
102. The grant (*EI* 31 (1955-56, A.S. Gadre): 299-304, l. 11, is mentioned by Veluthat (1975: 102). Mota Machiala is located near Amreli.
103. For the Madhuban plate, see *EI* 1 (1892, G. Bühler): 67-75, l. 9 and p. 74; for the Banskhera plate, see *EI* 4 (1896-97, id.): 208-11, l. 8.
104. On the meaning of *ghaṭikā*, a term erroneously identified with *maṭha*, see Tieken & Sato (2000) and the discussion in Chapter IV.
105. Reference is again to Gokhale (1980).

106. *Dīgha Nikāya*: 27.3 (p. 407).
107. *Sutta Nipāta*: I.7 (115); cf. p. 14.
108. *Dīgha Nikāya*: 4. 4 (p. 126).
109. Ibid.: 26 (p. 132).
110. *Dīgha Nikāya*, Ambaṭṭha Sutta 1.9-10 (p. 113). Other stories from the Canon may refer to the furious polemics that took place among *śramaṇa*-s. In a passage of the *Aṅguttara Nikāya* (XX.191; pp. 162-63), today's brāhmaṇas (*śramaṇa*-s of different persuasions were often brāhmaṇas by birth) are likened to dogs, the worst possible comparison. The comparison is made in order to demonstrate that they have nothing to do with the brāhmaṇas of yore, and convince those who identify themselves in the old virtues to find a way out—that indicated by the Buddha.
111. *Saṃyutta Nikāya*: IV.2.8 (vol. 1, p. 143).
112. *Majjhima Nikāya* b: 50.13 [i. 335] (p. 433; the 'Kinsman' is Brahmā). In the text, the brāhmaṇas go on comparing the monks to owls, cats and donkeys.
113. In *Divyāvadāna* a: XXXV (pp. 485 ff). On the composite nature of the *Divyāvadāna* and the chronological questions involved, see Andy Rotman's introduction to *Divyāvadāna* b: 12 ff., 15 ff. The majority of the stories depict an affluent urban society, and circulated in the early centuries AD.
114. See below, Chapters IV and VI. For the *nirgrantha*-s and the *ṛṣi*-s, see *Divyāvadāna* b: 266.
115. Ibid.: 229.
116. See O'Flaherty's introduction to *Manu*: xviii.
117. *Manu*: 9.225-26 (p. 222). G.P. Upadhyay (1979: 186) suggests that proselytising activities may be meant here.
118. *Manu*: 4.30 (p. 77).
119. Ibid.: 5.90 (p. 109).
120. M.M. Deshpande (1994: 97).
121. Kane (1930-62, I: 447 [*Yājñavalkya Smṛti* I, 273].
122. Legittimo in her introduction to the *Bodhisattva Womb Sūtra*, I: p. 2.
123. *Bodhisattva Womb Sūtra*, II: 56-57. In 21.4.8, 'spirit' is to be understood as *ātman*. The Chinese word used is *shen*, as Elsa Legittimo has kindly informed me.
124. *Arthaśāstra*: I, 10, 12.
125. *Kāma Sūtra*: V, p. 69; XXI, p. 234; XXVII, p. 290.
126. Ibid.: I.4.87 (p. 87).
127. Alain Daniélou, on whose translation I rely, maintains that the work was compiled in the fourth century but that it describes Mauryan customs (preface to *Kāma Sūtra*, p. 12); this is rather unlikely.
128. Schopen (2008).
129. *Daśakumāracarita*: 11.156-62 (pp. 440-43).
130. *Kathāsaritsāgara*: II, 5, 75-115 (vol. 1, pp. 102-3).

131. Cf. R.S. Sharma (2001: 61).
132. Cf. ibid.: 56. The arguments against the merchant class are summed up and discussed in Gokhale (1977).
133. See, e.g. Karashima (2001) and Daniel Boucher in the introduction to his translation of the *Rāṣṭrapālaparipṛcchā Sūtra* (pp. 52 ff., 64 ff.).
134. *Rāṣṭrapālaparipṛcchā Sūtra*: 178 (p. 138); cf. also 95 (p. 129).
135. Ibid.: 84, 180 (pp. 127, 138).
136. Kajiyama (2005: 71-88) has shown that this, on the authority of Haribhadra, is the appropriate definition of the Mahāyāna bodhisattva provided with altruism – a term not always suitable for the bodhisattva's behaviour.
137. *Ugraparipṛcchā*: 8D (p. 236).
138. See, e.g. ibid. 9A-F (pp. 237-40); 13A-B, G-I (pp. 247 ff.).
139. Yadava (1968: 75) on the authority of V.S. Agrawala's edition of the text; also, B.N. Mukherjee (1980-81: 42-43).
140. Yadava (1968: 75-76); V. Jha (1986-87: 22, n. 3).
141. Cf. V.S. Agrawala (1970: 17-18).
142. *Mahāvastu*: I.197 (vol. 1, p. 156).
143. *Abhisamayālaṅkāra*: I, 2, 3c, 5 (pp. 69-70).
144. Nattier in *Ugraparipṛcchā*: 77-78.
145. Ibid.: 78.
146. Ibid.: esp. 121 ff.
147. The acceptance of a certain number of traditional rites from at least the first-second century AD, including *homa*, is documented in the art of Gandhāra (Verardi 1994). In the monastic ambit, we assist to the introduction of the concept of the transfer of merit, a practice attested in inscriptions of the early centuries AD in Āndhra. See Hanumantha Rao's observations (Rao, B.S.L. Hanumantha 1990: 833, 835-36) and the Āndhra inscription collected in Rao, B.S.L. Hanumantha *et al.* 1998; for earlier textual evidence, see Kajiyama (2005*b*). The transfer of merit was theorised to correct a position that was cause for easy criticism and greatly favoured the Brahmanical model. The latter was always in favour of the second *āśrama* (Dutt 1924: 47-48, 57-60).
148. *Rāṣṭrapālaparipṛcchā Sūtra*: 99 (p. 130).
149. Ibid.: 179 (p. 138). Immediately below, they are said to serve as go-betweens; the point, however, is that they enter the houses wearing the monastic robe.
150. Ibid.: 180, 181, 183 (p. 138).
151. Ibid.: 190, 192 (p. 139).
152. Ibid.: 196, 198 (pp. 139-40).
153. *Xiyuji* a: XI (vol. 2, pp. 273-74).
154. *Rājataraṅgiṇī*: III.12.
155. See, first and foremost, though indirectly, Schopen (1997).
156. Hirakawa (1963: 79).
157. Richard S. Cohen (2000) has shown that *śākyabhikṣu* is a kinship term

connected with the rapport Śākyamuni-Rāhula-Sumati/Dīpaṃkara. Buddhabhadra, a donor of Ajanta cave 26 (it is at Ajanta that there is ample epigraphic evidence on *śākyabhikṣu*-s) refers to himself as a 'powerful and affluent bodhisattva, who desires mundane pleasures as well as ultimate liberation' (ibid.: 29), an unusual presentation. The explicit association of these *bhikṣu*-s with the Śākya family underlined by Cohen may indicate actual lineages of married priests seeking legitimation in precisely this kind of association. The existence of a Buddhist married clergy would be in accord with the religious climate of the orthodox Vākāṭaka house, whatever the patrons of the Ajanta caves may have been. At Ajanta there were *vihāra*-s for the dwelling monks, and the latter were rather numerous (see the calculations made by Spink 2005-7, V: 387). This would seem to rule out any association with householder monks, but for all that we know, we cannot exclude the possibility that fifth-century Ajanta was for them a temporary retreat.

158. See Shayne Clarke's discussion on the meaning of *asaṃvāsa* (not being in communion with one's own *saṃgha*) and his questioning our understanding of what it was to be a monk in India (Clarke 2009).
159. *Upāyakauśalya Sūtra*: 33-34 (p. 34). I quote from the briefer and earlier version of the work, known from a Tibetan translation (cf. Katz's introduction, pp. 17-18).
160. See the classical study by Pye (1978), and in particular the discussion on the term *upāya* (12-14).
161. *Upāyakauśalya Sūtra*: 20 (p. 29).
162. Ibid.: 44-45 (pp. 37-38).
163. Ibid.: 47 (pp. 38-39).
164. Bhandarkar (1913: 160 ff.). In the Nārāyaṇīya section of the Śānti Parvan, a typical text of the early Kali Age literature, we find Rudra, 'devoted to Yoga', together with Nārāyaṇa (see section CCCXLIX; vol. 10, p. 188).
165. Chhabra & Gai (1981: 242-44); Willis (2009: 33-34, 57).
166. Willis (2009).
167. Now in the National Museum, New Delhi. See it in Huntington (1985: 194).
168. Willis (2009: 55-56). For Varāha, see especially ibid. 41 ff, 79-81 (also, Gottfried Williams 1982: 40-49, pls. 34-39, 43 and Harle 1974: 9-10, 33-36; pls. 3-17). Willis (2009: 55) has been good enough to recall a minimal contribution of mine, but a clarification may be useful. The cave is unique in Indian art because the scene – an aquatic scene – runs uninterrupted along the three walls of the cave and on the bottom. The prototype, as far as the evidence goes, is the so-called Fish Porch of Tapa Shotor, Hadda (M. & Sh. Mustamandy 1969; Mustamandy 1972), destroyed in 1979, a chapel with an extraordinary aquatic landscape occupying the whole space that is deeply indebted to Hellenistic models, a sort of three-dimensional Nilotic scene that is likely to have also influenced the riverine imagery of early Pendžikent

in Sogdia. But it would be wrong to think that Udayagiri owes something to the art of Central Asia.

169. Ibid.: 37.
170. Hudson (2002: 145). See also below.
171. Willis (2009: 175 ff.).
172. *Devī Māhātmya*: 8.9-19 ff. (pp. 63 ff.).
173. The trident's 'essential feature is the triple metal pike in sharp points' (Rao, T.A. Gopinatha 1914-16, I: 8). Śiva first appears holding it and the club in north-western India on the coins of Maues (Banerjea 1956: 120-21) in the first quarter of the first century BC, and constantly holds it on Kuṣāṇa coins (Göbl 1984: 43-44). On Huviṣka's coins, he is also shown holding other weapons, namely the wheel, the club and the thunderbolt (ibid). The earliest relief of Śiva holding *triśūla* is also from the North-West (Härtel 1985: 392-96). In the Central Himalayas, Śiva appears with the trident/battle axe (*triśūla-paraśu*) on the Catreśvara type of Kuṇinda coins (M.P. Joshi 1989: 61-62), and in Gangetic India he is depicted with the trident in third-century Sāṃkāśya (Sankisa); cf. N.P. Joshi (1984: 49).
174. Ibid.
175. Harle (1974: pl. 54).
176. For the Mathurā icons and a general discussion see Kreisel (1986: 65 ff.).
177. The formation of the god Skanda/Subrahmaṇya and that of his iconography is too complex to be even simply touched on in this context. For a general information on his early forms and cult, the reader is referred to P.K. Agrawala (1967) and Chatterjee (1970), and for a discussion on his characteristics in south India, where he even assumes the role of Indra, to L'Hernault (1978; 1984).
178. N.P. Joshi (1986:19 ff.; 28 ff.; drawings 9-12).
179. *Vāyu Purāṇa*: II.11.47-48 (vol. 2, p. 573).
180. Ibid.: II.11.43-44 (vol. 2, p. 573).
181. Ibid.: II.11.21-34 (vol. 2, pp. 571-72).
182. Rao, T.A. Gopinatha (1914-16, I: 5).
183. Ibid.: I: 4. On *cakra* as a weapon in a Vishnuite context, see Begley (1973: 7-22). Vāsudeva's early icons, dating to the post-Kuṣāṇa period, come from Mathurā, the weapons he is provided with being a very large *cakra* and a gigantic *gadā* (K.S. Desai 1973: 8; figs. 1-3). Saṃkarṣaṇa and Vāsudeva Kṛṣṇa, two of the *pañcavīra*-s who contributed in shaping Viṣṇu's identity are depicted on Agathocles's coins (first half of the second century BC) holding club and plough and *cakra* and *śaṅkha* (?), respectively (Filliozat 1973: 113-23; Narain 1973: 113-23). For the iconographic relationship between Vāsudeva and Viṣṇu the reader is referred to Härtel (1987: esp. 586-87).
184. Rao, T.A. Gopinatha (1914-16, I: 3).
185. The *Vāyu Purāṇa* (II.6.61, 66; vol. 2, p. 516) calls him the lord of *daitya*-s, which are equated to the *asura*-s and *dānava*-s (II.6.63). The war against

Hiraṇyakaśipu is the first of the *devāsura* wars (below, Chapter V), something that may suggest the identification of this *asura* with Aśoka or, perhaps, with the last Mauryan emperor.

186. K.S. Desai (1973: 86-88).
187. See, as an early example, the sixth-century image kept in the Bharat Kala Bhavan in Benares (Biswas & Jha 1985: 52 and pl. III, 6, 6a). On the iconography of Narasiṃha see especially Ducrey Giordano (1977), where the *Narasiṃha Purāṇa* and the relevant passages from other texts are thoroughly examined. For Narasiṃha's myth, see Soifer (1992: esp. 73-111).
188. Hudson (2002: 145).
189. See Härtel (1992) and von Stietencron (2005: 131 ff.).
190. *Devī Māhātmya*: 2.19-30. This text has been attributed to the fifth-sixth century (Coburn 1984: 1), but a later date has been suggested (cf. Willis 2009: 176).
191. *ASIR* 10 (A. Cunningham): 50. Cunningham saw the relief in a better condition than it is now. See these two reliefs illustrated in Harle (1974: pls. 16-17).
192. Cave 5 according to the numeration of the Archaeological Survey of India. See this image in von Mitterwallner (1976: fig. 4).
193. Coburn (1984: 192-95) and id. in *Devī Māhātmya*: 22-23.
194. Harle (1974: 12-13, 38; pls. 27-30).
195. The reader is referred to the *Mythos-Debatte* of the 1980s and 1990s, which was set up by the publication in 1979 of *Arbeit am Mythos* by Hans Blumenberg.
196. Hübner (1990: 302, 459).
197. This was the concern of Karol Kerényi and Mircea Eliade, while Doniger O'Flaherty (1981: 9-12) particularly feared reductionism.
198. See a comment on this *Ṛgveda* myth in Kuiper (1983: esp. 50-51, 104-05).
199. On Vedic *asura*-s, see Hale (1986); predictably, it is with the *Atharvaveda* that we come closer to the use of the term *asura*-s understood as demons who oppose the gods. Archaeology, severely conditioned in pre-archaic India by the absence of funerary monuments, and of the large amount of materials they usually yield, has been of limited help in clarifying the traits of Vedic society at the level that would be necessary in this discussion.
200. There is a rich literature on this subject and related matters. For Rudra-Śiva, cf. in particular Gonda (1970: 1-17); Kramrisch (1981: passim).
201. On Vedic Viṣṇu and his three strides, cf. Gonda (1954: 55-72).
202. Cf. M. Dasgupta (1931).
203. V.S. Agrawala (1983: 1). On the Vedic connections of the goddess, in relation to the *Devī Māhātmya*, see Coburn (1984: 53 ff. and passim).
204. The increasing number of gender studies has caused several contributions on the goddess to be written, but a thorough investigation on the relationship between the neo-Brahmanical goddess and the Vedic female deities is

lacking. S.K. Lal (1980) has devoted a study to the Vedic goddesses who, in one form or another, have continued to be of significance in neo-Brahmanism.

205. Granoff (1984). The author, discussing religious biographies, has shown how this paradigm is persistent over time, providing also relatively recent examples.
206. See Kerényi introduction in Jung & Kerényi (1972: esp. 20-24).
207. *Vāyu Purāṇa*: II, 6.58-63 (vol. 2, pp. 515-16).
208. Ibid.: II, 6. 65-66 (vol. 2, p. 516). The sentence between inverted commas is uttered by Brahmā.
209. Hazra (1940: 24).
210. *Viṣṇu Purāṇa*: I.17.2-4 (vol. 1, p. 190).
211. Ibid.: I.17.6-7 (vol. 1, p. 190).
212. According to Hazra (1940: 25), the Māyāmohana story, reported also in other Purāṇas, did not originate earlier than AD 500.
213. *Viṣṇu Purāṇa*: III.17.37-44 (vol. 1, pp. 486-87).
214. Ibid.: III.18.13-20 (vol. 1, p. 490).
215. *Vāyu Purāṇa*: II.37.26-32 (vol. 2, p. 792).
216. Ibid. II.36.72 ff. (vol. 2, pp. 785 ff.). It is perhaps an interpolated passage, where the number of the *avatāra*-s is said to be ten, but no mention is made of the first and ninth.
217. Ibid.: II.36.80 (vol. 2, p. 785).
218. The *Viṣṇu Purāṇa*: XVIII.1 (vol. 2, p. 621) gives a similar, though not identical list of geographical names.
219. For the Brahmanical caves at Badami, see Burgess (1874:15-25); R.D. Banerji (1928); Soundara Rajan (1981: 47-72).
220. I interpret the material discussed by O'Flaherty (1971: esp. 297 ff.; 1976: 272 ff.) in this perspective, and I refer the reader to Chapter IV for an attempt at transposing this point on the historical level. O'Flaherty (1980) again discusses the question at length, but here the use of terms such as 'evil', 'sin', and even 'fall of man' leads us in a dimension alien to what is being discussed here, and somewhat questionable in itself.
221. Lippe (1972: 282-83); also, id. (1969-70: 8).
222. Lippe recalls a relief at Ranjim where 'the Brāhmin dwarf Vāmana is shown with *samghati*, curled hair and *usnisa*' (id. 1972: n. 31).
223. J.F. Fleet in Burgess (1874: 12-14); cf. also *IA* 10 (1881, id.): 57-59.
224. *IA* 3 (1874, J. Eggeling): 305-6; cf. also *IA* 10 (1881, J.F. Fleet): 57-59.
225. A.M. Annigere in Nagaraja Rao (1978: 232-33).
226. *IA* 10 (1881, J.F. Fleet): 61-62. I try here to elucidate the meaning of the first lines, unclear to J.F. Fleet.
227. V.S. Agrawala (1983: vi).
228. Ibid.: viii. The appellation *Mahābhāgavata*-s given to the *asura*-s applies to them as followers of the Buddha, addressed as Bhagavān (ibid.: 50). V.S. Agrawala recognised the Buddhists not only in the *asura*-s of the *Vāmana*,

but of the *Viṣṇu* and *Liṅga Purāṇa*-s (ibid. 4 and passim). He could have developed William Taylor's insights and reanalysed Rajendralala Mitra's contention regarding the story of Gayāsura, disclosing the historical aspects of Purāṇic narrations, but as one of the most distinguished representatives of the 'paradigm of Independence', he could not say everything he knew.

229. Longhurst (1936).
230. Id. (1938: 6). Only the upper part of the Nagarjuna Hill is visible today after the construction, in the 1960s, of a dam that caused the valley of Nagarjunakonda to be submerged by water. Some of the ancient monuments were reassembled at the end of an ambitious project the limitations of which, in today's perspective, have become increasingly evident. The *c.* 130 sites partially excavated in the 1920s and 1930s were systematically investigated between 1954 and 1960, and the research project had the merit of exposing a sequence going from the Lower Palaeolithic to the middle age. Unfortunately, no exhaustive report on the excavations relative to the Ikṣvāku phase has been published yet, the only sources available being Sarkar (1962) and Sarkar & Misra (1966).
231. Ibid.
232. Elisabeth Rosen Stone, mainly on the basis of stylistic evidence, has suggested to push forward the reign of the last known king of the Ikṣvākus, Rudrapuruṣadatta, until *c.* AD 325 (Rosen Stone 1994: 6-7).
233. Sircar (1939*b*: 10 ff.); id. in HCIP 2: 224.
234. In connection with these temples, we have, as at Udayagiri, Śiva, Kārttikeya and Viṣṇu, but the goddesses are conspicuous for their absence.
235. I follow the chronology suggested by Sarkar (1985: 31).
236. Sarkar & Misra (1966: 24-29). Cāṃṭamūla I was an *aśvamedhin* king who also performed *vājapeya* and other Vedic rituals (Sircar 1939*b*: 17 and id. in HCIP 2: 224), with the ensuing economic fallout in favour of the priests. In relation to the temple of Sarvadeva, Rosen Stone (1994: 12) underlines the fact that the related inscriptions are in pure Sanskrit, and not in Prakrit like the Buddhist inscriptions.
237. *EI* 20 (1929-30, J. Ph. Vogel): 19 (*āyaka*-pillar inscription B5). Cāṃṭaśrī may have inspired the figure of Śrīmālā, the queen of a famous early Mahāyāna text written in the third century for a Buddhist sect of Nagarjunakonda (Rosen Stone 1994: 13-16). This text was translated from various sources by A. Wayman & H. Wayman in 1974, and recently by Diana Y. Paul, who has underlined the importance of this *sūtra* for the Buddhist attitude towards women (D.Y. Paul 1974: 6-7). As regard patronage, we find the division of functions between the male and female members of ruling houses as late as the twelfth century (Chapter VI), and *The Lion's Roar*, representative of the Tathāgatagarbha theory, could help clarify the role of women, guiding us into a still unexplored territory. A part of the original Sanskrit text has recently surfaced, and has been edited and translated by Kazunobu Matsuda (*Śrīmālādevīsiṃhanādanirdeśa*, in Jens Braarvig,

ed., *Buddhist Manuscripts 1* (Manuscripts in the Shøyen Collection 1), pp. 65-76, Oslo 2000.

238. Sarkar & Misra (1966: 22). We inevitably think of those Indians who at the beginning of the second century were listening to the oration of Dio Chrysostomos in the theatre of Alexandria (see Chapter I).
239. Gandharan prototypes are very clearly observable in a number of reliefs, as for instance that illustrated in Rosen Stone (1994: pl. 111 and cover); the well-known guardian figure in Central Asian dress (ibid. pl. 232) is not simply a citation, but reflects a real knowledge of this class of people.
240. The date of this temple is discussed in ibid.: 8-9, 81-82.
241. Sankaranarayanan (1977: 205, 208).
242. Chhabra & Gai (1981: ll. 19-20, 22-23, pp. 213, 217).
243. On early Śrīparvata, see Sankaranarayanan (1977: esp. 205-10).
244. V.S. Agrawala (1963: 286).
245. *Rājataraṅgiṇī*: I.171.
246. Ibid.: I, 173.
247. Ibid.: I, 178.
248. Ibid.: I, 174-76.
249. Buddhism was introduced into Kashmir by Madhyāntika, a disciple of Ānanda, who, according to the oldest Chinese version of the legend, preserved in the *Ayuwang zhuan* (*Taishō* 50, 116a), found the resistance of a great *nāga*, who was eventually overcome by the supernatural power of the monk (cf. Funayama 1994: 367 and n. 1 on pp. 373-74; 369). Toru Funayama further observes that, according to Xuanzang, Kashmir was protected by *yakṣa*-s, and not by *nāga*-s who were often opposed to Buddhism (ibid.: n. 5 on p. 374; on *nāga* opposition to Buddhism see also N. Dutt 1939: 10-12). Funayama has proposed a reconstruction of the history of Buddhism in Kashmir comparing the evidence from the *Rājataraṅgiṇī* and Xuanzang's *Xiyuji*, the relevant passages of which he has translated anew. I follow also Witzler (1994), besides resorting to the other available sources.
250. *Rājataraṅgiṇī*: I, 181.
251. Ibid.: I, 184.
252. Wetzler (1994: 248) emphasises the fact that Gonanda recalls, with his name, the mythical founder of the Kashmiri kingdom. His would then be a re-enactment of a pristine state of virtue.
253. *Rājataraṅgiṇī*: I, 199-200.
254. Ibid.: I, 342-43.
255. Manu forbids brāhmaṇas to eat garlic, scallions, onions and mushrooms among other things (*Manu*: 5.5, p. 99). Khāsaṭā has not been identified.
256. *Rājataraṅgiṇī*: 2.5-14. I follow Wetzel (1994: 246 ff.), who identifies Gopāditya with Pratāpāditya, making possible the identification of his son with one Jaulaka presumed to be a son of Aśoka.
257. *Rājataraṅgiṇī*: 1.112.

258. Ibid.: 1.115-17.
259. Cf. Wetzler (1994: 250). Witzler mentions a passage ridiculing *Jātaka* tales, but at the *locus citatus* (cf. n. 105 on p. 285), I am unable, in the text available to me, to find anything else than Buddhist monks being ridiculed because they delight in indifference (*Pādatāḍitaka*: 65; cf. pp. 30-31).
260. Funayama (1994: 369-71).
261. The second edition of this book (R.C. Mitra 1981), to which reference is made here, was edited by D.C. Sircar, who did not add any new material.
262. Ibid.: 11.
263. *Xiyuji* a: I: (vol. I, pp. 98-99). Cf. Kuwayama (2002: 35 ff.).
264. *Xiyuji* b (vol. 2, p. 226; Watters amends Beal's translation here).
265. Kuwayama (2002: esp. 153 ff.); on the monuments of Bamiyan and their date, see Klimburg-Salter (1989).
266. Huisheng's narrative has reached us edited by Yang Xuanzhi in the fifth volume of the *Luoyang qielan ji* (*A Record of the Buddhist Monasteries in Luoyang*) dated *c.* AD 547-50. See Max Deeg's discussion in *Song Yun*: 65 ff.; cf. also Kuwayama (2002: 109).
267. *Song Yun*: 79.
268. Kuwayama (2002: 39-40). Kuwayama has questioned the widely accepted idea that the Hephthalites were responsible for the destruction of the Buddhist sites of Gandhāra and Uḍḍiyāna, showing that the collapse of Buddhist Gandhāra started later, to coincide with the shift westwards of the Trans-Himalayan route (ibid.: 41-42). To Kuwayama we also owe a thorough investigation of the historical-political situation of north-western India, Afghanistan and Tokharistan between the fifth and the ninth century based on both the Chinese sources, some of which he has translated for the first time, and of the archaeological evidence.
269. The plague erupted in the port of Pelusium in the Nile delta, near Alexandria, and spread rapidly thanks to the large amount and speed of traffic by sea. On the Justinian's plague, see Stathakopoulos (2004: 110 ff., 277 ff.) and Rosen (2007).
270. Xuanzang refers him to an impossibly early age, and probably attributes to him the deeds of other persecutors of the Law (*Xiyuji* a: IV, pp. 167-72).
271. *Rājataraṅgiṇī*: I, 307.
272. Cf. Aurel Stein's note to ibid. I, 289.
273. Sircar (1965*b*: 424-26; cf. note 6, p. 425) has explained the meaning of *abhaṅga*, which appears in the third line of the inscription.
274. Chappell (1980: 129-30).
275. Ibid.
276. Kuwayama (2002: 222-48) has attributed the whole set of Brahmanical marble sculptures from eastern Afghanistan to the Turki Ṣāhīs.
277. Rehman (1979: 47).
278. Callieri (2001); Filigenzi (2001).
279. van Lohuizen-de Leeuw (1959).

280. Sircar (1948: 11 ff.).
281. This process is documented by the Buddhist reliefs cut in the cliffs of the Swat River and its tributary from the seventh century onwards (Filigenzi (1997; 2000). On Swat, see also Chapter V. The history of the north-western regions in relation to the period preceding their Islamisation is still little known, but Elverskog (2010: 45) has too hastily concluded on the 'lack of Hinduisation' of north-western India, ignoring not only the role of the Turkī Ṣāhīs, but that of the Hindū Ṣāhīs, who controlled eastern Afghanistan and Gandhāra until the rise of the Ghaznavids.
282. An example could be Ranighat, in the hills north of Swabi. The excavation report has not yet been published but for the plates (Nishikawa 1994), though in the small brochure attached it is suggested that the site's life lasted until 'the end of the Ephtalite Era' (p. 12), too vague an indication. Some of the buildings, especially in the 'South-west Area', seem definitely late (Nishikawa 1994: pls. 73-76, 84); here the site acquired the aspect of a fortress (brochure, pp. 9-10). The site's name is spelt Ranigat.
283. As recalled by R.C. Mitra (1983: 7).
284. Corresponding to Sugh on the western Yamuṇa canal, north of Thanesar, commanding the passage of the river (*ASIR* 1, 1871, A. Cunningham: 291).
285. See Appendix 1.
286. These allegations, and others charging the Buddhist monks with sedition, immorality, economic liability and hypocrisy, are contained in the *Memorial Discussing Buddhism* (*Lun fo jiao biao*) that Xun Ji presented to Emperor Wu of the Southern Liang dynasty (AD 502-549). See Ch'en (1964: 127, 142-44).
287. Ibid.: 190-92. Xuanzang was born in *c.* AD 602, a generation after the events.
288. Xuanzang's *Jusheluo* [*Kü-che-lo*] according to Vincent Smith (in *Xiyuji* b; vol. 2: 341-42). The identification is not certain.
289. *Xiyuji* a: XI (vol. 2, pp. 269-70).
290. Ibid.: XI (vol. 2, pp. 270-71).
291. Xuanzang's *Molapo* is identified with the Mālavaka province of the Valabhī kingdom (see discussion in Jain 1972: 11-12).
292. *Xiyuji* a: XI (vol. 2, p. 261).
293. Ibid.: pp. 263-64.
294. Njammasch (2001: 200 ff.).
295. Copper-plate grant from Katapur near Mahua, dated Valabhī *saṃvat* 252 (Peterson 1895: 35-39, p. 37), where the statement is repeated thrice. The same words are found in a copper-plate from Jhara (ibid. 30-35). Śaṅkara, 'he who confers weal', is an epithet of Śiva.
296. Njammasch (2001: 279, 281). This author argues that the support given to the brāhmaṇas by the Maitraka kings between AD 525 and 590 is correlated with the difficulty of legitimising their sovereignty. The case of the Maitrakas

is parallel to that of the Cāḷukyas of Badami discussed above, the difference being that the geographical position of the kingdom of Valabhī allowed Harṣa to contain, during his reign, the phenomenon of brahmanisation.

297. *EI* 1 (1892, E. Hultzsch): 85-92, ll. 1-6.

298. *Xiyuji* a: XI (vol. 2, p. 267). The Jains appropriated this king, to whom the revival of Jainism was attributed. Cf. Lévi (1996*a*: 219).

299. Njammasch (2001: 278-79).

300. S. Tripathy (2000: 3-6).

301. Pāṇḍuvaṃśī or Somavaṃśī kings according to S.A. Banerji (1970: 17-18). The long reign of Mahāśivagupta Bālārjuna is assigned either to the first half of the seventh century or to *c.* AD 725-85 (see the matter discussed in A.M. Shastri (1985; 1995: esp. 144 ff.). Shastri is in favour of a late chronology, of which I am also convinced, and in this case, the identification of this king with the kṣatriya ruler of Xuanzang would be impossible. On Bālārjuna, see also below, Chapter V.

302. *Life*: IV (p. 135). After Bālārjuna, South Kosala was occupied by the Nalas (S.A. Banerji (1970: 19), an orthodox dynasty (HCIP 3: 188-90), but the picture is far from being clear (cf. for instance the confused description of the events provided by Singh Deo (1987: 158 ff.).

303. See Watters's criticism of too many approximate identifications proposed by nineteenth-century scholars and his observations on the reliability of *juan* X and XI in *Xiyuji* b: vol. 2, p. 233.

304. *Xiyuji* a: X (vol. 2, p. 221). Beal's identification of Dhānyakaṭaka with Dharaṇīkoṭa has been disproved; cf. *Xiyuji* b, X (vol. 2, p. 216); Bareau (1965).

305. *Xiyuji* a: X (vol. 2, p. 223).

306. Robert Sewell argued that the once Buddhist caves of Undavalli were probably appropriated by the brāhmaṇas, observing that 'In the Undavilli group the *Asuras* are represented as in actual conflict with the gods. The *Asuras* are raising their clubs and advancing to the attack, one of them especially eyeing the newly-created Brahma with open hostility depicted in his glance no less than in his attitude [. . .] we found that the Brahmans at Undavilli, of an age subsequent to that of the original stone sculptors, had partially bricked up the group of *Asuras*, so that their weapons were concealed. This piece of brick-work can be accounted for on no other assumption than that they desired to conceal to a certain extent the bold hostility of the demon figures [. . .]. They thought the antagonism too marked and tried to hide it' (Sewell 1878: 21). See the Undavalli caves described by Soundara Rajan (1981: 261 ff.).

307. *Xiyuji* a: X (vol. 2, p. 227). According to Vincent Smith (in *Xiyuji* b: 341), Xuanzang's Cōḷa country broadly corresponded to the Kadapa (Cuddapah) district in southern Andhra Pradesh.

308. Cf. Watters in *Xiyuji* b: vol. 2, p. 229.

309. *Xiyuji* a: X (vol. 2, p. 231).

310. Ibid (vol. 2, p. 229).
311. Hikosaka (1989: 21-26).
312. Hikosaka argues that they were attracted by Gupta patronage; they, rather, went to northern India during the period of Buddhist revival after the mid-fifth century, when the situation in the south started changing. Bodhidharma (on which see below, Chapter V) went as far as China, where he landed before AD 478; Dharmapāla spent the rest of his short life (AD 530-61) in Nālandā; Dharmagupta went to China in the sixth century (ibid.: 30 ff.), etc.
313. Fleet (1896: 316); Sircar (1939*b*: 155); Sastri, K.A. Nilakantha (1966: 102).
314. Sircar (1939*b*: 154).
315. Rao, T.N. Vasudeva (1979: v-vii, 175-77). On the religion of the Kaḷabhras, seen from the perspective of a mature Brahmanical system and through the eyes of the *Periya Purāṇam*, see Arunachalam (1979: 46 ff.).
316. Davidson (2004: 29).
317. *Life*: IV (p. 155).
318. It is at this point in history that the episode of Wang Xuance took place.
319. If we give credit to the late Deogarh inscription, which is perhaps a copy of an early text (HCIP 3: 128).
320. I follow Tripathi (1964: 196-97), who suggests for this ruler the dates *c.* AD 725-52. Thaplyal (1985: 79-80) suggests AD 720 as the date of his accession.
321. *Hui Chao*: 3 (p. 39).

CHAPTER IV

A Period Which is Not Pleasant to Contemplate

PRELIMINARY

The long period of hardships that Buddhism experienced from the mid-seventh century onwards was the result of the unrelenting effort of both the *vaidika* and theistic brāhmaṇas to prevent undesired social sectors from holding power or sharing it in the regions where they were settling in increasing number and with increasing determination. The social sectors representing themselves as Buddhist were incorporated, step by step and through the frequent use of violence, into the Brahmanical model of society. Only later on the Vajrayāna supplied a theoretical framework where the innovations introduced by the Mahāyāna groups that had compromised with the Brahmanical model of society were given full justification, or else opened with great determination towards the 'tribals' and the outcastes, pursuing the model of a non-*varṇa* state.

To frame the discussion that follows in a broader perspective, I should enter the debate on Indian feudalism, but I hesitate to do so because, while appreciating the results of decades of research, it is difficult for me to accept a historiographic approach based on a phenomenon – European feudalism – whose very existence is, for many an aspect, disputed. In Europe, the concepts of vassalage and fief are largely the work of scholars-ideologues who, from the sixteenth century onwards, have given a distorted interpretation of the social relationships based on customs, court judgements and imperial constitutions contained in the *Libri feudorum*. Composed in Lombardy between the twelfth and the early thirteenth century, they were integrated into the *Corpus iuris*, and had only vague connections with the law applied in the courts of the alleged feudal kingdoms of early medieval Europe, whose received history appears to be, in actual reality, a pseudo-history.[1]

The issue of a feudal India has been debated among Indian historians with renewed interest from the 1980s onwards, and opinions remain mixed.[2] In the Gupta and post-Gupta period no form of feudalism is observable; there was, rather, an exchange between the king, guardian of the *varṇa*-system, and the brāhmaṇas who, rewarded with lands, supported his authority and rights.[3] The point is that in many cases, and as late as the time of the Senas, the kings themselves were brāhmaṇas performing the duty of kṣatriyas, at least when major dynasties were concerned and when establishing the desired social order was difficult. This would show that the setting up of a 'feudal' hierarchy was not so much a matter regarding the relationships between the centre (an independent royal court) and brāhmaṇa landowners in the periphery, but between Brahmanical *gotra*-s as a whole and the tax and rent paying peasants. In the case of local rulers integrated into the *varṇa* system, the brāhmaṇas' dual role of intellectuals/administrators and priests was instrumental in determining their policy. Wherever the control over society was exercised from the beginning through a network of temples, the rulers were figureheads with little real power or authority outside of what was ceded to them by the temple priests.[4] Focusing on Kerala, M.G.S. Narayanan has recognised the existence of 'a bold and visible Brahman oligarchy, thinly disguised as a monarchy to satisfy the sentiments of the lawgivers of India',[5] a statement that has much weight and is worth developing. The settlement model, implemented by the Guptas, was exported and adapted wherever the brāhmaṇas would move. The Brahmanical revivalism of early medieval South India, crucial for the whole subcontinent,[6] was the work of settlers imbued with the ideology prevalent in fourth-fifth century northern India who had moved to the coastal plains of southern Deccan.

In this perspective, it is also difficult for me to accept the attempts at adapting the model of segmentary state proposed by Burton Stein for Tamiḻakam[7] to other Indian regions, or subscribe to the existence of the *sāmanta* feudalism. The latter mimics a system of relations – that between a small military elite and a large mass of subject peasantry – that has no real counterpart in India in the course of the crucial centuries going from the death of Harṣavardhana to the advent of Islam. I share the observations made long ago by D.C. Sircar, who observed that but for a few examples, there are no charters recording grants or land to people of the warrior class, and there is no mention of obligations of the feudal type.[8] The above constructs end up masking the identity of the real protagonists of Indian medieval history. To readdress the issue, we need to identify with clarity the forces in the field, trying to wipe away the foggy atmosphere that mystifies the logic of events.

The structural change that affected India with the strengthening of the agrarian society and the deteriorating of the proto-capitalist economy of the Buddhists that maximised the profits of trade is linked to the great sixth-century crisis in the Mediterranean and the Near East. The structural weakening of the West caused by Justinian's plague has been associated, in the West, with the ease with which the Muslims arrived quickly, almost without striking a blow, as far as the Maghreb:[9] they operated in a region fallen short of human resources. The setback must have been serious also in the subcontinent, as shown by Xuanzang's travelogue – but not for everybody. The orthodox not only had nothing to lose from the general collapse of trade, but had everything to gain instead. The agrarian model that identified them at the social level, brought to perfection through centuries of experience, compensated for the losses in macro-economical terms.

If any signs of change appear between the centre and the periphery, they are all to the advantage of the brāhmaṇas. If *ghaṭikā* is an abbreviation of *ghaṭikāsthāna*, 'custom house'[10] – this interpretation gains strength from the term being found for the first time in the *Arthaśāstra*, a Gupta work – the early prohibition for *bhaṭṭa*-s and *cāṭṭa*-s to enter the lands granted to brāhmaṇas points to some kind of exemption in addition to the known immunities. The *bhaṭṭa*-s and *cāṭṭa*-s were in-charge of the *ghaṭikāsthāna*-s, and the expression *achāṭabhaṭaprāveśya* is very frequently found in land grants, an early example being the royal charter of the Parivrājaka King Hastin who started his reign in AD 475.[11] Much remains to be investigated here. In a Kadamba inscription of AD 450, only *bhaṭṭa*-s are mentioned and not *cāṭṭa*-s.[12] This may suggest a rapid evolution of the institution, whose members, in the eighth century but possibly also before in places, not only had a role in the choice of rulers, but were also the performers of the *rājasūya*.[13] Granting lands with immunity from the entry of *cāṭṭa*-s and *bhaṭṭa*-s became the rule, and this means that an ever-growing number of lands did not contribute to the state coffers.

It is often repeated that the cause that brought about the decline of

Buddhism was the shifting of patronage, but this is, rather, an effect of the situation as it developed in the early middle age. The rulers were less and less free to dispose of their will and means, patronage becoming an independent variable in the hands of the orthodox. In the myth of Vāmana and Bali, Viṣṇu says flatly that once the Brahmanical rites are established, there should be no share to the *asura*-s.[14] The speech addressed by Bhīṣma to Yudhiṣṭhira in the Anuśāsana Parvan of the *Mahābhārata* would deserve a long comment: the king is not only invited to give the brāhmaṇas whatever they ask, but he is warned that '[w]hen angry they are like snakes of virulent poison'.[15] The king should regard the brāhmaṇas 'as fire covered with ashes'; blazing with penances, 'they are capable of consuming the whole earth'.[16] This is exactly what happened to their adversaries, and the kings knew it. Outside the literary realm, the crucial concept of the superiority of the first *varṇa* was developed with the utmost rigour by Kumārila Bhaṭṭa, one of the greatest opponents of Buddhism.

Violence played a major role in progressively preventing the trading class and the mid-lower and lower social groups from continuing to resort to Buddhism as to a hegemonic force. If the process of brahmanisation was slow – the situations greatly varied in the different parts of India – it was so because some of these groups obstinately resisted their expulsion from the social and political scene, and their opposition was difficult to put down. Moreover, the outlying, clan-based, non-agricultural communities that the brāhmaṇas intended to integrate into the *varṇa* system were not prone to surrender in a number of cases. This was particularly true in the upper Deccan and eastern India, where a part of the Buddhists, undergoing a profound transformation, not only remained faithful to their stand against the *varṇa* society, but radicalised their positions.

In a large part of the country, Buddhism ceased early enough to constitute a threat to the Brahmanical social order. Going through the *Biography on the Eminent Monks Who Went in Search of the Law in the Western Countries During the Great Tang Dynasty* written by Yijing at the end of the seventh century, it appears that the Chinese and Korean monks who came to India mostly sojourned at Bodhgayā, Nālandā, and in other monasteries of south Bihar.[17] North of the Ganges, they mainly sojourned in the Monastery of the Great Faith (*Xinzhesi*)[18] in the kingdom of Anmaluoba, identified with Vaiśālī, ruled by a Licchavi king.[19] Some monks visited Kuśīnagara and some other holy places outside Bihar,[20] but only a few ventured into north-western and western India and into the Deccan. We note an eastward shift of the Buddhist oecumene, a phenomenon that we shall examine again in a later chapter: in eastern India, open to South-East Asia and China, as well as to Tibet, it was possible to recreate the trading society that in the west and south had suffered a severe blow. Now many foreign monks arrived from East Asia by sea and not by land, and many travelled to Laṅkā without even touching India. Nevertheless, in Magadha Buddhism had succeeded in creating an impassable monastic network: '[e]verywhere there were monasteries', says Yijing,[21] and in fact, Ādityasena of the Later Guptas, an *aśvamedhin* king,[22] had to comply and had a monastery built at Bodhgayā.[23] In the years 670s-80s, there were a very large number of monks residing at Nālandā,[24] and the emergence of Pāla power in the eighth century would reinforce Buddhism. In particular, Pāla expansionism was instrumental in the strengthening and spreading of the Vajrayāna, which affected all the existing forms of the religion.

Even where Buddhism structured itself in such a way as to be compatible with Brahmanical principles, it remained a symbol for all anti-Brahmanical identities, and symbols, we constantly learn from history, must be destroyed. There is more than that, however. Starting from the eighth century, and more so in the eleventh and twelfth centuries, the Buddhists were perceived as joining forces with the Muslims. The orthodox were before an explosive mixture of loss of political power caused by the Islamic conquest and of radical anti-caste positions adopted by the Vajrayānists. This thwarted their centuries-long effort to establish full control over society. To eliminate Muslim power was impossible, but getting rid of the Buddhists and leaving the outcastes without political representation was feasible, and this is what happened. The most crucial facts took place in northern India, but what remained of the Buddhist élites in the rest of the country was equally beheaded.

Not considering the explanations provided by the most indulgent forms of Orientalism, the poor understanding of the long crisis and final downfall of Indian Buddhism depends on the tendency of projecting into early medieval and medieval India the hegemony over society that in actual reality the brāhmaṇas acquired very slowly and with great difficulty. The establishment of the 'state society', as it has become customary to call it, was a long, difficult process. Even in south India, the brāhmaṇas did not dominate society until a relatively late period. There were, in fact, a large number of peasant settlements of non-brāhmaṇas, individual landowners, military lords and old locality chiefs.[25] The new agrarian order was imposed, as documented by several copper-plate records and stone inscriptions, by either subjecting the pre-existing peasantry or replacing them by new peasant settlers,[26] and it would be naïve to believe that this happened without conflict. The new order was based on a more efficient management of landed-property and was provided with an ad hoc ideology.[27] It inevitably entailed the suppression of the Buddhists and Jains or the restructuring of their institutions. What took place from the mid-seventh century onwards was an extremely serious and long conflict, if progressively limited to the regions where the Buddhists showed themselves capable of hegemonising the strong resistance of the threatened natives and the have-nots. '*Varṇa* state society' would be a better expression than 'state society'. The latter expression ultimately implies that only one model of state and society was proposed in India, and this does not correspond to the dynamics of the Indian middle age. Brahmanism and caste system, rather than 'feudalism' are a better guidance to understanding the process by which the hierarchic structure of Indian society was held together, with some classes producing use value and some other classes appropriating and distributing the surplus among themselves. This is the reason why I prefer to draw attention on the slow but relentless acquisition of power by the brāhmaṇas, regardless of the nature of the 'feudal' relationship between a 'culture' and a 'periphery'.

It would be both difficult and misguiding to present the evidence in chronological order, not so much because the chronology of individual facts is, at times, uncertain, but because the logic of events is better understood if separate sets of evidence are examined. Within each set, facts repeat themselves with striking regularity, which betrays the slowness of Brahmanical normalisation and the presence of a permanently unsolved social question.

The evidence comes from written and archaeological sources, as well as by the subtle testimony of iconography. Literary sources are often plain-spoken, and there are plenty of them in the south: the difference between the majority of Sanskrit Purāṇas and such a work as the *Periya Purāṇam* (a poem on the lives of the Nāyaṉmār resorting to a narrative technique close to that employed in the hagiographic accounts of Christian saints), is very great. There are also a number of chronicles and tales reporting facts lacking Rankean status and resorting to stratified literary clichés. Their distance in time and space, and their being written in different languages is not, *per se*, a reason to consider them independent, one from the other and relating to separate events. They are the work of literate brāhmaṇas who, though settled in different parts of India, were bound together not only by the bonds of caste and faith but by what could be called the perception of forming a nation, if we attribute to this term one of its pre-modern meanings. Yet it would be difficult to question their fundamental veracity, even when they resort to repetitive *tópoi*, supernatural intervention, etc. They often contain informative details, and their repetitiveness betrays, once again, the existence of unsolved problems dragging on for centuries.

As to the hagiographical material, we still lack a clear picture, not to speak of easily available editions and translations; in particular, we still lack a methodology in dealing with them, especially as regards the possibility of seeing through the grain a series of stratified events. To make my point clear, I will take an example from the Tamil literature, which lies on relatively firmer grounds. It regards the chain of the developing hagiographic tradition regarding the Nāyaṉmār. In the first place, we have the material contained in the *Tēvāram* hymns, then Cuntaramūrtti Nāyaṉar's *Tiruttoṇṭar Tokai* ('*The Roll of the Holy Servants* [*of Śiva*]), which gives a short account of their lives (Cuntaramūrtti is the sixty-third Nāyaṉār). This work is the primary source of Nampi Āṇṭār Nampi's *Tiruttoṇṭar Tiruvantāti* (*The Holy* antāti *of the Holy Servants*), composed between AD 870 and 1118.Finally, we have Cēkkiḻār's *Periya Purāṇam*, written in the second quarter of the twelfth century.[28] If we had at our disposal only Cēkkiḻār's work, we would be inclined to believe that the events narrated in the *Periya Purāṇam* are the result of a late discourse, but it is not so, despite the fact that 'Cēkkiḻār is entirely incorporated into the *Tēvāram* and nobody after him has been able to read it except through him'.[29] The hymns written by the first three Nāyaṉmār, which seem to have been chanted in temples as early as the second half of the ninth century,[30] show that they were instrumental in the suppression of the *śramaṇa*-s. So steep is, in fact, the relationship between the *Tēvāram* hymns and the *sthala*-s, of which they give a sort of inventory, that '[t]he sense of the earth appropriated in the service of Śiva' may be considered a structural feature.[31] We face here the modalities of Brahmanical settlement, which implied violence. Considering these facts, we must be cautious in rejecting *all* the traditions regarding Śaṅkara and the other opponents of the Buddhists, or in considering them a mirror of exclusively late events and constructs, as is now often maintained. A balanced evaluation of the relevant material is, I think, necessary if we do not want simply to overturn the positions of nineteenth-century scholars,[32] often inclined to trust the hagiographical material *ad litteram*.

Things are easier with the epigraphic sources, after their exuberance is thinned and their metaphors and allegories are unveiled (this is often far from simple, but can be done to an extent): fortunately for us, many of them are dated or datable. Archaeological sources in a proper sense are rare: the Indian middle age is an archaeological blank. However, they are supplemented by the analysis of monuments, an extremely rewarding study matching the importance of iconographic analysis. The transformations to which monuments have been subject through time is revealing, little studied details (they are plenty) often being crucial.

THE LOGICIANS AND THE RIFT IN THE *BRĀHMAṆAVARṆA*

Chapter III closed with the death of Harṣavardhana, though not in compliance with the thesis that his reign constituted the last stage of India's classical age. We have rather emphasised the deep discontinuity that exists between his policy and that of the Guptas, and if his death marked the end of an epoch, it was so because it meant the impossibility for any Buddhist power or institution to be established without some form of Brahmanical control, with the exception of north-eastern India.

It seems appropriate to resume the discussion where it was left by past scholars and take up old issues fallen into oblivion. We can better assess the traditions associated with Kumārila Bhaṭṭa and be more accurate than the nineteenth-century scholars who first quoted the texts which provide evidence of the qualitative leap that the most important exponent of the *Pūrvamīmāṃsā* is said to have caused anti-Buddhist positions to make. To this end, it is necessary to reconsider the nature and impact of the doctrinal controversies that for centuries were a crucial test for the affirmation of one system over another. The subject is familiar to the students of philosophy, especially to epistemologists, but the historical dynamics of the public debates that frequently took place in appointed places have not thus far been highlighted. Historians have considered the question extraneous to their interests, but wrongly so.

Debates have a long tradition in India, and their animosity is known from early times, as shown by a passage of the *Aṅguttara Nikāya* where the Kālāmas of Kesaputta confessed that great was their confusion:

> Sir, certain recluses and brāhmins come to Kesaputta. As to their own view, they proclaim and expound it in full: but as to the view of others, they abuse it, revile it, depreciate and cripple it. Moreover, sir, other recluses and brāhmins, on coming to Kesaputta, do likewise.[33]

Public debates gained full acceptance when it was agreed upon that reasoning could not be opposed to the injunctions of the Veda,[34] and, we may add, when the theistic instances were made to converge into Vedic orthodoxy. The Vaibhāṣika, Sautrāntika, Vijñānavāda and Śūnyavāda schools were the object of a continuous, relentless critique,[35] but until the seventh-eighth century, and occasionally later, Buddhist logicians took part in public contests in opposition to both *vaidika* and theistic controversialists on an equal footing. The situation became serious when the theistic discriminating factor was introduced and acquired importance. Doctrinal debates became hot political issues, and the very development of Buddhist logic and Brahmanical critique can be construed as functions of the political confrontation characterising the Indian scene. That the stake was political can be deduced from a passage of Yijing, who arrived in India by sea in AD 673. Buddhist controversialists, after studying at Nālandā or in Valabhī and 'discuss[ing] possible and impossible doctrines', acquired confidence in themselves, and

> [t]o try the sharpness of their wit, they proceed to the king's court to lay down before it the sharp weapon (of their abilities); there they present their schemes and show their (*political*) talent, seeking to be appointed in the practical government. When they are present in the House of Debate, they raise their seat and seek to prove their wonderful cleverness.
>
> When they are refuting heretic doctrines all their opponents become tongue-tied and acknowledge themselves undone.[36]

Yijing describes exactly what Kumārila is reported to have maintained: that the Buddhist teachers with their own following used to propitiate kings and through them persuade people to accept Buddhism and discard the Vedic faith.[37] This seems to have been the role of such an authority as Nāgārjuna.[38] Xuanzang's account of the dispute between the Bodhisattva Guṇamati and Mādhava, a follower of the Sāṃkhya system – unreliable as it may be in relation to the actual protagonists of the story – shows the decisive role played by the king of Magadha in securing the victory to the Buddhists.[39] Diṅnāga (*c.* AD 480-530 or 540),[40] besides acquiring the fame of being an invincible controversialist (he was known as *tarka puṅgava*, 'a bull in discussion')[41] both in relation to the exponents of the other Buddhist schools[42] and to orthodox opponents,[43] had succeeded, in the south, in having 'most of the damaged centres of the Doctrine established by the earlier *ācārya*-s' reconstructed.[44] While the latter piece of information implies that destructions had previously taken place, pro-Buddhist patrons must have backed Diṅnāga's victory and implemented the reconstruction work. It is not important for us to establish whether the facts handed down really relate to Diṅnāga: they refer to a time when the Buddhists were still able, in the South, to buy their positions back with the decisive support of a king.

The pan-Indian arena where the *vādin*-s met has nothing in common with the set of Raphael's *School of Athens*, the conscious or unconscious model of philosophical discussion in the West. It was rather a set instrumental to an epoch-making transformation of Indian society, and it has been recognised that debates were not conducted with the aim of arriving at the truth, but in order to inflict a defeat on the opponents.[45] That they were staged 'as a form of entertainment',[46] should not make us forget that they were a very serious matter, which involved a radical change in the religious life of a given territory: in fact, the losers were compelled to renounce their religion or quit. Detailed rules had to be followed in the discussion, and the debates, which lasted for weeks or even months, could be either peaceful (*sandhāya*) or hostile (*vigṛhya*), and the assembly where they took place could be indifferent to the parties or committed to one side.[47] For certain aspects, these debates were similar to the disputations, questions and quodlibetal questions that took place very frequently in medieval Europe between the representatives of the most various philosophical schools, especially but not exclusively in universities.

In particular, they resemble, for the great crowd of people participating in them and watching, the solemn quodlibetal questions that were held twice a year, before Easter and before Christmas. For other aspects, however, they rather recall the trials of heretics, theatrically staged as public entertainments, that by late Roman antiquity had become ritualised and were not simply theological debates but legal trials.[48] The legal dimension of Indian debates eludes us, but as in late Roman antiquity we see the judicial experience appropriated by the bishops and an increasing overlapping of civil court and ecclesiastical court,[49] in India we see the judiciary pass under the control of the theistic movements.

The stakes must have already appeared high in Gupta times, when Vāṭsyāyana, the author of the *Nyāyabhāṣya*, criticised Nāgārjuna and, significantly, started clarifying the theistic doctrine of the early Nyāya *sūtra*-s,[50] thus acquiring the status of major representative of Gupta ideology. Uḍḍyoṭakara, author of the *Nyāyavārttika*, attacked Vasubandhu, Nāgārjuna and Diṅnāga,[51] but by the end of the sixth century or in the early seventh century, the political climate in northern and central India was still not always favourable to the orthodox. The brāhmaṇas still had to learn a lot from the Buddhists before being able, '[going] across the Vedas' – as we read in the *Mañjuśrīmūlakalpa* – to go round all over the country for controverting and exporting this technique 'over all the three Oceans', namely South-East Asia, engaging themselves in controversies.[52] The Buddhists were accused of not making any distinction between a logical argument and a tricky disputation: they used the term *vāda* to denote both these forms of argument.[53] However, as we know from the *Saddharmapuṇḍarīka Sūtra,* quoted in the earlier chapter, they were not the only ones to falsify the cards, and the brāhmaṇas did not behave differently.

After the death of Harṣavardhana, things started changing precisely with Kumārila Bhaṭṭa, who was more than a philosopher, as has been said.[54] He lived between *c.* AD 625 and 675,[55] or perhaps a little earlier, and in the first part of his life he studied for twelve years with various heterodox *guru*-s. Tradition has it that he betrayed his real beliefs protesting against his Buddhist teacher who ridiculed the Vedas, and his companions threw him headlong from the third floor of the residence where they lived.[56] The tradition of Kumārila having studied with a Buddhist *guru* sounds authentic on behalf of the fact that it would have been impossible for him, as has been noted, to learn such a text as the *Pramāṇasamuccaya* of Diṅnāga without the assistance of a Buddhist teacher:[57] the elliptical style of this extremely difficult work is typical of inner-directed groups. Only some centuries later were philosophical ideas set forth in an exposition that a general reader might understand.[58] This we should keep in mind if we want to understand what lies behind the seemingly naïve stories we will mention below.

As the tradition of Kumārila's suicide seems to imply, he probably was one of those extremely talented young brāhmaṇas looking for self-affirmation who soon after Harṣavardhana's death were quick to understand that Buddhism had no future and did not hesitate to put their knowledge at the service of rulers who were willing to enforce orthodox rule to the detriment of Buddhist political fortunes. Śaṅkara – or the tradition associated with him – recognised Kumārila 'as an incarnation of Guha born for the eradication of [the] Buddhists'.[59]

Kumārila's battle for the establishment of *apauruṣeyatā*, the non-human character of Vedic revelation, and *vedamūlatā*, the root-ness of the Veda, which certifies the orthodoxy of neo-Brahmanical positions, is rooted in a deep hostility towards Buddhism.[60] The Buddha, an irreligious man, taught practices opposed to the injunctions laid down in the Veda 'to the deluded men of the lowest caste'. As a kṣatriya, he was not entitled to impart any teaching and transgressed his own duties 'tak[ing] up the duties of the Brāhmaṇa'.[61] Leadership in society pertains *naturaliter* to the brāhmaṇas, and brāhmaṇa-ness is recognised by means of direct sense-perception handed down by an unbroken line of tradition.[62] Here Kumārila exerted tremendous pressure on the apostate brāhmaṇas (that is, all the possible contenders in public debates), who had accepted to defend and promote a teaching which was illegal and/or antinomial at its very root.

The most famous story regarding Kumārila's zeal in spreading orthodoxy is preserved in Mādhava's *Śaṅkara Digvijaya*.[63] An ordeal took place at the presence of King Sudhanvan, a supporter of the Buddhists who ruled in Dvārakā (Dwarka).[64] In a public controversy, Kumārila had defeated the Buddhists (compared to 'excited snakes trampled upon by a pedestrian' when they were addressed by the *bhaṭṭa*),[65] but the king, still unconvinced by his arguments, challenged the contenders 'to jump down unhurt from the top of yonder mountain', which Kumārila did without being hurt.[66] His adversaries claimed that he had saved his life thanks to his magical powers, so that Sudhanvan resorted to a variant of the pot-cum-snake ordeal, maintaining that he would inflict capital punishment on the party that failed it. Kumārila got through the test recognising Viṣṇu Anantaśayana in the cobra concealed in the vessel. A divine disembodied voice urged the king to carry out his promise, and he ordered his people that those who would not kill the Buddhists, including old men and children, from the bridge of Rāma to the Himalaya should be killed in turn.[67]

It is difficult to see Kumārila as a devout Bhāgavata, and there is little doubt that the story handed down to us was adjusted to meet later developments. Moreover, no king in the second half of the seventh century had the power to have a similar order obeyed. What is interesting for us to note, however, is that the order was not simply to oblige the heretics to leave the country, as was customary, but to have them killed. This detail appears in all the versions of the story. Kumārila's former *guru*, Sugata, was among the heretics sentenced to death, and was crushed in an oil-mill. Although Kumārila was only indirectly responsible for his death, the remorse for having caused the death of his *guru*, an extremely serious sin, led him to commit suicide. It took place at Ruddhapura/Rudrapura, a suburb of Prayāga,[68] allegedly in the presence of Śaṅkara.[69] There is nothing hagiographic in this tradition of Kumārila's suicide.

Kumārila's role in silencing the heretics is emphasised in other hagiographies, notably in Anantānandagiri's *Śaṅkaravijaya*,[70] who reports the exploits of the *bhaṭṭa* who came from the North:[71]

> He defeated countless Buddhists and Jains by means of different types of arguments in the various sciences. Having cut off their heads with axes, he threw them down into numerous wooden mortars and made a powder of them by whirling around a pestle. In this way he was fearlessly carrying out the destruction of those who held evil doctrines.[72]

The fact that the events related to Kumārila's life are all contained in the hagiographies of Śaṅkara (and, as regards the Buddhist side, in the sources used by Tāranātha) obliges us to be cautious and make the appropriate distinctions. The story of the pot-cum-snake ordeal sounds spurious when referred to the great polemicist, not to mention the ordeal of the jump from the cliff, but the tradition of Kumārila's suicide is unique and not easy to be dismissed as either a biased detail or a later interpolation.

In any case, debates appear to have been increasingly associated with ordeals, which were administered to the defendant.[73] There were clauses protecting the brāhmaṇas from the riskiest ones, such as the poison ordeal. As already said, the ordeals were run by the king or the judge appointed by him, and the place varied according to the caste of the defendant. It is not always clear which procedures were followed. P.V. Kane observes that the procedures of the water, fire and weight ordeals cited in Xuanzang's *Xiyuji* do not agree in several respects with the descriptions of the *smṛti*-s and digests, and that the poison ordeal described by the Chinese pilgrim has nothing in common with the *smṛti* poison ordeal.[74]

Since we know that the losers underwent punishment (leaving the territory, or even the death penalty), we must conclude that they were regarded as a judicial procedure, which in fact occurred only in the courts of kings and judges.[75] It remains to be determined whether these debates-ordeals took place after a formal plaint or, as it seems more likely, they were what may be called 'restorative ordeals'. In this case, those who were believed to have committed some wrongdoing, arranged for themselves to undergo an ordeal in order to test their innocence and restore their social priority status. This is, I think, the case which best suits our evidence. It should be added that *ānvīkṣikī*, the science of inferential reasoning, central to the doctrinal controversies, was not connected to philosophy, but pertained to the domain of *nītiśāstra* and *rājadharma*,[76] thus being strictly related to kingship. Finally, as regards the punishments inflicted upon the Buddhists, if our un-Rankean sources make us believe that they reflect twelfth- and early thirteenth-century events, there is other evidence, both literary and iconographical, as well as archaeological, advising us not to take them as simply reporting facts of the last hour. They describe late events that stratify on earlier facts of the same nature.

The numerous stories about this or that controversialist making his way into the opposite camp to steal the dialectical secrets of his opponents may not be as anedoctal as they seem at first when we become familiar with the historical context of which these accounts are a distant echo. Tāranātha reports that Kumārila defied Dharmakīrti (*c*. AD 600-60) after the latter had won the favour of a king: 'He demanded of the king, "Should I be victorious, Dharmakīrti is to be killed. If Dharmakīrti be victorious, I should be killed" '[77] – a proposal that Dharmakīrti refused (he did not want Kumārila to die), turning to the more traditional condition that whoever was defeated should accept the doctrine of the winner. Thus Dharmakīrti went to Kumārila's *āśrama* in south India in disguise and learnt 'all the secrets of philosophy'.

Jain sources depict similar situations. The second version of the biography of Haribhadra, a Śvetāmbara Jain who lived in the eighth century, initiator of what has been called Indian doxography,[78] is worth reporting. According to the earliest account of his life, two of his disciples went to study logic at Bodhgayā in disguise, and when they were discovered,[79] their Buddhist teacher caused them to be killed. Haribhadra, stricken with grief, responded to the Buddhist violence with a suicidal depression. In the second version, one of the two disciples (here turned into Haribhadra's nephews) suggests, to escape with his life, that he debates with the Buddhists and that if he wins he be set free, if not, that he be killed: he is defeated and killed. Haribhadra responded by making a cauldron of boiling oil and magically caused not only the person directly responsible for the death of his nephews, but seven hundred Buddhists to fly through the air and land in the cauldron, where they were scalded to death.[80] Haribhadra as a persecutor of the Buddhists is probably a later development connected to the dire twelfth-century crisis, but the story, besides mirroring a logic of rigged debates and violence, shows the importance of mastering the skills of the opponents. Being defeated, as we have seen, did not simply mean to have a laurel less to boast of. It should be noted that it would have been impossible for a king to get rid of *all* the brāhmaṇas if these were the losers – although due attention must be paid to the story reported by Xuanzang, according to which Harṣa banished five hundred brāhmaṇas 'to the frontiers of India'[81] – but to get rid of a few hundred monks, if not in the whole kingdom, least in the territory where the debate had been held, was feasible.

The controversy between the Buddhists and the eighth-century Digambara Jain Akaḷaṅka, who brought Jain logic to the level of sophistication of Buddhist and Brahmanical *vādin*-s and became the most effectual critic of Dharmakīrti, and whose *Tattvārthavārtthika* (*Rājavārttika*) is to these days a text used by advanced Digambara students,[82] took place in the crucial eighth century. The orthodox were taking advantage of the traditional enmity between Buddhists and

Jains and used the latter against the former.[83] Akaḷaṅka defeated the Buddhists severally, also resorting – the relevant sources are not Buddhist – to unfair systems. The *Pāṇḍava Purāṇa* of Vādicandra, a Jain work of the sixteenth century, reports that on one occasion the *ācārya* could not stand up to the arguments of a Buddhist antagonist until the point when he understood that it was Māyādevī who was prompting the Buddhist from within a jar and put an end to the advantage of his adversary by kicking the jar over with his foot.[84]

A variant of this story is found in the account of the dispute reported in a Tamil manuscript of the Mackenzie collection, either derived from the *Rājāvaḷī Kathe*, a Kannada work,[85] or from the earliest recorded version of Akaḷaṅka's life history related in Prabhācandra's *Kathākośa*,[86] a Digambara work of the second half of the eleventh century. The story is set in Kāñcīpuram, where the Buddhists, who 'ruled over one-third of the country forming the Daudacaranya', had their own temples. The ruling king was Hemaśītala, who has been identified – we are in the early decades of the eighth century – with Hiraṇyavarman, father of Pallavamalla Nandivarman.[87] The identification helps us in setting the story in context and makes us understand that later amplifications fuelled by new contrapositions have a firm root in the past.

The story as narrated here supplements the account of the controversy with an antecedent fact which seems to be an independent tale, and is worth reporting because it is a vivid testimony, with several others, of the relations existing between Buddhists and Jains.

> Two persons named Acalangan and Nishcalangan produced a persecution by privately writing in a *Bauddha* book that the *Jaina* system was the best one. A device was had recourse to in order to discover the authors; and, on being discovered, they were forced to flee for their life, hotly pursued; when Nishcalangan, by sacrificing his life, contrived to allow Acalangan to escape, charging him, on succeeding to spread their system. The *Bauddhas*, in the heat of the moment had tied a piece of flesh in all the *Jaina* fanes, with a *slóca* of contemptuous import. Acalangan after his escape put a vessel containing ordure in the *Bauddha* fanes, with another *slóca* in retaliation. Under these circumstances of discord, the *rája* ordered an assembly of *Bauddha*, and *Jaina*, learned men to dispute with each other, and to finish within a specified time, when he would himself embrace the victorious system, and put all of the opposite party to death by grinding them in oil-mills.[88]

The interventions of the deities follow, and eventually Akaḷaṅka unmasks and defeats the Buddhists: 'The king in consequence declared the *Bauddhas* to be conquered, to which they were compelled to accede', and Akaḷaṅka became the king's instructor. What really happened after Akaḷaṅka's victory is not clear. According to another version of the story, 'the conquered sect he [the king] bruised to death in oil-mills of stone', even though a number of Buddhists were made to adopt Jainism and others 'went to Ceylon by sea; where their power continues'.[89] According to yet another version, some Buddhists 'were intended to be put to death in large stone-oil-mills; but instead of that were embarked on board ships, or vessels, and sent to Ceylon'.[90] Phyllis Granoff has examined a later, more detailed version of the story in an attempt at typologising the divine intervention in debates,[91] and here, too, the narrative keeps the memory of king Hemaśītala/ Hiraṇyavarman, the ruler who tipped the balance of the situation in what is apparently the story's earliest layer. The defeat of the Buddhists in Kāñcī was an epoch-making event for the Jains, and the debate is mentioned in the Sravana Belgola epitaph of Mallisena in the second half of the eleventh century. Here Akaḷaṅka speaks in the first person as the advocate of a theistic religion:

> [...] because (*I*) felt pity for those people who, having embraced Atheism, were perishing, that, in the court of the glorious king Himaśītala, I overcame all the crowds of Bauddhas, most of whom had a shrewd mind, and broke (*the image of*) Sugata with (*my*) foot.[92]

From these and other stories, we realise that the contenders are all brāhmaṇas, all have the same curriculum and all are associated with a political milieu, and yet contraposition is so sharp as to be pushed as far as death. Tāranātha provides complementary evidence of the bitterness of interpersonal relationships, a crucial fact in small communities. In his account of Diṅnāga's life, he reports the reaction of Kṛṣṇa, a brāhmaṇa whose behaviour had already been extremely hostile:

> The *ācārya* returned and, staking their respective creeds, entered into a debate. The *tīrthika* was repeatedly defeated. He [Diṅnāga] said, 'You have now to accept the Law of the Buddha.' At this, he [Kṛṣṇa] threw enchanted dust, which burnt the belongings of the *ācārya* and even the *ācārya* himself narrowly escaped the fire. The *tīrthika* fled.[93]

We must assume that the Buddhist brāhmaṇas represented social groups whose interests could neither be reconciled with the tenets of the caste-bound Mīmāṃsakas nor with those of the theistic lot. The history of debates reveals an incurable split in the *brāhmaṇavarṇa*: if a part of the brāhmaṇas could not be admitted to live in one and the same territory, it was because they represented the intellectual leadership of an incompatible social model. This has little to do with the remote cleavage between brāhmaṇas and kṣatriyas, although the latter continued to contribute to fill the ranks of the Buddhist intelligentsia.[94] It rather was a new fracture, first brought to the fore by the Kali Age literature of the Gupta period. The use of the term *tīrthika*s to indicate the orthodox is perfectly justified: at the level of leadership groups, neither Tāranātha nor the orthodox chroniclers and hagiographers would have been able to distinguish between the two parties on the basis of *varṇa*.

Now we can better explain that apparently strange, inclusive myth according to which the *asura*s are high-caste rebels whom Viṣṇu and the other gods either annihilate or convert. Viṣṇu plays both the role of the enemy of the *asura*s and that of the deluder, thus encompassing the whole reality, because the latter is made to coincide with the *brāhmaṇavarṇa*, which is one by definition. It could not be admitted that two antagonist systems had generated from it: Hiraṇyakaśipu is a high-caste demon, but cannot be entitled to rule in Indra's place.

THE LOGIC OF THE SAINTS

Kumārila and Campantar are almost contemporary, but are carriers of different, if related instances. The *vaidika* Kumārila puts an end to his life by suicide; conversely, Campantar in his works appears as a triumphant, remorseless theist. Thus the defensive battle of the Buddhists had to unfold on two levels: they were under pressure from and they had to develop arguments against different adversaries. It is no accident that the Buddhist campaign against the theism of the Naiyāyikas was started in the seventh century by Dharmakīrti, who reacted against his contemporary Uḍḍyoṭakara, a Pāśupatācārya.[95] The latter maintained that *Īśvara* is the efficient cause of the universe and introduced the concept of inferential reason (*hetu*).[96]

In Tamiḻakam, the Nāyaṉmār in the first place and then the Āḻvārs entered, with great determination, in competition with the Buddhists at the level of the political representation of the lower segments of society. The Nāyaṉmār included a certain number of śūdras and women, not to count the untouchable Nantamar. The presence in their ranks of vaiśyas and petty chieftains is equally significant.[97] In northern India, however, where the events related to King Sudhanvan are set, and where Kumārila committed suicide, the 'impenetrable gloom' of the second half of the seventh century mentioned in Chapter III stands for a rather different story. The attempts at stemming the tide of the insurgency of the outcastes, disclosed by the story of Śaṅkara meeting the *cāṇḍāla* in Kāśī,[98] were not as successful, and this eventually led to the establishment of the Pāla dynasty in the central-eastern and eastern Ganges plains.

The young brāhmaṇa Campantar, one of the most popular saints of south India, lived in the second half of the seventh century,[99] being thus a younger contemporary of Kumārila Bhaṭṭa. His exploits fit well in a political climate where the conservative positions embodied by his Sivaite faith were increasingly popular: he quickly understood that action would pay. His half-legendary life (we can hardly believe in his exploits as a child) has its *raison d'être* in Sivaite propaganda and in the fight against the *śramaṇa*-s. The conversion from Jainism to Sivaism of King Arikēsari Parāṅkusa Māravarman, who ruled between AD 670 and 720[100] and the consequent suppression of the Jains of Madurai, is the best known of Campantar's exploits, if we want to give credit to it. The story is told at length in the *Periya Purāṇam*[101] and is represented in a number of reliefs and paintings throughout Tamil Nadu.[102] Its veracity as regards the final martyrdom by impalement of the Jains, better than in any written record or figurative scene, is attested to by the re-enactment that takes place every year in Tinnevelly, Tiruchendur, Kalugumalai and Vilattikulam in southern Tamil Nadu on the occasion of the Kaluvēttal (Impalement) festival associated with the Jains:

> The model of a human head is stuck on a spike and carried in procession. To lend spirit to the performance temple servants turn out with their bodies bedaubed with black and red paint; some suspend false tongues from their mouths and coil round their bodies the intestines of a sheep, or sit as if impaled on a stake; others appear to be hanging from gibbets, or have a leg bent double and tied up to suggest that it has been cut off; others again lie in pits in the ground, showing only what pretends to be a head cut from its body. The idea of the performance is to suggest mutilation [...].[103]

Campantar's struggle against the Buddhists is less known, yet the tenth verse of every hymn he wrote contains a thorough denunciation of the Buddhists and Jains.[104] He triumphantly asserts to have caused the head of a Buddhist *vādin* to roll on the ground by the potency of a song in the course of a controversy at Bōthi Maṅgkai/Būtamaṅkalam in Cōḷamaṇṭalam, tentatively identified with the native place of the *thera* Buddhadatta.[105] The amplification of the story provided by the *Periya Purāṇam* helps us clarify what may have really happened. When Campantar, welcomed by the local Sivaites with joyful music, arrived in town, the Buddhists of Būtamaṅkalam reported the news to their elder, and

> [...] Buddha Nandi of flawed
> And hateful heart, rose up in wrath, and circled
> By the crowd of Buddhists, came before the servitors
> And roared in wrath, thus: 'Tis only after vanquishing me
> In disputation, you can blare your triumphant instruments.'[106]

When Campantar's followers came to know that the saint had accepted the challenge,

> Burst out thus with the uncontainable utterance:
> 'May the head of Buddha Nandi roll down
> Slashed by thunder winged with lightning.'
> When the command of the Lord whose banner
>
> Sports the Bull was thus pronounced,
> Like the great thunder, the peerlessly puissant
> Mantric weapon—impossible to forfend –,
> Which annihilates all troubles that beset the way
> Of Saivism, by reason of the truth-laden
> Pronouncement of the divine serviteur,
> Rent asunder the head from the body of Buddha Nandi,
> The hair-splitting logomachist that came thither;
> Witnessing this the Buddhist crowds, struck with fear,
> Ran helter-skelter and quailed.
>
> The serviteurs of Siva who witnessed the plight
> Of the Buddhists and also the head and the trunk
> Of Buddha Nandi severed by the mantric weapon
> Of words, came before the godly child—the conferrer
> Of Triumph –, and humbly narrated
> The happenings; thereupon he said: 'The Lord
> Has ruled even thus to quell the opposing obstruction;
> So, may you all chant, "Hara, Hara".'[107]

Despite the death of their elder, the Buddhists insisted on a debate to be held, though not '[...] by flawless mantric disputation,/But by disputation through words',[108] and accompanied the *vādin* Cāri Buddha to the 'choultry *maṇṭapam*' where Campantar, 'who had the head/Of Buddha Nandi pulverized' was waiting.[109] A long debate on *mokṣa* followed, which ended with the victory of Campantar. The saint observed that the omniscience of the Buddha was hollow like his *mokṣa*, and so were 'the works in this connection'.[110] The Buddhists '[t]hat became clarified in their mind-heart/Neared the Sacred Brahmin child of Sanbai/And adored his roseate feet', and 'fell down prostrate before him and rose up/As Saivites', celestial flowers raining everywhere.[111]

Heads do not roll down by the potency of a *mantra*, and the story is transparent. The Sivaite crowd that welcomed Campantar caused the death of the Buddhist elder through an intimidatory act in order to condition the debate and preventively put the Buddhists with their backs to the wall. Nothing was left for them to do but to convert to Sivaism, and our thoughts go to an eighth-century relief from Tiruvalanjuli depicting two converts worshipping Śiva now in the Thanjavur Art Gallery.[112] Intimidations and preventive acts took place to avoid an open fight or a massacre.[113]

The south was largely Sivaite in the seventh century. Pāśupatas and Kāpālikas appear as important components of Kāñcī religious and social life in the *Mattavilāsa*, the play composed by the Pallava king Mahendravarman I (AD 571-630),[114] and Appar, the convert from Jainism and spiritual guide of Campantar, testifies that in the streets of Tiruvārūr, one could see 'Virati ascetics with matted hair,/brahmins and Śaivas,/Pāśupatas and men of the Kāpālika sect'.[115] The Kāpālikas, who in Kāñcī[116] presided over the Ekāmbiranātha Temple, seem to have originated in the south,[117] and in point of fact Śiva, in Appar's hymns, is very often depicted as wearing a garland of skulls and bearing a skull bow, and even as '[h]olding a garland of dead men's skulls in His hands', being thus seen in his *vāma* aspect of Bhairava.[118] The identification of these 'dead men' with the heretics is inevitable. We read, in fact, of the triumphant entry of Śiva in Valampuram (hence Tiruvalampuram), to the south of Chidambaram, 'whose streets are rich/In cloud-capped mansions', and which we may picture as a village only partly inhabited by Sivaite devotees like Campantar's Būtamaṅkalam. Here Śiva

Caused the huge heads of the warring Rakshasa
To fall on dust. Our Lord, the Lofty One gently pressed
His beauteous toes and crushed his heads and then
Graced Him [...][119]

The multi-headed Heresy, allegorised as a *rākṣasa*, is violently put with its back against the wall, and has to compromise. The followers of Śiva (the god in this hymn is described as 'ash-bedaubed' and '[s]urrounded by His Bhoota-Hosts')[120] have suppressed and intimidated the adversaries and have enthroned Śiva in the new temple. In this case, too, we are not dealing with dubious hagiographic material, although we can always suspect Appar's hymns to have been given their present form relatively later.

Although in the eighth-century Tamil Nadu Brahmanical power, in both its Sivaite and Vishnuite variants, was firmly established (the evidence from Kāñcīpuram is particularly strong), social resistance was still vigorous in places even in the ninth century, as is shown by the anti-Buddhist exploits of the brāhmaṇa Māṇikkavācakar (*c.* AD 862-85), author of the *Tiruvācakam*. The *Tiruvatāvūrar Purāṇam*,[121] which in the sixth canto gives a detailed account of his disputations with the Buddhists, reports that the saint, being unable to convince them in a great debate organised at Chidambaram, where the king of Laṅkā had come with his chief priest, resorted to his miraculous powers, first striking dumb the priest, and then making the king's dumb daughter to speak.[122]

According to the *Tiruviḷaiyāṭar Purāṇam*, the debate between the Sivaites and the Buddhists at Tillai (Chidambaram) was organised with the understanding that it would last a week. It was Śiva himself who, appearing to Māṇikkavācakar in the night, convinced the saint to take part in the debate. The following morning, Māṇikkavācakar went to the hall where the Buddhists were assembled, and asked them to speak about their God, their sacred book and the destiny waiting for those who followed their principles. The Buddhists discussed resorting to evidence and inference, but Māṇikkavācakar proved that not all their arguments were founded on evidence, and that they had lost. The Buddhists requested him to show his God by means of the evidence, but the saint observed that '[i]t is not possible to make a blind man see the shining sun. Our God is above everything. He only is visible to those who put themselves to his service, besmeared with ashes'. The Buddhists requested at least to establish, based on evidence, the relationship existing between Śiva and the ash, and agreed upon being grinded in an oil-mill if such a proof was given. Māṇikkavācakar took some dried cow-dung, put it in the fire and heated it. When it turned red, he took it out of the fire and showing it to the Buddhists said: 'The glittering body of our Śiva and the ash he is besmeared with are like this cow-dung reddened on fire and the ash layer covering it.'[123] Unable to counter this evidence, the Buddhists lost their cause, and the Cōḷa king who supported them, after the miracle performed by the saint who caused his dumb daughter to sing the praises of Śiva, made the Buddhists to serve the sentence they had previously accepted.[124]

By the end of the eighth century, the turn of the screw was felt in Koṅgu Nadu and Kerala, where the brāhmaṇas who had settled in the country developed into an organised, powerful community enjoying the patronage of the state.[125] The Nampūtiri brāhmaṇas, keepers of the Śrauta traditions and of the tenets of the *Pūrvamīmāṃsā*, are the best-known example of conservative orthodoxy. The brahmanisation of the country was given its myth of origin in the extermination of the kṣatriyas carried out by Paraśurāma and the resulting distribution of lands to the brāhmaṇas by the violent hero-god – a myth re-actualised in Purāṇic Brahmanism so as to sanctify the battle against the rulers who did not conform to Brahmanical order. The myth, which we will examine in the next chapter, was made to combine with the story of King Cēramāṉ Perumāḷ who after a debate at Trikkariyur, had the tongues of the Buddhists cut, as already reported in Chapter I. The Perumāḷs were a local lineage of kings who had been given kṣatriya status by the brāhmaṇas and who, at least from a certain period onwards, became staunch supporters of Brahmanism. The king of the story is probably to be identified with the eighth-century Cēramāṉ Perumāḷ of Makōtai (modern Kodungallur) in the Cēra country, known as the author of literary works.[126]

From this and the preceding evidence, the successful attempt of the brāhmaṇas to replace the *śramaṇa*-s at the court and play an undisputed political role emerges with great clarity. Conversions to Sivaism followed one another, not without difficulties at first.[127] The brāhmaṇas had perfectly understood the structural relationship between the king, the *saṃgha* and the laity, and every effort was made to undermine it. The following is a Kannada tale curiously reversing the story of the fourth Nāyaṉār, Meipporuḻ:

Mēporul-Nāyanār, a king or chief of the Lāda country, long waged war, unsuccessfully, with a Bauddha-raja: at length he took advice from Śaiva votaries; and, at their suggestion, disguised himself as a Śaiva ascetic, and with a Tambiran, went to the palace of the Bauddha king with a book in his hand. The king came out to meet him, and asked him what he wanted, to which the reply was that he came to teach him the contents of the book, and that if allowed to enter inside the palace, he would do so. Leave was granted, and, putting the book into the hands of the king, he told him to read; while the latter was doing so, the disguised chief took out a knife, and cut the king's throat. An alarm arose in the palace; and the Lāda chief prevailed on the warder of the palace to allow the Tambiran to escape out of the bounds of the country, before he should lose his own life. The god is represented as being pleased at this affair; and, appearing on his bullock-vehicle, gave tokens of favour, and beatitude to the said Mēporul-Nāyanār.[128]

Any discussion on the role played by the saints or philosophers-saints in the eradication of Buddhism would be incomplete without mentioning Śaṅkarācārya, but the deeds attributed to him are so many that it would be impossible to give an even sketchy presentation of the questions involved, and the reader is referred to the scattered reference we shall make of his deeds in this and the next chapter. Here we limit ourselves to recall a passage of Tāranātha, which demonstrates that his fame as eradicator of the heretics has not only been handed down by Hindu texts and oral tradition, which may have had all the interest in expanding the extent of his triumphs over the *śramaṇa*-s, but also by the Buddhists. Tāranātha, though emphasising Buddhist victories and the malice of the adversaries, recognises the superiority of orthodox *vādin*-s in a number of cases. The Lama recalls the distant events that took place in the south and seriously jeopardised the existence of the Law observing that, after a series of defeats suffered in debates with Kumārila and another brāhmaṇa which he calls Kaṇataroru, '[…] there were many incidents of the property and followers of the insiders being robbed by the *tīrthika*-s *brāhmaṇa*-s'.[129] In connection to a debate where Śaṅkara himself is told to have accepted the challenge of some young, unwise Buddhist *vādin*-s of a monastery in Bengal, the Lama says that 'the Buddhists were defeated and, as a result, everything belonging to the twentyfive centres of the Doctrine was lost to the *tīrthika*-s and the centres were deserted. About five hundred *upāsaka*-s had to enter the path of the *tīrthika*-s.'[130]

Doctrinal debates continued to be held long after the period considered in this section (seventh to ninth century). In the following chapters, we will give some more examples of debates that had become mere excuses to get rid of the opponents.

ELEPHANT HUNTING AND BEHEADING

Kumārila Bhaṭṭa was known as the Lion's Roar of Brahmanical learning,[131] an appropriation of the ancient Lion's Roar expounding the *Buddhavacana* from atop the Aśokan pillars and of the image of the teaching imparted by the learned Buddhists.[132] Kumārila's association with the lion is not simply a rhetorical expression, but is connected to his deep enmity towards the Buddhists, who were often mockingly called 'elephants' from – presumably – the form the Buddha had assumed to enter the womb of Māyādevī. Lions are the natural enemies of elephants, which they seize by the throat jumping on their back. In the *Śaṅkara Digvijaya* we read that 'When the elephants of Jaina and Buddhist heretics disappeared because of the roaming lion of Kumarila, the tree of Vedic wisdom began to spread everywhere with luxuriant foliage.'[133]

In the epigraphic record of medieval India, the equation Buddhists-elephants is common and explicit. At Raṇipadra (Ranod, in Shivpuri district of Madhya Pradesh; Map 3), an inscription datable to the end of the tenth or the beginning of the eleventh century accounting for the lineage of the Maṭṭamayūra ascetics of the now deserted but still standing *maṭha*, compares the Śākyas to elephants, and the Jains to jackals.[134] In Karnataka, we have both Brahmanical and Digambara Jain inscriptions attesting to this equivalence in the context of the new series of attacks against the Buddhists which took place in the eleventh and twelfth century. In an inscription from the Belur district of AD 1136, a Jain 'emperor of logicians', Vādībhasiṃha, is described as 'a lion to the elephant disputants'.[135] In an inscription from Sravana Belgola of AD 1100, Yaśakīrti, brother of the *guru* Vāsavacandra, is defined as 'the splitter of the frontal globes of the elephants, the Bauddha and other disputants'.[136] In an epigraph of AD 1163, a Digambara Jain *guru* is called 'destroyer of the rutting elephant the indomitable Bauddha',[137] the 'elephant(s) in rut' being a frequent, derogatory expression that, when applied to the Buddhists, is perhaps meant to stigmatise their immoral behaviour.

The best-known symbol of elephant hunting and killing in Purāṇic literature and figurative art is, easily, the Gajāsurasaṃhāramūrti of Śiva.[138] The myth is set in Benares, and is concisely narrated in the *Kūrma Purāṇa* in relation to the Kṛttivāseśvara Liṅga, the *liṅga* of the Lord who is clad in the garment of the skin:

Formerly a Daitya assumed the form of an elephant in this place and came near Bhava (Śiva) to kill those Brāhmaṇas who worship the Lord here everyday. O Excellent Brāhmaṇas, in order to protect those devotees, the three-eyed Mahādeva, favourably disposed to the devotees, appeared out of the Liṅga. Contemptuously Hara killed the Daitya of the form of an elephant with his trident. Its hide he made his robe. Hence the lord is Kṛttivāseśvara.[139]

Here the myth allegorises the clash between the Sivaite devotees and the *śramaṇa*-s, whose elder, the elephant, was killed as an intimidatory act aimed at dispersing his followers. An analysis of the myth at the symbolic level leads us to the same conclusion: the *gajāsura* is slain by Śiva at the beginning of his cosmic dance because the god has to remove all obstruction to the dance, the hide of the elephant being 'the symbol of covering and limitation (*āvaraṇa*) which on the plane of matter is known as *charman* and on the level of Praṇa or the life-force is known as *śarman*'.[140] The Buddhists-elephants are the major obstruction to the complete affirmation of Śiva, and they must be removed, or made to submit. Campantar, as early as the second half of the seventh century, clears up all doubts. In one of his hymns he says:

Those Buddhists and mad Jains may slander speak.
Such speech befits the wand'rers from the way.
But he who came to earth and begged for alms,
He is the thief who stole my heart away.
The raging elephant charged down at him;
O marvel! He but took and wore his hide;[141]

The association between the elephant killed by Śiva and the 'elephant of rut' of the epigraphic record is established in the hymns of Cuntarar, the great eighth-century Nāyaṉār. Ārūrar speaks of 'the elephant of the oozing must', of 'the black colour of the oozing must' and of 'the intoxication and pride of the elephant, thanks to this oozing'. The elephant is 'monstrous, fierce and big', and nobody 'could prevent its onslaught on the universe' before Śiva's exploit.[142] The use of sexual metaphors to describe the Buddhists and their behaviour seems thus to be rather early, antedating the epigraphic evidence.

The sections of the *Kūrma Purāṇa* dealing with *śivaliṅga*-s and the glorification of Benares[143] are additions of the Pāśupatas and do not seem to be earlier than AD 700,[144] but Campantar's verses may persuade us that the myth was already well known. Kāśī, like many towns which had known a spectacular growth in the first and second centuries AD, had been transformed – like Mathurā, Ujjayinī, Prayāga, and a number of other capital-multiplier towns – into a major *tīrtha*, the Pāśupatas being the most active promoters of this transformation.[145] Kāśī became a centre under strict Sivaite control. The scant amount of information on ancient Benares remarked in the preceding chapter becomes even scantier, and I know of no iconographic evidence that can help us to detail the formation of a myth that seems to have originated there. However, the distribution pattern of the myth in both its literary and iconographic form shows that events similar to those that took place in Benares were common. The myth is depicted, among many other places, in that sculptural *summa* of Śiva's exploits that is the eighth-century Cave XVI of Ellora.[146] In Tamil Nadu, it is narrated in the Sivaite *āgama*-s,[147] and here Śiva's destructive act retains a protracted potential of historical violence. Valuvur, a neighbourhood of Buddhist Nagapattinam,[148] is the reputed place of the killing of Gajāsura, and the exceptional Cōḷa bronze of Gajahāmūrti kept in the Vīrattēśvara Temple,[149] testifies to an event that saw one or more 'elephants' killed and Śaivaism established unopposed.[150]

The semantic ambiguity of figurative art makes an interpretation at the historical-political level convincing when other data are integrated in the discourse, and makes of it, in turn, a primary source of information when other data are wanting. The task is difficult in relation to aniconic imagery. The antinomy lions-elephants, or *vyāla*-s elephants, falls within the case of extremely ambiguous signifiers. The rampart lions attached to the bases of the pilasters decorating the angles of the main shrine of the Tālagirīśvara Temple at Panamalai, built by the Pallava king Narasiṃhavarman II (AD 700-28) are crushing the heads of small recumbent elephants, and the interposed inscribed band extols the king as 'vanquisher of the elephants'.[151] Are the elephants simply vanquished political enemies? In his inscription in the Rājasiṃheśvara Temple of the Kailāsanātha compound at Kāñcīpuram, the Pallava emperor, known as Rājasiṃha, after recalling that Puruṣottama (Viṣṇu) 'was born to rescue from the ocean of sin the sinking people, who were swallowed by the horrid monster, (*called*) the *Kali* age!',[152] defines himself 'that pious king of kings, who made all quarters obedient to his orders and who proved a royal lion [Rājasiṃha] to the dense troops of the elephants of his daring foes!'[153] The reference to the Kali Age convinces us to follow a precise track, especially when, among the panels showing Śiva triumphing over defeated *asura*-s and framed upon elephants heads, we see Śiva in his aspect of *yogin* seated under a tree in company of a couple of deer disturbingly similar to those of the Buddha's first sermon;[154] the elephant head below being a cut-off head (Fig. 3).[155]

The Vaikuṇṭha Perumāḷ Temple, built by Nandivarman II Pallavamalla (*c.* AD 730-95)[156] in the second half of the eighth century, is in accord with the prescriptions of the *Pāñcarātra Āgama*,[157] the Bhāgavatas having replaced the Sivaites in the court of Kāñcī. As in the Kailāsanātha temple, from the outer walls of both the *garbhagṛha* and the *maṇḍapa*, decorated with niches and a variety of images, protrude a long series of large-size, fierce rampant lions – technically, *vyālapāda* pilasters[158] – which seem to have the function of defending the place from the outside. This impression is strongly enhanced by the row of *vyālapāda* pillars of the *mālikā* cloister enclosing the temple, the back walls of which display the reliefs depicting the historical events related to the Pallava dynasty and to Nandivarman II.[159] Walking in the space between, the visitor is snarled at from both sides.[160]

Pallavamalla was a resolute persecutor of *śramaṇa*-s, and the evidence brought forward by Cadambi Minakshi with regard to the Buddhists is worth reporting. A panel in the western part of the cloister, to the right of the entrance, shows two men being impaled, the king sitting in a pavilion where judgement has been delivered (Fig. 4). They cannot be mistaken as ordinary criminals (impalement was customary in south India until the Vijayanagara period)[161] because the relief is located in the midst of other panels that have a bearing on the religious policy of the king. The panel to the right displays an Āḻvār (probably one the first three Āḻvārs) and a shrine resembling the Vaikuṇṭha Perumāḷ, the series being preceded by an image of Viṣṇu, arguably that installed in the temple. Minakshi observes that 'this row of panels represents nothing less than the establishment of Vaiṣṇavism on the destruction of the heretics'.[162] The Āḻvārs, particularly Tirumaṅkai and Toṇṭaraṭippoṭi, went very far in their anxiety to get

Figure 3: Śiva as *yogin* on cut-off elephant head.
Kāñcīpuram, Kailāśanātha Temple.

Figure 4: Pallavamalla Nandivarman II delivering judgement and impalement of Buddhists. Kāñcīpuram, Vaikuṇṭha Perumāḷ Temple.

rid of the *śramaṇa*-s and condition the policy of the rulers. Toṇṭaraṭippoṭi, who was born in a family of brāhmaṇas near Kumpakōṇam/ Kumbakonam in AD 726[163] and is therefore a contemporary of Pallavamalla, supported an extermination policy in one of his *Tirumālai* hymns:

> Oh Lord of Śriraṅga, our ears have become diseased by listening to the series of unceasing and unbearable slander of the so-called preachings of the Samaṇa ignoramuses and the unprincipled Śākyas. If you would only endow me with sufficient strength I shall deem it my duty to do nothing short of chopping off their heads.[164]

Minakshi has shown that the last few lines of the Udayendiram grant, mentioning the destruction of all persons whose observances were not in accordance to *dharma* (*anyān adharma kṛtyān*) do not refer to the Jains, but to the Buddhists.[165] The radical measures alluded to were preliminary to the donation of four pieces of *araṇya* land, with all the usual immunities, to the brāhmaṇa Kuḷacarman in the Kāñcivāyil village. The verses of Toṇṭaraṭippoṭi may be considered suggestive of the mechanisms usually followed when land distribution in favour of the brāhmaṇas took place in the myriad of villages dotting the plains. The Buddhists and the other heretics living in the villages were not simply obliged to leave but were killed – at least some of them – *sur-le-champ*,[166] that is, in the very place where they were carrying on their sinful life. What actually happened must have depended on how strong, at a local level, was the resistance of the peasants and of the low caste and outcastes. The land was appropriated and, made free from the presence of the former owners and their religious representatives, donated to the brāhmaṇas, village after village.

This process is substantiated by a few Pallava records where we find the expressions *kuṭi nīkki*, which means 'removing the earlier occupants' and *mun-peṟṟārai māṟṟi*, which has the same meaning. As observed by Kesavan Veluthat, both these expressions 'signify that the recipients of the land were at liberty to evict the earlier occupants of the land and settle it with new occupants of their own choice'.[167] It should be noted here that the 'inherent expansionism' of the land-granting system implemented by the Guptas, which had proved sustainable due to the vastness and even to the marginality of the territories to colonise,[168] had reached saturation, and that now there was much more ground for clashes and violence.

The evidence regarding Pallavamalla and the Āḻvārs is to be seen in relation to the other events that had already taken place in Kāñcīpuram, as for instance the defeat of the Buddhists by Akaḷaṅka and their expulsion during the reign of Hemaśītala/Hiraṇyavarman, discussed above. A controversy ending with the expulsion of the *śramaṇa*-s is said to have taken place also between the Buddhists and Śaṅkarācārya when the latter established the *śākta-pīṭha* of the Goddess Kāmākṣī.[169] The change in the structure of the society is reflected by the thorough transformation of their capital in the eighth century, when the Buddhist establishments were obliterated. T.A. Gopinatha Rao recognised a number of scattered Buddhist images exactly in the area of the Kāmākṣī Temple in Kāñcī,[170] and assumed that the latter was built on the place of a former Buddhist building.[171] Whatever the historical reliability of the traditions concerning the saint, the presence of Śaṅkara at Kāñcī, where he is also said to have established a famous *maṭha*,[172] seems well grounded. According to tradition, the saint had the plan of the town completely changed and shrines erected in such a way as to form a larger *śrīcakra* around the Kāmākṣī Temple.[173] Even if we do not want to believe in the direct involvement of Śaṅkara, the substance of things does not change. Only a small Buddhist community survived the dramatic years of the Brahmanical transformation of Kāñcīpuram: a Bauddhapaḷḷi and a merchant street are recorded as late as the thirteenth century.[174]

In Orissa the clash with the Buddhists was particularly violent and lasted as far as the sixteenth century, and aniconic imagery retained for long its deeper meaning, without turning into decorative imagery. In the temples of Bhubaneswar the lions-elephants opposition is striking, echoing on a smaller scale the lions-elephants opposition constitutive of the Kailāsanātha temple of Ellora, which is literally built on elephants, fiercely attacked by lions. We shall return to Ellora in the next chapter, concentrating here on Bhubaneswar. The square tassels in a row below the now empty niches on the *bāḍa* of the temple of Paraśurāmeśvara depict either elephants assailed and bitten into by lions or tamed elephants paying homage to the lion-king. This temple dates to the first half of the seventh century,[175] and has many iconographic peculiarities in common with the Vaitāl Deuḷ. Cāmuṇḍā, the *mātṛkā*-s and Kārttikeya are depicted on the outer walls of the *jagamohana* along with several other divinities and symbolic imagery.[176] Lakulīśa with his four disciples is present on the front façade of the superstructure, being thus given a prominent status. The original name of the temple was, in fact, Parāśarēśvara, from the *liṅga* enshrined in the *garbhagṛha* in the name of a famous Pāśupata teacher.[177] An image of Śiva Bhikṣāṭana, also present in the Vaitāl Deuḷ, among the images decorating the temple points to Śiva's exploit against Brahmā.

On the outer walls of the Vaitāl Deuḷ we observe panels depicting huge, fierce *vyāla*-s mounted by riders who have just defeated two-armed warriors, on whose identity we remain uncertain (Fig. 5). Long strings of pearls come out from their mouths.[178] Higher up, the rectangular tassels just above the *garbhagṛha* at the height at which the roof starts are decorated with pairs of elephants crushed by gnashing lions which are holding their paws on the elephants' heads. The *kīrtimukha*/lion-head from which hang strings of pearls, known from a number of Brahmanical temples, held a deep meaning before being transformed into a decorative motif. The *kīrtimukha* was transformed into a lion-face motif in Gupta and post-Gupta art, and the lion became a symbol of Śiva's wrath.[179] The 'large pearls hanging from the mouths

Figure 5: Strings of pearls seized by *vyāla*-s in the Vaitāl Deuḷ, Bhubaneswar.

of the lions acquired by 'breaking open the temples of the elephants' is a common literary metaphor,[180] but when we read it in a passage of the *Ādipurāṇa*, the ninth-century work of the Digambara Jinasena, where victory over delusion (*moha*) is alluded to,[181] it is probable that reference is made to the riches stolen from enemies, and, in context, to the destruction of Buddhist stūpas and institutions. A passage from Bu Ston's prophecy on the end of Buddhism seems to fit in this picture:

> The hosts of Māra and other foes of the Doctrine will appear there and become powerful. The kings, ministers, etc., will lose faith and will no more draw a distinction between virtue and sin. They will inflict wounds upon the Highest Doctrine, and will rob and carry away the property of the 3 Jewels and that of the Congregation. They will have no shame in committing sinful deeds and will destroy the images and sanctuaries, so that the objects of worship will grow scant.[182]

Regarding the later evidence at Bhubaneswar, I will limit myself to making a few observations on the Brahmeśvara and Rājarāṇī temples, built in the eleventh century, although clarifying the semantic ambiguity of these images is particularly difficult. The temple known today as Rājarāṇī is identifiable with the Sivaite temple of Indreśvara.[183] Its *jagamohana*, *pañcaratha* in plan, attracts attention because of the massive columns entwined by *nāga*-s flanking the entrance and the side balustraded windows. The front of the pedestals have the form of three lions riding as many tamed elephants, and the back that of fierce *vyāla*-s mounted by riders assailing diminutive elephants. A lion, arguably identifiable with the unknown ruler who had the temple built, towers on the top of the structure before the *kalaśa*. Mistaking for decorative features what is in fact an aniconic representation would be a serious misunderstanding, even considering that the iconographic decoration was left incomplete and that it was repaired from serious damages in 1903.[184] *Gajavyāla*-s, and in some cases rampart lions attacking men (*naravyāla*-s) are found in the recesses of the *deuḷ*, too.

Fierce *vyāla*-s mounted by riders going on with the hunt, while the dismounted ones trample on the elephants are observable in the Brahmeśvara Temple, erected by Kolāvatī Devī, mother of Uddyōta Kēśarī (*c*. AD 1040-65),[185] and in fact the motif has been long associated with the Kēśarī or Somavaṃśī kings.[186] The elephants crushed by the *yāli*-s are depicted as small, clumsy animals doomed to be defeated. The Somavaṃśīs were staunchly Sivaite, apparently acting under the influence of the Maṭṭamayūras, the already mentioned Sivaite sect that originated in central India.[187] The inscription (now lost) recording the construction of the Brahmeśvara Temple mentions King Janamejaya II Mahāśivagupta's difficult but victorious fight against the elephants of a political enemy,[188] a frequent expression. Political enemies are also mentioned in relation to his predecessor Uddyōta Mahābhavagupta IV, who caused 'numberless rājās to bow down their heads',[189] so that we would be inclined to refer the temple imagery to victorious wars and the construction of the temples as celebrating, besides the greatness of Śiva, their military power and glory. However, in the complex reality of Orissa that we shall examine below and in the next chapters, we should ask ourselves who those 'numberless rājās' and their supporters may have been. The social and political dynamics governing the relationships between Hindu kings and native chiefs characterising the history of the region up to the eighth-ninth century[190] had not much changed in the tenth and eleventh century. Although the process of *varṇa* state formation was more advanced, the social and religious implications of the military offensive of the Kēśarī kings supported by the Sivaite *ācārya*-s must be set in the geopolitical perspective of the fault line running along the Vindhyas and of the armed Buddhist response to Brahmanical expansionism.

MILITARY TRAINING

Attention has been drawn by several authors on the early testimonies on the large establishments where young brāhmaṇas from many parts of India were trained in a number of disciplines. They included the study of the Vedas, grammar, the science of logic – Mīmāṃsā, Sāṃkhya, Vaiśeṣika, Naiyāyika *darśana*-s, and, significantly, *Buddhadarśana* – but were also practicing archery and shield sport, and were engaged in crossing swords, handling arrows and different kinds of stakes, in fighting with spears and clubs and wrestling hand to hand and fist to fist. The evidence comes from a Jain work, the *Kuvalayamālā*, a *campū* composed by Uddyotanasūri in AD 779[191] that, despite being an unsympathetic source, is of particular interest. The hero of the romance, the prince Kuvalayacandra, arrives at Vijayāpurī on the western coast of the Deccan or in Kerala[192] in search of Kuvalayamālā, and is wrongly directed to a *caṭṭānam maḍham*, that is, a *maṭha* housing young brāhmaṇa students. It is here that the prince is struck by the great number of subjects taught. Uddyotana critically addresses the group of students who bring all their intelligence to recite the Vedas, and nothing else. They gave each other slaps on their curly hair and hit their plump limbs with brutal kicks; they shrugged their shoulders, and fattened on the alms of others their already ample flesh; they aspired to visit other people's women and were incredibly proud of their good fortune and beauty.[193]

Christine Chojnacki has warned us against considering the novel a reflection of the reality of the eighth century without reading the context,[194] but with regard to *maṭha*-s we have further evidence confirming Uddyotana's report. These *maṭha*-s were known in Kerala as *śālai*-s (from *śālā*), which were attached to temples.[195] Going by a Tamil inscription of King Karunantaṭakkan of the Yādava or Āy family dated AD 866,[196] the strict rules governing the *śālai*-s had started relaxing in the ninth century. In fact, the charter forbids the *caṭṭar*-s to keep concubines (as it would have been obvious for *brahmācārya*-s) and prescribes fines for a number of faults. Later sources prove the continued existence of arms-bearing brāhmaṇas and, at the same time, a further relaxation of the discipline.[197] The existence of orthodox schools throws light on the formation of the intellectual élite who opposed the Buddhist logicians in debates, but their most striking characteristic, however, is that the students underwent military training and made use of weapons, acting as a volunteer force in defending the properties of the school and the temple. This arms-bearing community of dedicated scholars must have constituted a formidable force.[198]

It was probably in one of these institutions that Śaṅkarācārya was trained.[199] His fame as controversialist[200] and his knowledge of Buddhism point to this conclusion. If the oversimplification of nineteenth-century authors, ready to saddle Śaṅkara with the extermination of the heretics in accord with the stories narrated in the hagiographies and handed over by local traditions, must be rejected, it remains to be understood why such stories have been so unanimously transmitted: there is a thread, we have suggested, that binds earliest events with those closer in time to the period when the literary sources were written. The *maṭha* where Śaṅkara is likely to have received his training and the *maṭha*-s he founded according to a unanimous tradition can be considered aggressive institutions and the members of his *maṭha*-s are likely to have played a part in the uprooting of the *śramaṇa*-s by taking action in a number of cases. The direct initiative of the ruler under Brahmanical pressure was not the only way to wipe out the power of the monasteries: the initiative could come from below, from militias organised by religious groups.

The question of the relationship between the *cāṭṭa*-s of the *maṭha*-s and those of the *ghaṭikā*-s, who are associated with *bhaṭṭa*-s, remains open. We have seen that *ghaṭikā* has been considered synonymous with *śālai/maṭha*,[201] but that it rather denotes an institution regulating trade where the seal of the dynasty was kept:[202] hence the role played by the *ghaṭikā* of Kāñcī in the selection and consecration of the new king Nandivarman II Pallavamalla in AD 732.[203] *Ghaṭikā*-s are associated with the establishment of the new orthodox powers, as is shown by the story of Mayūraśarman of Banavāsī, who eventually quarrelled with the persons responsible for the Kāñcī *ghaṭikā*:[204] after becoming king in his country, he is reported to have performed eighteen *aśvamedha*-s,[205] an inflated number that, in any case, indicates that the Kadamba *kula* was under strict Brahmanical control. An inflated number of *aśvamedha*-s are attributed to several Viṣṇukuṇḍin kings[206] after that *kula* became a bulwark of orthodox power with the conversion to Sivaism of Govindavarman (*c.* AD 422-62), who had formerly supported Buddhism.[207] This is not the case of Indrabhaṭṭārakavarman, to whom the re-establishment of Viṣṇukuṇḍin power after a serious crisis was due,[208] but his ascending the throne of Veṅgi in *c.* AD 526 is connected with the establishment of a *ghaṭikā*.[209]

With the present state of our knowledge, it is difficult to say if the *cāṭṭa*-s of the *ghaṭikā*-s were imparted military training as happened to those attached to *maṭha*-s. Brāhmaṇas proudly claimed kṣatriya role,[210] and we cannot exclude that kṣatriya training was imparted in other institutions besides *maṭha*-s. It is possible that a paramilitary force was established to guarantee the operations *bhaṭṭa*-s and *cāṭṭa*-s were responsible for. The association between the king and the brāhmaṇas of both the administrative machinery and the *maṭha*-s grew so close as to make the decisional level difficult for us to identify. The religious cleansing of the Kāñcīvāyil village under Nandivarman Pallavamalla discussed above probably needed the intervention of a regular army unit, because the land was granted by the king, and the same was probably true for the orders imparted by Mahendravarman I Pallava. Born a Sivaite, he joined the Jain monastery at Pāṭali (modern Cuddalore),[211] which he caused with other shrines to be destroyed when the first Nāyaṉār, Appar, reconverted him to his former creed.[212] Conversely, in such a case as that of Campantar entering Būtamaṅkalam, or of the Sivaites establishing their power at Valuvur, the use of militias is more likely.

The reason why *maṭha*-s fell gradually into a state of anarchy lies probably in the fact that their adherents, kept under control until when – the ninth century in the South – they were invested with the major objective of eradicating heresy, were no longer offered any major task. It is interesting to note that ranks tightened again when the situation became tense once more. Social dynamics tend to present themselves again almost unchanged, although in disguise, when a situation gets stuck in its fundamentals or evolves into a renovated contraposition of social models (this happened in the eleventh and twelfth century). It has been maintained that the groups of warrior ascetics of the Indian middle ages are not the gradual evolution of previously existing institutions but arose only after the Muslim conquest.[213] But this is not very likely. The presence of warrior ascetics in earlier times was better understood, though in a simplified way, by nineteenth-century observers. James MacNabb Campbell in 1896 observed that the Pāśupatas, identified with the Dasanāmīs because the latter were 'Nakuliśas in their discipline doctrines and habits',

> were ever ready to fight for their school and often helped and served in the armies of kings who became their disciples. Till a century ago these unpaid followers recruited the armies of India with celibates firm and strong in fighting. It is apparently to gain these recruits that so many of the old rulers of India became followers of the Pasupata school. To secure their services the rulers had to pay them special respect. The leaders of these fighting monks were regarded as pontiffs like the Bappa-pāda or Pontiff of the later Valabhi and other kings. Thus among the later Valabhis Śilāditya IV, is called Bārapādānudhyāta and all subsequent Śilāditya Bappapādānudhyāta, both titles meaning Worshipping at the feet of Bava or Bappa.[214]

ON THE FAULT LINE: THE *MAHĀVRATA* OF THE KĀPĀLIKAS

In Orissa we are in a position to appreciate both the pan-Indian unison in which the brāhmaṇas acted in connection with the creation of an agrarian society and the radicalisation of the social and political struggle involved in the process. The lands in the coastal plains of Orissa started being granted to the brāhmaṇas in the fourth and fifth centuries AD,[215] but complete acquisition of the land and the control over the whole territory was a long, strongly opposed process. There is a certain similarity with the situation in Tamil Nadu, even if we do not accept the theory of segmentary state adapted to the Orissan situation, but in Orissa the brahmanisation process was more difficult and painfully slow, which resulted in continuous warfare. Discussing the political-religious events of the region and the often convulsive, contradictory state of the affairs, we should never lose sight of the fact that it bordered Bihar and Bengal, which were under Pāla control. Pāla interference was continuous, even when the dynasty lost part of its power. Unlike Tamil Nadu, in Orissa the front of anti-Brahmanical forces could continue to look northwards, never giving up hope. The weight of non-brahmanised areas and the presence of numerous local chiefs in a territory with a weaker identity than Tamiḻakam, make of Orissa the best possible vantage point for the faultline, pretty much coinciding with the ridge of the Vindhya mountains, which was subjected to centuries of violent shaking. The ultimate objectives were the trans-Vindhyan plains of Magadha, the Mahanadi delta (a replica of the Kaveri delta), and Bengal. We lack the extraordinary directness of Tamil literary sources, reflecting an unequalled degree of self-confidence, but the directness of Orissan iconographic sources have probably no equal in the whole of India.

Let us go back again to the Vaitāl Deuḷ on the Bindusarovara at Bhubaneswar. At first, looking at the ithyphallic image of Lakulīśa accompanied by his four disciples[216] and, just below, at a relief with Śiva and Pārvatī on the southern side (the front part) of the superstructure, the affiliation of the temple seems evident. Nevertheless, it is the iconographic programme of the *garbhagṛha* that provides us with better clues to understanding the *raison d'être* of the temple. The presiding deity is Cāmuṇḍā, depicted at the centre of the back wall.[217] She tramples on a corpse, according to the iconography developed in the late eighth century.[218] Two series of *mātṛkā*-s, lesser in size, are found on both sides of the goddess along the back and side walls. The first is led by Vīrabhadra, the other by a deity analogous to the female aspect of the god. In the northern wall, next to an image of Gaṇeśa who has, among his attributes, a battle-axe, there is an ithyphallic Bhairava in his skeletal form (Atiriktāṅga Bhairava) wearing a garland of skulls (Fig. 6). The god, who wears a garland of skulls, 'sits in a fighting posture', resting the weight of his body on the left knee, and holds in the right hand a *kartrī* or sacrificial knife.[219] A severed head, with the feature of the Buddha, lies in front of him, and two chopped heads are depicted on a tripod on the pedestal, while a wild pig (?) is eating the remnants.[220] Among the other images in the *garbhagṛha*, stands out an unusual Gajāsurasaṃhāramūrti, with an ithyphallic Śiva engaged in killing Gajāsura with a knife, his elephant form being visible in the upper right corner.[221]

Outside the temple, just in front of the entrance to the *jagamohana*, there is a much worn, reworked Buddhist sculpture serving as the base of a *yūpa* (the socket on top was made to insert another stone or a wooden feature, Fig. 7),[222] testifying to the sacrifices – including human sacrifices – offered up to the goddess.[223] K.C. Panigrahi has shown, on textual basis, that the Cāmuṇḍā of the Vaitāl Deuḷ was known as Kāpālinī, and that the Vaitāl Deuḷ was a shrine of the Kāpālikas, its name being derived from the *vetāla*-s or spirits with the help of which they attained their *siddhi*-s.[224] The Kāpālikas, naked

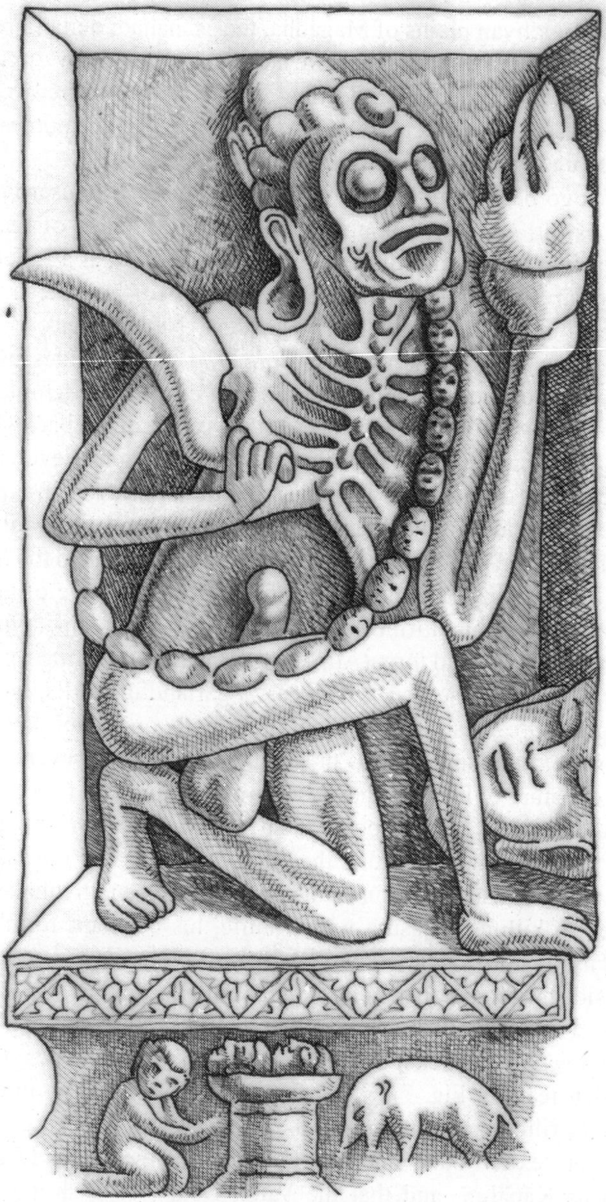

Figure 6: Bhairava in the *garbhagṛha* of the Vaitāl Deuḷ, Bhubaneswar.

Figure 7: *Yūpa* obtained from a Buddhist architectural fragment in front of the Vaitāl Deuḷ, Bhubaneswar.

and holding *khaṭvāṅga*-s, are actually represented in the *barāṇḍā* recess of the temple superstructure along with Śiva Bhikṣāṭana and *liṅgapūjā*.[225]

The Kāpālikas are unanimously reviled in the literature, and the struggle carried out by Śaṅkara against them is also well known.[226] Yet the fact that in the eighth century, high-level patronage was available for such a temple as the Vaitāl Deuḷ to be built indicates that their function in society was far from being marginal, and responded to a specific need. The influence of the Kāpālikas, already well established in Gupta time at the highest political level (Chapter III) grew exponentially wherever their services were required. On the basis of a somewhat later evidence (ninth-tenth century), it appears that whereas the Kālāmukhas took root in Tamil Nadu and lower Andhra Pradesh, where they often filled the role of royal chaplains, it was the Kāpālikas who emerged at a higher level of responsibility further north, as for instance in Candella territory.[227] The presence of Lakulīśa's on the Vaitāl Deuḷ suggests that there was a real ambiguity in the relationships between Kāpālikas and Pāśupatas, or at least between the former and some groups of the latter, and that probably it was not only a question of a mistaken identification of the two sects in later sources.[228] The fact that the Kāpālikas do not appear to have had any scriptures of their own points to their need to borrowing from other compatible traditions.[229] On the authority of Bavabhūti's *Mālatīmādhava* we know that in the eighth century the Kāpālikas were adepts of both Śiva and the goddess (in their *vāma*, 'left' shapes), since Aghorakaṇṭa and Kapālakuṇḍalā were about to sacrifice Mālatī to Cāmuṇḍā-Karālā:[230] the information fits the iconographical programme of the *garbhagṛha* of the Vaitāl Deuḷ. The cult of the goddess had gained ground, and Śiva would gradually be left in the background. Even Śiva's murderous Bhairava aspect would be slowly put aside to the advantage of the goddess and her multiplication in space through the *yoginī*-s.[231]

The presence and influence of the Kāpālikas remain, in part, obscure, but some light can be shed on the meaning of the *mahāvrata* that identified them as a distinct sect and bound them together as well as on the myth they were connected with. Their great vow was the penance for removing the sin of killing a brāhmaṇa, as prescribed in the *śāstra*-s. This meant carrying the skull of the person slain on a stick, like a flag, and taking a human skull as drinking vessel if – these are the textual prescriptions – the person killed was not an ordinary but a learned brāhmaṇa.[232] This is exactly the point: why should the Kāpālikas kill learned brāhmaṇas, and who could the latter ever be? It is extremely unlikely that their target were the *vaidika*-s or the theists imbued with ritualistic doctrine, and the only learned brāhmaṇas to be killed were the Buddhists – the apostate brāhmaṇas representing the antinomial élite, and especially the controversialists who kept the orthodox in check. David N. Lorenzen has maintained that the Kāpālikas adopted their vow in order to be at the same time the holiest of all ascetics and the lowest of all criminals, that which is lowest in the realm of appearance becoming a symbol for the highest in the realm of the spirit.[233] This may be true, but the evidence provided by the Vaitāl Deuḷ and the discussion made earlier in this chapter show that real people were killed, and the paradoxical position of the Kāpālikas cannot be considered as purely symbolic. The apparently split personality of the murderous ascetics finds an explanation in the equally split personality of Śiva, who turns to ascetic practices after casting off his *saṃhāra* aspects, that is, after slaying the *asura*-s/heretics.

In the *bhrūṇahan* (the killing of a learned brāhmaṇa) we discover the reason why the Kāpālikas created or made their own the myth of Śiva who cuts Brahmā's fifth head, an act providing for the same type of *mahāvrata* that identifies them. In the *Śiva Purāṇa* it is, significantly, Kālabhairava who commits the murder.[234] In the myth, known in various versions, Śiva is condemned to wander from *tīrtha* to *tīrtha* until he is delivered from his sin, symbolised by the head of Brahmā which remains magically attached to his body, in the Kapālamocana *tīrtha* in Benares.[235] In the same way, the Kāpālikas, who re-enact Śiva's deed, move from one place to the other ready to kill again, and once again be pardoned.

The suppression of the Buddhists is to be seen – as we shall better see in the next chapter – in relation to the subjugation of the local *rājā*-s, who mushroomed in Orissa after the crisis of the Bhaumakaras. They were ready to hold up their heads again whenever war was waged (for instance against the Cōḷas) even after the firm establishment of the Somavaṃśī dynasty by Yayāti I Mahāśivagupta (AD 922-55). Our working hypothesis is that the Buddhists actively entered the anti-Kēśarī front, trying to bind together local chiefs, tribal people, and, in the more developed areas, urban low caste people and outcastes to react against the policy of the dynasty. The radical measures taken by Yayāti I after gaining power deserve some attention. He is reputed to have invited ten thousand brāhmaṇas from Kanauj to settle in the region, where present-day brāhmaṇas claim descent from them, and to have performed ten *aśvamedha*-s at Jajpur.[236] The arrival of such a large number of new settlers implied the elimination of the previous landowners or users, and inevitably led to clashes. Yayāti made the town on the Baitarani (Vaitaraṇī) one of his major headquarters, and Yayātipura or Yayātinagara,[237] also known as Viraja/Virajā, at the centre of the Virajakṣetra,[238] grew into an important *tīrtha*.[239] An outlying part of the town was Guhiraṭikirā, the seat of power of the

Bhaumakaras,[240] which rose in the immediate neighbourhood of the Buddhist site of Khaḍipadā.[241]

THE BHĀGAVATAS AND PĀŚUPATAS OF NEPAL

In the eighth century, coherently with the majority of Indian regions (though differently from the plains south of the mountains, ruled by the Pālas), Nepal[242] underwent a major transformation. This may be considered, in part, a reaction against the Tibetan domination, an issue that has long been the subject of debate. Mary Shepherd Slusser, taking her cue from Sylvain Lévi, has maintained that there were either two periods of Tibetan domination, i.e. at the time of Narendradeva and in the first half of the ninth century, or one that lasted more than two centuries.[243] There are a number of arguments against the latter possibility, but it is quite probable that during the eighth and ninth centuries the Tibetans made their presence felt in Nepal raiding the valley from time to time.[244] Buddhism, though already seriously conditioned by Sivaism,[245] played a leading role until the second half of the eighth century.

The events which took place in Andigrāma (present-day Harigaon), which was part of the early town of Viśālanagara,[246] help us to clarify the picture, all the more so because they have been reconstructed on the basis of a strictly controlled excavation. The very name of Andigrāma has re-emerged thanks to a dedicatory inscription on a water drain dated AD 749[247] representing the latest piece of evidence associated with the Buddhist sanctuary that rose in the excavated area during the third occupation period (*c.* AD 640 – second half of the eighth century). The most significant remains of this phase are the foundations of a square-based stūpa (Stūpa 21) in the form of a grid-shaped chamber with nine square pits.[248] The monument, built with baked bricks, was completely dismantled some time after AD 749, and its foundations, which remained under the walking level, were covered by the new, large floor of a Vishnuite temple compound, in front of which a Garuḍastambha was erected (Fig. 8). The latter bears a famous, long but undated inscription – a hymn, actually – in praise of Dvaipāyana Kṛṣṇa or Vyāsa, the mythical *ṛṣi* credited with the composition of the *Mahābhārata*. An extremely violent earthquake destroyed the temple in the thirteenth or fourteenth century,[249] and the 1934 earthquake destroyed it again, but the Garuḍastambha has survived intact, despite

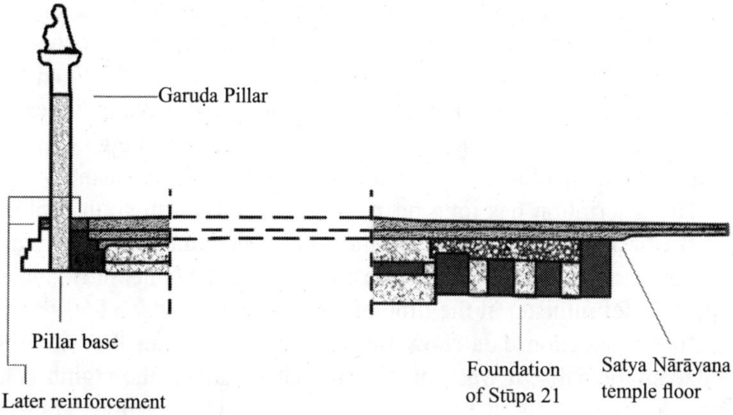

Figure 8: Harigaon Satya Nārāyaṇa, Kathmandu. Section showing foundation of Stūpa and Garuḍa Pillar.

the extensive work that was carried out all around subsequent to its original erection. A trial-trench at the base of the pillar has revealed three successive floors, the lowest of which is stratigraphically one and the same with the floor of the temple compound covering the stūpa remain. The bricks used or rather – on the evidence of the many wear marks displayed – re-used in the sub-structure on which the pillar stands are those plundered from the stūpa or from some other building of the Buddhist sanctuary.[250]

Dvaipāyana is praised in the inscription[251] because he has cured the evils that we have seen described and condemned in the Kali Age literature, at a time when 'men had taken to atheism' opposing the Veda and when 'leaning only upon their foolishness constantly, the false logicians were suppressing the truth'.[252] The 'false logicians' are the Buddhist controversialists whom we have seen prevail at first over the orthodox brāhmaṇas and then start being silenced. Those responsible for past evils are expressly said to be 'these disciples of the Sugata', further called 'crooked distorters of this world'.[253] The explicit reference to the Buddhists leaves no doubt as to the meaning of the metaphors employed in other parts of the hymn and suggests the actual meaning of a number of passages in other texts, both literary and epigraphic. Dvaipāyana is invited to destroy 'all this network of illusion like the Sun destroys darkness'.[254] He is the 'breaker of evils', and thanks to him the world was liberated 'from all evil passions, like the sky with dispelled darkness as the sun shines', and the 'thick clouds of illusion spread in the world' have been dissipated; the *ṛṣi* is further praised because he has broken 'the chains of the world'.[255] When, for example, Nandivarman Pallava appears in the Kasakudi Plates as having dispelled all darkness,[256] we realise, knowing the king's exploits that we have mentioned earlier in this chapter, what is meant.

The inscription has long been assigned to the fifth-sixth century on the basis of the alleged identification of the author of the hymn, the Anuparama mentioned in the last verse, with the father of Bhaumagupta, chief minister at the time of king Gaṇadeva (*c.* AD 560-65),[257] but the excavation data show that it cannot be earlier that AD 749. Palaeographically, it was not until the latter half of the eighth century that the Northern Brāhmī of the Licchavi inscriptions showed any sign of change.[258] The new date is also in keeping with the attribution, on stylistic ground, of the Garuḍa image to the seventh-eighth century[259] and, indeed, with the text itself.

The evidence from Andigrāma/Harigaon shows that the condemnation of Buddhism issued by the Bhāgavata representatives of neo-orthodoxy was not only theoretical and sermonising but took, once again, the form of very concrete measures. At Harigaon, the destruction of the Buddhist sanctuary was so radical that all the related material, not just the relics of Stūpa 21, was scattered and lost. With the exception of the inscribed water drain, which was found re-utilised in the last period of occupation of the site, the only objects pertaining to the Buddhist sanctuary found in the excavation were the handle of a lamp showing a Buddha in *bhūmisparśamudrā* and a small inscribed sealing exhibiting a stūpa.[260] The latter was sealed up in an interstice of the floor that interfaced the area of Stūpa 21, and resurfaced thanks to the wearing out of the brickwork. Important economic consequences were to follow the events that the evidence from the excavation partly illustrates. The lands owned by the monastery were transferred to the new temple, and in fact, in accord with a general pattern, the name of the place was changed into Harigaon, the village of Hari, that is, *Hari(mandira)-grāma*, 'the village of the temple of Hari', to be understood as the village whose revenues have been assigned to the maintenance of the temple of Viṣṇu.[261]

The Bhāgavatas were recognised as the authors of the Harigaon pillar inscription already by Sylvan Lévi.[262] Despite the fact that in some quarters they were still considered *sātvata*-s, low-caste, and the Pāñcarātra texts adopted by them invalid and non-Vedic,[263] their involvement in temple worship had made them extremely influential since Gupta times, and in eighth-century Nepal, as in Kāñcī, they succeeded in controlling kingship to the detriment of the Sivaites – a general trend in India. Nepal kingship would remain Vishnuite-oriented until its recent extinction. The period between the death of the last known Licchavi king, Jayadeva II (*c*. AD 750), and AD 879/80, marking the beginning of the Newār era, for which almost no information is available,[264] witnessed the consolidation of orthodox power. The so-called 'Transitional Period' (an over three-centuries long span of time, AD 879-1200) [265] may be understood as the real Licchavi period in Nepalese history. The dynasty, supported by the Bhāgavatas, remained stable for long, having nothing to fear from other models of kingship, as had happened between the fifth and the eighth century. The Buddhists had no hand in the matter now, and were obliged to accept the rules of *varṇāśramadharma*, while the Sivaites were integrated into the new political-institutional framework. In the valley of Kathmandu, the lack of epigraphic records from *c*. AD 750 to 1300 is not in itself a sign of 'decadence', reduced economic resources and the like, but rather a sign that the established ideology was successful in absorbing and controlling any conflict that might arise without the need to resort to propaganda and self-assuring eulogies. Bhāgavatism established itself as a powerful, unifying, and all-pervasive ideology and epigraphs no longer served any purpose, nor did any other records. History was, to a certain extent, reduced to ideology.

The role played by the Sivaites in curbing the power of the monasteries in the valley was not less effective. The evidence, carefully examined by Ulrich Wiesner, is provided by the transformation into *liṅga*-s of early votive stūpas.[266] Though provided with niches opening along the superimposed square and/or circular tiers into which they are subdivided, these stūpas bear no images, even though the profuse decoration of the niche frames imply the presence of icons. In the example from Chabahil,[267] there are twelve niches on each of the four levels, all empty, as is also the case of the votive stūpas shaped according to a different plan. In addition, the stūpas have no base nor finial, essential as the latter is for the cult. The majority of the stūpas have not been under continuous worship and are in a dilapidated state.

Some appear to be the result of the reassemblage of elements taken from different stūpas, and only in a few, exceptional cases, are the icons in the niches still present. Whenever, in modern times, the stūpas have been reactivated, they have been provided with a new finial and a base, because none of the Licchavi stūpas now situated in *vihāra*-s stand on their original bases.

The images once housed in the niches were carefully chiselled away, as is shown by the marks left on the back walls. This was not deemed to be necessary for the *kīrtimukha*-s, *kalahaṃsa*-s, *makara*-s and *kinnara*-s decorating the niche frames, because their semantic ambiguity did not identify them as Buddhist. Deprived of their most significant features, the stūpas started being revered as *liṅga*-s, according to a procedure documented in the narrative of a Nepalese pilgrim – recorded by Hodgson – who observed that the *caitya*-s to the north of the Mahābodhi Temple in Bodhgayā were worshipped as *liṅga*-s by the local brāhmaṇas after breaking off the *cūḍāmaṇi* from each.[268] Thus the present-day condition of the Licchavi votive stūpas is not the consequence of neglect over a long period, nor can the evidence they provide be construed as the outcome of a process of a long decline affecting the religion of Dharma, rather, they attest to 'a once-for-all and conscious act' and a 'centrally organized, large scale operation', in the course of which all the votive stūpas were systematically revised and adapted for the purposes of another cult.[269]

Oral traditions, widely current in Nepal, have afforded us the knowledge of the poor relationships between the Buddhists and the Brahmanical sects. A major clash between Hindus and Buddhists is insistently said to have occurred in Viśālanagara, the early town that included Andigrāma/Harigaon and where some of the Licchavi stūpas analysed by Wiesner are also located. The *vaṃśāvalī*-s contain a lot of information that, if properly understood and set in context, helps to get a non-stereotyped view[270] of the history of medieval Nepal and medieval India. With regard to the events that took place in Viśālanagara, the Buddhist *vaṃśāvalī* made known in 1877 by Daniel Wright in a somewhat amplified translation reports a version of the story that we would not expect to find in a Buddhist chronicle:

> Long before this time, out of hatred to Shankarāchārya, a party of one thousand Bānrās murdered seven hundred Brāhmans residing in Bisālnagara. The wives of these Brāhmans immolated themselves as Satīs, and their curses were so

powerful that the thousand murderers were burned to ashes. The spirits of these Satīs became so turbulent, that no one would venture to pass that way. The Rājā, therefore, in order to put a stop to this trouble, caused an emblem of Siva to be placed there by venerable pandits.[271]

These or similar events are likely to have taken place in the eighth century, to coincide with those described in relation to the destruction of Andigrāma, even though the chronicle, as we will see, interprets earliest facts in the light of the Vajrayāna transformation of Newār Buddhism.

Of great interest is the information provided by the Buddhist chronicle on the change that Buddhism was subjected to as a result of the alleged sojourn in Nepal of Śaṅkarācārya. To the latter is ascribed the restoration of worship in the temple of Paśupatinātha – a deep-rooted tradition according to which the *varaliṅga* installed there would be one of the five *liṅga*-s that the saint received from Śiva on Mount Kailāsa.[272] The fact that the temple cult has been administered for centuries by Nampūtiri brāhmaṇas cannot be taken as evidence of Śaṅkara's responsibility for the transformation of Nepal society, but raises the question of the extraordinary strength and influence of southern Brahmanism. Śaṅkara is said to have defeated 'the Buddhamārgīs' after ousting the Goddess Sarasvatī who, according to the usual *tópos*, was helping them in a debate from within a water jar:

Some of them fled, and some were put to death. Some, who would not allow that they were defeated, were also killed; wherefore many confessed that they were vanquished, though in reality not convinced that they were in error. These he ordered to do *hinsā* (i.e. to sacrifice animals), which is in direct opposition to the tenets of the Buddhist religion. He likewise compelled the Bhikshunīs, or nuns, to marry, and forced the Grihasthas to shave the knot of hair on the crown of their heads, when performing the *chūrā-karma*, or first shaving of the head. Thus he placed the Bānaprasthas (ascetics) and Grihasthas on the same footing. He also put a stop to many of their religious ceremonies, and cut their Brahmanical threads. There were at that time 84,000 works on the Buddhist religion, which he searched for and destroyed. He then went to the Manichūra mountain, to destroy the Buddhists there. Six times the goddess Mani Jōginī raised storms, and prevented his ascending the mountain, but the seventh time he succeeded. He then decided that Mahākāla, who was a Buddha and abhorred *hinsā*, should have animals sacrificed to him. Mani Jōginī or Ugra Tārinī was named by him Bajra Jōginī. Having thus overcome the Buddhists, he introduced the Saiva religion in the place of that of Buddha. [...]

Shankarachārya thus destroyed the Buddhist religion, and allowed none to follow it; but he was obliged to leave Bauddhamārgīs in some places as priests of temples, where he found that no other person would be able to propitiate the gods placed in them by great Bauddhamārgīs. [...]

Very few Bauddhamārgīs were left in the country now, and the Bhikshus began to intermarry with the Grihasthas.[273]

What follows in the text is at the same time moving and informative, and accounts for the transformation of Buddhist priesthood. The *bhikṣu*-s of the Cārumatī Vihāra,[274] 'who had married their aunts through fear of Shankarāchārya', are disheartened and uncertain about their future and that of their kinsfolk, who are unable to perform the crucial *cūḍākaraṇa* ritual.[275] Those who had been living as *bhikṣu*-s have been forced to live as *gṛhastha*-s, 'contented with the scanty means of livelihood' and keeping 'the things they know in their hearts': they are well aware that having to obey the rule about sacrificing animals, they shall commit 'a great breach' of the rules of their own religion. It was in that time that the stūpa of Svayambhū was established: the Śākya priests appointed for keeping up the worship were now made to follow 'the Tantra Shāstras', while the Buddhist *ācārya*-s (themselves *bhikṣu*-s – *gṛhastha*-s) took charge in turn of the *caitya*.[276]

In the preceding chapter we have contended that doctrinal changes and social adjustments originated from the situation with which Buddhism had to come to term, and many of the changes said to have been introduced by Śaṅkara's are seemingly earlier than the eighth century, but the process of transformation was certainly accelerated in that period. The *vaṃśāvalī*-s tell the truth in their own way. The monks were left without any choice but to comply or abjure.[277] The account of the Buddhist *vaṃśāvalī* shows that no exceptions were tolerated to a family-based society (the Brahmanical obsession with family had grown so strong that even the relationships between gods were normalised).[278] The normalisation of Buddhism meant, among other things, the elimination of an all-male or all-female life in communities based on positive law and the insistence on the *lex naturalis*.

The evidence regarding the destruction of books is also notable. That books were burnt when monasteries were attacked is a matter of course, but the passage of the *vaṃśāvalī*, however amplified the reported facts may be, implies ad hoc actions. The loss of the Sanskrit Canon and of many Mahāyāna works cannot be generically accounted for as the consequence of the disappearance of Buddhism from the Indian horizon. It was probably in the eighth and ninth centuries that a number of texts started being destroyed in India, where the violent upsetting of Buddhist life led the monks to concentrate on the new texts (the *tantra*-s) which provided a better description of the situation that Buddhism was now facing.

The *Bhāṣā Vaṃśāvalī*, a Hindu work, reports some of the facts also recorded in the Buddhist *vaṃśāvalī* after describing in paradoxical terms the religious conditions of the country at the time of King Vṛkṣadevavarman, an early king in which we can recognise, through the grain, rulers such as Narendradeva and Harṣavardhana:

> [...] the sect of the Buddhists became very powerful and built a Vihār called Punya-Vihār which was inhabited by their class, who used to throw leavings of their food and drink on Paśupatināth every evening and [...] next morning remove[d] it from his image and worship[ped] it. In this way [...] all the religious rites of Paśupati were there performed by their sect who were the sole Pujaris in Nepal; for the Rajahs and the people had all embraced Buddhism and plunged themselves in the ocean of Buddhamārga.[279]

In the Nepal Valley, Śaṅkarācārya was assisted, according to this *vaṃśāvalī*, by the Goddess Guhjeśvarī, and the saint defeated the Buddhists in debate, so that some of them 'fled the country, and others were slaughtered on the very instant and their sacred books were destroyed and burnt to ashes'.[280] It would be easy to discard the entire narrative as a cluster of late banality were it not for the fact that the archaeological evidence and the structure of Newār Buddhism convince us to dig more deeply into the nature of these sources. Later violence is the filter through which early violence is also handed over to us.

How tenacious in Nepal was the tradition of Śaṅkara as destroyer of the Buddhist religion and how far went the desire for revenge appears from a story, recorded by Brian Hodgson, set in Tibet:

> The Lamas are orthodox *Buddhamárgis*, and even carry their orthodoxy to a greater extent than we do. Insomuch, that it is said, that Sankara Achárya, *Siva-Márgí*, having destroyed the worship of Buddha and the scriptures containing its doctrine in Hindustan, came to Nepaul, where also he effected much mischief; and then proceeded to Bhot. There he had a conference with the grand Lama. The Lama, who never bathes, and after natural evacuations does not use topical ablution, disgusted him to that degree, that he commenced reviling the Lama. The Lama replied, "I keep my inside pure, although my outside be impure; while you carefully purify yourself without, but are filthy within;" and at the same time

he drew out his whole entrails, and shewed them to Sankara; and then replaced them again. He then demanded an answer to Sankara. Sankara, by virtue of his *yoga*, ascended into the heavens; the Lama perceiving the shadow of Sankara's body on the ground, fixed a knife in the place of the shadow; Sankara directly fell upon the knife, which pierced his throat and killed him instantly.[281]

NOTES

1. This is, in a nutshell, the thesis of the extremely analytic work of Susan Reynolds (2004). Reynolds does not discuss the Marxist, manorial feudalism that fuels the Indian debate, but warns against the too many models of feudalism used by Marxist scholars for the sake of comparison. They either are elaborations of models created in sixteenth-century France or include aspects of the phenomenon that are superficial or irrelevant from a Marxist point of view.
2. See, for instance, the contributions edited by D.N. Jha (1987; 2000; see, in the latter work, Jha's introduction, pp. 1-58) and Mukhia (1999). It was Harbans Mukhia who reignited the discussion on Indian feudalism in the late 1970s.
3. Willis (2009: esp. 161-63).
4. In Kerala, for instance; see Davis (2004: 35-36), with references.
5. Narayanan (2002: 116).
6. D.C. Sircar (1983), providing examples of brāhmaṇa settlers in the north-eastern regions under south Indian rulers, observed that the impact of the phenomenon would require careful consideration, but we still lack a comprehensive study on the matter.
7. Stein (1969; 1980). Stein's model has been vigorously criticised by many Indian historians (see, e.g. Narayanan (1988) and Veluthat (1993).
8. Sircar (1966: 58). For Sircar, the contrary evidence provided by Yadava (1966) was not sufficient to support the construct of a political structure equalled, in the twelfth century, to 'a network of vassal and suzerain relationship' (Sircar 1966: 84). On the *sāmanta*-s as rulers of little kingdoms, see S. Bhattacharya (1988, with reference to Bengal).
9. Rosen (2007: 3, 320-21). McNeill (1998: 137) thought that the bubonic plague might have originated either in Africa or north-eastern India, but western Africa is now being recognised as having been at the origin of the infection (Rosen 2007: 195-96).
10. Tieken & Sato (2000).
11. R.B. Pandey in *EI* 28 (1949-50): 264-67, l. 13 and p. 265. The Parivrājaka *mahārāja*-s controlled the territories of the Rewa-Satna region.
12. *EC* 4 (1898, Mysore Inscr. 2; B.L. Rice): 84-85, 136.
13. Hudson & Case (2008: 69-70). On *ghaṭikā*-s see also below in this chapter.

14. *Vāmana Purāṇa*: 10.81 (p. 162).
15. *Mahābhārata*, Anuśāsana Parvan: section LIX (vol. 11, p. 64).
16. Ibid.: section LX (vol. 11, p. 64).
17. There were monasteries 'everywhere' in the region (cf. *Eminent Monks* b: 49).
18. See ibid.: e.g. 11, 27, 40. Lahiri is not consistent in rendering the name of this monastery throughout his translation. Chavannes (*Eminent Monks* a: passim) has always Sin-tché, but we cannot follow him as regards the identification of the country where it was located (cf. n. 4 on pp. 18-19).
19. Cf. *Eminent Monks* c: 26-27. Thanks are due to Minoru Inaba for providing me with this information.
20. For Kuśīnagara, see *Eminent Monks* b: 42, 82.
21. Ibid.: 49.
22. HCIP 3: 127; Sinha (1954: 285) has emphasised the role played by Ādityasena as king of Magadha.
23. *Eminent Monks* b: 48-49.
24. *Yijing*: XXXII (p. 154).
25. Veluthat (1993: 17-18 and passim).
26. Ibid.: 15 and especially 222 ff., where Veluthat questions Burton Stein's paradigm. See also below in this chapter.
27. Cf. ibid. 201.
28. McGlashan (2009: 293-94). The *antāti* is a particular kind of verse. The date of the *Tēvāram* and of the early Nāyaṉmār has been the object of much discussion, and for a balanced assessment of the question I refer the reader to the sophisticated contribution of Gros (1984).
29. Ibid.: xliii.
30. For all that we know: cf. ibid. viii/xl.
31. Cf. ibid.: lvii-lviii.
32. This has been, to make an example, the position of David N. Lorenzen (1978: 65).
33. *Aṅguttara Nikāya*: III.7.65.ii (vol. 1, p. 171). Kesaputta is an unidentified locality in Kośala.
34. Vidyabhusana (1920: 36 ff.). Vidyabhusana's book has been criticised by many for its inaccuracies, from D.N. Shastri (1964: e.g. 98, n. 63) to Frauwallner (1982: 847) and Sung (2003: 8, n. 23), but he is one of the few providing information at the historical-hagiographical level that are relevant here. For some of the chronological questions related to the Buddhist logicians the reader is referred to Frauwallner (1982), the earlier literature – including F. Th. Scherbatsky's famous *Buddhist Logic* – being less utilizable today.
35. Kher (1992).
36. Yijing: XXXII.v (p. 177).
37. Gopinath Kaviraj in his introduction to *Tantravārttika*: vii.
38. Scherrer-Schaub (2007: 762-63). Scherrer-Schaub is well aware of the political role of the *vādin*-s and of the political fallout of philosophy.

39. *Xiyuji* a: VIII (vol. 2, pp. 108-09). On the reliability of the story, see Thomas Watters's observations in *Xiyuji* b (vol. 2: 108-09).
40. Cf. Hattori (1968: 4-6); Frauwallner (1982: 856-59).
41. Cf. Vidyabhusana (1920: 272).
42. Debates were also common among Buddhists of different persuasion; cf. for instance the debate between Vindhyavāsin and Buddhamitra, Vasubandhu's teacher, at the presence of King Vikramāditya, which resulted in the victory of the former and provoked Vasubandhu to challenge him; cf. Hattori (1968: 4 [Paramārtha's chapter on the life of Vasubandhu, *Posoupandou fashi zhuan*, in *Taishō* 2049, pp. 189b.24-190a.28]). The debates between Buddhist masters would be better understood if put in relation with the strategy to oppose the brāhmaṇas.
43. See several examples in *Tāranātha*: 66A-68A (pp. 181-85).
44. *Tāranātha*: 68A (p. 184).
45. S. Dasgupta (1932-55, I: 406-07).
46. John Taber in *Ślokavārttika*: xvii.
47. On the method of debate, see Vidyabhusana (1920: 28-35).
48. Humfress (2007: 248 ff.).
49. Ibid.: esp. 153 ff.
50. Vattanky (1978: 396-99); see also Kher (1992: 13 ff.). See Vidyabhusana (1920 : 117-23) for some information on Vātsyāyana.
51. Ibid.: 123-33.
52. *Mañjuśrīmūlakalpa*: [53], vv. 957-58 (§55, p. 76).
53. S. Dasgupta (1932-55, III: 512-13).
54. Eltschinger (2001: 7).
55. Chris Bartley in *EAP*: 303. See the different opinions on Kumārila's chronology in P.S. Sharma (1980: 13 ff., 16 ff.).
56. I follow Piantelli (1998: 149). Kumārila's life is known from the hagiographies of Śaṅkara and from Tāranātha. Śaṅkara's life has been reconstructed as convincingly as possible by Pande (1994: 73-98; 337-71) and Piantelli (1998: 93-206), who have provided a narrative of the saint's life after thoroughly discussing the literary sources, as well as by Bader (2000: 71-229), who has discussed the events of Śaṅkara's life putting eight hagiographies in close comparison. The introductory part of Anton Ungemach's edition and translation of Nīlakaṇṭha's *Śaṅkaramandārasaurabha* also provides a précis of the saint's life (Ungemach 1992).
57. Cf. Taber in *Ślokavārttika*: n. 76 on pp. 169-70.
58. H.H. Ingalls in Hattori (1968: vi-vii).
59. These are the words addressed by Śaṅkārācārya to the *bhaṭṭa* in the *Śaṅkara Digvijaya* (7.106-07, p. 79), on which see n. 63 below.
60. Eltschinger (2001: 7). As is known, in his *Ślokavārttika* Kumārila carried out a close critique of Buddhist epistemology. See also Kher (1992: 357-464).
61. *Tantravārttika*: I.iii.iii (vol. 1, p. 167).

62. Ibid. I.ii.i (vol. 1, p. 10). Here Kumārila responds, with unconvincing arguments, to the Buddhist criticisms of the naturalisation of the concept of caste. In addition to dialectics, the Buddhists did not lack sarcasm when they resorted to arguments of the type *mater semper certa, pater incertus* (cf. Eltschinger 2000: 79-80, discussing Candrakīrti); the Jains, Prabhācandra for example, also used similar arguments (*EJ* 6: 1525). On the question of the perception of *jāti* in Kumārila see Eltschinger (2000: 116 ff).
63. The *Śaṅkara Digvijaya* has been known to scholars as early as the beginning of the nineteenth century and has been frequently quoted, in the first place by Horace Wilson (see Chapter I). Piantelli (1998: 51-52 and n. 70 on pp. 68-69) seems to consider it a modern apocrypha, but Bader (2000: 53-62), rejecting the identification of Mādhava with Vidyāraṇya, considers it a work of the eighteenth century incorporating a vast amount of material from earlier hagiographies, judiciously collected from the best available sources by its author. Bader's considerations bring us nearer to a correct understanding of the information contained in these text. The translation of the *Śaṅkara Digvijaya* into English by Swami Tapasyananda is rather free, but a German translation of the first chapter (particularly relevant for Kumārila) is found in Deussen (1908: 181-89).
64. Piantelli (1998: 149); see also Bader (2000: 86).
65. *Śaṅkara Digvijaya*: 1.66 (p. 7).
66. Ibid.: 72-77 (p. 7). Since a similar story is referred to Udayana, a later adaptation of the story is likely. Udayana had defeated the Buddhist logicians in several contests, but on one occasion, being unable to convince them of the existence of God, took a brāhmaṇa and a Buddhist with him to the top of a hill. Falling down, the brāhmaṇa cried aloud 'there is God' and came to the ground unhurt; the Buddhist, crying 'there is no God', died of the fall (cf. Vidyabhusana 1920: 142; a different version of the story is reported by D. Bhattacharya 1987: 6). The contest-ordeal took place in Mithilā.
67. Deussen (1908: 188).
68. According to the *Bṛhacchaṅkaravijaya* mentioned by Piantelli (1998: 151). Other texts set the scene elsewhere.
69. For all its unlikelihood, the meeting points to Śaṅkara as Kumārila's heir in fighting the heretics.
70. For this work, his author and date (Anantānandagiri lived in the thirteenth century), see Telang (1876) and Bader (2000: 26-32).
71. According to some sources, Kumārila was born in northern India (regions vary, Bihar being the most likely option); according to others, including Tāranātha, he was born in the South like Śaṅkara.
72. Cf. Bader (2000: 215), quoting the *Śaṅkaravijaya* (eds Jayanarayaṇa Tarkapanchanana & Nabadwipa Chandra Goswami, Calcutta 1868), p. 173, ll. 5-8. Bader mentions a similar but briefer description contained in Cidvilāsa's *Śaṅkaravijayavilāsa* (ibid.: 86, n. 27).
73. I follow Kane (1930-62, III: 361 ff.).

74. Ibid. 376, n. 591. Cf. *Xiyuji* a: II (vol. 1, p. 84). As to the snake-in-the-jar ordeal, it was referred to among *mleccha*-s: it consisted in taking out a ring or coin with the hand from a jar in which a snake was placed; if there was no snake-bite or no effect from it, the person was declared innocent (Kane 1930-62, III: 366, n. 580; 367).
75. I arrive at these conclusions on the basis of David Brick's discussion on Devaṇa Bhaṭṭa and his *Smṛticandrikā*, composed in south India between AD 1150 and 1225 (Brick 2010: 30-31).
76. Hacker (1958: esp. 64-67). The horizon of Hacker's analysis is the *Artha-śāstra*, and his conclusions are all the more pertinent to the present discussion when we refer this work to the Gupta period.
77. *Tāranātha*: 90A (p. 232).
78. Qvarnström (1999).
79. An interesting detail of the story is that the teacher, looking for the culprits of the refutation of the Buddhist doctrines, had an image of the Jina drawn on the floor, knowing that a Jain would never tread on it. The students outsmart their teacher adding a line that converted the picture into that of the Buddha (cf. Granoff 1989: 112). The ordeal recalls the anti-Catholic practice of *fumi-e* introduced by Tokugawa Ieyasu and still in use in nineteenth-century Japan.
80. Ibid. 116-17. Phyllis Granoff recognises three distinct versions in Haribhadra's biography, which circulated independently and concurrently. She doubts whether these stories were attached to Haribhadra on the basis of the traditions regarding Akaḷaṅka.
81. *Xiyuji*: V (vol. 1, p. 221). The ban was in relation with the attempt at assassinating the king after that Harṣa had 'exhausted the treasury' to benefit the *śramaṇa*-s, leaving the brāhmaṇas empty-handed.
82. Jaini (1979: 83-84).
83. In the South, the Jains do not answer the stereotypical image of a community exclusively belonging to the merchant class, but were agriculturists (Zydenbos 1999: 198). It would be interesting to know how far back in time this trend went. The Digambaras may have sided with the brāhmaṇas in the reorganisation of the agrarian order as early as the Pallava period.
84. Vidyabhusana (1920: 186). As already seen, the goddess hidden in a pot to help a party is a *tópos* frequently met in the accounts of rigged debates. In the text and translation of the *Pāṇḍava Purāṇa* provided by Padmanabh S. Jaini, I only find mentioned the defeat of the Buddhists in debate by Akaḷaṅka. Cf. *Pāṇḍava Purāṇa*: I.21 (pt. 1, p. 109).
85. Cf. B.L. Rice in *EC* 2 (1889, Sravana Belgola): 45-46 (Introd.).
86. For this version of the story, see Granoff (1989: 113-14).
87. Sastri, S. Kuppuswamy (1937: 27). Hiraṇyavarman's position in Pallava succession is not clear (cf. HCIP 3: 262, 281), but he lived in the early decades of the eighth century. According to the *Akaḷaṅkacarita*, the learned Jain would have defeated the Buddhists in VS 700 (*EC* 2, rev ed. R. Nara-

simhacar 1923, Sravana Belgola: 84). The name of the ruler in Taylor's transliteration is Yemasithalan; the Daṇḍakāraṇya is the forest region described in the *Rāmāyaṇa* (for instance, *Rāmāyaṇa*, Kiṣkindhā Kāṇḍa: 61, p. 645); here it stands for the Tontaimantalam.

88. *Mackenzie Manuscripts* 1: 121-22.
89. Ibid.: 4: 260-61.
90. Ibid.: 4: 284. This is how the story ends according to the *Rājāvaḷī Kathe* (B.L. Rice in *EC* 2 (1889, Sravana Belgola): 46 (Introd.). According to the same work, as a young man Akaḷaṅka studied with a Buddhist teacher, Bhagavaddāsa, and fought the Sivaites; some versions set the debate at the court of the Rāṣṭrakūṭa king Sāhasatuṅga Dantidurga (mid-eighth century): see the intricate question discussed by Sastri, S. Kuppuswami (1937: 27-28).
91. Granoff (1985: 461-62).
92. *EI* 3 (1894-95, E. Hultzsch): 184-207, v. 23. Hultzsch naturally knew Taylor's account and B.L. Rice's material, but, characteristically, maintained that he would 'entirely ignore king Himaśītala of Kāñchīpura for historical purposes as long as no contemporaneous epigraphic records, but only legends, are available as proofs of his existence' (p. 187). Other medieval inscriptions keep memory of the event. An epigraph from Sravana Belgola of AD 1128 recalls the debate as follows: 'He by whom Tārā, secretly born in the earthen pot (*ghaṭa kuṭi*), was vanquished together with the Bauddhas, trouble of the false professors; doing reverence only to the gods; he who forced Sugata as penance for the faults to perform ablution with the pollen of his lotus feet; – such was Dēvākalaṅka paṇḍita, to whom is he not a refuge?)' (*EC* 2, 1889, Sravana Belgola, B.L. Rice: 134-40, 41-47; cf. p. 136). Rice wondered about the peculiarity of the detail of Tārā in the earthen pot, present in all the traditions: the goddess used to reply incognito to all the questions posed by Akaḷaṅka from within a pot of toddy, 'the intoxicating fermented juice of the palmyra palm' placed behind a curtain (ibid. 45, Introd.). An inscription of AD 1183 praises Akaḷaṅka in these terms: 'The glory of Akalaṅka-Dēva, by whom can it be described? by the blows of the sword of whose speech the unenlightened (*vibuddhi*) Buddha was slain' (*EC* 3, 1894, Mysore Inscr. 1, B.L. Rice: 89-90, 171-72; cf. p. 89).
93. *Tāranātha*: 67A (p. 183).
94. For instance, Candragomin, who, according to Tāranātha (75A, p. 200), was the son of a learned kṣatriya *paṇḍita*.
95. Vidyabhusana (1920: 604-5).
96. The reader is referred to the limpid article of Vattanky (1978). Dharmakīrti's arguments are at the basis of all later confutations, an example of which is found in the *Tarkabhāṣā* 20.1-2, with useful comments by Yuichi Kajiyama (2005: 282 ff.). See also P.G. Patil (2009) for a thorough presentation of the critique of the Īśvara-inference carried out by Ratnakīrti, 'gate-keeper' at Vikramaśīla in the eleventh century. While I sympathise with Patil's attempt

at transferring the Buddhist-Naiyāyika debate to the level of general philosophical discussion, and even with his pointing to the 'tiranny of social and cultural history' (p. 6), it should be remembered that Indian history is still too little known to forgo less traditional approaches than those offered by historical-philological studies. Not always have these shaped our idea of Indian history for the better.

97. See the Nāyaṉmār subdivided according to caste in Dehejia (1988: 154-55).
98. Pande (1994: 87); Piantelli (1998: 166-68).
99. I follow Dehejia (1988: 46).
100. He is generally known as Kūṉ Pāṇṭya in literary sources, but as Neṭumāṟan in the *Periya Purāṇam*.
101. The final ordeal and impalement of the Jains are described in *Periya Purāṇam*: 33.796-856 (vol. 2, pp. 154-65). K.A.Nilakantha Sastri refused the authenticity of the story ('This, however, is little more than an unpleasant legend and cannot be treated as history. There is no reason to believe that, even in those days of intense religious strife, intolerance descended to such cruel barbarities'; Sastri, K.A. Nilakantha 1966: 424). In some accounts, the Buddhists, and not the Jains, are the victims of Kūṉ Pāṇṭya (cf. *Mackenzie Manuscripts* 3: 8), but Buddhists and Jains are easily confused in later sources.
102. See a few temple reliefs in Verardi (1996: 222-27; pls. I-IV) and later paintings in L'Hernault (2006).
103. Pate (1917, I: 100).
104. Rao, T.N. Vasudeva (1979: 207); Champakalakshmi (1981: 255-56). Rao quotes several epithets by which Campantar calls the Buddhists in his hymns, a particularly interesting one being 'the Sākkyas who argue till death' (esp. pp. 216-18), obviously referring to the public debates.
105. Dikshitar, V.R. Ramachandra (1931: 689, n. 1). The place is probably present Budalur near Tirukkattupalli in Thanjavur district (Ramachandran 1954: 11). Thera Buddhadatta, who lived in the fifth century and ran several monasteries in both Sri Lanka and Tamil Nadu, is the author, among many other works, of the *Abhidhammāvatāra*. His connection with the Cōḷa-maṇṭalam during the Kaḷabhra rule has been underlined by Rao, T.N. Vasudeva (1979: 182-86).
106. *Periya Purāṇam*: 33. 906 (vol. 2, p. 176).
107. Ibid.: 33.908-10 (vol. 2, p. 177).
108. Ibid.: 33.911 (vol. 2, p. 178).
109. Ibid.: 33.913-14 (vol. 2, p. 178).
110. Ibid.: 33.924 (vol. 2, p. 181).
111. Ibid.: 33.925-26 (vol. 2, p. 181).
112. Inv. no. 89.
113. In the same locality, Campantar vanquished another Buddhist *vādin*, Śāriputra, and defeated once again the Buddhists at Sattamankai (Ramachandran 1954: 7, 10).

114. After his conversion, a *śuddha* Sivaite for Dehejia (1988: 37), but the fact that the farce ridicules the Buddhists and, to a lesser extent, the Kāpālikas and the Pāśupatas while no Jain appears on stage, may point to a pre-conversion chronology of the play. The particularly strong bias against the Buddhists is shown, at the beginning of the work, by the Kapālin associating the Buddhists to dogs ('I suspect a dog or a Buddhist friar has taken it'); eventually, the Madman gives back to the Kāpālika the skull he got 'from the most respectable dog belonging to a Caṇḍāla'. See *Mattavilāsa*: 706, 715.
115. *Poems to Śiva*: 182 [*Tirumuṟai* IV.20.3].
116. Lorenzen (1972: 50).
117. Ibid. 53.
118. *Appar Tirumuṟai* VI.13.5 (p. 100); cf. also VI.2.8-9 (pp. 14-15), etc. In VI.8.1, 'He is the mighty One of the crematory' (p. 60).
119. *Appar Tirumuṟai* VI.58.10 (p. 391).
120. Ibid: VI.58.3, 4 (pp. 387-88). *Bhūta*-s ('billions and billions'), accompany Śiva 'in sheer ecstasy' according to the *Periya Purāṇam*, I. 16 (vol. 1, p. 11).
121. Vadāvūrar was the saint's name as minister of the Pāṇṭya king Varakuṇa.
122. Rao, T.N. Vasudeva (1979: 229-30); cf. also Dikshitar, T.N. Ramachandra (1931: 690-91). The same story, summarised by Taylor, is reported in the 'Bauddha section' of the *Vātur Sthalapurāṇam* where the king of Sri Lanka and his followers become Sivaite converts (cf. *Mackenzie Manuscripts* 5: 343-44).
123. This passage corresponds to *Tiruviḷaiyāṭaṟ Purāṇam*: 64.97-108 as summarised and partly translated by Dessigane, Pattabiramin & Filliozat (1960: 100-01). The passages translated into French are the following: 'Il n'est pas possible de faire voir à un aveugle le soleil brillant, Notre Dieu est au dessus de tout. Il ne peut être visible que pour ceux qui se mettent à son service, en se frottant de cendre'; 'Le corps luisant de notre Śivaṉ et la cendre qu'il porte sur lui sont comme cette bouse de vache chauffée au rouge et la couche de cendre qui la couvre'. The *Tiruviḷaiyāṭaṟ Purāṇam* was written by Perumpaṟṟappuliyūr Nampi in the twelfth century, the edition followed by the authors being that of V. Cāminātaiyar, Madras 1927[2]. This work has a popular parallel in a text with the same title composed at the beginning of the sixteenth century by Parañcōti Muṉivar, on which the nineteenth-century paintings of Madurai are based. Finally, there is a Sanskrit translation in verse, the *Hālāsya Māhātmya*. For all these questions, cf. ibid. ii-iii.
124. Ibid.: 101 (*Tiruviḷaiyāṭaṟ Purāṇam*: 64.109-13).
125. Narayanan & Veluthat (1986: 259).
126. Zvelebil (1975: 142-43). According to the version of the *Kēralōtpatti* followed by P.C. Alexander, the Perumāḷ king who had converted to Buddhism was Paḷḷi Bāṇa Perumāḷ, who after being obliged to have the Buddhists mutilated, 'abdicated in great remorse and left for "Makkam"'

(Alexander 1949: 51). The common identification as *mleccha*-s of both Buddhists and Muslims, as well as of Christians, and the chronological inconsistencies of the chronicle make the evaluation of this and other passages of the *Kēralōtpatti* difficult. See the discussion by Alexander (ibid.: 51-61).

127. The traditions according to which Mahendravarman I Pallava and Arikēsari Parāṅkusa Māravarman were Sivaites who converted to Jainism, eventually reverting to Sivaism, reflect the climate of the period when they lived, a turning point in the history of Tamilakam.
128. *EC* 4, 1898 (Mysore Inscr. 2, B.L. Rice): 36.
129. *Tāranātha*: 87A (p. 226).
130. Ibid.: 86B-87A (pp. 225-26).
131. Pollock (2006: 55).
132. See the discussion by Anālayo (2009) on the lion's imagery in the teaching of the Buddha in the *nikāya*-s and in the Chinese *āgama*-s.
133. *Śaṅkara Digvijaya*: 1. 95-98 (p. 9).
134. *EI* 1 (1892, F. Kielhorn): 351-61, l. 41.
135. *EC* 5/1, 1902 (Hassan Inscr., B.L. Rice): no. 17 (cf. trans. p. 51).
136. *EC* 2, rev. ed. 1923 (Sravana Belgola, R. Narasimhachar): no. 69; p. 35, trans. section.
137. Ibid.: no. 63; p. 15, trans. section.
138. See the iconographic evidence and the relevant texts on this myth collected in Melzer (2002).
139. *Kūrma Purāṇa*: I.32.16-18 (vol. 1, p. 253).
140. V.S. Agrawala (1984*a*: 41). Agrawala further states: 'The elephant is the symbol of the universal the Mahat and was transformed as Gajāsura, the elephant-demon, in the Purāṇa story whose Āsuric form was bent in order to bring him into the rhythmic mould of the yajña'.
141. Kingsbury & Phillips (1921: no. 18; p. 27). The killing of the elephant is very frequently recalled in the poems of Campantar's elder companion, Appar; see for example *Appar Tirumuṟai* VI.4.8 ('Is He the One who destroyed/the ichor-abounding and haughty tusker [...]', p. 32), VI.8.7 ('He is Kaapaali who mantled Himself/In the tusker's hide and joyed at it', p. 64); etc.
142. See Rangaswamy (1990: 348-49).
143. *Kūrma Purāṇa*: I.31-34 (vol. 1, pp. 246-47).
144. Hazra (1940: 73).
145. V.S. Agrawala (1984*a*: 47).
146. Regarding the Gajāntaka panel, Soundara Rajan (1981: 193) observes that 'the main episode is almost overpowered by the attendant figure sculpture suggesting only ritual significance but a conceptual degeneration'.
147. Rao, T.A. Gopinatha (1914-16, II: 150-52).
148. Nagapattinam, known for the famous bronzes (Ramachandran 1954),

survived as a Buddhist site until the fifteenth-sixteenth century (see, for instance, Bronze no. 84 in ibid. 60-61).

149. Rao, T.A. Gopinatha (1914-16, II: 150, 153-54 and pl. XXXI).
150. Valuvur as the place where the elephant was flayed is recorded by Nampi Ārūrar (Rangaswamy, M.A. Dorai 1990: 354 [*Tēvāram* 7.10.1]).
151. Longhurst (1930: 5-6). See the section of the *adhiṣṭhāna* of the Panamalai Temple in Meister & Dhaky 1983: 48, fig. 30a)
152. *SII* 1 (1890, E. Hultzsch): v. 8 (p. 14).
153. Ibid.: v. 11.
154. The panel is part of the decoration of the *ardhamaṇḍapa* (Rea 1909: 39; pl. LXII).
155. See also the cut-off elephant heads in the *adhiṣṭhāna* (Meister & Dhaky 1983: pl. 30).
156. For the chronology of this king, see HCIP 3: 262-63.
157. Hudson (2002: 134).
158. Meister & Dhaky (1983: 71).
159. Minakshi (1941).
160. I find it difficult here to follow Hudson & Case (2008: 63-64) who, although rightly refusing the idea that the 'Pallava-style lions' are 'merely adornments', suggest them to allude to the conquering power of Durgā embodied by the king. For all the complexity of mature, inclusive Bhāgavatism, Durgā seems to me to be out of place here, and we should rather recall the inherent leonine nature of Viṣṇu, betrayed by both the lion-head he displays in his crown (below, note 173) and by his Narasiṃha, *vāma* aspect.
161. Minakshi (1938: 172).
162. Ibid.
163. Cf. Chari (1997: 11, 26-27).
164. Dikshitar, V.R. Ramachandra (1931: 692, n. 4; cf. also Rao, T.N.Vasudeva 1979: 235). The Tamil text, also quoted by Minakshi (1938: 172) runs: *Veṟuppoṭu camaṇar muṇṭar vitiyil cākkiyarkaḷ ninpāl/Poṟuppariyanakaḷ pēsil pōvatēnōyatāki/Kuṟippeṉakkaṭaiyumākil kuṭumēl, talayaiyānkē/ Aṟuppatē karumam kaṇṭāy arankamānakaruḷānē*. As an example of the difficulty in interpreting these and similar passages, I report the observations kindly provided to me by François Gros. Line 1: according to some commentators, *muṇṭar* refer to the Sivaites, who would thus be included, coherently with the strong sectarian nature of Tamil Vishnuism, among the enemies to eradicate; line 2: *pōvatēnōyatāki* decomposes as *pōvat(u)-ē* ('this will go, will end' + emphatic *ē*) and *nōy-atu-āki* (an illness this having become). Three interpretations are possible: (a) *pōvatu* (to go, to leave) can be understood, with reference to the blasphemers, as 'to be ruined, to be destroyed': this is the interpretation accepted for the translation above; (b) the Vishnuite devotees, affected by the blasphemers as by an illness, will die; (c) The devotees, being unable to endure the sufferance caused by the

evil plans of the blasphemers, will leave covering their ears; line 3: there is a variant for *kuṟipp(u)eṉakku aṭaiyum*, that is, *kuṟippiṉukku aṭaiyum* ([the question being of] reaching one's aim). However, the Āḻvārs speak very often in the first person in their poems, also for reviling the heretics; line 4: the commentaries underline the advisability of immediate justice, and the text may thus be understood that the heretics are to be killed in the very place where they have blasphemed. A tentative French translation would thus be: 'Qu'avec répulsion, Camanar, crânes-rasés, infortunés Cakkiyar, sur Toi/Tiennent des propos intolérables, cela finira, certes, comme un mauvais mal;/Mais s'agissant d'atteindre mon but,—si possible—le karma, voyez-vous,/Est bien de leur trancher la tête sur-le-champ. Ô Lui-qui-réside dans la grande Cité d'Arangam !'

165. Minakshi (1938: 171). The grant was published by Thomas Foulkes (*IA* 8, 1879: 273-84; cf. l. 74, p. 276).
166. Cf. n. 164 above.
167. Veluthat (1993: 224).
168. Willis (2009: esp. 158-59).
169. Rao, T.A. Gopinatha (1915: 128); Champakalakshmi (1996: 398).
170. See now the few known images from the town and the district of Kāñcīpuram in Fukuroi (2002).
171. The learned scholar noted that while in his times the Jain temples of Kāñcī were still in existence, there were no relics of the places and objects of worship of the Buddhists (Rao, T.A. Gopinatha 1915: 128).
172. As is known, there is a bitter dispute between the Kāñcī and Śṛṅgerī *maṭha*s as to which of the two is Śaṅkara's original monastery. Sankaranarayanan (1995: 293) observes that the street where the Kāñcī *maṭha* is located bears the name *cālai teru* (Salai Street), that is, a street marked by the presence of a *cālai/śālai*, that is, a *maṭha*. Kāñcī was probably Śaṅkara's last sojourn (Piantelli 1998: 192 ff.; Pande 1994: 342, 359-60).
173. Piantelli (1998: 192).
174. Champakalakshmi (1996: 398).
175. Panigrahi (1961: 26 ff.); Meister, Dhaky & Deva (1988: 256).
176. The most complete description of the iconographies profusely displayed in this temple is, to this day, that of Panigrahi (1961: 69-77), though it is not an iconographical study in a proper sense.
177. Ibid.: 224-25.
178. Donaldson (1976) provides other examples from the temples of Bhubaneswar.
179. V.S. Agrawala (1965: 235 ff). A similar, subtle allusion, harking back to *sandhyābhāṣā* in literary texts, may be seen in the early crowns of Viṣṇu decorated with lion heads and strings of pearls, pointing to the parallel role of the Bhāgavatas in curbing the power of the heretics.
180. See for instance *Kādambarī* : 57 (cf. p. 39 of the trans.).

181. I read the passage in Kramrisch (1946, II: 336, n. 118); cf. *IA* 14, 1884 (K.B. Pathak): 105 [*Ādipurāṇa*: XXI. 231-32]; 'temples' has the sense of 'frontal globes'. On Jinasena, see below, Chapter VI.
182. *Bu ston*: fol. 132 a-b (p. 173). The great Tibetan scholar (AD 1290-1364) places these events before an ephemeral recovery of the religion and the appearance on the Indian horizon of three kings, 'neither of Indian, nor of Chinese descent', but 'Yavana, Pahlika and Çakuna'.
183. Panigrahi (1961: 94-95).
184. Ibid.: 97.
185. See the Ananta Vāsudeva inscription in R. Mitra (1875-80, II: 150-52).
186. Ganguly (1912: 203).
187. Panigrahi (1981: 238-39). The temples of Kadwāhā, their religious seat in Gopakṣetra (then Candella territory), which dates back to the tenth and eleventh centuries, were erected by their *ācārya*-s with the support of the local rulers. On the Maṭṭamayūras, see Mirashi (1955: cli ff.); Pathak (1960: 32-34) is not in agreement with Mirashi's identifications, and believes Maṭṭamayūra to be located in Panjab. See, however, Willis (1997: 80).
188. R. Mitra (1875-80, II: 151 [l. 2]). Mahāśivagupta ruled between AD 1065 and 1085.
189. Ibid.: 151-52 (l. 10).
190. Kulke (1986: 127-29).
191. *Kuvalayamālā*: 150.20-151.6 (vol. 2, pp. 439-41); for the date of the work, see Chojnacki in ibid. vol. 1, 64.
192. Chojnacki, following A.N. Upadhye, editor of the manuscript, identifies Vijayāpurī with Vijayadurg, due north of Goa (cf. *Kuvalayamālā* II: 436, n. 1388), but Krishnan (1970), followed by other authors, has proposed the identification with ancient Kāntaḷūr – probably Thiruvananthapuram (see below).
193. *Kuvalayamālā* II: 151.15-16 (vol. 2, p. 442).
194. Chojnacki in *Kuvalayamālā* I: 23, 244.
195. Krishnan (1970: 347-48). The *Kuvalayamālā* (150.15-20; vol. 2, pp. 439-40) clearly distinguishes between *maṭha* and temple. In fact, the prince mistakes at first the former for the latter, until a passerby tells him that it was not a temple but an educational institution.
196. Rao, T.A. Gopinatha (1920, I: 19-34; cf. p. 33). The plate is about the establishment of a *śālai* at Kāntaḷūr, identified by him with Valiyasali, a locality in Tiruvananthapuram (Krishnan 1970: 349-50).
197. Veluthat (1975: 100).
198. Narayanan (1970: 128).
199. Ibid.: 129. Almost all the sources agree in locating Śaṅkara's birthplace at Kālaṭi in the Ernakulam district (Bader 2000: 79). The reader is referred to ibid (313 ff.) for the construction of the myth of Śaṅkara as a restorer of Brahmanism by both hagiographers and modern nationalists.

200. With regard to the tradition of Śaṅkara's challenge to the Buddhists, see *Tāranātha*: 90B-93A, pp. 232-37, for his repeated debates (two of which after being reborn) with Dharmakīrti at Nālandā.
201. It is this perspective that Narayanan (1970) and Veluthat (1975) have developed their interpretations. There is much to be kept here, but the whole question must be rediscussed.
202. Tieken & Sato (2000) and above.
203. Ibid.: 217 (the authors have re-translated the relevant passage of the Vaikuṇṭha Perumāḷ label inscription in n. 20 on pp. 221-22).
204. See the Talagunda pillar inscription of the Kadamba king Śāntivarman (*c.* AD 450-75) that contains this early reference to a *ghaṭikā*: the relevant passage has been retranslated in ibid.: 213-14.
205. Moraes (1931: 16).
206. Sankaranarayana (1977: 2 ff.).
207. Ibid.: 37-40, 45. If the Sivaite temple of Srisailam was erected on the ruins of a Buddhist establishment, Govindavarman may have been the king responsible for the radical transformation of the site (ibid. 40).
208. Ibid.: 66.
209. Ibid.: 236.
210. In the Kasakudi plates, Nandivarman says of one of his ancestors that '[t]hough born from a race of Brāhmaṇas, he possessed in the highest degree the ,valour of the Kshatriyas, which was inherent in him' (*SII* 2/3 [1895, E. Hultzsch]: 342-61: v. 18).
211. Cf. Aiyangar, S. Krishnaswamy (1923: 237).
212. It should be kept in mind that – as recalled by Gros (1984: xiii) – our only source for all this is the *Periya Purāṇam*: 'The Kadava king who came to con the falsity/Of the Jains who knew not the way to salvation,/Came by truth; he razed all the shrines/And mutts of the Jains at Pataliputra, and with/Their spoils brought to Tiruvatikai, raised the temple/Gunaparaveechharam for the brow-eyed Lord' (26.146; vol. 1, p. 291). The temple of Guṇadhārīśvara is located at Tiruppatirippuliyur, Cuddalore, which before becoming a Jain and then a Sivaite centre, was a centre of Buddhism (cf. Ramachandran 1954: 11). It was to Mahendravarman's patronage, as shown by Ramaswamy (1975), that the Sivaite monuments of Māmallapuram were erected (against Ramaswamy's chronology, see e.g. Rabe (1997).
213. Lorenzen (1978: 64).
214. Campbell (1896: 84). On this recurring formula in Maitraka inscriptions see Njammasch (2001: 8 ff.). Dyczkowski (1988: 200, n. 53) has underlined the dependency of the Dasanāmīs from previous traditions (though obviously not as early as the Sivaite groups of Valabhī).
215. U. Singh (1993: 29). The author gives a full account, based on the epigraphic evidence, on land distribution in the various parts of the region.
216. A thorough analysis on Lakulīśa on early Sivaite temples of Orissa is provided by D. Mitra (1984: 103-18; for Bhubaneswar, pp. 106 ff.).

217. For this condensed iconographic description, I follow Panigrahi (1961: 78 ff.) and Donaldson (2002, I: 109-10). For other Orissan temples presided over by Cāmuṇḍā, see ibid. 417 ff..
218. See the typology proposed by Donaldson (1991: 122ff.), whose interpretation develops on an exclusively symbolical level.
219. In the words of Panigrahi (1961: 80), 'a large knife usually seen in a butcher's shop'.
220. Ibid.
221. Ibid.
222. This is how I interpret the piece (Panigrahi rightly maintains that it is 'the remnant of a *yūpa*', ibid. 234). For Mohapatra (1982: 39), a Buddha image was carved on the sacrificial post as an insult to him (the images are two, actually), but it is definitely a reused piece. As to Donaldson, he is reticent on this point. According to Panigrahi (1961: 80), one of the images in the *garbhagṛha* 'is definitely that of Amoghasiddhi [...] the left hand – the right one is broken – holds a vase and the deity is seated in *yogāsana* with an attendant on each side and a canopy of seven serpent hoods over the head'. If the identification is correct, it must be assumed that the relief was re-used here from an earlier or contemporary Buddhist shrine, reinterpreting the iconography. A careful examination of the slab would be necessary to form an opinion on this point.
223. Panigrahi (1961: 234); Donaldson (2002, I: 108).
224. Panigrahi (1961: 233).
225. Donaldson (2002, I: 108; III: fig. 627).
226. The reader is referred to Lorenzen (1972: 31 ff.) for an appraisal of the information available in both the *Śaṅkara Digvijaya* and the *Śaṅkaravijaya*. See also Dyczkowski (1988: 29-30).
227. Dagens (1984: 26-27). In Tamil Nadu and lower Andhra Pradesh the Kālāmukhas were replaced by the Pāśupatas from the twelfth century onwards (ibid.: 41, 46-47).
228. See Lorenzen's analysis of a passage of the *Rājataraṅgiṇī* (Lorenzen: 1972: 66-67). The *vrata* of the Pāśupatas consisted in the besmearing of and sleeping over ashes, as explicitly said in the *Pāśupata Sūtra*: I.1-9, 2-17 (pp. 25-26). The *vrata*-s, which included several other unsocial behaviours, were to be kept secret (ibid.: IV: 2-7, p. 30). The Pāśupatas hated the Kāpālikas (Sircar 1948: 10, n.1), but contexts and chronology should be carefully evaluated.
229. Dyczkowski (1988: 27).
230. *Mālatīmādhava*: Act V (pp. 94-97/41 ff.). Bhavabhūti naturally cuts out for himself the position of an observer completely alien to the compromises between high-caste, orthodox brāhmaṇas and *vāmācāra*-s (on this, see the next chapter).
231. This trend is shared by other Sivaite groups (Dyczkowski 1988: 13). In the south, Bhairava did not acquire the gruesome aspect he has in central and

northern India because his adversaries were successfully got rid of in a relatively short time. To a certain degree, this is true also for Cāmuṇḍā, the *mātṛkā*-s, and the *yoginī*-s. See the evidence from southern Andhra Pradesh provided by Dagens (1984, I: 58-60 for Bhairava; 181 ff. for the *mātṛkā*-s and Cāmuṇḍā; cf. the relevant photographs in the second volume).

232. Lorenzen (1972: 74-77; cf. esp. p. 75).
233. Ibid.: 77.
234. *Śiva Purāṇa*, *Rudrasaṃhitā*: II.xxxiv.52 (vol. 1, p. 434).
235. I refer again the reader to Lorenzen (1972: 77-81), who examines the version of the *Matsya Purāṇa* and provides references to other relevant material. As for the myth, see it analysed from quite a different point of view, and unsatisfactorily for me, by O'Flaherty (1980: 277 ff.; 1981*b*: 123 ff.).
236. Panigrahi (1981: 80). This fact is extraordinary, since *aśvamedha*-s had long been replaced by the neo-Brahmanical rituals.
237. D.C. Sircar in *EI* 28 (1949-50): 180.
238. See the *Virajā Māhātmya* and U.N. Dal's introduction to the text.
239. As early as 1836, Markham Kittoe noticed 'a number of Jain and Buddhist figures in different places scattered around' in the town (Kittoe 1838: 55). Outside Jajpur, he saw 'a very large tank and a high mound around it, on which there are traces of there having been buildings in former years. [...] The mounds are now covered with jungle and brambles. I remarked a figure of Buddh under a large banyan tree, it was all besmeared with sendoor (red lead) and worshipped by the villagers as the thakoor (Mahadeo); there were other pieces of sculpture scattered about in different directions' (ibid. 201).
240. The Buddhist Bhaumakaras had to yield, in course of time, to Sivaite pressure. The mechanism observed at Nagarjunakonda (Chapter III) is, significantly reversed: Sivaite patronage is assigned to the female representatives of the dynasty, as is documented for the temple of Madhaveśvara, built in the seventh century thanks to the patronage of Mādhavadevī, the wife of king Śubhākara I (D.C. Sircar in *EI* 28, 1949-50: 179-85, ll. 3-4 and p. 182). On the Bhaumakaras as active participants in the furtherance of the Buddhist faith, see Donaldson (2001: 5-7).
241. See the complex matter summed up by S. Tripathy (2000: 54-59).
242. Here Nepal is considered in its proper sense, as the valley of Kathmandu.
243. Shepherd Slusser (1982, I: 34).
244. Ibid.: 35. D.R. Regmi has reacted vigorously against Lévi's conjecture that Tibet held control over Nepal into the ninth century, i.e. until the new era of AD 879 (Lévi 1905-8, II: 171 ff.), arguing that Nepalese subjugation lasted until AD 704, when the Tibetan king was defeated and killed in battle by the Nepalese (Regmi 1969: 218-19). Petech (1984: 25) is even more restrictive in judging the available information 'confused', holding that 'the Tibetan ascendancy in Nepal waned during the decades after 651'.

245. Narendradeva, already mentioned in Chapter II, is a good example of the compromise Buddhist kings had come to. He was a devotee of Lord Paśupatinātha and on his coins (known as 'Paśupati coins') there always is a bull, standing or recumbent.
246. As known to the *vaṃśāvalī*-s. It lay to the northeast of the town of Kathmandu of Malla times, and the residence of the Licchavi kings of the fourth and fifth century AD, as well as the Kailāsakūṭabhavana of Aṃśuvarman were probably located there.
247. Inv. no. HSN 142. See the text and translation of the inscription in Verardi (1992, I: 143-44).
248. The stūpa seems to have been built according to the rules laid down in the *Mañjuśrīvāstuvidyā Śāstra* or in a similar text. See ibid., I: 72-78.
249. It could be the earthquake which took place in NS 375 (AD 1255) recorded in the *Gopālarājavaṃśāvalī*: fol. 26 (p. 129).
250. For the stratigraphic evidence, see Verardi (1992, I: 88-90). What was carried out at Andigrāma was made easier by the fact that the Buddhist buildings were made of bricks. The plundering of brick structures and the re-use of bricks is very common in the alluvial plains, where this building material is normally used. This largely accounts for the lesser number of temples and other ancient edifices in the plains of northern India.
251. I follow Regmi's translation (Regmi 1984, I-II: no. XXVII).
252. Ibid.: l. 21 and 27, respectively.
253. Ibid.: l. 42 and 50, respectively.
254. Ibid.: l. 54.
255. Ibid.: l. 63-71.
256. Cf. *SII* 2/3 (1895, E. Hultzch): 345-61, v. 71 (p. 359).
257. Regmi (1984, III: 72).
258. Cf. Verardi (1992, I: 24).
259. Pal (1974: pl. 10).
260. Inv. nos. HSN 31, 58 (Verardi (1992, I: 143).
261. For the names of Andigrāma and Harigaon, see discussion in ibid.: I: 21, n. 48.
262. Lévi (1905-8, III: 32).
263. S. Dasgupta (1932-55, III: 14-15, 18-20); cf. above, Chapter II.
264. See for instance the considerations of the editors and translators of the *Gopālarājavaṃśāvalī* (p. VIII); Pal (1974: 7); etc.
265. Shepherd Slusser (1982, I: 41).
266. Wiesner (1980).
267. The Cārumatī Vihāra set of stūpas in the Chabahil village, now part of modern Kathmandu.
268. Hodgson (1874: 135-36). See also the testimony of Cunningham in Chapter I, n. 66.
269. Wiesner (1980: 171).

270. Ibid.: 172.
271. *History of Nepal* a: 159-60. 'The word Bandya, the name of the Buddhámargí sect [...] is metamorphosed by ignorance into Bánra, a word which has no meaning' (Hodgson 1874: 51); the *bandya*-s/*vandya*-s include all the Buddhists of Nepal (ibid. 63). The custom of *satī* is documented in Nepal as early as AD 464 (cf. Michaels 1993: 22-23).
272. Pande (1994: 348); Piantelli (1998: 48; 179).
273. *History of Nepal* a: 119-20.
274. Above, n. 267. That the site was erected by Aśoka's daughter Cārumatī may not be credible, but the main stūpa is an early one, as is shown by a brick inscription in Aśokan *brāhmī* (Verardi 2004: 43-44).
275. See it described in Vaidya (1986: 14 ff.); cf. also Gellner (1992: 199-202).
276. *History of Nepal* a: 121-23. The story accounts for the two classes of married monks of Newār Buddhism, the Vajrācāryas and the Śākyas. See below, Chapter VI.
277. A case of an abjuration antedating any possible journey of Śaṅkara to Nepal (we are in the second half of the seventh century) is probably that of a Chinese monk descended from a high family. Yijing reports that while his companion returned to the lay state, he went to reside in the temple of Śiva, arguably that of Paśupatināth. So I interpret the evidence in *Eminent Monks* a: 18-19, pp. 50-51. *Eminent Monks* b: 30-31, has instead: 'There were two other monks in Nepal. [...] One of them later on, entered the family life again. They lived at the great Rājavihāra'.
278. Kārttikeya and Gaṇeśa, for instance, were made at first the sons of Śiva and then given consorts. This is especially significant for Gaṇeśa, a combination of child-ascetic-eunuch which is 'an explicit denial of adult male sexuality' (Courtright 1985: 111); Gaṇeśa's *śakti* is Gaṇeśānī.
279. *History of Nepal* b: 38.
280. Ibid.: 39. Bikrama Jit Hasrat, after expressing his doubts on Śaṅkara's visit to Nepal, observes that 'the debates and struggles by the two creeds referred to in the text, have relation to what occurred in the plains of India, where the prosecution of the Buddhists was furious—root and branch eradication in fact'.
281. Hodgson (1874: 48).

CHAPTER V

Battlefields and *Yajña*-s

THE BLOOD OF THE *ASURA*-S

The *devāsura* wars were devastating for both the demons and the gods. Already the *Vāyu Purāṇa* acknowledges the exhaustion they resulted in and the misfortune they brought upon the people.[1] In later Purāṇas, weapons multiply and blood flows freely. In the massacre which took place in the war against the *asura* Kālakeya, the enemies of the gods had their heads 'broken with pestles',[2] and 'the whole earth with mountains, forests and groves was flooded with blood'.[3] In the war against Bala and Namuci, both 'gods and demons showered blood oozing': arms and legs were cut off, and 'abdomens cut-off lay in hundreds on the ground. Crores of thousands of elephants, horses and demons fell variously on the ground in the stream of blood. From there, inauspicious rivers flew there', and 'a great ocean of blood due to many other beings falling therein' was formed: the entire earth 'was having the stream of blood'.[4]

In the battle against Tripura's son, 'gods of great might, fell down with their bodies covered with streams of blood'.[5] Even Gaṇeśa was wounded, and fought back with his body 'moistened with blood'.[6] In the battle against Bala, the bodies of both the *asura* and Indra were 'moistered with blood spreading forth' like 'the blossomed Kiṃśuka trees in the spring'.[7] In the Kālakeya war the allegory becomes transparent: the gods-brāhmaṇas need medical treatment, and Dhanvantari moves to the battlefield carrying medicines, thanks to which 'the gods that were dead in the great war, again came back to life'.[8] The four major *asura*-s who were then fighting, Madhu, Dhundhu, Sunda and Kālakeya, 'had mastered the science of all weapons',[9] a detail that indicates that the heretics had developed a system of defence and fought back. Their historical identity is disclosed in a passage of the *Brahmāṇḍa Purāṇa*: 'Formerly, in the battle between the Devas and the Asuras, the Asuras were defeated. They created the heretics, like Vṛddhaśrāvakīs, Nirgranthas, Śākyas, Jīvaskas and Kārpaṭas',[10] who do not follow *varṇāśramadharma* and discard 'the *trayī* or triple Veda, declared as the protective covering for all living beings',[11] being thus considered *nagna*-s, nudes.

The myth of the Deluder, as already suggested, does not only emphasise the fact that the *asura*-s' power derives from God, as no being in the *triloka* exists independently from an act of creation (that very creation denied by Buddhism), but points to the theoretical difficulty to admit that apostate brāhmaṇas could exist. Admitting this was tantamount to declaring that the whole *varṇa* system was groundless. The issue became central in post-Gupta times and in fact we meet an increasing number of high-caste *asura*-s in the literature. Mahiṣa's status, for instance, is raised in the course of time; he is said to have been born from the involuntarily emitted semen of the *ṛṣi*, Sindhudvīpa,[12] an enemy of Indra and father of another *asura*, Vetrāsura.[13] Nothing reminds us here of the destructive, early agrarian buffalo-demon. Gaja becomes Mahiṣa's son in later works, and he performs penance meditating on Brahmā, who grants him the boon of being immune from death by men or women overwhelmed by lust.[14] Tāraka, doomed to be killed by Skanda, does penance to propitiate Śiva and gets a boon to the effect that none other than a son born to Śiva should be able to kill him.[15] This amounts to saying that only brāhmaṇas (allegorised as gods) are entitled to get rid of other brāhmaṇas (allegorised as *asura*-s). Myths over time tend to clarify the caste identity of the *asura*-s because we are now in the epoch of doctrinal debates in which brāhmaṇas of different belief oppose each other in a tough struggle. The blood that in the texts flows more and more abundantly is not symbolical, but metaphorical, and refers to a real clash.

The *asura*-s repeatedly said to have dispossessed the gods, taken possession of the *triloka* and harassed the brāhmaṇas are of high caste. The *asura* kings belong to patrilinear lineages and are assisted by courageous relatives (like Hiraṇyakaśipu's brother Hiraṇyākṣa) and their rule lasts for a long time (eons in the expanded temporal perspective of neo-Brahmanical literature). They are *cakravartin*-s who have displaced Indra after conquering all the rival kings on earth, thus mirroring the kings of the Kali Age. Twelve *devāsura* wars are listed, sometimes rather confusedly as is the case of the early *Vāyu Purāṇa*, which had to accommodate them in a Bhāgavata perspective,[16] and in later texts in a rather extended way. In the *Vāyu Purāṇa* the initial 'great friendship' between *deva*-s and *asura*-s is, significantly, acknowledged.[17] The reference is to an epoch when heresy did not yet threaten the identity of the first *varṇa*. Only later, 'a terrible, violent dispute' arose between them, causing 'horrible devastation' to both parties.[18] Far from denying history, this Purāṇa speaks very clearly: all we need is a code to enter the archives.

The slaying of Hiraṇyakaśipu takes place at the end of the first *devāsura* war, and I have already suggested that the great *asura* may be identified with either Aśoka or the last Mauryan emperor. The exploit of Śiva against Tripura, included in the early list of the *Vāyu Purāṇa*, should be also considered an early *devāsura* war: Śiva's fight against Andhaka, where the role of the *mātṛkā*-s is fundamental, is alluded to,[19] but no mention is made of the role of Skanda in the Tārakāmaya.[20] In the *Vāyu Purāṇa* and dependent texts no mention is made of the war against Mahiṣa, and we can conclude that the myth of the buffalo-demon started being interpreted as an allegory of the eradication of heresy only at a later date, and/or that it developed in a region foreign to the Bhāgavatas. These early myths indicate that the wars against the heretics were fought from the beginning by the Bhāgavatas and Pāśupatas, who acquired power by this means.

The escalation of violence that took place from the second half of the seventh century is best illustrated by the great Sivaite myths, one of which, that of Śiva Gajāsuramardana, we have already discussed in the earlier chapter. The story of the *asura*-s of the three towns is narrated in the Karṇa Parvan of the *Mahābhārata*. The root of the evil lies in the defeated Tārakāsura, whose three sons, Vidyunmālī, Tārakākṣa and Kamalākṣa, practising austere penances that caused their bodies to become emaciated, obtained from Brahmā the boon of residing in three cities. These shall eventually transform into one and be only destructible by means of a single shaft. The *asura* architect, Maya, built a golden city set in heaven, a city of silver in the air, and one of iron on the earth, of which the three *asura* brothers became the kings. The towns, with wide streets, houses, mansions and lofty walls and porches, attracted millions upon millions of people from every side, 'desirous of great prosperity'. Having received further boons, the wicked *dānava*-s (a class of malign beings equated with the *asura*-s) ceased to show respect for anybody, afflicting the *triloka*. Though impartial to all creatures, Brahmā decided that the unrighteous should be slain, and that the task of destroying the triple city should be conferred upon Īśāna. Mahādeva asked the gods for half of their *śakti*, to add to his own strength: Viṣṇu, Agni and Soma became his shaft, Brahmā the charioteer and the Vedas the steeds. Before the armed god, the three cities became united, and Śiva sped the shaft at the triple city, which began to fall down. 'Burning those *Asuras*, he threw them down into the Western Ocean. Thus was the triple city burnt and thus were the *Danavas* exterminated by Maheswara [...]'.[21]

The story betrays the hostility towards urban life and enrichment: the three kings have an asuric nature just because they promote wealth and 'millions' of unmonitored people benefit for it escaping the control of the gods/brāhmaṇas. The destruction of the triple town is a metaphor for the collapse of the rich towns of the heretics, and in the fire that eventually destroys them we make out the fires that destroyed their symbols, the Buddhist monasteries.[22]

The battle against Andhaka, who had become king of the *asura*-s, is a further step leading Śiva towards his final dance. It is, at the same time, a story of destruction and submission. There are several versions of the myth, one of the most extended narratives being that of the *Kūrma Purāṇa*.[23] The Pāśupata recasting of the original Pāñcarātra text would date the passage to the eighth century.[24] No mention, however, is made here of the *asura*'s faculty of regenerating, nor are the *mātṛkā*-s associated with Śiva. We find these features in the *Padma Purāṇa* that, in accord with the *Kūrma Purāṇa* ends the story with the submission and conversion of the demon/heretic. The narrative lingers over the initial defeat of Śiva who, falling on the earth, causes the three worlds tremble and the disjoined constellations go in various directions:[25] the power of the heretics is at its apex. With the help of the other gods, Śiva, who wears the elephant's hide (the trophy of his previous battle against Gajāsura) succeeds in wounding Andhaka, but from the *asura*'s blood

> hundreds and thousands of Andhakas sprang up. When they were being pierced, other fearful Andhakas sprang up from their blood, and they occupied the entire world. Then the god of gods having seen that deceitful Andhaka, created the Mothers to drink his blood. [...] Then the destroyer of Tripura pierced the demon with his trident. The Mothers then drank the blood that flowed out.[26]

In this version of the myth, the bloodless *asura* do not die, and instead of reviving the fight, start praising Śiva, asking his mercy for having gone to the battlefield: '[t]hus praised with respect, Śiva gave him the position of his attendant and named him "Bhṛṅgīriṭī"'.[27] Here the *mātṛkā*-s perform their function of drinking the blood of the multiplying *asura*-s assigned to them by the *Devī Māhātmya*,[28] and Śiva is obliged to recognise their crucial role: alone, he would not have been able to defeat the *asura*. This is an important step in finding new means to silence the Buddhists.

The task that the *mātṛkā*-s and Śiva carry out jointly is best appreciated at Ellora, where Andhaka's story is repeatedly depicted. In Cave 15, the Daśāvatāra Cave, the Andhakāsuravadhamūrti panel combines the Gajāntaka and Andhakāri stories: as Śiva goes to fight with the *asura*, he wears the elephant skin, the head of the elephant appearing to his left, and the legs and tail to his right. The *mātṛkā*-s are condensed in the frightening figure of Kālī/Cāmuṇḍā collecting the blood spilt in a bowl.[29] In the Laṅkeśvara Cave, the stories are depicted in two separate panels. Śiva transfixes Andhaka with his long *śūla* while Cāmuṇḍā is seated with a dagger in her hand.

The nearby *yajñaśālā* is the litmus paper of the Andhaka myth, and a very peculiar place. Alongside the three walls of the rectangular hall, due perhaps to the patronage of the Rāṣṭrakūṭa queens, identified in the three female figures, two-handed and without vehicles, depicted on the eastern wall,[30] we find Śiva as Kāla along with Kālī, Gaṇeśa, and the *mātṛkā*-s. Kāla is seated and holds a hand and a foot on the corpses of two *asura*-s under the impassive gaze of the goddesses to his left, Aparājitā and Durgā (Fig. 9).[31] The *asura*-s are not armed, as we would expect them to be, they are naked. This detail contextualises the myth and reveals their true identity:[32] they are naked because they are deprived of the cloth of the Vedas. Their hairdo, made in small, regular curls, is unmistakably remindful of the curly Buddha heads of the late and post-Gupta period. The *yajñaśālā* may be interpreted as the stone rendition of the temporary structure erected outside the temple where the *asura*-s/heretics were or had been actually executed (if we want to approach with caution the problem raised by the existence of a similar secluded room and by the iconographies), or else can be the real place where special *yajña*-s were performed.

During the seventh and early eighth century, the latest and most ambitious Buddhist rock-cut monuments of western Deccan were made precisely at Ellora,[33] a tangible sign of the renewed presence of the heretics in the region. Early royal Brahmanical patronage had declined during the second decade of the seventh century, and local patronage is probably responsible for the Buddhist phase to begin.[34] It reached its peak by the later years of the century with the Do Thal and Tin Thal caves. Buddhism had probably remained popular in the Ellora-Aurangabad region since the days of Hariṣeṇa's(?) patronage at Ajanta,[35] and it can be further maintained that in the seventh and early eighth century the Buddhists succeeded in carving out a space in the large territory between present-day Maharashtra, Andhra Pradesh up to Orissa,[36] in the attempt to unite with Magadha and the North-East.

Rāṣṭrakūṭa power was established on firm orthodox positions by Dantidurga. The initial part of the Samangarh and other inscriptions allude to Viṣṇu and Brahmā and mention Hara.[37] Dantidurga's uncle and successor, Kṛṣṇa I (*c.* AD 756-72) was the creator of the Kailāsa

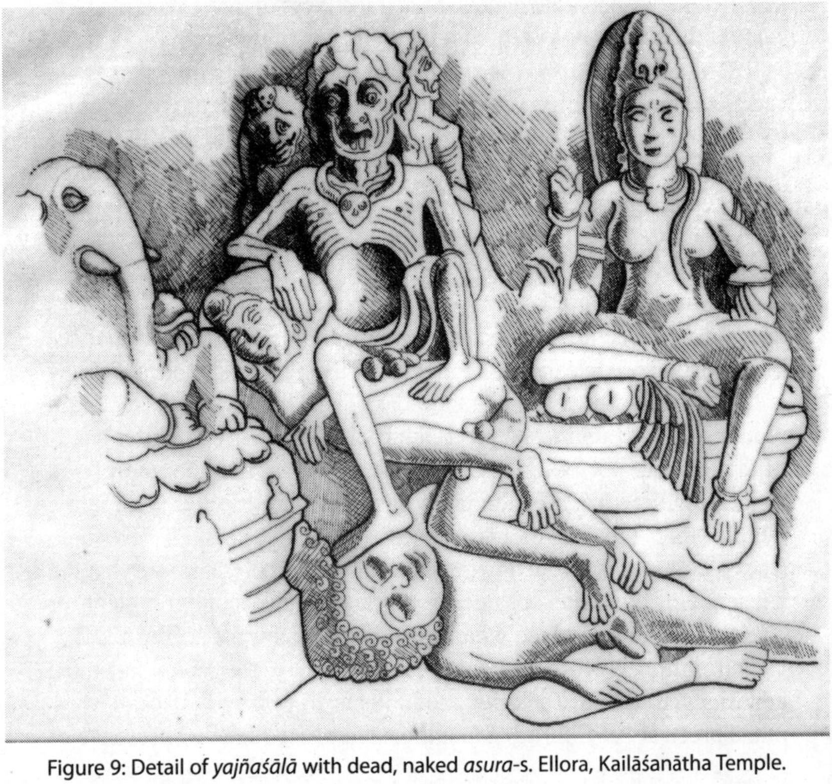

Figure 9: Detail of *yajñaśālā* with dead, naked *asura*-s. Ellora, Kailāśanātha Temple.

Temple, arguably planned and begun by Dantidurga.[38] The eradication of heresy, judging from the general iconographical layout of the Daśāvatāra Cave and the Kailāsa Temple as well as from the decision to occupy an area already taken up by the Buddhists, was one of the main objectives of the dynasty. On the capital of a pillar in Cave 15 we can still see a seated Buddha, and below a panel depicting a *pūrṇaghaṭa* and devotees.[39] Rock-cut monuments were excavated starting from the top of the rock formation, and it is clear that the Buddhists were obliged to interrupt their project: excavations had not yet reached the level of the court, which made the creation of the present pavilion possible. It is there that we find Dantidurga's inscription. The enormous amount of violence implicit in the iconographies of Ellora, and the unparalleled assertiveness of the monuments erected by the Rāṣṭrakūṭas rule out that they 'peacefully assumed control of the region around Ellora'.[40] Śiva's transmutation into his *vāma* aspects of Kāla and Bhairava and his association with the *mātṛkā*-s, shown by the skulls he wears as trophies in his fight against Andhaka, points to a situation similar to that observed in eighth-century Bhubaneswar.

The Śiva myths end with the dance of the God, who triumphs over his many enemies. Some aspects of the dance, usually overshadowed by an excess of symbolical interpretations, are worth considering. The dance is briefly mentioned in the *Vāmana Purāṇa* after the God's exploit against Andhaka: Śiva has purified himself, has been immersed in meditation, and finally, holding a lance, has started dancing, with the *gaṇa*-s and the gods who begin to dance with him. Then, 'having danced to the utmost of his desire, he again made up his mind for battle with the demons'.[41] Śiva's dance is, therefore, strictly associated with his wars against the *asura*-s, and his two most famous dances make this point clear.

In the *tāṇḍava* dance, pertaining to the tāmasic, or better to say, *vāma* aspect of the god, he appears as Bhairava or Vīrabhadra, the forms he assumes in association with the *mātṛkā*-s. This dance is performed in cemeteries and burning grounds, and it is at Ellora, Elephanta and Bhubaneswar that, as first observed by T.A. Gopinatha Rao, it found a sculptural rendition.[42] The *Liṅga Purāṇa* clarifies the connection between Śiva, the goddess(es) and the *asura*-s. The set is the cremation ground, 'full of corpses and ghosts', and here Kālī, who has killed the *asura* Dāruka, starts dancing 'in the midst of ghosts, happily along with yoginīs' after seeing Śiva's *tāṇḍava* dance at dusk.[43] Considering the context, in both Bhubaneswar and Ellora[44] the meaning of the dance cannot escape us: the God rejoices because the heretics have been exterminated. We shall see below the role played by Cāmuṇḍā/Kālī in central and north-eastern India, when she takes Śiva's place.

The meaning of Śiva as Naṭarāja becomes clear in context. The great temple at Tillai/Chidambaram, a privileged place in the meditation and predication of the Nāyaṉmār, was already famous in the days of Campantar.[45] Māṇikkavācakar defeated the Buddhists there, and there he died. It is not inappropriate to take back to the eighth and ninth century the popularity of the Naṭarāja cult that became so widespread with the Cōḷas. It was at Chidambaram that, according to tradition, the *Tēvāram* was discovered, and when we consider the role played by the Tamil saints in the extirpation of heresy, we must conclude that Śiva's final dance seals up the relatively – in the South – short period during which all efforts were channelled into silencing the heretics by expropriating their lands and free activities. Later tradition lost interest in past events and actualised Śiva's enemies. In the *Kōyil Purāṇam*, the *ṛṣi*-s whom Śiva meets in the forest of Tillai are identified with the Mīmāṃsakas,[46] and Muyalaka, the malignant dwarf created by the heretic sages upon whom the God presses his foot breaking his back before starting his dance, is in turn identified with the Apasmārapuruṣa on which the dancing God stands. The fight against the *śramaṇa*-s was now a thing of the past. The force of the myth lies in its faculty of being continuously reinterpreted and allegorised, but in the prostrate, miserable *asura* trampled by the Naṭarāja we recognise, in the first place, the Buddhists and Jains of the preceding centuries.[47]

In Chapter II we briefly discussed the context in which the Vālmīki *Rāmāyaṇa* was seemingly created. One among the several layers of meaning discernible in the poem alludes, perhaps, to the defeat of the heretics. We cannot subscribe to Wheeler's apodictic statement reported in Chapter I on the identification *tout court* of the *rākṣasa*-s with the Buddhists: this is a contention that needs good arguments to be taken into consideration. Verifying this hypothesis in relation to the Vālmīki poem is difficult at the present state of our knowledge, but an analysis of the Bhāgavata construal of the story in relation to the composition of the first and seventh *kāṇḍa*-s, would probably be rewarding. Rāvaṇa is a *brahmarākṣas* said to have obtained a boon of invulnerability by Brahmā[48] in the same way as the *asura*-s do in Purāṇic literature, beginning with Hiraṇyakaśipu. There is an attempt at unifying all the forces opposing the orthodox in the perspective examined above and in Chapter III: in the early middle age, the poem took a meaning (which, with reasonable certainty, it preserved henceforth for quite a long time) that is possible to retrieve.

Vimalasūri's *Paumacariyam*, a Jain work composed in Gupta or post-Gupta time, is a programmatic re-writing of the *Rāmāyaṇa*.[49] The evidence it provides on the political lineages of the Vindhya region and on the conflicts caused by the colonisation of previously unexploited territories have been analysed by Thapar,[50] but the work has more to say. Vimalasūri's *Pratirāmāyaṇa* makes sense only if we take it as a radical protest and defence against an epic tradition that had been given an increasingly unacceptable interpretation by the Bhāgavatas, arguably accompanied by pressure and violence. Situations and statements in the *Paumacariyam* cannot be construed as being only functional to emerging lineages and standard political operations but go deeper into the heart of Indian history. Vālmīki is accused of having written lies and absurdities, and in Vimalasūri's work, the brāhmaṇas are the heretics and expounders of false scriptures (*kuśāstravādin*-s) who have acquired pre-eminence through fraud. Significantly, Rāvaṇa, a handsome and pious Jain, is a protector of Jain temples (which, we must assume, needed protection). This work, with its strong critique, reverses the Brahmanical allegations against those responsible for the collapse of society in the Kali Age, and Vimalasūri's positions should be examined in this perspective.

Vimalasūri rejects the idea that the *rākṣasa*-s, led by Rāvaṇa, are inferior beings who have the habit of eating meat and drinking blood and marrow; they are, on the contrary, highly civilised beings adhering to the vow of *ahiṃsā*. The Vidyādharas of Laṅkā, Rāvaṇa's dynasty, were named *rākṣasa*-s after a famous Vidyādhara. Why did Vimalasūri radically change this aspect of the story? Why did he transform the *rākṣasa*-s into pious people practising *ahiṃsā*? The answer is found at the beginning of the work, when Śreṇika, the king of Magadha, says: 'How could Rāvaṇa and other Rākṣasas *who were good Jainas* [my emphasis], eat and drink human flesh and blood without any disgust and compunction? Oh! The *Rāmāyaṇa* that has been written is false and foul and distorted […]'.[51] From this passage it appears that in Vimalasūri's times the *rākṣasa*-s of Vālmīki were identified with the heretics, like the *asura*-s and *daitya*-s, and that Vimalasūri, instead of uselessly disproving the arguments of the orthodox one by one, decided to write a counter-*Rāmāyaṇa*, attributing an entirely different nature to Rāvaṇa and his followers. The Buddhists are also identified with the *rākṣasa*-s. In a Tibetan version of Rāma's story found in Dunhuang, and therefore composed between AD 787 and 848, Laṅkāpura is situated in the midst of the ocean,[52] and it is naturally there that the *rākṣasa*-s lived. It is not by chance that Somadeva contends that the fault with the South is that it borders on the *rākṣasa*-s.[53]

The oral tradition, still lingering about in the nineteenth century, also points to the identification of the *rākṣasa*-s with the *śramaṇa*-s. J.A.C. Boswell, describing the Undavalli Caves in Guntur district, reports that the chief tradition of Palnad 'relates to the wars between the Devatas and Rākshasas', and that 'the country is spoken of as the land of the Rākshasas', the term 'being commonly used to designate the Buddhists'.[54] In actual fact, it designated also the Jains, as shown by the lore of the village of Bahayudam 'just across the Kṛishṇa', taking its name from one 'of the Rākshasa leaders'. In fact, '[t]he cave temples are always pointed out as remains of the Rākshasas, and the people continuously speak of Rākshasas and Jainas in connection with each other'.[55]

Rāvaṇa was the enemy of Rāma's righteous rule, and making him the leader of the heretics and the enemy of the eternal law of the gods gives the extent of the obsessive climate of medieval India. The gods are now those assembled on Mount Kailāśa presided over by Śiva, and the transformation of the head of the *rākṣasa*-s into a powerful *asura* actually takes place. It was an attempt of the Sivaites at appropriating an extremely popular story that the Bhāgavatas had made their own at a much earlier date. The object of Rāvaṇa's fury is not Rāma, but Śiva, and in fact, again at Elephanta and Ellora, we witness Rāvaṇa's attack on the mountain of the gods.[56] His threat is real, because Kailāsa is made to quake from its very foundations. *Rākṣasa*-s and *asura*-s jeopardise the Brahmanical order of society in exactly the same way.

THE MASSACRE OF THE KṢATRIYAS AND THE BATTLE OF BODHGAYĀ

The Narasiṃha *avatāra* shows the role played by the Bhāgavatas in the battle against the *asura*-s also after the Guptas. The images from the seventh to the ninth century present us a terrifying god: he does not simply kill Hiraṇyakaśipu and his brother, but disembowels them. The Purāṇic narratives emphasise his role expanding and detailing the story.[57] In Vishnuite circles, the attitude towards the Buddhists was ambiguous and dictated by the circumstances. We have seen this with Vāmana and Bali, and we see it to a greater degree with the attempt at incorporating, in places, the surviving Buddhists. The priestly attempt at making the Buddha an *avatāra* of Viṣṇu denying the Buddha any separate identity and legitimacy never gained popularity. Kumārila did not admit that the Buddha was an *avatāra*,[58] and Francis Buchanan actually reports that Vishnuite brāhmaṇas, and probably any brāhmaṇa in Madurai, never worshipped this *avatāra*, nor was Viṣṇu ever invoked by the name or in the form of Buddha.[59] Two other Viṣṇu *avatāra*-s deserve our attention, Paraśurāma and Kalki, both seldom represented as independent deities,[60] and generally depicted only in the *avatāra* stele. Their role as destroyers of the heretics was limited in space and time (Paraśurāma is an *āveśāvatāra*, or temporary descent of Viṣṇu), but their interventions were crucial.

It would be misleading to consider Paraśurāma as one and the same being as the Bhārgava Rāma of the *Mahābhārata*, exterminator of Arjuna Kṛtavīrya (in the Vana Parvan) or of his sons (in the Śānti Parvan) and of the whole race of the kṣatriyas against whom he carries out twenty-one mortal attacks.[61] In the *Mahābhārata*, the hero has no axe to fight against the kṣatriyas, he is not known as Paraśurāma, and he is not considered an *avatāra* of Viṣṇu.[62] Only in the late formative stages of the epic Bhārgava Rāma acquires the characteristics he has in the Purāṇic literature, which tries to bring the epic into line with subsequent tradition.[63] Purāṇic Brahmanism actualised the myth and regarded Rāma as a divine manifestation whose purpose was to clear the earth of the oppressive kṣatriyas of the present day,[64] not of those of a distant past: kṣatriya kings supporting Buddhism were ruling at the time of Xuanzang.[65] Śiva's intervention, a later addition to the *Mahābhārata*,[66] allows Paraśurāma's education and training to be construed as an episode of the *devāsura* war, and helps us to clarify who the kṣatriyas he exterminates may have been. The story finds its natural place in the Purāṇas, which deal with it at length, as for instance the *Brahmāṇḍa Purāṇa*.[67] In the *Padma Purāṇa*, it is Viṣṇu who gives Rāma the axe and other weapons,[68] specifying that his mission is to kill 'the wicked great kings' who 'cause a burden to the earth'.[69] In this case, the identification of the kṣatriyas with the *asura*-s and the unrightful kings becomes quite explicit.

If Paraśurāma superimposes on Bhārgava Rāma blurring the latter's identity and becoming the actor of a different play, we need to re-discuss a question that seemed already settled. The best known scenario of Paraśurāma's exploits is early medieval Kerala, recounted in the *Kēralōtpatti* and a number of other medieval and late medieval accounts. The role of Paraśurāma, that is, of the brāhmaṇas in arms, in establishing the new agrarian order in Kerala has been denied on the ground that the god's exploits are associated with places in Saurashtra, Gujarat and Maharashtra. These 'legends' would allude to settlements of brāhmaṇas of the Kāśyapa and Bhārgava clans on the western coast of the Deccan and to their migration further south, but as to Kerala we would simply be in the presence of the migration of a myth with no bearing on the actual situation.[70] Nevertheless, the Purāṇic Paraśurāma acts quite differently from the Bhārgava hero and in a different context, and local traditions in Kerala appear to be a restructured myth, being evidence of a new, different series of events. The Purāṇic identification of the kṣatriyas with the *asura*-s and the present-day adhārmic kings of the present day points to a recasting of Paraśurāma's story in, approximately, an eighth-century context. The massacre of the kṣatriyas and the ensuing distribution of lands to the brāhmaṇas palpably alludes to the elimination of the *rājā*-s who still supported the heretics and the adhārmic society.

The Malayalam manuscripts of the Mackenzie collection that deal with the myth recount that Paraśurāma 'formed the country and located therein the Brahmans, in sixty-four villages' and the Brahmans introduced King Cēramāṉ Perumāḷ,[71] under whose rule, as we have reported in Chapter I, the Buddhists were expelled from the country after having their tongues cut at the end of a debate. Another account of the same story specifies that Paraśurāma – projected in the distance of myth – did not establish any images or fanes, which were erected later on by Cēramāṉ Perumāḷ and the brāhmaṇas.[72] This is a quite accurate account of how the brāhmaṇas settled. Finally, the section of a Tamil manuscript book on the 'Jainas of Tondamandalam' specifies that the kṣatriyas exterminated by Paraśurāma were Jains,[73] thus providing further evidence that the post-*Mahābhārata* version of the Paraśurāma myth is a variant of the *devāsura* war: the target here being not the apostate brāhmaṇas, but the petty kings that must be removed.

The *Kalki Purāṇa*, classed among the *upapurāṇa*-s, is a little known text in both India and the West. It is a late, patched work, its *post quem* being the beginning of the eighteenth century.[74] In some parts of the work, the matter dealt with has hardly anything to do with the Kalki *avatāra*, as for instance the insert with the story of Rāma,[75] the battle against the *asura* Śumbha,[76] and several other passages. However, this Purāṇa, or, as it has been called, this 'pseudo-biography',[77] includes a narrative that overtly points to the Buddhists as the enemies which Viṣṇu's last *avatāra*, Kalki – he who makes the filth disappear from the world – has descended on earth to destroy.

The Purāṇa opens with a description of the evils of the Kali Age, when the brāhmaṇas have become perverted (the usual allusion to apostate brāhmaṇas) and the śūdras make business appropriating other people's richness.[78] The text clearly identifies the Kali Age – at the end of which Kalki appears to re-establish the Brahmanical social order – with the age of Buddhist hegemony in medieval Magadha. To put an end to this situation, Viṣṇu is born in human form at Śambhala,[79] and performs his duty of young brāhmaṇa, and then marries Padmā, Śiva's daughter, who gives him two sons.

It is at this point that an extraordinary piece of narrative begins. Kalki is ready to leave with his army for the town of Kīkaṭa,[80] which, from both the Purāṇic literature and the inscription found by Wilkins in 1788 is identifiable with Bodhgayā and its region.[81] The text speaks of two Buddhist centres opposing Vedic *dharma* and, at the same time, of a town whose activities were associated with the world of the dead – an allusion to Gayā. Its depraved inhabitants had abandoned the traditional rites and only cared for material goods, women, food and drink. As soon as the Buddhists heard about the coming of Kalki, they left the town at the head of their armies.[82] In the ensuing battle, at first Kalki is knocked down and brought away unconscious by his companions, but after recovering his senses, he kills thousands of Buddhists and enemies, and meets at last the Buddhist leader of the army, with whom he has a short dialogue. After a hand-to-hand struggle, Kalki breaks his back, and the defeated chief rolls down into a nearby pond.[83] But the battle continues, because the brother of the dead leader, Śuddhodana, is ready to attack Kalki's army. He is knocked down by a companion of Kalki, but picks himself up and goes seeking the Goddess Māyā for help.[84] At this point there is an interesting passage: the Buddhists draw up again in battle order behind the goddess accompanied by 'millions of outcastes'.[85]

This is one of those rare occurrences where the social implications of the anti-Buddhist struggle are overtly admitted. A little below in the text, the Buddhists are said to be black skinned, including Śuddhodana,[86] something that again brings us on the right interpretive track. In the inscriptions of the Pāla kings, otherwise so similar to those of the other Indian rulers, there are details which take us by surprise. In the Nālandā copper-plate of Devapāla (*c.* AD 800-40),[87] the most powerful of the Pāla kings, the enumeration of the people assembled in the villages of the Rājagṛha and Gayā districts which formed the object of the endowment registered in the charter closes with 'the *Mēdas*, the *Andhrakas* and the *Chāṇḍālas*'.[88] The Bhagalpur copper-plate inscription of Nārāyaṇapāla (*c.* AD 854-930), who defines himself a 'staunch Buddhist'[89] and, at the same time – for the reasons discussed in relation to Harṣavardhana – maintains to have built 'thousands of temples' of Śiva, includes the 'Brāhmaṇas upto Meḍas, Āndhras and Caṇḍālas' among the people he favours,[90] Meḍas and Andhras being untouchable natives.[91] We cannot but think of these people when we read of the black Śuddhodana who momentarily leaves the battlefield to summon Māyā and the outcastes.

Proceeding with the narrative, we discover that Māyā was none other than Lakṣmī,[92] and the Buddhists are massacred.[93] The wives of the dead men, beautiful and courageous though depraved, after seeing the bodies of their husbands thrown here and there like pieces of wood, decide at first to continue the battle, not convinced by the speech of Kalki who would like them to surrender and become part of his folk.[94] But suddenly the weapons of their husbands – the swords, the arrows – start talking with the voice of the dead, who recognise in Kalki the Lord. Hearing the weapons to talk in these terms, the womenfolk abandon all their illusions and ask the protection of the resplendent God, who receives them among his devotees.[95]

It is difficult for us to say to which event(s) the narrative alludes. There are a few realistic details, as for instance the allusion to the existence of two centres of anti-Brahmanical propaganda and of two Buddhist armies, even though the text describes a single battlefield. The mention of two Buddhist centres of learning arguably refers to two of the Buddhist 'universities' of Magadha. We know that the army of the orthodox Senas attacked the monasteries, as the following passage from a Nālandā inscription suggests:

> In the illustrious Sōmapura there was the ascetic Karuṇaśrīmitra, so called on account of his compassionate disposition, abundance of merits, and his efforts towards the welfare and happiness of living beings; who, when his house was burning, (*being*) set on fire by the approaching army of Vaṅgāla, attached (*himself*) to the pair of lotus feet of the Buddha, (*and*) went to heaven.[96]

A battle took place probably at Vikramaśīla in Bihar: as we shall see in the next chapter, the monastery was appropriated by the orthodox some time in the twelfth century, an episode during a more general fight for the control of the region.

The events narrated in the *Kalki Purāṇa* may thus refer to the Sena period, when what remained of Pāla power collapsed. Other scenarios are possible. Bodhgayā was the repeated target of anti-Buddhist attacks arguably to coincide with the establishment of Gayā as the place *par excellence* of *śrāddha* rituals. The first to appropriate the site had been the Sivaites, who had occupied it even before Śaśāṅka (Appendix 1). Even under Pāla rule these attempts continued: in the 26th year of Dharmapāla (*c.* AD 796), a *caturmukhaliṅga* was installed by one Keśava at Campaśa, to the south of the Mahābodhi Temple, 'for the benefit of the descendants of *snataka*-s residing at Mahābodhi'.[97] In the ninth century the Bhāgavatas-Pāñcarātras gained control on Gayā-kṣetra, as is shown by the commencement of iconographic production in Gayā proper.[98] The story of Gayāsura killed by Viṣṇu's mace that we have repeatedly mentioned, is an example of the attacks carried out by the Vishnuites, and Viṣṇu Gadādhara, first mentioned in an inscription of Viśvāditya Viśvarūpa, exponent of a Brahmanical family ruling over Gayā datable to AD 1058,[99] confirms the frightful nature of the god. At Gayā, according to the *Vāmana Purāṇa*, a king called Gayā performed an *aśvamedha*, a *naramedha* and a *mahāmedha*, and these rituals appear associated with the instalment of the god in the Gadādhara Temple: with his 'sharp axe' he had hewn 'the tree of great sin'.[100] Whether the rulers of Gayā were of a low-class Brahmanical order, and thus identifiable with the Gayāvāla brāhmaṇas who made their living on gifts presented in the *śrāddha* ceremonies, or brāhmaṇas of higher social standing, remains uncertain:[101] what is clear is that the Pāla kings could not always control all their territories. Southern Magadha was the object of constant warfare and changed hands several times, as for instance at the time of the Gurjara-Pratihāra invasion of the north-eastern regions at the time of Bhoja I (AD 836-85): the region was to remain under orthodox control for some time.[102] Both scenarios fit the narrative of the *Kalki Purāṇa*, which expressly mentions the Buddhists calling to arms the outcastes. This was the policy that the followers of Vajrayāna adopted from at least the eighth century – from when Buddhism could no longer count on the urban and trading bourgeoisie that had formed its backbone. It is also possible that the text combines the traditions of events that took place in different localities and at a different time.

The memory of the conflict that had Bodhgayā at stake survived in the oral tradition, gathered by Colonel Mackenzie's Jain *paṇḍita* during the latter's visit to Gayā in March 1821. It clearly reflects the point of view of the brāhmaṇas.

> South-west of the temple of Saraswatī is a ruined city of the Bauddhas, with the remains of an ancient fort. It is said, that in former times, when the Bauddhas had possession of the country, they destroyed the old city of Gayā, and established another city called Bauddha Gayā, of which these are the vestiges; they erected here a large Bauddhālayam or temple of Buddha, with nine storeys, making the height of the temple 108 feet. [...]
>
> During the government of the Bauddhas, having destroyed old Gayā, and broken the images of all the temples of the Hindus, they carried the Gayāwālā Brahmaṇs to their new city, or Bauddha Gayā and put them in confinement, to compel them to transfer all the ceremonies of pilgrimage to the latter place. In this way some of the Gayāwālās were destroyed; but some escaped in distant countries. The Bauddhas established themselves, and ruled here for about 700 years in the Vikramaśaka. [...]
>
> [...] When the government of the Bauddhas had ceased, all the Gayāwālās that survived returned to the former Gayā and repeopled it. Travellers then resorted to the ancient Gayā; and the city of the Bauddhas was deserted, and overrun with jungle. At last a Bairāgi, who arrived at the ruined city of Bauddha Gayā, found the dilapidated temple, and he took up his abode there.[103]

This tradition derives in part from the *Gayā Māhātmya* and conforms to the generally accepted but unsupported opinion that in antiquity Gayā played the same role as major *pitṛtīrtha*[104] as it did in medieval and modern times. It cannot be doubted that Gayā was an important place in ancient Magadha: Śākyamuni would not otherwise have chosen it as the site of his Awakening. Yet the hypothesis that Gayā acquired the role that is still its own as a result of the establishment of the holiest among all Buddhist places cannot be easily discarded. The evidence provided by Benimadhab Barua in support of the thesis that Gayā was, *ab origine*, a Vishnuite *tīrtha* is not convincing.[105] The reassessment of the evidence made by Debjani Paul is also marred by inconsistencies, even if we give the weight it deserves to the argument that neither archaeology and art history nor the epigraphic evidence mean that much when we deal with immaterial culture (the *śrāddha* rituals).[106]

That funeral rites are a crucial issue in the acquisition of hegemonic power over society and that *śrāddha*-s were not only an effective, but a recurrent means for establishing Brahmanical supremacy, can be seen from the creation of other *śrāddha* centres pretending direct affiliation with Gayā. This is the case of Jajpur in Utkala, which became the regional *śrāddha* centre when the Somavāṃśīs dispossessed the former Buddhist Bhauma sovereigns.[107] The battle of Gayā proved that the *śrāddha* issue was worth fighting for,[108] and that it was so advantageous that it was worth exporting the model. *Śrāddha*-s are strictly related to the birth of sons destined to ensuring a male descendant who can perform them after the death of one's own father. This creates a birth-death circularity within the family system that perfectly fits the Brahmanical system.

The Gayāsura myth, if we give credit to the testimony of '[t]he only person of the sect of the Buddhas' met by Francis Buchanan at Gayā in the winter of 1811-12, always appeared to the Buddhists as a fabrication of the brāhmaṇas. It is quite possible that Rajendralala Mitra's interpretation of the Gayāsura myth, which appears at first purely euhemeristic, is based on a tradition handed down to the few Buddhists still surviving in Bodhgayā at the time.[109]

ON THE FAULT LINE: BHAIRAVA, THE GODDESS, THE *YOGINĪ*-S

It has been observed that if Indian art could be valued anew, without taking account of the heavy load of symbolism accumulated in the course of time mainly through interpretations of Brahmanical and Buddhist texts and of modern scholarship, 'its violent and sometimes outright aggressive character would become terribly apparent'.[110] Karel

R. van Kooj has shown that the iconographic representations of terrifying and bloody scenes are modelled on real battlefield behaviour, and are not the remnants of what is labelled as 'primitive' society or tribal culture. For these aggressive iconographies to be created, high patronage and complex theorisation were required, and considering them the result of subaltern cultures is nothing but an easy escape from the real question. The cruelties of which warriors are capable at the end of heavy combat, when – as noted by van Kooj – they 'start dancing on the battlefield, trampling their enemies under their feet, ripping open their bellies and drinking their blood', are those we have observed in Śiva who starts dancing after slaying the *asura*-s, of Narasiṃha ripping open the belly of Hiraṇyakaśipu, of the goddesses drinking the blood of the vanquished enemies, etc.

It is more difficult for me to agree with van Kooj when he connects violent warfare with the rise of city culture. The rise of Indian cities in the third-second century BC certainly implied violence, as violence had characterised the rise of the earlier chiefdoms or *janapada*-s, but the appearance of the violent Brahmanical gods is not connected with the rise of cities in a proper sense but with the establishment of *tīrtha*-s and the transformation into *tīrtha*-s of former manufacturing and trading towns. Van Kooj's scenario becomes true and reveals all its drama if we speak of temple towns replacing the old, decaying cities of a de-urbanised country. This is exactly the scenario of late ancient and medieval India, when the brāhmaṇas persevered, slowly and painstakingly, in establishing their power.

As already observed, Orissa and the adjoining regions of Bihar, Jharkhand, Chhattisgarh and Madhya Pradesh are privileged vantage points. Here the logic of the battlefield appears with gruesome evidence from the eighth century onwards, and an additional analysis of the sources at our disposal (especially the iconographic sources, which are the most explicit) should persuade us that the battlefield in question was where Brahmanical power was at stake. The first attempt of the Pāśupatas at establishing Bhubaneswar as a *tīrtha* probably goes back to the time of Śaśāṅka, who conquered Utkala and Koṅgoda (northern and southern Orissa) at the beginning of the seventh century.[111] The *Ekāmra Purāṇa*, a work of the Āgamic Pāśupatas,[112] preserves the information about the conquest of the country by Śaśāṅka, of whom it speaks in glowing terms,[113] and credits the king of Gauḍa with having made Lord Tribhuvaneśvara the presiding deity of the place.[114]

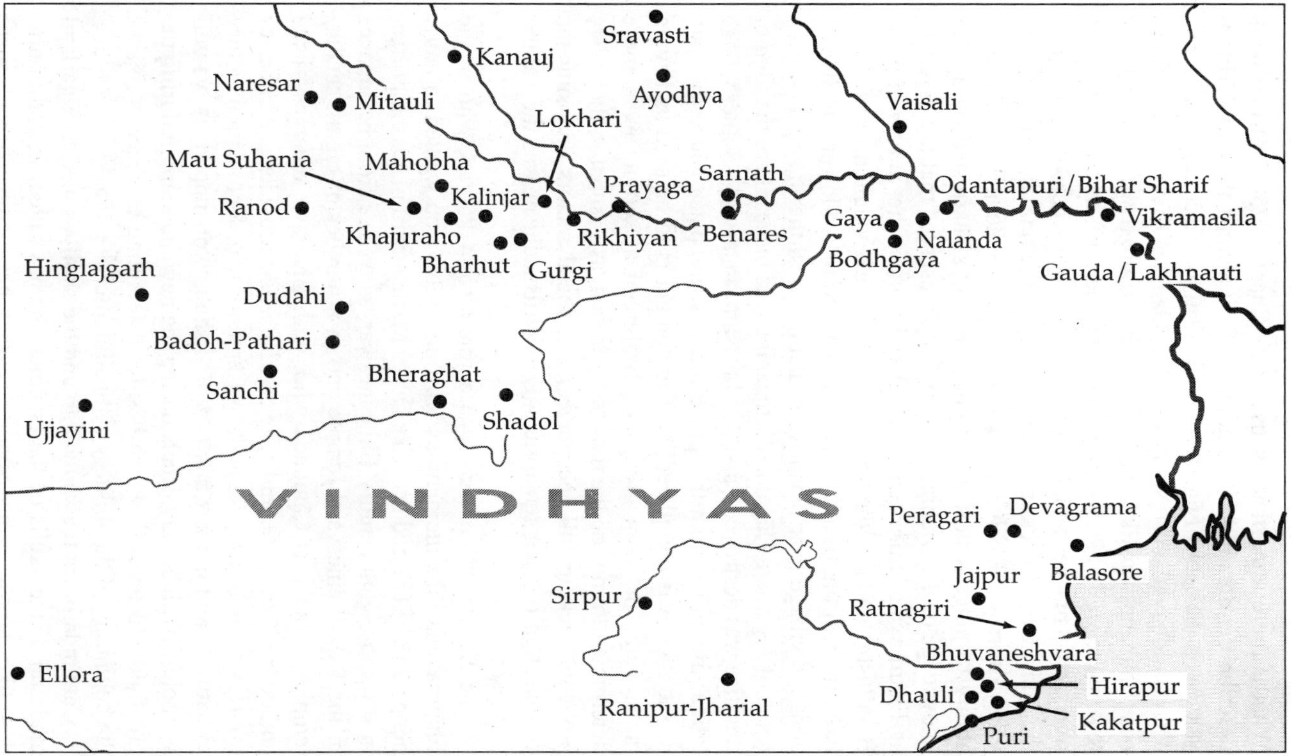

Map 3: Northern and eastern slopes of the Vindhyas, eighth century to thirteenth century.

What is more important for us is that Chapters 25-32 of this work describe the dreadful war waged by Śiva against the *asura* Hiraṇyākṣya on the bank of the river Gandhavatī for the control of Ekāmra. The Gandhavatī corresponds to the Gangua River, which flows near Bhubaneswar-Ekāmra. Hiraṇyākṣya, advised by Śukra, had tried to stop the *yajña* that the gods wanted to perform on the bank of the river, and at first he and his *asura* followers had succeeded in defeating the gods. Only Śiva's intervention caused the final defeat of Hiraṇyākṣya's army.[115] Krishna Chandra Panigrahi, a scholar whose unbiased ability to judge historical-religious facts was sharpened by a deep knowledge of the Brahmanical tradition, observed that the *devāsura* at Ekāmravana mirrored 'a conflict between the Śaivas and the Buddhists', and that the text, as 'a Śaiva work, would have certainly liked to term the Buddhists as demons and the followers of Śiva as gods'. A village near Khandagiri, Panigrahi further noted, bears the name of Jagamara [Jāgamarā], meaning 'the place where the *jāga* or sacrifice was destroyed', and that Jagasara [Jāgasarā], another village 'about five miles from this place', means 'the place where the *jāga* or sacrifice was completed'.[116] The conflict is to be seen as having taken place between groups of Brahmanical settlers even more determined to impose the new order in that, as Pāśupatas, they were probably seeking full acceptance, and social sectors opposing the colonisation of their territories of which Buddhism was the natural catalyser.

The *Ekāmra Purāṇa* assigns a role also to Parvatī, who in the Ekāmravana kills the demons Kīrti and Vāsa who wanted to enjoy her person.[117] The goddess, like Durgā Mahiṣamardinī, was important in seventh-eighth century Bhubaneswar, as we see from her images in the Paraśurāmeśvara Temple and in a number of eighth-century temples,[118] but it is Cāmuṇḍā who, with Bhairava, emerges as the embodiment of battlefield. The *Agni Purāṇa* provides a number of impressive invocations to address Cāmuṇḍā in order to obtain victory in battle,[119] and in the *Kālikā Purāṇa* she is worshipped, as we will see below, with bloody rituals during the new moon night during the great autumn festival, which besides celebrating the harvest, marks the beginning of the military campaign after the rains.

Cāmuṇḍā bears the *khaṭvāṅga* and the skull, as well as a garland made up of the skulls of the enemies she has killed. In addition to this, like the victorious Śiva, she wraps herself up in an elephant skin.[120] Looking at the images of the goddess scattered all over Orissa, we identify two models as regards the bodies she tramples on.

1. In a number of cases, the body is that of a naked man. Warriors are never naked in Brahmanical art,[121] and the naked bodies depicted in the Cāmuṇḍā stele have nothing in common with the idealised naked warriors – both vanquishers and vanquished – of Classical and Renaissance art. Their nudity is that of the naked *asura*-s killed by Bhairava and the *mātṛkā*-s in the *yajñaśālā* of the Kailāsanātha Temple of Ellora. Once again, the dead men are naked because those represented are meant to be those who do not wear the triple cloth of the Veda. Iconographies bring to the fore the importance of this point, which remains implicit in the texts. The nakedness of the heretics (not necessarily men of religion) is emphasised, here as at Ellora, by bringing their genitals into focus, notably so in later images, dating to the period when the mutual fury of the opposing forces, aggravated by the destabilising Muslim presence, reached its climax. The late tenth-early eleventh century stele in the dilapidated Bhīmeśvarī Temple at Peragari, a village in the Mayurbhanj district, shows the dead enemy with upraised penis – the target of a jackal waiting for corpses (Fig. 10).[122] The now broken stele is divided into two parts, almost equal in size, the upper one with Cāmuṇḍā seated displaying the elephant skin, the lower one with the very large image of the dead man (in keeping with the recommendations of the *Agni Purāṇa*, which prescribes a corpse of immense size as *vāhana* of the goddess).[123] He has a short beard, moustache, and bulging eyes, suggesting an *asura*, but 'his hair is closely cropped or shaved, producing a nearly bald effect, and his ears are elongated in the manner of a Buddhist deity'.[124] His erect penis and the animal's muzzle lie along an axis at the centre of the lower part of the relief, and this detail captures the eye of the observer. A similar effect has been looked for in the late eleventh-century stele in the Dhakulei Ṭhakurānī Temple of Pratapnagari (Cuttack district), even though here the lower part of the scene occupies less than one-fourth of the stele, and the intended message is less clear.[125] How can we interpret this message? The penis is not affected by the rigor mortis (which starts a few hours after death), but since the corpse is laid face down, the blood flowing to it results in an erection. This is the very moment these iconographies

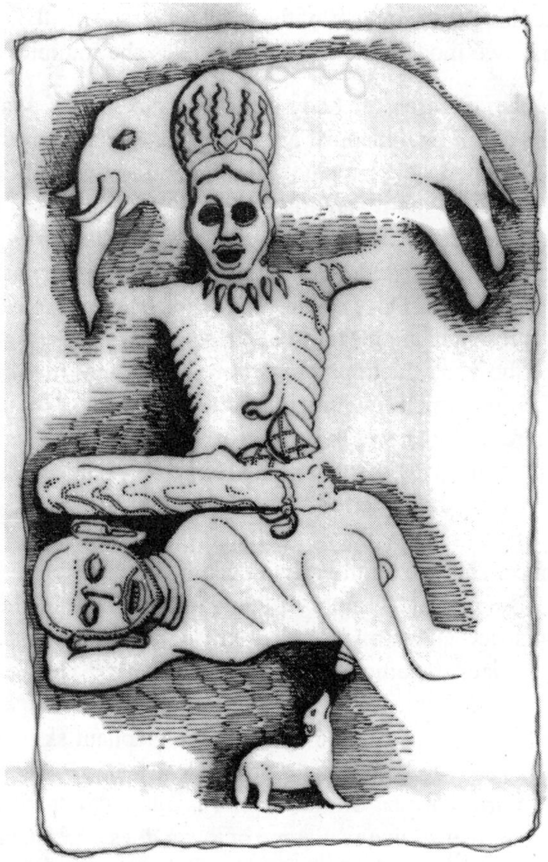

Figure 10: Cāmuṇḍā on dead, naked *asura*. Peragari, Orissa.

malignantly depict, significantly adding the detail of the jackal that is on the verge of seizing the penis with its teeth. These images intend to clarify that the *asura*-s are really dead, perhaps also alluding to the immodest behaviour imputed to the Buddhists.

2. In the second model, the dead body is that of a dead warrior, as shown in certain cases by the short sword in the sheath that he wears slipped into the waist belt.[126] In some case, as in a late tenth-century stele from Devagrama on the Sona River in Balasore district, the dead man is a richly clothed personage wearing a necklace and bracelets, and with a flamboyant hairdo, easily identifiable as a native *rājā* (Fig. 11).[127] Long, often curly hair, characterise the

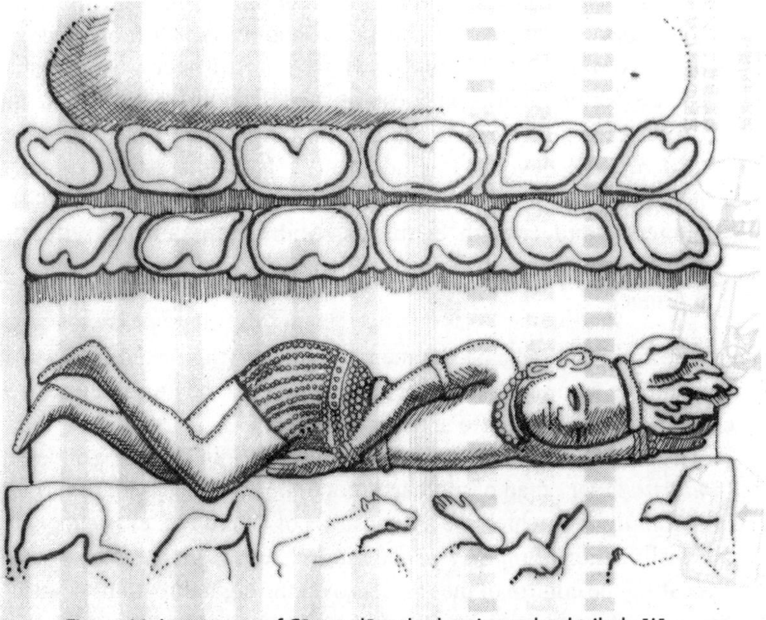

Figure 11: Lower part of Cāmuṇḍā stele showing a dead tribal *rājā*. Devagrama, Orissa.

'tribal', unorthodox kings,[128] and one inevitably thinks of the Śabara general in the *Kādambarī*, who had 'a mass of hair whose ends curled and which hung over his shoulders'.[129] In other cases, the princely status of the dead men, or of the men asking for mercy, is indicated by the pointed headgear.[130] Thanks to the parallelism of the iconographies, we can interpret these princely figures as those of local *rājā*-s supporting Buddhism. We know of several minor rulers who adhered to Buddhism in Orissa: at an undetermined date, one Nāgeśa, son of 'king' Jaleruha, was converted to Buddhism, and the brāhmaṇa minister of one king Indrabala became a Tantric Buddhist.[131] King Indrabala, in turn, was converted into a Tantric Buddhist by Nāgeśa.[132] One king Muñja attained the position of *vidyādhara siddha* together with one thousand followers.[133] Broadening the perspective to Bengal, we see in action the same mechanism. We read in the *dPag bsam ljon bzang* of the Candra 'tribal' kings who embraced the cause of Buddhism. Prakāśa Candra became a convert to Tantric Buddhism,[134] and the first king of the lineage, Hari Candra, embraced Buddhism with one thousand followers and, like his Orissan peer, obtained the position of *vidyādhara siddha.*[135] One Sundara Hatsi reigned over various tribes of the Naṅgaṭa hills and established Buddhism,[136] and in the Chittagong hills, Vāvalā Sundara, a king of the Chakama tribe, also became devoted to Buddhism.[137] It is interesting for us to note that in the revival of the Mahiṣamardinī iconographies of the eleventh and twelfth centuries, Mahiṣa, in accord with the textual developments noticed above in this chapter, is depicted as a prince.[138]

The fight to eradicate the men of religion (the naked *asura*-s) is one and the same with the struggle to eradicate the non-brahmanised chiefs who were ready to support them.

The *Agni Purāṇa* describes a series of eight female goddesses (*ambāṣṭaka*, or octad of mothers), not to be confused with the *sapta*- or *aṣṭamātṛkā*-s, which are a hypostasis of Cāmuṇḍā, as is shown by the qualification of *śmaśanajā* and *raudrā* they are given.[139] This octad, indicating the control of the goddess over the eight directions of space, can be considered, in turn, as the unit generating the sixty-four *yoginī*-s, mentioned for the first time, as far as the textual evidence is concerned, in the *Agni Purāṇa.*[140] Their temples were built throughout the territory stretching from eastern Rajasthan to Orissa, and their cult was connected to royalty.[141] This brings us back to Cāmuṇḍā, whose close connection to kingship is implicit in her role as goddess of the battlefield. It has been observed that the trampling motif in Indian and Tibetan art is always associated with the theme of victory and war, whether in a mythological or theological framework, and that the gods and goddesses so represented 'are meant to protect royal dynasties, royal cities or the warrior class'.[142] However, I do not think that we can consider the battlefield – endemic as warfare was in medieval India – as a unifying factor for explaining sets of monuments and iconographies that remain different one from the other, though seemingly related by gruesome effects. We need rather to clarify which wars are represented in the different situations.

The succession one/eight/sixty-four, from Cāmuṇḍā to the octad of *mātṛkā*-s to the sixty-four *yoginī*-s,[143] and the related variants of the rituals, may be understood as an expansion and diversification of the goddess's power. The *yoginī*-s are related, in all likelihood, to the worsening of the confrontation between Brahmanical and anti-Brahmanical forces ignited by the rise of Pāla power. The goddesses depicted in the earliest of the *yoginī*-s enclosures, that of Hirapur in the vicinity of Bhubaneswar[144] share many of the features of Cāmuṇḍā and Bhairava examined above. Some *yoginī*-s trample on corpses,[145] and others are dancing or standing on severed heads.[146] The latter cannot be always taken as evidence of the self-immolation of the warriors to Bhairava or the goddess.[147] The Bhairava depicted in the Vaitāl Deuḷ (Fig. 6) is clearly responsible for the death of the man whose head, modeled on that of the Buddha, lies on his left: he has just severed it with the knife he holds in his right hand. In the lower part of the relief there would be no animal feeding on limbs if the two severed heads on the tripod were those of two heroic self-immolated warriors. The nude female deity in the Kiñcakeśvarī Temple at Khiching who holds a severed head with her lowered left arm, has clearly cut it herself with the sword that she holds raised up with her right hand.[148]

That the severed heads are those of very peculiar enemies is shown in two stele, one doubtfully from Orissa, the other from Bihar. The eleventh-century relief with Bhairava (Fig. 12), the four-armed, dancing God bears rosary, *ḍamaru*, *triśūla* and plays *vīṇā*. He wears snakes as wristlets, armlets and necklace, and additional serpents are visible in his hair. He is dancing on five severed heads that are not simply 'skull-like'[149] but are those of Buddhist monks. The *vīṇā* the God is playing is probably made with one of the skulls.[150] The five shaven heads are piled up to suggest a larger number of victims than that actually depicted, and we cannot help but think of butchery of the type mentioned by Īśvara Dāsa at a later time (Chapter VI). It was not only a question of the adversaries of *varṇāśramadharma* hegemonised by Buddhism being killed in battle, but of the members of the *saṃgha* being decimated on occasions. For iconographies to be so explicit and renouncing their semantic ambiguity, we must be facing a final showdown where the cards are on the table. Metaphorical transpositions were no longer believable. This is what the Buddhists would do, in turn, in developing the iconographies of Vajrayāna.

The same can be said of the stele from Bihar representing Cāmuṇḍā (Fig. 13).[151] The goddess is sitting on a lotus seat under a pipal tree, and her destructive power is amplified by her having ten arms. She is recognisable not only by her skeletal aspect, but also by the elephant

Figure 12: Bhairava dancing on severed heads of Buddhist monks. Orissa (?).

skin she holds with her two upper arms. Her main offensive weapons are a sword and a long spear. Around her neck is not hanging a garland of skulls but a string to which the heads she has just severed (twelve in number) are appended by the hair. The lotus seat on which she is seated rests on a dead body, easily recognisable as that of the Buddha from his face, showing *ūrṇā* and long ears, and by the creases in the neck. The body is nude (which the Buddha never is), to show his status of heretic. Several severed heads hang from the tree under which

Figure 13: Cāmuṇḍā seated on dead Buddha. Bihar.

the goddess is seated, and a few others in the basin at the centre of the lower part of the stele, together with amputated legs and arms. Two of the heads in the foreground show an *uṣṇīṣa*, while the other two, including that depicted upside down, wear a short beard and moustache. On both sides of the basin, the animals of prey are feeding on corpses, strongly foreshortened. The arms of the corpse on the right are amputated, and it is being attacked by two jackals and a vulture that has just started eating the penis of the dead man.[152] Cāmuṇḍā's owl stands on the stretched right palm of the corpse lying to the left of the basin. The stele is, at the same time, a first-hand documentation of what happened in places after the tenth century and a symbolic funeral of Buddhism: the Buddha lies dead, and Cāmuṇḍā sits under the pipal tree, the symbol of Awakening and antinomial society.

The presence of severed heads and human limbs in association with vessels in the images of Bhairava and Cāmuṇḍā suggests that the victims were ritually killed and their limbs severed for their blood to be offered to the deities. These *balidāna*-s are associated with the *vāmācāra* or *vāmabhāva*, the 'left method' by which even the Brahmanical deities can be worshipped when they assume – as in our case – their heterodox 'left' shapes.[153] The *sādhaka*-s or adepts belonged to groups like the Kāpālikas and Bhairavas,[154] but an important point to remember is that brāhmaṇas, normally only associated with the *dakṣiṇabhāva* or performance of the five *mahāyajña*-s, could take part, though only once and through others, to the heterodox form of worship such as the offering of intoxicating liquors.[155] This detail discloses how interdependent were, in actual reality, the representatives of Purāṇic Brahmanism and those very groups that the Purāṇas condemned, as is also evident from many of the Purāṇic passages we have quoted and from the very existence of extremely fine works such as the Cāmuṇḍā stele, implying high patronage. Van Kooj adds the 'Ḍāmaras' to the list of heterodox *sādhaka*-s, and landlords are probably meant,[156] obviously interested in the cleansing activity.

Regarding the *balidāna* offered to the goddess, the study of the material contained in the *Kālikā Purāṇa*, which allowed us to provide the above comments, is of particular interest. The work is datable to the mid-ninth century,[157] and the rituals it describes are consistent with the questions discussed here, although this Purāṇa may not be directly related to them. Different rules for the containers of the sacrificial blood are listed, and a king, for instance, is required to use metal and clay containers that, when filled with human blood, are to be placed in front of the goddess.[158] For the human sacrifice or *mahābala* the prescriptions, understandably, multiply.[159] An interesting detail of the ritual is the consecration of *khaḍga*, the sword by which the victim is beheaded, and its being called *dharmapāla*, protector of *dharma*.[160] This epithet attributed to the *khaḍga* goes back to the *Viṣṇudharmottara Purāṇa*,[161] something that sheds more light on the meaning of iconographies showing gods and goddesses provided with this weapon, starting from the early Skanda examples. Much remains to be investigated in this direction in order to understand, for example, the difference between *khaḍga* and the butcher knife used by Bhairava and sometimes preferred by Cāmuṇḍā. A frightening image of the goddess in the Daśāśvamedha Ghāṭ at Jajpur keeps the knife raised with her upper right hand, while holding by the hair the head she has just cut with her lower left hand. She is seated on a naked *asura* in *añjalimudrā* seeking grace.[162]

As already observed, the Buddhists succeeded in carving out a space in the large territory between present-day Maharashtra and Andhra Pradesh up to Madhya Pradesh and Orissa in the attempt to unite with the North-East. It was in the regions of the central and eastern Vindhyas, on the southern slope of the mountains towards the plain, that the temples of the *yoginī*-s started being built from the ninth century onwards. They dotted the landscape (see Map 3) from Hinglajgarh in easternmost Rajasthan to Hirapur in the vicinity of Bhubaneswar, passing through the region of Gwalior-Lalitpur (Naresar, Mitauli and Dudahi), Bundelkhand and Baghelkhand (Khajuraho, Gurgi, Mau Suhania and, in the southernmost reaches of present-day Uttar Pradesh, Lokhari and Rikhiyan), and the territory stretching from Jabalpur (Bheraghat and Shahdol) to innermost Orissa (Ranipur Jharial).[163] The evidence suggesting the existence of *yoginī*-s temples in Bengal[164] is of particular interest, because they make us understand that the Pāla territories were being increasingly eroded and lost for the religion of Dharma.[165] The sanctuaries of the murderous goddesses are to be seen in relation to the new stance that Vajrayāna Buddhism took on the violent attempts at suppressing the religion. The *siddha* movement and the organisation of assemblies and rituals in the form of *gaṇacakra*-s and other group-oriented religious practices,[166] which needed no fixed places of worship, were a strong response to the forced abandonment of monasteries and temples (we have seen above the case of Ellora). We will focus on what has been called non-institutional Buddhism below, and here we concentrate on the organised reaction against the recruitment of untouchables and 'tribals' by the Buddhists in a territory that constitutes the faultline of Indian medieval history.

In these regions, the *maṇḍala*-s of the *yoginī*-s overlap too closely in both chronological and geographical terms to the likely activities of the *siddha*-s to be a coincidental phenomenon. The severed heads of the iconographies are those of the followers of the early *siddha*-s, whose ritual circles were imitated and replaced not only by parallel rituals but by solidly built temples erected thanks to the patronage of local rulers determined to put an end to social anarchy and impose Brahmanical order on society by extreme means. The two phenomena are diachronic, not synchronic, at least in their early developmental stage, and that they both largely drew on the 'tribal substrate' is not a reason to consider them interchangeable, nor is it particularly meaningful in terms of political history. It is obvious that, in a given place, competing systems utilise largely similar means. The fact that Sivaite *tantra*-s came into evidence some time in the ninth to tenth centuries,[167] while canonical as well as exegetical references to tribal and outcaste people are frequent in esoteric Buddhist texts from the beginning,[168] also points to a precise chronology of the events. The Kaula *cakra*-s of the *yoginī*-s[169] are modelled on the *gaṇacakra*-s and betray the determination to replace the Buddhists in the control of the native populations.

The particularity of the temples of the *yoginī*-s is that they are open-air enclosures, either quadrangular in plan as at Khajuraho and Mau Suhania near Chhatarpur[170] or more often circular, unlike any other class of Indian temples. Their *maṇḍala*-shaped aspect, usually resorted to as an explanation for their existence is too generic a feature, and helps to explain at most that we are dealing with sacred places where ritual activities were performed. In accord with the dictate of the texts that Bhairava be at the centre of the circle of *yoginī*-s,[171] shrines or round pavilions rose at the centre of the enclosures, arguably housing an image of the God and his retinue.[172] Vidya Dehejia has contended that only already dead human beings were offered to the goddesses (*śava sādhanā*), and that the ritual killing of humans was excluded.[173] But procuring 'beautiful' corpses 'not injured in any way, and not defaced or marked in any manner', and even 'still sweet-smelling'[174] was hardly a feasible thing, and it is preferable not to rely upon normative textual dictates to provide an explanation as regards, in particular, the early, elusive *yoginī*-s enclosures,[175] based on the relationship between Śiva and the goddess(es) discussed above: at Ranipur-Jharial, the circle was presided over by Śiva as Naṭarāja and by Cāmuṇḍā dancing on a corpse.[176] The enclosures appear *prima facie* as developments of earlier spaces such as the *yajñaśālā* of Ellora, and in fact the earliest ones are quadrangular in plan. The enclosures appear as ritualised *assommoirs* where special opponents were got rid of, it being otherwise difficult to account for their isolated location and special iconographic features.

Inimical armies were defeated in battle, and both soldiers and military commanders were killed, but the logic underlying the battlefield is different in that it presupposes openly conducted operations. The battlefield was sacralised, but was under everybody's gaze: there was no need for secrecy, quite the opposite. But different wars were also waged, more similar to guerrilla wars, whose military chiefs and political leaders had to be suppressed, and this happened according to different procedures. Early enclosures point to *yajña*-s amplifying the specialised slaughtering of heretics and their supportive *rājā*-s that we have seen performed by Bhairava and Cāmuṇḍā. The holy terror that the local people still show for the remains of the *yoginī* temples is nothing but a memory of what was performed there,[177] and cannot be explained by the memory of the battlefield, bloody though this may have been.[178]

We have already mentioned the immaterial activities of the *siddha*-s, but we should also bear in mind that Buddhist sites are not lacking throughout the whole Vindhya region, and that traces of Buddhism survive in the places occupied by the *yoginī* enclosures or at a short distance from them.[179] A careful assessment of their chronology would be of great help for understanding how Buddhist and Brahmanical India interface in these territories. Suffice it here to recall the two major sites of Sanchi and Bharhut, which we do not generally associate with later Buddhism, but which lasted until the twelfth century.[180] The temple at Bharhut, in particular, which underwent reconstruction in about AD 1100, displayed Vajrayāna iconographies with the subjugation of Brahmanical deities[181] showing that the Buddhists did not give up, and when circumstances allowed it, reacted vigorously. It has been recently confirmed that '[s]culptural remains recorded in photographs of the site, taken during Cunningham's excavation, many of which have been preserved in the modern village of Bharhut, include both Buddhist and Brahmanical carvings': this would indicate that 'at least by the Kalachuri period the site was being used by both Buddhist and Brahmanical religious groups'.[182] Late Bharhut may be described as a Buddhist stronghold surrounded by inimical forces, and its survival through compromise and revolt would deserve further investigation. Farther north-east, in a still safe area, there was Bodhgayā.

PACIFIED KINGDOMS

The Candella kingdom may be taken as the epitome of the *pax brahmanica* in northern India. The sources at our disposal, both scriptural and iconographical, allow us to re-create a context where all the enemies of the Brahmanical sociey had been defeated and the new orthodoxy – born out from the synthesis of Vedic thought and of the Pañcarātra and Śaiva Siddhānta systems – could display all its effects.

Jejākabhukti, later known as Bundelkhand, had seen the establishment of orthodox Gupta power like the other regions of central-northern India, but the discovery made by Cunningham at Khajuraho of the pedestal of 'a colossal draped figure' inscribed with the Buddhist formula, which he dated to the seventh century,[183] indicates that Buddhism had regained ground. If the kingdom of Zhizhituo mentioned by Xuanzang[184] is to be identified with Jejākabhukti,[185] this must have happened at the time of Harṣavardhana: the kingdom was Buddhist only on behalf of his king, a brāhmaṇa who firmly believed in the Three Jewels, while most of its inhabitants were unbelievers, and only a few honoured the Buddhist Dharma. There were 'several tens' of monasteries, but the priests were few, whereas the *deva* temples, about ten in number, were frequented by some thousand followers. The situation depicted by Xuanzang points to the typical capacity of Harṣavardhana of shifting the balance of power in his favour even in the presence of adverse social and religious conditions. The Buddha image now in the site museum is an eighth-century work,[186] and its presence suggests that the region of Khajuraho was included in those territories of central and upper Deccan that the Buddhists had managed, between the seventh and the eighth century, to make, in part, their own. Their presence was hegemonic in the region at the time of the early Pāla rulers, and in fact, until the ninth century there is no visible trace of other religious groups, although the presence of Sivaites is to be assumed.

In was around AD 900 that a temple of the sixty-four *yoginī*-s was built at Khajuraho,[187] something that introduces us into a new scenario. Its presence suggests a *devāsura* war to have been fought. The memory of the events related to the brahmanisation of the region in which the Candellas, as feudatories of the Pratihāras, had played a leading role was well present to the new independent dynasty when, from the tenth century onwards, the temples of Khajuraho were constructed. On the high plinth (*vedībandha*) of the Kandarīya Mahādeva Temple, built in the second quarter of the eleventh century,[188] open out nine niches that, being placed at eye level, the devotees could observe from close up when circumambulating the temple. Proceeding clockwise from the *ardhamaṇḍapa,* they display the images of Gaṇeśa, the *saptamātṛkā*-s and Vīrabhadra, which we have seen directly connected with the extirpation of heresy since Gupta times and, in a visually terrifying way, in the *yajñaśālā* of Ellora. The *saptamātṛkā*-s include a ferocious Cāmuṇḍā dancing on a corpse. These images are the symbolic base upon which the Temple, with its complex theological conceptualisation, stands: without the war waged against the opponents of orthodoxy, the erection of the temple would not have been possible. Not only the Śivaites, but also the Bhāgavatas-Pañcarātras contributed to the religious cleansing of Jejākabhukti, as is apparent from the dedicatory inscription of the Lakṣmaṇa Temple, built in the first half of the tenth century during the reign of King Yaśovarman (*c.* AD 925-50) and consecrated under Dhaṅga in AD 954. The inscription opens invoking protection upon Vāsudeva, whose breast is 'marked with scars by the swords of the Daityas':[189]

> May that Vaikuṇṭha protect you, who, frightening the whole world with his roaring, as boar and as man-lion, slew the three chiefs Asuras, Kapila and the rest, (*who were*) terrible in the world, (*and who*) possessed one body which by the boon of Brahman enjoyed freedom from fear (*and*) could be destroyed (*only*) by (*Vaikuṇtha*) having assumed those forms.[190]

Both Vāsudeva and Vaikuṇṭha (a form of Viṣṇu developed by the Bhāgavatas-Pañcarātras that by this time had acquired the complex, esoteric nature of the highest personal God) are considered under their aspect of destroyers of the *daitya*-s/*asura*-s. They act according to the mechanisms we know from the Purāṇic literature. To make the point clear, the story of Trivikrama and Bali is also recalled at the beginning of the inscription.[191] If we look at the Candella temples from this perspective, the interpretation of the architectural and iconographical world of Khajuraho (in particular of the Lakṣmaṇa and Kandarīya Mahādeva temples) proposed by Devangana Desai[192] becomes even more meaningful. The Pañcarātra and Śaiva Siddhānta systems, which made them symbols of cosmic order on earth,[193] are the protagonists of Brahmanical normalisation.

Kṛṣṇa Miśra's *Prabodha Candrodaya*, or *The Rise of the Moon of Awakening*[194] is a mine of information, and is quite explicit. This morality play in six acts was composed at the Candella court between AD 1050 and 1116,[195] and more precisely during the reign of King Kīrtivarman (*c.* AD 1070-98), before whom it was staged at the instance of Śrī Gopāla, his military commander in the war against the Cedis.[196] The play depicts the pacified situation reached after a religious war. For the achievement of peace, the different forces of Brahmanism, unified and hierarchised in the perspective of the Advaita Vedānta, are explicitly declared to have jointly fought. In fact, the *śāstra*-s 'born from the Vedas, though they are opposed to each other internally, unite together to over-throw the non-believers (in the Vedas) and protect the Vedas'.[197] Śraddhā (Faith), one of the main characters of the morality, recalls the past, separate wars, and makes them appear as what they really were – one and the same generalised conflict. In the context where the play was composed, there were no reasons to conceal the real identity of the slaughtered adversaries. It was addressed to a small, sophisticated circle of people who perfectly knew the dynamic of events. It was no longer the time to allegorise historical facts for the benefit of a large audience of devotees as in the case of the Purāṇas. Thus Faith, after evoking the battlefield, tells plainly what was the consequence of the defeat for the survivors:

> There the rivers of abundant blood as their waters flew, whose mud was pieces of flesh (lying) in plenty, were covered with wretched birds; the huge elephants which were shattered by the arrows and were scattered (here and there) formed the rocks, and stopped their speed, whose ear-ornaments were the umbrellas fallen here and there that looked like haṁsa birds.
>
> In that great and fierce battle, the materialist who is opposed to both the parties

(the Vaidika and Advaitika) was placed in the front by the heretics and was killed in the conflict (between two armies). The other anti-Vedic schools were destroyed by the flow of the ocean of Vedic thoughts. The Buddhists entered the almost barbarous countries of Sindhus, Gāndhāras, Pārasīkas, Māgadhas, Āndhras, Hūṇas, Vaṅgas, Kaliṅgas etc. The heretic Digambaras (Jaina), Kāpālikas and others live hidden in the Pāñcālas, Mālavas, Ābhīras and Āvarta near the ocean, which (countries) abound in illiterates. The logic of the anti-Vedic schools shattered by the Mīmāṁsā accompanied by Nyāya had the same fate of the (heretic) śāstras.[198]

It is interesting for us to note that besides the Buddhists, the Kāpālikas were also proscribed: by the late eleventh century they had already accomplished their task, and could be declared *personae non gratae*. In the play, the Kāpālika threatens to kill the Digambara Jain, accused of insulting Śiva by calling him a magician: 'I shall please the wife of Bharga (Śiva) with the blood springing out in thick foaming streams of bubbles from the throat which is cut with this frightful sword, along with the host of ghosts called by the booming sound of the Ḍamaru.'[199]

These words depict the social-religious dynamics described in the preceding section and in Chapter IV, the *modus operandi* of the Kāpālikas (and possibly of other *vāma* groups) being obviously known to Kṛṣṇa Miśra. He treats them better than the Buddhists and the Digambaras, but the climate had changed, and Śraddhā, in fact, declares, 'I abhor the sight of battles full of violence', and wants to leave Benares, the place of the battlefield.[200] There were probably deeper implications in the decision of jettisoning the Kāpālikas. The butchers they recruited to carry out the religious cleansing must have come from the most unclean and unruly sectors of society, something that could no longer be tolerated in a successfully reformed society where even the lowest of the low had to conform to a strict code of behaviour.

Some of the erotic reliefs on the temples of Khajuraho are to be understood as mocking scenes depicting the Digambara Kṣapaṇika monks,[201] ridiculed by the sophisticated Candella intelligentsia. It is difficult to know the precise reason that brought about the expulsion of the Digambara Jains from the kingdom. The temple of Pārśvanātha (originally dedicated to Ādinātha) is contemporaneous with the Lakṣmaṇa Temple,[202] whose construction was initiated by Yaśovarman in about AD 950,[203] and the Ādinātha Temple belongs to the group of developed temples, being thus dated to around the mid-eleventh century.[204] The place that the Brahmanical deities have in the iconographical programme of these Jain temples is too central for them to be considered ancillary presences.[205] The Jains living in Khajuraho between *c.* AD 950 and 1050 were a community integrated willy-nilly within the Brahmanical order, having not only accepted the normalisation of society and *varṇabheda* but the control of *Jainadharma* and temple service, according to a process that we will discuss in the next chapter. The fact that Cunningham found the Buddha image mentioned above 'lying amongst the ruins' outside the Ghaṇṭāi Temple, a ruined Jain building roughly contemporary with the temple of Pārśvanātha,[206] may suggest that the Digambaras erected it on the site of a former Buddhist establishment, after actively taking part in its destruction as was happening elsewhere.[207] Something, however, must have happened after AD 1050 for Kṛṣṇa Miśra to include the Digambaras among the enemies of the Brahmanical order, but we have no clue on the reasons why the pact between the two parties, always in jeopardy, was eventually broken. We can only argue that it was during Kīrtivarman's reign that the expulsion of the Jains took place.

A relief on the Devī Jagadambā Temple (Fig. 14) deserves a comment. According to an untenable theory advanced by Alain Daniélou, it would represent a king hailing a monk in a most friendly (and, we may add, unusual) way, ascribing it to a set of iconographies revealing Indian tolerance towards homosexual behaviour.[208] The bearded man is better identified as a Kāpālika ascetic, raising his right hand to hit the Digambara Jain (but he could be a Buddhist, because of the virtual nakedness of all *śramaṇa*-s) who is asking for mercy and is ready to convert. Threat and mockery go together in this relief,[209] which reveals the various levels through which normalisation was reached: the Jains and the Buddhists are killed or obliged to convert, but the Kāpālikas are, in turn, mocked and got rid of.

The main target of Kṛṣṇa Miśra are the Buddhists. Immediately after the passage mentioned above, Viṣṇubhakti asks Śraddhā news of Mahāmoha, the delusion through which Viṣṇu has generated heresy:

Faith: Goddess, it is not known where Great Delusion has hidden himself along with the Obstacles of Yoga.

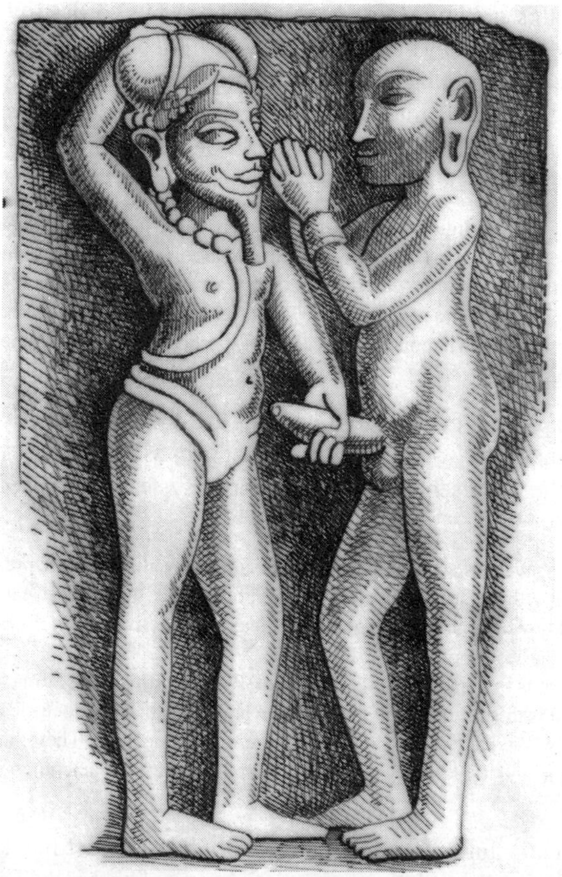

Figure 14: A Kāpālika threatening a naked ascetic in the Devī Jagadambā Temple, Khajuraho.

> *Delusion of Viṣṇu*: If so the great danger is still there. He should be destroyed. A wise person desiring lasting good will not be careless and leave behind remnants of fire, debt and enemy.[210]

Moha, significantly, has made Benares his capital, and has explained to one of his sons and accomplices, Dambha (Deceit), that 'the city named Vārāṇasī is the best place in the world to attain liberation', and that he must go there 'and try to obstruct the path of the liberation of all the four castes'.[211] Deceit explains in turn to Ahaṃkāra (Egoism) that 'Vārāṇasī is the birth place of knowledge and spiritual awakening', and that this is why Mati (Reason), who wants to destroy Moha's family, 'wishes to stay there permanently'.[212] Moha, that is, the Buddha, has made Benares, that is to say, Sarnath, where he first preached, the place of false awakening. Therefore, King Viveka (Discrimination) fights against Moha with the assistance of the orthodox *darśana*-s.

In Act III, the Buddhist *bhikṣu* presents himself as follows:

> How good is the religion of the Buddha where there is (sensual) enjoyment as well as liberation. For—(living in) beautiful houses, (possessing) prostitutes who are to their liking, (having) food of their taste at any time they desire, (sleeping on) soft beds, they who meditate with faith (on Buddha) spend the nights bright with moon light, with happiness derived from sporting with young women offering their bodies.[213]

The *bhikṣu* is even ready to accept the doctrine of the Kāpālikas for the sake of sexual pleasure, proving himself the most debased among the representatives of the three systems criticised by the author:

> How often have I ardently embraced widows with swelling breasts, pressing their big breasts with my arms with great passion! but by the Buddhas I swear a hundred times that nowhere have I attained such pleasure as derived from the embrace of big swelling bosom of this Kāpālinī.
>
> Excellent is the practice of the Kāpālika. Praiseworthy is the Soma Siddhānta. Wonderful is this religion. Oh good sir, we have forsaken the doctrine of Buddha completely. We have accepted the doctrine of Parameśvara. Therefore, you are my teacher and I am your disciple. Initiate me into the teachings of Parameśvara.[214]

This caricature of what are apparently householder monks echoes and amplifies the old accusations of immoral behaviour. The *bhikṣu* of the play (whether a real monk or a priest) is the personification of the whole Buddhist community, which is condemned en bloc. We know that in the eleventh century a Buddhist community was living within the Candella territory, at Mahobā, the cradle of the dynasty and one of its capital towns.[215] The stele found near the Kirat Sagar, now kept in the Archaeological Museum in Lucknow, are dated on epigraphic basis to the eleventh-twelfth century,[216] and may be considered as creations of the community that was obliged to quit. Judging from an exceptional, sixty-four-armed image of Cāmuṇḍā, as well as from the other numerous rock-cut images of the goddess observable at Mahoba,[217] the departure of the heretics did not take place peacefully. Other Buddhist communities were present in the kingdom. We have mentioned Bharhut in the section above, and groups of Buddhists were still living in the Gopeśvara Hills in Datia district and in Damoh district.[218] That the Buddhists fled to Magadha, Vaṅga, Kaliṅga and Āndhra is credible (although by the end of the eleventh century only a few Buddhist strongholds were extant in the two latter regions), but that they would take refuge in Sind and Gandhāra can only be understood as having found there a temporary shelter before moving to more suitable places.[219]

We have mentioned the war waged by the Candellas against the Cedis. We are generally unable to go beyond military history, but some scattered information help us in getting a deeper insight on the social dynamics of this region during this period. The Rewa inscription of Malayasiṃha (a 'feudatory' of the Kalacuris-Cedis) of the end of the twelfth century testifies that this *rājā* supported Buddhism.[220] The policy followed by the local chiefs may not have always been coincidental with those of the 'central' power, and only a thorough survey of the archaeological evidence could throw more light into the stratifications of Indian history. In the above-mentioned inscription of Yaśovarmàn of AD 954, which opens with the mention of the war against the *asura*-s, there is a passage about the Candella prince Rāhila, father of Harṣa (the real founder of Candella power), who ruled in the second half of the ninth century.[221] We read that Rāhila was

> [...] never tired, at the sacrifice of battle, where the terribly wielded sword was the ladle, where the oblation of clarified butter was made with streaming blood, where the twanging of the bow-string was the exclamation *vashaṭ*, *(and)* at which exasperated warriors marching in order were the priests, successful with his counsels (as with sacred hymns) sacrificed, like beasts, the adversaries in the fire of enmity, made to blaze up by the wind of his unappeased anger.[222]

Here warfare is viewed in terms of the performance of sacrifice, and the passage has been taken as further evidence of the strict orthodox policy followed by the Candellas: the literal likeness between the priestly and princely sacrifices 'fully drives home the hold of Vedic rituals on the upper classes'.[223] It was approximately at the time of Rāhila that the temple of the sixty-four *yoginī*-s of Khajuraho was built, and we wonder about the real nature of a battlefield being made 'sacred': which kind of war was that waged by Rāhila?

The radical change that the *pax brahmanica* brought to the Indian landscape is best illustrated by the new geography that was created. The Purāṇas and the appended *māhātmya*-s provide ample evidence of *kṣetra*-s presided over by a Brahmanical deity. The process of renaming every corner of India was as long as different were the dynamics that led to the final control of the brāhmaṇas over the whole subcontinent. The new names given to regions, provinces, towns, neighbourhoods and crossroads accomplished the task of cleansing the past, whose memory either disappeared or was distorted. What the Purāṇas do not tell us, or recount only indirectly, is that the new toponyms replaced, one after the other, the place names of the geographical horizon of the open society. The establishment of a new geography is by no means unique to India, but here it was carried out with a radicalism that has few parallels.[224] Buddhist geography was cancelled, and to such a degree that, despite the enormous efforts made in the last two centuries to retrieve the ancient toponyms, to date we are still ignorant of the ancient names of many a Buddhist site, and are unable to identify many a place known from the texts. The Brahmanical occupation of the whole country did not simply come to be a substitution and appropriation of past realities, but to a real extent implied the reset of all the other histories of India: the power and importance of medieval Brahmanical myths lie here.

A WAY OUT FROM THE SIEGE: THE BUDDHIST REACTION

The *Guhyasamāja Tantra* is regarded as the earliest *tantra* and the revered source of all the subsequent esoteric scriptures of the Buddhists. Its date has been the object of much debate among scholars,[225] but the second half of the eighth century is now generally acknowledged as the period of its composition.[226] The aim of this *tantra* is declared in the first chapter: no one can succeed in obtaining perfection through processes that are difficult and painful; but one can succeed easily through the satisfaction of all desires.[227] In the fifth chapter, the Bhagavān Mahāvairocana declares that outcastes, workers and similar people find perfection in this *yāna*. This means of salvation is likewise for those who do not respect the life of the others, who delight in telling falsehood, who steal other people's property, who continuously take recourse to sensual pleasures, and who feed on excrements and urine. It is the *yogin* lusting after his mother, sisters and daughters who attains the greatest perfection.[228]

Paradoxical as these statements may have intended to be,[229] the attack on social institutions and commonly accepted behaviour contained in these and other passages of the *Guhyasamāja Tantra*, is radical. In this text, the society appears *prima facie* as an entirely collapsed, broken-up entity, or, better to say, the text appears as something that actively brings about the establishment of such a society: the addressees of the initiates are the murderers, thieves, liars, immoral and incestuous persons, the defamers. At the same time, the metaphors and the rituals created to make them the protagonists of the Buddhist survival strategy are plunged in an astonishing, dazzling light, something that lends the text that de-historicised character, which made a symbolical interpretation possible. The *Guhyasamāja Tantra* appropriates, magnifies, and extols the social subjects that Brahmanical texts had been reviling as responsible for the disastrous situation of the Kali Age. Even the bodhisattvas attending the *saṃgīti* where the Bhagavān explains the new 'secret' doctrine are scandalised, and to such a degree that they fall down motionless from the shock: only when, at the instance of the Tathāgatas, they are touched by the light emanating from the Sublime Being, they are reanimated and take their seats again.[230] The shocked bodhisattvas represent the traditional upper caste elite of Buddhist monasticism that was invited to adjust to a strategy they found difficult to adhere to, but that, in the new situation, the Buddhist masters, unable to respond to the reorganised, differentiated Brahmanical elites, could no longer refuse. Traditional Mahāyāna had brought the religion of Dharma to a dead end.

For such a text as the *Guhyasamāja* to be written, conditions of social strain and a desperate will to react, although kept 'secret' (*guhya*), must be assumed, and these conditions are those of extreme hardships described in this and in the preceding chapter. In many parts of India the monasteries had been, and still were, the target of attacks; many had been destroyed, appropriated or had been forcibly deserted; even where Buddhism still held its positions, violence was always possible. This situation could not but generate a general lack of confidence in the political and social praxis adopted in the past, and a stronger contrast towards the wicked world.[231] We must carefully consider the political perspective of the late eighth and early ninth century: it is the period of the great Pāla emperors, which makes us understand that the response of the Vajrayāna was political, perfectly rational and well-coordinated, capable of uniting the various, weakened bits of Indian Buddhism once the resistance of which the author of the *Guhyasamāja Tantra* is aware was overcome.

Two survival strategies were developed. The first, which we shall discuss in the next chapter and awaits investigation, was a mimetic strategy strengthening the status of the already existing married clergy, entrusted with the administration of *saṃskāra*-s. It could no longer be looked down upon, but was called to participate in the common cause. The Buddhist priesthood paralleled that of the brāhmaṇas and of the Jains. The second survival strategy was based on the interdependence of non-institutional Buddhism, as it has been called,[232] and the monasteries of north-eastern India.

In the hostile territories, the *siddha*-s developed a model of social presence that did not require a permanent residence. The locations where they performed their rituals and imparted their teaching could hardly be the object of aggressions. They were out-of-the-way places, at the far-edge of the inhabited areas, and the *gaṇacakra*-s and other ritual groups assembled at night. These settings were not merely bizarre, sorcerous locations, a folkloric scenario, but a necessity and a strategic choice. By the eighth century Buddhist recruitment in the upper castes must have turned extremely difficult in large parts of the country. The social origin of the eighty-four *siddha*-s, for all the inadequateness of the sample, mirrors the impasse. The support of the commoners, and their contribution to restock the ranks of the *saṃgha* had equally faded away for the radically changed economic situation. The opening to the lowest segments of society was a necessity.

In the eighth century, the political resistance against caste brāhmaṇas had concentrated in the North-East. Gopāla (*c.* AD 750-70), founder of the Pāla dynasty, was a śūdra according to the *Mañjuśrīmūlakalpa*, and rose to power when 'the people [were] miserable with the Brahmins'.[233] He was not the first low-caste king to rule in India: when it was in their interest, the brāhmaṇas had no difficulty in clearing dubious social origins, but the case was different here. The expression *kāmakārī* found in the initial verse of Pāla inscriptions – a eulogy of both Buddha and Gopāla, indicates those who do not acknowledge any control and act wilfully.[234] This does not so much refer to local unruly chiefs, but to the brāhmaṇas who fomented them. In the eighth century, the constant presence of the Tibetans strongly conditioned the political events in north-eastern India: they probably played an important role in placing a Buddhist king on the throne.[235] From a geo-strategic standpoint, we have a powerful Buddhist block similar to that created by Harṣavardhana, although its centre of gravity was more to the east, in Magadha and Bengal, thus showing a further withdrawal from India proper, but included the trans-Himalayan and trans-delta countries.[236] As mentioned above, the rise of the new Vajrayāna strategy must be seen in the perspective of a renewed confidence fuelled by the existence of a strong political power that was giving hope for the future. With Dharmapāla (*c.* AD 765-800) and Devapāla (*c.* AD 800-40), but also with the latter's successors,[237] it seemed that the whole of northern India, and even parts of the south, could be restored to the religion of *dharma*. A *caitya* was seemingly built on the ashes of Devapāla, whom the Buddhists must have honoured as a real *cakravartin*.[238] The activism of the early *siddha*-s, their apparent ubiquity and interrelationship with the monasteries finds an explanation in this new political scenario: they could be active in the hostile periphery because they had a strong point of reference in a powerful state severally threatening the Brahmanical kingdoms.

There is a strong discrepancy between the great number of texts testifying to the activity of the *siddha*-s and the material traces of their presence, which until the tenth century are non-existent. The widely accepted opinion that it was in Uḍḍiyāna that the *siddha*-s first appeared and the earliest Vajrayāna texts were composed,[239] is not documented by the material evidence. At the iconographical level, too, there is no evidence of the early responses elaborated in the texts against Brahmanical abuse.[240] The iconographies that would develop from the tenth century onwards define yet another situation – one where the Muslim presence kindled new hopes.

Attention has been called on the *Sarvatathāgatatattva Saṃgraha*, an esoteric Buddhist text codified in the eighth century where we find the story of the subjugation of Maheśvara, perhaps 'the most influential myth of esoteric Buddhism'.[241] Vajrapāṇi, the master of mysteries,[242] warns the *tathāgata*-s against the existence of criminals such as Maheśvara and other gods. Summoned by a *mantra*, they appear on Mount Sumeru, where Maheśvara displays his wreath and cruelty in the form of Mahābhairava – the reader knows why – and is annihilated by Vajrapāṇi, with whom the other gods take refuge. Brought back from the dead, Maheśvara again opposes Vajrapāṇi's attempt at subduing him, until when, dragged stark naked with his consort Umā and stepped on by the bodhisattva, abandons his form of Mahādeva and is reborn, and enters the *maṇḍala* with another name, like the other gods.[243] A text of the Cakrasaṃvara cycle, the *Guhyagarbhatattvaviniścaya*, introduces Heruka who 'seizes Maheśvara and his entire retinue, rips out their internal organs, hacks their limbs to pieces, eats their flesh, drinks their blood, and makes ritual ornaments from their bones'.[244] After having been digested and excreted into an ocean of muck, Maheśvara and the other gods are revived and accepted into the *maṇḍala*. An escalation is observable: in the first case, the power of the *mantra*-s is sufficient to subdue Śiva and the other gods, while in the second Heruka makes Narasiṃha's technique his own for dismembering his opponents. We face different situations here, the latter one aggravated by the increasingly complicated game of the late eleventh and twelfth century.

As an example of the early strategy at the level of monastic Buddhism, I will mention the case of the sanctuary of Tapa Sardar near Ghazni in south-eastern Afghanistan. The sanctuary was entirely rebuilt according to a much modified plan towards the end of the seventh century after a big fire had caused extensive damages in AD 671-72, when the territory from Bost and al-Rukhaj up to Kābul was overrun by the Muslims.[245] Its reconstruction was possible thanks to the patronage of the rulers of Zābulistān, the *eltäbar*-s of Ghazni Khuras and his son and successor Alkhis, whose safety, like that of the other rulers of the Buddhist kingdoms of western Central Asia and Kashmir, depended on Tang protection.[246] The period of Tang hegemony can be circumscribed between the reign of Empress Wu Zhao (reigning from AD 690 to 705, actually a break in Tang rule), and the withdrawal of the Tang to China proper after the mid-eighth century. In the newly erected sanctuary, a series of chapels opened around the main stūpa. In Chapel 23, an image of a goddess modelled on the eight-armed Durgā Mahiṣamardinī was added on a sidewall[247] after the end of Tang hegemony. By the mid-eighth century, a Kabul shah and ruler of Uḍḍiyāna, Śrī Ṣāhī Khiṃgāla or Khiṅgila had become a supporter of the Brahmanical faith; in AD 765 he had an image of Gaṇeśa made in Gardez, in Logar.[248] The Sakāwand Temple, mentioned in several Muslim sources, which attracted Hindu worshippers 'from the most remote parts of Hindustan'[249] was probably already in existence.[250] The Durgā image of Tapa Sardar points to the reaction of the Buddhists to the new state of things. The goddess, subjugated by the new powerful Vajrayāna gods, is now at the service of Buddhism with a different name. A similar case, to remain on the mountains barring India to the North-West, is that of the goddess Lakṣaṇā at Bharmour in the upper Ravi region of Chamba. The eighth-century bronze is *prima facie* that of Mahiṣamardinī, but the deity has acquired the characteristics of an esoteric Buddhist goddess, whose temple the Buddhist inhabitants of the region still regard as a shrine of Vajravārāhī.[251]

The early *siddha*-s, documented in the first decades of the eighth century,[252] originated and were especially active in apparently de-structured territories. Uḍḍiyāna, a short distance from Zābulistān, is a case in point. This region found itself at the periphery of the Ṣāhī agrarian state centred on Udabhāṇḍapura (present-day Hund) on the right bank of the Indus in Gandhāra, although, as we have already seen, the orthodox considered it one of the major Sivaite *pīṭha*-s.[253] The main stūpa of the sanctuary of Butkara, near Saidu Sharif, was enlarged and reconstructed several times. The fifth stūpa, built at the end of the seventh or the beginning of the eighth century, passed through intensive changes mirrored by three phases, its appearance growing ever shabbier and its workmanship coarser. After becoming 'a very poor affair', it perhaps crumbled wholly or in part and was abandoned, and its life ended in the tenth century.[254] The excavations at Butkara were extremely accurate, yet the attention paid to the phases of abandonment was lesser than that devoted to the Gandharan period, and possible clues on the elusive presence of Vajrayāna ascetics are not available.[255] Should we imagine a setting for King Indrabhūti, Padmasambhava and the early *siddha*-s, as well as for the author of the *Guhyasamāja Tantra*, we should think of a landscape with residual monastic presence and tiny communities up in the valley to which the new teachings were imparted. As conjectured by Giuseppe Tucci, the effigies of the symbols utilised by the *siddha*-s may have been painted on the walls of chapels and temples closed to all but the initiates, as is still the custom in Tibet.[256]

The composition of many important texts is accounted for by the continuous exchange of spiritual and material experiences between the *siddha*-s and the north-eastern monasteries. In AD 783 Dharmapāla begun his northern Indian campaign, and conquered or overran Panjab and the North-West (*Yavana* and *Gandhāra*).[257] This opened a channel of communication between regions that were in the process of being brahmanised and the eastern Gangetic territories. The distance between institutional and non-institutional Buddhism must have been negligible in the given situation. The *siddha* movement is hardly distinguishable from institutional Buddhism, whose representatives were the first to turn non-institutional: the earliest *siddha* was Saraha, the author of the *Dohākośa*, or so runs the story. He was a monk at Nālandā towards the end of the eighth century, and took a new name after he started living as an arrow-maker in the company of a girl of that profession. Rāhulabhadra, before espousing the cause of the lower classes and become a *siddha*, had been a *bhikṣu*, a pupil of Haribhadra, in turn a pupil of Śāntarakṣita.[258] There is evidence showing that *saṃgha* members participated in *gaṇacakra*-s, and *bhikṣu*-s and *śramaṇera*-s also took the role of the *gaṇayaka* presiding over the gathering, being preferred over laymen. Abhayākara Gupta, abbot of the Vikramaśilā monastery, recognised that the *gaṇacakra* was an authentic method for attaining enlightenment.[259] Naturally, it took a long time for all the shocked bodhisattvas of the *Guhyasamāja Tantra* to revive, and in fact we are dealing with a centuries-long process.

Attention has been called to Sirpur (Śrīpura) in South Kosala, in the Upper Mahanadi Valley (Raipur district of Chhattisgarh): an image of Vajrasattva and the inscriptional evidence on the use of *mantra*-s suggest the early involvement with *siddha* traditions.[260] The history of Buddhism at Sirpur must be seen within a complex mechanism of antagonism and destruction. The main temple with the attached monastery built by the monk Ānandaprabhu during the reign of Mahāśivagupta Bālārjuna is reported to have been appropriated later on by the Sivaites, who carried out extensive repairs and changes. Other smaller monasteries were to fall to the same fate.[261] The chronology of the events is uncertain, given that the absolute chronology of the Pāṇḍuvaṃśī kings, as we have seen in Chapter III, is not known. Things are even more difficult to disentangle because there are two Brahmanical temples at Sirpur, those of Lakṣmaṇa and Rāma, attributed by some to the same chronological horizon as the Buddhist buildings.[262] The inscription of queen Vāsaṭā, mother of Bālārjuna, who had the Lakṣmaṇa Temple built, provides us with an unexpected picture of the events. It opens with an invocation to Puruṣottama, and then extols the exploits of Narasiṃha – the *vāma* aspect of Viṣṇu – whose nails are told to have torn through the mass of dark clouds and revealed the stars, 'like a lion who, having overcome that storehouse of darkness, – the elephant, jumps about scattering brilliant pearls' torn from his temples.[263] We already know the meaning of these words, alluding to the confiscation of the wealth of Buddhist shrines. The text further clarifies the events, describing the god's fight with Hira nyakaśipu. Here we see Narasiṃha stealing Śiva's job:

As if bearing the jaws like a beautiful conch and the tongue like a sword, with the face burning like the discus *(and)* with the eye-brows *(as if carrying)* the mace, this form of Vishṇu born for devouring, like sins, the demons, presented the appearance of the god of death.[264]

The inscription points to the Bhāgavatas as early adversaries of the Buddhist community in the Sirpur territory, and in fact, Queen Vāsaṭā claims to have been the shelter of the four *varṇa*-s and to have checked the spread of the sins characteristic of the Kali Age.[265] It is a scenario we have seen recurring with great frequency. Then the Bhāgavatas (to which *siddha* identity is indebted)[266] seem to disappear from the scene. Vāsaṭā's son, Bālārjuna, made endowments to Śiva temples[267] but a donation of a village to the monks of the small monastery of Taraḍaṃśaka is also recorded,[268] not considering the fact that he allowed Ānandaprabhu to build a monastery in the capital. He resorted to that balanced policy which satisfied the Sivaites and the Buddhists alike, Śiva being, for the latter, nothing but a *deva*. The changed religious scenario, with the withdrawal of the Bhāgavatas, and the policy followed by Bālārjuna would be consistent with the eighth-century scenario that saw the rise of Pāla power, and a late chronology for Bālārjuna seems thus more likely. The Buddhist sculptural production, which includes the well-known bronzes,[269] is attributed to the eighth century, and it was only some time after the reign of Bālārjuna that the Buddhist-Sivaite compromise came to an end. The large amount of Sivaite plaques found in the upper levels of the main monastery and of other *vihāra*-s points to the occupation of the complex by Sivaite ascetics, even though it is not clear if this event is marked by an interface of destruction or by layers of abandonment or by both things. In South Kosala, the *siddha*-s were probably present both in the late seventh and early eighth century, when the Buddhists were trying to create a corridor between central Deccan and Magadha, as well as much later, when the Sivaites took a firm root in the region. The temples of the *yoginī*-s were eventually built to oppose their activities in the frame of generalised guerrilla warfare.

In the map of the probable sites of *siddha* activity provided by Ronald M. Davidson,[270] we see them concentrated in the middle and lower Ganges plains and Orissa, with small pockets in other areas, notably so in Kashmir and in the mountains of Panjab and in the Godavari and Krishna deltas. The map probably depicts a late phase, because the presence of the *siddha*-s shrank in the hostile territories after the weakening of Pāla power, and tended to concentrate in the North-East where, as we shall see in the next chapter, the final game was played out. It may be of interest to note that Dhanyakaṭaka, where the Buddha was said to have revealed the new doctrine to the king of Śambhala and where Buddhism survived until the fourteenth century,[271] was part of the territories overrun by Dharmapāla. Other sites could be added to the list, as for instance Panhale Kaji (ancient Praṇālaka) in southern Konkan, where the Vajrayāna *siddha*-s dwelling in a group of caves between the tenth and the twelfth century were later supplanted by the Nātha *siddha*-s, who adapted the caves to the Brahmanical faith.[272]

In the myth of the subjugation of Maheśvara by Heruka, violence becomes openly part of the Buddhist defense strategy. The symbolisation and ritualisation of the stages of this process, testified to by a large number of texts and iconographies, should not lead us to believe that it was limited to symbolic actions, an all too common mistake. The *maṇḍala* is the conceptualisation of a physical, territorial space where the brāhmaṇas and their allies must be reduced to impotence for the Buddhists to survive and recreate that Dharma Kingdom which lies at the root of political Buddhism. The *Guhyasamāja Tantra* explicitly invites concentration on the three-pronged *vajra* 'that paralyzes all the non-Buddhist teachers' projecting it on the head of the enemy, which will not prevail against the *buddhasainya*, the Buddha's army.[273] As to Vajrapāṇi, if his task was to reinforce the law and prevent the Maheśvaras of the world from overwhelming the monasteries at the symbolical level,[274] new followers of Buddhism existed who could protect them in actual reality. Violence is explicitly recognised as having a value, as in the case of one Viromaṇi, a Buddhist *yogī* who greatly enhanced the cause of Tantric Buddhism by suppressing the *tīrthika*-s.[275]

We wonder whether the Buddhists waited until the eighth century and favourable political conditions to respond to threats. They certainly encouraged the resistance of the social groups endangered by the occupation of lands and of the harassed traders community: in an inscription from Baijnath, we read that those alone can be considered true merchants whose wealth is lent to Śiva, the others being 'miserable traders' who fill their pockets and 'run to and fro somewhere in the nearest country'.[276] Had physical reaction against outer attacks started at an early date? Here we enter an unexplored territory, the few sources being either indirect or disputed. The tradition of martial arts and fighting bodhisattvas of Eastern Asia is thought to date back to Bodhidharma, who would have introduced them in the early sixth century after leaving India. The earliest sources on this misty figure are the *Memoir on the Buddhist Monasteries in Luoyang* (*Luoyang quielan ji*), composed by Yang Xuanzhi in AD 557-60, [277] according to which he was a blue-eyed Iranian (that is, a Buddhist monk of western Central Asia), and the more authoritative *Continued Biographies of Eminent Monks* (*Xu Gaoseng Zhuan*),[278] written in AD 645 by Daoxuan, who revised the text in AD 667. According to this biography, which draws from the *Damolun*, a treatise ascribed to Bodhidharma himself,[279] he was a brāhmaṇa from south India who arrived in China by sea and settled in Luoyang, where his teaching was not well received: he was left with only two disciples, Huike and Daoyu. The association of Bodhidharma with the Shaolin monastery, where he is said to have practised wall contemplation (*biguan*) for nine years, thus establishing Chan Buddhism in China, is far from being certain. The generally accepted theory according to which martial arts were developed by Buddhist monks in India before being transmitted to China along with the other features of Buddhist teaching is also doubtful.[280] There is no patent evidence supporting the hypothesis that in the fifth century or earlier some form of military discipline had developed in Indian Buddhist monasteries, and yet the silence of the sources should not prevent us from investigating the question a little further, especially knowing that armed exercises were practised in Sivaite *maṭha*-s.

Śākyamuni, as a young kṣatriya, had practised the exercises typical of his *varṇa*,[281] and although the scriptures condemn any form of physical violence,[282] a docetist interpretation of the Buddha results in considering every act of his life as an example to follow on occasions, and consider physical dexterity as complementary to spiritual training. The theory of skilful means (*upāya*) helped, in turn, to justify the behaviour of monks subject to difficult circumstances. The *Upāyakauśalya Sūtra* recounts the story of the compassionate captain of the ship (the Lord himself in a previous life) who, knowing that the merchants on board are about to be killed by a robber, decided to deliberately slay the failed criminal with a spear, 'with great compassion and skill in means', to avoid the murder and save the thug from hell. For this good action, *saṃsāra* was curtailed for him by one hundred thousand eons.[283] Stewart McFarlane, discussing certain aspects of East Asian Buddhism, has quoted a passage of Asaṅga's *Bodhisattvabhūmi* where the bodhisattva is ready to be reborn in hell for killing those potentially responsible for the slaying of innocent beings. The text continues as follows:

> So too is the Bodhisattva where there are kings or great ministers who are excessively cruel and have no compassion for beings, intent on causing pain to others. Since he has the power, he makes them fall from command of the kingdom, where they cause so much demerit. [...] If there are thieves and bandits who take the property of others, or the property of the Saṅgha or a *stūpa*, making it their own to enjoy, the Bodhisattva takes it from them [...]. So he takes it and returns it to the Saṅgha or to the *stūpa*. By this means, the Bodhisattva, though taking what is not given, does not have a bad rebirth, indeed much merit is produced.[284]

Who were the unworthy rulers against whom the Buddhist community, led by the bodhisattva, is urged to take action? Asaṅga lived in the fourth century, and the target could be no other than the Guptas and the local chiefs who oppressed the religion. The 'thieves and bandits' seizing the property of the monasteries and destroying the stūpas in order to grab the gold of the reliquaries (the lions' pearls of the preceding chapter) authorised reaction. If skilful means deploy a range of methods for the salvation of the multitude,[285] they are even more justified for saving the religion.[286] There are examples in the late *pāramitā* literature where he who kills will attain Awakening. The translators and commentators of Amoghavajra's *Prajñāpāramitānaya Sūtra* had difficulties in explaining a passage introducing the idea of the permissibility of killing,[287] thus inaugurating a symbolic interpretive approach that has not only permeated non-Indian Buddhist traditions but also modern scholarship. The incident that occurred in Tibet in AD 842 may throw light on how Buddhist monks could act. King gLang dar ma, who followed an anti-Buddhist policy, had ordered all the monasteries to be closed and the monks to disrobe. A monk, dPal gyi rdo je, concealing his bow and arrow in the sleeves of his cloak, presented himself before the king and killed him[288] according to the *drag las* (*abhicāra*) ritual.[289]

Krodha Vighnāntaka images make an early appearance as attendants of bodhisattvas in the iconographies. The earliest known examples of wrathful deities are from Caves 6 and 7 at Aurangabad, and are datable to the second half of the sixth century. Other early examples, datable to the seventh century, are from Ellora and Sarnath.[290] The risk of arranging the evidence ex-post, in a sort of evolutionary chain, is always very high in history, but the early emergence of deities having the visible task of defending the bodhisattvas from outside dangers is something that deserves the greatest attention:[291] by that time, an enormous amount of violence had already been exercised against the *śramaṇa*-s.

In China, seditions, rebellions and *jacqueries* stirred up or inspired by the Buddhists were numerous.[292] It was not uncommon, when central power weakened, to see monks descended from the common people form armed bands. As early as AD 445, a number of bows, arrows, lances and bucklers were discovered in a monastery in Chang'an,[293] which may mean either that the monks took active part in the revolt or that the monastery was used as a depot by external rebels. Similar events may have occurred also in those parts of India where political chaos reigned. In India, the aggressive affirmation of the *buddhasainya* is observable in Vajrayāna literature, and the armed defence of Dharma appears to be a major concern of the *siddha* literature.[294] When the hopes raised by the Muslims who had started crushing Brahmanical power vanished, and the struggle for survival became fiercer than ever, the texts do not hesitate to speak out, putting aside much of the symbolic apparatus. We read in the *Hevajra Tantra* how we must expect to behave: procedures are rather simplified.

> Such slaying is done from compassion, after one has supplicated one's *guru* and master (and is directed against) those who bring harm to the doctrine or injure one's guru or other buddhas.
>
> One should imagine such a one as a victim face-downwards, vomiting blood and trembling with his hair unloosed. One should then imagine a needle of fire as entering his rear, and the seed-syllable of fire in his heart. By envisaging him thus, one slays him in that instant, for in this rite there is no need of oblations or a performance of a sequence of gestures [. . .].[295]

It is not certain that esoteric ritual gatherings originated from tribal practices. Even Tantric visualisation techniques do not have any connection with them.[296] The Buddhists had always been in strict contact with the lower castes and the natives. The reader certainly remembers the tattooed personages emerging, so to say, from the forest, sculpted on the *vedikā* of the stūpa at Bharhut mentioned in Chapter II. In the early centuries BC/AD, and in many parts of India even later (in Tamil Nadu, for instance), the Buddhists and the followers of other *śramaṇa* groups not only stood for the natives, but *were* the natives, even though the intellectuals of the *saṃgha* were often of high caste. They had no conflicting economic interests, as was to happen with the brāhmaṇas. Few stories give us the sense of the attitude of the 'tribals' towards a Buddhists-led society than that of Harṣavardhana in search of his sister who asks and obtains their help. According to the *Harṣacarita*, the king entered the Vindhya forest, where he roamed for many days until he met Vyāghraketu, son of the tributary chief of the forest Śarabhaketu. He was accompanied by the nephew of Bhūkampa, a general of the Śabaras and the lord of all the village chiefs of that part of the Vindhya range, Nirghāta by name. And Nirghāta 'laid his head on the ground and made his obeisance and offered the partridge and hare as his present'.[297]

Some Gandharan reliefs, too, bring us into the little explored universe of the interrelationships between the Buddhist monastic élite and the natives. One of them displays two Nāga princes who, at the head of two separate groups, throw something out of the basket held by their wives onto an incense burner, while an apparently wild dance is performed all around to the sound of wind and percussion instruments.[298] Several other music and dance scenes attested in Gandhāra show that the recommendations of the *Vinaya* had not many chances to be applied in a number of monasteries.[299] The apparently orgiastic festivals of early Gandhāra have been considered rationalised representations of the pleasures waiting the devotees in the most accessible heavens of the *cakravāla* cosmology.[300] As to the scenes on the Buner stair-raiser reliefs, they would represent sacred dance dramas, 'part of a dionysiac or bacchic celebration' during which 'the emblematic chest, the holy container, is brought on stage as focus for the dramatic action'.[301] This interpretation has never been questioned, probably because its implications have not been fully understood.

The *yakṣa/guhyaka* Vajrapāṇi, the constant companion of the

Gandharan Buddha, is a figure equally difficult to set in place. From the one side, we must avoid projecting his later characteristics into an early set of iconographies, but, from the other, we cannot help noticing that the functions he seems to perform are not mentioned in the canonical texts. Who and why, in Gandhāra, endorsed Vajrapāṇi's presence?[302] The sensation remains that there is a link somewhere, lost in the seven or eight centuries separating early Mahāyāna from early Vajrayāna – a long period during which the religion of Dharma appears to be still a largely unknown phenomenon.[303]

NOTES

1. *Vāyu Purāṇa*: II.35.87 (vol. 2, p. 767).
2. *Padma Purāṇa*: I.65.85-89a (vol. 2, p. 822).
3. Ibid.: I.65.89b-92a (vol. 2, p. 822).
4. Ibid.: I.67.10-21 (vol. 2, p. 828). The inauspicious rivers, as glossed by the translator, are streams of blood.
5. Ibid.: I.74.30 (vol. 2, p. 845).
6. Ibid.: I.74.19-20 (vol. 2, p. 844).
7. Ibid.: I.67.34-36 (vol. 2, p. 829).
8. Ibid.: I.65.94-95 (vol. 2, p. 823).
9. Ibid.: I.65.60 (vol. 2, p. 820).
10. *Brahmāṇḍa Purāṇa*: 2.3.38b-42 (vol. 2, p. 541).
11. Ibid.: 2.3.35-38a (vol. 2, p. 541).
12. *Varāha Purāṇa*: 95.18-21 (vol. 1, p. 97).
13. Ibid.: 28.6-16 (vol., 1, pp. 97-98). Vetrāsura succeeds in vanquishing Indra.
14. *Śiva Purāṇa, Rudrasaṃhitā*: 5.57.17-18 (vol. 2, p. 1055).
15. Ibid.: 3.15.41 (vol. 2, p. 531); *Brahmāṇḍa Purāṇa, Lalitā Māhātmya*: 11.7-17 (vol. 4, pp. 1074-75).
16. *Vāyu Purāṇa*: II.35.68-104 (vol. 2, pp. 765-68). A similar list is given in the *Brahmāṇḍa Purāṇa* (II.3.72.72-88; vol. 3, pp. 908-9; cf. also the table provided by G.V. Tagare in the introduction, p. lv) and in the *Matsya Purāṇa* (47.36), usefully commented upon by V.S. Agrawala (1963: 145-46).
17. *Vāyu Purāṇa*: II.35.69 (vol. 2, p. 765).
18. Ibid.: II.35.71 (vol. 2, p. 765).
19. The text says that in the course of the eight wars the *deva*-s defeated the *asura*-s and the *rākṣasa*-s 'who were Andhakārakas' (ibid.: II.35.83-84; vol. 2, pp. 766-67).
20. 'Virocana, the son of Prahlāda, always attempted to kill Indra. In the Tārakāmaya war he was killed by Indra by means of his exploits' (ibid.: II.35.80; vol. 2, p. 766).

21. *Mahābhārata*, Karṇa Parvan: XXXIII-XXXXIV (vol. 7, pp. 74-82).
22. We have already recalled that V.S. Agrawala contended that the Tripura myth has a historical basis, and that one of the cities that took fire fell on Srisailam (above, Chapter III), marking the ruins of Āndhra Buddhism.
23. *Kūrma Purāṇa*: I.131b ff. (vol. 1, pp. 154 ff.).
24. Hazra (1940: 71).
25. *Padma Purāṇa*: I.46.31b-36 (vol. 2, p. 639).
26. Ibid.: I.46.75-84a (vol. 2, pp. 642-43).
27. Ibid.: I.46. 84b-93a (vol. 2, pp. 643-44).
28. *Devī Māhātmya*: 8.40-62 (pp. 66-67). Here the bloodthirsty *mātṛkā*-s fight against the *asura*-s (above, Chapter III), but no mention is made of Andhaka. All the *asura*-s are slain.
29. See this panel described by Soundara Rajan (1981: 172-73; pl. LXXXXVIIIA).
30. S.K. Panikkar (1988: 305).
31. The identification of the *mātṛkā* between Kāla and Durgā is uncertain, but see S.K. Panikkar (1988: 304-5).
32. A de-historicised interpretation of the Andhaka myth such as that provided by O'Flaherty (1973: 190-92), who emphasises Andhaka's lust (which he uses to weaken Śiva), turns paradoxically into a reductionist operation.
33. On the Buddhist caves of Ellora see Malandra (1997); cf. also Huntington (1985: 268-74).
34. In this, I follow Spink (1967: 22).
35. Ibid.
36. Cf. Malandra (1997: 91).
37. See the Samangarh plates in *IA* 11 (1882, J.F. Fleet): 108-15.
38. Huntington (1985: 341).
39. I am grateful to Claudine Bautze-Picron for reporting to me this important detail, which would otherwise have escaped me. See the carving on http://www.elloracaves.org/index.php [Cave 15]. Cave 27, too, was begun as a Buddhist excavation (cf. Spink 1967: 13, n. 8).
40. Malandra (1997: 61). To this author we owe a thorough study of the Buddhist caves; she has emphasised the aspects of continuity between the Buddhist and the second Brahmanical phase of Ellora, but her conclusions point to the opposite: 'Ellora's latest Buddhist caves should be seen as early Rāṣṭrakūṭa-period monuments, although there is neither evidence nor need to assume that they were directly sponsored by the Rāṣṭrakūṭa themselves' (ibid.: 61-62).
41. *Vāmana Purāṇa*: 43.74 (p. 381).
42. Rao, T.A. Gopinatha (1914-16, II: 234).
43. *Liṅga Purāṇa*: 106.15-28 (vol. 2, pp. 580-81).
44. For Elephanta, a Sivaite complex equally due to Rāṣṭrakūṭa patronage, the reader is referred to Collins (1991).

45. Rao, T.A. Gopinatha (1914-16, II: 229-30).
46. Ibid., II: 235. The *Kōyil Purāṇam* is the Tamil version of the *Cidambara Māhātmya*, and is attributed to Umāpati, an exponent of the Śaiva Siddhānta School (see D. Smith 1996: esp. 31 ff.).
47. On Śiva Naṭarāja the reader may be referred to Sivaramamurti's profusely illustrated book (Sivaramamurti 1974), but he will not find anything that has been discussed here. As for A.K. Coomaraswamy's 'The Dance of Śiva', published for the first time in New York in 1918, it is a plagiarism of the first part of the chapter 'The Dance of Śiva' of T.A. Gopinatha Rao's most learned book (vol. 2: 231 ff.).
48. *Rāmāyaṇa*, Uttara Kāṇḍa: 10 (pp. 1246-49).
49. What follows is based on Narasimhachar (1939); U.P. Shah (1983); Kulkarni (1990); Thapar (2000: 647-78).
50. Thapar (2000: 660 ff.).
51. Cf. Narasimhachar (1939: 579 [*Paumacariyam*: II, 112-14]).
52. de Jong (1983: 164).
53. *Kathāsaritsāgara*: III, 4, 55-59 (vol. 1, p. 151). Although it is possible that Laṅkā was identified with a region in the Vindhyas to serve political aims (we have seen how frequent was the manipulation of facts and even myths), it certainly was, *in primis* and at least from the early middle ages, the name of the island in the Indian Ocean: see the Mahānāman inscription (above Chapter III, n. 11). On the location of Rāvaṇa's Laṅkā and the bizarre opinions of many historians on the matter, see V.V. Mirashi (1975: 205-19).
54. *IA* 1 (1872, I.A.C. Boswell, ed. Jas. Burgess): 153.
55. Ibid. 154.
56. For Elephanta, see the iconographical analysis provided by Collins (1991: 41 ff.); at Ellora, Ravaṇa is depicted a number of times; cf. e.g. Soundara Rajan (1981: pls. XXV A, LI B, CIII B).
57. For an expanded version of the myth, see *Padma Purāṇa*: I.45 (vol. 2, pp. 623-36).
58. Cf. Kane (1930-62, II: 721-22; V, 914, 924, 993, 1025).
59. Buchanan (1807, I: 144). The explanation provided to Buchanan is worth reporting, because it reveals the deep contempt brāhmaṇas continued to nourish towards Buddhism long after its disappearance: in a version of the Tripura myth where Viṣṇu, not Śiva, conquers the triple town, the god 'took upon himself the form of a beautiful young man, and became *Budha Avatára*. Entering then into the cities, he danced naked before the women, and inspired them with loose desires; so that the fortress, being no longer defended by the shield of purity, soon fell a prey to the angels' who had asked the god to take action. The story is known from a number of sources in Tamiḻakam.
60. Independent images of Paraśurāma are not lacking in the south; see Champakalakshmi (1981: 115-16).
61. See Paraśurāma's exploits against the kṣatriyas in *Mahābhārata*, Vana Parvan,

section 116 (vol. 3, pp. 249-50); Śānti Parvan, section 49 (vol. 8, p. 99). For the twenty-one massacres, see Aśvamedha Parvan, section 29 (vol. 12, pp. 51-52).

62. R. Goldman (1972).
63. Ibid.: 164.
64. Ibid.
65. See for instance the kings of South Kosala (*Xiyuji*: X; vol. 2, p. 209) and that of Valabhī (ibid.: XI; vol. 2, p. 267).
66. R. Goldman: 159-60.
67. *Brahmāṇḍa Purāṇa* 2.3.25.38-47 (vol. 2, pp. 613-14). In this Purāṇa Śiva provides Rāma with a chariot, two quivers of arrows, a bow and a coat of mail, but not with an axe.
68. *Padma Purāṇa*: VI.241.42-44 (vol. 9, p. 3218).
69. Ibid.: VI.241.40-41 (vol. 9, p. 3218).
70. Narayanan & Veluthat (1986: 257).
71. *Mackenzie Manuscripts* 2: 490.
72. Ibid.: 493.
73. *Mackenzie Manuscripts* Suppl.: 73.
74. Hazra (1958-63, I: 308).
75. *Kalki Purāṇa*: III.iii.23-30 (pp. 95-101).
76. Ibid.: III.vi.44-49 (pp. 112-13).
77. Granoff (1984: 299).
78. *Kalki Purāṇa*: I.i.23-30 (p. 25). The description continues at length until the end of the first *aṃśa*.
79. Ibid.: I.ii.4. (p. 27).
80. Ibid.: II.vi.40 (p. 76).
81. For Wilkins's inscription, see Chapter I. The *Padma Purāṇa* (I.11.64; vol. 1, p. 100) says that 'The holy Gayā is in the Kīkaṭa country'.
82. *Kalki Purāṇa*: II.vi.41-45 (p. 76). The text has 'The Buddhists and Jains', but it is clear from the narrative that here Jains is a synonym of Buddhists.
83. Ibid.: II.vii.1-27 (pp. 77-79).
84. Ibid.: II.vii.28-36 (pp. 79-80).
85. Ibid.: II.vii.36-38 (p. 80).
86. Ibid.: III.i.3 (p. 85).
87. Here and below, I follow the chronology of the Pāla kings provided by S.C. Bhattacharya (2005-06: 65).
88. *EI* 17 (1923-24, Hirananda Shastri): 310-27, ll. 32-33 and p. 325.
89. *paramasaugata*; see Mukherji & Maity (1967: 167, 174: l. 28).
90. Ibid.: l. 37, pp. 168, 175.
91. Ibid.: 182.
92. *Kalki Purāṇa*: II.vii.43 (p. 80).
93. Ibid.: III.i.1-10 (pp. 85-86).
94. Ibid.: III.i.14-26 (pp. 86-87).
95. Ibid.: III.i.27-41 (pp. 87-88).

96. *EI* 21 (1931-32, N.G. Majumdar): verses 2-3. Somapura is identified with Paharpur in present-day Bangladesh. Whatever the relationship between the house of Karuṇaśrīmitra and the monastery (we will see below how difficult it is to give a standardised description of Vajrayāna monasteries), it must have been in the close vicinity of the latter.
97. Barua (1931-34, I: 231); Mukherji & Maity (1967: 110-14). The *snātaka*-s are erudite brāhmaṇas of Sivaite orientation.
98. There are neither images nor shrines earlier than the eighth-ninth century in Gayā (Asher 1988: 74-75).
99. R.D. Banerji (1915: 78, v. 9); D.C. Sircar in *EI* 36 (1964-65): 81-94, v. 9.
100. *Vāmana Purāṇa*: 50.15 (pp. 424-25). The text speaks of these sacrifices having been performed a hundred and even a thousand of times. The mention of a *naramedha*, a human sacrifice, deserves some serious thinking in the light of what we will discuss in the next section.
101. D.C. Sircar in *EI* 36 (1964-65): 83-84; Chatterjee (1965). The Vishnuite appropriation of the Mahābodhi Temple (Appendix 1) may go back to this period.
102. Not for so long a period as maintained in the past, however, following the recent identification of Mahendrapāla, formerly identified with the Gurjara-Pratihāra king, with the elder son of Devapāla. On the new identification, see G. Bhattacharya (2000: 407 ff, 431 ff.) and the comments provided by S.C. Bhattacharya (2005-06) who has re-edited the Jagjibanpur inscription. According to a provisional chronology, Mahendrapāla reigned between *c.* AD 840 and 856 (S.C. Bhattacharya) or between AD 847 and 862 (see the chronological question summarised by Bautze-Picron (forth: Chapter VII). Warfare affected Magadha even later than the time of Bhoja. An incident connected with Atīśa, which took place in AD 1041, can be recalled. Karṇa, son of the Kalacuri king Gāṅgeya and future monarch, waged war against Magadha, then ruled by Nayapāla. Karṇa's troops sacked some Buddhist establishments and killed four ordained monks and an *upāsaka*. The state of war and the attacks ceased after a treaty was signed thanks to the good offices of Atīśa (*Atīśa New Biography*: 97 ff.; Mirashi 1955: xci-xcii).
103. *IA* 31 (1902): 73-74. The 'Extracts from the Journal of Colonel Mackenzie's Pandit of His Route from Calcutta to Gaya in 1820' (pp. 65-75) were edited by Jas. Burgess.
104. On *śrāddha* rituals, see Kane (1930-62, IV: 334 ff.).
105. Barua's contention is that the *Gayā Māhātmya* distinguishes three stages of manifestation of the existence of Viṣṇu, the earliest (when rocky hills and peaks were venerated) and the second (the period of *liṅga*-s and *Viṣṇupada*-s) preceding the stage testified by the iconographic production (Barua 1931-34, I: 57 ff.) – the only one we have evidence of. Leaving aside all other considerations, the worship of hierophanies and symbols are not, *per se*, a sign of an early chronology (in India they have survived

alongside a major iconic production). One of the passages of the Vana Parvan quoted by Barua mentions the God with the trident and the practice of besmearing oneself with ashes (ibid.: 70-74; cf. verses 91-92), a Pāśupata practice. Several points of Barua's work were criticised by Kane (1930-62, IV: 649 ff.).

106. Debjani Paul's thesis is that Gayā as a *pitṛtīrtha* was not a creation of the Bhāgavatas, but the result of an early, conscious speculation on Ṛgvedic Viṣṇu. The large, single human footprint in the Viṣṇupada Temple to the west of the river Phalgu would reflect the original Trivikrama myth, untouched by Purāṇic updating. It is a fascinating idea, and one I am not averse to. The point, however, is not whether Gayā is an early *tīrtha*, but if it always was a privileged place for both Vishnuite worship and *śrāddha*-s or else became the centre of the rituals of the dead only later in history and, in this case, why this happened. Some of Paul's statements are not consistent: the *pada*-s on the Padaṇa Hill to the north of Mumbai would be Rāma's footprints, and if Rāma's footprints were venerated as early as the first century AD, 'that of Viṣṇu must have been in worship from a much earlier time' (Paul 1985: 140). The gap in the evidence between early and medieval Gayā, the lack of any Gupta remains and the fact that the town was a 'complete waste' at the time of Faxian's visit (*Faxian* b: 53) cannot be ascribed 'to both human and natural devastations' as for instance fatal earthquakes (Paul 1985: 133). The argument (derived from Kane 1930-62, IV: 650; cf. also Jacques in his introduction to *Gayā Māhātmya*: XXV) is aporetic, and earthquakes, contrary to what these authors think, are an excellent source for the archaeologist, since destruction implies abandonment and reuse.

107. The rituals take place where the navel of the dead Gayāsura is supposed to be located. See above, Chapters I and IV.

108. The question of the control of funeral rites in relation to the fortunes of Buddhism would deserve a careful study, and not only in relation to India. Here Buddhism lost its battle, as also happened in China, whereas in countries with weaker opponents, the Buddhists succeeded in controlling the world of the dead. In Japan, for instance, they still keep their positions.

109. For Buchanan and R. Mitra, see Chapter I.

110. van Kooj (1993: 379).

111. Panigrahi (1981: 39). We know from the epigraphic sources that in AD 619 Śaśāṅka was the overlord of Koṅgoda, which he probably held until his death. It was only in AD 643 that Harṣavardhana undertook his expedition to the region.

112. Hazra (1951: 70). The work is assignable to the tenth-eleventh century according to Hazra (ibid.: 75), but Panigrahi (1961: 22) considers it not earlier than the fourteenth century.

113. Id. (1981: 114 ff.); Hazra (1951: 73-74).

114. Panigrahi (1961: 31, 219).

115. Ibid.: 215; cf. also Hazra (1951: 73).
116. Panigrahi (1961: 215). Jagamara is just to the east of Khandagiri.
117. Hazra (1951: 73).
118. For the Vaitāl Deuḷ, see above, Chapter IV; see the images of Mahiṣamardinī in the Uttareśvara and Mohinī temples on the bank of the Bindusarovara (Donaldson 2002, III: figs. 81-83).
119. '[...] *Om phaṭ om*. Pierce open. *Om*. Cut with the trident. *Om* kill with the mace. *Om* strike with the stick. *Om*. Cut with the disc. *Om*. Break with the spear. Stake with the teeth'; etc. (*Agni Purāṇa* 135.1; quoted passage on vol. 2, p. 399).
120. '[...] One who is clad in the hide of an elephant! One who is besmeared with flesh! One whose terrific tongue is licking!'; etc. (ibid.: 135; p. 398).
121. See for instance the friezes with the *Rāmāyaṇa* and *Mahābhārata* scenes stretched across the *maṇḍapa*-s of the Pāpanātha Temple at Pattadakal and in other eighth-century Cāḷukya temples. Cf. for instance the iconographic documentation accompanying Wechsler (1994).
122. It is usually maintained that a change in the iconography of Cāmuṇḍā takes place when the corpse replaces the owl as her *vāhana*. The owl, however, is a bird of prey, and in fact is often represented with other animals of prey (dogs, jackals, wild pigs, etc.) devouring the corpse (see for instance Donaldson 2002, III: figs. 257, 261, etc.). The early Cāmuṇḍā stele are allusive, not as explicit as later ones, but their meaning is the same. In the image of Cāmuṇḍā in the *garbhagṛha* of the Vaitāl Deuḷ, it is a dog which starts feeding on the corpse, while the owl is perched nearby (ibid.: fig. 249).
123. de Mallmann (1963: 153).
124. Donaldson (1991: 123).
125. Id. (2002, III: fig. 264).
126. See, for instance, the eighth-ninth-century stele published by Donaldson (2002, III: figs. 257, 258, 260). One of them is in the Kālikā Temple in Bhubaneswar, another in the temple of Bhagavatī at Banpur (Khorda district).
127. Ibid.: III: fig. 274.
128. Several examples can be found in Donaldson, one being that of the Mahiṣāsura killed by Durgā in a stele from Kanheivindha in Balasore district (ibid.: III: fig. 115; also, Pani 1988: pl. 9).
129. *Kādambarī*: 55 (p. 38).
130. See the Cāmuṇḍā stele from the Kapoteśvara temple at Nathuavara (Cuttack district) and from the Kālī Temple at Someśvara at Ranipur-Jharial, as well as the Bhairava stele from the Kapilas Hill, Dhenkanal district (Donaldson 2002, III: figs. 266, 267, 293).
131. *dPag bsam ljon bzang*: I. 94 (Index: liv-lv).
132. Ibid.: I.94 (Index: cxl).
133. Ibid.: I.87 (Index: lxxxv).

134. Ibid.: I.115 (Index: liii).
135. Ibid.: I.65, 84 (Index: lxx, cxxxv).
136. Ibid.: I.123 (Index: lvii, cxxviii).
137. Ibid.: I.123 (Index: lxx).
138. Donaldson (2002, III: figs. 107-111).
139. de Mallmann (1963: 154-55).
140. *Agni Purāṇa*: 52 (vol. 1, pp. 138-39), 146.3-21 (vol. 2, pp. 420-23). According to de Mallmann (1963: 181), the passage of *Agni Purāṇa* 52 where the goddesses are led by Vīrabhadra and encircle Bhairava reveals a cosmological and astral influence, whereas the later passage of *Agni Purāṇa* 146 witnesses that a Tantric conception had already taken place.
141. Dehejia (1986: 85-86). The evidence is particularly convincing in relation to the eighty-one *yoginī*-s at Bheraghat, arguably built by the Kalacuri king Yuvarāja I (AD 915-45) near Tripuri, the capital town of the dynasty (ibid. 138-39).
142. van Kooj (1999: 267).
143. There are variants, as the eighty-one *yoginī*-s temple at Bheraghat (this number is envisaged in the *Matottara Tantra*; see Dehejia (1986: 51) and the forty-two *yoginī*-s temple at Dudahi (ibid.: 51-52, 141-42).
144. Dehejia (1986: 95 ff.). The Hirapur temple is dated on stylistic ground to around AD 900.
145. Donaldson (2002, III: figs. 461, 462, 475).
146. Ibid.: figs. 454-456, 477.
147. Cf. van Kooj (1999: 266 ff.).
148. Donaldson (2002, III: fig. 442).
149. I follow the description given by Donaldson (2002, I: 454). The relief is kept in the Norton Simon Museum, Pasadena (California, USA).
150. The reader probably remember that William Taylor wondered about the 'enigmatic meaning' of the skull of the *asura* used for the head of Śiva's *vīṇā* (Chapter I).
151. New Delhi, National Museum, inv. no. 63.939.
152. Here we do not have a paradigmatic stand as at Peragari, because our attention does not focus on the corpse, and because the birds of prey start devouring carcasses from the usual parts (eyes, etc.).
153. van Kooij (1972: 8-9).
154. Ibid.: 9.
155. Ibid.: 29.
156. (Sircar 1971: 300, on the authority of the *Rājataraṅgiṇī*); *dāmara*-s (not *ḍāmara*-s) are mentioned as a people in the *Bṛhatsaṃhitā*: 14.30 (cf. id. 1967: 98, n. 20).
157. See B.N. Shastri's in *Kālikā Purāṇa*: vol. 1, pp. 66-67, at the end of a detailed discussion.
158. Cf. Chisato Maeda's précis of the sacrifice (Maeda 2007: 254, with corrections to B.N. Shastri and van Kooij's translations).

159. Ibid.: 255-56.
160. *Kālikā Purāṇa*: I.55.17a (vol. 2, p. 663).
161. B.N. Shastri in *Kālikā Purāṇa*: I, pp. 61-62.
162. See this image in Donaldson (2002, III: fig. 442).
163. The reader is referred to Dehejia (1986) for a description of the principal temples. Dehejia's study resorts to explanations at the symbolic level and yields sometimes to misleading generalisations ('The circle is of great importance in the Buddhist world', p. 40; etc.), but remains an invaluable reference work. See also Das (1981). For Hirapur and Ranipur Jharial, see Donaldson (2002, II: 661 ff., 665 ff.; III: figs. 452-523, 524-549).
164. Dehejia (1986: 79).
165. See the images of Cāmuṇḍā clustering in the Dinajpur region and in the adjoining districts of Rajshahi, Naogaon and Bogra (Melzer 2008-9: 142). Images of the goddess cluster also in present-day Begusarai district of Bihar, north of the Ganges (Sahai 1985-86).
166. On the latter, see Shizuka (2007: xii, 403-4).
167. Davidson (2002: 206).
168. Ibid.: 226 (see the *loci* cited by the author in n. 205).
169. The reader is referred to Dehejia (1986: 31 ff.) and, for a general evaluation of the *Kaula Tantra*-s, to Dyczkowski (1988: 59 ff.).
170. For the temple of Khajuraho, see Deva (1990, I: 25-29; map and elevations in vol. 2) and D. Desai (1996: 81 ff.). For the identification of the remains at Mau Suhania, cf. ibid.: 85-87.
171. Dehejia (1986: 35).
172. Ibid.: 40. For Khajuraho, cf. D. Desai (1996: 86-90).
173. Dehejia (1886: 59).
174. According to the requirements of the *Matottara Tantra*; cf. ibid.: 59.
175. Different layers of meaning in the sets of *yoginī*-s sculptures are observable. See for instance the naked, but also the dressed male figures subjugated by the *yoginī*-s in the later sculptural production: they are by no means dead and seem rather to ask to be pardoned (see the two stele from Hinglajgarh and the princely figures from Shahdol in ibid. 154, 155 and 163, 167, respectively).
176. Donaldson (2002, II: 670).
177. Dehejia (1986: ix), referring to the deep sense of fear and awe inspired by these places, observes that secrecy is kept to such an extent that 'the very existence of the Yoginī temple at Hirapur became public knowledge only as recently as the year 1953'.
178. Later enclosures, or later use of early ones may have served a wider range of operations. From the epigraphic evidence of twelfth-century south India, we learn that the *yoginī*-s are gratified 'with draughts of blood out of the skull of Kalapāla', a local king who died in battle at the time of the early conquests (AD 1115) of the Hoyṣala king Viṣṇuvardhana. Cf. *EC* 5 (Hassan district): no. 58, dated AD 1117, from Belur district (pp. 56-58 of the English trans., cf. p. 57).

179. Hirapur is located near Dhauli, which continued to be an important Buddhist site even in later times (see the next chapter). At Bheraghat a '[f]igure of Dharmma, a 4-armed female [...] with a small figure of Buddha in the head-dress' was mentioned by Cunningham among the sculptures he saw in the temple built at a later date within the enclosure (*ASIR* 9: 62); for Khajuraho, see the section below. Buddhist icons have surfaced from several sites around Vidiśā, either transformed into Sivaite or Jain places of worship in the eighth century; see for instance the Buddhist stele from Badoh-Pathari made known by Casile (2009: 197 and pl. 78, 1).
180. The lack of interest for the late phases of archaeological sites, often recalled in these pages, has affected, in particular, the sanctuaries whose early monuments have magnetised the attention of researchers. The sole pre-occupation of Alfred Foucher in his study of Sanchi's late production was that 'the latest of the images at the local museum offer[ed] us nothing really tāntric' (Marshall & Foucher 194, I: 255). Even less interested was Foucher about the 'statuettes', some of which depicting Śiva, Durgā and Gaṇeśa, because their fragments were mostly 'useless from an iconographical point of view'. See Marshall's description of the late monuments of the site in ibid, I: 72 ff.
181. *ASIR* 9 (A. Cunningham): 3.
182. Hawkes (2006, I: 77). There probably were two Buddhist temples at Bharhut, one near to the stūpa, and the other on the summit of the hill (ibid. 76, 84).
183. *ASIR* 2 (A. Cunningham): 414.
184. *Xiyuji* a: XI (vol. 2: 271 [*Chi-ki-to*]).
185. *ASIR* 2 (A. Cunningham): 412-13.
186. See the image in D. Desai (1996: 22, fig. 20). The Buddha head appears as having been wantonly defaced (Agarwal 1964: 211-12).
187. Ibid.: 91; the temple dates to the second half of the ninth century according to Deva (1990, I: 26).
188. Ibid.: 147-48. D. Desai (1996: 43; 2000: 53) suggests that it was built by King Vidyādhara after repelling the attacks of Maḥmūd of Ghazni.
189. The temple was erected by King Dhaṅga's father Yaśovarman (*EI* 1, 1892, F. Kielhorn: 122-35, v. 3); see thc inscription re-edited by Sircar (1983: 258-67).
190. *EI* 1 (1892, F. Kielhorn): 122-35, v. 1. Kāpila was a demon eventually assimilated by Viṣṇu in his tetracephalic aspect of Vaikuṇṭha (de Mallmann 1963: 21).
191. *EI* 1 (1892, F. Kielhorn): 122-35: v. 2. D. Desai (1996: 104) is aware of the emphasis on Vaikuṇṭha as Daityāri, but has no further elaborated on this point.
192. D. Desai (1984; 1996); her short guidebook to Khajuraho is also useful (id.: 2000). To explain the religious milieu of Khajuraho, Desai (esp. 1996) has emphasised the role played by the twilight language (*sandhyābhāṣa*), similar

to that used by Kṛṣṇa Miśra in his *Prabodha Candrodaya*, and by sculptural puns (*śleṣa*).

193. D. Desai (1996: 53 ff, 57 ff., 151-52).
194. I follow Sita K. Nambiar, to whose introduction to the play I refer the reader (cf. pp. 2-3).
195. See Hultzsch in *EI* 1 (1892): 218.
196. S.K. Mitra (1977: 99, 179).
197. *Prabodha Candrodaya*: V.9 (p. 125).
198. Ibid.: V.10-11 (p. 127). Regarding the less familiar names, Pārasīka is Persia, the land of the Ābhīras corresponds to the south-eastern part of Gujarat, and Āvarta corresponds to Saurashtra. As for the Hūṇas, Punjab is probably meant (cf. Sircar 1971: 108). Buddha Prakash has discussed the matter at length, emphasising the fact that after Harṣavardhana the Hūṇas set up a number of principalities that played a notable part in history (Prakash 1965: 170); however, he identified them with the former rulers of Kābul and Zābul, which modern research has shown were of Turkish origin.
199. *Prabodha Candrodaya*: III:15 (p. 79).
200. Ibid.: V.3 (p. 119).
201. D. Desai (1996: 51-52).
202. Deva (1990: 57-58).
203. D. Desai (1996: 99).
204. Deva (1990: 192-93, 210). D. Desai (1996: 34) dates it to *c.* AD 1075.
205. Id. (2000: 73) says that 'It is still unclear' why the Pārśvanātha Temple 'contains images of Krishna, Rama, Balarama, Vishnu, and Shiva on its exterior wall', and K.K. Shah (1988: 170) has noted the absence of episodes associated with the Tīrthaṃkaras and the 'repetition' of Brahmanical iconography. Images of Sarasvatī and Lakṣmī are found inside the temple, in the *antarāla* (Deva 1990: 63; the reader will find a detailed description of the temple iconography in ibid. 65 ff.). Images of Brahmanical gods are also found in the temple of Ādinātha (ibid. 214 ff.).
206. Ibid.: 250-51. In the beginning, Cunningham (*ASIR* 2: 414) thought that this Jain temple was a Buddhist building.
207. See above, Chapter IV and below, Chapter VI.
208. Daniélou (1973: 73-74).
209. Ascetics performing various sexual acts are mockingly represented at Khajuraho and elsewhere (D. Desai 1985: 77-79), but we do not know which ascetics were meant in the various contexts.
210. *Prabodha Candrodaya*: V.11 (p. 129).
211. Ibid.: II.1 (p. 27).
212. Ibid.: II.12 (p. 37).
213. Ibid.: III.9 (pp. 70-71).
214. Ibid.: III.18-19 (pp. 82-83). On the term *Soma Siddhānta* applied to the doctrine of the Kāpālikas, see Lorenzen (1972: 82-83).
215. A tradition regarding the origin of the Candellas is preserved in the *Mahobā*

Khaṇḍ, for which see S.K. Mitra (1977: 14 ff). Mahobā as an archaeological site was studied by Cunningham (*ASIR* 2: 439-59; *ASIR* 21: 70-74), but the site still awaits proper investigation.

216. K.N. Dikshit (1921:1). The inscription on the pedestal of Siṃhanāda Avalokiteśvara refers to Chītnaka, son of the painter Sātana, as the donor, and the Tārā inscription mentions another relative of Sātana's. The image of Padmapāṇi bears no inscription (ibid.: 2-3). Cf. also S.K. Mitra (1977: 203-04).
217. K.K. Shah (1988: 66; fig. 13). See the image of the sixty-four-armed goddess, of which only the upper part is preserved, also in id. (1977). It would deserve a careful study.
218. Id. (1988: 166, 168).
219. In Sind, the early region of India conquered by the Muslims, some Buddhist communities survived until the tenth century (van Lohuizen-de Leuw 1975). Gandhāra, as we have seen in Chapter III, had turned into an orthodox kingdom even before the Ṣāhī rule, and at the time of Kṛṣṇa Miśra was overrun by the Muslims, opposed by the Hindū Ṣāhīs. The ambiguous relationship between the Buddhists and the Muslims, which might account for Kṛṣṇa Miśra's list of countries where the Buddhists fled, will be dealt with in the next chapter.
220. *EI* 19 (1927-28, R.D. Banerji): 295-99.
221. See what is known on this ruler in S.K. Mitra (1977: 33).
222. *EI* 1 (1892, F. Kielhorn): 122-35: v. 17.
223. K.K. Shah (1988: 131). With the Candellas, Vedic scholars were welcomed in Jejākabhukti with unprecedented favour.
224. New Christian names replaced the old ones in large parts of Europe, but a large number of place names (from Rome to Paris to London) remained unchanged.
225. Benutosh Bhattacharya put forward a number of reasons suggesting a date to the third, or maximum the fourth century, pointing to Asaṅga as the author of the text (B. Bhattacharya 1931: xxxiv ff.). The latter attribution was questioned by Alex Wayman, who, however, was also in favour of a fourth-century date (Wayman 1977: 99). The German translator of the work, Peter Gäng, suggested a date from the third to the seventh century (cf. *Guhyasamāja Tantra*: 101). Tucci, however, maintained that only a date between the end of the seventh and the eighth century was possible (see below n. 239).
226. Davidson (2002: 198, 217).
227. *Guhyasamāja Tantra*: I (p. 42).
228. Ibid.: V (pp. 133-34).
229. Cf. Gnoli in *Nāropā*: 30.
230. *Guhyasamāja Tantra*: V (p. 134).
231. I make my own, adapting his words to this context, a statement by Tucci (1958: 282).
232. Davidson (2002: esp. the last three chapters).

233. *Mañjuśrīmūlakalpa*: [53], vv. 883-84 (cf. § 49 on p. 72).
234. R.C. Majumdar (1943: 102-3).
235. Ibid.: 125, n. 2.
236. The north-western wing of this block, formed by the Buddhist kingdoms of western Central Asia, soon collapsed after the retreat of the Tang from Xinjiang in the second half of the eighth century. See below.
237. See above. For the chronology, I follow S.C. Bhattacharya (2005-6: 65), but other dates have been proposed: Dharmapāla, *c.* AD 775-812; Devapāla, *c.* AD 815-55 (cf. Bautze-Picron forth: Chapter 7).
238. Maitreya (1987: 81).
239. Gnoli in *Nāropā*: 26, 50. In particular, the *Guhyasamāja Tantra* would have been composed there (Tucci 1949: 212 ff.); according to Tucci, '[t]here is only one point on which the traditions agree: namely that the *Guhyasamāja* was revealed to king Indrabhūti in Uḍḍiyāna; the meaning of this, for us, is that the *Guhyasamāja* was elaborated in the Swat Valley, in or about the epoch of this personage, which seems to be, more or less, the end of the VIIth and the beginning of the VIIIth century AD' (p. 213).
240. Tucci (1958: 284, 323) already wondered why no artistic manifestations reflected the presence of Vajrayāna Buddhism in Swat.
241. Davidson (1991: 200).
242. On Vajrapāṇi in the context of Vajrayāna Buddhism, see Lamotte (1966: 149 ff.).
243. Cf. the passage translated into English by Davidson (ibid. 200-02). For a de-contextualised description of the 'myth' of the subjugation of Maheśvara, see Iyanaga (1985).
244. Ibid.: 203.
245. Kuwayama (2002: 181-82); Verardi & Paparatti (2005: 432). The *tapa* is a natural stronghold near the desolate pass of Dahana-ye Sher barring the southern route towards Wardak and Kābul-Kapiśi and towards Logar, and has a commanding position. It was probably selected by 'Ubayd Allāh, as a military outpost, as often happened later and up to the present (Verardi 2010: 231-32).
246. Verardi & Paparatti (2005: 434 ff.). As in Semireche and Kashmir, they probably counted on the presence of political and religious staff of Han origin or Han obedience, something that is mirrored by the surprising physiognomic change affecting the sculptural production, which displays distinct Chinese features (ibid. 432-33, 438-40). In Kashmir, the prime minister of Lalitāditya Muktāpīḍa, Caṅkuṇa, was a Chinese officer sent by Emperor Xuangzong as an adviser to King Candrāpīḍa (AD 715-25). He was a Sino-Tokharian, and a fervent Buddhist (*Rājataraṅgiṇī*: IV. 211 ff.). Lalitāditya's extraordinary career might not have been possible without Chinese political and military advice. When in the 740s the Tibetans put Kashmir with its back against the wall, he pleaded for Chinese assistance. Conversely, the stability and power of Kashmir were crucial for the Chinese

struggle against the Arabs and the Tibetans. Lalitāditya, a supporter of Brahmanism, was one of those Indian rulers heavily exposed to diverging political-religious pressure.

247. The finds from this chapel are published in Taddei & Verardi (1978: 47 ff.).
248. Kuwayama (2002: 257).
249. *Muslim Historians*: 172; cf. Rehman (1979: 12-13). There is a fort in the present-day Sakawand village, near Baraki Barak (on the route connecting Logar to Wardak), and the site is perhaps to be identified with the Sakawand of the sources. This part of Logar (Baraki Barak, Pul-i Alam, Charkh) is extremely lush, and suitable for an agrarian *kṣetra*.
250. The temple was destroyed by the Muslims towards the end of the ninth century (ibid), when the region was under the rule of the Hindū Ṣāhīs. In Logar, no trace of the 'Chinese phase' is observable in the huge site of Kafir Kot (at a short distance from Ghazni as the crow flies), consisting of a town and a series of monasteries (Verardi 2007*a*: 239 ff). The site seems to have been abandoned by the late seventh century, probably in connection to the change of religious policy of the Turki Ṣāhīs in the region.
251. Handa (1994: 209-11; pl. 50).
252. Davidson (2002: 170, 203).
253. Above, Chapter III. This may indicate that the suppression of the Buddhists was particularly difficult in this region. We lack an analysis of the modalities according to which the *pīṭha*-s were established and of the reasons why they are hierachised in major and minor *pīṭha*-s.
254. Faccenna (1980-81, I: 126-27, 173).
255. The last phase of a given site is the first to be brought to light (the excavator may leave some parts of the upper deposit unexcavated for later controls). The archaeologists who start working *in terra incognita* may find themselves faced with evidence difficult to evaluate before the levels that interest them more are reached. An excavation is always problem-oriented, whether explicitly or not, and the excavations in Swat had as their principal aim that of unearthing early Gandharan buildings and sculptures. No relevant information has come from the levels of the small habitation area near the sanctuary stratigraphically related to the fifth reconstruction of the stūpa (ibid., IV: esp. 736-37).
256. Tucci (1958: 284). In Swat, where after AD 700 the human environment was not favourable as in Tibet, we should only think of chapels and temples built of perishable material or of abandoned monasteries.
257. Banerji (1915: 50-51).
258. Prakash (1965: 265-66), drawing on Rāhula Sānkṛtyāyana's introduction to the *Dohākośa* (Patna 1957, in Hindi). See Kurtis R. Schaffer's recent assessment of Saraha's life based on the Tibetan literary tradition in *Dohākośa*: 49 ff.
259. Shizuka (2007: 402-5, English summary of chapters 6-8; 2008: 192-93).

The author discusses, in particular, the evidence from the eighth section of the *Saṃvarodaya Tantra*, and further argues that *maṭha*-s or shrines for Tantric gatherings existed in monastic compounds to allow Vajrayāna *bhikṣu*-s to meet and not be hindered by their religious opponents in the monastery (id. 2007: 405, English summary of chapter 9).

260. Davidson (2002: 276).
261. *IAR* (1954-55: 24, 26; 1955-56: 27); Ghosh (1989, II: 411); M.G. Dikshit's reconstruction of the events in *IAR* and other publications has been criticised by S.L. Katare (1959) in the name of the 'complete harmony that prevailed between the various religions' (p. 7). The absence of a final excavation report prevents me from further investigating the matter.
262. Meister, Dhaky & Deva (1988: 235-36); A.M. Shastri (1985).
263. *EI* 11 (1911-12): 184-201, v. 1 (the last words are integrations of Rai Bahadur Hira Lal, editor and translator of the text).
264. Ibid.: v.3.
265. Ibid.: vv.18-19.
266. Gnoli in his introduction to *Nāropā* maintains that Vishnuite influence on the *siddha*s is greater than that of the Sivaites (p. 50).
267. Cf. Singh Deo (1987: 153-54).
268. *EI* 23 (1935-36, V.V. Mirashi): 113-22 (Mallar plate). Mallar is located in the Bilaspur district.
269. M.G. Dikshit (1955-57); Śarmā & Śarmā (1994).
270. Donaldson (2002: map 4 on p. 314).
271. We know of repairs carried out at Amaravati as late as AD 1344 (Knox 1992: 16). In the tenth century, a Śiva temple was built a few hundred meters from the stūpa (ibid.: 15-16), and when the latter fell into disuse, small shrines were constructed with re-used materials. The documentation is scanty because of the loss of Walter Elliot's papers (ibid.: 227-29), and it is not clear which kind of shrines they were. They may have been connected to the activities of the *siddha*-s.
272. Deshpande (1986). This author observes how the intellectual and iconographic traditions of eastern India became increasingly manifest in western Deccan, where Vajrayāna activity is manifest, besides the well-known site of Kanheri, at Kondivte and Mahad (ibid.: 16). At Panhale, an image of Mahācaṇḍa-roṣaṇa (a form of Acala), closely resembling an analogous image from Ratnagiri, is notable (ibid.: 46-50). Deshpande's analysis fits the scenario we have tried to outline, where the Vajrayāna is strictly dependent on the political fortunes of the Pālas.
273. Here I follow the translation of the *Guhyasamāja Tantra* XIII.67-68 provided by Davidson (2002: 193-94); cf. *Guhyasamāja Tantra*, p. 196.
274. Davidson (2002: 197). Davidson sees clearly that the attacks on the Buddhist monasteries, especially by the Sivaites, were real, and in his *Indian Esoteric Buddhism* upholds this opinion in a number of occasions (cf. for instance pp. 191-94).

275. *dPag bsam ljon bzang*: I.111 (Index: lxxii).
276. *EI* 1 (1892, G. Bühler): 97-118, line 30. Baijnath is located in Himachal Pradesh.
277. *Luoyang qielan ji*, in *Taishō* 2092.51.999-1022. For this work, see above, Chapter III.
278. *Xu Gaoseng Zhuan*, in *Taishō* 2060.50.425a-707a.
279. For both a translation of the *Damolun* and Bernard Faure's précis on Bodhidharma, the reader is referred to *Damolun* (1986).
280. McFarlane (1995: 195-96).
281. Archery was a popular game played by young Śākyas, as shown by the story of Siddhārtha's arrow causing a spring to rush forth (cf. e.g. *Lalitavistara*: XII, pp. 147-49; *Life of the Buddha*: 19).
282. See Demiéville (1973: 261 ff.); McFarlane (1995: 195-96).
283. *Upāyakauśalya Sūtra*: 132-135 (pp. 73-74).
284. McFarlane (1995: 194), quoting from Unrai Wogihara's edition of the text (Tōkyō 1930-36, 165-7).
285. Pye (1978: 4).
286. It is now admitted that stories like that reported above and those discussed in Chapter III have provided the basis for Mahāyāna Buddhist participation in violence (P. Williams 2009: 152), although Williams gives examples exclusively taken from contemporary history.
287. Matsunaga (2008: 152-53).
288. Shakabpa (2010, I: 112-13; 163-64).
289. Ruegg (1981: 223). The episode, played down by Kapstein (2000: 11-12), is considered a fabrication by Yamaguchi (1996); even for Waddell (1934: 34), 'the incident forms a part of the modern Lāmaist masquerade'.
290. Linrothe (1999: esp. 33-37).
291. The reader is referred to Linrothe's study (note above) for the ample documentation provided, even though the author restricts his analysis to the realm of symbols.
292. Demiéville (1973: 271).
293. Ibid.
294. Davidson (2002: 194).
295. *Hevajra Tantra*: II.ix.3-6 (vol. 1, pp. 116-17).
296. Donaldson (2002: 129).
297. *Harṣacarita*: VIII.261 (p. 232).
298. See it in Kurita (1988-90, II: 509). The relief is 81 cm long, but is far too low (12 cm) in proportion to have served as the base of an image. This is also excluded by the lower mouldings, which also rules out the possibility that it was a stair-riser. The relief decorated perhaps the lower part of a square-based stūpa.
299. We read in the *Cūḷavagga* that once the *bhikkhu*-s went to a festival in Rājagṛha where there was music with dancing and singing, incurring the criticism of the people. The Lord said, 'Monks, you should not go to see

dancing or singing or music. Whosoever should go, there is an offence of wrong-doing' (*Cūḷavagga*: V.2.6 (p. 145).

300. Carter (1992: 57-58).
301. B. Goldman (1978: 194, 196).
302. Lamotte (1966: esp. 120 ff.). The early Gandharan representations showing Vajrapāṇi as protector of the Buddha go back to the first century AD.
303. There are more questions left open in Gandhāra, whose social and religious panorama is more varied than we usually believe. Giuseppe Tucci published an early ritual object that he referred to a Sivaite milieu. It is a three-sided stand with a cavity depicting a young man raising his hands, in the act of masturbating and, in the last scene, in a state of rest. Tucci interpreted it as either pertaining to a ritual performed by the follower of the *akulavīra* method or as an *arghyapātra* that was first filled with alcoholic substances and next with *kuṇḍagolaka*, i.e. the male and female fluids, which were consumed by the initiate. We are, however, in the first or second century AD (Tucci 1968). We know that Sivaism had an early grip on society from Kuṣāṇa coinage (above, Chapter II) and that it was fully structured at the time of Xuanzang's journey. One of Xuanzang's *deva* temples in Kapiśi is certainly Tapa Skandar (Kuwayama 2002: 165).

CHAPTER VI

The Days of Reckoning

THE HOUSEHOLDER MONKS

When discussing Indian Buddhism we never associate it, despite all its segmentations, with a married clergy. Even when discussing the Vajrayāna, the emphasis is on *siddha*-s and the doctrinal transformation that took place in the large monasteries of north-eastern India, where the monks, as is apparent from the monasteries provided with rows of individual cells, continued to live in a community.[1] This is, I think, a serious mistake in judgement. In mediaeval India there were numerous Buddhist communities under the guidance of a married clergy, and Newār Buddhism stands as a fossil guide, as it were, for us to understand a crucial development of the religion. The habit of considering Nepal as a separate entity from the rest of north-eastern India (something that can be done, to a degree, only from the thirteenth-fourteenth century onwards) misrepresents the real religio-historical situation. Moreover, while scholars have been able to offer a depiction of contemporary Newār Buddhism,[2] the attempt at interpreting it diachronically and at investigating its origin is still at an initial stage.

As is known, Newār Buddhism structures itself around two classes of householder monks, the Vajrācāryas and the Śākyas, both of which undergo a monastic initiation, through which they become members of the monasteries run by their fathers. The Vajrācāryas also undergo the rite of consecration as Tantric masters, which confers on them a higher status. Only the Vajrācāryas, who in Newār society form a caste parallel to that of the brāhmaṇas, are entitled to act as temple priests and guardians of the public deities. The intricate stratification of Newār Buddhism (here simplified to the extreme), is the litmus paper of the complex, dramatic history of medieval Buddhism *tout court*. In the Śākya householder monks (the *Śākyabhikṣu*-s) we recognise the householder bodhisattvas who were mentioned in Chapter III, with ranks reinforced by the monks who were obliged to disrobe in the eighth century as a consequence of the attempt at eradicating Buddhism from the Valley, and in the Vajrācāryas (this would explain their higher status) the product of the Vajrayāna of the great monasteries. The interaction of two priesthoods sharing the same characteristic of married life and consequent hereditary functions and ownership of the *vihāra*-s (the *bāhā*-s and *bahī*-s) but having a different origin, and their existence side by side with the Brahmanical institutions within a restricted territory explain the conundrum of Newār Buddhism and, to a large extent, the intricacy of its rituals. This form of Buddhism is not a later deterioration of the Buddhism of the great eastern monasteries, and there are reasons to believe that Nepalese Buddhism has been supported by householder monks since its inception,[3] thus being a tradition having its origin in the Mahāyāna and in the duress of Indian history.

There is an interesting passage in the *Bhāṣā Vaṃśāvalī* on the compromise eventually arrived at in the Valley (here, as usual, Śaṅkara is held responsible for these developments):

> Afterwards, Śaṅkarācārya went to Vajra Yoginī in order to extirpate in the like manner her worship and followers. A debate ensued, but in the end it was settled by mutual agreement of both the religionists that henceforth both mārgas or sects should have equal access to the temple and can offer goat sacrifices. From that day the Śaiva, the Vaiṣṇava and the Tāntrica sects became powerful, and their principles and rites came to have much influence over the practices of even the Buddhists, so that the Bandyas or orthodox Buddhamārgīs were appointed to discharge their duties in the temple of the Devīs, where without the killing of the goats the deity is not pleased, though this is quite contrary to the tenets of the Bandyas.[4]

Despite these adjustments, if we trust the few scholars who between the end of the nineteenth and the beginning of the twentieth century visited Nepal with cognizance of the case, the Buddhist priests were subject to the ire of the brāhmaṇas, and were considered *anācaraṇīya*.[5] Sylvain Lévi wrote that at the time of his sojourn Buddhism was dying in the Valley.[6] Only the opening of the country in the early 1950s reversed the trend, even though Newār Buddhism was to face the challenge of other forms of the religion – that brought by the Tibetan refugees from the 1960s onwards and the one that came along with the revival of Theravāda Buddhism.

As for the rest of India, we mentioned in Chapter III the testimonies of both the *Rājataraṅgiṇī* and Xuanzang regarding the early existence of a married clergy. Once the existence of the phenomenon is admitted, it will probably be possible to obtain more evidence from the existing sources. The Vajrayāna sanctioned this state of affairs, although we lack at present any sort of information regarding the early doctrinal apparatus brought into play in, presumably, the eighth-ninth century. We learn from Tāranātha that family lineages of Tantric masters were established in Kashmir. The famous Ratnavajra, son of a brāhmaṇa converted to Buddhism after having been defeated in a debate, was succeeded by his son Mahājana, and the latter by his own son Sajjana.[7] Ratnavajra was probably born in AD 940; Mahājana was a collaborator of Mar pa's, and Sajjana, in turn, had a son, Sukṣmajana.[8] In the *dPag bsam ljon bzang* we read of a Buddhist master, Maitripa, who had kept a wife,[9] and of Hadu, a householder monk who lived by ploughing.[10]

In twelfth-century Bengal the masses were almost entirely left in the hands of the Buddhist priests, both married and unmarried, the former probably predominating in number,[11] despite the importance of the monasteries. Scholars of pre-Independence and pre-Partition Bengal considered the Vajrayāna as having been the form of religion of the middle class and the married Buddhist clergy.[12] Modern Bengal still bears testimony of past events and of relatively recent transformations. The priests of the Kaivartas have been considered the descendants of the Buddhist married clergy,[13] and other social groups such as the Karas, the descendants of the learned and married Buddhist priests.[14]

In eastern India, the Buddhists and the Pāla rulers had understood the advantage that a married clergy could be to hold control over society, and the patronage of large monasteries went hand in hand with the strengthening of the secular clergy. The brāhmaṇas could be defied on their own ground, and the reason why it took so long to eradicate Buddhism in this part of India is probably that, thanks to the presence of householder monks, it had taken root socially as it had never done before in any other part of the country. Here, in fact Buddhism survived the destruction and abandonment of the monasteries that, as we shall see, took place under the Senas. A married clergy meant living side by side with the common people in every village in the attempt at opposing the rigid caste system of the brāhmaṇas or interpreting it at one's own advantage. By the mid-twelfth century, when King Vallālasena (*c.* 1158-79) took a census of the descendants of the five progenitors of the Rāḍhiya and Vārendra brāhmaṇas who had initially come to Bengal from Kanauj, he found only eight hundred families in all. They lived mostly on grants of lands made to them by the *rājā*-s, or by fees for services rendered to the state. They rarely interfered with other people's religion, and we know of defections from but of no additions to their ranks.[15] Clearly, brāhmaṇas from other regions of India had also moved to both Vārendra and Rāḍha and to other parts of Bengal as well,[16] but their grip on society was not as firm and universal as it was in the Deccan and in other parts of the North.

The archaeological evidence should be also carefully questioned. The Vajrayāna monastery under excavation at Adi-Badri in Haryana, about 40 km west of Ambala as the crow flies, does not correspond in plan to any known monastic establishment of the tenth-twelfth century, the individual cells being conspicuous for their absence.[17] Its size, too, indicates that it is not a traditional monastery. How should we regard the numerous, late Buddhist establishments that from the epigraphic material we know existed in the territories where the Buddhists, after the destruction of the monastic life, had long since become a small minority?[18] In a Western Cāḷukya inscription dated AD 1021, Akkādevī, elder sister of King Jayasiṃha III is praised for having practised the religious observances prescribed by the rituals of Jina, Buddha, Ananta (that is, Viṣṇu) and Rudra.[19] The three systems were thus placed at the same level and regarded as being interchangeable. This can only be explained assuming that they were structured in the same way in relation to the mechanisms of the *varṇa* state, whatever mental reservations the *śramaṇa*-s might have had. In AD 1065, at Baḷḷigāve (Belgami in Shimoga district, not far from Banavasi), the *daṇḍanāyaka* Rūpabhaṭṭayya recorded the erection of the Jayantipura Bauddha *vihāra* and the land grants for the worship of Tārā Bhagavatī, Keśava, Lokeśvara and Buddhadeva with their attendant gods, and for the distribution of food to the *yoginī*-s, *kuśalī*-s and *saṃnyāsī*-s.[20] A Telugu-Cōḍa chieftain of Nellore, feudatory of Rājarāja III Cōḷa (AD 1216-43) refers in an inscription to the merchant community and to the Buddhapaḷḷi of Kāñcīpuram.[21] In the last case, we do not know which deities were worshipped and which rituals were performed, but the situation was probably similar to the preceding examples. If, in places, Buddhism was accepted as part of the established religious order, it was because it had restructured itself as a subaltern system. The Dambal inscription of AD 1095-96 reports that two *vihāra*-s, of the Buddha and Tārā Devī, had been built by the merchant guilds of Dharmavoḷal (Dambal) and Lokkiguṇḍi (Lakkundi), respectively. The donations of the Cāḷukya queen Lakṣmadevī were destined, among other things, to provide food and clothes for the *bhikṣu*-s, and for the support of the *pujārī*.[22] The queen hoped that those who preserved that act of religion 'obtain[ed] the reward of fashioning the horns and hoofs of a thousand tawny-coloured cows from gold and silver, and giving them [...] to a thousand Brāhmaṇs, well versed in the four *Vēdas*'.[23] This points to an entirely brahmanised context. We also wonder what the 'Heruka temple', whose site Buddhagupta, the *guru* of Tāranātha, saw in Rajasthan in the sixteenth century, may have been like.[24]

It is possible to understand these developments by turning to the changes that took place in medieval Jainism. In the preceding chapters, we mentioned only in passing the persecutions and intimidations suffered by the Jain communities at the hands of the orthodox. Much should be added, since the social reverses caused by these persecutions, leading ultimately 'to the all but complete obscuration of all traces of Jainism' are very often recorded in local traditions, such as for instance in the Āndhra-Karnāṭa region.[25] Jainism survived in India, however,[26] and it is in the different destiny of Jainism that Buddhism's later history finds, in part, an explanation.

The Jains, like the Buddhists, had constantly to confront the orthodox. They succeeded in handling the task of perpetuating their faith and retaining the spirit of their tradition through compromise, even during the most calamitous circumstances,[27] preserving, among other things, all the texts – something that Indian Buddhism could not do. Where they could – in Nepal – it was because the *saṃgha* disguised itself socially and was not overwhelmed by Vajrayāna political extremism. The Digambaras, for instance, organised their community along the lines of the caste system and introduced new sets of *kriyā*-s. All worldly practices were accepted as long as there was no loss of pure insight and violation of the *vrata*-s. The first point was particularly difficult to accept, but was formalised in the *Ādipurāṇa* of Jinasena (*c.* AD 770-850), where Ṛṣabhanātha appears as the one who instituted caste division responding to the lawlessness and disorder of the world, a sort of Jain Brahmā. His son Bharata introduced the notion of hereditary *jaina brāhmaṇa*-s, entrusted with the care of temples and the performance of elaborate rituals. As for the *upādhye*-s (*upādhyāya*-s), they are said to have developed out of a group of laymen or of brāhmaṇas converted to Jainism, but represent most probably an adaptation to the model of Brahmanical priesthood. In any case, the system became almost as rigid as that of the orthodox. The śūdras were excluded from taking part to higher religious functions, even though, in opposition to orthodox practice, they could perform a number of *saṃskāra*-s.

Crucial rituals such as marriage were celebrated by brāhmaṇas, and this, as already mentioned in Chapter III, put at risk the integrity of the communities organised around *śramaṇa* groups. Jinasena's integration of Brahmanical *saṃskāra*-s into the Jain system safeguarded its autonomy. The only *saṃskāra* the Jains could not accommodate with was *śrāddha*, since the food offering to the spirit of the dead meant sacrificing animals.[28] The use of the five ritual elements, apparently identical to that of the orthodox, was markedly different from the doctrinal point of view; in the *pūjā*, for instance, no deity was (and is) really present. The Jains tried to keep their distance from Brahmanical beliefs and organisation of society, resorting to a number of subtle doctrinal distinctions, which were ultimately capable of preserving their endangered identity. However, they created a system parallel to the Brahmanical system, centred on temples and rituals. The governing bodies of the Jain communities were, for the Digambaras, the *bhaṭṭāraka*-s and for the Śvetāmbaras the *caityavāsī*-s. We can form an idea of the extent to which Jain institutions were integrated within the Brahmanical world from certain recurrent expressions used by local rulers in granting villages to the new Jain temples. I limit myself to recalling two short inscriptions from the Coorg district, dated to AD 888 and 978, respectively. The expression the rulers resort to in both cases is the same used in a number of occasions with reference to grants made to the orthodox: who destroys the gift 'destroys Bāraṇāsi, a thousand Brāhmans and a thousand tawny cows, and is guilty of the five great sins'.[29]

Jain conformism caused ancient rivalries to surface, and the Jains became thus instrumental in the destruction of the last Buddhist strongholds in the Deccan when northern India started being affected by the violent Vajrayāna survival strategy which resorted to low castes and outcastes. The Jains held tight to the positions they had conquered, and did not embark on risky adventures. Fearing for themselves, they were more Catholic than the Pope on occasions, not only charging the Buddhists with accusation of heresy but throwing on them the blame for stirring up social revolt.[30] We have seen a few examples of anti-Buddhist exploits carried out by the Jains in Chapter IV. The need they felt to recollect the ancient triumphs over the Buddhists, those of Haribhadra and Akaḷaṅka (of which we know the usual outcome) were equalled by the then contemporary triumphs, obtained either by the Jain *guru*-s or by sympathetic kings like Jayasiṃhadeva II of the Western Cāḷukyas.[31] I limit myself to resorting to the words of R.C. Mitra:

> In an inscription of 1036 AD, the Cālukya king Jayasiṁhadeva is called "a fierce and powerful tiger to all evil speakers and a submarine fire to the Bauddha Ocean" and in a later record of 1136 AD his Guru Vādirājendra is remembered as one to whom "Sugata lost his reputation for omniscience and Lokāyata was blinded by the destruction of the system he had erected." The inscription of 1077 AD extols a Jain Guru Vādisiṁha at whose entrance into the hall of debate "even Buddha becomes unenlightened". […] In another inscription of 1077 AD the Jain Guru Ajitasena who was patronised by Vikrama Sāntaradeva (a feudatory of Hoysala Tribhuvanamalla) is qualified as the submarine fire in drying up the Bauddha doctrine. In the Mudgere 22 inscription of 1129 AD Gaṇḍa-Vimuktasiddhāntadeva, whose lay disciple was a feudatory of Hoysala Tribhuvanamalla, is explicitly called "an enemy to the water-lilies, the Śākyas and the cause of destruction of the moonlight, the Cārvākas, and the opener of the lotuses, the excellent Bhavyas or Jains."
>
> […] In 1145 AD Śubhakīrtideva was described as the thunderbolt to the mountains, the Bauddhas who had been inflated by excessive pride which was humiliated by the Jain disputant. The inscription 63 (39) Śravaṇa Belgola of 1163 AD is in commemoration of Devakīrti Paṇḍitadeva, the illustrious *Mahā-maṇḍalācārya* who was the destroyer of the rutting elephant, the indomitable Bauddhas, by the deep and terrific roar of the lion, his unrestrained voice. The inscription No. 64 (40) of the same year qualifies Devacandra-munipa as another thunderbolt to the mountain, the Bauddhas. In 1176 AD, Udayacandra Paṇḍita is called the wild fire to the forest, the Bauddhas, and another Jain scholar Damānandin is, like Bhavadeva-Bhaṭṭa of Bengal, described as the Agastya to the ocean that is the Bauddhas.[32]

In reconstructing Jain medieval history there is a grey area regarding not so much the Digambara *bhaṭṭāraka*-s, celibate clerics engaged in a quasi-householder lifestyle,[33] but the ultimate meaning of the continual debate over whether Mahāvīra had always been a celibate (the position of the Digambaras) or had married (as maintained by the Śvetāmbaras). The discussion can hardly have been only purely theoretical, being rather stirred up by serious social reasons connected to the strained conditions to which the two main branches of Jainism and their subdivisions were subjected. A survey on the modern Jain community sheds some light on the way Jainism restructured itself. The *upādhye*-s are temple priests who can give up their profession and become laymen. Conversely, laymen can become priests. The village priests (*grāmopādhye*-s) are married, and in their families the office of priest is hereditary. They meet their religious and caste obligations to the *dharmādhikārī*, a higher priest who practices an ascetic life.[34] We see in place a strategy aimed at preserving the main tenets of the religion in a situation where one is obliged to capitulate before the principle of reality.[35]

One of the main reasons why the Buddhist householder monks disappeared from India lies in the fact that, contrary to Jainism, Buddhism had expanded its presence outside India: the Himalayan valleys and Tibet, in particular, represented an easy way out and a place that gave the illusion of a transitory exile. The householder monks, squeezed between the brāhmaṇas, the Muslims and the Jains, threw in the sponge, and either became assimilated or fled as the Vinaya monks and the *siddha*-s had done before them, leaving the common people to their fate.

The still living traditions of Tibet, Korea and Japan, which is impossible for me to discuss as would be necessary, should be placed in relation to the model established by the lineages of Indian householder monks. It is significant that the 'white *saṃgha*' of the rNying ma pa, the sNgags pa, are entitled to perform the rites of passage, exorcisms and divinations for their communities according to the teachings transmitted through family lineages. The rNying ma pa were not involved in the monastic reform promoted by Atīśa, and only to a limited degree in the general reorganisation of Tibetan Buddhism,[36] and continued to represent an earlier Buddhist tradition dating to the eighth century,[37] the epoch when the existence of a Buddhist married clergy was, in all likelihood, an established fact in India. Other Tibetan lineages, such as the Sa skya 'khon, reflect a compromise between the tradition of the married priesthood and Vinaya ordination, and allow marriage for the lineage-holders. We cannot explain these facts by resorting to the trite argument of local conditions, which are of course real, but must be seen as growing from other original roots. Similar explanations are particularly weak with regard to Tibetan Buddhism, which has made all the received traditions its own, trying to mediate incompatibilities.

Newār, Tibetan, Korean and Japanese Buddhist traditions, to which we may also add Balinese Buddhism, where lineages of married monks have always existed, may be compared to the lands that continue to emerge after the sinking of a continent. Their legitimacy, at least historically, is much greater than is usually believed.

SOCIAL AND SEXUAL INSUBORDINATION

Edward Conze, in his *Buddhist Thought in India*[38] refused to discuss Tantric Buddhism. He contended that two kinds of Buddhism existed, that of the monks and that, more and more predominant, of the laymen. Tantrism originated within the latter, in which Conze declared himself not to be interested. The *Hevajra Tantra* was for him 'of slight literary merit, composed by members of the lower classes, who knew Sanskrit only imperfectly'; this *tantra* attempted 'to combine the lofty Mādhyamika-Yogācāra philosophy with the magical and orgiastic rites current in Indian villages living on the level of the Old Stone Age'.[39] It is all water under the bridge now, and if we cite Conze, it is because he was one of the first scholars to comprehend the structural link existing between Buddhism and the doctrines of the Gnostics,[40] which, in principle, would have made him better qualified than any other to address the matter. However, he did not question the historical reality that caused the *tantra*-s to be composed, thus missing the point: an antinomial doctrine can change beyond (apparent?) recognition because, in the impossibility of developing its potentialities, it remains anchored to a destiny of social opposition or to irrelevance. Indian history as it unfolded from Gupta times onwards progressively cornered Buddhism, either in a subaltern role or in a role of violent social revolt doomed to failure.

The history of the lowermost castes and the untouchables in early historical and medieval India has not attracted sufficient attention.[41] In general, what we know of the subaltern classes, not to speak of the lowermost social groups, depends on sources that do not mention, or mention only incidentally, or overtly refuse to record their life, yet modern scholars have devoted a considerable number of studies to slavery in the Greek and Roman world and to the peasant world of ancient and medieval China. Indian written sources are much richer than any others in this regard and subaltern groups are not always silent. Archaeology would be a crucial source of information, since the mass of subordinate people – the large majority of the population – have inevitably left traces of their activities, but historical archaeologists seem to be at a loss to interpret the huge amount of 'minor' finds coming from sites of habitation and connect them with the activities of the élite groups. They are regarded as products of contexts they do not empathise with.[42] The problem is even more serious for the epoch dealt with in this book, because medieval archaeology in a proper sense barely exists in India.[43]

Modern historians have also examined the attempts of the subaltern classes to change their condition, and such events as the revolts of the helots in Sparta, the servile wars in second-first century BC Italy, or the social revolts in mediaeval Europe have been the object of a number of works.[44] The social conditions of the insurgents and the historical contexts vary, but a common destiny of strict subordination, lack or denial of rights and lack of representation binds them together. Similar concerns are still rare in India because of a preconception that holds back research: the brāhmaṇas would create a social system where the conflict rate was extremely low, though at the price of reinforcing the caste system and creating the barrier of untouchability.[45] We are face to face with an ideological taboo paralleling that of the religious tolerance that would have reduced religious conflicts to a minimum. Orientalism welded up to Brahmanical ideology has created the umpteenth Indian mirage. Even modern scholars of Muslim India, in criticising the biased idea of an egalitarian Islam, seem to think that the weaker sections of Indian society had no consciousness of their condition.[46] These assumptions must be questioned, especially with regard to the medieval period.

There are recognised exceptions. The first is the revolt of the Kaivartas in Vārendra (North Bengal), which took place in about AD 1075. A part of the Kaivartas[47] were boatmen-peasants deprived of their plots of land given as service tenure and were subject to heavy taxes. Under the guidance of their chief Dibboka, they initiated a revolt, routing the army hastily organised by the Pāla king Mahīpāla II. Although the peasants fought naked with bows and arrows riding buffaloes, Mahīpāla was slain and the Kaivartas established their headquarter in a suburb of Gauḍa, one of the Pāla capitals. It was destroyed when Rāmapāla assembled a new army and crossed the Ganges.[48] R.S. Sharma has maintained that the peasant dimension of the Kaivarta problem has been overlooked, while other scholars have denied that it was a revolt of the Kaivarta caste.[49] That the revolt took an organised form with the participation of different social groups remains an event of considerable interest, even when the particular, decentralised structure of the Pāla state is taken into account. In northern India, the fragmentation of political power was almost complete in the eleventh century,[50] and we must expect revolts to have been frequent. Politically fragmented areas also characterised several regions in the preceding centuries – Orissa, for example.

Social unrest and revolts occurred also after the establishment of a firm Brahmanical rule.[51] The case of the Vīraśaivas or Liṅgāyatas is well known. In twelfth-century Deccan, the Vīraśaivas rejected the authority of the Vedas, developing a fierce hostility against the brāhmaṇas from whose conception of family and society they significantly distanced in such issues as child-marriage and treatment of widows (who were allowed to remarry), and founded their movement on the *guru*-disciple relationship.[52] This radical movement was joined by artisans and members of the service castes (washermen, barbers, potters, weavers, carpenters, tanners and cremation ground watchmen) as well as by people with unrespectable professions (burglars, prostitutes, and pimps).[53] For all his willingness to accept people of the lowest layers of society, Basava (AD 1106-68) was highly critical of their 'unclean' habits, and the new adepts were requested to radically change their life, a non-vegetarian diet and liquor-drinking not being considered to be in accordance with the path of the *liṅga*.[54] Basava gave his imprint to the sect and kept it in check, channelling the social anger of the adepts against the Jains and Buddhists.[55] An inscription of AD 1184 describes the Mahāmaṇḍaleśvara Vīrapuruṣadeva, a feudatory of Vīra Someśvara IV (the last king of the Western Cāḷukyas) as a forest-fire of the Jain religion, 'a destroyer of the Bauddha religion', 'a demolisher of Jaina *basadis*', and 'establisher of the Śivaliṅga-siṃhāsana'. He is further stated to have destroyed several *samaya*-s in a number of places, almost all identified.[56] Kings could hardly escape the pressure of the violence exerted upon the Jains by Vīraśaiva saints such as Ekānta Rāmayya, who after performing a miracle, had a Jain shrine destroyed and the Jains forcibly converted.[57] In the *Paṇḍitārādhya Caritra* of Pālkuriki Somanātha (the author of the Telugu *Basava Purāṇamu*) we read that at the end of the debate between Paṇḍitārādhya and a Buddhist dialectician, the disciples of the former killed the monk.[58]

If the scenario we have disclosed in the preceding chapters has any historical validity, it appears that between the eighth and the twelfth century the strongest opposition to the *varṇa* state society and the most serious revolts, of both the peasant world and the non-caste groups, were hegemonised by the Buddhists. Historians have been unable to enter this perspective because they are convinced that Buddhism turned, *sic et simpliciter*, into a theistic, caste religion, and because they have remained prisoners of the commonplaces on the Vajrayāna. Here we lack the level of analysis that has been devoted to early Buddhism and the useful distinctions that have helped us to rescue it from the Weberian swamp. It does not represent the (re)emergence of a 'substrate', the nature of which remains unspecified; it is, rather, a question of a large mass of people extraneous and hostile to Brahmanical rules to which the Buddhists gave representation and a chance. It is impossible to quantify their number, but those who resisted brahmanisation in the still 'free' territories and those that had nothing to lose in the disputed regions on the faultline must have been very numerous. We can imagine their reaction when the armies raised by the orthodox kings started being defeated by the Muslims, one battle after the next, and the situation of law and order started to disintegrate.

When we read in the *Sekoddeśa* that there is no greater sin than the lack of concupiscence, that non-concupiscence is to be avoided because from it originates sorrow, and from the latter originates death,[59] we are clearly in front of a total rejection of *nómos* and to a call for open social rebellion. The *siddha*-s and the Vajrayāna monks, consciously or unconsciously, utilised sex as a most powerful instrument to introduce social anarchy and revolt. We have the tendency to believe that the disruptive consequences of the non-observance of sexual norms have been weighed up only by the moderns, but it is certainly not so. The example *a contrariis* of the brāhmaṇas opposing the sexual (im)morality of the outsiders is there to prove it. An extreme case in medieval India was that of the Nīlāmbaras, the Buddhist 'blue-clad' ascetics, so-called because they would unite sexually with a woman under a cloak of blue colour.[60] They were expelled from Kashmir by King Śaṅkaravarman (*c.* AD 883-902), which probably indicates that they did not take much care to keep their sexual activity secret. The orthodox Jayantabhaṭṭa censured their behaviour as anti-social maintaining that a religious tradition is valid when it is supported by a large majority of people, is accepted by the learned, and is free from any eccentricity and actions unbecoming.[61] Several Buddhist masters would have agreed with Jayantabhaṭṭa on censoring the Nīlāmbaras and the literal interpretation of the Tantric texts,[62] but would have continued not to subscribe to the introduction or the reinforcement of the *varṇa* state society.

The process which eventually led to the formulation of the Cakrasaṃvara and Kālacakra cycles reached its climax in the twelfth and early thirteenth centuries,[63] when overt sexual iconographies complemented the iconographies showing the new Buddhist deities trampling on Brahmanical gods. An early example is the ninth-tenth century image of Saṃvara in *yuganaddha* from Nālandā, and mention can be made of a later six-headed and sixteenth-armed image of Hevajra with Nairātmyā from Paharpur[64] and of a less known, diminutive Hevajra-Nairātmyā stele from Murshidabad datable to the eleventh-twelfth century.[65] A small bronze image of Saṃvara embracing Vajravārāhī probably from Orissa can equally be mentioned.[66] It is difficult to say how many images of this type became lost when monastic life collapsed, especially metal images kept in secret shrines.[67] If a comparison is possible with the loss of scriptures, they must have been very numerous.

The *siddha*-s and, in part, the Vajrayāna monks, addressed outcastes, 'tribals', and women, and this was a call to arms. Abhayadatta's *Lives of the Eighty-four Siddhas*, written in the late eleventh or early twelfth century and known to us thanks to a Tibetan translation, makes extraordinary reading if we focus on the social ambience depicted: the stories are set in small towns and villages, along rivers, on the seashore and in the jungle. We are also transported to the outskirts of small settlements, such as the neighbourhood of a cemetery where packs of wolves howling at night frighten Śalipa,[68] and in taverns, like that where the tavern-girl waits on Virūpa with a glass of wine and a plate of rice.[69] In the humble feminine universe, we meet fish-market women, as in the story of Lūyipa,[70] wine-selling women, as in the story of Ṭeṅgipa,[71] girls who are the object of unjustified gossiping,[72] prostitutes who go to the banks of the Ganges to bathe.[73] We read of people as poor as Khandipa, who made his clothes by collecting scraps from the garbage piles and patching them together,[74] and we catch a glimpse of an entire world, reading about Tilopa stuffing himself at a wedding and, not yet replete, morally obliging his disciple Nāropa to steal a pot full of food when the guests of the householder were not paying attention.[75] All the people we meet in the text drink wine willingly,[76] to mark the distance of their world from that of the *jāti*-s under Brahmanical control. There are stories where social destitution couples with illness and old age. Kucipa, a low-caste man working in the fields has a neck tumor,[77] Rāhula, himself low-caste, is old and unable to control his bodily functions,[78] and yet they are initiated by the *yogin*-s.

The lọw and outcaste people had – as is obvious but, as said above, not always understood – a clear perception of their condition. In the story of Ḍombipa, set in Magadha, a group of low-caste singers come to the capital, offering to sing and dance for the king. When he asks for the young daughter of a singer, the latter says, 'We are of low caste, denigrated and shunned by other classes of people'.[79] These groups, coming into contact with the Vajrayāna Buddhists realised that their behaviour and way of life, far from being in contrast with the requirements of a high system, were accepted and promoted as part of its doctrine. For the eighth-century Sivaites of Tamiḻakam, the inclusion of a handful of low casters and outcastes among the Nāyaṉmār had been sufficient to extend their social base and bring the situation under political control, violence having preventively eliminated and paralysed the opponents, and as to the Vīraśaivas, the lọw-caste proselytes were requested to change their life radically (with Cenna Basava, the śūdras had to wait twelve years to be initiated).[80] The situation was entirely different in the Vajrayāna, since the have-nots, structured by the *siddha*-s and, to an increasing extent, by the Vajrayāna monks, were accepted *as they were*, becoming the protagonists of the political scene, which in fact the *siddha*-s strongly influenced.[81] It is obvious, however, that even a text such as the *Caturaśīti-siddhapravṛtti* is the product of Buddhist intellectuals, whose structuring presence is visible everywhere.

The early *siddha*-s have been compared, from the phenomenological point of view, to such ascetics as the Kāpālikas. The social landscape would also have been the same.[82] The excommunication fulminated against the Kāpālikas by the *smārta* and *śrauta* brāhmaṇas in a number of works would also lead us to consider the two phenomena close to each other. However, phenomenological aspects may conceal deep divergences in the goals, and we must avoid what we may call the phenomenological trap.[83] The Kāpālikas certainly proselytised in the lower social groups, but the height of their fortune coincided with the recruitment of thugs to carry out the religious cleansing epitomised by the exploits of their gods, Bhairava, Cāmuṇḍā and the Mothers. We could call their presence, in classical Marxist terms, a contradiction within the Brahmanical world. But *smārta* and *śrauta* brāhmaṇas needed them, and we could say in simpler terms that one may need the executioner, but we avoid socialising with him. The recruits of the Kāpālikas represented social groups destined to be incorporated in the *varṇāśramadharma* at the lowest possible level. Conversely, the Buddhist *siddha*-s, with the support of the monasteries, based their project on the possibility of transforming the natives and the outcastes into the new lay devotees, who would then continue to carry out their usual lives. The dwelling of a *siddha*, a shrine, and when possible a monastery, would give them the possibility of representing themselves as Buddhists, upgrading their identity without changing their lives.

The eruption onto the scene of the mass of people whom the Vajrayāna gave a new identity and a cause to fight for caused a tightening of Brahmanical sanctions. Significantly, women and wine drinkers came under attack, as we learn from the later Kali Age literature (which we must keep distinct from the early one, whose target, as we have seen in Chapter III, was the trading community). The *Bṛhannāradīya Purāṇa* includes the following statements:

A twice-born man who, being invited by a Śūdra, takes his meal, is known as a drinker of wine and thrown outside (the pale of) all (Śrauta and Smārta) Dharma [14.39].

One who salutes a Liṅga or even an image of Viṣṇu worshipped by women, lives in Raurava hell with a crore of his generations up to the end of a *kalpa* [14.58].

Neither women nor those not invested with the sacred thread, nor the Śūdras, O lord of men, have the right of touching (an image of) Viṣṇu or Śaṃkara [14.60].

There is no atonement for those who … have association with Śūdra women, (and) nourish their body with food received from Śūdras, … [14.66-67].[84]

The *Bṛhaddharma Purāṇa*, a work particularly useful for the reconstruction of the social and religious history of Bengal,[85] describes the Kali Age of its time. It is interesting for us to note that the *pāsaṇḍa*-s are said to have created 'their own gods by dint of their own intellect' and preach 'their own faiths with a spirit of rivalry', something that perfectly depicts the plethora of the new Vajrayāṇa gods. In addition, the text remarks that the *yavana*-s have become powerful, so that the gods have left this earth, which will 'be crowded only by Mlecchas'.[86] Here the text alludes to the Muslims, whose presence appears inextricably connected with the misdeeds of the Buddhists.

In his poem *Narottama Vilāsa* ('The Life of Narottama', a famous Vishnuite saint of sixteenth-century Bengal), Narahari Cakravarti describes the horrors of Tantrism:

Who can count their crimes? The blood of goats and buffaloes stain each house. Many of them hold in one hand the heads of men severed from the body and in another a sword and dance in frightful ecstasy. If any body falls in their way, he is sure to meet with death at their hands. There is no way to avoid the frightful doom—not even if he be a Brahmin. All of them are addicted to meat and wine and are lost to all sense of sexual morality.[87]

The passage, and the whole poem, betrays the intention to close with the era of carnage that in Bengal accompanied and followed the Muslim conquest. Even Visnuism had turned to disallowed strategies, although Tantric initiation among the brāhmaṇas was regarded as a subsidiary initiation designed more for women and śūdras, who had no claim to Vedic initiation. Conversely to the earlier, competing Sivaite strategy, it was a strategy of social recovery conterminous with the disappearance of Buddhism.[88]

As shown in the earlier chapter, violence was no longer a taboo for the Buddhists: it was part of their strategy, together with sexual unruliness and a conscious resorting to social revolt. It is a mistake to consider the incitements to revolt contained in the texts and the manifestations of violence in both texts and iconographies as purely symbolic. They are literal or metaphorical, not symbolic. As metaphors, through the analogical process, texts and iconographies transfer the violence committed by the Buddhists on the *tīrthika*-s to those carried out on the Brahmanical gods by the new Buddhist deities. That a symbolic interpretation started developing at an early stage is not particularly significant, because it was largely the work of trans-Himalayan Buddhists who had to adapt the received tradition to a context where there were no *tīrthika*-s. The Vajrayāna was considered part of the true teaching of the Buddha, and neither texts nor images could be changed: they could only be interpreted. These interpretations have their own legitimacy, and so deep and influential as to have generated an entire symbolic universe, extending from Tibet to Japan, but we must distinguish between Indian Buddhism and the violent world where it developed and the forms it took when it was received outside India.

In contrast to the non-monastic, compromising Mahāyāna developments, the Vajrayāna movement recovered the antinomial stance of early Buddhism. Only by understanding this can we pick-up the threads of the troubled path of Indian Buddhism. In a situation that could not be more different from that described in Chapter II, we discover an unexpected continuity, something which the brāhmaṇas were always aware of.

SIND AS A TEST

The death of Harṣavardhana marks a divide also in the history of Sind, as elsewhere in northern India. A Buddhist dynasty had ruled the kingdom until the 640s. Its history has been reconstructed on the basis of the *Fatḥnāma-yi Sind*, or *Chachnāma*, of Xuanzang's travelogue, and of the information contained in a few other, later sources such as the *Tuḥfat al-kirām.*[89] The metropolitan region (Xuanzang's *Xinduo*) was the territory around Brahmaṇābād, where the majority of the followers of Buddhism lived. The other region of Sind where the Buddhist population was preeminent was Budhīya, the main towns of which were Qandābīl (Gandava) in the north and Sīwistān (Sehwan) in the south. The śūdra king mentioned by Xuanzang[90] was Sīhara (Sahira II) of the Sīharsī dynasty,[91] who fell in battle against the Arabs in AD 643.[92] The establishment of the Brahmanical dynasty of Yayyati [Yayāti]/Jajja/Chach[93] fits very well into the picture of the second half of seventh-century India. The Buddhists lost their political status and were removed from their posts, with the exception of the *šamanī* ruler of Armābil (Bela), a friend of Yayāti, and of Buddharakṣita (Bhandarkū/Buddha Rakū/Butt Rakū *šamanī*), a friend of the former ruler

Agham Lohānā and minister of King Dāhir in Brahmaṇābād at the beginning of the eighth century.[94]

The *Fatḥnāma-yi Sind* describes a long standoff between Yayāti and the Buddhists, who did not give in. The new brāhmaṇa ruler had threatened to kill Buddharakṣita: 'If I succeed in taking this fort, I shall seize the Samaní, take off his skin, give it to low-caste people to cover drums with it and to beat them till it was torn to pieces.'[95] He was informed that the monk had 'attained sublimity and perfection', and that 'in magic and enchantments' he was so clever as to submit men to his will; by means of his talismans, he could provide himself with all he wanted. Thus Yayāti, when the war waged to conquer Brahmaṇābād came to a stalemate, decided to begin negotiations, still warning his men, 'when I have done speaking and look towards you, you should draw your swords and sever his head from his body'.[96]

Candra, who succeeded his brother Yayāti in AD 671, presumably undertook a more decided action against the Buddhists. The *Fatḥnāma-yi Sind* reports that '[h]e strengthened and promulgated the religion of monks (*nasik*) and hermits (*ráhib*)', but from the statements that follow it appears that Brahmanical ascetics, probably the Pāśupatas, are alluded to, and that a fierce war was waged: 'He brought many people together with his sword, and made them turn back to his faith'. The impression that he carried out a religious normalisation is strengthened by the fact that '[h]e received many letters from the chiefs of Hind'.[97] It is the epoch of Kumārila Bhaṭṭa and Appar, when kings were under the increasing pressure of both the *vaidika* and theistic brāhmaṇas. King Candra was known as a devotee who spent 'his whole time with other devotees in his temple in the study of religion'.[98] The excavations at Banbhore, identified with the port town of Daybul/Debal, besides bringing to light an early eighth-century mosque (the oldest in the subcontinent), affected the pre-Muslim levels. They revealed the presence of a *śivaliṅga in situ* and of a *liṅga* and a few carved architectural features re-used in the area of the mosque,[99] which appears to have been built on the place of a Sivaite temple. In Sind historical excavations have come to a complete stop[100] and no further evidence is available, but the picture, though partial, is a familiar one: Sind was a Buddhist kingdom dotted with large stūpas and monasteries,[101] where the presence of the Sivaites was limited,[102] and in the second half of the seventh century the Brahmanical offensive commenced. Here, however, with the arrival of the Arabs, the Buddhists unexpectedly came up trumps.

Muḥammad b. Qāṣim started his rapid conquest of Sind in AD 711, winning one battle after the other. After occupying Debal, he conquered Nīrūn (Hyderabad), Sīwistān and Rāor (Rāwar), and then Brahmaṇābād, Alōr (Rohri) and Multān (in Panjab). The Buddhists decided to collaborate and submit.[103] The minister Buddharakṣita advised King Dāhir, Yayāti's successor, against organising the defence of Debal. As long as the king was alive, he argued, no enemy could live in peace, while a dead king would mean the end of the kingdom. His advice, he insisted, rested on the fact that the king should be safe and the kingdom secured.[104] Was Buddharakṣita suggesting a guerrilla strategy instead of a risky open battle? Did he aim, if we accept the identification of Debal with Banbhore, at cutting down the power of the Pāśupatas, who had taken foot in the area?[105] Dāhir, who had also heard of the brave Arab 'Ilāfī soldiers,[106] followed Buddharakṣita's advice. At Nīrūnkōṭ, Buddharakṣita surrendered to Muḥammad b. Qāṣim on the terms given in a letter from al-Ḥajjāj, the governor of Iraq who had decided on the expedition. He opened the gates of the fort and welcomed Muḥammad with presents and provisions for his soldiers. Regardless of this, Muḥammad b. Qāṣim ordered a mosque to be built 'in the place of the idol-temple of Budh'.[107] Buddharakṣita accompanied Muḥammad b. Qāṣim to Mauj, identified with Lakhi (to the north-West of Sukkur, on the left bank of the Indus).[108] Here the officer appointed by Bajhara, cousin of Dāhir and governor of Sīwistān, was a *šamanī*,[109] while Bajhara himself was-in charge of the fort.[110] The *šamanī*-s sent him the following message:

> We people are a priestly class, our religion is peace and our creed is good will (to all). According to our faith, fighting and slaughtering are not allowable. We will never be in favour of shedding blood [...]. We have come to know that Amīr Hajjāj, under the order of the Khalīfah, instructed them to grant pardon to those who ask for it. So when an opportunity offers, and when we consider it expedient, we shall enter into a solemn treaty and binding covenant with them. The Arabs are said to be faithful to their words. Whatever they say they act up to and do not deviate from.[111]

Bajhara did not comply and the fight commenced. Then the monks sent a message to Muḥammad b. Qāṣim who, certain of the Buddhist support, ordered the assault until when Bajhara was obliged to leave. The message was this:

All the people, whether agriculturists, artisans, merchants or other common folk, have left Bachehrā's side and do not (now) acknowledge allegiance to him, and Bachehrā has not sufficient men and material of war, and can never stand against you in an open field, or in a struggle with you.[112]

The ruler of Budhīya, where Bajhara had fled, was Kāka, son of a *šamanī* whose ancestors had migrated from the Audaṇḍa Vihāra in Bihar,[113] that is, Odantapurī.[114] He opposed the plan of a night attack on the Arab forces on the pretext that 'seers and hermits' had read in their books that the country would be conquered by the army of Islam. The night attack failed, and Kāka reached the Arab camp, where Muḥammad b. Qāṣim offered him a robe of honour. After that, Kāka sided with the Arabs to curb the resistance of 'those who remained stubborn and disobedient'.[115]

The final battle for the conquest of Nīrūnkōṭ and Brahmaṇābād was a long and bloody one. At least six thousand soldiers were beheaded, whereas the prisoners 'who belonged to the classes of artisans, traders and common folk were let alone'.[116] The evidence is rather confusing, and we are in doubt whether the thousand men 'with their heads and beards clean shaved' who approached Muḥammad b. Qāṣim to ask permission to continue worshipping their 'idols' after being given the status of *dhimmī*-s, were Buddhist monks or brāhmaṇas in mourning for the death of their king.[117] The text has *brahman*, but speaks invariably of their institutions as *khāna-yi buddha*, *butkhāna-yi buddha* and *'imārat-i buddha*.[118] Moreover, when after the conquest the 'brāhmaṇas' complained about the fact that 'the keepers of idol-houses and temples became poor and needy, as they depended for their living on the gifts and charities of the people, and the people, through fear of the Mussalman soldiery, did not continue their offerings',[119] Muḥammad b. Qāṣim allowed them 'to go about begging at the doors of houses, with a copper bowl, and collecting corn in it, and to utilise such corn in any way they liked'.[120] Buddhist monks are likely to be alluded to here. The *šamanī*-s and their Jāṭ followers of Musthal/Manhal in the neighbourhood of Sāwand(ar)ī, identified with Thul Mir Rukan,[121] were also given full assurance regarding the liberty of leading their usual life if they paid the due taxes. The *šamanī*-s Bavād and Budhinī were appointed as officers-in-charge of the local population.[122]

It thus appears that whenever the Buddhists were in a position to condition the course of political events or take autonomous decisions, they considered the Arabs a better alternative to the Brahmanical rulers, for all the limitations and costs that the freedom they granted implied. Something serious must have happened for the Buddhists to change their position with respect to the recent past (King Sīhara, as we have seen, seems to have died fighting the Arabs in AD 643). This can only have been the duress and strain they had been subjected to during the rule of the new dynasty of brāhmaṇa kings. Any interpretation of the events deriving from a modern, national approach to history is out of the question. Indian society, as we have seen, was not only segmented but vertically split at the highest political level and at the level of the intelligentsia.

The best analysis of the relationship between the Arabs and the Buddhists and of the merging of the latter into the trade community of Islam has been provided by Derryl N. Maclean. He has shown that in the primary sources Buddhist communities are mentioned without exception in terms of collaboration, and that there is not one example of an individual Buddhist or a group of Buddhists who did not collaborate. Conversely, Hindu communities rarely collaborated until after the conquest of Brahmaṇābād, and even then only sparingly.[123] Collaboration reveals those socioeconomic features of Buddhism that we have described in Chapter II: the Arab sources mention the Sindhi Buddhists either in a list with merchants and artisans or in connection with commerce. The Buddhists were waiting for some action that would improve their fortunes,[124] although they actually were held in a dramatic grip. Conversely, the brāhmaṇas received their primary support, as expected, from rural areas,[125] and in fact, in keeping with their rural origins, the brāhmaṇa kings of Sind had shown little understanding of regulated inter-regional commerce.[126]

The Buddhists used their financial expertise for the benefit of the Arabs,[127] but their expectations of the revival of inter-regional trade and of the mercantile sector of the Sindhi economy were only partly fulfilled, although the capital generated in Arab Sind was substantial.[128] The point is that, although both Arab conquest and settlement did not imply conversion but, rather, submission, the Buddhists were *dhimmī*-s, second-class citizens and followers of an inferior religion.[129] The Buddhist merchants found it increasingly difficult to compete with Muslim merchant on an equal footing in the revived commerce, and there was a negative change in their share of the accumulation of surpluses. Within a relatively short time, the Arabs not only gained their own expertise in eastern commerce, but displaced the Buddhists as the dominant urban, mercantile class, settling in existing cities and expanding them, and building new cities like Manṣūra. Unequal competition also meant the decline of the Buddhists ability to process the articles of inter-regional trade, which was to the advantage of the Arabs.[130]

The turning point was, once again, the Tang retreat from Central Asia, which gradually passed under the control of the Arabs, allowing them to re-structure trade, progressively cutting out all competitors. With their long experience, the Buddhists countered the growing hegemony of the Arabs in the west at those places where their institutions were still safe and their economic activities not discriminated against, as in the cis- and trans-Himalayan block formed by north-eastern India and Tibet and, in a spectacular way, in easternmost India and south-eastern Asia up to Cambodia and Java. This extraordinary success of the Buddhists at the height of Pāla rule[131] cannot hide the fact that their pushing northwards and eastwards marked, as already noted, a departure from the Indian scene. East of the Indus and up to the territories under Pāla rule or influence, the Buddhists were no longer free to carry out their traditional work, or even to live freely. They were squeezed by a pincer movement the responsibility for which – the Muslims in the West and the *tīrthika*-s in India, – acted independently of each other to meet later on a compromise that meant the end of the religion of Dharma.

The political and economic dynamics observed in eighth-century Sind are probably the same as those that acted in other regions of western India where the Muslims started their armed advance. The *rtbyl* (*eltäbir*, a Turkish title) of Zābulistān and Kābul, two of the Buddhist kingdoms of western Central Asia under Tang protection, fought against the Arabs throughout the seventh and eighth century, succeeding, to a certain degree, to defer their advance, already hampered by political difficulties within the Muslim front.[132] Yet the roads were frequently blocked, as is also witnessed by Chinese pilgrims.[133] When, by the mid-eighth century, the Turki Ṣāhīs of Kābul had to grant more and more concessions to the Sivaites, the Buddhists are likely to have experienced a period of duress. No written records exist, unlike in Sind and north-eastern India, which might have helped us to decipher the situation, but archaeology provides us with some important clues.

In the Upper Arghandab Valley, just south of the Lake Nawor, in the districts of Qarabagh-e Ghazni and Jaghuri, there are several groups of Buddhist caves. They started being excavated at the foot of the mountain barrier off the great southern Hindukush route in order to re-direct trade. The earliest caves are datable to the second half of the seventh century, when there must have been the conviction that the normal route would not be practicable for quite a long period but, at the same time, with the sense that the investment would pay off. The final caves excavated, of imposing dimensions and all unfinished, are datable to the ninth century. By that time, the new dynasty of the Hindū Ṣāhīs, ruling in Kābul, may have created a barrier to the east and south, preventing the Zabulite merchant community from moving freely to Wardak, Logar and Kābul. The Upper Arghandab route, through which Bamiyan could be reached, acquired an even greater importance.[134] When, however, at the end of the tenth century, the battle between Sabuktigīn and Jayapāla that took place between Ghazni and Lamghan[135] put an end to the Ṣāhī rule, the Buddhists had already given up their attempt at carving out an autonomous space for themselves. There is no trace of them south of the Hindukush after AD 860.[136] By that time, the Arabs had created a new network of trade routes through present-day Afghanistan that connected Sind and Multan to Central Asia skipping brahmanised Gandhāra, and the Buddhist merchant community had thus started to give in.

An important point to consider are the dynamics that brought monastic life to an end, and the behaviour of Buddhist monks as a social group. From Sind, the monks moved to other parts of Buddhist South Asia, especially to north-eastern India,[137] a slow process that lasted about three centuries.[138] In south-eastern Afghanistan, they dissolved much earlier because of the strengthening of Ṣāhī rule. With the exception of the rock sanctuaries of the mountain route, the last Buddhist sanctuaries came to an end with the 'Chinese phase' described in the preceding chapter. Only at Tapa Sardar a later phase is attested when, some time after AD 750, the Durgā-shaped goddess described in Chapter V was added to one of the chapels. The first to benefit from the collapse of Tang hegemony in the region were the Hindū Ṣāhīs, not the Muslims.[139] The mountain region of the Upper Arghandab remained the only place where for some time the Buddhists tried to survive as a religious community, and not just only as a trading community.

THE GAME OF THE *TĪRTHIKA*-S

In Madhyadeśa and in eastern India, the series of events set in motion by the arrival of the Muslims and their gradual territorial conquests initially took place according to the lines observed in Sind, but there was soon a dramatic crescendo that brought things to a very different finale. We can distinguish three phases, set in a loose chronological sequence according to circumstances and geographical areas:

First phase. For long, from the time of the inroads made by Maḥmūd of Ghazni, the orthodox kings fought against the Turuṣkas convinced that they would be able, soon or later, to defeat and drive them out. The Buddhists tried, in places, to benefit from the situation weakening the orthodox front: they stirred up the lower classes to jeopardise the Brahmanical control over society, and sided with the Muslims in a number of cases. Social unrest reached its peak in the twelfth century.

Second phase. The *tīrthika*-s realised that they would never defeat the Turuṣkas in battle and that it was a glaring blunder to allow the Buddhists to be their only interlocutors. From then on, their efforts were aimed at separating the two parties and striking hard at the weakest, better-known party, the Buddhists. They pursued their objective with the greatest determination, writing, particularly in Magadha, a most obscure and appalling page in history, a sort of implosion of Indian history, the consequences of which are felt to these days.

Third phase. The political compromise between the orthodox powers and the Turuṣkas which allowed the former to survive and re-organise (as for instance in Mithilā) in exchange for a temporary but fundamental alliance that allowed the invaders to settle in other parts of northern India. The strategy adopted by the *tīrthika*-s once they understood the ineffectiveness of any armed policy against the Muslims, was perfectly rational. Only coming to terms with them would allow them to retain an operational political space. Getting rid of their Indian adversaries and re-establishing an acceptable level of social order was a prerequisite for them to play the defensive-conservative role that would characterise them in the following centuries.

As observed by Buddha Prakash, one of the few historians who has given a credible if incomplete account of the events, the 'spectacular establishment of Muslim rule in northern and eastern India' was largely due to the 'atmosphere of rancour and rivalry, acquisitiveness and aggrandisement, in religion and politics [...]'.[140] In Magadha, on the eve of the Muslim invasion, 'political instability was aggravated by the religious antagonism between the Buddhists and the non-Buddhists, the sectarian rivalries between the sects of the Buddhists, untouchability and caste-rivalry, and priestcraft and exactions and demands of the temple priests from the lower classes'.[141]

In the twelfth century, evidence of a significant Buddhist presence in the middle Ganges plain is provided by the religious policy followed by the Gāhaḍavālas, who ruled over the region from Benares. They stood as champions of Brahmanism from the very beginning,[142] and the majority of their grants record *brāhmadāna*-s.[143] The western part of their territories had been lost for the Buddhists for a long time. The Chinese pilgrim Jiye, who left China for India in AD 964 with a group of three hundred monks, reports that at Kanauj there were plenty of stūpas and temples, but there were neither monks nor nuns.[144] Yet, in AD 1128-29 king Govindacandra, gratified by the *mahāpaṇḍita* Śākyarakṣita from Utkala and his disciple Vāgīśvararakṣita from the Cōḷa country, donated six villages to the community of *śākyabhikṣu*-s of the Jetavana at Śrāvastī.[145] The mention of the *śākyabhikṣu*-s would suggest it to be a community of householder monks: the royal donation makes sense in this perspective.

In AD 1119-20, one of Govindacandra's vassals, a member of the Vāstavya family, had a dwelling for the Buddhist ascetics erected at Jāvṛṣa/Ajāvṛṣa,[146] identified with Śrāvastī, where the inscription attesting to the donation was found.[147] Two of Govindacandra's four queens were Buddhist. The first was Kumāradevī, who depicted herself as 'the streak of the moon among the stars' in the king's harem and donated a *vihāra* to the *sthavīra* of the Buddhist community of Sarnath to honour the Dharmacakra Jina, whose image was also restored by her 'in accordance to the way in which he existed in the days of Dharmāśōka'.[148] The other Buddhist queen was Vāsantadevī.[149] Neither of the two Buddhist queens is described as having been endowed with all the royal prerogatives (as *paṭṭamahādevī* or *samastarājaprakriyopetā*), while each of the two Hindu queens received this honour,[150] but finding here and at this date the division of tasks between the ruler and his queens we first met at Nagarjunakonda is interesting, although it probably has to do with subaltern Buddhist groups. The Buddhist queens supported the *śākyabhikṣu*-s seen as a pendant of the brāhmaṇa priests.

Govindracandra faced an extremely difficult situation. He was exposed to the attacks by the Muslim rulers of Panjab, to whom he paid tribute, from the west,[151] and to those of the hardliner Senas from the east. The social sectors controlled by the Buddhists were, arguably, not negligible in places, and it was in Govindracandra's interest to maintain social order and halt the spread of the most intransigent wing of the Vajrayāna. His successor Jayacandra (*c.* AD 1170-93) found himself in a serious impasse, and opted for a policy strongly supportive of the Buddhist communities. The penultimate king of the Gāhaḍavāla dynasty was called 'a worshipper of Kṛṣṇa' on the day of his installation as *yuvarāja*,[152] but the Bodhgayā inscription of AD 1185 is a eulogy of the *siddha* Śrīmitra, his *dīkṣāguru*. The *siddha* had had the merit to guide 'the rulers of earth addicted to the wrong path' and make them 'renowned for the worship of Śrīghana', i.e. the Buddha, and had 'restored the discipline and recovered the numerous collection of lost scriptures and others of the same kind, belonging to the illustrious site of the Mahābodhi'.[153] Jayacandra owned a white elephant, an animal laden with precise symbolism in Buddhism, which eventually became a possession of Shihāb al-Dīn Ghūrī.[154] All the forces in the field were converging towards Magadha, and the impending clash with the Senas drove Jayacandra towards Buddhism in the attempt to find support among its followers in the region – Magadha – that was becoming the magnet attracting all the contradictions of India.

The forces set in motion by the Vajrayāna were important enough, and Jayacandra seems to have decided to count on them. His praise of Śrīmitra and his mentioning the recovery of lost scriptures, reveals a real involvement and does not seem due to episodic circumstances. Jayacandra was accused of having invited or assisted Shihāb al-Dīn Ghūrī against Pṛthvīrāja III, the powerful Cāhamāna king of Ajmer and Delhi (unless, of course, it was a minister of the latter king who betrayed his master).[155] The state of uncertainty and confusion fell to the level of intrigue and personal interest. Subhāgadevī, a concubine of Jayacandra's, hatched a plot to invite the Muslims to invade Kanauj in order to favour her own son in the dynastic rush.[156] In the end, Jayacandra's defeat at the hands of Lakṣmaṇasena[157] marked a turning point in the history of the region.

The collapse of the Pāla state at the hands of the Senas, the Karṇāṭas of Mithilā and, to a degree, the Gāhaḍavālas, meant the collapse of Indian Buddhism. The last Pāla king Govindapāla had been overthrown in Gayā by either Vallālasena or the Gāhaḍavāla king Vijayacandra (*c.* 1155-70)[158] in an action the details of which are perhaps those narrated in the *Kalki Purāṇa* (Chapter V). As already said, the Buddhists were numerous in the region. Tāranātha reports that whereas after the death of Dharmapāla the majority of the kingdoms of northern India had seen the growth of *tīrthika*-s and *mleccha*-s, '[i]n Magadha the Buddhists were greater in number than before, because of the increase of the *saṃgha*-s and *yogī*-s'.[159] The destiny of Buddhism would have been different if hardliners such as the Senas and Karṇāṭas had not prevailed, but it would have been impossible for these dynasties – after finding a compromise solution with the Turuṣkas – to consolidate their power without planning a radical extirpation of Buddhism. While the Muslims were advancing towards the middle and eastern Ganges Valley, the concern of the Senas was to establish *varṇāśramadharma*. As an example, we see how Vallālasena (*c.* 1158-79) upgraded the Kaivarta fishermen to the status of śūdras in exchange for their traditional job (they became, arguably, peasants) and how, conversely, he refused to accede to their demands to be further promoted socially allotting the degraded Vyāsokta brāhmaṇas as their priests.[160] The lay devotees of the merchant class apparently drew upon themselves the wrath of the king.[161] Vallabha Āḍhya, a Buddhist and the richest merchant and banker of Bengal, leader of the Sonār-Vaniās who had always financed Vallālasena, refused to do so when the king showed the intention to march against Magadha: this caused the Vaniās to be forcibly expelled. Those who remained in Bengal were degraded: brāhmaṇas were prohibited from teaching them and officiating for them.[162] The Senas began a radical administrative-territorial overhaul of the conquered territories, with emphasis on *grāma*-s, which, judging from the 'camps of victory' established within each of them,[163] were milestones in the creation of a caste agrarian society. The largest concentration of the new administrative centres is found in the *nāvya* or navigable sector of Vaṅga and the Khāḍi contiguous to the estuarine mouth of the Bay of Bengal,[164] which may be construed as the determined attempt at curbing down trade.

Tāranātha provides us with the following information, rather confusedly referred to as the time of the 'four Sena kings':

> Then came the Turuṣka king called the Moon in the region of Antaravedi in-between the Gaṅgā and the Yamunā. Some of the monks acted as messengers for this king. As a result, the petty Turuṣka rulers of Bhaṃgala and other places united, ran over the whole of Magadha and massacred many ordained monks in Odantapurī. They destroyed this and also Vikramaśīla.[165]

Antaravedī, 'the area within the sacrificial ground', is the region bounded by the Ganges in the north, the Yamuna in the south, Kuru-kṣetra in the west and Prayāga/Allahabad in the east,[166] and Bhaṃgala corresponds to east Bengal and the adjacent regions.[167] The Turuṣka king Candra is identifiable with Quṭb al-Dīn Aybak, since in the Turkic languages Aybeg ('Aibak in Arabic) means 'Lord of the Moon'.[168] Quṭb al-Dīn, founder of the 'Slave dynasty', helped his master Muḥammad Ghūrī and captured several cities, including Delhi; two years later he conquered Kanauj and Benares by defeating Jayacandra Gāhaḍavāla, and in 1202 he besieged the fortress of Kalinjar in the Candella territory, and then took possession of Mahobā.[169] The Turuṣka kings of Bhaṃgala have been identified with the chiefs of small trading communities of Persian origin settled in the Gangetic ports and deltaic regions tolerated by the Senas as allies ready to attack the Buddhists of Magadha in concert with them and the Turuṣkas.[170]

Regarding the monasteries of Odantapurī and Vikramaśīla, Tāranātha provides us with an additional piece of information:

> During the time of these four Senas, the number of *tīrthika*-s went on increasing even in Magadha. There also came many Persian followers of the *mleccha* view. To protect Odantapurī and Vikramaśīla, the king even converted these partially into fortresses and stationed some soldiers there.[171]

The four Sena kings were Lavasena, Kāśasena, Maṇitasena and Rāthikasena.[172] Since they succeeded Lakṣmaṇasena (AD 1185-1206),[173] they ruled locally when the two monasteries were no longer in existence.[174] It was probably the last Pāla king Govindapāla, who had been ruling over the region, who took the measures attributed by

Tāranātha to the Sena kings, since Odantapurī had been one of the Pāla capitals:[175] the place had withstood repeated onslaughts of Vallālasena.[176] Further measures aimed at defending the site may have been taken at the time of Lakṣmaṇasena by the local Chinda rulers, of which something will be said below.

The relationship between Govindapāla's fortified camp and the monastery is not clear,[177] but the latter was probably included within the defences. The Muslims attacked it, as narrated in a famous passage of the *Ṭabaqāt-i Nāṣirī*:

Having been honoured with such notice and favour [by Sulṭān Quṭb al-Dīn] he [Ba<u>kh</u>tyār-i <u>Kh</u>aljī] led a force towards Bihār, and ravaged that territory.

He used to carry his depredations into those parts and that country until he organised an attack upon the fortified city of Bihār. Trustworthy persons have related on this wise, that he advanced to the gateway of the fortress of Bihār with two hundred horsemen in defensive armour, and suddenly attacked the place. There were two brothers of Far<u>gh</u>ānah, men of learning, one Niẓām-ud-Dīn, the other Ṣamṣām-ud-Dīn (by name), in the service of Muḥammad-i-Ba<u>kh</u>t-yār; and the author of this book met with at Lakhaṇawatī in the year 641 H., and this account is from him. These two wise brothers were soldiers among that band of holy warriors when they reached the gateway of the fortress and began the attack, at which time Muḥammad-i-Ba<u>kh</u>t-yār, by the force of his intrepidity, threw himself into the postern of the gateway of the place, and they captured the fortress, and acquired great booty. The greater number of the inhabitants of that place were Brahmans, and the whole of those Brahmans had their heads shaven; and they were all slain. There were a great number of books there; and, when all these books came under the observation of the Musalmāns, they summoned a number of Hindūs that they might give them information respecting the import of those books; but the whole of the Hindūs had been killed. On becoming acquainted (with the contents of those books), it was found that the whole of that fortress and city was a college, and in the Hindūī tongue, they call a college Bihār.[178]

The Muslims seem to have been unaware of the real nature of the fortified monastery, and seem to have been genuinely upset when they discovered the truth. The episode – a trap prepared at the expense of the Buddhists – was arguably part of the Sena strategy. In fact, if we credit Minhāj with the fortress being without armed forces (as was discovered), we must necessarily think that the Turuṣkas were directed to a place that at the time was not defended. Minhāj's concern to explain to his readers that Bakhtyār-i Khaljī was not responsible for a massacre that had manifestly raised horror and protests is palpable. The gravity of the destruction of the Odantapurī library far exceeds, to make a modern example, that of the library of the Leuven University, *furore teutonico diruta* in 1914, because fraud added to the savageries of war. While the latter are generally recognised and denounced, the former continues, undetected, its destructive action.

The *dPag bsam ljon bzang* (whose first part deals with the rise, progress, and downfall of Buddhism in India) reports that the destruction of the Ratnodadhi Library at Nālandā was also a deliberate action of the *tīrthika*-s. The Ratnodadhi was a nine-storeyed building where the *Prajñāpāramitā Sūtra*-s and the Ṭantric works were preserved. The damages inflicted by the Turuṣka raids on the temples and *caitya*-s of the monastic town had been repaired by Muditabhadra, and a new temple was erected by Kukuṭa Siddha, minister of 'the king of Magadha'. During a sermon delivered there, two young novices threw in disdain washing water on two indigent *tīrthika* mendicants who had appeared in the place. The latter spent twelve years propitiating the sun, and eventually performed a *yajña*, after which they threw live embers and ashes from the sacrificial pit into the monastic buildings. This produced a great conflagration that consumed the Ratnodadhi.[179] That two *tīrthika*-s alone could cause a devastating fire is not, in itself, incredible (arson is the easiest of crimes), but it is unlikely that they spent twelve years preparing a solitary attack. We must set the story in the right perspective, which is better done in the light of the archaeological evidence.[180]

Behind Monasteries 7 and 8, on the eastern row of *vihāra*-s, rises a Brahmanical temple, probably Sivaite,[181] clearly out of place with regard the general layout of the monastic town, juxtaposed as it is 'in a somewhat hostile position and facing the opposite direction towards east, as against the monasteries facing west'.[182] Moreover, the temple was entirely built with huge dressed stone, unlike the Buddhist buildings, which were all made of backed bricks. The intent of emphasising the distance separating the temple from the Buddhist buildings from the architectural and sculptural point of view is evident.[183] The temple was first built around the mid-seventh century, as shown by the reliefs that decorate it.[184] It was rebuilt two centuries later, and the old reliefs were reinstalled in the new building. This is consistent with the political history of Magadha, where the situation, for the Buddhists, came to a head after the death of Harṣavardhana, and which fell in the hands of the *tīrthika*-s after the weakening of the Pālas in the second half of the ninth century. Monastery 1, the first of the eastern row of *vihāra*-s, was reconstructed nine times, in particular after the devastating fire that occurred in the ninth century.[185] The stratigraphic relationships between the two phases of the Sivaite temple and the structural phases of Monasteries 7 and 8 are not known, even less so the relationships with the phases of Monastery 1, the best documented. Thus we lack the objective evidence for understanding what may have happened.[186]

Besides the evidence from Temple 2, several seals have come to light mentioning some *agrahāra*-s and bearing Brahmanical symbols.[187] It has been contended that the site was not exclusively Buddhist,[188] but it is preferable to say that the monastic town went through periods of crisis and setbacks. The 'sequence of occupation and destruction, desertion and re-habilitation' that have been observed, for instance, in Monasteries 1 and 4,[189] points to a complex history of destruction, abandonment and reoccupation. The chronology of the site, especially from the second half of the ninth century onwards, is poorly understood, and prevents us from suggesting a more precise correlation with political-religious events. Even the evidence provided by Cunningham regarding the wanton destruction of stūpas (Chapter I) is set in a chronological limbo. We face the usual problem of the scanty attention paid to the upper layers and to the last phases of abandonment of archaeological sites. What we can say is that after the death of Harṣavardhana the monasteries were abandoned and the Pāśupatas occupied the site. The rise of the Pālas in the mid-eighth century meant the resurgence of Nālandā, which, especially with Dharmapāla and Devapāla reached the peak of its fortune. The second half of the ninth century, when the Sivaites rebuilt their temple, was again a difficult period for the monastic community. One of the layers of ashes in Monastery 1 and the evidence of fire in other parts of the site are the result of unknown events that took place in about that time. We do not know when the monasteries that Dharmasvāmin found empty in 1234-35 (only two of them 'were in a serviceable condition' at the time of his visit) were deserted,[190] and one of the upper layers of ashes found in the excavation can be tentatively related to the fire lit by the *tīrthika*-s that destroyed the Ratnodadhi.

If Odantapurī and Vikramaśīla outgrew Nālandā, this may have depended on their safer position. Although Tāranātha maintains that the origin of Odantapurī owed nothing 'to the grace of any king or minister',[191] it is difficult to explain its extraordinary growth and popularity on the exclusive basis of patronage from below.[192] It is located at a very short distance from Nālandā, and the site, as already said, was a Pāla stronghold, where the court used to encamp.[193] The place must have been well protected, and Bakhtyār-i Khaljī's option to establish its military outpost there depended on its known, favourable position.

Here comes the case of the attack on Vikramaśīla, the great centre of Vajrayāna learning founded by King Dharmapāla identified with the site of Antichak, situated in the Bhagalpur district of Bihar on the right bank of the Ganges.[194] It is commonly but groundlessly maintained that, like Odantapurī, it was attacked, and even destroyed, by Bakhtyār-ī Khaljī: a *lectio facilior* of the events has been given, *in primis*, by Tāranātha and other Tibetan historians. Bakhtyār never passed through the place in his march from Bihar Sharif towards Nadiya in Bengal, where Lakṣmaṇasena resided at the time. To avoid the Sena forces posted to intercept him, he took the Jharkhand route and then passed through Birbhum, thus following a southern route to fool his enemies.[195]

The destruction of the Buddhist monastery was due to very different causes. Excavating the monastery's third-phase structures, 'represented by shoddy walls constructed of stone rubble and bricks', it became apparent that

> [c]uriously enough a few Buddhist deities like Mahakala and goddess Tara were found to have been used as building material for the construction of the walls. A number of sculptures both of the Brahmanical and Buddhist deities were recovered from the excavation. The former include Mahishasuramardini, Chamunda, Uma-Mahesvara, Vishnu, Seshasayi Vishnu, Manasa, Yama Ganesa and Surya, while the latter consisted of mutilated Avalokitesvara, Bodhisattva-Padmapani and goddess Tara […].[196]

A big fire had destroyed the monastery,[197] the Buddhist images were broken into pieces and used as building material, and on the interfaced ruins a Brahmanical temple was built, to be later abandoned. The Buddhist images were found 'kept flat upside down in the masonry' to raise the height of the new walls, which points to 'an element of hatred and vengeance' against Buddhism; '[r]eligious rivalry was one of the fundamental causes of the destruction of the University […]'.[198] It is interesting to note that before the final attack on the monastery, other attempts had taken place to destroy it. An inscription on a pillar stump refers to the fact that a local chief, Sahura of Campā, had dispelled a planned attack by 'the rulers of Baṅga'[199] – evidently, the Senas. If we have a better knowledge of what really happened at Antichak, it is because excavations, though far from satisfactory, have been more accurate than those carried out in other monastic sites until the 1930s. More attention than usual was paid to the site's later phases and to the phases of abandonment, a rewarding strategy. Vikramaśīla is not an isolated case, however. The case of Sarnath, analysed in Appendix 2, is another case in point.

When the *tīrthika*-s started using the Muslims to get rid of the Buddhists, the latter found themselves in a fight on two fronts. We read in Tāranātha some instances of Buddhists taking action against the Turuṣkas by making use of magic. Riripa, a disciple of Nāropa, performed a magical rite on the street somewhere to the west of Benares when the Gar log army (the army of the Turuṣkas) materialised: 'When the Gar-log-s reached there, they saw only dead bodies and the ruins full of stones and wood and the soil upturned. So they went back'.[200] Riripa 'made big offerings to Cakrasaṃvara' when 'Vikramaśīla was once attacked by the Turuṣka army', so that the latter was struck by terrible thunder four times. This killed their chief and many brave soldiers and thus they were repelled.[201] That the Buddhists had to fight on two fronts is clear from the fact that the same Riripa is said to have defeated in debate 'eight *tīrthika* rivals': 'six of them [he] turned dumb and two blind', though later on he released them.[202]

Līlāvajra, a *vajrācārya* from Vikramaśīla, on hearing the rumour of an impending Turuṣka invasion, defeated their soldiers by drawing the *Yamāricakra*. 'After reaching Magadha – Tāranātha reports – the soldiers became dumb and inactive and remained so for a long time. Thus they were turned away.'[203] The Lama further says that Līlāvajra's fifth successor, Kamalarakṣita, was about to hold a *gaṇacakra* when he 'encountered the minister of the Turuṣka king of Karṇa of the west, who was then proceeding to invade Magadha with five hundred Turuṣkas'.[204] The latter 'plundered the material for *sādhanā*, but when he came near the *ācārya* and his attendants,

> [Kamalarakṣita] became angry and threw at them an earthen pitcher full of charmed water. Immediately was generated a terrible storm and black men were seen emerging from it and striking the Turuṣkas with daggers in hand. The minister himself vomited blood and died and the others were afflicted with various diseases. Excepting one, none of them returned to their country.[205]

From what Tāranātha reports immediately after ('This made both the *tīrthika*-s and Turuṣkas terror-stricken'), we realise once again that the Buddhists were fighting on two fronts, something which they would not be able to stand for long. In fact, the *yogī*-s started to secede, and in the case reported by Tāranātha, they seceded to the *tīrthika*-s:

> At that time, most of the *yogī* followers of Gaurakṣa were fools and, driven by the greed for money and honour offered by the *tīrthika* kings, became the followers of Īśvara. They used to say, 'We are not opposed even to the Turuṣkas.' Only a few of them belonging to the Naṭeśvarī-varga remained insiders.[206]

The Gaurakṣa/Gorakṣa of the text is probably the ninth of the eighty-four *siddha*-s;[207] the secession took place at the time of the 'four Sena kings'.

When Dharmasvāmin, who went to India from Nepal against the advice of his companion scholars,[208] arrived in Magadha, destruction was almost complete. Between 1234 and 1235, he sojourned at Nālandā, where only two monasteries, as said above, 'were in a serviceable condition'.[209] Before reaching there, he stopped at Bodhgayā, and the account of his short stay throws light on the real situation:

> [...] the place was deserted and only four monks were found staying (in the Vihāra). One (of them) said, "It is not good! All have fled from fear of the Turushka soldiery". They blocked up the door in front of the Mahābodhi image with bricks and plastered it. Near it they placed another image as a substitute. They also plastered the outside door (of the temple). On its surface they drew the image of Maheśvara in order to protect it from non-Buddhists. The monks said, "We five do not dare to remain here and shall have to flee."[210]

The monks decided to remain for the night, but '[h]ad the Turushkas come, they would not have known it'. What requires an explanation in Dharmasvāmin's account is that the monks, for all their fear of Muslim attacks, felt safer camouflaging the Buddhist temple as a temple of Śiva. Why did they? The only plausible explanation is that by so doing they hoped to be spared in the event of a Turuṣka assault. The strategy of the orthodox, reversing the early alliance system, had been successful: their temples were now spared and the Turuṣkas were encouraged to attack the establishments of the Buddhists, arguably indicated as a treacherous and immoral lot.

Another example of the Indian contradictions and of the treacherous plans that were being organised is the inconclusive attack, recorded by Dharmasvāmin, that the Muslims made from their newly built outpost of Odantapurī/Bihar Sharif against what remained of Nālandā. There was no comprehensible reason for the Muslims to organise an attack, since no commandant of a fortress could afford the luxury of engaging three hundred men to attack a religious centre, which, in any case, he would have let his men sack after a battle or a siege as was customary. Yet, Dharmasvāmin reports that when 'suddenly some three hundred Turushka soldiers appeared, armed and ready for battle', the monks hid themselves, and the soldiers went back, keeping prisoner two lay supporters of the Abbot 'for several days'.[211] The residents of the monastery had been informed that the Turuṣkas would soon come to kill them. The Muslim commander of Bihar Sharif had summoned a lay relative of the Abbot, Jayadeva, and had detained him and other members of his family, but Jayadeva succeeded in sending the following message to the monastery:

> The Brāhmaṇa lay-supporter wishes to tell the Guru and disciples, that he had been detained by the officer who said that he, (Jayadeva), had honoured numerous monks attending on the Guru. Now they shall surely kill the Guru and his disciples. Flee![212]

The most likely explanation of this apparently strange story is that the commander of Bihar Sharif, though encouraged to assault the residents of Nālandā (by whom is an easy guess), gave the game away so that the Buddhists could save themselves. He knew Jayadeva to be a friend of the monks, as his words prove, and let him free so that he could inform the monks. Moreover, when the soldiers arrived in the monastic town, they did not make any real search and went back.

Moving down from Nepal to the plains and returning home, Dharmasvāmin passed through Tirhut (Tīrabhukti) and its capital Simraongarh (near Birganj in the central Nepalese Tarai). As underlined by A.S. Altekar, the kingdom of Mithilā, ruled at the time by the young King Rāmasiṃha of the Karṇāṭa house, kept its independence thanks to the alliance that his father, Narasiṃha, had made with Sulṭān Ghiyāth al-dīn 'Iwaẓ, to whom he paid tribute. Narasiṃha helped the Sultan to capture the whole of South Bihar, the heart of Buddhist India. It was not by chance that Muḥammad Bakhtyār-i Khaljī in his expedition to Bengal had taken the southern route, submitting parts of Purnea and sparing the kingdom of Mithilā.[213]

In this region, doctrinal controversies had continued to take place at the highest level. Nyāya commentators such as Vācaspati Miśra (ninth century) and Udayana (the tenth-century author of the *Ātmatattvaviveka*, a thorough confutation of Buddhist doctrines) still felt the urge to carry out a critique of Buddhist positions.[214] Nor could the virtual extinction of Buddhism in the early thirteenth century shake off the traditional hatred of the Maithila scholars for the apostates, and the brāhmaṇas 'treated the Buddhists, and not the Muslims, as their worst enemies' as late as the fourteenth century.[215] Jyotirīśvara Kaviśekharācārya, the learned minister of King Harisiṃhadeva (AD 1279-1325),[216] denounced the Buddhists as 'degraded and dangerous' in his *Varṇaratnākara*, and applauded Udayana's stand against them as 'pleasant and commendable'.[217] Mithilā's 'national' poet Vidyāpati, in the second tale of his *Puruṣaparīkṣā*, accounts for the alliance between 'Alā al-Dīn Khaljī (AD 1296-1316) and Sakrasiṃha/Śaktisiṃha.[218] One of Vidyāpati's early poems is dedicated to Sulṭān Ghyāth al-dīn A'ẓam of Bengal, who extended patronage to him,[219] and this most famous among the Maithili intellectuals considered the Sharqī ruler of Jaunpur Ibrāhīm Shāh (AD 1402-40), to whom he paid a visit, second only to God, and his capital a second Amarāvatī or Indrapurī. He persuaded him to organise a military expedition to put an end to the chaotic conditions prevailing at the time in Mithilā.[220]

Upendra Thakur mentions an obscure episode that is worth recording, since it is evidence of the radical enmity that the *tīrthika*-s nourished against the Saugatas. After the death of Śivasiṃha (the most famous king of the Oinavāra family who ruled over Mithilā in the first half of the fifteenth century), a local ruler of northern Mithilā, Purāditya of Raj Banauli, massacred the Buddhists and their patron, King Arjuna of Saptari,[221] a region now in the eastern Nepalese Tarai.[222] Despite the deluge of 'national' (*lege* 'Brahmanical') literature stating the opposite, the relationships between the Muslim rulers and the Brahmanical states of post-conquest India were often good.[223] Only later on did conditions change.

THE SIṂHALA MONKS

The thirteenth-century dynasty of rulers with names ending in *-sena* holding power in Gayā may not be related to the Sena dynasty. They may be identified, allowing for some discrepancies from Tāranātha's account, with the representatives of the Chinda family, known to have ruled locally as feudatories as early as the tenth or eleventh century. The territory over which they ruled was known as Pīṭhī, from Vajrāsana Pīṭha, namely Bodhgayā.[224] That they acknowledged the suzerainty of the Muslims[225] is more than a hypothesis. One of the Chinda rulers, Buddhasena, known to Tāranātha, was the ruling *rājā* at the time of Dharmasvāmin's journey.[226] His son Jayasena is known for having granted a village to the Siṃhala monk Maṅgalasvāmin for the maintenance of the Vajrāsana and his attached residence in AD 1283.[227] At that time Maṅgalasvāmin was thus the abbot in-charge of the holy place. The Siṃhala monks had been associated with the Vajrāsana for a long time: in the *Da Tang Xiyu qiu fa gao seng zhuan*, Yijing maintains that the Vajrāsana and the Mahābodhi temple 'had been erected by the king of Ceylon', and that '[i]n olden days the monks coming from Ceylon always remained in this Temple':[228] the reader probably remembers the story that associates Bodhgayā with Laṅkā as early as the time of Samudragupta (Chapter III). The monastery had probably grown as a centre of Theravāda learning since the time of Mahānāman[229] and the sojourn at the Vajrāsana of Buddhaghoṣa and Dharmapāla in the fifth century. The *saṃghārāma* of Laṅkā was an important one, rising just to the west of the Mahābodhi Temple,[230] and from Xuanzang's description we know what it was like in the first half of the seventh century.[231]

The question of the role played in the thirteenth century by the Siṃhala monks in the very centre of Buddhist spiritual power and of their relationship with the Sena rulers and other Indian kings is difficult to answer. In AD 1150-51, the *bhaṭṭa* Dāmodara had erected a shrine with an image of the Buddha with the assent of Aśokacalla, *rājā* of the Khasa country in the Sapādalakṣa Hills in Panjab. Provisions were made for the offerings, entrusted to the members of the Sri Lankan monks' assembly.[232] As late as AD 1286, the Tibetan monk Grub thob O rgyan was in Bodhgayā, where he repaired the northern side of the temple, bestowing all the donations he received upon the Mahābodhi. At that time, there were five hundred *yogī*-s with him, and during the work he remained with them to the north of the temple. The other three sides of the temple were repaired by three other persons, one of whom acted on behalf of the king of Laṅkā.[233] One of the last Theravādin monks who taught at Bodhgayā seems to have been the

Laṅkān Ānandaśrī towards the end of the thirteenth century, before he went to Tibet, where he translated Pāli texts into Tibetan.[234] The learning centre of the Ceylonese did not favour the Buddhist masters with a different doctrinal orientation, even though a Tibetan *lo tsa ba*, Sangs-rgyas grags, had succeeded in holding the Vajrāsana throne.[235] What is striking in all this is the virtual disappearance from the scene of the *Indian* Buddhists.

With regard to the dominance exercised by the Sri Lankans, Tāranātha reports on an episode that he attributes to the time of Dharmapāla, but which is probably later:

In a temple of Vajrāsana there was then a large silver-image of Heruka and many treatises on Tantra. Some of the Śrāvaka Sendhava-s of Siṅga island and other places said that these were composed by Māra. So they burnt these and smashed the image into pieces and used the pieces as ordinary money.[236]

At the time of Dharmasvāmin's visit, the hostility towards the Mahāyānists-Vajrayānists was palpable:

When the Guru Dharmasvāmin visited the Vajrāsana-Saṅgha-Vihāra carrying an Indian manuscript of the *Ashtasāhasrikā-Prajñāpāramitā*, the keeper, a Śrāvaka, enquired, "What book is it?" The Dharmasvāmin answered that it was the *Prajñāpāramitā*. The Śrāvaka said, "You seem to be a good monk, but this carrying on your back of a Mahāyāna book is not good. Throw it into the river!" He had to hide it.[237]

Bodhgayā seems to have been appropriated by the Siṃhala monks. Inside the three great gates giving access to the Mahābodhi Temple and the Vajrāsana, only the sacristans could sleep. The point is that there were 'three hundred sacristans native of Ceylon, who belong[ed] to the Śrāvaka school; others (schools) ha[d] no such right'.[238] The influence gained by the *śrāvaka*-s in the course of time had certainly its good reasons, but the exclusion of Indian Buddhists from control of the Vajrāsana is surprising, and we cannot explain it only in terms of inter-Buddhist rivalry. How could foreign monks get the better of their Indian doctrinal opponents without enjoying strong political support? The more reasonable explanation is that, once the site was cleansed of the Indian opponents of orthodox rule, the Siṃhala monks were granted the privilege of being the only authorised keepers of the Vajrāsana. They had no following in India and were not a threat at the social level. They were probably also under the menace of being sent back to their island. Who could not be intimidated or stopped by the Sinhalese monks and their protectors were the Śivaites. In the fourteenth century, they remained the masters of the field.

THE LAST BUDDHISTS OF ORISSA AND BENGAL

Images of Heruka, rare though they are, appear in the tenth-eleventh century at Sarnath, Nālandā and in Bengal,[239] and those of Trailokyavijaya trampling on Śiva and Pārvatī, of Aparājitā and Parṇaśavarī defeating Gaṇeśa, as well as that of Saṃvara are documented from the same period onwards. Parṇaśavarī, an emanation of Amoghasiddhi and a healing goddess, appears in Bengal as having been attacked by Gaṇeśa, now prostrated at the bottom of the stele with a sword and a shield.[240] We are not accustomed to associate Gaṇeśa with violence, but the reader will remember his presence in the *yajñaśālā* of Ellora (Fig. 9): the Buddhists knew better. Parṇaśavarī was associated with the notorious Śabara tribals, confirming the mode of Buddhist proselytising. The lineage of the Candra kings, mentioned in the previous chapter, exemplifies, in easternmost India, the line of resistance against Brahmanical dominance. Connections with a local god are also assumable for Saṃvara,[241] which a stele from thirteenth-century Orissa shows trampling on Śiva and Cāmuṇḍā, thus disclosing the goddess's responsibility in the elimination of the Buddhists.[242] Cāmuṇḍā holds a *kartrī* in her right hand, the very instrument she holds in an Orissa stele mentioned in Chapter V and by Bhairava in the *garbhagṛha* of the Vaitāl Deuḷ in Bhubaneswar – hardly a coincidence. Cāmuṇḍā appears, significantly, as a member of Māra's army.[243] Of great interest are the ferocious, naked *devī*-s surrounding Heruka/Hevajra in the *pañcaḍāka* and other *maṇḍala*-s described in the *Niṣpaññayogāvalī* and in the *Sādhanamālā*, notably so the outcastes Ḍombī and Cāṇḍālī. The latter wears a garland and a crown of skulls and dances on the prostrated Nirṛti,[244] the daughter (or consort) of Adharma abusively inhabiting the *aśvattha* or Bodhi tree – which reminds us of the Cāmuṇḍā of Fig. 13.

The iconographic explosion in north-eastern India in such a late period requires an explanation. Texts could be written and rituals performed thanks to the sole intellectual and organisational capacity of the Buddhist erudite, but for images to be painted, sculpted or cast, and shrines to be built, patronage and resources were needed. We must assume that in eastern India the Buddhist laymen were convinced that there were still good chances for the religion of Dharma to survive and prosper and for financial investment to be repaid. This conviction depended on their judgement of the political dynamics of the moment. It appears that, besides counting on the support of new followers, the men of religion and the lay élite considered the Muslim attacks on Brahmanical power an opportunity for creating or widening their political-religious space.

The conquest of western Bengal opened the road to Orissa to the Muslims. Rājarāja III of the Eastern Gaṅga dynasty (AD 1198-1211/12) was paralysed by the first inroads of the Turuṣkas into Jājnagar/Jajpur in Utkala, prized for its elephants. Military reaction started with his son Anaṅgabhīma III (AD 1211/12-38), when the kingdom was already paying tribute to Ghyāth al-Dīn 'Iwaẓ.[245] Muslim power was not to be firmly established in Orissa until as late as 1568, when it was annexed by the Karrānī Sulṭāns of Bengal.[246] Orissa was, once again, and for different reasons, on the faultline, but the final eradication of the Buddhist communities was the exclusive concern of the native ruling elite.

There are both literary and archaeological sources documenting the blows struck upon Buddhism, although their fragmentary and debatable nature often makes the dynamics of the events and their chronology uncertain. Much evidence comes from the Prachi Valley, the alluvial plain south-east of Bhubaneswar, where Buddhism had exercised an overwhelming influence during the Bhaumakara rule.[247] The non-systematic way with which the evidence has been collected makes its classification and interpretation tentative, and much work is needed to render it unquestionable.[248] However, to affirm that in the Prachi Valley the majority of the Buddhist buildings were either abandoned or destroyed, and that the number of Brahmanical shrines springing up almost everywhere were built on or near them, seems correct. As early as the 1950s, N.K. Sahu noticed that 'most of the Buddhist images in this region have been badly damaged and mutilated'.[249] Destruction and appropriation took place under the rule of both the Somavaṃśīs and Eastern Gaṅgas. Later events, also testified by the literary evidence, are particularly relevant because they bear on the latest Vajrayāna phase of Indian Buddhism.

Some of the best evidence comes from the architectural peculiarities of the Pūrṇeśvara stone temple of Bhillideuli, a village in the valley of the Kadua (a tributary of the Prachi River) near Kakatpur. It was built in the early twelfth century[250] on a Buddhist brick *vihāra*, a portion of which was spared to serve as a temple *maṇḍapa*. The two small temples of Kedāreśvara and Kaṇṭeśvara were also constructed making use of the Buddhist structures.[251] In the same locality, a *liṅga* appears to have been shaped by sculpting a stūpa,[252] according to a practice that we have seen well documented in Gayā and Nepal. At Pitapara, near Madhava in Puri district, the Aṅgeśvara Temple seems equally to have been built on Buddhist remains, as is shown by a road section yielding bricks and a Buddhist image.[253] The village is supposedly named after the Indian *siddha* who first obtained the Kālacakra in Śambhala,[254] and the twelfth-century Brahmanical temple would thus have replaced a Vajrayāna shrine. A similar case is that of the Someśvara Temple in the Sauma or Dahikhia village near Kakatpur,[255] where an image identified as Tārodbhava Kurukullā is worshipped as the Goddess Lalitā. In the *Prācī Māhātmya*,[256] the place is associated with the victory of Viṣṇu, armed with the *sudarśana cakra* given to him by Someśvara, over the powerful *daitya* Namuci who threatened the existence of the *deva*-s.[257] This is an interesting case of the great Purāṇic allegories being adapted to a local reality. Evidence of a late Buddhist presence comes from Belpada. The village deity is a Buddhist male deity trampling on Śiva who lies recumbent on the ground with his head raised by his left hand.[258] The Dakṣiṇeśvara Temple at Bagalpur, rising on the ruins of a Buddhist temple, as shown by the numerous Buddhist image preserved in its precincts, may not have been built on the remains of a Bhaumakara sanctuary, but on a later establishment.[259] Unfortunately, we do not have the plans of these buildings, and cannot make any hypothesis on the kind of monks they accomodated.

The numerous Buddhist images preserved by the Agikhia Maṭha at the Agni Tīrtha in the Sohagpur village, greatly praised in the *Prācī Māhātmya*, show the former affiliation of this establishment with Buddhism. An accidental digging brought to light a stūpa on which a shrine of Sudarśana was built. This and other *maṭha*-s, such as the Kuṇḍhei Maṭha near Bajapur and the Taila Maṭha near Madhava, where Buddhist images are also observable, belong to the Rāmānuja *sampradāya* and were built on former Buddhist buildings.[260]

A similar situation, also documented by the written sources, is observable also elsewhere in the vicinity of Bhubaneswar, as for instance in the region of low hills crossed by the Daya River and honeycombed with Buddhist caves. The best-known site in the area is Dhauli, with the famous Aśoka inscription and the unfinished rock-cut image of an elephant, symbolising the Buddha.[261] Buddhist remains are numerous at Aragarh/Airagarh, and include a two-storeyed, flat-roofed temple on the hill top and late Vajrayāna images.[262] As in the Prachi Valley, a panorama of mutilated images is observable. A story from the *Mādalāpāñji*, a chronicle of the temple of Puri with a complex textual history,[263] resorts to the usual repertory as far as the dynamics of the confrontation between the *tīrthika*-s and the Buddhists are concerned, but is credibly set in this area. The episode took place at the time of the Gaṅga king Rājarāja II (AD 1171-94), known to the *Mādalāpāñji* as Madana Mahādeva:

> Buddhist monks were residing in eightyfour caves, excavated by them on the Aragaḍa and Dhauli hills in Pāraṅga *daṇḍpāṭa*. They claimed omniscience. One day the queens of the king (also) said that they were omniscient. Hearing this, the king said that Brahmins were superior to the Buddhists and Brahmins should be put to a test in order to ascertain who were omniscient and whose words were true.[264]

The snake-in-the-pot ordeal was performed by order of the king, and the *tīrthika*-s turned out to be the winners. According to a version of the story, '[...] the king attempted to smash the heads of the Buddhists to death. But at this moment the Buddhists cursed the king and (then) entered the forest after leaving the caves.'[265] According to another recension, 'this king built [the] Alāranātha. He killed the Buddhists. This king was engaged in the construction of the *Baḍa Deaula*.'[266]

We know from Tāranātha that doctrinal debates between *tīrthika*-s and Buddhists were common at a late period,[267] but there are aspects that are still in an area of shade. In the *mukhaśālā* of the Lakṣmī Temple within the Puruṣottama-Jagannātha Temple compound in Puri, datable to the twelfth century like the main shrine, there is a painting showing how a Vishnuite theologician converts a Buddhist monk into Vishnuism at the point of his dagger.[268] It is difficult to establish which event is alluded to, and the time when it took place,[269] but the forced conversion is probably connected to the struggle for power that led to the construction of the present-day temple of Puri on the ruins of Buddhism, and perhaps on those of an actual Buddhist temple.[270] A forced conversion is attributed to Caitanya Mahāprabhu (AD 1486-

1534), whose preaching was to shape the religious world of eastern India well into modern times. Several works were devoted to the narration of his life and deeds. The most famous is the *Caitanya Caritāmṛta*, composed by Kṛṣṇadāsa Kavirāja Gosvāmī (AD 1528-1615/20),[271] where the following story is reported:

On hearing of His scholarship the skeptics came to Him, boastfully bringing their pupils with them. In a lonely forest a very learned Buddhist professor held forth dogmatically on the nine doctrines of his church before the Master. Though the Buddhists are unfit to be talked to or even to be looked at, yet the Master argued with him to lower his pride. The very Buddhist philosophy of nine tenets, though rich in logical reasoning, was torn to pieces by the Master's vigorous logic. The great philosophers were all vanquished; the audience tittered; the Buddhists felt shame and alarm. Knowing that the master was a Vaishnav, the Buddhists retired and hatched a wicked plot. They placed before the Master a plate of unclean rice, describing it as Vishnu *prasād*. But just then a huge bird swooped down and carried off the plate in its beak! The rice falling on the bodies of the Buddhists was [openly] rendered impure; the plate fell down slanting on the Buddhist professor's head, cutting it open, and throwing him down in a fit. His disciples lifted up their voices in lamentation, and sought the Master's feet imploring Him, "Thou art God incarnate! O forgive us! Out of Thy grace revive our teacher." The Master replied, "Cry out, all of you, Krishna's name. Pour the word loudly into your teacher's ears, and he will recover." They did it, the professor rose up and began to chant *Hari! Hari!* He did reverence to the Master saluting Him as Krishna, to the wonder of all. After this playful act the son of Shachi vanished; none could see him.[272]

Not differently from the story of Campantar at Būtamaṅkalam mentioned in Chapter IV, the conversion takes place as a consequence of an act of intimidation, in this case a wounding. The place, the time, and the religious convictions of the converter are different, but the dynamic of forced conversions remains the same. We do not know exactly where the episode attributed to the Vishnuite saint took place. Caitanya went to preach in south India, where he is reported to have made many converts among the Buddhists and the Jains. True though it is that Buddhist communities survived in Tamil Nadu,[273] the episode may reflect some event that took place at the time of the Gajapati king Pratāparudra (*c.* AD 1497-1540).

The attacks against the Buddhists carried out by the Sivaites through the Somavaṃśī rulers and by the Vishnuites through the Gaṅga kings were largely effective. Yet in Orissa, if we have to judge from the length of the conflict, the opposition of the Vajrayānists was almost as effective. Miserable as it may look, the reconstruction of the main stūpa of Ratnagiri – one of the largest monasteries in the forest hills of the Cuttack district – took place long after the thirteenth century,[274] and some Buddhist groups survived, especially in Utkala, until they succumbed to the new Vishnuite wave roused exactly by Caitanya and the other reformers of the sixteenth century. In 1510, Caitanya, whose family was original from Jajpur, set out for Puri, where he was to reside for a very long time.[275] He greatly influenced Pratāparudra, to whose reign the facts narrated in the *Caitanya Bhāgavata* of Īśvara Dāsa[276] are likely, once again, to refer. This Bengali work, written towards the end of the sixteenth century, reports that out of seven hundred Buddhist monks, six hundred and sixteen were put to death by a 'Kēśarī king'.[277] The remainder asked for protection from Padmāvatī, whom we know to have been, in the reality, the queen of Pratāparudra. The king sided with the brāhmaṇas, and the usual trial of the snake in the jar took place. 'Thirty two of the Buddhists were clubbed to death and the surviving few fled to Bāṅki and took shelter in the caves of the Mahāparvata hill.'[278] The leader of the Buddhist was Vīrasiṃha, the greatest *siddha* of his times,[279] and the story, recounted in Chapter 53 of the *Caitanya Bhāgavata*, has been rendered by Prabhat Mukherjee as follows:

> One day the queen Pādmavatī went to offer worship to the image [of Narasiṃha]. At the temple she met Vīra Siṃha. She overheard his philosophical expositions and began to weep. "Why dost thou weep", questioned the Buddhist leader. "Hast thou mercy upon me" replied the queen, "and let me serve thee". But the Brahmins were loath to tolerate the ascendancy of Vīra Siṃha. Forthwith they repaired to the king's palace and reported, "There is a Buddhist Brahmin, heterodox in his conduct. The chief queen hath received religious instruction from such a person. Hearing this, the king became angry. He reprimanded his wife for her action but Pādmavatī held her ground.[280]

Eventually Vīrasiṃha yielded to the spiritual power of Caitanya, acknowledging him as the embodiment of the Buddha and casting himself at the feet of the Master.[281] Pratāparudra's persecution against the Buddhists makes sense only assuming that there were Buddhist groups that could still stir social protest locally, although religious hatred can explain the suppression of even insignificant minorities when new-formed élites are anxious to establish their power, as was the case of the Caitanya brāhmaṇas.

Jayānanda Dāsa's *Caitanyamaṅgala* provides evidence of the uprooting of the Buddhists (called *yavana*-s) living in the Piralya village in Navadvīpa/Nabadwip, the 'nine islands' on the Hooghly to the north of Kolkata where Caitanya's birthplace, Minapur/Mayapur, is located. Such a piece of information probably represents only the tip of the iceberg of what happened in Bengal.[282]

Nagendranath Vasu made an interesting attempt at identifying the social identity of the sixteenth-century Buddhists of Mayurbhanj, pointing to the Bāthuris (or Bāhuris/Bāuris, or Bātulas) as the 'tribals' who, in consequence of Pratāparudra's blow, took refuge in the impregnable hilly part of the region and slowly gave up their ancient beliefs adapting themselves to the new religious reality.[283] The images found at Similipal and Adipurgarh, where they ruled, include Prajñāpāramitā and Aśokāntā Mārīcī, and a *Bātula Mahātantra* has been attributed to them.[284] They were legitimised to represent their former Buddhist kinfolk thanks to a compromise with the orthodox sanctioned by a myth based on a pun between *śaṅkha* (Viṣṇu's weapon) and *saṃgha*. Viṣṇu killed Saṃghāsura but gave the *śaṅkha* to the elder member of the community to the detriment of those who had opposed his intervention.[285]

Although Mukundadeva (AD 1560-68), the last independent king of Orissa,[286] seems to have supported the Buddhists who were still living in his territories,[287] the game was up. By fair means or foul, the social groups left without a voice were incorporated into the main stream of Brahmanical India. In Bengal, two thousand five hundred *bhikṣu*-s and *bhikṣuṇī*-s assembled at Khaddaha/Khardaha, now in the northern periphery of Kolkata, surrendered themselves to Vīracandra Prabhu, a disciple of Caitanya's.[288] The contemptuous title of *naḍā naḍau*, 'the shaved couple', reserved to them, was later applied to the lower members of Vishnuite society, the so-called Sahajīyā Vaiṣṇavas,[289] 'converted' from Buddhism.

The process leading to the forced merging of the Buddhists into the hegemonic neo-Visnuism of Bengal and Orissa is outside the scope of this work, which aims only at documenting how even the final dissolution of Buddhism in the sixteenth century was not a 'natural' phenomenon, but a process largely conditioned by political pressure and religious violence. Haraprasad Shastri, one of those Bengali intellectuals who knew a number of texts little known or little utilised by Indologists,[290] maintained that the brāhmaṇas were not slow to take advantage of the fact that for the Muslims all the Indians were 'Hindus', making it appear 'that the Buddhists did not exist'.[291] As had happened in Magadha, '[a]ll the intellectual followers of Buddhism were either massacred or compelled to fly away from the country.'[292] The Dharmites, or followers of the Dharma cult, were persecuted by caste Hindus and used to rejoice when the latter were abused by the Muslims: these had been sent by the Lord to save the Dharmites of Bengal from the hands of the orthodox.[293]

A considerable proportion of the people who had found representation in Buddhism turned to Islam. I can make my own the words of Ambedkar quoted in Chapter I, even though I do not believe in the social thaumaturgic power of Islam. It is not by chance that in modern, undivided India, the majority of the Muslims were concentrated in those regions where the process of brahmanisation had not been completed by the time of the Muslim conquest: the West and the North-East.[294] The recent historiographic trend according to which the Muslim conquest brought little or no change in the structure of Indian society, though partly justified by the recurrent claim that all the evils of India arise from Islam and, conversely, that Islam was an instrument of social redemption and justice, tends to project the past into the boundaries of the present-day Republic of India. The Muslim conquest remains an epoch-making event, which irreversibly transformed a relevant part of the Indian world: towns were founded or reshaped – from Peshawar to Delhi – whose very layout unmistakably associates them to the Muslim oecumene, and in the west the peasant population was to follow. Only in Bengal could the Vishnuites contain the phenomenon of the shift of the population towards Islam by adopting a *Realpolitik* that reversed many of the principles advocated by the Vishnuite religious élite for centuries.

In the sixteenth century, the process of assimilation, by either the Hindus or the Muslims, came to a successful end. It was up to the British, a couple of centuries later, to catch the echo of still recent events and start unearthing the relics of a deceased world. Of Indian Buddhism, otherwise, we would have said that *etiam periere ruinae*.

NOTES

1. The most spectacular among the late monasteries of Bengal is Paharpur/Somapura in Bangladesh excavated by K.N. Dikshit (1938); below in this chapter we will discuss some evidence regarding Nālandā, Odantapurī and Vikramaśīla.

2. The fascination with Newār organisation of society and with rituals have caused a number of studies to be written in the last few decades. Toffin (1984) and Lienhard (e.g. 1989) have provided many useful insights. A comprehensive study is that of Gellner (1992; also 2001: 106-33), and Locke (1985) provides much precious information on the structure and nature of Newār Buddhism; Locke (1980), though mainly focused on the cult of Avalokiteśvara-Matsyendranāth, is also recommended.
3. Locke (1985: 6, 483-84) has also reacted against the 'semantic or theological bias' of most modern writers as regards *vihāra* as a term and as an institution in Newār Buddhism, which constitutes a real *saṃgha.*
4. *History of Nepal* b: 39.
5. H. Shastri in Vasu (1911: 19). Shastri further observed that since not all the descendants of the married clergy could find sufficient work as priests, they took 'to such arts and callings as would bring respectable wages without hard manual labour', and were now goldsmiths, carpenters and painters. See also Lévi (1905-8, I: 226).
6. 'J'ai fait des bouddhistes du Népal une triste expérience. De la rue je vois ou j'entrevois par la porte basse, dans la cour rectangulaire d'une maison, une façon de stûpa. C'est ici un vihâra, cela promets des pandits, des moines, une bibliothèque. Allez-y voir. Les vihâras d'ici servent de logement à des pères de famille entourés de leur progéniture et qui y exercent un métier ou n'y font rien du tout. Ils ne savent rien que les seuls noms des neuf *dharmas* népalais. [...] Le bouddhisme se meurt ici ; stûpas et çaityas se rencontrent partout encore, mais à l'intérieur de la ville ils sont abandonnés et à demi ruinés' (ibid.: II: 325). (I had a sad experience of the Buddhists of Nepal. From the street, I see or perceive through the low door, in the rectangular courtyard of a house, the form of a stūpa. There is a vihāra here, and this for me means pundits, monks, and a library. Let us go and see. But here the vihāras serve the purpose of accommodating family men surrounded by their offspring and there carrying out their job, or doing nothing at all. All they know are the names of the nine Nepalese *dharmas*. [. . .] Buddhism is dying here; stūpas and caityas are still everywhere, but inside the city they are abandoned and half ruined). Cf. ibid. It is not clear why Lévi expected a doctrinal discussion from the residents of a *bahī* he had just caught a glimpse of, his conceitedness becoming open racism in the following lines on the Tibetans, and yet the sense of abandonment and desolation conveyed by his description sounds convincing.
7. *Tāranātha*: 117B-119A (pp. 301-02). That Ratnavajra was the son of Haribhadra is disputed (Naudou 1980: 168).
8. *Tāranātha*: 118B-119A (p. 302).
9. *dPag bsam ljon bzang*: I.119 (Index: xlvii).
10. Ibid.: I.98 (Index: cxxxiv).
11. H. Shastri (1911: 4).
12. Ibid.: 13.

13. Ibid.: 15.
14. Ibid.: 18.
15. Ibid.: 3-4.
16. Majumdar (1943: 579 ff.).
17. Cf. Dwivedi & al. (2005-06).
18. The reader will find the evidence regarding the surviving Buddhist communities in the south and in other Indian regions in R.C. Mitra (1981).
19. *IA* 18 (1889, J.F. Fleet): 270-75, ll. 18-19. Cf. R.C. Mitra (1981: 108).
20. *EC* 7/1 (Shimoga district 1): 112, 197-98. B. Lewis Rice saw the temple site, from where he retrieved the image of Tārā (ibid.: 20 and pl. between pp. 20-21 in the Introduction). See other Buddhist images (Belgami, nos. 72, 77-79) at http://dsal.uchicago.edu/images/aiis/aiis_search.html?depth=Get+Details&id=18278
21. Cf. R.C. Mitra (1981: 116).
22. *IA* 10 (1881, J.F. Fleet): 19-21. Fleet translates 'bhikshugaḷ' with 'religious mendicants'; he probably explains too much, assuming that *bhikṣu*-s must necessarily have been mendicant monks.
23. Ibid.: 22-25.
24. Tucci (1971, II: 310).
25. Ramaswamy Ayyangar & Seshagiri Rao (1922, I: 31).
26. See Granoff (2000) for a plurality of literary examples on their position as an oppressed religious minority.
27. This sketchy reconstruction of later Jain history follows Jaini (1979: 285 ff.) and takes into account the contributions of a few other scholars cited below. A detailed knowledge of the events as they progressed over time and of the transformation of medieval Jainism will be available only when learned Jains resolve to disclose that portion of Jain history that is still in darkness.
28. An early nineteenth-century report on Jain customs written by Alexander Walker, attests to the fact that in Gujarat the 'Shrimala Bramans' performing the marriage rites for the Jains, also performed 'the ceremonies of Shrad for the Shravacas who employ them' (Bender 1976: 119).
29. *EC* 1 (*Coorg Inscriptions*): no. 2 from Biliur (pp. 52-53, 31), no. 4 from Peggur (pp. 53, 32). The reference is to the revised edition of the work due to B.L. Rice, corresponding to ASI, New Imperial Series 39 (Madras 1914).
30. H.H. Wilson, as we have seen in Chapter I, noted that the overthrow of the Buddhists coincided with the highest pitch of power and prosperity attained by the Jains.
31. According to HCIP 5: 434, Vāgbhaṭa wrote his *Neminirvāṇa* at the time and under the protection of this king, who reigned between AD 1015 and 1043. Vāgbhaṭa writes that there are only three gems in the world, namely, Aṇahilapura city, King Jayasiṃhadeva, and his Śrīkalaśa elephant.
32. R.C. Mitra (1981: 113-14); the references are to *EC* 7 (Shimoga district, AD 1036 inscription), *EC* 5 (Hassan district, AD 1136 inscription), *EC* 8 (for

the two inscriptions of AD 1077, Shimoga district), *EC* 6 (Kadur district, AD 1129 inscription), *EC* 2 (Sravana Belgola, first and rev. ed.). Mudigere is located near Chikmagalur. Agastya is the mythical missioner and coloniser of the regions located to the south of the Vindhyas identified with the Vedic seer.

33. Sanghavi (1980: 320); Dundas (2002: 123-24).
34. Sanghavi (1980: 99). On the function of the *upādhyāya*-s as teachers and their position in the hierarchy see *EJ* 5: 1173; 21: 5668 (what interests us here is touched upon only indirectly).
35. The adoption of an inclusive paradigm still prevents clarity on a number of crucial questions. P. Dundas writes, for instance, that '[. . .] we may discover that, on closer examination, categories and reifications such as 'Jainism' and 'Hinduism' melt away and, in the end, we find ourselves confronting a socio-religious continuum which can only be described as 'South Asian' (*EJ* 6: 1534).
36. Atīśa maintained that Tantric practices were incompatible with *brahmacarya*, and therefore also with the life of the *bhikṣu*-s, and acted accordingly (cf. *Atīśa New Biography* 49, p. 427). This is probably to be read against the background of the canonisation of Tibetan Buddhism and of the marginalisation of the old schools whose scriptures lacked the legitimacy traced to Indian Sanskrit texts. Davidson (2005: 108 ff.) has questioned the extent of Atīśa's influence in Tibet, especially from the mid-eleventh century onwards.
37. Snellgrove (1987: 397). On other non-celibate priestly lineages in Tibet, see Samuel (1995: esp. 288-89).
38. Conze (1983). The book was first published in 1962.
39. The rational content of Tantric meditations – Conze contended – is negligible; Tantric texts are written in a code and cannot be understood in the absence of the *guru*; the secretness of the doctrines is an impassable barrier; finally, with the *tantra*-s, 'the tribal imaginations of the Hindu race re-assert themselves', and only a thorough knowledge of the Brahmanical scriptures would allow us to understand the mythological figures occurring everywhere (ibid.: 270-73).
40. Above, Chapter II. Going back to times earlier than Conze's, it is to be regretted that the history of India has mostly been written by English scholars adhering to the upper class ideology of their country and by brāhmaṇas. The moral code of both brāhmaṇas and Englishmen as regards the universe of sex was the least appropriate to give an unprejudiced appraisal of the social behaviour, past and present, of the classes escaping Brahmanical control. I will not dwell upon English prudery (half true, half imaginary), since the literature existing on the subject is redundant. From people who thought or let others believe that crossing the Channel was a plunge into sin we could not expect a trustworthy description of the habits of Indian lower social groups. The English, we read in the records, often deemed the brāhmaṇas oleaginous, deceitful and greedy, but beyond criticism as far as sexual moral

was concerned. Scholars like H.H. Wilson and M. Monier-Williams, on behalf of their religious convictions, not only censored the Indian life of their time, but India past. Wilson's reaction to B.H. Hodgson's reports from Kathmandu and his final verdict on degenerated Buddhism (Chapter I) mirrors his fears not less than his disgust for the behaviour of English lower classes, whose members would not have been shocked at all crossing the Channel. The creation of 'Tantrism', a term implying reprehensible sexual behaviour, took place in this cultural context.

41. A major work remains R.C. Sharma (1980), but it does not cover the middle age.
42. Archaeological finds in India often tell an entirely different story than that narrated in the texts, and it is extremely difficult to make the two types of sources meet. The finds consist mainly of small terracotta objects, some cultic (animal figurines, for instance) and others pertaining to the sphere of the relations of production (the so-called 'pottery discs', the counters made out of reworked potsherds in the shape of geometrical figures, etc.). The former have not been studied as components of complex assemblages, and so their meaning escapes us (see an attempt at interpreting them in Verardi (2007: 192 ff.); as regards the latter, see the author's discussion in ibid.: 235 ff.).
43 As for the medieval monuments restored by the Archaeological Survey, they convey a sense of unreality, set as they are in luscious gardens strongly contrasting with the present and, presumably, past human landscape, standing out in a fabulous, a-historical perspective trimming down cultural differences and cancelling contexts.
44. In Graeco-Roman antiquity slavery was generally considered an accidental and not a natural condition, a notable exception being Aristotle (see Ellen Meiskins Wood in Settis: 618). Slaves were by no means untouchables. Even in Sparta, the helots, who were the physical target of Spartan warring aristocrats, enjoyed some rights and were freed on occasions (Spartans lived in constant terror of helot uprisings, however; Baltrusch 2002: 30; Ducat 1990: 129 ff. for the Helots' revolts). For the Roman world, I refer the reader to Bradley (1989) and Grünewald (1999), but a vast, specific literature exists on Spartacus (who in modern Europe became a symbol of resistance and social redemption even before Karl Marx). The revolt led by him against the Roman Republic involved the uprising of peasants and of the slaves-shepherds of the Apennines. Cohn (2006) provides a panorama of the revolts in medieval Europe, including the radical, sub-proletarian revolt of the Ciompi in fourteenth-century Florence.
45. This construct owes much, I think, to Ashok Rudra, who at the end of a paper in which he criticised the very concept of Indian feudalism, interpreted the history of medieval India as being characterised by ideology rather than violence (Rudra 1981: 2144-5). I would suggest that it was characterised by both.

46. See e.g. Eaton (2009: 193 ff.). One of Eaton's polemical targets is what he calls the Protestant vision underlying the concept of conversion. While it is true that the history of India has been and is mostly written by Protestant scholars, the concept of 'conversion' is much older than any Protestant reform movement, being at the very root of Christianity (St. Paul).
47. For the difficulties met in defining the Kaivartas historically see Dutt (1933: 533-34).
48. *Rāmacarita*: II, 39-42 and Haraprasad Shastri's introduction, pp. 13-14. The name of the 'capital' of the rebels was Ḍamara, corresponding to present-day Damarnagar (cf. R.D. Banerji 1915: 91). The revolt has been discussed by R.S. Sharma (1965: 268; 1988: 9 ff.) and Maitreya (1987: passim). This author has highlighted the dense presence of hidden references and allusions present in the *Rāmacarita*, a difficult text (when understood, they help to decrypt the relevant epigraphic material); hence a reasoned criticism of Sastri's pioneer work (36 ff., 46 ff.). The text of the *Rāmacarita* has been edited several times (see e.g. the edition provided by R.C. Majumdar, R. Basak & N. Banerji (*Rāmacarita śrīsandhyākaranandinviracitam*, Varendra Research Museum, Rajshahi 1939), and Radhagovinda Basak's revision (and translation) of Haraprasad Sastri's edition, Calcutta 1969. A recent work, which I have been unable to see before handing over the manuscript to the publisher, is Sylvain Brocquet, *La geste de Rāma : poème à double sens de Sandhyākaranandin (Introduction, texte, traduction, analyses)*, Collection Indologie 110. Institut Français d'Indologie-EFEO. Pondichéry 2010.
49. R.S. Sharma (1988: 9); Maitreya (1987: esp. 37, n. 1; 46).
50. R.S. Sharma (1988: 156). Bengal-Bihar was split up into about ten principalities at the time of the Kaivarta revolt.
51. See the examples given in ibid.
52. For the Vīraśaivas, the reader is referred to E.P. Rice (1921: 52 ff.), Schouten (1991), on which see the detailed, perhaps too severe review by Zydenbos (1997), and Nandi (2000).
53. I take this list from V. Narayana Rao and G.H. Roghair's introduction to the translation of the *Basavapurāṇamu* (p. 9), where these people act as protagonists.
54. Schouten (1991: 39-41).
55. Basava was the brāhmaṇa prime minister of the Kalacuri king Bijjala, a supporter of the Jains, who ascended the throne in AD 1156. In the *Basavapurāṇamu*, a Telugu work of the thirteenth century written by the Vīraśaiva devotee Pālkuriki Somanātha, a convert from Buddhism, Sāṅkhyatoṇḍa, complains of having been born in a polluted house (that of his Buddhist parents) and wishes Śiva to destroy 'the three antivedic traditions, Jaina, Buddhist and Cārvāka', something that eventually becomes true (*Basavapurāṇamu*: VI, pp. 205-6). That the story derives from the *Periya Purāṇam* (39, 3639 ff.; cf. vol. 2, pp. 339 ff.), where the name of the devotee is, signifi-

cantly, Cākkiyaṉār, adds to the evident brahmanisation of the text. On the brahmanisation of Vīraśaivism, see the introduction to *Basavapurāṇamu*, pp. 15 ff. and Schouten (1991: 40 ff.). Nandi (2000: 470) contends that it would be naïve to suppose that the Vīraśaivas and the Jains, expressions of the same class of traders and merchants, 'attacked one another merely from a sense of religious rivalry', but religious identity was, and is, a powerful means of division and hatred when duly channelled, irrespective of class identity. For the forced conversion from Jainism to Vīraśaivism, see Zydenbos (1997: 530).

56. *ASIAR* 1929-30 (Hirananda Sastri): 171. The destroyed *samaya*-s were at Pariyaḷige, Aṇiḷevāḍa (Anhilvad in Gujarat), Uṇukallu (Unkal, in the suburbs of Hubli), Sampagāḍi (Sampagaon in Belgaum district), Ibbalūru (Ablur in Dharwar district?), Māruḍige (Maradigi, Dharwar), Aṇampūr (Alampur, near Kurnool), Karahāḍa (Karad, Satara district), Kembhāvi and Bammakūṛu.
57. See Ablur Inscription E (*c.* AD 1200) in *EI* 5 (1898-99, J.F. Fleet): 237-60, cf. ll. 43-50.
58. Cf. Hiremath (1994: 89), who mentions (without giving any reference) a Kannada version of this Telugu work.
59. *Sekoddeśa*: 135, 138-39 (pp. 146-47); cf. *Nāropā*: pp. 124-25.
60. For a tradition regarding the early origin of the blue robes in connection to the moral lassitude of a Saṃmitīya monk, see Sâṅkṛtyâyana (1934: 216).
61. Ruegg (1981: 221-22). The *Purātanaprabandha Saṃgraha*, cited as evidence by Ruegg, is a thirteenth-century work according to which it was Bhoja, king of Mālavā, and not Śaṅkaravarman of Kashmir, who expelled and killed the Nīlāpaṭas (as they are called in this text). When they were asked if they were hale and hearty, they replied, 'How can a wearer of blue clothes be happy unless all the inmates of the world are turned into women, all the mountains are turned into heaps of meat and all the rivers are turned into currents of wine' (Prakash 1965: 319). They claimed to act as Ardhanārīśvara, and when Bhoja's daughter asked for advise, they told her to eat and drink, since 'the past never returns', the body being 'a mere aggregate of elements' (ibid.).
62. Cf. Ruegg (1981).
63. The *Kālacakra* cycle was developed in north-western India, as testified by Bhadrabodhi (cf. Gnoli in *Nāropā*: 15); on its structural link with the *Guyhasamāja Tantra*, see Tucci (1971*b*, II: 339).
64. K.N. Dikshit (1938: 55; pl. XXXVIIIc); Saraswati (1977: LXII; fig. 175).
65. D. Mitra (1997-98: 381-82; fig. 1 on p. 391). See also the fragmentary image of Hevajra and consort from eastern India now in the Newark Museum (Linrothe 1999: 270).
66. Ibid.: 288.
67. Bronze images were usually melted down, and those that have reached us are mainly from hoards (Kurkihar in Bihar, Achutrajpur in Orissa, and a few others).

68. *Caturaśītisiddhapravṛtti*: 96-97.
69. Ibid.: 29.
70. Ibid.: 24.
71. Ibid.: 122.
72. Ibid.: 211-12.
73. Ibid.: 257.
74. Ibid.: 106-07.
75. Ibid.: 94-95.
76. The weaver Kāṇhapa buys food and wine for five pennies; Nāropa's family is one of wine-sellers; 'Have you been drinking wine?' asks the *guru* to a servant; etc. (ibid.: 83, 93 and 229, respectively).
77. Ibid.: 131-33.
78. Ibid.: 163.
79. Ibid.: 34.
80. Schouten (1991: 42-43).
81. Davidson (2002: 171). Davidson's chapter on 'Siddhas and the "Religious Landscape"' (pp. 169 ff.) is a strongly recommended reading. Here and there, as already done in the preceding chapter, we are complementing Davidson's book with some extra information.
82. Davidson (2002: 203 ff.).
83. There are analogies with the case of the Buddhist and Upaniṣadic ascetics, on whose alleged similarities see Chapter II.
84. *Upapurāṇa*-s, I: 324-25. I have corrected a misprint in 14.60. Then, the early warnings against socialising with Buddhist people are reiterated: 'The Bauddhas are called Pāsaṇḍins, because they decry the Vedas. So, a twice-born man, if he has (any) regard for the Vedas, must not look at them. (One acquires sin), in case one enters the house of a Bauddha knowingly or unknowingly. There is no escape (from sin), (if one does so) knowingly. This is the decision of Śāstras' [14.69-71] (ibid.: 326-27).
85. Ibid, II: 488-89, 550.
86. *Bṛhannāradīya Purāṇa*: III.19, in ibid., II: 550-51.
87. *Narottama Vilāsa*: VII (Sen 1911, II: 412, with Bengali text). An English version of the poem by Dravida Das is available at the website http://www.salagram.net/parishad7.htm
88. H. Shastri (1911: 11).
89. The reader is referred to Lambrick (1973: 136 ff.; 155 ff.).
90. *Xiyuji* a: XI (vol. 2: 272).
91. Maclean (1989: 6).
92. Lambrick (1973: 150-51).
93. Cf. N.A. Baloch's notes to *Fatḥnāma-yi Sind* a (p. 33).
94. Dani (1979: 58-59, 60-61) argues that they might be the same person; on a possible scribal error preventing us from clarifying the identity of Buddharakṣita see Maclean (1989: 51). Armābil is identified with Bela in Las Bela district (Baluchistan). In the conglomerate cliffs at Gondrani (Shahr-e Rogan),

15 km or so to the north north-west of Bela, there is a group of Buddhist caves, later transformed into dwellings, typically giving onto a river valley, the Purali Valley. They are mentioned in *Gazetteer Baluchistan* (p. 189). The ruler of this region was, according to the *Fatḥnāma-yi Sind*, a *šamanī*, perhaps the descendant of the governor of Harṣavardhana (Dani 1979: 60).

95. *Fatḥnāma-yi Sind* b: 33-34.
96. Ibid.: 34-35. Things went in an entirely different way, however; the monk not only had his life spared, but the brāhmaṇa had to comply with his requests. Questioned on his behaviour, Yayāti confessed that, sitting with the monk, he could see no signs of magic or jugglery, but that he had a horrible and ghastly apparition: 'Its eyes were fiery and full of anger, its lips thick, and its teeth pointed like spears. It had rods in its hands, sharp and piercing like a diamond (and it waved them), as if it was about to strike some person with them. I saw it and felt afraid, and I dared not speak to it so has to be heard by you' (ibid.: 36). The weapon held by the ghost is reminiscent of a *vajra*, and this, together with his behaviour, may point to the existence of some already developed means of defence.
97. *Fatḥnāma-yi Sind* b: 39.
98. Ibid.: 39-40. On Candra, cf. Lambrick (1973: 175-77).
99. F.A. Khan (1964: 53; pls. XVI B, XVII). On the mosque, see Ashfaque (1969). Banbhore/Debal is located to the east of Karachi, on the route to Thatta. On its identification with Debal, see Ghafur (1966).
100. All interest in the field of historical archaeology ceased in Sind in the early 1920s after the discovery of Harappa and Mohenjo Daro. Since then, but for a few sporadic studies, little or no attention has been paid to the early historical and medieval period.
101. The reader must still refer to Cousens (1929), but there are a number of chronological questions that are open. To give an example, Cousens dated the stūpa of Mirpur Khas to the fourth century (p. 96), but a late fifth century date for the panels that once decorated it is more reasonable (Huntington 1985: 205). Van Lohuizen-de Leeuw (1975: 162-64) attributed them to the sixth century.
102. Xuanzang states that at the time of his visit there were over thirty *deva* temples in Sind against several hundred monasteries with ten thousand monks (*Xiyuji* a: XI; vol. 2: 272).
103. Maclean (1989: 51); see below.
104. Dani (1979: 61-62).
105. According to al-Balādhurī, there was huge stūpa in Debal (ibid.: 63), and in this case, the identification of the ancient port town with Banbhore would be difficult, since no evidence of Buddhist monuments has come from the excavations. If al-Balādhurī is right, Buddharakṣita may have tried to protect an important Buddhist site. Dāhir wrote to Muḥammad b. Qāṣim: 'You have conquered a place which is the home of traders and artisans', not a strong

fort (ibid.: 62-63), and the *Fatḥnāma-yi Sind* associates traders and artisans with the Buddhists (ibid.: 57; see below).

106. Dani (1979: 62).
107. *Fatḥnāma-yi Sind* b: 92.
108. Cf. N.A. Baloch's notes to *Fatḥnāma-yi.Sind* a (p. 77).
109. Ibid.
110. Dani (1979: 64).
111. *Fatḥnāma-yi Sind* b: 93.
112. Ibid.
113. Dani (1979: 65).
114. Cf. Harbans Mukhia in *Tāranātha*: 442; *Ṭabakāt-i Nāṣirī*, I: 491.
115. *Fatḥnāma-yi Sind* b: 96-97.
116. Ibid.: 164.
117. *Fatḥnāma-yi Sind* b: 164. We will see below that other Muslim sources, too, describe the Buddhist monks as 'shaven-head Brahmans'.
118. Dani (1979: 66).
119. *Fatḥnāma-yi Sind* b: 167-68.
120. Ibid.: 169.
121. See the stūpa in this locality described by Cousens (1925: 98-99).
122. *Fatḥnāma-yi Sind* b: 173.
123. Maclean (1989: 51-52). Maclean subscribes to the hypothesis that the shaven-headed monks of Brahmaṇābād were brāhmaṇas, but I consider this interpretation unlikely.
124. Ibid.: 67.
125. Ibid.: 60.
126. Ibid.: 65.
127. Ibid.: 58.
128. Ibid.: 68.
129. Ibid.: 49-50. Yohanan Friedman (1977: 331-32) has interpreted the obligation imposed by 'Imrān b. Mūsā, appointed to the governorship of Sind in AD 835/36, on non-Muslim Jāts that they each be accompanied by a dog, as a way of humiliating *dhimmī*-s.There was the precedent of Muḥammad b. Qāṣim, who had confirmed that very obligation, introduced by the brāhmaṇa rulers.
130. Maclean (1989: 70 ff.).
131. The enthusiastic support given to Buddhism by the rulers of easternmost India as early as the end of the seventh century can be appreciated reading Yijing's description of Samataṭa and his king; cf. *Eminent Monks* b: 84-86. Only later, even in these regions their success started being undermined by the competition of the Arabs, who would gain the upper hand in the trade between India and China in the tenth century; cf. Sen (2003: 166-68).
132. The recurrent expeditions against the Buddhist kingdoms south of the Hindukush and the resistance of the latter, starting with the AD 656-57 campaign of 'Abd al-Raḥmān, who was the first to capture Kābul, are best

recounted in the *Tārikh-i Sīstān*: esp. 67 ff., 75 ff., 84 ff., 122 ff. Here we find the term *zunbīl*, a misreading of *rtby/eltäbir* used until recently.

133. See *Eminent Monks* b apropos of Xuan Zhao (p. 15).
134. On these groups of caves and the historical problems involved, see Verardi & Paparatti (2004).
135. Rehman (1979: 136ff.).
136. This is the latest possible date for the caves of Tapa Zaytun, planned on an unprecedented scale and left unfinished. AD 860 marks the beginning of the military operations of Yaq'ūb b. Laith, which in a very short time put an end to the uncertainties of two centuries of only partial successes of the Islamic forces in a large part of present-day Afghanistan.
137. Maclean (1989: 54).
138. Several finds from Buddhist Sind are datable to the ninth-tenth century (cf. van Lohuizen-de Leeuw 1975).
139. In previous occasions I have maintained that the sanctuary was abandoned on the arrival of Ibrahim b. Jibril in AD 795 cf. i.e. Verardi & Paparatti (2005: 441-42), but it is an assumption depending on the received paradigm that there were only two historical players in medieval North-West and that the Buddhists of eastern Afghanistan were driven away by the Muslims.
140. Prakash (1965: 215).
141. CHB II/1: 32.
142. Niyogi (1959: 200).
143. Ibid.: 203-4; cf. the list of the Gāhaḍavāla inscriptions, pp. 245 ff.
144. *Jiye*: 256.
145. *EI* 11 (1911-12, D.R. Sahni): 20-26.
146. *IA* 17 (1888, F. Kielhorn): 61-64; cf. l. 15-16; cf. Niyogi (1959: 258).
147. F. Kielhorn reports that William Hoey had found the inscription in the Jetavana mound, 'in the ruins of an essentially Buddhist building with monastic cells'. It is difficult to say what the building was like; in the inscription we read that the dwelling was *vihāravidhinā*, 'after the manner of convents'.
148. *EI* 9 (1907-8, S. Konow): 319-28, v. 20-23. On the meaning of v. 22-23, see discussion on p. 320.
149. Ibid.: 321.
150. Niyogi (1959: 199).
151. HCIP 5: 51.
152. *EI* 4 (1896-97, F. Kielhorn): 117-20, l. 19.
153. N. Sanyal (1929: cf. in particular ll. 7, 11; see also Niyogi 1959: 198, 210, 260). Śrīmitra (Mitrayogi or Jagan Mitrānanda) is the author of a letter (*Candrarājalekha*) addressed to Jayacandra (cf. Sâṅkṛtyâyana 1934: 227). His works were translated into Tibetan, where he is known as bsTan pa gsal ba'i sgron me.
154. Niyogi (1959: 198).
155. Prakash (1965: 196).

156. Ibid.: 198. Subhāgadevī came to greet the conqueror, but Shihāb al-Dīn 'despised her, spat on her face and handed her over to a man of low caste for being killed' (ibid.: 199; Prakash quotes a Prakrit work, the *Purātana-prabandha Saṃgraha*).
157. HCIP 5: 54.
158. CHB I/2: 272.
159. *Tāranātha*: 123B (p. 314). Magadha, for Tāranātha, naturally means south Bihar; Tirhut or Mithilā (North Bihar) is mentioned among the kingdoms where the number of *tīrthika*-s had increased.
160. Cf. Risley (1891, I: 377).
161. See Vedāntaśāstri (1956: 73).
162. H. Shastri (1911: 21-22). Vallālasena is reported to have been a follower of the Vajrayāna initially, and to have become a staunch Sivaite later in his life.
163. R. Sanyal (2008-9: 101).
164. Ibid.: 102.
165. *Tāranātha*: 125B (p. 319). According to other translations of this passage, King Candra acted 'with the help of some Bhikṣus, who were the king's messengers'; also, more explicitly, 'Some monks helped him acting as spy'. Cf. Prakash (1965: 203).
166. Cf. Sircar (1971: 303).
167. S.C. Sarkar (1942), quoted in Harbans Mukhia's note to *Tāranātha* (p. 444).
168. Prakash (1965: 203-4). Mukhia hesitates, wrongly I think, between Quṭb al-Dīn Aybak and Muḥammad Ghūrī (cf. *Tāranātha*: 442). The latter marched beyond the Panjab in 1190-91 and in 1192 his troops defeated Pṛthvīrāja III, who was put to death, thus laying the foundation of Muslim power in northern India.
169. These events are very well known, and I refer for brevity to Majumdar, Raychaudhuri & Datta (1967: 270-71).
170. Harbans Mukhia's note to *Tāranātha* (pp. 443-44).
171. *Tāranātha*: 125A (p. 318).
172. On the later Sena kings, see Majumdar (1943: 248-50).
173. For Lakṣmaṇasena's dates, I follow CHB II/1: 31.
174. Bakhtyār b. Khaljī conquered the Sena capital in Bengal in AD 1204 (Eaton 1993: 32-33), and Odantapurī was the first stronghold he took possession of. See below.
175. M.M. Ali (1406 H/1985, I A: 50).
176. Ibid.
177. M.M. Ali (ibid) maintains that Odantapurī was 'dominated by a Buddhist monastery'.
178. *Ṭabaqāt-i Nāṣirī*, I: 551-52. Lakhaṇavatī (Lakhnauti) corresponds to Gauḍa/Gaur and, *lato sensu*, to western Bengal.

179. *dPag bsam ljon bzang*: I. 92, quoted by Vidyabhusana (1920: 516). I read in the index under the heading 'Kakuta Sidha': 'While a religious sermon was being delivered in the temple that that he had erected in Nālanda, a few young monks threw washing water at two *Tirthika* beggars. The beggars being angry, set fire on the three shrines of Dharmagañja, the Buddhist University of Nālandā, viz. – Ratna Sāgara, Ratna Rañjaka including the nine-storeyed temple called Ratnodadhi which contained the library of sacred books' (Index: i).

180. The site is too large and complex to allow for even a simple presentation of the questions left open by the excavations carried out from the winter 1915-16 throughout the 1920s. The methodological flaws and the rush in bringing the ruins to light have seriously jeopardised the possibility to reassess the evidence. In no case the opinion should be accepted according to which in the twelfth century the monastic town was flourishing as it did between the seventh and the ninth century. Only Indian and British scholars, who have at their disposal all the documentation, are in a position to re-examine the evidence. Access to archives is limited for other scholars, and that to storehouses impossible. Excavations have been recently resumed in the area, with interesting result. See, for instance, Saran & al. (2008), who have identified the site of Juafardih with Kulika, the birthplace of Maudgalyāyana.

181. Deva & Agrawala (1950); see some of the images in B.N. Misra (1998, II: 71 ff.).

182. Patil (1963: 328). Several other scholars have made this observation.

183. A similar case is that of the Turkī and Hindū Ṣāhī marble production in south-eastern Afghanistan, which breaks completely and *pour cause* with the Buddhist coroplastic tradition.

184. Deva (1980: 83).

185. The best presentation of the phases of this building is by Page (1923: 8-13) and Ḳuraishī (1931: 70-77). J.A. Page and M. H. Ḳuraishī were superintendents of the Central Circle of the Archaeological Survey of India, and contributed with reports on the ongoing excavations in the *ASIAR* throughout the 1920s. Page was a conscientious archaeologist, well aware of the problems posed by the site's stratigraphy and periodisation. He was unable to tackle them because the documentation at his disposal when he took office was defective (Page 1923: 13-14). The earliest, brief excavation reports by D.B. Spooner were published by the Asiatic Society in Kolkata, and some others appeared in the *Annual Reports of the Archaeological Survey of India, Eastern and Central Circle*.

186. One of the main problems we face for understanding the stratigraphy of the site and, consequently, its chronology, is that the layers observed within each monastery and temple were not put in mutual relationship, the only partial exception being the 'Devapāla level', which is referred to in some

reports. The seventh-century temple is roughly contemporary with Ādityasena and the Aphsad temple near Wazirganj, east of Gayā, on which cf. Asher (1980: 53).

187. Sastri (1942: 28, 83). Sastri suggested that that the temple could be a Sūrya Temple (ibid.: 8, 83).
188. Ibid.
189. *ASIAR* 1921-22 (J.A. Page): 20 (Monastery I); 1922-23 (id.): 106-07. The circumstance that the remains of Nālandā were composed of 'a sequence of structures erected one upon the other after intervals of ruin and desertion' greatly complicated the measures taken for their preservation (*ASIAR* 1923-24, id: 23). No temporary preservation measures were taken at the time, and the restoration and partial reconstruction of the structures followed each excavation campaign. This prevented even conscientious archaeologists such as Page from re-examining the whole site at the very end of the work, which often came, as at Nālandā, after several years from the first campaign. Gathering up all the threads became impossible.
190. On Dharmasvāmin's testimony, see below in this section.
191. *Tāranātha*: 103B (p. 264). According to the Lama, the monastery was founded at the time of Gopāla (*c.* AD 750-70) or Devapāla.
192. Odantapurī served as a model for the construction of the bSam yas monastery, the first in Tibet. Odantapurī was famous for the initiation into the *Guhyasamāja Tantra*, and this may have created the tradition that it was founded 'from below'.
193. From the Guptas onwards, Indian dynasties did not have a real capital. The latter was one and the same thing with the seat of the Court, which was always on the move because of the continuous state of war. This state of affairs caused a number of 'capitals' to be built, though rarely recognisable as such.
194. Excavations have been in progress at Antichak, first identified with Vikramaśīla by Nundolal Dey (1909), since the early 1960s. From 1971-72 onwards the works, previously entrusted to the University of Patna, have been carried out by the Archaeological Survey of India. A comprehensive report of the excavations is lacking, (it is expected in 2011), and we must resort to the progress reports published on *IAR* from the 1971-72 to the 1981-82 issue.
195. Chaudhary (1978: 217-18); on Bakhtyār's Jharkhand route see also Majumdar (1943: 32, 223).
196. *IAR* 1974-75: 7. Cf. also Verma (2001: 304).
197. *IAR* 1971-72: 4.
198. Chaudhary (1978: 229-30). Others have continued to blame Bakhtyār-i Khaljī and the followers of Islam for it (Prasad 1987: 89-90). Even specialists of Muslim history of India, while rightly trying to restore the truth of facts, continue to mechanically accept the vulgate (cf. Eaton 2000: table 10.1).
199. Verma (2001, II: 303). Verma is reticent; from the one side, he maintains

that 'the destruction of the monastery was completed by a planned attack by some outer elements' – here he seems to point to the Senas of Bengal – and from the other recalls that the Tibetan sources report that 'the Turks destroyed the monastery and constructed a fort there' (pp. 303-04). The Tibetans (see Tāranātha above in the text) ended up accepting the manipulated version of the events provided by the *tīrthika*-s. A case like that of Odantapurī was probably not isolated and, once an understanding was reached with the orthodox, the Muslims had per force to contribute directly to the destruction of other sites.

200. *Tāranātha*: 120B (p. 306). This would have happened at the time of King Nayapāla (AD 1038-55), when the Pāla kingdom was indeed shaken to its very foundations (Majumdar 1943: 148), but not on account of the Muslims.
201. Ibid.: 121A (p. 307).
202. Ibid.
203. Ibid.: 127B (p. 328).
204. Ibid. Karṇa (*Karṇa) is a re-Sanskritisation of the Prakrit *Kannara* (Sircar 1971: 309), a term used for the Senas, whose origins were in Karnataka.
205. Ibid.: 128A (p. 328).
206. *Tāranātha*: 125B-126A (p. 320).
207. Prakash (1965: 211) is certainly wrong in identifying the *yogī*-s with the followers of Gorakhnāth and in considering them as connivers in the sack of the Buddhist establishments. Not on this evidence.
208. Dharmasvāmin: III (p. 57).
209. Ibid.: X (p. 91).
210. Ibid.: V (p. 64).
211. Ibid.: X (p. 94).
212. Ibid.: X (p. 93).
213. A.S. Altekar's introduction to *Dharmasvāmin*: xiv. Narasiṃhadeva used to go to Kanauj with his uncle Malladeva, and fought for Ghyāth al-Dīn after the death of Jayacandra (Chaudhary 1970: 238).
214. On these two philosophers see Vidyabhusana (1920: 133-47) and D. Bhattacharya (1987: 1-11 and passim and 143 ff., respectively). Mention has been made of Udayana in Chapter IV.
215. Thakur (1964: 125).
216. On the death year of Harisiṃhadeva, see Petech (1984: 115-16).
217. Cf. ibid. Thakur quotes a passage (p. 39) from the *Varṇaratnākara*, ed. S.K. Chatterji & B. Misra (Bibliotheca Indica 262), The Asiatic Society, Calcutta 1940.
218. This king, who succeeded Rāmasiṃha II on the throne of Mithilā, helped 'Alā-al-dīn in the momentous conquest of Ranthambor in Rajasthan, which fell in 1301 (Chaudhary (1970: 45; 243-45). Chaudhary's chronology of the Karṇāṭa kings has been corrected by Petech (1984: 207-12). Vidyāpati (*c.* 1352-1448) is the well-known poet and writer who gave a substantial

contribution to the development of the eastern Indian languages. He wrote the *Puruṣaparīkṣā* under the orders of King Śivasiṃha, mentioned above in the text. Chaudhary (1970: 230 ff.) has clarified the importance of this work as a source of history.

219. CHB, II/1: 377.
220. Chaudhary (1970: 71; 1976: 51).
221. Thakur (1964: 125-26). Thakur mentions the episode also in the first edition (1956) of his *History of Mithila* on p. 374, but has expunged it in the second revised edition of 1988, in keeping with his drawing near to nationalist, if not fundamentalist, positions. On Śivasiṃha, cf. Thakur (1988: 247 ff.); Chaudhary (1970: 72 ff.).
222. Cf. Chaudhary (1970: 75-76).
223. As recognised by some authors, though not with the necessary capacity to grasp the political importance of some of the information at our disposal; see e.g. K.L. Srivastava (1980: 136 ff.).
224. On the Senas of Pīṭhī, see Ray (1931-36, I: 383); R.C. Majumdar (1943: 259-61); CHB: I/2: 275.
225. Ray (1931-36, I: 383).
226. *Dharmasvāmin*: V (pp. 64-65); X (p. 90).
227. *IA* 48 (1919, N.G. Majumdar): 43-48. Some of the questions raised by the inscription have been discussed by Majumdar (1943: 259-60) and H.N. Ansari in CHB, II/1: 79-80, among others. We do not know which relationship existed between 'the Sena kings' and the *rājā*(-s) of Gayā; a certain Vanarāja held power in Gayā in 1268 (ibid. 78, and esp. note 131, pp. 101-2).
228. *Eminent Monks* b: 51.
229. Tournier (forth.) has shown that Mahānāman positions himself as the heir of a lineage devoted to the transmission of the teachings received from Mahākāśyapa.
230. Cunningham (1892: 42 ff. and pl. 20); Barua (1931-34, II: 32 ff.).
231. *Xiyuji* a: VIII (vol. 2: 133).
232. The inscription recording these events was first made known by Cunningham (1892: 78-79), and then re-edited by V.V. Vinavinoda (*EI* 12, 1913-14: 27-30, which includes the inscription of Aśokacalla's brother).
233. *Chos 'byung mkhas pa'i dga' ston*, II: p. 915, 14. The monk is reported to have stayed three years in Bodhgayā, to have gone back to Tibet and have returned to Bodhgayā; the episode is mentioned in relation to his second sojourn. I thank Christoph Cüppers for providing me with the translation of this passage.
234. On Ānandaśrī as translator, see Skilling (1993: 86 ff.).
235. Sangs rgyas grags 'was a [lineage-] holder of all *tantra* divisions. Since he had the highest realisation, his insight was even higher as that of [his teacher] Abhaya. He became the abbot of Bodhgayā and Nālendra and took great care there of students from Tibet. He himself translated the great commentary to the *Kālacakra* and gave instructions into it. In short, he was a Tibetan

who occupied the Dharma throne of Bodhgayā and his deeds for liberation are unconceivable [by us]' (Sangpo Khetsun 1973-90, IV: 280; thanks are due to Christoph Cüppers for providing me with the translation from the Tibetan). From the *Blue Annals* (X.39b-40a, vol. 2, p. 837) we know that he was one of the translators of the *Kālacakra*.

236. *Tāranātha*: 109A (p. 279).
237. Dharmasvāmin: V (pp. 73-74). The Tibetan monk takes revenge for this behaviour reporting the story of a Śrāvaka teacher who, being carried away by a river, resorted to Tārā, the bodhisattva invoked by the Mahāyānists to save people: duly invoked, Tārā appeared and saved him (ibid.: 75).
238. Ibid.: 73.
239. For Sarnath and Nālandā, see Saraswati (1977: LVIX-LX; figs. 171, 172); for Bengal, see Bhattasali (1929: 35-37; pl. XII).
240. On this goddess see especially Bhattasali (1929: 58-61); for her healing powers, see also M. Shaw (2006: 188-202).
241. Davidson (2002: 214).
242. See a similar, much earlier image from Ratnagiri published in D. Mitra (1981-83, II: 429-30; pl. CCCXXVIIIA, reproduced by Davidson 2002: 215, fig. 13).
243. The large fragment of a mid-twelfth century stele from Lakhi Sarai in Bangladesh depicting the enlightenment of the Buddha, vividly shows Cāmuṇḍā and Brahmā as members of Māra's army; Brahmā, as one of the 'four Māras', dominates the scene, running angrily away (Bautze-Picron 1996: 125-27, figs. 18-22).
244. The reader is referred to Bhattacharyya (1958: esp. 309 ff.), to whom the publication of both the *Niṣpaññayogāvalī* and the *Sādhanamālā* in the Gaekwad Oriental Series are due. Cf. also de Mallmann (1975: 136-37 for Cāṇḍālī; 159-60 for Ḍombī). The spectacular groups of sculptures photographed by Alexander von Staël-Holstein in winter 1926-27 in the Baoxianglu temple in the garden of the Cining Palace in the Forbidden City in Beijing and published by Clark (1937) best exemplify the *maṇḍala*-s and *sādhana*-s described in the texts. The circle of Gaurī is also mentioned in the *Hevajra Tantra* (I.viii.14), where Cāṇḍālī is given an important role (ibid.: I.i.31 and Snellgrove's comment in the Introduction, pp. 36-37).
245. Neither R.D. Banerjee (1930-31: 255-56; 258 ff.) nor Rajaguru (1968-72, I: 47 ff.) give any credit to this statement of the *Ṭabakāt-i Nāṣirī*: XX.viii (vol. 1, pp. 587-88), but they are probably wrong. On Anaṅgabhīma III, see Kulke (1993: 17-32).
246. M.M. Ali (1406 H/1985, I A: 244-46); Eaton (1993: 140-41).
247. P.K. Ray (1975: 52); Tripathy (1988: 53).
248. The evidence is found in Tripathy (1988). The flaws of the work and its lack of academic paraphernalia should not prevent scholars from considering it a useful source of information in certain cases. The Prachi Valley and the adjoining areas have been the object of a thorough survey by Donaldson

aimed at retrieving the architectural and iconographical evidence (see Donaldson 1985, esp. I: 371 ff. 438 ff.; II: 682 ff.; 2001: 79 ff.; 2002: esp. I, 138 ff., 163 ff.).

249. Sahu (1958: 215).
250. Donaldson (1985, I: 371).
251. Tripathy (1988: 297, 300). The identification of these structures as those pertaining to the Kuruma monastery, on which see D. Mitra (1978: 21, n. 2), is wrong. Cf. Donaldson (2001: 83).
252. Ibid.: 150.
253. Ibid.: 323-24. This temple has been described by Donaldson (1985, II: 682-83).
254. Ibid.: 323. Tāranātha knows him as Piṭo *ācārya* (*Tāranātha*: 113B, p. 289), the *Blue Annals* (X. 4*b*; vol. 2, p. 761) as Piṇḍopa. For more details, see the translator's note in *Tāranātha*, p. 289.
255. Donaldson (1985, I: 438-39) describes the images, datable to the late eleventh and twelfth century, now part of the modern brick structure.
256. On the Oriya and Sanskrit versions of this *māhātmya*, see Tripathy (1988: 1259 ff.).
257. Tripathy (1988: 402-03). The literary references to the *sudarśana cakra* can be found in W.E. Begley (1973: 7 ff., 23ff.). Donaldson (2002: 696) dates the Someśvara Temple to the eleventh century.
258. Tripathy (1988: 156). That the Buddhist deity raises his right hand in the attitude of administering a slap is doubtful.
259. Ibid.: 249. Tripathy considers the numerous Buddhist images observable at the site as belonging to the Bhaumakara period, but Donaldson (2001: 85) assigns the image of a crowned Buddha in the temple compound to the tenth century.
260. Tripathy (1988: 187-88). Further evidence comes from Kopari in Balasore district, whose ruins were seen in 1871 by John Beames: 'These ruins exhibit the traces of an ancient Buddhist temple, and *vihára* or monastery [...]. The Buddhist temple appears to have been destroyed and its materials used to erect a Brahmanical temple dedicated to Shiva [...]. Later than these supervened the present Vishnu worship, now the prevailing type of Hinduism in Orissa [. . .]'; see Beames (1871: 248). Cf. Pani (1988: 252).
261. See Mohapatra (1986, I: 99-102) for the other remains at the site.
262. Ibid.: I: 30-32; Panda (2007: 21-22).
263. Kulke (1993: 136-58, 159-91).
264. *Mādalāpāñji*: 34 (first *pāñji*).
265. Ibid.
266. Ibid.: 35 (third *pāñji*). The *Baḍa Deaula* is the temple of Jagannāth in Puri; on the Alāranātha temple at Brahmagiri, south-east of Puri, see Mohapatra (1986, I: 84-85).
267. Above in this chapter, and *Tāranātha*: 116B (p. 287), 118B (p. 301), 121A (p. 307); etc.
268. Tripathy (1988: 188).

269. Tripathy puts the painting in relation to the presence at Puri in the twelfth century of the four great Vishnuite saints Rāmānuja, Viṣṇusvāmi, Nimbārka and Mādhavācārya (ibid). The dates of Rāmānuja (*c.* 1077-1147) would fit the picture, as would the sojourn in Puri of Viṣṇusvāmi in the later decades of the twelfth century, when he established a *maṭha* (Rath 1987: 97-98). However, Mādhavācārya lived much later, and the chronology of Nimbārka is uncertain.
270. The question was raised by several authors in the nineteenth century (see e.g. R. Mitra 1975-80, II: 176 ff.), and has been entirely dropped by modern researchers. It certainly deserves to be discussed again.
271. I follow Dimock and Stewart in their introduction to *Caitanya Caritāmṛta* a: 26-32.
272. *Caitanya Caritāmṛta* b: II. 9. 47-63 (p. 106); the translator, Jadunath Sarkar, follows the Gauḍīya Maṭha edition (Calcutta 1926-27). The 'skeptics' of the text are the *pāṣaṇḍī*-s. I make use of Sarkar's translation because of the caveats at quoting long passages from the Harvard translation; the reader will find the passage in *Caitanya Caritāmṛta* a: Madhya Līlā, 9.40-57 (pp. 464-65).
273. Nagapattinam, as already seen (Chapter IV, n. 148), survived as a Buddhist site until the fifteenth century and beyond (cf. Ramachandran 1954: 18-19).
274. D. Mitra (1981-83, I: 41).
275. See Caitanya's life summarised by Sen (1911, I: 414 ff.); see also Dimock and Stewart in *Caitanya Caritāmṛta* a: 10 ff.
276. It is a Bengali work of the early seventeenth century, very important for the study of neo-Vishnuism. According to P. Mukherjee (1940: 87-89) Īśvara Dāsa 'shows a wonderful capacity of gathering information, however absurd they might be', but 'there is nevertheless a basis of hard fact in his statements'. The manuscript of his work is very rare, and Bibekananda Banerji, whom I thank for having tried to find for me a copy, was unable to find any, either in the library of the Asiatic Society or elsewhere in Kolkata.
277. Ibid.: 53; Mahtab (1947: 63-64).
278. P. Mukherjee (1940: 53); cf. also Mahtab (1947: 63-64) and Panigrahi (1981: 234). Banki is located in the Cuttack district, and there is still a thick forest to the south of it.
279. P. Mukherjee (1940: 62); Sahu (1958: 178-79).
280. P. Mukherjee (1940: 61).
281. Ibid.: 62, with reference to *Śūnya Saṃhitā* XI.
282. *Piralyā grāmete vasye yatek yavane | Ucchanna karilā Navadvīper brāhmaṇe* || (*Caitanyamaṅgala*: 14.11-12). Bibekananda Banerji kindly transliterated for me the text from Bengali. On the reliability of this work, see the different opinions of Sen (1911, I: 471-77) and P. Mukherjee (1940: 114-15).
283. Vasu (1911: cxvi ff.).

284. Ibid. cxxv, cxxxiv. Adipurgarh or Adipura corresponds to Edapura, where the queen of King Rāmapāla had a temple built for the *ācārya* Abhayākara Gupta (Sahu 1958: 170-71). Similipal (Vasu's Simlipala/Simlipada) must be a village in the Similipal hills of Mayurbhanj district.
285. Vasu (1911: cxx-cxxi). This is the interpretation I give of the rather confused evidence provided by the author.
286. On this king, see Banerjee (1930-31, I: 341 ff.); Panigrahi (1981: 182-84).
287. *dPag bsam ljon bzang*: I.123 (Index: lxxxxv); cf. Vasu (1911: cxxi-cxxii, clxv).
288. D.C. Sen (1917: 36). Sen reports an anecdote which makes us understand how strong, a century ago, still was the perception that the end of Buddhism was a recent and painful phenomenon: 'A distinguished European friend of mine once went to Khaddaha [...] to the place where these people had assembled, and referred to the spot as marking the death of Buddhism in Bengal; for here the last vestige of Buddhistic powers surrendered itself and was incorporated with Vaiṣṇavism' (ibid).
289. D.C. Sen (1911, I: 45).
290. They include the *Śūnya Purāṇa* and the *Dharmamaṅgala*-s.
291. H. Shastri (1911: 14).
292. Ibid.
293. Das Gupta (1969: 266).
294. The point is well understood by Eaton (2009: 194), who, however, draws wrong conclusions maintaining that 'having never been fully integrated into a Brahmin-ordered society, there was no logical way that peoples of these areas could have sought escape from an oppressive Hindu social order'. Of course, there was, since people knew very well what was going to happen to them with the establishment of *varṇāśramadharma*. Islam was little known, but was one way out. Eaton misses the point because he entangles himself in the piddling matter of what is conversion, what is religion, what is change (here, I think, there is a methodological problem): once one has accepted some of the strongly identifying features of Islam such as circumcision, one starts representing himself as a Muslim and *being* a Muslim (Hindus, or 'Hindus' if one prefers, will also consider you such). Naturally, grey areas exist, but they can be better explored resorting to the concept of subaltern culture. Subaltern classes have only partial access to the higher formulations of the systems of which they are part, hence their nebulous position at times. On the other hand, syncretism is the borrowing from another religion that the upper representatives of a given system consciously implement for political reasons; it is a typical operation from above.

APPENDICES

APPENDIX 1

The Brahmanical Temple of Bodhgayā

As is known, the Buddha attained Awakening under a pipal tree near Gayā. The site became sacred: a throne (the *vajrāsana*) was placed under the tree and a shrine (the *bodhighara* or Bodhi-tree shrine) was built around the tree and the throne. Later on, the *bodhighara* was replaced by a tall brick temple (Fig. 15), whose construction implied the uprooting of the tree. In the course of time, the brick temple underwent many alterations, until when, in 1880, underwent a complete

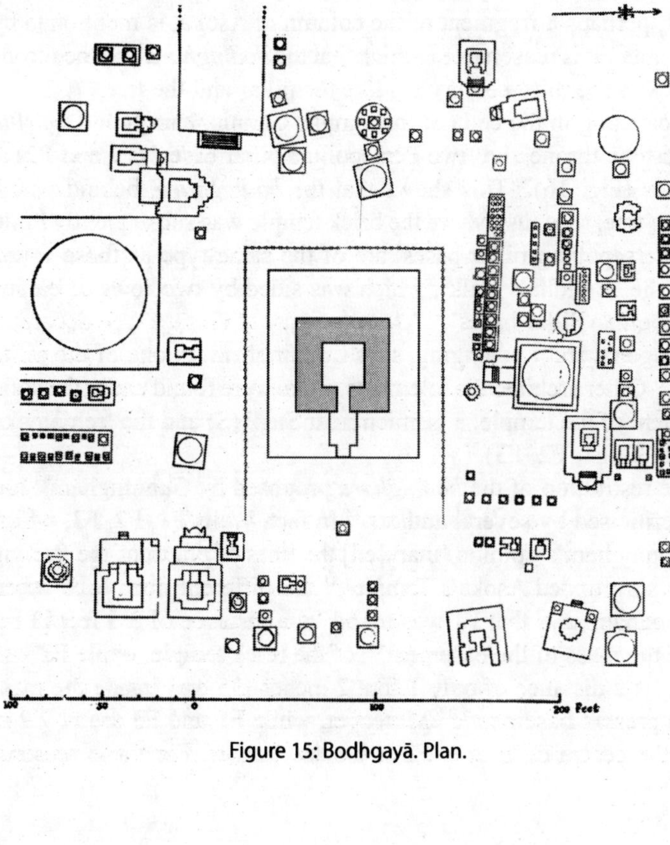

Figure 15: Bodhgayā. Plan.

restoration.[1] Despite the fact that the documentary evidence comes only from pre-1880 drawings and photographs[2] and from a limited number of descriptions and reports,[3] doubts can be raised on the answers given until now to these questions: when was the brick temple built? Why? By whom was it rebuilt and altered?

THE *BODHIGHARA*

The *bodhighara* is represented on the Prasenajit Pillar in the Bharhut railing:[4] the throne and the tree are surrounded by an open pavilion; outside, stands the Aśoka pillar, crowned by an elephant capital. Alexander Cunningham discovered some of these architectural features excavating the strata underlying the brick temple. A sandstone slab (V2 in Cunningham's plan),[5] found under the western buttresses of the building and attributed to the third century BC,[6] was, according to Cunningham, the cover-slab of the *vajrāsana.*[7] A 'replanted fragmentary pillar', perhaps a fragment of the column of Aśoka, is mentioned by S.P. Gupta.[8] It is reasonable to think that the *bodhighara* and the throne go back to the third century BC, like the pillar and the tree.

Excavating in the cella of the temple, Cunningham found, *in situ*, a sandstone throne and 'two Persepolitan pillar bases' (P1 and P2) at its sides (Fig. 16).[9] This shows that the *bodhighara*, behind which was the tree, rose just where the brick temple was subsequently built. The 'Persepolitan pillar bases' are of the same type as those found along the 'Buddha's walk', which was sided by two rows of eleven 'Persepolitan Pillar-bases'.[10] A female figure of Kuṣāṇa type decorates an octagonal shaft belonging, says Cunningham, to one of the pillar bases.[11] Other architectural elements *in situ* were found under the solid basement of the temple: a 'semicircular Step' (S) and the 'remains of old walls' (F1, F2, F3).[12]

The restitution of the *bodhighara* proposed by Cunningham[13] has been criticised by several authors.[14] In fact, Walls F1, F2, F3, which in Cunningham's opinion 'mark[ed] the lines of plinth of the Railing which surrounded Asoka's Temple',[15] are different from each other. Cunningham says that F1 was found 'at a distance of 3½ feet [1 m] inside the mass of the basement'[16] of the brick temple, while F2 was found 'at a distance of only 1 foot 2 inches [35 cm] inside the mass of the present basement'.[17] Moreover, while F1 and F3 are at 7.9 m from the centre of throne, F2 is located farther. For these reasons,

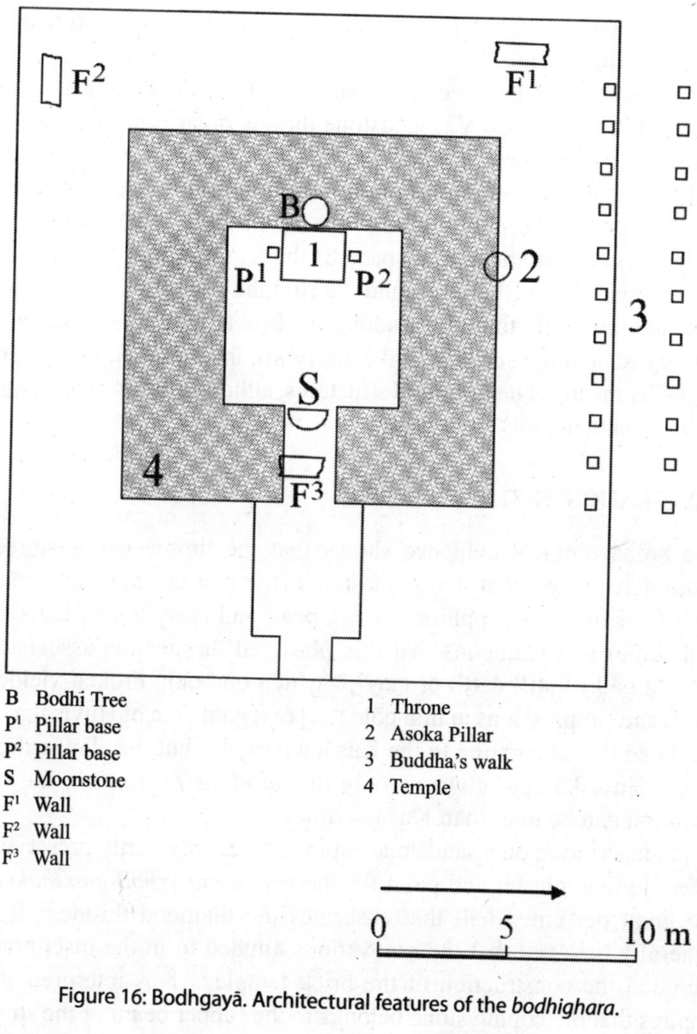

Figure 16: Bodhgayā. Architectural features of the *bodhighara*.

Walls F1, F2, F3 cannot be regarded as the plinths of one and the same railing.

The sandstone uprights and crossbars now visible, dated to the first centuries BC/AD, would have also pertained to the *bodhighara*.[18] However, they were not found in their original position, but were discovered in the veranda of the Mahant's residence, in the rubbish mounds in the vicinity of the site, or re-used in the railing built around the brick temple.[19] Therefore, we do not know to what structure they originally belonged.

The few other architectural elements of the *bodhighara* so far discovered (cover-slab V2, sandstone throne, pillar bases P1 and P2, Walls F1, F2, F3, step S, Buddha's walk) belong to different periods, and consequently the original plan of the shrine cannot be identified. The distance between the centre of the throne and the threshold stone (step S) is *c.* 6 m, the sacred space of the temple being thus at least 12 m^2 large. Walls F1, F2, F3 and the Buddha's walk are outside this area and are likely to be later additions. Probably, between the third century BC and the second-third century AD, the *bodhighara* was enlarged by means of new pillared structures, although the original layout of the sanctuary was preserved.

RESTORATION OF THE *BODHIGHARA*

The archaeological evidence shows that the throne was restored. Cunningham says that it was plastered (the plaster contained small fragments of coral, sapphire, crystal, pearl and ivory bound together with lime) and maintains that this plastered throne was associated with 'a ball of stiff earth or clay',[20] which on being broken yielded relics and 'impressions in thin gold [...] of a gold coin of Huvishka'.[21] He dated this restoration to the Kuṣāṇa period,[22] but the clay sealing of the Huviṣka coin gives us only the *terminus post quem*: the restoration can be later than Kuṣāṇa times.

An inscription on a sandstone coping stone, only partly preserved, refers to new plaster and paint for the *vajrāsana-vṛhad-gandhakuṭi*, the great perfumed hall that enshrines the diamond throne.[23] It is generally believed that the renovations alluded to in the inscription included the construction of the brick temple.[24] This interpretation implies that the coping stone belongs to the 'upper beam of the stone railing around the temple'.[25] However, its size does not correspond to that of the uprights of the railing,[26] and when the latter was set around the temple, a new floor was also laid where the coping stone was reused.[27] It is thus more plausible that the coping stone was an architectural feature associated with the *bodhighara* and that the inscription refers to the restoration of the tree-shrine, and not to the construction of a temple. Asher dates the inscription to the Gupta period,[28] and it is reasonable to think that the restoration of the *bodhighara* was realised in the fourth-fifth century and was carried out either by the monks from Laṅkā after king Meghavarṇa complied with the requests of Samudragupta and offered him precious stones to obtain permission for the monks to reside at Bodhgayā or by their successors.

THE BRICK TEMPLE

According to Cunningham, the restoration of the throne was contemporaneous with the construction of the brick temple. Myer, among others, has accepted Cunningham's opinion and maintains that 'it seems probable that the renovation and enlargement of the throne coincided with a drastic rebuilding which replaced the open pillared Bodhi-tree shrine with a tall tower-like structure, most likely of brick'.[29] Myer attributes the temple to the Kuṣāṇa period on the basis of the Kumrahar plaque, whose inscription in Kharoṣṭhī script was dated to the Kuṣāṇa epoch by Sten Konow.[30] According to Myer, '[w]hatever the identity of the temple represented on the plaque [. . .] it is probable that the Kushāna temple at Bodh-Gayā was of a very similar type'.[31] However, the temple is characterised by a very high corbelled, triangular opening or window above the door,[32] whereas the temple depicted on the plaque displays only a large, arched doorway, being thus smaller than the temple of Bodhgayā. Myer also resorts to the travelogue of Faxian for dating the temple to the Kuṣāṇa period, referring to the term 'tower' in Samuel Beal's translation.[33] But no mention is made of a temple-tower in the text: Faxian's towers are the stūpas that the pilgrim says were erected in memory of various events of the life of the Buddha.[34] Therefore, the temple was built *after* Faxian's visit in AD 404.

An important point is that the construction of the brick temple implied the removal of the Bodhi-tree and its separation from the throne (Fig. 17). How has this fact been explained? According to Malandra, the '[r]elocation of the tree may have not been problematic since [...] it was the *vajrasana* (adamantine or diamond seat), not the tree, that was intended to be the exact centre of the *bodhimanda*, place of the enlightenment'.[35] But is it really so? And was there really a throne in the cella of the temple?

When Cunningham excavated the cella of the temple, he identified four floors (Aśoka floor, plaster floor, sandstone floor, granite floor)

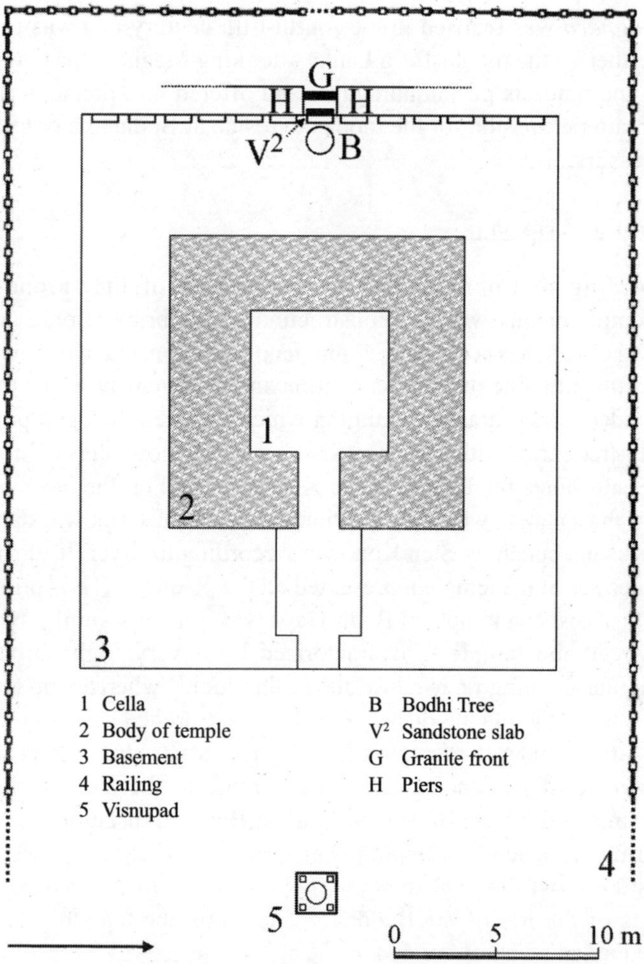

Figure 17: Bodhgayā. Schematic plan of Brahmanical Temple at the time of Vishnuite restoration.

and three thrones (from the bottom: sandstone throne, plastered throne, basalt throne).[36] In the section and prospect he published,[37] the sandstone throne rests upon the Aśoka floor of the *bodhighara* and the plastered throne rests upon the plaster floor. Cunningham believes that this plastered throne belongs to the brick temple, his opinion, not based on stratigraphic data, voicing the feeling that 'the plaster-faced Throne was lengthened at the northern end by 19 inches [48.26 cm] so as to place it exactly in the middle of the present Chamber' (i.e. the cella of the temple).[38] However, the size of the cella is not so certain. For Cunningham, 'the original cella of the Buddha Gaya temple was nearly square',[39] its side being '20 feet 4 inches [6.2 m]',[40] but Rajendrala Mitra says that 'repeated measurements showed the results to be different from what General Cunningham had arrived at'.[41] According to Mitra, the cella was 'originally a cube of about 22 feet [6.7 m]'.[42] It can be added that the *bodhighara* has a slightly south-eastern orientation, while the brick temple has an eastern orientation, and that the sandstone throne has the same orientation as the *bodhighara*.[43] The 'plaster-faced Throne' does not appear in any of the plans provided by Cunningham, nor, consequently, is its relationship with the cella of the temple clear. If the throne was simply re-plastered, it is reasonable to think that it kept the same orientation of the sandstone throne and that the re-plastering was part of the restoration of the *bodhighara* made in the fourth century.

What about the stratigraphical position of the sandstone floor? Cunningham says that when he removed the plaster facing of the plastered throne, he found the ball of clay with the relics resting 'on the upper plastered floor'[44] and 'just below the sandstone floor'.[45] Therefore, the sandstone floor is later than the plastered throne, and if it is, there was no throne associated with it, because the basalt throne (the last one) stood on the granite floor.[46] It would seem that there was no throne in the cella of the temple with which both the sandstone and the granite floors are associated until the basalt throne, a 'large pedestal of black basalt',[47] was installed.

The literary sources testify to the same fact. In his account of Bodhgayā, Xuanzang does not say that the *vajrāsana* was in the cella. He saw the tree behind the temple and the *vajrāsana* under the tree, within an enclosure:[48] inside the temple there was a statue of the Buddha, not a throne.[49] As is known, Xuanzang recounts how some time before his visit (probably around AD 600), King Śaśāṅka uprooted the tree and ordered the statue of the Buddha in the cella to be replaced by an image of Maheśvara. Here, too, no mention is made of a throne inside the temple: a statue was standing there instead. Myer tries to explain this fact saying that '[t]he builders of the new brick temple very probably made explicit the function of the altar as Throne or Buddha-seat by installing an actual image of the Buddha',[50] but there is the additional problem of the sandstone slab that Cunningham found outside the temple just where the tree must have been replanted (V^2 in Fig. 17). According to Myer, the cover-slab 'was removed from an earlier position, possibly within the old *Bodhi-garha*, and installed beneath the tree, where it served to complete the traditional relationship between Tree and Throne even though the altar-throne within the temple was identified as the true Vajrāsana'.[51]

This somewhat convoluted explanations show the difficulty in explaining actions that are actually incomprehensible: building a brick temple and uprooting a tree (presumably a very large one), replanting the tree in a rather awkward position behind the new building, placing the throne both under the tree and in the cella, installing a statue in the cella in order to explain the meaning of the throne, etc. The simplest of all questions has not been posed: why was a temple built? Why had it become necessary for the Buddhists to replace the *bodhighara* with a temple? Did they really build it? The question has not been posed because no one has questioned the nature of the temple. Was it really Buddhist?

We can reconstruct its shape on the basis of the plan published by Cunningham in 1871,[52] which is closer to the actual state of the temple before the restoration of 1880 than the two plans that Cunningham published later on. In the plan published in 1873,[53] there is a stairway in the south-east corner, which never existed.[54] In the plan published in 1892,[55] the temple is smaller and the railing is more distant from it: it is in the position it was given in 1880. In the 1892 plan, there are also the four-pillared portico and the four towers built in 1880. According to the 1871 plan, the basement had a width of about 23.7 m,[56] and the body of the temple was *c.* 14.3 × 14.3 m large.[57] According to Mitra, the square cella was *c.* 6.7 × 6.7 m.[58] The access to the cella was through a narrow room or corridor, preceded by a larger room. Cunningham says that there was also a portico, to which a 'facing was added to carry the vaulted arch'.[59] Since the doorway was also modified, we do not know how it was in the beginning.[60]

A building very similar to the temple of Bodhgayā is the temple of Bhitargaon, generally dated to the fifth century.[61] Its plan includes a porch, an *ardhamaṇḍapa* or ante-room, a passage and the sanctum. The sanctum (4.62 m^2) has a pointed ceiling, built of bricks laid in corbelled courses, the distance between its centre and the floor being 7.59 m. The body of the temple measures 10.74 × 12.43 m, and the *śikhara* is 9.81 m high.[62] The temple of Bhitargaon is Sivaite: the cella, accessed through a series of rooms, as is typical of Brahmanical temples, housed a *liṅga*. The temple of Bodhgayā is larger than that of Bhitargaon, but has the same plan. When was it built? Could have it been a Brahmanical temple in origin?

At the time of Xuanzang's visit (AD 637), the temple was in existence and, as reported by the pilgrim, it already existed at the time of Śaśāṅka at the beginning of the seventh century. Therefore, it must have been built between AD 405 (after Faxian) and AD 600 (before Śaśāṅka), during the same period that saw the construction of the temple of Bhitargaon. If the brick temple of Bodhgayā was originally a Brahmanical temple, we can explain why the throne was found outside it: the Buddhists, after taking again possession of Bodhgayā, replanted the tree behind the temple and placed the old cover-slab of the *vajrāsana* under the tree, on a new base.[63] They also adorned the western side of the basement with 13 niches where they installed Buddhist statues.[64] The reconversion of the temple also meant setting up an image of the Buddha in the cella.

At the beginning of the seventh century, Śaśāṅka did nothing else than re-establishing Śiva's worship in Bodhgayā, causing the tree to be cut and the image in the cella be replaced. At the time of Xuanzang's visit and under the Pāla dynasty,[65] the site was again under Buddhist control, although the discovery of a four-faced Mahādeva testifies that the Sivaites were again in Bodhgayā, at least for some time, in the late eighth century AD.[66]

THE VISHNUITE RESTORATION OF THE TEMPLE

A railing was set around the temple (Fig.17), made of uprights of different periods and materials: sandstone uprights of the first century BC/AD, an upright with a female figure of the Kuṣāṇa period[67] and many granite uprights dated to the fifth-sixth century AD. It is generally believed that the granite uprights were expressly made when the railing was set around the temple, as an addition to the old sandstone uprights, whose number was not sufficient to complete the circle,[68] and consequently the placing of the railing is dated to the fifth-sixth century AD.[69] Nevertheless, it seems illogical that the granite uprights were not made of the same size as the sandstone uprights and that, because of their different size, the railing was laid in a rather uneven way.[70] It is more probable that both the sandstone and the granite uprights were taken from the ruined monuments of Bodhgayā. A photograph published by Barua[71] shows one of the sandstone uprights whose decorated medallion was drilled to create the socket hole where a crossbar had to be inserted. This indicates that the railing was not set up by the Buddhists. It rather seems that it was set in place all around the temple to separate it from the large area crowded with Buddhist shrines and votive stūpas in order to create an empty space around the building (Fig. 15). Mitra maintains that the area between the railing and the temple was paved with bricks on the south, the west and the north, and with flags of granite on the east, and that it was 'perfectly clear'.[72] To the north and south, the railing is 4.5 m distant from the temple basement (1871 plan), but on the western side, it is at a distance of 4.5 m from Piers H and the granite front of squared stone G,[73] which cover the *vajrāsana* and the niches containing Buddhists sculptures (Fig. 17).[74] On the eastern side, the railing has not been traced. Here, the granite floor was found up to a distance of 10 m from the temple door.[75]

The granite floor, laid both in the cella and in the area in front of the temple, is made, in part, of architectural fragments from the *bodhighara*: for example, three sandstone 'coping stones'[76] and a 'Persepolitan base [. . .] placed upside down so as to present its broad flat bottom as a part of the pavement'.[77] A fourth coping stone of the same type as those reused in the granite floor was reutilised, 'split into two slabs',[78] in the roof of the pavilion which protects a stone bearing two footprints carved on its upper surface. Was it a Viṣṇupad or a Buddhapad? The first hypothesis is more credible because Cunningham explains that the 'round stone which formerly stood in front of the Temple with the feet of Vishnu sculptured on its face [. . .] was originally the hemispherical dome of a Stûpa'.[79] Mitra says that the pavilion 'was improvised with stones which originally belonged to other temples'[80] and that 'the foot-marks in question are of Hindu origin, and were put up by the Hindus to reduce the place and its old associations to the service of their creed'.[81]

The Viṣṇupad, the granite floor and the railing, made of re-used materials, were probably executed in the same period, to which the re-decoration of the *śikhara* is also attributable. The *śikhara* was also drastically remodelled, the new tower design being 'clearly related to the early Hindu temples',[82] something which shows that the 're-builders at Bodh-Gayā were working under strong Hindu influence'.[83] Believing that the restoration was a Buddhist work, Myer tries to explain this fact invoking 'a synthesis of strong local traditions [...] with current architectural tendencies'.[84] The re-use of Buddhist architectural fragments, betraying 'an element of hatred and vengeance'[85] (for example, re-utilising them in the floor or defacing their decoration) as at Sarnath and Vikramaśīla, shows instead that it was not carried out by the Buddhists.

Vishnuite and Sivaite sculptures have been found all over the site (Viṣṇu, Umāmaheśvara, Gaṇeśa, etc.).[86] They have been dated from the ninth to the eleventh century AD. The restoration goes probably back to this period, and much remains to investigate on the alternating hegemony exercised on the site by the Vishnuites and the Sivaites (see the stele with Cāmuṇḍā on the dead Buddha, Fig. 13, and the 'battle of Bodhgayā').

BURMESE MISSIONS

Before the restoration of 1880, there is evidence that the temple underwent other important changes, characterised by the use of basalt and vaulted structures. According to Cunningham, the use of basalt became common from the tenth-eleventh century onwards.[87] It was used on the western side of the temple, where a 'massive addition was made to the buttress, forming a great niche in the middle [...]. The west facing of this work formed a grand entrance of richly carved basalt'.[88] This is perhaps an attempt to re-establish the worship of the tree, rooted behind the temple. It was probably in this period that the basalt pedestal or throne was placed on the granite floor inside the cella.[89] The construction of vaulted structures is probably coeval.[90] According to Myer, vaults of this type are 'very common in Burma during the period of Pagān domination'.[91] In the cella, the walls supporting the vault stood on the granite floor, reducing the width of the cella to 3.9 m.[92] The basalt throne is exactly of the same size.

Mitra says that 'the vaulted roof of the first storey is levelled on the top, and made the floor of a second-storey room, which, like the first, is oblong and covered by a vaulted roof'.[93] The 'second-storey room' was reachable through a great vaulted porch,[94] in which two stairs on both sides led to a 'terrace', 4 m broad.[95] What was the use of the 'second-storey room'? According to Mitra, there was a brick throne similar to the basalt throne in the temple cella.[96] However, the 'second-storey room' was not reachable when Mitra visited the site, due to the collapse of the porch. Buchanan says that: '[s]everal of the people [...] remember the porch standing, and have frequently been in the chambers [...]. The middle chamber has a throne, but the image has been removed'.[97] According to Myer, it was not a room, but a 'broad vaulted arch projecting from the face of the tower [that] presumably formed part of a large niche or shallow chamber on the upper level'.[98] Climbing up to the terrace was necessary in order to reach the tree behind the temple.[99] Mitra explains that 'as earth and rubbish accumulated round the original tree, people from time to time built raised terraces and covered up its roots, so that the tree in a manner rose with the rise of the ground-level'.[100] When Cunningham visited the site, the terrace from which the tree sprung was at the same level as the upper floor of the temple.[101]

A Burmese inscription carved on a basalt slab dated to the eleventh or fourteenth century[102] records a restoration of the temple. Myer also recalls the '[t]ailing inscription' mentioning that 'King Kyanzittha (1048-1112), founder of the powerful dynasty ruling at Pagān, sent an embassy to Bodh-Gayā to rebuild the temple'.[103] The presence of Buddhist devotees at the site in the fourteenth century is perhaps witnessed by 'rudely carved figures kneeling in adoration after the manner of the Burmese *Shiko*'[104] carved on the granite floor 'both inside the temple and in the court-yard outside'.[105] These works may represent the last attempt to reconvert the temple to the Buddhist faith. After that, the site was abandoned, until it became property of the Sivaite Mahants.

NOTES

1. The temple was rebuilt on the basis of a stone model found by Cunningham during the excavation (Cunningham 1892: 25; pl. XVI).
2. Published by Losty (1991).
3. Buchanan (1936, I: esp. 149 ff.); R. Mitra (1864, 1878); *ASIR* 1 (A. Cunningham): 4-12; *ASIR* 3 (id.): 79-105; Cunningham (1892).
4. Cunningham (1879: pl. XIII, outer face).
5. Id. (1892: pl. XI).
6. Huntington (1985: 51).
7. Cunningham (1892: 19).
8. S.P. Gupta (1980: 26).

9. Cunningham (1892: 4-5, pl. II). According to Cunningham (ibid.: 19), the cover-slab found outside the temple was originally located on this throne.
10. Ibid.: 8-10.
11. Ibid.: pl. IV. For similar sculptures dated to the Kuṣāṇa period, see Asher & Spink (1989).
12. Cunningham (1892: pl. II).
13. Ibid.
14. Recently by Myer (1958: 280-81) and Malandra (1988: 14-16).
15. Cunningham (1892: 5).
16. Ibid.: 7.
17. Ibid.
18. Ibid.: 11; R. Mitra (1878: 72); Myer (1958: 288); Malandra (1988: 16).
19. R. Mitra (1878: 72-73).
20. Cunningham (1892: 20).
21. Ibid.
22. Ibid.: 21.
23. Malandra (1988: 17); see also, Cunningham (1892: 22-23); Barua (1931-34, II: 71); Myer (1958: 291).
24. Cunningham (1892: 22); Malandra (1988: 17); Myer (1958: 291).
25. Myer (1958: 291).
26. *ASIR* 3 (A. Cunningham): 98. Later, Cunningham (1892: 22-23) implicitly considered the coping stone as belonging to the railing around the brick temple.
27. *ASIR* 3 (A. Cunningham): 98, pl. XXIX; see below.
28. Asher (1980: 28).
29. Myer (1958: 283).
30. Konow (1926). Sten Konow, like Vincent Smith, did not believe the plaque to represent the temple of Bodhgayā. Similar doubts have been expressed more recently by B.N. Mukherjee (1984-85), who has noticed the existence of a second inscription; it is in Brāhmī, and dates to the first century AD.
31. Myer (1958: 284).
32. Well visible in a pencil drawing by Thomas and William Daniell dated March 1790 (British Library Online Gallery, Shelfmark: WD1727).
33. Myer (1958: 283); Malandra (1988: 17) resorts to the same argument to date the temple to the Gupta period.
34. *Faxian* a: 126-32 (p. 555). Faxian adds that there were three monasteries.
35. Malandra (1988: 14). Myer (1958: 286) simply says that 'the temple ceased to be a *Bodhi-ghara* and became a *Vajrāsana-gandhakuṭi*, or Diamond-throne Temple, centering around the altar-throne'.
36. Cunningham (1892: pl. VI).
37. Ibid.: pl.VI.
38. Ibid.: 5.
39. *ASIR* 3 (A. Cunningham): 84. Cunningham explains that the width of the

cella was reduced, later on, to 13 feet, 'supposing that, when the vaulted roof was added to the chamber, a new wall, 3½ feet thick, was built against the north and south sides to carry the vault' (ibid.).

40. Ibid.: 83.
41. R. Mitra (1878: 76).
42. Ibid.
43. See Cunningham (1892: pl. II).
44. Ibid.: 20.
45. Ibid.
46. Ibid.: 4.
47. *ASIR* 3 (A. Cunningham): 83.
48. *Xiyuji* a: VIII (vol. 2, pp. 115-16): 'In the middle of the enclosure surrounding the *Bôdhi*-tree is the diamond-throne'.
49. Ibid.: vol. 2, p. 122.
50. Myer (1958: 286).
51. Ibid.
52. *ASIR* 1 (A. Cunningham): pl. IV.
53. *ASIR* 3 (A. Cunningham): pl. XXV.
54. R. Mitra (1878: 64).
55. Cunningham (1892: pl. XI).
56. Cunningham mentions the existence of a basement only when he speaks of Walls F1, F2, F3, etc. 'under the basement of the present Temple' (ibid.: 5). We can establish the width of the basement from the 1871 plan, whereas the original length is more difficult to determine because of the additions made over time to the basement both on the eastern and western sides.
57. *ASIR* 1 (A. Cunningham): 5; *ASIR* 3 (id.): 81.
58. R. Mitra (1878: 76).
59. *ASIR* 3 (A. Cunningham): 82.
60. Losty (1991: 238, 241).
61. Zaheer (1981); Michell (1977: 96); Huntington (1985; 213-214); Harle (1986: 116). Myer (1958: 285, n. 45) dates it to the sixth century.
62. Zaheer (1981); see also the temple described by Meister, Dhaky & Deva (1988: 36-37).
63. A. Cunningham (1892: 20).
64. Ibid. 18-19.
65. Cunningham says that 'the whole mass of sculpture that now exists being of the medieval period, during the flourishing rule of the Pâla kings' (ibid.: 54).
66. Ibid.: 63-64. P.R. Myer (1958: 297) says that 'by the late eighth century part of the Bodh-Gayā area was already given over to the devotees of Maheśvara (Śiva)'.
67. *ASIR* 3 (A. Cunningham): 89; Cunningham (1892: 12, pl. VII). For similar sculptures from Mathurā, cf. Huntington (1985: 156).
68. Myer (1958: 288); Malandra (1988: 19).

69. Ibid.
70. *ASIR* 3 (A. Cunningham): 90; R. Mitra (1878: 72).
71. B. Barua (1931-34, II: 19).
72. R. Mitra (1878: 75).
73. See the 1892 plan (Cunningham 1892: pl. XI) for Piers H and Granite Front G, and the 1871 plan (*ASIR* 1: pl. IV) for the original position of the railing.
74. Cunningham (1892: 25).
75. *ASIR* 1 (A. Cunningham): pl. IV; *ASIR* 3 (id.): 87.
76. Ibid. 98.
77. Cunningham (1892: 5).
78. *ASIR* 3 (A. Cunningham): 98.
79. Cunningham (1892: 56-7). The Viṣṇupad has been dated to the fourteen century because it bears an inscription dated AD 1308 (ibid), but the latter can be later than the artefact.
80. R. Mitra (1878: 100).
81. Id. (1864: 181); R. Mitra (1878: 100) also says that '[t]he carvings are said to be impressions of Buddha's feet, and bear certain marks or symbols, which, however, are not character[i]stic of a Buddha'.
82. Myer (1958: 292).
83. Ibid.: 293.
84. Ibid.
85. Chaudhary (1978: 229).
86. See Huntington Archive, http://www.huntingtonarchive.osu.edu/ (photographs taken in the temple compound and in the site museum). Some sculptures were drawn by D'Oyly in 1824 (Losty 1991: fig. 9), and were seen by Buchanan in 1827 (1936, I: 152; 155 ff.), Cunningham (*ASIR* 3 : 105) and R. Mitra (1878: 99-100).
87. A. Cunningham (1892: 25).
88. Ibid.: 25, pl. XI: E.
89. Ibid.: 4. Cunningham (*ASIR* 3: 100); R. Mitra (1878: 71). Cf. the works carried out at the site in the thirteenth century; above, Chapter VI.
90. These structures have been described by R. Mitra (ibid.: 82, 83, 85).
91. Myer (1958: 296).
92. Cunningham (1892: 81-82).
93. R. Mitra (1878: 85).
94. Losty (1991: fig. 2).
95. R. Mitra (1878: 85, 87-91); Buchanan (1936, I: 154).
96. R. Mitra (1878: 83).
97. Buchanan (1936, I: 154).
98. Myer (1958: 296).
99. On the terrace there was 'a fine walk round the temple, leading […] to a large area behind, on which is planted a celebrated pipal tree' (Buchanan 1936, I: 153).

100. R. Mitra (1864: 174-75); id. (1878: 92-93).
101. *ASIR* 3 (A. Cunningham): 80.
102. According to Malandra (1988: 21-22) it dates back to AD 1086; according to Myer (1958: 295-97), it is dated AD 1306.
103. Ibid.: 296.
104. *ASIR* 1 (A. Cunningham): 9.
105. Ibid.

APPENDIX 2

Sarnath: A Reassessment of the Archaeological Evidence with Particular Reference to the Final Phase of the Site

The place where the Buddha preached his first sermon, the Deer Park at Isipatana, became one of the main centres of Buddhist worship. The destruction of Sarnath is generally ascribed to the Muslim invaders, but the archaeological evidence suggests that around the mid-twelfth century the Buddhists were forced to leave and that an imposing Sivaite temple was erected on the site. Other discontinuities are observable in the history of the site, and here a general reassessment of the evidence is proposed.

THE EXCAVATIONS

The discovery of Sarnath goes back to the end of the eighteenth century, when the site became a source of building materials. In 1794, the so-called Jagat Singh stūpa was brought to light (Fig. 18), allowing the ruins to be identified as those of a Buddhist sanctuary.[1] This discovery did not stop the exploitation of the ruins: 'all portable antiquities were removed by the excavators, and the exposed ruins and carved stones were left an easy prey to those in search of building materials'.[2] The last large-scale robbing took place at the end of the nineteenth century, when the construction of the railway 'created a great demand for bricks and stones, to be broken up for railway ballast'.[3] Documented excavations had started in 1835, when Alexander Cunningham brought to light a number of buildings, including three stūpas (Jagat Singh, Dhamekh and Chaukhandi), the so-called Monastery L and Temple M.[4] In 1851, Markham Kittoe resumed Cunningham's work and explored the areas to the north of the Jagat Singh and Dhamekh stūpas. He also started excavating the so-called Monasteries V (or Hospital) and VI.[5] After Kittoe's death, the work was continued by Edward Thomas.[6]

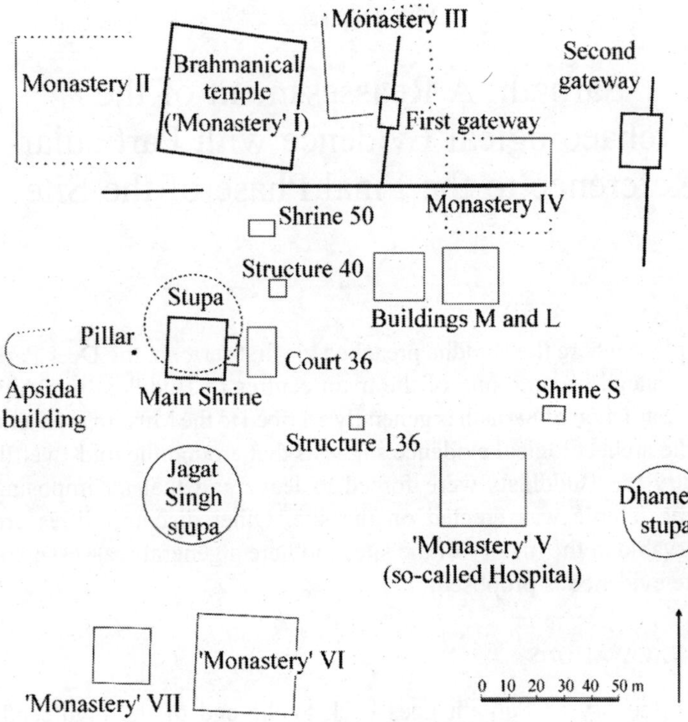

Figure 18: Sarnath. General plan.

In November 1900, a watchman was appointed to the site and some years later major excavations were undertaken by Frederick Oscar Oertel, who continued the excavation of the three main stūpas and started that of the Main Shrine. He discovered the remains of the Aśoka pillar, the lion capital, and the foundations of Building R (also known as Stūpa 22).[7] As for John Marshall, at first he resumed Kittoe and Oertel's works, bringing to light a great number of small shrines and stūpas around the Main Shrine, and subsequently started the excavation of the northern area, which had been less affected by previous works. He found four buildings, identified as monasteries (nos. I-IV), and two gateways.[8] In November 1914, Harold Hargreaves resumed the excavation of the Main Shrine and the surrounding area. One of his major achievements was the discovery of an apsidal building, located to the west of the Aśoka pillar.[9] The last important excavations, during which various areas were exposed and restorations made, were carried out under Daya Ram Sahni's supervision. Sahni wrote only brief reports on the work done.[10]

The excavations were carried out before the introduction of the stratigraphic method, and consequently the archaeological strata were not clearly identified and recorded. Structures pertaining to different periods appear side by side in the plans, as if belonging to one and the same horizon. Although the majority of the monuments have not been dated with precision, it is possible, nevertheless, to identify the main phases of the site, from Aśoka to the Gāhaḍavāla dynasty in the twelfth century.

THE EARLY SANCTUARY

The main structures of the Mauryan and Kuṣāṇa periods are the Aśoka pillar and the Jagat Singh stūpa. What was probably another stūpa was located where the Main Shrine was later built.[11] In fact, during the excavation of the Main Shrine, a 'solid mass of brickwork' consisting of 'odd and even ornamented bricks' was discovered at – 0.70 m below the floor. The structure was dismantled, 'brick by brick, layer by layer' to a depth of – 2.75 m, 'when only earth was found'.[12] The same solid mass of brickwork was also found north of the Main Shrine, at a depth of – 0.30 m from the walking level. [13] As this mass of brickwork was located near the Aśoka pillar, it is reasonable to identify it with the stūpa built by Aśoka. Another important shrine belonging to an early period is the apsidal building,[14] whose entrance faced the Aśoka pillar.

Near the apsidal building (which soon 'fell into decay'),[15] Hargreaves discovered an area packed with stone fragments ranging 'from Maurya times to the 1st Century BC.'[16] In his opinion, 'some of the monuments [...] had undoubtedly been wilfully destroyed while others, especially railing pillars, had clearly suffered the ravage of fire'.[17] Hargreaves dated the re-use of stone fragments as filling material to level the ground to the Gupta period.[18]

Three Brahmanical sculptures, now in the site museum, are datable to the Gupta age, providing evidence that the followers of the neo-Brahmanical movements had established themselves in Sarnath. One of the sculptures (the exact finding spot is unknown) represents Viṣṇu with Gadadevī and Cakrapuruṣa and can be dated to the fifth century.[19] The other sculptures were discovered in the so-called

Hospital: a small female figure representing an *āyudhapuruṣa* of Viṣṇu and the Dwarf *avatāra*.[20] During the excavation of the 'Hospital', the remains of two distinct buildings came to light, one on the ruins of the other. The first was dated 'to the early Gupta period':[21] it is 'a quadrangle' (*c.* 18 × 14 m) bound to the east, west and south by low parapets, on which stood a row of columns. The northern portion of the monument, devoid of columns, was not excavated. The function of the building was not ascertained and Marshall only observed that 'the building was not the ordinary type of monastery'.[22]

A similar case is that of Court 36 (*c.* 14 × 8 m), which 'cannot be earlier than the fourth or fifth century'.[23] The entrance was in the middle of the east wall, while a projection in the form of a solid platform was present in the west wall. The south, east and north walls 'were furnished on the outside with a stone railing comprising 74 uprights and 108 cross-bars [. . .]. In order to secure the rails in position against the face of the wall, the interstices between the uprights and the cross-bars were filled in with brickwork'.[24] According to Marshall, 'it is obvious [...] that the railing [...] originally surrounded some earlier building and was shifted here at a later date'.[25] The railing, formed by plain uprights and crossbars, had probably encircled the Aśoka stūpa,[26] which was behind the court. Fencing a court by means of the dismantled elements of a stūpa railing is hardly something that we can ascribe to the Buddhists.

A small structure in brickwork (no. 136 in Sahni's plan),[27] located between the so-called Hospital and Court 36, was probably a Brahmanical shrine. Unlike the Buddhist votive stūpas (which display a square or cross-shaped base), it consisted of a central square body with four smaller square projections at each corner. In plan, it is strongly reminiscent of the Daśāvatāra Temple at Deogarh,[28] though much smaller in size.

Towards the end of the Gupta period, the site was again occupied by the Buddhists. An intense building activity and a great artistic output characterise this phase, during which some of the best sculptures ever made in India were produced. Small votive stūpas and shrines, several of which rebuilt more than once, mushroomed around the Aśoka pillar and the Jagat Singh stūpa.[29] The damaged Buddhist structures underwent some repairs: the monolithic *harmikā* originally surrounding the umbrella of the Aśoka stūpa, for example, had been probably thrown down when the monument was destroyed in the

Gupta period to build Court 36.[30] Some time later, the *harmikā* was repaired with bricks and used to encircle a small stūpa, which was located just south of the Aśoka stūpa.[31]

The area around the Dhamekh stūpa[32] was also crowded by votive shrines.[33] To the north of the Dhamekh stūpa, monuments nos. 71-80 have been attributed to the long period going from the Gupta epoch to the eleventh or twelfth century AD.[34] There were three monasteries (nos. II, III and IV) in the northern area[35] and two other edifices (nos. VI and VII) were built in the southern area.[36]

A peculiar structure (no. 50 in Sahni's plan) displays a pillared hall that was built reusing the sculptured uprights of a railing.[37] Marshall observed that 'the pots are sunk so far into the floor as to conceal part of their sculptured relief'.[38] It appears, once again, that non-Buddhist occupants had appropriated the site, at least in part. Brahmanical temples with pillared *maṇḍapa*-s were already common in the eighth century AD,[39] and the building may belong to this epoch.[40] That groups of brāhmaṇas were present at Sarnath is shown by two Brahmanical sculptures attributable to the early medieval period.[41]

Summing up, we can say that the history of Sarnath in the early middle age is marked by discontinuities. The site was magnificently adorned during the Mauryan and Kuṣāṇa periods, but under the Guptas the major monuments were damaged or destroyed, and Brahmanical buildings (Court 36, Structure 136) were built in front of the Buddhist ones, presumably abandoned. After the Buddhist revival, the site appears to have been appropriated once again, and a small Brahmanical shrine (no. 50) to have been built in the area between the Mauryan stūpa and the monasteries.

THE LATE SANCTUARY

The last Buddhist monuments of Sarnath, probably built in the first half of the twelfth century, are Stūpa 22 and Buildings L and M. Large Stūpa 22 (R in Oertel's plan) was built on high ground in the area of the apsidal temple.[42] Buildings L and M (Oertel's plan)[43] stand on the same high ground to the south of Monastery IV.[44] Building M (a temple, according to the excavator) has a cross-shaped plan and was decorated with statues and bas-reliefs. A few meters to the north, in a small detached room at a depth of – 1 m below the walking level, 'about 60 statues and bas-reliefs in an upright position all packed closely together'[45] were discovered. These sculptures had been probably carried to Sarnath and momentarily stored before being set in place,[46] but the work was stopped due to the insurgence of a new 'time of persecution':[47] in the same period, the buildings in the southern area (nos. V, VI and VII, identified as monasteries) were destroyed by fire. As regards the destruction of Monastery VI, 'the conflagration had been so sudden and rapid as to force the monks to abandon their very food'.[48] Small Monastery VII 'probably fell a prey to the same conflagration'.[49] The edifice built in the '8th-9th century' on the so-called Hospital (or Monastery V) was also set on fire.[50] While the southern area was abandoned, the central and northern areas underwent a complete reconstruction, attested to by two impressive buildings: the Main Shrine and the so-called Monastery I.

THE MAIN SHRINE

The Main Shrine[51] was built on the Aśoka stūpa. The square hall (18.2 × 18.2 m) displays projecting bays (the chapels to the south, north and west and the entrance portico to the east), thus creating a *triratna* design. The impressive thickness of the walls (3 m) was 'evidently intended to carry a massive and lofty superstructure'[52] and a large portion of the interior was later built-up 'possibly to help in upholding the roof'.[53] The shrine was built with re-used materials: for example, late-fifth century doorjambs were re-used in the doorway[54] and the plinth was faced with ancient, irregularly set-up stones. Only a headless Buddha image comes from this building: it was found in the south chapel, but was not 'the original image in this shrine, as it look[ed] much too small for its position'.[55]

Around the Main Shrine, a vast area was paved with a concrete floor made of re-used stones, 'some of [which] were mere undressed blocks, while others were elegantly carved'.[56] At a distance of 18 m from the eastern façade, the floor step abutted on a broad pathway, called Approach Way or Courtyard.[57] It was *c*. 90 m long, paved with concrete and 'enclosed in a brick wall on the north, south and east sides, the greater part of which ha[d] fallen down. The interior of the court was approached by a double stair-case in the middle of the east wall, which [was] built up with stone slabs of different periods'.[58]

The court appears nearly free from structures: in the area to the south of the Main Shrine, Oertel noted some remains on the floor, but 'nothing of importance',[59] and near the Aśoka pillar, votive stūpas were found only below the floor.[60] In the northern area, the floor level was devoid of structural remains[61] and, to the east of the Main Shrine, only a few structures have been associated with the concrete floor.[62] Further east, Sahni excavated two rows of votive stūpas (nos. 82-104), without unfortunately giving any detailed information.[63] It is evident that the impressive building activity involving the erection of votive stūpas and shrines that had characterised the post-Gupta and Pāla periods (with an interlude in the eighth century) broke off after the construction of the Main Shrine: only a few structures were erected in the vast court after the concrete floor was laid down. The Main Shrine, built on a stūpa, made of re-used building materials taken from the Buddhist monuments and situated in a large empty courtyard, can be properly understood when we start considering it a Brahmanical temple.

THE SO-CALLED MONASTERY I

The so-called Monastery I, dating 'from the 12th century AD',[64] was built on Buddhist monasteries. It is a walled compound subdivided into two courtyards, both accessible through huge gateways, provided with richly carved bastions of chiselled brick and stone combined. The second gateway does not seem to mark the limits of the compound, because 'two parallel walls one on each side of the gateway stretch towards the east, indicating, no doubt, the existence of other courts beyond'.[65] In the western half of the first courtyard, an imposing building was excavated in 1907, when a portion of its massive elevated platform ('brick plinth') was brought to light.[66] On the eastern side, the doorjambs of a large doorway were identified, placed at a distance of 8.8 m one from the other and 'apparently occupied by a broad flight of steps leading up to the plinth'.[67] The platform was divided into 'rows of chambers' by cross foundation walls. Marshall interpreted these 'chambers' as a series of rooms pertaining to a Buddhist monastery (Fig. 19).[68] It is evident, however, that the 'chambers' were not arranged in single rows. The bases of seven pillars indicate that this part of the building was a vast pillared hall, *c.* 10.6 m long, that must have had four or six pair of pillars supporting the roof.[69] At the western end, a small flight of steps gave access to a large quadrangle (*c.* 21 x 21 m) labelled as 'courtyard' or 'inner court'. According to

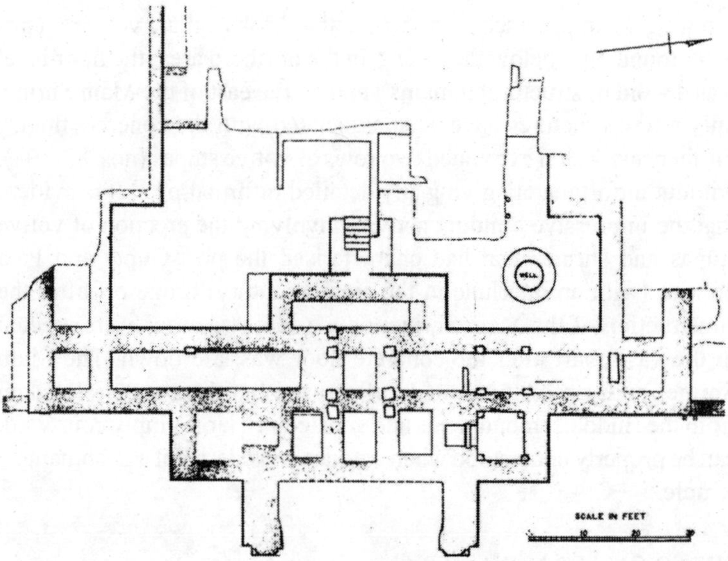

Figure 19: Sarnath. So-called Monastery I.

the Marshall, the floor of the courtyard was 1.8 m lower than the floor of the eastern hall,[70] but it appears that the lower floor actually pertains to an earlier building on which the so-called Monastery I was built. The floor pertaining to 'Monastery I' was probably unintentionally removed by the excavators during the clearing of the 'vast array of massive stones'[71] fallen on it. A brick well in the north-eastern corner is associated with the lower floor, because its low parapet was 'about one foot above the level of the courtyard'.[72] The identification of the building as a monastery, based on 'its rows of chambers, its paved courtyard and its well'[73] is untenable: the 'rows of chambers' are the foundations of a pillared hall, while the paved courtyard and the well clearly belong to an earlier edifice—probably a real Buddhist monastery.

The 'inner court' is provided with flights of steps also on the southern and northern sides, leading to the other parts of the building. The exposed walls of the southern and northern areas follow a plan similar to that of the eastern hall. In the area to the west of the 'inner court', a spacious floor was uncovered. According to the excavators, 'near the middle of this floor is the stone base of a column *in situ*, carved in identically the same style as the column bases and other architectural members found on the eastern side of the monastery; and traces of another column also were found having existed to its south. These columns must have been intended to carry an architrave and roof, and we may assume therefore that there was a large pillared hall or portico on this side of the monastery'.[74] Marshall had the intention to complete the clearance of the building during the following season but never resumed the work.

Some years later, Monastery I started being called 'Dharmacakra-Jinavihāra',[75] with reference to the donation of a *vihāra* by Kumāradevī, the Buddhist wife of the Gāhaḍavāla king Govindacandra, recorded by an inscription found to the north of the Dhamekh stūpa.[76] The Kumāradevī hypothesis has been accepted by scholars,[77] despite the fact that the inscription is not associated with the monastery,[78] but they do not agree on the nature of the edifice, whether it is a monastery or a temple. H.W. Woodward Jr. believes it to be a monastery, even if he maintains that it 'differs from a traditional one in having such a high basement and in not having cells in single, simple rows'[79] and is well aware of the similarity between 'Monastery I' and the Duladeo temple at Khajuraho. Sahni observed that the building had 'a curious plan which has not yet been noticed on any other Buddhist site',[80] and claimed that the structure was a temple, '(1) because in plan it differ[ed] essentially from the monasteries known to us […], (2) the structural arrangement [wa]s such as to afford little room for actual residential cells, (3) no other monastery known to us [wa]s preceded by such extensive courts with elaborate gateways […], and (4) builders of monasteries seldom lavished such exuberant ornament on their works'.[81] Sahni's remarks open a perspective that has not been sufficiently explored. There is no doubt that the building was a temple, but the analysis of the finds shows that it was not a Buddhist building.

It has been observed that 'all the stone-work employed in this building appears to have been expressly made for it, for it is all carved and chiselled exactly in the same style'.[82] Only a few pieces are inventoried and illustrated in the excavation reports and in Sahni's catalogue,[83] but their peculiar 'flat and stencil' decoration is easily identifiable: the main motifs are bands of scrollwork, pot-and-foliage, lotus petals, chess pattern and a motif with warriors alternating with lions.[84] Foliate and geometrical designs are found in both Buddhist and Brahmanical monuments, but what about the sculptures and the architectural fragments of the 'Monastery'? At least fourteen Brahmanical images were discovered in the area [85] and their presence has not been explained. Marshall and Konow mention some of these images without any comment;[86] Woodward does not make any reference to them at all. Sahni is the only scholar who has provided some information. Going through his catalogue, we see that Jamb Stone Df48 has 'borders of musicians and lions attacked by warriors' to the sides of a central face showing a Brahmanical goddess.[87] The fragment 'must have belonged to a Brahmanical temple at Sarnath'.[88] The same motif ('border of warriors alternating with lions') decorates Door-jamb Df41, one of the architectural features ascribed to the 'Buddhist Monastery I'.[89] The finding spot of Df41 is the same of Df48: the first outer court of 'Monastery I'. Sahni maintains that they belong to different monuments: Df41 to a Buddhist temple (the so-called Monastery I) and Df48 to a Brahmanical temple (of which no trace would have remained). The impasse can be solved only identifying Monastery I with the 'Brahmanical temple at Sarnath'. The above examples are not the only ones. In the site museum, several late medieval architectural fragments with Brahmanical figures display the decorative motifs and the peculiar 'flat and stencil' style observable in the architectural fragments ascribed to 'Monastery I'.[90]

Only two Buddhas in *dharmacakramudrā* are stylistically compatible with Monastery I.[91] However, they are not in contrast with the Brahmanical iconographic developments of the period, because they may represent Śiva as a teacher, an iconography cast on Buddhist models already popular in the eighth century AD.[92] It would not be surprising to see the Śaivaites appropriating the fundamental symbol of the site – the Buddha's teaching – in their own temple at Sarnath. The name by which we know the place, derived from Sāraṅganātha or Lord of the Deer, may not allude to the Buddha but to Śiva, one of whose attributes is the deer.[93]

As scholars have a priori excluded that the Brahmanical sculptures found in 'Monastery I' had any relation to it, we find it associated with a limited number of sculptures. Sahni mentions three female figures: Bf4 and Bf5, which 'might be representations of the river goddesses Gangā and Yamunā' and Bf6, which represents 'Śrī or Lakshmī'.[94] However, these images fit better a Brahmanical temple, as noted by Sahni himself.[95] The Makara Gargoyle,[96] attributed to 'Monastery I', is also typical of many Hindu temples.[97] 'Monastery I', built in the twelfth century AD, not only is a temple, as maintained by Sahni, but a Brahmanical one, as shown by the sculptures and architectural fragments associated with it.

As regards the Buddhist sculptures and fragments found in the area, they span from the 'Gupta style' period to the '10th-11th centuries'.[98] None of them (at least the illustrated ones)[99] has any stylistic relation with the architectural fragments of 'Monastery I'. Moreover, they are all 'injured', 'defaced', 'damaged', 'disfigured', 'having the face cut away', 'head missing', 'faces peeled off',[100] etc. It is probable that they were used by the Sivaites as building material, as at Vikramaśīla (Chapter VI).

The temple was probably built in the second half of the twelfth century. It has been suggested that the Gāhaḍavālas moved their capital from Kanauj to Benares in order to profit from the religious prestige that was connected with it. Whereas Kanauj was a political capital, Benares had evolved into the holiest of *tīrtha*-s. Choosing Benares as the seat of their power, the Gāhaḍavālas proclaimed themselves as 'protectors of the (North) Indian holy places' and at the same time promoted a 'holy war' against the Muslim invaders.[101] Many shrines and bathing places were built thanks to royal patronage, especially in the northern part of the city, at a very short distance from Sarnath.[102] No donation to the Buddhists is recorded in Benares, where a large number of inscriptions attest to the donations made to the brāhma nas.[103] An inscription from Gangaikondacholapuram shows that a member of the Gāhaḍavāla family visited the new temple of the Cōḷas with the purpose of making a grant.[104] It is probably not a coincidence that the Sarnath temple stands within a *prākāra* (*c*. 200 × 60 m) of about the same size as that of Gangaikondacolapuram (*c*. 180 × 100 m).[105] The entrance is filtered by two large *gopura*-s, typical of Cōḷa temples. Marshall observed that 'judging from the massiveness of its foundations, this gateway would seem to have something like a South India *gopuram* – an analogy which is reflected in the diminishing size of the gateways as one approaches the central building'.[106] For all its similarity with Cōḷa temple architecture, the decorative features of the Sarnath temple are closely related to the Candella art of Khajuraho, and especially to the temple of Duladeo, dated to *c*. AD 1100-50.[107] The aim of the Gāhaḍavālas was to reproduce the grandeur of south

Indian temples preserving, at the same time, the stylistic features of the northern temples, probably due to skilled workers arguably coming from Jejākabhukti.

The temple of Sarnath (Fig. 20) stood on a high platform, like the Khajuraho temples (1.70 m at Sarnath, 1.52 m the Duladeo temple). It is neither rectangular nor square, but adjusts itself to the form of the temple. A large door (8.8 m) on the eastern side gave access to a long *mukhamaṇḍapa*. The *mahāmaṇḍapa* (the so-called 'inner court') is rather large (*c.* 21 × 21 m)[108] because it occupies the courtyard of the earlier monastery. The original floor of the *mahāmaṇḍapa*, as already said, was unintentionally removed during the excavations, and the evidence regarding the position of the roof-supporting pillars is consequently lost. Marshall, who was convinced that the 'inner court' was the open-sky courtyard of a Buddhist monastery,[109] stated at the same time that 'ceiling slabs and other architectural members were found among the debris in the courtyard'.[110] According to Sahni,

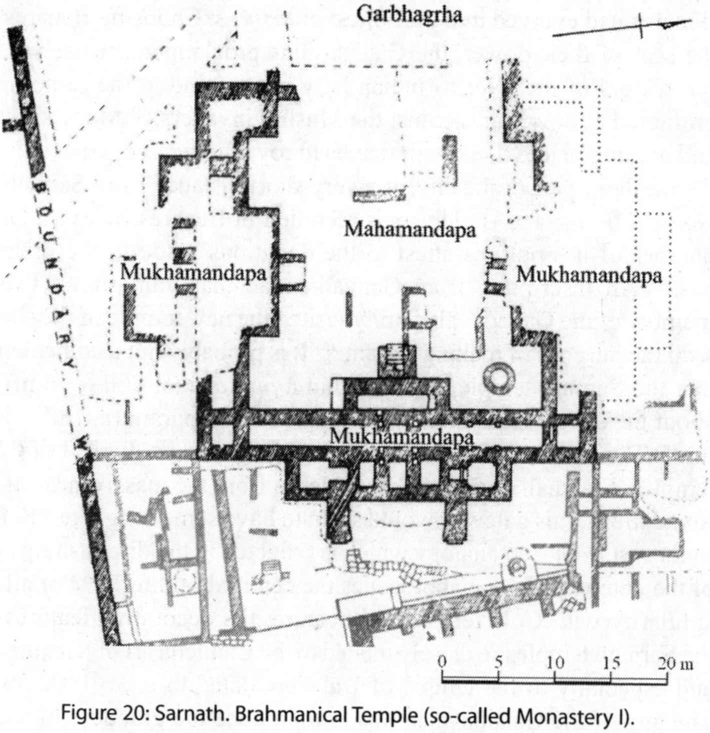

Figure 20: Sarnath. Brahmanical Temple (so-called Monastery I).

a slab with a conventional lotus flower, lying on the floor of the inner court, was 'employed as a roof slab'.[111]

On the northern and southern sides of the *mahāmaṇḍapa*, there were two more *mukhamaṇḍapa*-s,[112] one leading to the Main Shrine, the other to the lake. The southern hall was excavated in part and its perimeter could be outlined, but the northern hall (probably identical to the southern one) was not excavated because the structure was damaged due to the sloping ground.[113] A 'great drain' (1.8 m deep, 1 m wide), built on the ruins of the earlier Monastery II, was observed in the western area. It was probably connected to the unexcavated *garbhagṛha* because it 'appears to have carried off all the water' from the building.[114] The drain was again excavated by Sahni, who assumed that it was a 'subterranean passage [...] which led into a very small shrine'.[115] As mantained by Sahni himself, it would be a unique example in Indian architecture, either Buddhist or Hindu: in fact, only the 'Mughal forts often contain secret passages'.[116] The drain hypothesis is more likely and fits the requirements of a Brahmanical temple.[117]

BRAHMANISED SARNATH

The project undertaken by the rulers of Benares involved a complete transformation of the Buddhist sanctuary. It affected the central part of the site, with the stūpa of Aśoka as the first target of the works. The railing that encircled the stūpa and the *harmikā* had already been dismantled in the Gupta period and now a Brahmanical temple (the Main Shrine) was built on the stūpa. The capital and the broken shaft of the Aśoka pillar were found on the concrete terrace set around the Main Shrine[118] and it is probable that the pillar was split up in this period and turned into a *liṅga*.[119]

The Main Shrine and the associated large floor were built re-using the architectural fragments of the Buddhist edifices. The reused slabs are often placed upside down 'with an element of hatred and vengeance',[120] as happened at Vikramaśīla. Even in the temple of the 'Monastery I' area, built with new building stones, a railing pillar of the '1st century BC.'[121] was used as a step in the stairs of the eastern entrance.

A wall, partly excavated by Sahni,[122] was built to separate the court of the Main Shrine from the southern area, where the Buddhist buildings (so-called Monasteries V, VI, VII) were destroyed by fire.

Another wall separated the central court from the northern one, but there is a large door[123] that connected the Main Shrine to the 'Monastery I' temple. In the northern court, the innermost *gopuram* is on the same axis as the 'Monastery I' temple, while the outermost one is aligned with the Main Shrine. It is thus probable that the outermost *gopuram* gave access to both the northern and central courts. The other Buddhist structures still standing were converted into Brahmanical shrines. For example, an image of Tryambaka Śiva was discovered in Structure 40, situated on the way connecting the 'Monastery I' temple to the Main Shrine.[124] A Sivaite image (neither dated nor published, but described as a two-armed Śiva image of the Tryambaka type) was found in the *garbhagṛha* of a shrine in the south-eastern corner of the court of the Main Shrine (Shrine S in Fig. 18). Sahni maintained that the shrine was Buddhist in origin and later 'appropriated for Brahmanical purpose'.[125]

The Brahmanical project at Sarnath was never completed, as attested by the finding of numerous unfinished carvings[126] and sculptures in the 'Monastery I' temple area, among which a colossal image of Śiva[127] now in the site museum.

NOTES

1. *AsRes* 5 (1798): 131-32. See Chapter I.
2. *ASIAR* 1904-5 (F.O. Oertel): 64.
3. Ibid.
4. *ASIR* 1 (A. Cunningham): pls. XXXII, XXXIII.
5. Kittoe's work was never published; some of his observations are mentioned in ibid.: 116, 124-26, 128.
6. Thomas (1854).
7. *ASIAR* 1904-5 (F.O. Oertel): 59-104.
8. *ASIAR* 1906-7 (J.H. Marshall & S. Konow): 68-101; 1907-8 (id.): 43-80.
9. *ASIAR* 1914-15 (H. Hargreaves): 97-131.
10. *ASIAR* 1916-17 (D.R. Sahni): 14-15; 1917-18 (id.): 5-6; 1918-19 (id.): 4-5; 1919-20 (id.): 26-27.
11. The Main Shrine 'marked the site of some more ancient structure' (*ASIAR* 1914-15, H. Hargreaves: 105).
12. Ibid.: 105.
13. Ibid.: 106.
14. The structure was ascribed to the 'Late Maurya period' as its 'foundations [we]re only 1′ 9″ [53.34 cm] above the Maurya level and no earlier remains exist[ed] beneath' (ibid. 109). These stratigraphic observations are rudimental, and the building is most probably a later structure.

15. Ibid.
16. Ibid.: 111, pls. LXV-LXIX.
17. Ibid.: 111.
18. However, Hargreaves says that the deposition 'may not necessarily synchronize with the destruction of the monuments' (ibid.).
19. See this sculpture in the Digital South Asia Library, Accession no. 1753. Compare with the Viṣṇu image from Unchdih in the Allahabad Museum, dated to the early fifth century (P. Chandra 1970: 97-98, no. 223; pl. LXXX); Harle (1974: 46; fig. 61) attributes it to the mid-fifth century.
20. They are included in Sahni's catalogue (1914: Bh19 and Bh17 entries on pp. 167-68); Sahni suggested a medieval chronology. Bh19 is illustrated in the Digital South Asia Library, Accession no. 1754.
21. *ASIAR* 1907-08 (J.H. Marshall & S. Konow): 62.
22. Ibid.
23. *ASIAR* 1906-07 (J.H. Marshall & S. Konow): 79.
24. Ibid.: 78-79.
25. Ibid.: 79.
26. '[T]he few parts of the railing so far discovered are quite plain, but its age is determined by the Mauryan inscription on the cope-stone' (ibid.).
27. Sahni (1923: 22); see also Digital South Asia Library, Accession nos. 25645, 25652.
28. Gottfried Williams (1982: 130-36).
29. *ASIAR* 1904-05 (F.O. Oertel): 71; 1906-07 (J.H. Marshall & S. Konow): 70, 73, 78, 80. The Jagat Singh stūpa also underwent several reconstructions (*ASIAR* 1907-08, id.: 65).
30. According to Sahni (1923: 21), the *harmikā* 'was thrown down by a violent earthquake'. K. Kumar (1985-86: 12) says instead that it was destroyed 'by accidental damage or deliberate vandalism which perhaps took place in the wake of the Hun invasions'.
31. It was discovered by Oertel, 'built up in the foundation and wall of the south chapel' in the Main Shrine (*ASIAR* 1904-05: 67-8). K. Kumar (1985-86: 12) says that 'the railing [. . .] was repaired with bricks. It is interesting to note that even today a brick carved in the late Gupta style is visible in the western arm'.
32. The Dhamekh stūpa has long been dated to Gupta times, but is instead a seventh-century work (Gottfried Williams 1982: 168-69).
33. They were brought to light by Kittoe and subsequently destroyed (*ASIAR* 1907-08, J.H. Marshall & S. Konow: 59).
34. Ibid.: 60.
35. Ibid.: 54-59; *ASIAR* 1906-07 (id.): 85.
36. Thomas (1854); Sahni (1923: 16-17); *ASIAR* 1917-18 (id.): 5. In Sahni's plan, Monastery VI (south of the stūpa) is given no. V and Monastery V (so-called Hospital) is given no. VI.
37. *ASIAR* 1907-08 (J.H. Marshall & S. Konow): 69 and pl. XX.
38. Ibid.: 70.

39. Relatively large entrance *maṇḍapa*-s are already present in seventh-century temples, from Alampur to Saurashtra (Meister, Dhaky & Deva 1988: e.g. pls. 381, 658).
40. The structure was found buried in ashes (*ASIAR* 1907-08, J.H. Marshall & S. Konow: 70). According to Sahni (1923: 28), the 'heaps of ashes and charred wood [...] might be remnants of *Agni-hotras*, performed by adherents of the Brahmanical faith'.
41. These are an image of Sarasvatī playing the lute (*ASIAR* 1904-05, F.O. Oertel: 86, fig. 9; Sahni 1914: 150, Bf27; Digital South Asia Library, Accession no. 5806) and an image of Agni (Digital South Asia Library, Accession no. 5798; Huntington Archive no. 1657). Some other Brahmanical sculptures (not illustrated) were inventoried by Sahni (1914): Bh6, Bh9, Bh10, Bh11 (medieval period); Bh5, Bh8, Bh18.
42. The stūpa was dismantled to allow for the excavation of the lower strata (*ASIAR* 1904-05, F.O. Oertel: 70; *ASIAR* 1914-15, H. Hargreaves: 109).
43. *ASIR* 1 (A. Cunningham): 120, pls. XXXII-XXXIII; *ASIAR* 1904-05 (F.A. Oertel): pl. XV. These buildings were dismantled between 1905 and 1907 and do not appear in the plans published by Marshall and Konow (*ASIAR* 1906-07: pl. XVII; *ASIAR* 1907-08: pl. XI).
44. In the upper strata some walls were unearthed, pertaining to temporary habitations, typical of the phases of abandonment (*ASIR* 1, A. Cunningham: 122).
45. Ibid.
46. A similar case is documented at Sanghol in Ludhiana district (Panjab) where 117 railing pieces manufactured in Mathurā were found piled near the main stūpa (S.P. Gupta 1985: 19, 23). It is hardly believable that the stūpa railing was dismantled to 'preserv[e] the sculptural wealth from further destruction at the hands of the marauding invaders'.
47. *ASIR* 1 (A. Cunningham): 123. The sculptures, left by Cunningham lying on the ground, were taken away and 'thrown into the Barna river under the bridge, to check the cutting away of the bed between the arches' (ibid.).
48. Ibid.: 128. Several inscribed miniature stūpas were found inside the building and were dated 'between the 7th and the 10th century' (Thomas 1854: 474). Other uninscribed stūpas were discovered 'mingled with the debris in the open court, generally at the level of the original surface, showing that their date is not later than that of the destruction of the building itself' (ibid.: 475).
49. Sahni (1923: 17).
50. *ASIAR* 1907-08 (J.H. Marshall & S. Konow): 62; *ASIR* 1 (A. Cunningham): 125.
51. According to the excavator, it can 'hardly be earlier than the eleventh century AD.' (*ASIAR* 1914-15, H. Hargreaves: 97).
52. *ASIAR* 1904-05 (F.O. Oertel): 67.

53. Ibid.
54. Gottfried Williams (1982: pl. 99).
55. *ASIAR* 1904-05 (F.O. Oertel): 67.
56. *ASIAR* 1906-07 (J.H. Marshall & S. Konow): 77.
57. Ibid. 76-77.
58. Sahni (1923: 22).
59. *ASIAR* 1904-05 (F.O. Oertel): 67.
60. *ASIAR* 1906-07 (J.H. Marshall & S. Konow): 73.
61. *ASIAR* 1914-15 (H. Hargreaves): 106-07.
62. Small square plinths nos. 25, 26, 29, 31, 33, 34, 35 (*ASIAR* 1906-07, J.H. Marshall & S. Konow: 77-78).
63. Sahni (1923: 23); *ASIAR* 1918-19 (D.R. Sahni): 5.
64. *ASIAR* 1907-08 (J.H. Marshall & S. Konow): 43.
65. Ibid.: 46.
66. Ibid.: 43.
67. *ASIAR* 1906-07 (J.H. Marshall & S. Konow): 83.
68. Ibid.: 82.
69. The excavators recognised that 'the central chamber of the eastern side may thus be supposed to have done duty as a hall' (ibid.: 83).
70. Sahni (1923: 29). The excavators observed that the flights of steps 'start[ed] from a slightly higher level than the floor of the courtyard' and tried to explain this incongruity saying that the steps 'must therefore have been put in later' (*ASIAR* 1907-08, J.H. Marshall & S. Konow): 44.
71. *ASIAR* 1906-07 (id.): 83.
72. Ibid.
73. Ibid.: 82.
74. *ASIAR* 1907-08 (J.H. Marshall & S. Konow): 44.
75. Sahni (1923: 28).
76. *ASIAR* 1907-08 (J.H. Marshall & S. Konow): 60, 76-80. Cf. also Chapter VI.
77. See Woodward (1981: 11).
78. Building M, which rises near to the place where the inscription was discovered, can be identified as the *dharmacakrajinavihāra*. This hypothesis has been recently suggested by B.R. Mani (2005-06).
79. Woodward (1981: 12).
80. Sahni (1923: 29).
81. Ibid.: 32.
82. *ASIAR* 1906-07 (J.H. Marshall & S. Konow): 83.
83. Sahni (1914: Df36-41, Df44, Dg32-34, Dg28, Di110-Di114, Di117, Di135-136, Di139-140, Di143-168, Dk34).
84. Some other fragments, stored in the site museum, display the same decoration and probably pertain to Monastery I (Digital South Asia Library, Accession nos. 28773, 25811, 25637, 25638, 25639, 25640, 25983, 5849).

85. Sahni (1914: Bh1, Bh2, Bh3, Bh7, Bh12, Bh13, Bh14, Bh15, Df34, Df42, Df48, Df49); *ASIAR* 1906-07: pl. XXIX, d; *ASIAR* 1907-08 (J.H. Marshall & S. Konow): 48, no. a48.
86. Ibid.: 48, 52.
87. Sahni (1914: 244).
88. Ibid.
89. Ibid.: 243; *ASIAR* 1906-07 (J.H. Marshall & S. Konow): pl. XXVI, 6.
90. Digital South Asia Library, Accession nos. 5847, 5848 (lions-warriors motif, lotus medallion), 5802, 5841 (pot-and-foliage motif), 5838, 5842 (bands of scrollwork), 5840 (lotus medallion).
91. Digital South Asia Library, Accession no. 5759 (find spot not documented); Dk4 (Sahni 1914: 266; *ASIAR* 1906-07, J.H. Marshall & S. Konow: 77, pl. XXIII, 8) from the area to the east of Main Shrine.
92. Cf. Donaldson (1999).
93. We have seen him, in Kāñcī, displacing the Buddha from his seat, the deer of the First Sermon lying below him under a tree (Chapter IV, Fig. 4).
94. Sahni (1923: 32; 1914: 142; pl. XVI).
95. Sahni (1914: 142)
96. *ASIAR* 1906-07 (J.H. Marshall & S. Konow): 94, pl. XXVI, 2; Sahni (1914: Di110-Di114); Digital South Asia Library (no. 5829).
97. See for instance Donaldson (1985, II: figs. 2518-2519).
98. *ASIAR* 1907-08 (J.H. Marshall & S. Konow): 47-53.
99. Sahni (1914: Bc39, Bd11, De5, Df22, Df29, Dk53).
100. Ibid. Bb30, Bb40, Bb52 Bb120, Bb178, Bb186, Bb192, Bb213, Bb219, Bb227, Bb238, Bb271, Bc6, Bc12, Bc14, Bc24, Bc43, Bc119, Bc202, Bc206, Bd28, Bd32, Bd36, Bd44.
101. Bakker (1996: 38-39).
102. Ibid. note 32.
103. Niyogi (1959: 243 ff.).
104. *ASIAR* 1907-08 (J.H. Marshall & S. Konow): 228.
105. The temple of Gangaikondacholapuram has been published by Pichard & al. (1994): see temple map in vol. 2, pl. 5.
106. *ASIAR* 1907-08 (J.H. Marshall & S. Konow): 45.
107. Deva (1990: 240).
108. The Duladeo *mahāmaṇḍapa* is much smaller: 5.60 × 5.60 m (ibid.: 244).
109. *ASIAR* 1907-08 (J.H. Marshall & S. Konow): 43.
110. *ASIAR* 1906-07 (id.): 83; Sahni (1923: 29).
111. Sahni (1914: 261; Di117). Later, Sahni (1923: 30) maintained that 'the inner courtyard was open to the skies'.
112. Cōḷa temples are often equipped with more than one entrance. *Mukha-maṇḍapa*-s are necessary in a temple surrounded by an enclosure because they 'have the function of an entrance pavilion, conceived as a monumental entrance, leading to a ritually defined space, as opposed to a physically

delineated precinct bounded by an architectural enclosure wall' (Wagoner 2001: 173).

113. *ASIAR* 1907-08 (J.H. Marshall & S. Konow): 43.
114. Ibid.: 46.
115. Sahni (1923: 31).
116. Ibid.: 31.
117. See for instance the medieval Śiva temple of Balikeśvara (district East Nimar, Madhya Pradesh) in which a covered drain built in bricks connected the sanctum to a circular *kuṇḍa*, receiving the *abhiṣeka* water (*IAR* 1987-88: 61).
118. Sahni (1914: 31).
119. Many examples of Aśoka pillars used as *Śivaliṅga*-s are enumerated by S.P. Gupta (1980: 27).
120. Chaudhary (1978: 229).
121. Sahni (1914: 213, Da32).
122. Id. (1923: 22).
123. *ASIAR* 1907-08 (J.H. Marshall & S. Konow): 68.
124. *ASIAR* 1906-07 (id.): 80-81, pl. XXIII,11; Sahni (1914: Bh4); Digital South Asia Library (no. 5809). For Tryambaka as a form of the eleven Rudras, see Rao, T.N. Gopinatha (1914-16, II: 390).
125. *ASIAR* 1918-19 (D.R. Sahni): 15. In relation to the 'Saiva sculptures', Sahni says that they 'show how completely the site of Sarnath must have been Brahmanized in later periods'.
126. Marshall states that Monastery I 'had not long been built when destruction overtook it', and that 'the discovery, to the west of the monastery, of a number of unfinished carvings of identically the same pattern as those belonging to the structure, suggests that the superstructure may not have been actually completed when ruin overwhelmed it' (*ASIAR* 1906-07, J.H. Marshall & S. Konow: 84).
127. Sahni 1914: Bh1, pl. XVIII.

Bibliography

[This bibliography is ordered in three sections (*Data Archive*, *Texts*, *Modern Sources and Studies in History, Religion and Philosophy*), of which the first two are further divided in sub-sections. The articles published in some journals and collections (*The Indian Antiquary*, *Epigraphia Indica*, *Annual Reports of the Archaeological Survey of India*, and a few others) are not listed in the bibliography, but their authors and the year of publication are cited in the notes to the texts. Only academic institutions (universities, museums, etc.), some difficut to track even with the help of the World Wide Web, are mentioned as publishers. Journals cited only once are not included in the list of abbreviations.]

ABBREVIATIONS

AA *Artibus Asiae*. Dresden-Leipzig, Ascona-New York, Zürich-Washington.

ABORI *Annals of the Bhandarkar Oriental Research Institute*. Bhandarkar Oriental Research Institute, Poona 1917-92.

AI *Ancient India*. Bulletin of the Archaeological Survey of India, 1946-62/63. New Delhi.

AION *Annali dell'Istituto Orientale di Napoli*. Napoli.

AITMS Ancient Indian Tradition & Mythology Series/Purāṇas in Translation. Delhi.

ArsOr *Ars Orientalis*. Washington.

ArtsAs *Arts Asiatiques*. Paris.

ArtBull *The Art Bullettin*. A Quarterly Published by the College Art Association of America. New York.

ASI Archaeological Survey of India, New Delhi.

ASIAR *Archaeological Survey of India. Annual Reports*. Calcutta, Delhi 1902-03 [1904]-1938-39 [1941].

ASIR *Archaeological Survey of India Reports*, ed. Alexander Cunningham & al. Simla, Calcutta, 1871-85 (Index vol. 1887).

AsRes *Asiatick Researches; or, Transactions of the Society Instituted in Bengal, for Inquiring into the History and Antiquities, the Arts, Sciences, and Literature, of Asia*. Calcutta 1788 [Jan. 1789]-1839.

ASWIR *Archaeological Survey of Western India Reports*. London 1874-83.

BSOAS *Bullettin of the School of Oriental and African Studies*. University of London.

CHB *The Comprehensive History of Bihar*, ed. Bindeshwari Prasad Sinha & al., 3 vols. in 6 tomes. K.P. Jayaswal Institute, Patna 1974-87.

CII *Corpus Inscriptionum Indicarum*. ASI. Oxford, New Delhi.

EAP *Encyclopaedia of Asian Philosophy*, ed. Oliver Leaman. London 2001.

EC *Epigraphia Carnatica* (Mysore Archaeological Series), ed. B[enjamin] Lewis Rice. Bangalore, Mangalore 1886-1905. Rev. ed. B.L. Rice, Ramanujapuram Narasimhacar & al. Bangalore.

EFEO Ecole Française d'Extrême-Orient. Paris.

EI *Epigraphia Indica*, 1892-1977/78. Calcutta, New Delhi.

EJ *Encyclopaedia of Jainism*, ed. Nagendra Kr. Singh, 30 vols. New Delhi 2001.

EITA Encyclopedia of Indian Temples Architecture. New Delhi.

EW *East and West*. IsMEO/IsIAO, Rome.

HCIP The History and Culture of the Indian People, vols.: 2 (*The Age of Imperial Unity*, 1968^4 [1951]), 4 (*The Age of Imperial Kanauj*, 1964^2 [1955]), 5 (*The Struggle for Empire*, 1966^2 [1957]), gen. ed. R[amesh] C[handra] Majumdar. Bombay.

HistRel *History of Religions*. University of Chicago.

HJAS *Harvard Journal of Asiatic Studies*. Cambridge, Mass.

IA *The Indian Antiquary,* A Journal of Oriental Research in Literature, Languages, Folklore, etc., etc. Bombay 1872-1933.

IAR *Indian Archaeology. A Review.* ASI.

IHQ *The Indian Historical Quarterly*. Calcutta 1925-63.

IHR *The Indian Historical Review*. New Delhi.

IIJ *Indo-Iranian Journal*. Leiden.

IsIAO Istituto Italiano per il Medio ed Estremo Oriente, Roma.

IsMEO Istituto Italiano per l'Africa e l'Oriente, Roma. [Merged in the above]

JAIH *Journal of Ancient Indian History*. University of Calcutta.

JAOS *Journal of the American Oriental Society*. Ann Arbor.

JASB *The Journal of the Asiatic Society of Bengal*. Calcutta 1832-1904.

JBORS *Journal of the Bihar [and Orissa] Research Society*. Patna 1915-61.

JIABS *The Journal of the International Association of Buddhist Studies*. University of Wisconsin, Madison.

JIP *Journal of Indian Philosophy*. Dordrecht.

JISOA *Journal of the Indian Society of Oriental Art*. Calcutta.

JOIB *Journal of the Oriental Institute of Baroda*. Maharajah Sayajirao University, Baroda.

JPTS *Journal of the Pāli Text Society*. London.

JRAS *Journal of the Royal Asiatic Sociey of Great Britain and Ireland*. London.

JRASB *Journal of the Royal Asiatic Society of Bengal*. Calcutta 1935-50.

LK *Lalit Kalā*. A Journal of Oriental Art, Chiefly Indian. Lalit Kalā Akademi, New Delhi.

MJLS *Madras Journal of Literature and Science*. Madras Literary Society and Auxiliary of the Royal Asiatic Society, Madras 1833-89/94.

MASI	Memoirs of the Archaeological Survey of India. Calcutta, New Delhi.
Numen	*Numen.* International Review for the History of Religions. Leiden.
PA	*Pakistan Archaeology.* The Department of Archaeology and Museums, Karachi.
PIFIP	Publications de l'Institut Français d'Indologi, Pondichéry.
PIHC	*Proceedings of the Indian History Congress.*
PTS	The Pali Text Society, Oxford.
SAA	*South Asian Archaeology. Proceedings of the International Conferences of South Asian Archaeologists in Western Europe.*
SAS	*South Asian Studies.* The British Association for South Asian Studies, London.
SBB	Sacred Books of the Buddhists. The Pali Text Society, Oxford.
SBE	Sacred Books of the East, translated by Various Scholars and edited by F. Max Müller (50 vols). Oxford 1879-1910.
SII	*South Indian Inscriptions*, ed. Eugen Hultzsch, 1890-1903. Madras.
SOR	Serie Orientale Roma. IsMEO/IsIAO, Roma.
SocSci	*Social Scientist.* New Delhi.
SRAA	*Silk Road Art and Archaeology.* Institute of Silk Road Studies, Kamakura 1990-2004.
WSTB	Wiener Studien zur Tibetologie und Buddhismuskunde. Universität Wien.

DATA ARCHIVE

(A) Archaeological and Numismatic Sources, Reports and Gazetteers

Agrawala, Vasudeva S. (1984*b*), *Varanasi Seals and Sealings*, ed. Prithvi Kumar Agrawala. Varanasi.

Allchin, F. Raymond, with contributions from George Erdosy & al. (1995), *The Archaeology of Early Historic South Asia: The Emergence of Cities and States*. Cambridge.

Ashfaque, S.M. (1969), 'The Grand Mosque of Banbhore'. *PA* 6, pp. 182-209.

Barba, Federica (2004), 'The Fortified Cities of the Ganges Plain in the First Millennium BC'. *EW* 54, pp. 223-50.

Beames, John (1871), 'The Ruins at Kopari, Balasore District'. *JASB* 40, pp. 247-50.

Bechert, Heinz (1961), 'Aśokas "Schismenedikt" und der Begriff Sanghabedha'. *Wiener Zeitschrift für die Kunde Südasiens* 5, pp. 19-52.

Begley, Vimala & al. (1996), *The Ancient Port of Arikamedu: New Excavations and Researches 1989-1992*, vol. 1 (EFEO, Mémoires archéologiques 22). Pondichéry.

Bopearachchi, Osmund & Marie-Françoise Boussac eds (2005), *Afghanistan, ancien carrefour entre l'est et l'ouest. Actes du colloque international, Musée Henri-Prades-Lattes, 5-7 mai 2003*. Indicopleustoi, Archaeologies of the Indian Ocean 3. Turnhout.

Buchanan, Francis (1807), *A Journey from Madras through the Countries of Mysore, Canara, and Malabar*, 3 vols. London.

——— (1936), *An Account of the Districts of Bihar and Patna in 1811-1812*, 2 vols. The Bihar and Orissa Research Society, Patna. Calcutta.

[——] Buchanan Hamilton, Francis (1819), *An Account of the Kingdom of Nepal and of the Territories Annexed to this Dominion by the House of Gurkha*. Edinburgh.

Burgess, James (1874), *Report of the First Season's Operation in the Belgâm and Kaladgi Districts. January to May 1874*. ASWIR 1. London 1874.

——— (1883), *Report on the Elura Cave Temples and the Brahmanical and Jaina Caves in Western India, Completing the Results of the Fifth, Sixth, and Seventh Seasons' Operations of the Archaeological Survey, 1877-78, 1878-79, 1879-80*. ASWIR 5. London.

Callieri, Pierfrancesco (2001), 'Excavations of the IsIAO Italian Archaeological Mission in Pakistan at Bīr-koṭ-ghwaṇḍai, Swat: The Sacred Building on the Citadel', in C. Jarrige & Vinçent Lefèvre, eds., pp. 417-25.

Chakrabarti, Dilip K. (1999), *India, an Archaeological History: Palaeolithic Beginnings to Early Historic Foundations*. New Delhi.

——— (2001), *Archaeological Geography of the Ganga Plain: The Lower and the Middle Ganga*. New Delhi.

Cousens, Henry (1929), *The Antiquities of Sind with Historical Outline*. ASI, Imperial Series 46. Calcutta.

Cribb, Joe (1998), 'Western Satraps and Satavahanas: Old and New Ideas of Chronology', in Amal Kumar Jha & Sanjay Garg, *Ex moneta: Essays on Numismatics, History and Archaeology in Honour of Dr. David W. MacDowall*, 2 vols., I, pp. 167-82. New Delhi.

——— (2005), 'The Greek Kingdom of Bactria, its Coinage and its Collapse', in O. Bopearachchi & M.-F. Boussac, eds, pp. 207-25.

Cunningham, Alexander (1854), *The Bhilsa Topes; or, Buddhist Monuments of Central India: Comprising a Brief Historical Sketch of the Rise, Progress, and Decline of Buddhism, with an Account of the Opening and Examination of the Various Groups of Topes around Bhilsa*. London.

——— (1863), *Abstract Report of Operations of the Archaeological Surveyor to the Government of India during the Season of 1861-62*. *JASB* 32, Supplementary I. (Also, in *ASIR* 1, pp. 1-130.)

——— (1879), *The Stūpa of Bharhut: A Buddhist Monument Ornamented with Numerous Sculptures Illustrative of Buddhist Legend and History in the Third Century* BC. London.

——— (1892), *Mahābodhi or the Great Buddhist Temple under the Bodhi Tree at Buddha-Gaya*. London.

——— (1963), *The Ancient Geography of India. I, The Buddhist Period, Including the Campaigns of Alexander, and the Travels of Hwen-Thsang*. Varanasi. (London 1871).

Dagens, Bruno (1984), *Entre Alampur et Śrīśailam. Recherches archéologiques en Andhra Pradesh*, 2 vols. PIFIP 67.

Deyell, John S. (1990), *Living Without Silver: The Monetary History of Early Medieval North India.* Oxford University Press, New Delhi.

De Simone, Daniela (forth.), 'A Tentative Map of Mauryan Pataliputra: The Limits Defined by the "Palisade"'. *SAA* 2010.

Dwivedi, I.D. & al. (2005-06), 'Archaeological Investigation in and around Adi-Badri in Yamuna Nagar District of Haryana'. *History Today: Journal of History and Historical Archaeology* 6, pp. 54-63. New Delhi.

Faccenna, Domenico (1980-81), *Butkara I (Swāt, Pakistan) 1956-1962*, 5 vols. (vol. 5.2 is a portfolio). IsMEO Reports and Memoirs 3. Rome.

Falk, Henry (2006), *Aśokan Sites and Artefacts. A Source-book with Bibliography.* Museum für Indische Kunst, Berlin, Monographien zur Indische Archäologie, Kunst und Philologie 18. Mainz am Rhein.

Filigenzi, Anna (2001), 'Stone and Stucco Sculptures from the Sacred Building of Bīr-koṭ-ghwaṇḍai, Swat, Pakistan', in C. Jarrige & V. Lefèvre, eds, pp. 453-61.

Ghosh, A[malananda], ed. (1989), *An Encyclopaedia of Indian Archaeology*, 2 vols. New Delhi.

Göbl, Robert (1984), *System und Chronologie der Münzprägung des Kušansreiches* (Österreichische Akademie der Wissenschaften, Phil.-Hist. Kl.). Wien.

Hawkes, Jason Derek (2006) *The Buddhist Stupa Site of Bharhut and its Sacred and Secular Geographies*, 2 vols. (Ph. D. thesis). Department of Archaeology, University of Cambridge.

Härtel, Herbert (1987), 'Archaeological Evidence on the Early Vāsudeva Worship', in Gherardo Gnoli & Lionello Lanciotti, eds, *Orientalia Iosephi Tucci Memoriae Dicata* (Serie Orientale Roma 56), 3 vols., pp. 573-87. Roma.

Hoey, W[illiam] (1892), 'Set Mahet'. *JASB* 61 (Part 1, extra number), pp. 1-64.

Jarrige, Cathérine & Vincent Lefèvre eds, *SAA 2001*, 2 vols. Paris.

Jayaswal, Vidula (1991), *Kushana Clay Art of the Ganga Plains: A Case Study of Human Form from Khairadih.* Delhi.

——— (2009) *Ancient Varanasi: An Archaeological Perspective (Excavations at Aktha).* New Delhi.

Joshi, Maheswar P. (1989), *Morphogenesis of Kuṇindas: A Numismatic Overview.* Almora.

Katare, S.L. (1959), 'Excavations at Sirpur'. *IHQ* 35, pp. 1-8.

[Khan, F.A.] (1964), 'Excavations at Banbhore'. *PA* 1, pp. 49-55.

Khare, D. (1967), 'Discovery of a Vishnu Temple near the Heliodoros Pillar, Besnagar, Dist. Vidisha (M.P.)'. *LK* 13, pp. 21-27.

Kumar, Krishna (1985-86), 'Date and Significance of a Stupa Shrine at Sarnath'. *JISOA* n.s. 15, pp. 8-15.

Ḳuraishī, Muḥammad Ḥamīd (1931), *List of Ancient Monuments Protected under Act VII of 1904 in the Province of Bihar and Orissa.* ASI, New Imperial Series 51. Calcutta.

Lal, B[raj] B[asi] (1993), *Excavations at Śṛṅgaverapura (1977-86),* vol. I. MASI 88.

Longhurst, A[lbert] H[enry] (1938), *The Buddhist Antiquities of Nāgārjunakoṇḍa, Madras Presidency*. MASI 54.

Losty, Jeremiah P. (1991), 'The Mahābodhi Temple Before its Restoration', in Gouriswar Bhattacharya, ed., Akṣayanīvī. *Essays Presented to Dr. Debala Mitra in Admiration of her Scholarly Contributions*, pp. 235-57. Delhi.

Lyding Will, Elizabeth (1991), 'The Mediterranean Shipping Amphoras from Arikamedu', in Vimala Begley & Richard Daniel De Puma, eds, *Rome and India: The Ancient Sea Trade*, pp. 151-56. University of Wisconsin, Madison.

MacDowall, David W. (2005), 'The Role of Demetrius in Arachosia and the Kabul Valley', in O. Bopearachchi & M.-F. Boussac, eds, pp. 197-206.

Mani, B.R. (2005-06), 'The Enigmatic Monastery of Kumāradevī at Sarnath: New Identification'. *Prāgdhārā. Journal of the U.P. State Archaeological Department* 16, pp. 157-64. Lucknow.

Marshall, John & Alfred Foucher [1940], *The Monuments of Sāñchī*, with the Texts of Inscriptions Edited, Translated and Annotated by N[ani] G[opal] Majumdar, 3 vols. [Calcutta].

Mitra, Debala (1981-83), *Ratnagiri (1958-61)*, 2 vols. MASI 80.

Mitra, Rajendralala (1864), 'On the Ruins of Buddha Gayā'. *JASB* 33, pp. 173-87.

——— (1875-80), *The Antiquities of Orissa*, 2 vols. Calcutta.

——— (1878), *Buddha Gayá, the Hermitage of Śákya Muni*. Calcutta.

Mohapatra, R.P. (1986), *Archaeology in Orissa (Sites and Monuments)*, 2 vols. Delhi.

Mukherjee, B[ratindra] N[ath], with the assistance of T.N. Raychaudhuri (1990), *The Indian Gold: An Introduction to the Cabinet of Gold Coins in the Indian Museum*. Calcutta.

Mustamandy, Shabiye [1972], *The Fishporch*. Information and Culture Ministry, Archaeology Institute. Kabul.

[——] Mostamindi, Shaïbaï & Mariella Mostamindi (1969), 'Nouvelles fouilles a Haḍḍa (1966-67) par l'Institut Afghan d'Archéologie'. *ArtsAs* 19, pp. 15-36.

Narain, A.K. (1976-78), *Excavations at Rājghāt (1957-58; 1960-65)*, 5 vols. Banaras Hindu University. Varanasi.

Nishikawa, Koji, ed. (1994), *Ranigat: A Buddhist Site in Gandhara, Pakistan, Surveyed 1983-1992*, vol. 2 *(plates)*. Kyoto University, Kyoto.

Page, J[ames] A[lfred] (1923), 'Nalanda Excavations'. *JBORS* 9, pp. 1-22.

Patil, D[evendrakumar] R[ajaram] (1963), *The Antiquarian Remains in Bihar*. K.P. Jayaswal Institute, Patna.

Prasad, Ram Chandra (1987), *Archaeology of Champā and Vikramaśīlā*. Delhi.

Sahni, Daya Ram (1914), *Catalogue of the Museum of Archaeology at Sārnāth*, with an Introduction by J.Ph. Vogel. Calcutta.

——— (1923), *Guide to the Buddhist Ruins of Sarnath, with a Plan of Excavations and Five Photographic Plates*. Calcutta.

Saran, S.C. (2008), 'Excavations at Juafardih and Its Identification with Kulika'. *Purātattva* 38, pp. 59-73. Indian Archaeological Society, New Delhi.

Sarkar, H. (1962), 'Some Aspects of the Buddhist Monuments at Nāgārjunakoṇḍa'. *AI* 16, pp. 65-85.

——— (1985), 'The Nāgārjunakoṇḍa Phase of the Lower Kṛṣṇā Valley Art: A Study Based on Epigraphical Data', in F.M. Asher & G.S. Gai, eds, pp. 29-40.

Sarkar, H. & B.N. Misra (1966), *Nagarjunakonda*. ASI.

Sarma, I.K. (1994), *Paraśurāmēśvara Temple at Gudimallam (A Probe into its Origins)*. Nagpur.

Sastri, T.V.G., M. Kasturibai & M. Veerender (1992), *Vaddamanu Excavations (1981-85)*. Birla Archaeological and Cultural Research Institute, Hydrabad.

Sewell, Robert (1878), *Antiquities of the Kistna. First Report – Bezwada and Undavilli—Archaeological Report on Antiquities near Bezwada, Kistna District—in Government of Madras, Public Department, 1st November 1878, No. 1620*. Madras.

Shaw, Julia (2004), 'Nāga Sculptures in Sanchi's Archaeological Landscape: Buddhism, Vaiṣṇavism and Local Agricultural Cults in Central India, First Century BCE to Fifth Century CE'. *AA* 64, pp. 5-59.

Shaw, Julia & John Sutcliffe (2001), 'Ancient Irrigation Works in the Sanchi Area: an Archaeological and Hydrogeological Investigation'. *SAS* 17, pp. 55-75.

——— (2005), 'Ancient Dams and Buddhist Landscapes in the Sanchi area: New Evidence on Irrigation, Land use and Monasticism in Central India'. *SAS* 21, pp. 1-24.

Singh, Birendra Pratap (1985), *Life in Ancient Varanasi: An Account Based on Archaeological Evidence*. Delhi.

Singh, Upinder (1988), *The Discovery of Ancient India: Early Archaeologists and the Beginnings of Archaeology*. Delhi.

Srivastava, K[rishna] M[urari] (1996), *Excavations at Piprahwa and Ganwaria*. MASI 94.

Thomas, Edward (1854), 'Note on the Present State of the Excavations at Sárnáth'. *JASB* 23, pp. 469-77.

Vasu, Nagendranāth (1911), *The Archaeological Survey of Mayurabhanja*. Calcutta.

Verardi, Giovanni (1992), *Excavations at Harigaon, Kathmandu: Final Report*. (IsMEO Reports and Memoirs 25), 2 vols. Rome.

——— (2004), 'Les recherches archéologiques au Népal', in *Le Népal. Au pays de Kathman du*. Dossiers d'archéologie 293, pp. 40-45. Dijon.

——— (2007*a*), 'The Archaeological Perspective [in Afghanistan]', in Giandomenico Picco & Antonio Palmisano eds, *Afghanistan. How Much of the Past in the New Future*, pp. 221-52. Quaderni di 'Futuribili' (Istituto di sociologia internazionale di Gorizia & International University Institute for European Studies). Gorizia.

——— (2007*b*), *Excavations at Gotihawa and Pipri, Kapilbastu District, Nepal*. IsIAO. Roma.

——— (2010), 'Issues in the Excavation, Chronology and Monuments of Tapa Sardar', in Michael Alram & al. eds, *Coins, Art and Chronology II: The First Millennium* CE *in the Indo-Iranian Borderlands*, pp. 341-55. Vienna.

Verardi, Giovanni & Elio Paparatti, with an Appendix by Minoru Inaba (2004), *Buddhist Caves of Jāghūrī and Qarabāgh-e Ghaznī, Afghanistan*. IsIAO Reports and Memoirs, n.s. 2. Rome.

——— (2005), 'From Early to Late Tapa Sardār: A Tentative Chronology'. *EW* 55, pp. 405-44.

Verma, B.S. (2001), 'Excavations at Antichak: The Ruins of the Ancient Vikramśīla University', in I.K. Sarma & B. Vidyadhara Rao, eds., *Śrī Subrahmaṇya Smṛtī. Essays on Indian Pre-history, Proto-history, Archaeology, Art, Architecture, Epigraphy, Numismatics, Crafts, Iconography and Conservation (Dr. Raviprolu Subrahmanyam Commemoration Volumes*), 2 vols., pp. 299-308. New Delhi.

(B) Epigraphy

Asher, Frederick M. & G[ovind] S[wamirao] Gai, eds (1985), *Indian Epigraphy. Its Bearing on the History of Art*. American Institute of Indian Studies, New Delhi.

Barua, Benimadhab [Beni Madhab] (1946), *Asoka and His Inscriptions*, 2 vols. Calcutta.

Basak, Radhagovinda (1959), *Aśokan Inscriptions*. Calcutta.

Bhattacharya, Suresh Chandra (2005-6), 'The Jagjibanpur Plate of Mahendrapāla Comprehensively Re-edited'. *JAIH* 23, pp. 61-125.

Chhabra, Bahadurchand & Govind Swamirao Gai (1981), *Inscriptions of the Early Gupta Kings* [J. Fleet]. Rev. Devadatta Ramakrishna Bhandarkar. *CII* 3. ASI [re-edition of Fleet 1888].

Cohen, Richard S. (1997), 'Problems in the Writing of Ajanta's History: The Epigraphic Evidence'. *IIJ* 40, pp. 125-48.

Didri, Henri (2002), 'Indiens et Proche-Orientaux dans une grotte de Suquṭrā (Yémen)'. *JA* 290, pp. 565-610.

Falk, Henry (2001), 'The *yuga* of Sphujiddhvaja and the Era of the Kuṣāṇas'. *SRAA* 7, pp. 121-36.

Fleet, John Faithfull (1888), *Inscriptions of the Early Gupta Kings and Their Successors* (*CII* 3). Calcutta.

Gershevitch, Ilja (1979), 'Nokonzok's Well'. *Afghan Studies* 2, pp. 55-73. London.

Ghafur, Muhammad Abdul (1966), 'Fourteen Kufic Inscriptions of Banbhore, the Site of Daybul'. *PA* 3, pp. 64-90.

Göbl, Robert (1965), *Die drei Versionen der Kaniška-Inschrift von Surkh Kotal. Neuedition der Texte auf verbesserter technisch-epigraphischer und paläographischer Grundlage*. Österreichische Akademie der Wissenschaften, Phil.-Hist. Kl., Denkschriften 88. Wien.

Hultzsch, E[ugen], ed. (1925), *Inscriptions of Aśoka. CII* 1. Oxford.

Joshi, M.C. & Ram Sharma (1991-93), 'A Reassessment of Ghosundi or Nagari Epigraph of Parasariputra Gajayana'. *JISOA*, n.s. 20-21, pp. 56-59.

Konow, Sten (1926), 'The Inscription on the So-called Bodh-Gaya Plaque'. *JBORS* 12/2, pp. 179-82.

Lüders, Heinrich (1961), *Mathurā Inscriptions*. Unpublished Papers Edited by Klaus L. Janert. Abhandlungen der Akademie der Wissenschaften in Göttingen, Phil.-Hist. Kl., Dritte Folge 47. Göttingen.

Lüders List = Lüders, Heinrich (1912), *A List of Brāhmī Inscriptions from the Earliest Times to about AD. 400 with the Exception of those of Aśōka* (Appendix to *EI* 10).

Mirashi, Vasudev Vishnu (1982), 'Did Candragupta II Sell His Own Palaces at Vidiśā?' *ABORI* 63, pp. 221-23.

Mukherjee, B[ratindra] N[ath] (1984-85), 'Inscribed "Mahabodhi Temple" Plaque from Kumrahar'. *JISOA*, n.s. 14, pp. 43-46.

Mukherji, Ramaranjan & Sachindra Kumar Maity (1967), *Corpus of Bangal Inscriptions Bearing on History and Civilization of Bengal*. Calcutta.

Norman, K[enneth] R[oy] (1990*a*), 'Aśoka and Capital Punishment', in id., *Collected Papers* 1, pp. 200-09. PTS.

——— (1990*b*), 'Notes on Aśoka's Fifth Pillar Edict' in id., *Collected Papers* 1, pp. 68-76. PTS.

——— (1992), 'Aśoka's "Schism" Edict', in id., *Collected Papers* 3, pp. 191-218.

——— (1994), 'Aśoka and Saṅghabedha', in id., *Collected Papers* 5, pp. 207-29.

Peterson, Peter [1895], *A Collection of Prakrit and Sanskrit Inscriptions*. Published by the Bhavnagar Archaeological Department under the Auspices of His Highness Raol Shri Takhtsingji [...] Maharaja of Bhavnagar. Bhavnagar.

Rao, Hanumantha, & al. (1998), *Buddhist Inscriptions of Andhradesa*. Ananda Buddha Vihara Trust. Secunderabad [Hyderabad].

Regmi, Dilli Rahman (1983), *Inscriptions of Ancient Nepal*, 3 vols. New Delhi.

Salomon, Richard (1991), 'Epigraphic Remains of Indian Traders in Egypt'. *JAOS* 111, pp. 731-36. New Haven.

Sanyal, Niradbandhu (1929), 'A Buddhist Inscription from Bodh-Gaya of the Reign of Jayaccandradeva', V.S.124x. *IHQ* 5, pp. 14-30.

Sastri, Hiranand (1942), *Nalanda and its Epigraphic Material*. MASI 66.

Schneider, Ulrich (1978), *Die grosse Felsen-Edikte Aśokas. Kritische Ausgabe, Übersetzung und Analyse der Texte*. Freiburger Beiträge zur Indologie 11. Wiesbaden.

Sims-Williams, Nicholas (2004), 'The Bactrian Inscription of Rabatak: A New Reading'. *Bullettin of the Asia Institute* 18, pp. 53-68. Bromfield Hills.

Sims-Williams, Nicholas & Joe Cribb (1995-96), 'A New Bactrian Inscription of Kanishka the Great', in *SRAA* 4, pp. 75-142.

Sircar, D[inesh] C[handra] (1965*a*), *Indian Epigraphy*. Delhi.
——— (1965[2]*b*), *Select Inscriptions Bearing on Indian History and Civilization*, vol. 1: *From the Sixth Century BC to the Sixth Century AD* Calcutta (1st edn 1942).
——— (1983*b*), *Select Inscriptions Bearing on Indian History and Civilization*, vol. 2: *From the Sixth to the Eighteenth Century AD* Delhi.
Strauch, Ingo & Michael D. Bukharin (2004), 'Indian Inscriptions from the Cave Ḥoq on Suquṭrā'. *AION* 64, pp. 121-38.
Taddei, Maurizio & Giovanni Verardi (1978), 'Tapa Sardār. Second Preliminary Report'. *EW* 28, pp. 33-136.
Thaplial, Kiran Kumar (1985), *Inscriptions of the Maukharīs, Later Guptas, Puṣpabhūtis and Yaśovarman of Kanauj*. Indian Council of Historical Research, Delhi.
Tieken, Herman (2000), 'Aśoka and the Buddhist *Saṃgha*: A Study of Aśoka's Schism Edict and Minor Rock Edict I'. *BSOAS* 63, pp. 1-30.
Tieken, Herman & Katsuhiko Sato (2000), 'The Ghaṭikā of the Twice-Born in South-Indian Inscriptions'. *Indo-Iranian Journal* 43, pp. 213-23.
Tournier, Vincent (forth.), 'The Elder Mahākāśyapa, His Orthodox Lineage, and the Wish for Buddhahood: Some Considerations on and around the Bodhgayā Inscriptions of Mahānāman', in Tansen Sen, ed., *Buddhism Across Asia: Networks of Material, Intellectual and Cultural Exchange. Proceedings of the Conference Held on 16-18 February 2009*. Institute of Southeast Asian Studies, Singapore.
Tripathy, Snigdha (2000), *Inscriptions of Orissa*, vol. II (*Inscriptions of the Bhauma-Karas*). Indian Council of Historical Research, New Delhi.
Vigasin, A[leksej] A[leksejevič] (1993-94), 'Aśoka's Third Rock Edict Reinterpreted'. *IHR* 20, pp. 16-21.

(C) Art-Historical Source Materials and Studies

Agarwal, U. (1964), *Khajurāho Sculptures and Their Significance*. Delhi.
Agrawala, Prithvi Kumar (1967), *Skanda-Kārttikeya (A Study in the Origin and Development)*. Monographs of the Department of Ancient Indian History, Culture and Archaeology 3. Banaras Hindu University. Varanasi.
Agrawala, R.C. (1969), 'Unpublished Yaksha-Yakshī Statues from Besnagar'. *LK*, pp. 47-49.
Agrawala, Vasudeva S. (1965), *Studies in Indian Art*. Varanasi.
——— (1977), *Gupta Art (A History of Indian Art in the Gupta Period, 300-600 A.D.)*. Varanasi.
Asher, Frederick M. (1980), *The Art of Eastern India, 300-800*. University of Minnesota, Minneapolis.
——— (1988), 'Gaya: Monuments of the Pilgrimage Town', in J. Leoshko, ed., pp. 74-88. Bombay.

Asher, Frederick M. & Walter Spink (1989), Maurya Figural Sculpture Reconsidered. *ArsOr* 19, pp. 1-25.

Auboyer, Janine & Herbert Härtel (1971), *Indien und Südostasien* (Propyläen Kunstgeschichte 16). Berlin.

Bakker, Hans (1997) *The Vakatakas: An Essay in Hindu Iconology*. Gonda Indological Studies 5. Groningen.

Banerjea, Jitendra Nath (1956²), *The Development of Hindu Iconography*. University of Calcutta.

Banerji, R[akhal] D[as] (1928), *Basreliefs of Badami*. MASI 25.

Bautze-Picron, Claudine (1996), 'From God to Demon, from Demon to God: Brahmā & Other Hindu Deities in Late Buddhist Art of Eastern India'. *Journal of Bengal Art* 1, pp. 109-35. Dhaka.

——— (2002), '*Nidhi*s and Other Images of Richness and Fertility in Ajanta'. *EW* 52, pp. 225-84.

——— (forth.[2011]), *The Forgotten Place: Stone Sculpture at Kurkihār*. ASI.

Begley, W[ayne] E[dison] (1973), *Viṣṇu's Flaming Wheel: The Iconography of the Sudarśana-Cakra*. New York.

Bhattacharyya, Benoytosh (1958²), *The Indian Buddhist Iconography: Mainly Based on* The Sādhanamālā *and Cognate Tāntric Texts of Rituals*. Calcutta.

Bhattacharya, Gouriswar (2000), *Essays on Buddhist, Hindu, Jain Iconography & Epigraphy*, ed. Enamul Haque. Studies in Bengal Art Series 1. Dhaka.

Bhattacharya, Swapna (1988), 'On the Concept of Sāmantas in Early Medieval Bengal (*c*. 5th-13th Centuries AD.)', in K.K. Das Gupta, P.K. Bhattacharyya & R.D. Choudhury, eds, Sraddhañjali: *Studies in Ancient Indian History (D.C. Sircar Commemoration Volume)*, pp. 75-81. Delhi.

Bhattasali, Nalini Kanta (1929), *Iconography of Buddhist and Brahmanical Sculptures in the Dacca Museum*. Dacca.

Biswas, T.K. & Bhogendra Jha (1985), *Gupta Sculptures, Bharat Kala Bhavan*. Banaras Hindu University, Varanasi.

Carter, Martha L. (1992), 'Dionysiac Festivals and Gandhāran Imagery'. *Res orientales* 4 (= *Banquets d'Orient*), pp. 51-60. Bures-sur-Yvette.

Casile, Anne (2009), *Temples et expansion d'un centre religieux en Inde centrale. Lectures du paysage archéologique de Badoh-Paṭhāri du 5e au 10e siècle de notre ère*. Ph.D. thesis, La Sorbonne-Paris 3. Paris.

Champakalakshmi, R[adha] (1981), *Vaisnava Iconography in the Tamil Country*. New Delhi.

Chandra, Pramod [1970], *Stone Sculpture in the Allahabad Museum: A Descriptive Catalogue*. American Institute of Indian Studies, Poona.

Clark, Walter Eugene, ed. (1937), *Two Lamaistic Pantheons: From Materials Collected by the Late Baron A. von Staël-Holstein*, 2 vols. Harvard-Yenching Institute Monograph Series 3 & 4. Cambridge, Mass.

Coomaraswamy, Ananda (1927), *History of Indian and Indonesian Art*. Leipzig-New York-London.

——— (1935), *Elements of Buddhist Iconography*. Harvard University Press, Cambridge, Mass.
——— (1956), *La sculpture de Bharhut*. Annales du Musée Guimet, Bibliothèque d'art, nouvelle série 6). Paris.
Daniélou, Alain (1973), *La sculpture érotique hindoue*. Paris.
Dass, Meera I. & Michael Willis (2002), 'The Lion Capital from Udayagiri and the Antiquity of Sun Worship in Central India'. *SAS* 18, pp. 25-45. London.
Dehejia, Vidya (1986) *Yoginī Cult and Temples: A Tantric Tradition*. National Museum, New Delhi
Desai, Devangana (1984), 'Placement and Significance of Erotic Sculptures at Khajuraho', in M.W. Meister, ed., 1984, pp. 143-55.
——— (1985²), *Erotic Sculpture of India: A Socio-Cultural Study*. New Delhi.
——— (1997), *The Religious Imagery of Khajuraho*. Franco-Indian Research Private Ltd., Mumbai.
——— (2000), *Khajuraho*. Oxford University Press, New Delhi.
Desai, Kalpana S. (1973), *Iconography of Visnu (in Northern India, upto the Mediaeval Period)*. New Delhi.
Deshpande, M[adhusudan] N[arhar] (1986), *The Caves of Panhāle-Kājī (Ancient Praṇālaka): An Art Historical Study of Transition from Hinayana, Tantric Vajrayana to Nath* Sampradāya *[Third to Fourteenth Century AD]*. MASI 84.
Deva, Krishna (1980), 'Stone Temple (No. 2) at Nālandā'. *JISOA*, n.s. 11, pp. 80-84.
——— (1990), *Temples of Khajuraho*, 2 vols. ASI. New Delhi.
Deva, Krishna & Vasudeva S. Agrawala (1950), 'The Stone Temple at Nālandā'. *Journal of the Uttar Pradesh Historical Society* 23, pp. 198-212. Lucknow.
Dey, Nundolal (1909), 'The Vikramasilā Monastery'. *JASB*, n.s. 5, pp. 1-13.
Dikshit, K[ashinath] N[arayan] (1921), *Six Sculptures from Mahoba*. MASI 8.
——— (1938), *Excavations at Paharpur, Bengal*. MASI 55.
Dikshit, M[oreshwar] G[angadhar] (1955-57), 'Some Buddhist Bronzes from Sirpur, Madhya Pradesh'. *Bullettin of the Prince of Wales Museum* 5, pp. 1-11. Bombay.
Donaldson, Thomas E. (1976), 'Development of the *Vajra-Mastaka* on Orissan Temples'. *EW* 26, pp. 419-33.
——— (1985), *Hindu Temple Art of Orissa*, 3 vols. Leiden.
——— (1991), 'The Śava-Vāhana as Puruṣa in Orissan Images: Cāmuṇḍā to Kālī/Tārā'. *AA* 51, pp. 107-41.
——— (1999), 'Lakulīśa to Rājaguru: Metamorphosis of the "Teacher" in the Iconographic Program of the Orissan Temple', in P.K. Mishra, ed., *Studies in Hindu and Buddhist Art*, pp. 129-54. New Delhi.
——— (2001), *Iconography of the Buddhist Sculpture of Orissa*, 2 vols. Indira Gandhi National Centre for the Arts. New Delhi.
——— (2002), *Tantra and Śākta Art of Orissa*, 3 vols. New Delhi.

Ducrey Giordano, Ferruccio (1977), *Di alcune rappresentazioni iconografiche dell'*avatāra *di Narasiṃha alla luce del* Narasiṃhapurāṇa *e di altre fonti* (Memorie dell'Accademia Nazionale dei Lincei, Classe di Scienze morali, storiche e filologiche, serie VIII, vol. 20, fasc. 1). Roma.

Fergusson, James (1876), *History of Indian and Eastern Architecture: Forming the Third Volume of the New Edition of the 'History of Architecture'.* London.

——— (1884), *Archaeology in India with Especial Reference to the Works of Babu Rajendralala Mitra.* London.

Fergusson, James & James Burgess (1880), *The Cave Temples of India.* London.

Filigenzi, Anna (1997), 'Buddhist Rock Sculptures in Swat, North Pakistan', in R. Allchin & B. Allchin, eds., with the assistance of Gill Elston & Oleg Starza-Majewski', *SAA 1995*, 2 vols., pp. 625-35. Cambridge, New Delhi.

——— (2000), 'Marginal Notes on the Buddhist Rock Sculptures of Swat', in M. Taddei & G. De Marco, eds., *SAA 1997*, 3 vols., pp. 1065-85. Rome.

Filliozat, Jean (1949), 'Les échanges de l'Inde et de l'empire romain aux premiers siècles de l'ère chrétienne'. *Revue historique* 73, pp. 1-29. Paris.

——— (1973), 'Représentations de Vāsudeva Saṃkarṣaṇa au IIe siècle avant J.C.' *ArtsAs* 26, pp. 113-23. Paris.

Fukuroi, Yuko (2002), 'The Remaining Stone Images of Buddha in Tamiḻnāḍu'. *The Mikkyō Zuzō (The Journal of Buddhist Iconography)* 21, pp. 1-15. Association for the Study of Buddhist Iconography. Kyoto.

Ganguly, Mano Mohan (1912), *Orissa and her Remains: Ancient and Medieval (District Puri).* With an Introduction by J.G. Woodroffe. Calcutta-London.

Goldman, Bernard (1978), 'Parthians in Gandhāra'. *EW* 28, pp. 189-202.

Gottfried Williams, Joanna (1982), *The Art of Gupta India: Empire and Province.* Princeton.

Gupta, S[warajya] P[rakash] (1980), *The Roots of Indian Art (A Detailed Study of the Formative Period of Indian Art and Architecture: Third and Second Centuries* BC *– Mauryan and Late Mauryan).* Delhi.

Gupta, S[warajya] P[rakash], ed. (1985), *Kushāṇa Sculptures from Sanghol (1st-2nd Century* AD*): A Recent Discovery.* National Museum, New Delhi.

Handa, O[ma] C[anda] (1994), *Buddhist Art & Antiquities of Himachal Pradesh Upto 8th Century* AD. New Delhi.

Harle, J[ames] C. (1974), *Gupta Sculpture: Indian Sculpture of the Fourth to the Sixth Centuries* AD. Oxford.

——— (1986), *The Art and Architecture of the Indian Subcontinent.* New Haven-London.

Härtel, Herbert (1985), 'A Śiva Relief from Gandhāra', in Karen Frifelt and Per Sorensen, eds, *SAA 1985.* (Scandinavian Institute of Asian Studies, Occasional Papers 4), pp. 392-96. London-Riverdale.

——— (1992), 'Early Durga Mahisasuramardini Images: A Fresh Appraisal', in T. S. Maxwell, ed., *Eastern Approaches: Essays on Indian Art and Archaeology,* pp. 81-89. Delhi.

Härtel, Herbert & Wibke Lobo (1984), *Schätze Indischer Kunst* (Staatliche Museen Preussischer Kulturbesitz, Museum für Indische Kunst). Berlin.

Hudson, D. Dennis & Margaret H. Case (2008), *The Body of God: An Emperor's Palace for Krishna in Eighth-Century Kanchipuram*. Oxford University Press, New York.

Huntington, Susan L., with contributions by John C. Huntington (1985), *The Art of Ancient India, Buddhist, Hindu, Jain*. New York-Tokyo.

Joshi, N[ilakanth] P[urushottam] (1984), 'Early Forms of Śiva', in M.W. Meister, ed., 1984, pp. 47-61.

——— (1986), *Mātṛkās: Mothers in Kuṣāṇa Art*. New Delhi.

Khan, Abdul Waheed (1964), 'An Early Sculpture of Narasimha (Man-Lion Incarnation of Vishnu Found from the Coastal Andhra along with Pañcha Vīras)'. *Andhra Pradesh Government Archaeological Series* 16. Hyderabad.

Klimburg-Salter Deborah (1989), *The Kingdom of Bamiyan* (Istituto Universitario Orientale, Series Major 5). Naples-Rome.

Knox, Robert (1992), *Amaravati: Buddhist Sculpture from the Great Stūpa*. British Museum, London.

Kramrisch, Stella (1946), *The Hindu Temple*, 2 vols. Calcutta.

Kreisel, Gerd (1986), *Die Śiva Bildwerke der Mathurā-Kunst. Ein Beitrag zur frühinduistischen Ikonographie*. Stuttgart.

Kurita, Isao (1988-90), *Gandhāran Art: 1. The Buddha's Life Story; 2. The World of the Buddha*. Tokyo.

Leoshko Janice, ed. (1988), *Bodhgaya, the Site of Enlightenment*. Bombay.

L'Hernault, Françoise (1978), *L'iconographie de Subrahmaṇya au Tamilnad*. PIFIP 59.

——— (1984), 'Subrahmaṇya as a Supreme Deity', in M.W. Meister, ed., 1984, pp. 257-70.

——— (2006), 'L'enfant-saint qui fait empaler les ennemis de Śiva. La narration figurée d'un épisode de la vie de Campantar à Tirupputaimarutur et à Avutaiyarkovil (Tamilnadu)'. *AION* 66, pp. 123-38.

Linrothe, Rob (1999), *Ruthless Compassion: Wrathful Deities in Early Indo-Tibetan Esoteric Buddhist Art*. London.

Lippe, Ashwin (1969-70), 'Additions and Replacements in Early Chālukya Temples'. *Archives of Asian Art* 23, pp. 6-23. New York.

——— (1972), 'Early Chālukya Icons'. *AA* 34, pp. 273-330, 282-83.

——— van Lohuizen-de Leeuw, J[ohanna] E[ngelberta] (1959), 'An Ancient Hindu Temple in Eastern Afghānistān'. *OrArt*, n.s. 5, pp. 61-69.

——— (1975), 'The Pre-Muslim Antiquities of Sind', in id., ed., *SAA 1975*, pp. 151-74. Leiden.

Longhurst, A[lbert] H[enry] (1936), *The Story of the Stūpa*. Colombo.

——— (1930) *Pallava Architecture, Part III (The Later or Rājasimha Period)*. MASI 40.

Malandra, Geri H. (1988), 'The Mahabodhi Temple', in J. Leoshko, ed., pp. 10-28.

——— (1997), *Unfolding a Maṇḍala: The Buddhist Cave Temples at Ellora*. New Delhi.

de Mallmann, Marie-Thérèse (1963), *Les reinsegnments iconographiques de l'Agni Purana* (Annales du Musée Guimet, Bibliothèque d'études 67). Paris.

——— (1975), *Introduction à l'iconographie du tântrisme bouddhique*. Bibliothèque du Centre de recherches sur l'Asie Centrale et la Haute Asie 1. Paris.

Meister, Michael W., ed. (1984), *Discourses on Śiva: Proceedings of a Symposium on the Nature of Religious Imagery*. Bombay.

Meister, Michael W. & M[adhusudan] A[milal] Dhaky, eds (1983), EITA*: South India, Lower Drāviḍadēśa*, 2 vols. American Institute of Indian Studies, New Delhi-Philadelphia.

——— (1991), EITA*: North India, Period of Early Maturity, c.* AD *700-900*, 2 vols. American Institute of Indian Studies. New Delhi-Princeton.

Meister, Michael W., M[adhusudan] A[milal] Dhaky & Krishna Deva, eds (1988), EITA*: North India, Foundations of North Indian Style, c. 250* BC-AD *1100*, 2 vols. American Institute of Indian Studies. New Delhi-Princeton.

Melzer, Gudrun (2002), *Gajasaṃhāramūrti und Andhakāsuravadhamūrti in der Ikonographie Śivas*. Ph.D. thesis. Freie Universität, Berlin.

——— (2008-9), 'The Wrathful Śiva and the Terrifying Great Goddess in Eastern Indian Art: Andhakāri, Bhairava, and Cāmuṇḍā'. *JAIH* 25, pp. 132-69.

Michell, George (1977), *The Hindu Temple*. Chicago.

Minakshi, C[adambi] (1941), *The Historical Sculptures of the Vaikuṇṭhaperumāḷ Temple, Kāñchī*. MASI 63.

Misra, B[haskara] N[atha] (1987-89), 'Śakrāditya, the First Historical Patron of Nālandā'. *JISOA* 16-17, pp. 26-32.

——— (1998) *Nālandā*, 3 vols. Delhi.

Mitra, Debala (1984), 'Lakulīśa and Early Śaiva Temples in Orissa', in M.W. Meister, ed., 1984, pp. 103-18.

——— (1997-98), 'Notes on Heruka/Hevajra and a Few Images of This Vajrayāna Deity'. *SRAA* 5, pp. 377-93.

——— von Mitterwallner, Gritli (1976), 'The Kuṣāṇa Type of the Goddess Mahiṣāsuramardinī as Compared to the Gupta and Mediaeval Types', in *German Scholars on India, Contributions to Indian Studies*, ed. Cultural Department of the Embassy of the Federal Republic of Germany, 2 vols, II, pp. 196-213. Bombay.

Myer, Prudence R. (1958), 'The Great Temple at Bodh-Gayā', *ArtBull* 40, pp. 277-98.

Narain, A.K. (1973), 'The Two Hindu Divinities on the Coins of Agathocles from Ai Khanum'. *Journal of the Numismatic Society of India* 35, pp. 113-23. Varanasi 1973.

Pal, Pratapaditya (1974), *The Arts of Nepal, I: Sculpture*. Leiden.

——— (1986), *Indian Sculpture*, vol. I, *Circa 500* BC-AD *700 (A Catalogue of the Los Angeles County Museum of Art Collection)*. Los Angeles.

Panikkar, Shivaji K. (1988), 'Sapta-mātṛkā Sculptures at Ellora: An Iconological Analysis', in Ratan Parimoo, Deepak Kannal & Shivaji Panikkar, eds, *Ellora Caves: Sculptures and Architecture*, pp. 291-309. New Delhi.

Panigrahi, Krishna Chandra (1961), *Archaeological Remains at Bhubaneswar*. Calcutta.

Paul, Debjani (1985), 'Antiquity of the Viṣṇupāda at Gaya: Tradition and Archaeology'. *EW* 35, pp. 103-41.

Pichard, Pierre & al. (1994), *Vingt ans après Tanjavur, Gangaikondacholapuram*. EFEO, Mémoires archéologiques 20. Paris.

Ramachandran, T.N. (1954), *The Nāgapaṭṭiṇam and Other Buddhist Bronzes in the Madras Museum = Bullettin of the Madras Government Museum*, n.s. 7/1. Madras.

Prasad, Ram Chandra (1987), *Archaeology of Champā and Vikramaśilā*. Delhi.

Rabe, Michael D. (1997) 'The Māmallapuram *Praśasti*: A Panegyric in Figures'. *AA* 57, pp. 189-241.

Ramaswamy, N[allathagudi] S[riṇivasa] (1975), *Mamallapuram*. Tamil Nadu State Department of Archaeology. Madras.

Rao, T.A. Gopinatha (1914-16), *Elements of Hindu Iconography*, 2 vols. in 4 tomes. Madras.

——— (1915), 'Bauddha Vestiges in Kanchipura'. *IA* 44, pp. 127-29 and pls.

——— (1920), *Travancore Archaeological Series Published under the Orders of the Government of Travancore*, vol. II: *Tamil and Vetteluttu Inscriptions on Stone and Copper-plates*. Trivandrum.

Ray, P.K., ed. (1975), *Archaeological Survey Report. Prachi Valley*. Orissa State Archaeology, Bhubaneswar.

Rea, Alexander (1909), *Pallava Architecture*. ASI, New Imperial Series 34. Madras.

Rosen Stone, Elizabeth (1994), *The Buddhist Art of Nagarjunakonda*. Buddhist Tradition Series 25. Delhi.

Rosenfield, John M. (1967), *The Dynastic Arts of the Kushans*. University of California Press. Berkeley.

Sahai, Bhagwant (1985-86), 'Some Images of Chāmuṇḍā from the District of Begusarai'. *The Journal of the Bihar Purāvid Pariṣad* 9-10 (Prof. V.A. Narain Commemoration Volume), pp. 267-73. Patna.

Sarcar, H. (1986), 'Beginnings of Saivism in South India with Special Reference to Date of Gudimallam Linga', in Kalyan Kumar Ganguli & S.S. Biswas, eds., *Rūpāñjali: In Memory of O.C. Gangoly*, pp. 115-21. Calcutta.

Śarmā, M. & D.P. Śarmā (1994), 'Sirpur ki kāṃsya pratimoṃ par Nālandā Pāl kalā śaulī prabhāv'. *Purātan* 9 (Special Issue, *The Art of Chhattisgarh*), pp. 119-25. Bhopal.

Sclumberger, Daniel, Marc Le Berre & Gérard Fussman (1983), *Surkh Kotal en Bactriane*, vol. 1: *Les temples : architecture, sculpture, inscriptions*, 2 tomes. Mémoires de la Délégation Française en Afghanistan 25. Paris.

Shah, K[irit] K. (1977), 'A Unique Image of Cāmuṇḍā'. *Prachya Pratibha. Journal of Prachya Niketan* 5/2, pp. 43-44. Bhopal.

Sharma, B.N. (1976), *Iconography of Sadāśiva*. New Delhi.

Shastri, Ajay Mitra (1985), 'The Date of the Lakṣmaṇa Temple at Sirpur', in F.M. Asher & G.S. Gai, eds, 1985, pp. 105-09.

Shaw, Miranda (2006), *Buddhist Goddesses of India*. Princeton University Press, Princeton.

Shimada, Akira (2006), 'The Great Railing at Amaravati: An Architectural and Chronological Reconstruction'. *AA* 66, pp. 89-134.

Sivaramamurti, C[alambur] (1974), *Nāṭarāja in Art, Thought and Literature*. National Museum, New Delhi.

Soundara Rajan, K.V. (1981), *Cave Temples of the Deccan*. ASI.

Spink, Walter [M.] (1958), 'On the Development of Early Buddhist Art in India'. *Art Bull.* 40, pp. 95-104.

——— (1967), *Ajanta to Ellora*. Center for South and Southeast Asian Studies, University of Michigan/Marg Publications. [Bombay].

——— (1967), 'Ellora's Earliest Phase'. *Bullettin of the American Academy of Benares* 1, pp. 11-22. Varanasi.

——— (1992), 'The Achievement of Ajanta', in A.M. Shastri, ed., *The Age of the Vākātakas*. New Delhi.

——— (2005-07), *Ajanta: History and Development*, 5 vols. Leiden-Boston.

Srinivasan, Doris M. (1984), 'Significance and Scope of Pre-Kuṣāṇa Śaivite Iconography', in M.W. Meister, ed., 1984, pp. 32-46.

Tucci, Giuseppe (1949), *Tibetan Painted Scrolls*, 2 vols. and portfolio. Libreria dello Stato, Roma.

——— (1968), 'Oriental Notes III. A Peculiar Image from Gandhāra'. *EW* 18, pp. 289-92.

Verardi, Giovanni (1994), Homa *and Other Fire Rituals in Gandhāra* (Suppl. no. 79 to *AION* 54, 2). Napoli.

Wagoner, Phillip B. (2001), 'Kannaḍa Kalla Upparige (Stone Palace): Multistoried Entrance Pavilions in Pre- and Early Vijayanagara Architecture', *ArsOr* 31, pp. 169-83.

Wechsler, Helen J. (1994), 'Royal Legitimation. Ramayana Reliefs on the Papanatha Temple at Pattadakal', in Vidya Dehejia, ed., *The Rama Legend in Art* (= *Mārg* 45/3), pp. 27-42. Bombay.

Wiesner, Ulrich (1980), 'Nepalese Votive Stūpas of the Licchavi Period: The Empty Niche', in A.L. Dallapiccola ed., in collab. with S. Zingel-Avé-Lallemant, *The Stūpa: Its Religious, Historical and Architectural Significance*, pp. 166-74. Beiträge zur Südasienforschung, Südasien Institut, Universität Heidelberg 55. Wiesbaden.

Willis, Michael D. (1997), *Temples of Gopakṣetra: A Regional History of Architecture and Sculpture in Central India, AD 600-900*. The British Museum, London.

——— (2009), *The Archaeology of Ritual: Temples and the Establishments of the Gods*. Cambridge.

Woodward, Hiram W. Jr. (1981), 'Queen Kumāradevī and Twelfth-Century Sārnāth'. *JISOA*, n.s. 12-13, pp. 8-24.

Zaheer, Mohammad (1981), *The Temple of Bhītargāon*. Delhi.

TEXTS

(A) INDIAN AND TIBETAN

Abhisamayālaṅkāra

Conze, Edward, tr. (1979), *The Large Sutra on Perfect Wisdom, with the Divisions of the* Abhisamayālaṅkāra. Edward. Delhi (Or. ed. Berkeley 1975).

Agni Purāṇa

The Agni Purāṇa. Translated and Annotated by N[atesa] Gangadharan, 4 vols. AITMS. Delhi 1984-87.

Aṅguttara Nikāya

The Book of the Gradual Sayings (Aṅguttara Nikāya) or More-Numbered Suttas, 5 vols. Trans. F[rank] L[ee] Woodward & E[dward] M. Hare, with an Introduction by Mrs. [Caroline A.F.] Rhys Davids. PTS, 1932-36.

Appar Tirumurai

Tirumurai the Sixth (St. Appar's Thaandaka Hymns). Tamil Text with English Translation by Sekkizhaar Adi-p-Podi T.N. Ramachandran. International Institute of Saiva Siddhanta Research of Dharmapuram Aadheenam. Dharmapuram, [Mayiladuturai] 1995.

Arthaśāstra

Kangle, R.P. (1960-65), *The Kauṭilīya Arthaśāstra*, 3 vols. (Part I: *A Critical Edition with a Glossary;* Part II: *An English Translation with Critical and Explanatory Notes;* Part III: *A Study*). University of Bombay.

Aśokāvadāna

John S. Strong, *The Legend of King Aśoka: A Study and Translation of the* Aśokāvadāna. Delhi 1989.

Atīśa New Biography

A New Biography of Atīśa Compiled in Tibetan from the Tibetan Sources by Nagwang Nima. Revised, Edited and Condensed by Lama Chimpa, in Alaka Chattopadhyaya, *Atīśa and Tibet: Life and Works of Dīpaṃkara Śrījñāna in Relation to the History and Religion of Tibet. With Tibetan Sources Translated under Professor Lama Chimpa.* Calcutta 1967.

Basavapurāṇamu
Śiva's Warriors. The Basava Purāṇa *of Pālkuriki Somanātha.* Translated from the Telugu by Velcheru Narayana Rao, Assisted by Gene H. Roghair. Princeton University Press, Princeton 1990.

Blue Annals
The Blue Annals, tr. George N. Roerich, 2 vols. Calcutta 1949.

Brahmāṇḍa Purāṇa
The Brahmāṇḍa Purāṇa. Translated and Annotated by G[anesh] V[asudeo] Tagare, 5 vols. AITMS. Delhi 1983.

Bodhisattva Womb Sūtra
Elsa I. Legittimo (2005-6) Synoptic Presentation of the *Pusa chu tai jing* (PCJ), the Bodhisattva Womb Sūtra. *Sengokuyama Journal of Buddhist Studies* 2, pp. 1-111 (Part I, Chapters 1-14) and 3, pp. 1-177 (Chapters 15-38). International College for Postgraduate Buddhist Studies, Tokyo.

Bu ston
The History of Buddhism in India and Tibet by Bu-Ston, Companion Volume to the Jewellery of Scripture. Translated from Tibetan by E[ugène] Obermiller. Heidelberg 1932.

Caitanya Caritāmṛta a
Caitanya Caritāmṛta *of Kṛṣṇadāsa Kavirāja.* A Translation and Commentary by Edward C. Dimock, with and Introduction by Edward C. Dimock and Tony K. Stewart, ed. T.K. Stewart. Department of Sanskrit and Indian Studies, Harvard University. Cambridge, Mass. 1999.

Caitanya Caritāmṛta b
Chaitanya's Life and Teachings From His Contemporary Bengali Biography the Chaitanya-charit-amrita. Translated in English by Jadunath Sarkar. 3rd Edition, Revised and Enlarged by the Addition of His Life as Householder from the *Chaitanya-Bhagabat.* Calcutta 1932.

Caturaśītisiddhapravṛtti
Buddha's Lions. The Lives of the Eighty-four Siddhas. Caturaśīti-siddha-pravṛtti *by Abhayadatta. Translated into Tibetan as* Grub thob brgyad cu rtsa bzhi'I lo rgyus *by sMon-grub Shes-rab.* Translated into English by James B. Robinson. Berkely 1979.

Caitanyamaṅgala
Jayānanda, *Caitanya-maṅgala*, eds Bimanbehari Majumdar & Sukhamay Mukhopadhyay. The Asiatic Society, Bibliotheca Indica 293. Calcutta 1971.

Chos 'byung mkhas pa'i dga' ston

Dpa'-bo gtsug-lag phreng-ba, *Chos 'byung mkhas pa'i dga' ston* [*A Scholar's Feast*], 2 vols. Varanasi 2003.

Cūḷavagga

The Book of the Discipline (Vinaya-Piṭaka), Volume 5 (Cullavagga). Translated by I.B. Horner. PTS 1992.

Daśakumāracarita

What Ten Young Men Did, by Dandin. Translated by Isabelle Onians. The Clay Sanskrit Library, New York University-JJC Foundation 2005.

Devī Māhātmya

Thomas B. Coburn, *Encountering the Goddess: A Translation of the* Devī-Māhātmya *and a Study of Its Interpretation.* State University of New York, Albany 1991.

Dharmasvāmin

Biography of Dharmasvāmin (Chag lo tsa-ba Chos-rje-dpal), a Tibetan Monk Pilgrim. Original Tibetan Text Deciphered and Translated by Dr. George Roerich [...]. With a Historical and Critical Introduction by A.S. Altekar. K.P. Jayaswal Research Institute, Patna 1959.

Dīpavaṃsa

Hermann Oldenberg, *The* Dīpavaṃsa: *An Ancient Buddhist Historical Record.* London-Edinburgh 1879.

Dīgha Nikāya

Thus I Have Heard: The Long Discourses of the Buddha, Dīgha Nikāya. Translated from the Pali by Maurice Walshe. London 1987.

Divyāvadāna a

The Divyāvadāna, a Collection of Early Buddhist Legends Now First Edited from the Nepalese Sanskrit MSS. in Cambridge and Paris, by E.B. Cowell and R.A. Neil. The University Press, Cambridge, 1886.

Divyāvadāna b

Divine Stories. Divyāvadāna, Part I. Translated by Andy Rotman. Boston 2008.

Dohākośa

Kurtis R. Schaffer, *Dreaming the Great Brahmin: Tibetan Traditions of the Buddhist Poet-Saint Saraha.* Oxford University Press, New York.

Gayā Māhātmya

Gayāmāhātmya. Edition critique, traduction française et introduction par Claude Jacques. PIFIP 20, 1962.

Gopālarājavaṃśāvalī

The Gopālarājavaṃśāvalī, eds Dhanavajra Vajrācārya & Kamal P. Malla. Nepal Research Centre Publications 9. Wiesbaden 1985.

Guhyasamāja Tantra

Peter Gäng tr. (1988), *Das Tantra der verborgenen Vereinigung: Guhyasamaja-Tantra*. Munich.

Harṣacarita

The Harṣa-carita of Bāṇa. Translated by E[dward] B[yles] Cowell & F[rederick] W[illiam] Thomas. The Royal Asiatic Society, London 1897.

Hevajra Tantra

David L. Snellgrove ed. & tr. (1959), *The Hevajra Tantra. A Critical Study*, *2* vols. London Oriental Series 6. Oxford University Press, London.

History of Nepal a

Daniel Wright (1877), *History of Nepāl*. Translated from the Parbatiyā by Munshī Shew Shunker Singh and Pandit Shrī Gunānand, with an Introductory Sketch of the Country and People of Nepāl by the Editor. Cambridge.

History of Nepal b

History of Nepal as Told by Its Own and Contemporary Chroniclers. Edited with a Prolegomena by Bikrama Jit Hasrat, with a Foreword by Donovan Williams. Hoshiarpur 1970.

Liṅga Purāṇa

The Liṅga-Purāṇa. Translated by a Board of Scholars, ed. J[agdish] L[al] Shastri, 2 vols. AITMS. Delhi 1973.

Mādalāpāñji

Mādalāpāñji: The Chronicle of Jagannath Temple (Rājabhoga Itihasa), tr. K.S. Behera & A.N. Parida. Bhubaneswar 2009.

Nāropā

Nāropā, *Iniziazione-Kālacakra*. Translated by Raniero Gnoli & Giacomella Orofino. Milano 1994.

Kādambarī

Bāṇa's Kādambarī [Pūrvabhāga Complete]. Edited with New Sanskrit Commentary 'Tattvaprakāśikā'. Introduction, Notes, and a Literal English translation by M.R. Kāle. Delhi 1968[4].

Kālikā Purāṇa

The Kālikāpurāṇa *(Text, Introduction & English Trans. with Shloka Index)*. Translated by B[iswa] N[arayan] Shastri; ed. Surendra Pratap. Delhi 1992.

Kalki Purāṇa

Le Kalki-Purāna. Première traduction du sanskrit en langue occidentale de Murari Bhatt et Jean Rémy, suivi d'une étude d'André Preau. Préface de Jean Varenne. Bibliothèque de l'Unicorne, Milano 1982. [Translation of the Sanskrit text ed. Śrī Jīvānanda Vidyāsāgara Bhaṭṭācharya, Calcutta 1860.]

Kāma Sūtra

Vātsyāyana, Kāma Sūtra. Commentario Jayamangalā in sanscrito di Yashodhara ed estratti di un commentario in hindi di Devadatta Shāstrī, ed. Alain Daniélou. Como 1997 (tr. from the French edition, Paris 1992).

Kathāsaritsāgara

Somadeva, L'oceano dei fiumi dei racconti. Translated Fabrizia Baldissera, Vincenzina Mazzarino & Maria Pia Vivanti, 2 vols. Torino 1993.

Kūrma Purāṇa

The Kūrma Purāṇa. Translated and Annotated by G[anesh] V[asudeo] Tagare, 2 vols. AITMS. Delhi 1981.

Kuvalayamālā

Christine Chojnacki, *Kuvalayamālā: roman jaina de 779 composé par Uddyotanasūri,* vol. 1, Etude; vol. 2, Traduction et annotations. Indica et Tibetica 50. Marburg 2008.

Lalitavistara

Histoire du Bouddha Çakya Mouni [*Rgya Tch'er Rol Pa, ou Développment des yeux*], traduit du Tibétain par Ph[ilippe]-Ed[ouard] Foucaux. Paris 1860.

Life of the Buddha

The Life of the Buddha and the Early History of His Order: Derived from Tibetan Works in the Bkah-hgyur and Bstan-hgyur, Followed by Notices on the Early History of Tibet and Khoten. Translated by W. Woodville Rockhill. Trübner Oriental Series, London 1884.

Mackenzie Manuscripts 1

Taylor, William (1838*a*), 'Examination and Analysis of the Mackenzie Manuscripts Deposited in the Madras College Library'. *JASB* 7, pp. 105-31, 173-92 (also, *MJLS* 7, pp. 1-51).

Mackenzie Manuscripts 2

Taylor, William (1838*b*), 'Second Report of Progress Made in the Examination and Restoration of the Mackenzie Manuscripts'. *JASB* 7, pp. 371-414, 469-521 (also, *MJLS* 7, pp. 277-378).

Mackenzie Manuscripts 3

Taylor, William (1838*c*), 'Third Report of Progress Made in the Examination of the Mackenzie MSS., with an Abstract Account of the Works Examined'. *MJLS* 8, pp. 1-86.

Mackenzie Manuscripts 4

Taylor, William (1838*d*, 1839*a*), 'Fourth Report of Progress made in the Examination of the Mackenzie MSS., with an Abstract Account of the Works Examined'. *MJLS* 8 (1838), pp. 215-305; 9 (1839), pp. 1-52.

Mackenzie Manuscripts 5

Taylor, William (1839*b*), 'Fifth Report of Progress made in the Examination of the Mackenzie MSS., with an Abstract Account of the Works Examined'. *MJLS* 9, pp. 313-76; 10, pp. 1-42.

Mackenzie Manuscripts 6

Taylor, William (1839*c*, 1844-45), 'Sixth Report of Progress Made in the Examination of the Mackenzie MSS., with an Abstract Account of the Works Examined'. *MJLS* 10 (1839), pp. 388-432; 13 (1844-45), pp. 57-115.

Mackenzie Manuscripts Suppl.

Taylor, William (1847, 1850), 'Analysis of Mackenzie Manuscripts, Supplement'. *MJLS* 14 (1847), pp. 112-59; 16 (1850), pp. 55-101.

Mackenzie Manuscripts (Mahalingam)

Mahalingam, T[eralundur V[enkatarama] ed. (1972-76), *Mackenzie Manuscripts. Summaries of the Historical Manuscripts in the Mackenzie Collection, Volume 1 (Tamil and Malayalam) & Volume 2 (Telugu, Kannada and Marathi).* University of Madras, Madras.

Mahābhārata

The Mahabharata of Krishna-Dwaipayana Vyasa. Translated into English Prose from the Original Sanskrit Text by Kisari Mohan Ganguli, 12 vols. Delhi 1970. (Or. ed. Calcutta 1883-96).

Mahāvastu

The Mahāvastu. Translated from the Buddhist Sanskrit by J.J. Jones, 3 vols. (Sacred Books of the Buddhists 16). The Pāli Text Society, London 1949.

Mālavikāgnimitra

The Mālavikāgnimitram of Kālidāsa. With the Commentary of Kāṭayavema, Various Readings, Introduction, Translation into English and Critical and Explanatory Notes by M.R. Kale. Revised by Jayanand L. Dave & S.A. Upadhyaya. Bombay 1960.

Mālatīmādhava
Bhavabhūti's Mālatīmādhava. With the Commentary of Jagaddhara. Edited with a Literal English Translation, Notes, and Introduction by M[oreshvar] R[amchandra] Kāle. Delhi 1967[3].

Majjhima Nikāya
The Middle Length Discourses of the Buddha: A Translation of the Majjhima Nikāya. Translated from the Pāli; Original Translation by Bhikku Ñaṇamoli. Translated, Edited and Revised by Bhikku Bodhi. Somerville 1995.

Mañjuśrīmūlakalpa
K[ashi] P[rasad] Jayaswal, *An Imperial History of India in a Sanskrit Text [c. 700 BC–c. 770 AD], with a Special Commentary on Later Gupta Period. With the Sanskrit Text Revised by Rāhula Sānkṛityāyana.* Patna 1937.

Manu
The Laws of Manu: With an Introduction and Notes. Translated by Wendy Doniger with Brian K. Smith. London 1991.

Mattavilāsa
Matta-Vilāsa: A Farce by Mahendravikrama-varman. Translated by L.D. Barnett. *BSOS* 5 (1930) pp. 697-717.

Nīlamata
A Study of the Nīlamata: Aspects of Hinduism in Ancient Kashmir, ed. Yasuke Ikari. Institute for Research in Humanities, Kyoto University, Kyoto 1994.

Pādatāḍitaka
Pādatāḍitaka/The Kick, in *The Quartet of Causeries by Śyāmilaka, Vararuci, Śūdraka & Īśvaradatta*; Edited and Translated by Csaba Dezso & Somadeva Vasudeva, pp. 2-161. The Clay Sanskrit Library, New York.

dPag bsam ljon bzang
Pag sam jon zang. History of the Rise, Progress and Downfall of Buddhism in India, by Sumpa Khan-po Yece Pal Jor [Sum–pa mKhan-po ye-shes dpal-'byor ye shes dpal'byor], ed. Sarat Chandra Das, 2 vols. Calcutta 1908.

Pāṇḍava Purāṇa
Padmanabh S. Jaini, 'Pāṇḍava Purāṇa of Vadicandra: Text and Translation'. *JIP* 25 (1997), pp. 91-227, 517-59; 27 (1999), pp. 215-78.

Pāśupata Sūtra
Pāśupata Sūtra, in Raniero Gnoli tr., *Testi dello Śivaismo*, pp. 25-33. Torino.

Periya Purāṇam

St. Sekkizhaar's Periya Puranam. Translated by T.N. Ramachandran, 2 vols. Tamil University. Thanjavur 1990-95.

Poems to Śiva

Poems to Śiva: The Hymns of the Tamil Saints. Translated by Indira Viswanatan Peterson. Princeton 1989.

Prabodha Candrodaya

Sita K. Nambiar, *Prabodhacandrodaya of Kṛṣṇa Miśra (Sanskrit Text with English Translation, a Critical Introduction and Index)*. Delhi 1971.

Rājataraṅgiṇī

Kalhaṇa's Rājataraṅgiṇī: *A Chronicle of the Kings of Kaśmīr*. Translated, with an Introduction, Commentary, and Appendices by Marc Aurel Stein, 3 vols. Delhi 1961 (vols. 1-2) & 1988 (vol. 3). Or. ed. Bombay-Leipzig 1892 (text) & Westminster 1900 (tr.).

Rāmacarita

Ramacarita: A Historical Record of the Pal Dynasty by Sandhyakara Nandi, ed. Mahamahopadaya Haraprasad Sastri (Memoirs of the Asiatic Society of Bengal 3, pp. 1-56). Calcutta.

Rāmāyaṇa

Le Rāmāyaṇa de Vālmīki, eds Madeleine Biardeau & Marie-Claude Porcher. Bibliothèque de la Pléiade, Paris 1999.

Rāṣṭrapālaparipṛcchā Sūtra

Daniel Boucher, *Bodhisattvas of the Forest and the Formation of the Mahayana: A Study and Translation of the* Rāṣṭrapālaparipṛcchā-sūtra. University of Hawa'i Press, Honolulu.

Saddharmapuṇḍarīka Sūtra a

Le Lotus de la Bonne Loi, traduit du Sanskrit, accompagné d'un commentair et de vingt et un memoires relatives au Buddhisme, par M.E. Burnouf. Paris 1852.

Saddharmapuṇḍarīka Sūtra b

The Saddharma-Pundarīka or the Lotus of the True Law. Translated by H[endrik] Kern. SBE 21, Oxford 1884.

Saṃyutta Nikāya

The Book of the Kindred Sayings (Saŋyutta-Nikāya) or Grouped Suttas. Translated by Mrs. [Carolina Augusta Foley] Rhys Davids & F[rank] L[ee] Woodward, 1917-30, 5 vols. Pali Text Society, London.

Śaṅkara Digvijaya
The Traditional Life of Sri Sankaracharya by Madhava-Vidyaranya. Translated by Swami Tapasyananda. Sri Ramakrishna Math, Madras [1978]. [Based on the edition published in the Anandasrama Sanskrit Series 22, Poona 1891].

Śatapatha Brāhmaṇa
The Śatapatha-Brāhmaṇa According to the Text of the Mādhyandina School. Translated by Julius Eggeling, 5 vols. Delhi 1963 (London 1882).

Sekoddeśa
Giacomella Orofino, *Sekoddeśa: A Critical Edition of the Tibetan Translations. With an Appendix by Raniero Gnoli on the Sanskrit Text.* SOR 72, 1994.

Śiva Purāṇa
The Śiva Purāṇa. Translated and Annotated by a Board of Scholars, ed. J[agdish] L[al] Shastri, 4 vols. AITMS. Delhi 1970.

Ślokavārttika
A Hindu Critique of Buddhist Epistemology: Kumārila on Perception. The 'Determination of Perception' Chapter of Kumārila Bhaṭṭa's Ślokavārttika. Translation and Commentary by John Taber. London/New York 2005.

Sutta Nipāta
The Group of Discourses (Sutta-Nipāta), vol. 2. Revised Translation with Introduction and Notes by K[enneth] R[oy] Norman. Pali Text Society Translation Series 45. Oxford 1992.

Tantravārttika
Kumārila Bhaṭṭa, Tantravārttika. A Commentary on Śabara's Bhāṣya on the Pūrvamīmāṁsā Sūtras of Jaimini. Translated into English by Mahamahopādhyāya Gangānātha Jhā, 2 vols. Asiatic Society of Bengal, Calcutta 1924.

Tāranātha
Tāranātha's History of Buddhism in India. Translated from Tibetan by Lama Chimpa Alaka Chattopadhyaya, ed. Debiprasad Chattopadhyaya. Simla 1970.

Tarkabhāṣā
Kajiyama, Yuichi, *An Introduction to Buddhist Philosophy: An Annotated Translation of the Tarkabhāṣā of Mokṣākaragupta*, in Kajiyama (2005), pp. 189-360. (Originally publ. in *Memoirs of the Faculty of Letters, Kyoto University* 10, 1966, pp. 1-173. Kyoto).

Ugraparipṛcchā
A Few Good Men: The Bodhisattva Path According to The Inquiry of Ugra

(Ugrapariprcchā). *Study and Translation by Jan Nattier*. Institute for the Study of Buddhist Traditions, University of Hawa'i. Honolulu 2003.

Upaniṣad

Upaniṣad. Translated by Carlo Della Casa. Torino 1976.

Upapurāṇa-s

Hazra, R[ajendra] C[handra], *Studies in the Upapurāṇas*, 2 vols (I, *Saura and Vaiṣṇava Upapurāṇas*; II, *Śākta and non-Sectarian Upapurāṇas*). Calcutta Sanskrit College Research Series 2 (1958) & 22 (1963). Calcutta.

Upāyakauśalya Sūtra

The Skills in Means (Upāyakauśalya) Sūtra. Translated by Mark Katz. Delhi 1994.

Vāmana Purāṇa

The Vāmana Purāṇa with English Translation. Edited by Anand Swarup Gupta; Translated by Satyamsu Mohan Mukhopadhyaya & al. All India Kashiraj Trust, Varanasi 1968.

Varāha Purāṇa

The Varāha Purāṇa. Translated and Annotated by S. Venkitasubramonia Iyer, 2 vols. AITMS. Delhi 1985.

Vāyu Purāṇa

The Vāyu Purāṇa. Translated and Annotated by G[anesh] V[asudeo] Tagare, 2 vols. AITMS. Delhi 1975.

Vimalakīrtinirdeśa

L'enseignement de Vimalakīrti (Vimalakīrtinirdeśa). Traduit et annoté par Etienne Lamotte. Bibliothèque du Muséon 51. Louvain-Leuven 1962.

Virajā Māhātmya

The Glory that was Virajaksetra (Virajakṣetramāhātmya) by Upendra Nath Dhal. Delhi.

Viṣṇu Purāṇa

The Viṣṇu Purāṇa: A System of Hindu Mythology and Tradition. Text in Devanagari, English Translation, Notes and Appendices, etc. Translated from the Original Sanskrit and Illustrated by Notes Derived Chiefly from Other Purāṇas by H[orace] H. Wilson, Enlarged and Arranged by Nag Sharan Singh), 2 vols. Delhi 1980.

Yuga Purāṇa

John E. Mitchiner, *The Yuga Purāṇa, Critically Edited, with an English Translation and a Detailed Introduction.* The Asiatic Society. Kolkata 2002[2].

(B) Chinese

Damolun

Le traité de Bodhidharma, première anthologie du bouddhisme chan. Traduction et commentaire [par] Bernard Faure. Saint-Amand-Montrond 1986.

Eminent Monks [Da Tang Xiyu qiu fa gao seng juan] a

Mémoire composé à l'époque de la grande dynastie T'ang sur les réligieux éminents qui allèrent chercher la loi dans les pays d'occident par I-Tsing, traduit en Français par Edouard Chavannes. Paris 1894.

Eminent Monks [Da Tang Xiyu qiu fa gao seng juan] b

Chinese Monks in India, Biography of Eminent Monks Who Went to the Western World in Search of the Law During the Great Tang Dynasty, by I-ching. Translated by Latika Lahiri. Delhi 1986.

Eminent Monks c

Kiroku Adachi (tr. and com.) *Daitō Sai'iki Guhō Kōsōden.* Tōkyō 1942.

Faxian a

Max Deeg, *Das Gaoseng-Faxian-Zhuan als religionsgeschichtliche Quelle. Der älteste Bericht eines chinesischen buddhistischen Pilgermönchs über seine Reise nach Indien mit Übersetzung des Textes.* Wiesbaden 2005.

Faxian b

The Travels of Fa-hsien (399-414 AD), or Record of the Buddhistic Kingdoms. Retranslated by H[erbert] A[llen] Giles.

Life

Samuel Beal, *The Life of Hiuen-Tsiang by the Shaman Hwui Li, with an Introduction Containing an Account of the Works of I-Tsing.* London 1911.

Hui Chao

The Hye-Ch'o Diary: Memoir of the Pilgrimage to the Five Regions of India. Translated by Jan Yun-Hua, Lawrence W. Preston, Iida Shotaro & Yang Han-Sung. Berkeley-Seoul 1984.

Jiye

E. Huber, L'itinéraire du pèlerin Ki-ye dans l'Inde. *Bulletin de l'Ecole Française d'Extrême-Orient* 2, pp. 256-59. Paris.

Shuijingju

Petech, Luciano (1950), *Northern India According to the Shui-Ching-Chu.* SOR 2. Roma.

Song Yun [Huisheng]

Max Deeg, 'A Little-Noticed Buddhist Travelogue – Senghui's Xiyu-ji and its Relation to the Luoyang-jialan-ji', in Birgit Kellner *& al.* eds (2007), pp. 66-76.

Yijing

A Record of the Buddhist Religion as Practised in India and the Malay Archipelago (AD 671-695) by I-Tsing. Translated by J[unjirō] Takakusu, with a Letter of F[riedrich] Max Müller. Oxford 1896.

Wang Xuance

The Mission of Wang Hiuen-ts'e in India (Les Missions de Wang-Hiuen-Ts'e dans l'Inde). Written in French by M. Sylvain Levi, Translated from the Original French by S.P. Chatterjee; Edited with Notes by B[imala]C[hurn]Law. Indian Geographical Society, Calcutta 1967.

[Da Tang] Xiyuji a

Si-Yu-ki. *Buddhist Records of the Western World, Translated from the Chinese of Hiuen Tsiang (AD 629) by Samuel Beal*, 2 vols. London 1884.

[Da Tang] Xiyuji b

Thomas Watters, *On Yuan Chwang's Travels in India, 629-645 AD*, ed. T.W. Rhys Davids & S.W. Bushel; with two Maps and an Itinerary by Vincent A. Smith, 2 vols. London 1904-05.

(C) Greek and Latin

Adversus Haereses

S. Ireneo di Lione, *Contro le eresie.* Translated by Vittorino Dellagiacoma, 2 vols. Siena 1996[3].

Acts of Thomas

The Acts of Thomas. Introduction, Text and Commentary by A[lbertus] F[rederick] J[ohannes] Klijn (Supplements to Novum Testamentum 5). Leiden 1962.

Adversus Valentinianos

Contro i Valentiniani, in Claudio Moreschini, tr., *Opere scelte di Quinto Settimio Florente Tertulliano*, pp. 897-940. Torino 1974.

De haeresibus

Liguori G. Müller, *The De Haeresibus of Saint Augustine: A Translation with an Introduction and Commentary.* The Catholic University of America Patristic Studies 90. Washington, D.C. 1956.

De mortalitate

On the Mortality, in *Ante-Nicene Christian Library VIII. The Writings of Cyprian, Bishop of Carthage,* vol. 1: *Containing the Epistles and Some of the Treatises*, pp. 452-68.Translated by Alexander Roberts & James Donaldson. Edinburgh 1882.

Lógoi

Dio Chrysostom, with an English Translation by J[ames] W[ilfred] Cohoon [and H. Lamar Crosby], 5 vols. The Loeb Classical Library, London-Cambridge, Mass. 1932-51.

Naturalis Historia

Gaio Plinio Secondo, Storia Naturale. Edited by Gian Biagio Conte in coll. with Alessandro Barchiesi & Giuliano Ranucci, 6 vols. Torino 1982-88.

Periplus

The Periplus Maris Erythraei, Text with Introduction, Translation, and Commentary by Lionel Casson. Princeton University Press, Princeton 1989.

Stromata

Clemente Alessandrino, *Gli Stromati. Note di vera filosofia.* Translated by Giovanni Pini. Milano 1985.

Systema brahmanicum

Paolinus a S. Bartholomaeo, *Systema brahmanicum liturgicum mythologicum civile.* Romae 1791.

(D) ARABIC AND PERSIAN

Fatḥnāma-yi Sind a

Fathnamah-i-Sind: Being the Original Record of the Arab Conquest of Sind. Persian Text. Edited, with Introductions, Notes and Commentary by N.A. Baloch. Institute of Islamic History, Culture and Civilization, Islamic University. Islamabad 1983.

Fatḥnāma-yi Sind b

The Chachnamah: An Ancient History of Sind, Translated from the Persian by Mirza Kalichbeg Fredunbeg. Karachi 1900.

Muslim Historians

The History of India as Told by its own Historians: The Muhammadan Period. Edited from the Posthumous Papers of the Late H.M. Elliot by John Dowson, vol. 2. London 1869.

Ṭabaqāt-i Nāṣirī

Ṭabaḳāt-i-Nāṣirī: A General History of the Muhammadan Dynasties of Asia Including Hindustan from AH *194 (810* AD*) to* AH *658 (1260* AD*) and the Irruption of the Infidel Mughals into Islam by Maulānā, Minhāj-ud-Dīn, Abū-'Umar-i-'Uṣmān.* Translated from Original Persian Manuscripts by Major H[enry] G[eorge] Raverty, 2 vols. The Asiatic Society, Calcutta 1881.

Tārīkh-i Sīstān

The Tārikh-e Sistān. Translated by Milton Gold. SOR 48. Roma 1976.

(E) OTHERS

Manichaen Texts

Gnoli, Gherardo, ed., assisted by Andrea Piras (2003) *Il Manicheismo*, vol. I. *Mani e il Manicheismo*. Fondazione Lorenzo Valla, [Milano].

MODERN SOURCES AND STUDIES IN HISTORY, RELIGION AND PHILOSOPHY

Abs, Joseph (1926), 'Beiträge zur Kritik heterodoxer Philosophie-Systeme in der Purana-Literatur', in Willibald Kirfel, ed., *Beiträge zur Literaturwissenschaft und Geistesgeschichte Indiens. Festgabe Hermann Jacobi zum 75. Geburtstag (11. Februar 1925) dargebracht von Freunden, Kollegen und Schülern*, pp. 386-96. Bonn.

Agrawala, Vasudeva S. (1963) *Matsya Purāṇa: A Study [Matsyapurāṇānuśīlanam] (An Exposition of the Ancient Purāṇa-Vidyā)*. All-India Kashiraj Trust. Varanasi.

——— (1964) *The Wheel Flag of India, Chakra-dhvaja*. Banaras Hindu University, Varanasi.

The Deeds of Harsha [Being a Cultural Study of Bāṇa's Harshacarita]. Redacted and edited by P.K. Agrawala. Varanasi.

——— (1970) *India as Described by Manu*. Varanasi.

——— (1983²) *Vāmana Purāna: A Study*. Banaras Hindu University, Varanasi. (1st edn. 1964).

——— (1984²*a*) *Śiva Mahādeva, the Great God (An Exposition of the Symbolism of Śiva)*. Varanasi (1st edn. 1966).

Aiyangar, S. Krishnaswami (1923) *Some Contributions of South India to Indian Culture*. University of Calcutta.

Alakhoon, Hector (1980) *The Later Mauryas, 232* BC *to 180* BC. New Delhi.

Alexander, P[adinjarethalakal] C[herian] (1949) *Buddhism in Kerala*. Annamalai University Historical Series 8. Annamalainagar.

Ali, Daud (2007), 'Violence, Courtly Manner and Lineage Formation in Early Medieval India'. *Soc. Sci.* 35, pp. 3-21.

Ali, Muhammad Mohar (1406 H/1985) *History of the Muslims in Bengal.* vol. IA: *Muslim Rule in Bengal (600-1170/1203-1757)*; vol. IB: *Survey of Administration, Society and Culture.* Imam Muhammad Ibn Sa'ūd Islamic University, Riyadh.

Allen, Charles (2003) *The Search for the Buddha: The Men who Discovered India's Lost Religion.* New York.

Ambedkar, B[himrao Ramji] (1987), 'The Decline and Fall of Buddhism', in V. Moon, ed., *Writings and Speeches, 3: Revolution and Counter-Revolution in Ancient India*, pp. 229-38. Bombay.

Anālayo (2009), 'The Lion's Roar in Early Buddhism: A Study Based on the *Ekottarika-āgama* Parallel to the *Cūḷasīhanāda-sutta*', *Chung-Hwa Buddhist Journal* 22, pp. 3-23. Taipei.

Arunachalam, M[uthiah] (1979), 'The Kalabhras in the Pandiya Country and Their Impact on the Life and Letters'. *Journal of the Madras University* (Section A, Humanities) 51, pp. 1-168.

Bader, Jonathan (2000), *Conquest of the Four Quarters: Traditional Accounts of the Life of Śaṅkara.* New Delhi.

Baechler, Jean (1988), *La solution indienne. Essai sur l'origine du régime des castes.* Paris.

Bagchi, P[rabodh] C[handra] (1946), 'Kṛmiśa and Demetrius'. *IHQ* 22, 2, pp. 81-87.

Bakker, Hans (1986) *Ayodhyā,* Part I: *The History of Ayodhyā from the 7th Century* BC *to the Middle of the 18th Century, its Developments into a Sacred Centre with Special Reference to the* Ayodhyāmāhātmya *and to the Worship of Rāma according to the* Agastyasaṃhitā. Groningen Oriental Studies 1, University of Groningen.

——— (1996), 'Construction and Reconstruction of Sacred Space in Vārāṇasī'. *Numen* 43, pp. 32-55.

Baltrusch, Ernst (2002). *Sparta.* Bologna. (*Sparta. Geschichte, Gesellschaft, Kultur.* München 1998).

Banerji, R[akhal] D[as] (1915), *The Pālas of Bengal* (Memoirs of the Asiatic Society of Bengal 5/3, pp. 41-113). Calcutta.

——— (1930-31), *History* of *Orissa from the Earliest Times to the British Period,* 2 vols. Calcutta.

Banerji, S.A. (1970), *Traces of Buddhism in South India (c. 700-1600* AD*).* Calcutta.

Bareau, André (1963), *Recherches sur la biographie du Buddha dans les Sūtrapiṭaka et les Vinayapiṭaka anciens: de la quête de l'éveil à la conversion de Śāriputra et de Maudgalyāyana.* Publications de l'EFEO 53. Paris.

——— (1965), 'Le site de la Dhānyakaṭakā de Hiuan-Tsang'. *ArtsAs* 12, pp. 21-82.

——— (1979), 'Ayodhyā et Mithilā dans les textes canoniques du bouddhisme ancien'. *Indologica Taurinensia* 7, pp. 75-82. Torino.

Barua, Benimadhab (1931-34), *Gayā and Buddha-Gayā*, 2 vols. Calcutta.

Basak, Radhagovinda (1967²), *History of North-Eastern India: Extending from the Foundation of the Gupta Empire to the Rise of the Pāla Dynasty of Bengal (c. AD 320-760).* Calcutta.

Basham, A[rthur] L[lewellyn] (1951), *History and Doctrines of the Ājīvikas: A Vanished Indian Religion.* London.

Bailey, Greg & Mary Brockington, eds. (2000), *Epic Threads: John Brockington on the Sanskrit Epics*. New Delhi.

Bandyopadhyay, Sekhar (2004), *Plassey to Partition: A History of Modern India.* New Delhi.

Bechert, Heinz (1986), 'Zur Buddhismus-Interpretation Max Webers', in *Max Weber e l'India. Atti del convegno internazionale su 'La tesi weberiana della razionalizzazione in rapporto all'Induismo e al Buddhismo'* (Goethe Institut of Turin and Cesmeo, Turin 24-25 November 1983), pp. 23-36. Torino.

Bechert, Heinz, ed. (1991-92), *The Dating of the Historical Buddha. Die Datierung des historischen Buddha* (Symposien zur Buddhismusforschung 4, 1 and 2; Abhandlungen der Akademie der Wissenschaften in Göttingen, Phil.-Hist. Kl., dritte Folge, 189). Göttingen.

Bender, Ernest (1976), 'An Early Nineteenth Century Study of the Jains'. *JAOS* 96, pp. 114-19.

Bhandarkar, R[amakrishna] G[opal] (1913), *Vaiṣṇavism, Śaivism and Minor Religious Systems*. Strassburg.

Bhattacharya, Benoytosh (1931), Introduction to: *Śrī Guhyasamāja Tantra, or Tathāgataguhyaka*, pp. i-xxxviii. Gaekwad's Oriental Series 53. Oriental Institute, Baroda.

Bhattacharya, Dineshchandra (1987²), *History of Navya-Nyāya in Mithilā.* Mithilā Institute of Post-Graduate Studies and Research in Sanskrit Learning, Darbhanga (2nd edn., ed. Shridhar Tripathi).

Bhawe, Shrikrishna (1939), *Die Yajus' des Aśvamedha Versuch einer Rekonstruktion dieses Abschnittes des Yajurveda auf Grund der Überlieferung seiner Fünf Schule.* Bonner Orientalische Studien 25. Stuttgart.

Bianchi, Ugo, ed. (1967), *Le origini dello Gnosticismo. Colloquio di Messina, 13-18 aprile 1966* (Studies in the History of Religions, Supplements to *Numen* 12). Leiden.

Boucher, Daniel (2006), 'Dharmarakṣa and the Transmission of Buddhism to China', in *China at the Crossroads: A Festschrift in Honor of Victor H. Mair = Asia Maior*, 3rd s., 19, pp. 13-37. Taipei.

Bradley, Keith Richard (1989), *Slavery and Rebellion in the Roman World, 140 BC-70 BC* Batsford and Indiana University Press, Bloomington-London.

Brick, David (2010), 'The Court of Public Opinion and the Practice of Restorative Ordeals in Pre-Modern India'. *JIP* 38, pp. 25-38.

Brockington, John L. (1984), *Righteous Rāma: The Evolution of an Epic*. Oxford.

Bronkhorst, Johann (1998²), *The Two Sources of Indian Asceticism*. Delhi.

Brown, Percy (1956³), *Indian Architecture (Buddhist and Hindu Periods)*. Bombay.

Brown, Peter (1969), 'The Diffusion of Manicheism in Roman Empire'. *Journal of Roman Studies* 59, 92-103. London.

——— (1975), *Religione e società nell'età di Sant'Agostino*. Torino. (*Religion and Society in the Age of Saint Augustine*, London 1967).

——— (1992), *Il corpo e la società. Uomini, donne e astinenza sessuale nel primo cristianesimo*. Torino. (*The Body and Society: Men, Women and Sexual Renunciation in Early Christianity*, New York 1988).

Burnouf, Eugène (1844), *Introduction à l'histoire du buddhisme indien*. Paris.

——— (1852), *Le lotus de la bonne loi. Traduit du sanskrit, accompagné d'un commentaire et de vingt et un mémoires relatifs au Bouddhisme*. Paris.

Burrow, T[homas] (1968), 'Cāṇakya and Kauṭalya'. *Annals of the Bhandarkar Oriental Research Institute* 48-49, pp. 17-31.

Cameron, Averil (1993), *The Later Roman Empire: AD 284-430*. London.

Cancik, Hubert (1984), 'Gnostiker in Rom. Zur Religionsgeschichte der Stadt Rom im 2. Jahrhundert nach Christus', in Jacob Taubes, ed. (1984), pp. 163-84.

Champakalakshmi, R[adha] (1996) *Trade, Ideology and Urbanization: South India, 300 BC to AD 1300*. New Delhi.

Chanda, R[amaprasad] (1929), 'Puṣyamitra and the Śuṅga Empire'. *IHQ* 5, pp. 393-407, 587-613.

Chappell, David Wellington (1980), 'Early Forebodings of the Death of Buddhism'. *Numen* 27, pp. 122-54.

Chari, S.M. Srinivasa (1997), *Philosophy and Theistic Mysticism of the Āḻvārs*. Delhi.

Chatterjee, Asim Kumar (1970) *The Cult of Skanda-Kārttikeya in Ancient India*. Calcutta.

——— (1972-73), 'Vimalasūri's Paümacarya'. *JAIH* 6, pp. 105-15.

Chatterjee, R. (1965), 'Members of a Medieval Brāhmaṇa Family Ruling in Gayā, and Their Religious Activity'. *Journal of the Asiatic Society* 7, pp. 7-11. Calcutta.

Chattopadhyaya, Brajadulal (1994), *The Making of Early Medieval India*. Oxford University Press, New Delhi.

[Choudhary] Chaudhary, Radhakrishna (1956), 'Heretical Sects in the Purāṇas'. *ABORI* 37, pp. 234-57.

——— (1970), *History of Muslim Rule in Tirhut (1206-1765 AD)*. The Chowkhamba Sanskrit Studies 72. Varanasi.

——— (1976), *Mithilā in the Age of Vidyāpati*. Chaukhamba Oriental Research Studies 1. Varanasi.

——— (1978), 'Decline of the University of Vikramaśīla'. *Journal of Indian History* 56, pp. 213-35. Trivandrum.

Ch'en, Kenneth (1952), 'Anti-Buddhist Propaganda during the Nan-Ch'ao'. *HJAS* 15, pp. 166-92. Cambridge, Mass.

——— (1954), 'The Economic Background of the Hui-Ch'ang Suppression of Buddhism'. *HJAS* 19, pp. 67-105. Cambridge, Mass.

——— (1964) *Buddhism in China: A Historical Survey*. Princeton.

Clarke, Shayne (2009), 'When and Where is a Monk No Longer a Monk? On Communion and Communities in Indian Buddhist Monastic Law Codes'. *Indo-Iranian Journal* 52, pp. 115-41.

Cohen, Richard S. (2000), 'Kinsmen of the Son: *Sākyabhikṣu*s and the Institutionalization of the Bodhisattva Ideal'. *HistRel* 40, pp. 1-31.

Cohn, Samuel Kline (2006), *Lust for Liberty: The Politics of Social Revolt in Medieval Europe, 1200-1425: Italy, France, and Flanders*. Harvard University Press, Cambridge, Mass.-London.

Coburn, Thomas B. (1984), *Devī-Māhātmya: The Crystallization of the Goddess Tradition*. Delhi.

Collins, Charles D. (1991), *The Iconography and Ritual of Śiva at Elephanta*. Delhi. (State University of New York Press 1988.)

Das, H.C., assisted by D. Panda (1981), *Tāntricism: A Study of the Yogini Cult*. New Delhi.

Conze, Edward (1955), *Il buddhismo*. Milano (*Buddhism: Its Essence and Development*, Oxford 1951).

——— (1967), 'Buddhism and Gnosis', in Bianchi (1967), pp. 651-67.

——— (1983[2]), *Buddhist Thought in India: Three Phases of Buddhist Philosophy*. London.

Coomaraswamy, Ananda K. (1909), *Essays in Indian Nationalism*. Colombo.

——— (1916), *Buddha and the Gospel of Buddhism*. London-New York.

——— (1943), *Hinduism and Buddhism*. New York.

Couliano, Ian P. (1989), *I miti dei dualismi occidentali. Dai sistemi gnostici al mondo moderno*. Milano. (*Les gnoses dualistes d'Occident*, Paris 1989.)

Courtright, Paul B. (1985), *Gaṇeśa: Lord of Obstacles, Lord of Beginnings*. New York-Oxford.

Daffinà, Paolo (1977), 'India e mondo classico: nuovi risultati e prospettive'. *Annali della Facoltà di Lettere e Filosofia* 10, pp. 9-33. Università di Macerata.

——— (1995), *Le relazioni tra Roma e l'India alla luce delle più recenti indagini* (Conferenze IsMEO 7). Roma.

Dange, Sadashiv Ambadas (1967), 'A Folk-Custom in the Aśva-medha'. *JOIB* 16, pp. 323-35.

Dani, A[hmad] H[asan] (1979), 'Buddhists in Sind as Given in the Chachnamah', in Heinz Mode & Hans-Joachim Peuke, eds., *30 Jahre unhabhängiges Sri Lanka. Studien zur Kulturgeschichte Südasiens*, pp. 54-70. Martin-Luther-

Universität, Halle-Wittenberg, Halle. (Also, in *Journal of Central Asia* 2, 1979, pp. 25-37.)

Dasgupta, Mrinal (1931), 'Early Viṣṇuism and Nārāyaṇīya Worship'. *IHQ* 7, pp. 343-58, 655-79.

Dasgupta, Surendranath (1932-55) *A History of Indian Philosophy*, 5 vols. Cambridge.

Das Gupta, Shashibhusan (1969³), *Obscure Religious Cults*. Calcutta.

Davidson, Ronald M. (1991), 'Reflections on the Maheśvara Subjugation Myth: Indic Materials, Sa.skya-pa Apologetics, and the Birth of Heruka'. *JIABS* 14, pp. 197- 235.

——— (2002), *Indian Esoteric Buddhism: A Social History of the Tantric Movement*. Columbia University Press. New York.

——— (2005), *Tibetan Renaissance: Tantric Buddhism in the Rebirth of Tibetan Culture*. Columbia University Press. New York.

Davis, Donald R. Jr. (2004), *The Boundaries of Hindu Law: Tradition, Custom and Politics in Medieval Kerala*. Corpus iuris sanscriticum et fontes iuris Asiae meridianae et centralis 5. Torino.

Dayal, Har (1932), *The Bodhisattva Doctrine in Buddhist Sanskrit Literature*. London.

Deeg, Max (1995-97), 'Origins and Development of the Buddhist Pañcavārṣika. Part I: India and Central Asia; Part II: China'. *Nagoya Studies in Indian Culture and Buddhism, Saṃbhāṣā* 16 (1995), pp. 67-90; 18 (1997), pp. 63-96. Nagoya.

Deeg, Max & Iain Gardner (2009), 'Indian Influence on Mani Reconsidered: The Case of Jainism'. *International Journal of Jaina Studies* 5/2, 2009, pp. 1-30. School of Oriental and African Studies, University of London. [Online resource].

Dehejia, Vidya (1988), *Slaves of the Lord: The Path of the Tamil Saints*. New Delhi.

Demiéville, Paul (1973), 'Le Bouddhisme et la guerre. Post-scriptum à l'«Histoire des moines guérriers du Japon» de G. Renondeau', in *Choix d'études bouddhiques 1929-70*, pp. 261-299. Leiden.

——— (1974), 'L'iconoclasme anti-bouddhique en Chine', in *Mélanges d'histoire des religions offerts à Henri-Charles Puech*, pp. 17-25. Paris.

Deo, S[hantaram] B[halchandra] (1954-55), *The History of Jaina Monachism from Inscriptions and Literature* (= *Bullettin of the Deccan College Research Institute* 16). Poona.

De Romanis, Federico (1996), *Cassia, cinnamomo, ossidiana. Uomini e merci tra Oceano Indiano e Mediterraneo*. Roma.

Deshpande, Madhav M. (1994), 'Brahmanism versus Buddhism: A Perspective of Language Attitudes', in N.N. Bhattacharyya ed., *Jainism and Prakrit in Ancient and Medieval India: Essays for Prof. Jagdish Chandra Jain*, pp. 89-111. Delhi.

Dessigane, R., P.Z. Pattabiramin & Jean Filliozat (1960), *La légende des jeux de Çiva à Madurai*, 2 vols. PIFIP 19.

Deussen, Paul (1908), *Allgemeine Geschichte der Philosophie, mit besonderer Berücksichtigung der Religionen* I/3. Leipzig.

Dikshitar, V.R. Ramachandra (1931), 'Buddhism in Tamil Literature', in B.C. Law, ed., pp. 673-98.

——— (1951), *The Purāṇa Index*, 3 vols. Madras.

Doresse, J[ean], K[urt] Rudolph & Henri-Charles Puech (1988), *Gnosticismo e Manicheismo* (Storia delle religioni, ed. Henri-Charles Puech, 8). Roma-Bari. (*Histoire des religions*, Paris 1970-76, 2, pp. 364-645).

Drijvers, Han J.W. (1984), 'Athleten des Geistes. Zur politischen Rolle der syrischen Asketen und Gnostiker', in Jacob Taubes (1984), pp. 109-20.

Ducat Jean (1990), *Les Hilotes*. Suppléments au *Bulletin de correspondance hellénique* 20. École Française d'Athènes, Athènes-Paris.

Dumont, Paul-Emile (1927), *L'aśvamedha. Description du sacrifice solennel du cheval dans le culte védique d'après les textes du Yajurveda blanc (Vājasaneyisaṃhitā, Śātapatabrāhmaṇa, Kātyāyanaśrautasūtra)*. Société belge d'études orintales. Paris-Louvain.

Dundas, Paul (2002^2), *The Jains*. London-New York.

Dutt, Nalinaksha (1933), 'Notes on the Kayasthas, Namasudras, Baidyas, Vyasa or Gaudadya Brahmans, Kaivarttas and Mahishyas, Patnis, Shahas and Telis and Tilis', in A.E. Porter, ed., *Census of India 1931*, Vol. V: *Bengal and Sikkim*, Part I, *Report*, pp. 524-38. Calcutta.

——— (1939), Introduction [Buddhism in Kashmir] to: *Gilgit Manuscripts*, ed. Nalinaksha Dutt with the assistance of D.M. Bhattacharya and Vidyavaridhi Pt. Shivnath Sharma, vol. 1, pp. 3-45. Calcutta.

Dutt, Sukumar (1924), *Early Buddhist Monachism*. London.

Dyczkowski, Mark S.G. (1988), *The Canon of the Śaivāgama and the Kubjikā Tantras of the Western Kaula Tradition*. State University of New York, Albany.

Eaton, Richard M. (1993), *The Rise of Islam and the Bengal Frontier*. University of California Press, Berkeley-Los Angeles.

——— (2000), 'Temple Desecration and Indo-Muslim States', in D. Gilmartin & Bruce B. Lawrence, eds, *Beyond Turk and Hindu: Rethinking Religious Identities in Islamicate South Asia*. University Press of Florida. Gainesville.

——— (2009), 'Shrines, Cultivators, and Muslim "Conversion" in Punjab and Bengal, 1300-1700'. *The Medieval History Journal* 12, pp. 191-220. Sage Journals Online.

Edgar, John Ware (1880), 'The Development of Buddhism in India'. *The Fortnightly Review* 27, pp. 801-21. London.

Eliade, Mircea (1982), 'Spirito, luce e seme', in id. *Occultismo. stregoneria e mode culturali. Saggi di religioni comparate*, pp. 105-40. Firenze. (*Occultism, Witchcraft and Cultural Fashions*, Chicago 1976).

Elst, Koenraad (1991), *Ayodhya and After: Issues before Hindu Society*. New Delhi.

Eltschinger, Vincent (2000) *'Caste' et philosophie bouddhique. Continuité de quelques arguments bouddhiques contre le traitement réaliste des dénominations sociales*. WSTB 47. Wien.

——— (2001), *Dharmakīrti sur les* mantra *et la perception du supra-sensible*. WSTB 51. Wien.

Elverskog, Johan (2010), *Buddhism and Islam on the Silk Road*. University of Pennsylvania Press, Philadelphia.

Esoteric Buddhist Studies = Esoteric Buddhist Studies: Identities in Diversity. Proceedings of the International Conference on Esoteric Buddhist Studies, Koyasan University, 5 Sept.-8 Sept. 2006, 2 vols. Kōyasan University 2008.

Filoramo, Giovanni (1993²), *L'attesa della fine. Storia della Gnosi*. Roma-Bari.

Fleet, John Faithfull (1896), 'Dynasties of the Kanarese Districts of the Bombay Presidency from the Earliest Historical Times to the Musalmán Conquest of AD 1318'. *Gazetteer of the Bombay Presidency*, ed. James M. Campbell, 2 vols., I/2, pp. 277-584. Bombay.

Forte, Antonino (1971), 'Il P'u-sa cheng-chai ching e l'origine dei tre mesi di digiuno prolungato'. *T'oung Pao* 57, pp. 103-34. Paris.

——— (2005²), *Political Propaganda and Ideology in China at the End of the Seventh Century*. Italian School of East Asian Studies, Kyoto.

Forte, Antonino & Jacques May (1979), 'Chōsai', in *Hōbōgirin* 5, pp. 392-407. Paris-Tōkyō.

Franco, Eli, ed. (1996), *Mémorial Sylvain Lévi*. (Landmarks in Indology. A Reprint Series). Delhi (Paris 1937).

Frauwallner, Erich (1982), 'Landmarks in the History on Indian Logic', in Gerhard Oberhammer & Ernst Steinkellner, eds., *Kleine Schriften*, pp. 847-70. Glasenapp-Stiftung 22. Wiesbaden.

Friedman, Johanan (1977), 'A Contribution to the Early History of Islam in India', in Myriam Rosen-Ayalon, ed., *Studies in Memory of Gaston Wiet*, pp. 309-32. Hebrew University of Jerusalem.

Funayama, Toru (1994), 'Remarks on Religious Predominance in Kashmir: Hindu or Buddhist?', in *Nīlamata*, pp. 367-76.

Fussman, Gérard (1988), 'Central and Provincial Administration in Ancient India: The Problem of the Mauryan Empire'. *IHR* 14, pp. 43-72.

——— (2006-7), 'Les Guptas et le nationalism indien'. *Annuaire du Collège de France* 107, pp. 696-712. Paris.

Gardner, Iain (2005), 'Some Comments on Mani and Indian Religions According to the Coptic *Kephalaia*', in Alois van Tongerloo & Luigi Cirillo eds, *Il Manicheismo: Nuove prospettive della richerca* (Quinto congresso internazionale di studi sul Manicheismo, Atti; Manichaean Studies V), pp. 123-35. Turnhout.

Gellner, David N. (1992), *Monks, Householder, and Tantric Priest: Newar Buddhism and its Hierarchy of Ritual.* Cambridge.

——— (2001), *The Anthropology of Buddhism and Hinduism: Weberian Themes.* Oxford University Press, New Delhi.

Gokhale, Balkrishna Govind (1969), 'The Early Buddhist View of the State'. *JAOS* 89, pp. 731-38. Ann Arbor.

——— (1977), 'The Merchant in Ancient India'. *JAOS* 87, pp. 125-30. Ann Arbor.

——— (1980), 'Early Buddhism and the Brahmanas', in A.K. Narain, ed., *Studies in the History of Buddhism*, pp. 67-80. Delhi.

Ghosh, A. (1973), *The City in Early Historical India.* Institute of Advanced Studies. Simla.

Golden, Peter B. (1992), *An Introduction to the History of the Turkic People: Ethnogenesis and State-Formation in Medieval and Early Modern Eurasia and the Middle East.* Wiesbaden.

Goldman, Robert [P.] (1972), 'Some Observations on the Paraśu of Paraśurāma'. *JOIB* 21, pp. 153-65.

——— (1984), 'Introduction' to *The Rāmāyaṇa of Vālmīki: An Epic of Ancient India*, vol. I, *Bālakāṇḍa*, eds id. & Sally J. Sutherland, pp. 1-59. Princeton University Press, Princeton 1984.

Gonda, Jan (1954), *Aspects of Early Viṣṇuism.* Leiden.

——— (1970), *Viṣṇuism and Śivaism: A Comparison.* London.

Granoff, Phyllis (1984), 'Holy Warriors: A Preliminary Study of Some Biographies of Saints and Kings in the Classical Indian Tradition'. *JIP* 12, pp. 291-03.

——— (1985), 'Scholars and Wonder-Workers: Some Remarks on the Role of the Supernatural in Philosophical Contests in Vedānta Hagiographies'. *JAOS* 105, pp. 459-67.

——— (1989), 'Jain Lives of Haribhadra: An Inquiry into the Sources and Logic of the Legends'. *JIP* 17, pp. 105-28.

——— (2000), 'Being in the Minority: Medieval Jain Reactions to Other Religious Groups', in Joseph T. O'Connell, ed., *Jain Doctrine and Practice: Academic Perspectives.* University of Toronto. (Also, in *EJ* 3, pp. 685-706).

Green, Henry A. (1985), *The Economic and Social Origins of Gnosticism.* Society of Biblical Literature, Dissertation Series 77. Atlanta.

Gregory, Peter N. & Patricia B. Ebrey (1993), 'The Religious and Historical Landscape', in id., eds., *Religion and Society in T'ang and Sung China*, pp. 1-44. University of Hawaii Press, Honolulu.

Grierson, George (1908), 'The Narayaniya and the Bhagavatas'. *IA* 37, pp. 251-62, 373-86.

Gros, François (1984), Introduction ['Pour lire les Tēvāram'/'Towards Reading the Tēvāram'] to: *Tēvāram. Hymnes Śivaïtes du pays tamoul*, vol. I, *Ñāṉacampantar*, eds. T.V. Gopal Iyer & François Gros, pp. v-xxxvi/xxxvii-lviii. PIFIP 68/1.

Grünewald, Thomas (1999), *Räuber, Rebellen, Rivalen, Rächer. Studien zu latrones in Römischem Reich*. Akademie der Wissenschaften und der Literatur, Mainz. (English trs. *Bandits in the Roman Empire: Myth and Reality*, London 2004).

Gupta, Paramesvara Lal (1974), *The Imperial Guptas*, 2 vols. Varanasi.

Habib, Irfan & Faiz Habib (1989-90), 'Mapping the Mauryan Empire'. *PIHC 50 (Golden Jubilee Session)*, pp. 57-79. Gorakhpur.

Habib, Irfan & Vivekanand Jha (2004), *Mauryan India* (A People's History of India 4). New Delhi.

Hale, Wash Edward (1986), *Ásura in Early Vedic Religion*. Delhi.

Hardy, R. Spence (1853), *A Manual of Bud[d]hism in Modern Development, Translated from Singhalese MSS*. London.

Harnack, Adolf von (1921), *Marcion: das Evanzelium vom fremden Gott. Eine Monographie zur Geschichte der Grundlegung der Katholischenkirche*. Leipzig.

Harvey, G.E. (1925), *History of Burma*. Calcutta.

Hattori, Masaaki (1968), Introduction to: *Dignāga, On Perception, being the Pratyakṣapariccheda of Dignāga's Pramāṇasamuccaya from the Sanskrit Fragments and the Tibetan Version*, pp. i-xi. Harvard Oriental Series 47. Cambridge, Mass.

Hazra, R[ajendra] C[handra] (1940), *Studies in the Purāṇic Records on Hindu Rites and Customs*. Dacca.

——— (1951), 'The Ekāmra-Purāṇa, a Work of Orissa'. *The Poona Orientalist: A Quarterly Journal Devoted to Oriental Studies* 16, pp. 70-76. Poona.

Heesterman, J[an] C. (1957), *The Ancient Indian Royal Consecration: The Rājasūya Described According to the Yajus Texts and Annoted*. Disputationes Rheno-Trajectinae 2.'s-Gravenhage.

Henning, W[alter] B[runo] (1945), 'The Manichaean Fasts'. *JRAS*, pp. 146-64.

Hikosaka, Shu (1989), *Buddhism in Tamilnadu: A New Perspective*. Institute of Asian Studies. Thiruvanmiyur, Madras.

Hirakawa, Akira (1963), 'The Rise of Mahāyāna Buddhism and its Relationship to the Worship of Stūpas', Translated from the Japanese by Taitetsu Unno. *Memoirs of the Research Department of the Tōyō Bunkō* 22, pp. 57-106. Tōkyō.

Hiremath, R.C. (1994), *Buddhism in Karnataka*. New Delhi.

Hodgson, Brian H[oughton] (1874), *Essays on the Languages, Literature, and Religion of Nepal and Tibet together with Further Papers on the Geography, Ethnology, and Commerce of those Countries*. London.

Houben, Jan E.M. & Karel R. van Kooij, eds (1999), *Violence Denied: Violence, Non-Violence and the Rationalization of Violence in South Asian Cultural History*. Leiden-Boston-Köln.

Hudson, [D.] Dennis (2002), 'Early Evidence of the Pāñcarātra', in Katherine Anne Harper & Robert L. Brown, eds, *The Roots of Tantra*, pp. 133-67. State University of New York, Albany.

Humfress, Caroline (2007), *Orthodoxy and the Courts in Late Antiquity*. Oxford University Press, Oxford.

Hunter, William Wilson (1896), *Life of Brian Houghton Hodgson, British Resident at the Court of Nepal*. London.

Hübner, Kurt (1990), *La verità del mito*, Milano 1990 (*Die Wahrheit des Mythos*, München 1985).

Iyanaga, Nobumi (1985), Récits de la soumission de Maheśvara par Tralokyavijaya —d'après les sources chinoises et japonaises, in Michel Strickmann, ed., vol. 3, pp. 633-745.

Jain, K. Chand (1972), *Malwa through the Ages (From the Earliest Time to 1305 AD)*. Delhi.

Jaini, Padmanabh S. (1979), *The Jaina Path of Purification*. Delhi (University of California, 1979).

Jayaswal, K[ashi] P[rasad] (1933), *History of India (150 AD to 350 AD)*. Lahore.

Jha, D[wijendra] N[arayan], ed. (1987), *Feudal Social Formations in Early India*. Delhi.

——— (2000), *The Feudal Order: State, Society and Ideology in Early Medieval India*. New Delhi.

Jha, Vivekanand (1986-87), 'Caṇḍāla and the Origin of Untouchability'. *IHR* 13, pp. 1-36. New Delhi.

Jung, C.G. & K. Kerényi (1972), *Prolegomeni allo studio scientifico della mitologia*, Torino. (*Einführung in das Wesen der Mythologie*, Amsterdam 1941).

Joshi, Hari Ram (1997), 'Nepalese Culture of Post-Ancient Times', in Giovanni Verardi ed., with the assistance of Andrea A. Di Castro & Riccardo Garbini, *Nepalese and Italian Contributions to the History and Archaeology of Nepal. Proceedings of the Seminar Held at Hanuman Dhoka, Kathmandu, on 27-28 January 1995* (IsIAO Reports and Memoirs, Series Minor 2), pp. 29-36. Roma.

Kajiyama, Y[uichi] (2005), *Studies in Buddhist Philosophy (Selected Papers)*, eds Katsumi Mimaki & al. Kyoto.

Kane, Pandurang Vaman (1930-62), *History of Dharmaśāstra (Ancient and Medieval Religious and Civil Law)*, 5 vols. in 8 tomes. Poona.

Kapstein, Matthew T. (2000), *The Tibetan Assimilation of Buddhism: Conversion, Contestation, and Memory.* Oxford University Press, New York.

Karashima, Seishi (2001), 'Who Composed the *Lotus Sutra*? Antagonism between Wilderness and Village Monks'. *Annual Report of the International Research Institute for Advanced Buddhology at Soka University for the Academic Year 2000*, pp. 143-79. Tokyo.

Keay, John (1988), *India Discovered: The Recovery of a Lost Civilization*. Glasgow. (Or. ed. Leicester 1981).

Kejariwal, O.P. (1988), *The Asiatic Society and the Discovery of India's Past, 1784-1838*. Oxford University Press, New Delhi.

Kellner, Birgit & al. eds (2007), Pramāṇakirtīḥ: *Papers Dedicated to Ernst Steinkellner on the Occasion of His 70th Birthday*, 2 vols. WSTB 70. Wien.

Kennedy, J. (1902), 'Buddhist Gnosticism, the System of Basilides'. *JRAS*, pp. 377-415.

Kern, H[endrik] (1896), *Manual of Indian Buddhism*. Strassburg.

Khare, D. (1967), 'Discovery of a Vishnu Temple Near the Heliodoros Pillar, Besnagar, Dist. Vidisha (M.P.)'. *LK* 13, pp. 21-27. New Delhi.

Kher, Chitrarekha V. (1992), *Buddhism as Presented by the Brahmanical Systems*. Delhi.

Kingsbury, F[rancis] & G[odfrey] E[dward] Phillips (1921), *Hymns of the Tamil Śaivite Saints*. Calcutta.

Kippenberg, Hans G. (1970), Versuch einer soziologischen Verortung des antiken Gnostizismus. *Numen: International Review for the History of Religions* 17, pp. 211-31. Leiden.

——— (1984), Gnostiker zweiten Ranges: zur Institutionalisierung gnostischer Ideen als Anthropolatrie, in Jacob Taubes, ed., pp. 121-40.

van Kooj, Karel R. (1972), 'Introduction' to: *Worship of the Goddess According to the Kālikāpurāṇa,* Part I: *A Translation with an Introduction and Notes on Chapters 54-69*, pp. 1-37. (Orientalia Rheno-Traiectina 14). Leiden.

——— (1993), 'Iconography of the Battlefield: Narasiṁha and Durgā', in Asko Parpola & P. Koskikallio, eds, *SAA 1993*, pp. 379-87. Helsinki.

——— (1999), 'Iconography of the Battlefield: The Case of Chinnamastā', in J.E.M. Houben & K.R. van Kooij, eds, 1999, pp. 249-74.

Kosambi, D[amodar] D[harmananda] (1950), 'On a Marxist Approach to Indian Chronology'. *ABORI* 31, pp. 258-66.

——— (1965), *The Culture and Civilization of Ancient India in Historical Outline*. London.

——— (1975²), *An Introduction to the Study of Indian History*. Bombay.

Kramrisch, Stella (1981), *The Presence of Śiva*, Princeton.

Krishnan, K[ogandannalur] G[anapati] (1970), 'Caṭṭāṇam Maḍham: Its Identification'. *JOIB* 19, pp. 346-50.

Kuiper, F[rans] B[ernard] J[acob] (1983), *Ancient Indian Cosmogony: Essays Selected and Introduced by John Irwin*. Delhi.

Kulkarni, V[aman] M[ahadeo] (1990), *The Story of Rāma in Jain Literature (as Presented by the Śvetāmbara and Digambara Poets in the Prakrit, Sanskrit and Apabrahṁśa Languages)*. Saraswati Oriental Studies 3, Ahmedabad.

Kulke, Hermann (1986), 'Royal Temple Policy and the Structure of Medieval Hindu Kingdoms', in Anncharlott Eschmann, Hermann Kulke & Gaya Charan Tripathi, eds, *The Cult of Jagannath and the Regional Tradition of Orissa*. New Delhi (Heidelberg 1978).

——— (1993), *Kings and Cults: State Formation and Legitimation in India and Southeast Asia*. New Delhi.

Kuwayama, Shoshin (2002), *Across the Hindukush of the First Millennium: A Collection of Papers*. Institute for Research in the Humanities, Kyoto University, Kyoto.

Lal, Shyam Kishore (1980), *Female Divinities in Hindu Mythology and Ritual* (Publication of the Centre of Advanced Studies in Sanskrit, Class B, no. 7, University of Poona). Pune.

Lambrick, H[ugh] [Trevor] (1973), *Sind before the Muslim Conquest* (History of Sind Series 2). Hyderabad.

Lamotte, Etienne (1953), 'Les premières relations entre l'Inde et l'Occident'. *La nouvelle Clio. Revue mensuelle de la découverte historique* 8, pp. 83-118. Paris.

——— (1958), *Histoire du Bouddhisme Indien, des origines à l'ère Saka*. Louvain. (English tr. *History of Indian Buddhism*, 1988. Louvain-la-Neuve).

——— (1966), 'Vajrapāṇi en Inde', in *Mélanges de sinologie offertes à Monsieur Paul Demiéville* (Bibliothèque de l'Institut des Hautes Etudes Chinoises 20), pp. 113-59. Paris.

——— (1988), *History of Indian Buddhism from the Origins to the Śaka Era*. Publications de l'Institut Orientaliste de Louvain 36. Louvain-la Neuve. (*Histoire du Bouddhisme indien de l'origine à l'ère Śaka*, Louvain 1958).

Lassen, Christian (1847-62), *Indische Alterthumskunde*, 5 vols. (four parts and appendix) Leipzig-London.

Law, Bimala Churn (1935), *Śrāvasti in Indian Literature*. MASI 50.

Law, B[imala] C[hurn], ed. (1931), *Buddhistic Studies*. Calcutta.

Lévi, Sylvain (1905-08), *Le Népal, étude historique d'un royaume hindou*, 3 vols. Paris.

——— (1996*a*), 'Les donations religieuses des rois de Valabhī', in Franco, ed., pp. 218-34.

——— (1996*b*), 'L'inscription de Mahānāman à Bodh-Gaya. Essai d'exégèse appliquée à l'épigraphie bouddhique', in Franco, ed., pp. 343-54.

Lienhard, Siegfried (1989), 'The Monastery and the Secular World: Saṅgha-Buddhism and Caste-Buddhism'. *JAOS* 109, pp. 593-96.

Lipsey, Roger, ed. (1977-78), *Coomaraswamy* (vol. 1: *Selected Papers, Traditional Art and Symbolism*; vol. 2: *Selected Papers, Metaphysics*; vol. 3: *His Life and Work*). Bollingen Series 89. Princeton.

Literary and Historical Studies in Indology. Delhi.

Liu, Xinru (1988), *Ancient India and Ancient China: Trade and Religious Exchanges, AD 1-600*. New Delhi.

Locke, John K. (1980), *Karunamaya: The Cult of Avalokitesvara-Matsyendranath in the Valley of Nepal*. Tribhuvan University, Kathmandu.

——— (1985), *Buddhist Monasteries of Nepal: A Survey of the Bāhās and Bahīs of the Kathmandu Valley*. Kathmandu.

Logan William (1887), *Malabar Manual*, 2 vols. Madras.

Lorenzen, David N. (1972), *The Kāpālikas and Kālāmukhas: Two Lost Śaivite Sects*. University of California, Berkeley-Los Angeles.

——— (1978), 'Warrior Ascetics in Indian History'. *JAOS* 98, pp. 61-75.

de Lubac, Henri (1987²), *Buddhismo e Occidente*. Milano. (*Le rencontre du bouddhisme et de l'Occident*, Paris 1985² [1952]).

Mackenzie, W. Colin (1952), *Colonel Colin Mackenzie, first Surveyor-General of India*. Edinburgh.

Maclean, Derryl N. (1989), *Religion and Society in Arab Sind*. Monographs and

Theoretical Studies in Sociolgy and Anthropology in Honour of Nels Anderson 25. Leiden.

Maeda, Chisato (2007), 'Sacrifice in the *Kālikā-purāṇa*', in *Esoteric Buddhist Studies*, pp. 253-56.

Mahtab, H[arekrushna] (1947), *The History of Orissa*. University of Lucknow.

Maitreya, Akshay Kumar (1987), *The Fall of the Pāla Empire*, with an introduction by D.C. Sircar. University of North Bengal.

Majumdar, R[amesh] C[handra], ed. (1943), *The History of Bengal*, vol. I: *Hindu Period*. Dacca.

Majumdar, R[amesh] C[handra], H.C. [Hemchandra] Raychaudhuri & K[alikinkar] Datta (1967^3), *An Advanced History of India*. London-Basingstoke.

Manteuffel, Tadeusz (1986^2), *Nascita dell'eresia. Gli adepti della povertà volontaria nel medioevo*. Firenze. (*Narodziny herezij. Wyznawcy dobrowolnego ubóstwa w średniowieczu*, Warszawa 1964).

Matsubara, Mitsunori (1994), *Pāñcarātra Saṃhitās & Early Vaiṣṇava Theology, with a Translation and Critical Notes from Chapters on Theology in the Ahirbudhnya Saṃhitā*. Delhi.

Matsunaga, Yūkei (1985), 'On the Date of the *Mañjuśrīmūlakalpa*', in Michel Strickmann, ed., vol. 3, pp. 882-94.

——— (2008), 'Indian Thought and Japanese Thought: Concerning the *Prajñāpāramitānaya Sūtra*', in *Esoteric Buddhist Studies*, pp. 149-53.

McFarlane, Stewart (1995), 'Fighting Bodhisattvas and Inner Warriors: Buddhism and the Martial Traditions of China and Japan', in Tadeusz Skorupski & Ulrich Pagel, eds, *The Buddhist Forum, volume III, 1991-1993. Papers in Honour and Appreciation of Professor David Seyforet Ruegg's Contribution to Indological, Buddhist and Tibetan Studies*, pp. 185-210. New Delhi.

McGlashan, Alastair R. (2009), 'Introduction' to: The *Tiruttoṇṭar Tiruvantāti* of Nampi Āṇṭār Nampi, *JIP* 37 [pp. 291-310], pp. 291-94.

McNeill, William H. (1998), *Plagues and People*. New York (1st edn 1976).

Menon, K.P. Padmanabha (1924-37), *History of Kerala Written in the Form of Notes on Visscher's Letters from Malabar*, ed. T.K. Krishna Menon, 4 vols. Ernakulam.

Meyer, J[ohann] J[akob] (1937), *Trilogie altindischer Mächte und Feste der Vegetation. Ein Beitrag zur vergleichenden Religions-und Kulturgeschichte, Fest- und Volkskunde*, 3 vols. in 1. Zürich-Leipzig.

Michaels, Axel (1993), 'Widow Burning in Nepal', in Gérard Toffin, ed., *Nepal Past and Present: Proceedings of the France-German Conference, Arc-en-Senans, June 1990*, pp. 21-45. Paris.

Miller, James Innes (1974), *Roma e la via delle spezie*. Torino. (*The Spice Trade of the Roman Empire: 29 BC to AD 641*. Oxford 1969).

Minakshi, C[adambi] (1938), *Administration and Social Life under the Pallavas*. University of Madras. Madras.

Mirashi, Vasudev Vishnu (1955), 'Introduction' to: *Inscriptions of the Kalachuri-Chedi Era*, vol. 1, pp. i-cxciii. ASI, Ootacamund 1955.

Mishra, Suresh Chandra (1989), 'A Historiographical Critique of the Arthaśāstra of Kauṭilya'. *Annals of the Bhandarkar Oriental Research Institute* 70, pp. 145-62. Poona.

Misra, B.N. (1987-89), 'Śakrāditya, the First Historical Patron of Nālandā'. *JISOA* n.s. 16-17, pp. 26-32.

Misra, Maria (2007), *Vishnu's Crowded Temple: India Since the Great Rebellion*. London.

Mital, Surendra Nath (2000), *Kauṭilīya Arthaśāstra Revisited*. Centre for Studies in Civilizations, Project of History of Indian Science, Philosophy and Culture 11. New Delhi.

[Mitra, Dilip Kumar, ed.] (1978), *Rajendralala Mitra (150th Anniversary Lectures)*. The Asiatic Society. Calcutta.

Mitra, Rajendralala (1885), *Centenary Review of the Asiatic Society, 1784-1884*. Part I: *History of the Society*. Calcutta.

Mitra, R.C. (1981²), *The Decline of Buddhism in India*. Santiniketan (1st edn. 1954).

Mitra, Sisir Kumar (1977²), *The Early Rulers of Khajurāho*. Delhi.

Monier-Williams, Monier (1877), *Hinduism*. Society for Promoting Christian Knowledge. London.

——— (1889), *Buddhism in its Connection with Brāhmanism and Hindūism, and in its Contrast with Christianity*. London.

Mookerji, Radha Kumud (1966⁴), *Chandragupta Maurya and His Times*. New Delhi.

Moraes, George M. (1931), *The Kadamba Kula: A History of Ancient and Mediaeval Karnataka*. Bombay.

Mukherjee, B[ratindra] N[ath] (1980-81), 'Revenue, Trade and Society in the Kuṣāṇa Empire'. *IHR* 7, pp. 24-53.

Mukherjee, Prabhat (1940), *The History of Medieval Vaishnavism in Orissa*. Calcutta.

Müller, Max (1895), 'Preface' to: J.S. Speyer, tr., *The Gātakamālā, or Garland of Birth-Stories by Ārya Śūra* (SBB 1), pp. vii-xvii. London.

Nagaraja Rao, M.S., ed. (1978), *The Chalukyas of Badami (Seminar Papers)*. The Mythic Society. Bangalore.

Nakamura, Hajime (1987), *Indian Buddhism: A Survey with Bibliographical Notes*. Delhi.

Nanda, Rajni (1992), *The Early History of Gold in India*. New Delhi.

Nandi, R.N. (2000), 'Origin of the Vīraśaiva Movement', in D[wijendra] N[arayan] Jha, ed., pp. 469-86.

Narasimhachar, D.L. (1939), 'The Jaina Rāmāyaṇas'. *IHQ* 15, pp. 575-94.

Narayanan, M.G.S. (1970), 'Kandalur Salai: New Light on the Nature of Aryan Expansion in South India'. *PIHC*, pp. 125-36. Calicut.

——— (1988), 'The Role of Peasants in the Early History of Tamilakam in South India'. *SocSci* 16, pp. 17-34.

——— (2002), 'The State in the Era of the Cēramān Perumāḷs of Kerala', in

R[adha] Champakalakshmi, Kesavan Veluthat & T.R. Venugopalan (2002) *State and Society in Pre-Modern South India*. Thrissur.

Narayanan, M.G.S. & Kesavan Veluthat (1986), 'A History of the Nambudiri Community in Kerala', in Frits Staal, ed. in collaboration with C.V. Somayajipad & M. Itti Ravi Nambudiri, *Agni: The Vedic Ritual of the Fire Altar*, 2 vols, II, pp. 256-78. Delhi.

Naudou, Jean (1980), *Buddhists of Kaśmīr*. Delhi (*Les bouddhistes kaśmīriens au Moyen Age*. Annales du Musée Guimet, Bibliothèque d'étude 68, Paris 1968).

Njammasch, Marlene (2001), *Bauern, Buddhisten und Brahmanen. Das frühe Mittelalter in Gujarat*. Asien- und Afrika-Studien der Humboldt-Universität zu Berlin 2. Wiesbaden.

O'Flaherty, Wendy Doniger (1971), 'The Origins of Heresy in Hindu Mythology'. *HistRel* 10, pp. 271-333.

——— (1980²), *The Origins of Evil in Hindu Mythology*. University of California Press, Berkeley-Los Angeles.

——— (1981*a*), *Sexual Metaphors and Animal Symbols in Indian Mythology*. Delhi (University of Chicago 1980).

——— (1981*b*), *Śiva: The Erotic Ascetic*. Oxford University Press, Oxford (*Asceticism and Eroticism in the Mythology of Śiva*, London-New York 1973).

O'Malley, L[ouis] S[ydney] S[tuart] (1903), 'Gayā Śrāddha and Gayāwāls'. *JASB* 73, pp. 1-11.

Otness, Harold (1998), 'Nurturing the Roots for Oriental Studies: the Development of the Libraries of the Royal Asiatic Society's Branches and Affiliates in Asia in the Nineteenth Century'. *International Association of Orientalist Librarians Bullettin* 43, pp. 9-17. Cornell University, Ithaca.

Pagels, Elaine (2005), *Il vangelo segreto di Tommaso. Indagine sul libro più scandaloso del cristianesimo delle origini*. Milano. (*Beyond Belief: The Secret Gospel of Thomas*, New York-Toronto 2003).

Panda, S.K. (2007), 'Rise and Fall of Buddhism on Daya Basin'. *Orissa Review*, Dec., pp. 20-23. Orissa State Portal, Bhubaneswar.

Pande, Govind Chandra (1994), *Life and Thought of Śaṅkaracārya*. Delhi.

Pani, Subas, chief ed. (1988), *Glimpses of History and Culture of Balasore*. Orissa State Museum, Bhubaneswar.

Panigrahi, Krishna Chandra (1981), *History of Orissa*. Cuttack.

Patil, Parimal G. (2009), *Against a Hindu God: Buddhist Philosophy of Religion in India*. Columbia University Press, New York.

Pargiter, F[rederick] E[den] (1913), *The Purāṇa Text of the Dynasties of the Kāli Age, with Introduction and Notes by –*. London.

Pathak, V[ishwambhar] S[haran] (1960), *History of Śaiva Cults in Northern India from Inscriptions (700 AD to 1200 AD)*. Varanasi.

Paul, Diana Y. (2004), 'Introduction' to: *The Sutra of Queen Śrīmālā of the Lion's Roar, Translated from the Chinese (Taishō Volume 12, Number 353) by –*, pp. 5-7. BDK [Bukkyo Dendo Kyokai] English Tripiṭaka 20-1. Numata Center for Buddhist Translation and Research. Berkeley.

Petech, Luciano (1974), 'Alcuni dati di Chih Sêng-tsai sull'India', in *Gururāja-mañjarikā. Studi in onore di Giuseppe Tucci*, 2 vols, II, pp. 551-58. Istituto Universitario Orientale, Napoli (also in id., *Selected Papers on Asian History*. SOR 60, pp. 313-21.

——— (1984^2), *Mediaeval History of Nepal (c. 750-1482)*. SOR 54. Roma.

Piantelli, Mario (1998), *Śaṅkara e il Kevalādvaitavāda*. Roma (rev. edn of *Śaṅkara e la rinascita del Brāhmaṇesimo*, Fossano 1974).

Pollock, Sheldon (2006), *The Language of the Gods in the World of Men: Sanskrit, Culture and Power in Premodern India*. University of California Press, Berkeley-Los Angeles.

Prakash, Buddha (1965), *Aspects of Indian History and Civilizations*. Agra.

Przyluski, Jean (1967), *The Legend of Emperor Aśoka in Indian and Chinese Texts*. Calcutta. [*La légende de l'empereur Açoka (Açoka-avadāna) dans les textes indiens et chinois*]. Annales du Musee Guimet 32, Paris 1923.

Puech, Henri-Charles (1985), *Sulle tracce della Gnosi. I. La Gnosi e il tempo. II. Sul Vangelo secondo Tommaso*. Milano. (*En quête de la Gnose. I. La Gnose et le temps et autres essais. II. Sur l'Evangile selon Thomas. Esquisse d'une interprétation systématique*, Paris 1978).

Pye, Michael (1978), *Skilful Means: A Concept in Mahayana Buddhism*. London.

Quinet, Edgard (1842), *Le génie des religions*. Paris.

Qvarnström, Olle (1999), 'Haribhadra and the Beginning of Doxography in India', in N.K. Wagle & Olle Qvarnström, eds, *Approaches to Jaina Studies: Philosophy, Logic, Rituals and Symbols*, pp. 169-210. Centre for South Asian Studies, University of Toronto.

Rajaguru, S.N. (1968-72), *History of the Gaṅgas*, 2 vols. State Museum, Bhubaneswar.

Rajan, Chandra (2006), Appendix to: *Kālidāsa, The Loom of Time: A Selection of His Plays and Poems. Translated from the Sanskrit and Prakrit with and Introduction by –*, pp. 307-15. London (New Delhi 1989).

Rajan, K. (2008), 'Situating the Beginning of Early Historical Times in Tamil Nadu: Some Issues and Reflections'. *SocSci* 36, pp. 40-78.

Ram, Rajendra (1981), 'Life and Works of Kashi Prasad Jayaswal', in J[ata] S[hankar] Jha, ed., *K.P. Jayaswal Commemoration Volume*, pp. 59-72. Patna.

Rao, B.S.L. Hanumantha (1990), 'Mahayana in Early Inscriptions of Andhra'. *PIHC (51st Session)*, pp. 832-37. Calcutta.

Rao, T.N. Vasudeva (1979), *Buddhism in the Tamil Country*. Annamalai University, Annamalainagar.

Ramaswami Ayyangar, M.S. & B. Seshagiri Rao (1922), *Studies in South Indian Jainism*, 2 vols. Madras.

Rangaswamy, M.A. Dorai (1990^2), *The Religion and Philosophy of Tēvāram, with Special Reference to Nampi Ārūrar (Sundarar)*. University of Madras.

Rath, Asoka Kumar (1987), *Studies on Some Aspects of the History and Culture of Orissa*. Calcutta.

Raychauduri, H. (1938³), *Political History of Ancient India: From the Accession of Parikshit to the Extinction of the Gupta Dynasty*. Calcutta.

Rehman, Abdur (1979), *The Last Two Dynasties of the Śāhis (An Analysis of Their History, Archaeology, Coinage and Palaeography)*. Quaid-i-Azam University, Islamabad.

Reynolds, Susan (2004), *Feudi e vassalli. Una nuova interpretazione delle fonti medievali*. Roma. (Rev. Italian edn of *Fiefs and Vassals*, Oxford 1994.)

Rhys Davids, T[homas] W[illiam] (1881), *Lectures on the Origin and Growth of Religion as illustrated by Some Points in the History of Indian Buddhism* (The Hibbert Lectures). London.

——— (1896*a*), 'Persecution of the Buddhists in India'. *JPTS 1894-1896*, pp. 87-92.

——— (1896*b*), 'Further Note on Persecutions of Buddhists in India'. *JPTS 1894-1896*, pp. 107-11.

Rice, E[dward] P[eter] (1921), *A History of Kanarese Literature*. Calcutta-London.

Risley, H[erbert] H[ope] (1891), *The Tribes and Castes of Bengal: Ethnographic Glossary*, 2 vols. Calcutta.

Rosen, William (2007), *Justinian's Flea: The First Great Plague and the End of the Roman Empire*. New York.

Rost, R[einhold] ed. (1862-71), *Works of the Late Horace Hayman Wilson*, 12 vols. London.

Rudolph, Kurt (1977*a*), 'Das Problem einer Soziologie und 'Sozialen Verortung' der Gnosis'. *Kairos. Zeitschrift für Religionswissenschaft und Theologie* 19, pp. 35-44. Salzburg.

——— (1977*b*), *Die Gnosis. Wesen und Geschichte einer spätantiken Religion*. Leipzig.

Rudra, Ashok (1981), 'Against Feudalism'. *Economic and Political Weekly* 16/52, pp. 2133-46. Bombay.

Ruegg, David S. (1981), 'Deux problèmes d'exégèse et de pratique tantrique', in Michel Strickmann, ed., vol. 1, pp. 212-27.

——— (1995), *Ordre spiritual et ordre temporal dans la pensée bouddhique de l'Inde e t du Tibet. Quatre conférences au Collège de France*. Publications de l'Institut de Civilisation Indienne 64. Paris.

Sahu, N[abin] K[umar] (1958), *Buddhism in Orissa*. Utkal University, [Bhubaneswar].

Samuel, Geoffrey (1995), *Civilized Shamans: Buddhism in Tibetan Societies*. Smithsonian Institution, Washington.

Sanghavi, Vilas Adinath (1980²), *Jaina Community: A Social Survey*. Madras.

Sangpo, Khetsun (1973-90), *Biographical Dictionary of Tibet and Tibetan*

Buddhism, 12 vols. Library of Tibetan Works and Archives. Dharamsala. [In Tibetan.]

Sâṅkṛtyâyana, Râhula (1934), 'Recherches bouddhiques, par le bhikṣu – (de Bénarès)'. *JA* 225, pp. 195-230.

Sankaranarayanan, S. (1977), *The Vishṇukuṇḍis and Their Time (An Epigraphical Study)*. Delhi.

——— (1995), *Śrī Śaṅkara: His Life, Philosophy and Relevance to Man in Modern Times* (The Adyar Library General Series 14). Madras.

Sanyal, Rajat (2008-09), 'Geo-Polity in Early Medieval Bengal under the Sena Rule: Re-Reading Epigraphic Sources'. *JAIH* 25, pp. 94-113.

Sastri, S. Kuppuswami & al. eds (1937), *New Catalogus Catalogorum: A Complete and up-to-date Alphabetical Register of Sanskrit and Allied Works and Authors*. University of Madras.

Sastri, K.A. Nilakantha (1966[3]), *A History of South India from Prehistoric Times to the Fall of Vijayanagar*. Bombay.

Scharfe, Hartmut (1993), *Investigations in Kauṭalaya's Manual of Political Science*. Wiesbaden. (Rev. edn. of *Untersuchungen zur Staatsrechtslehre des Kauṭalya*, Wiesbaden 1968).

Scherrer-Schaub, Cristina (2007), 'Immortality Extolled with Reason: Philosophy and Politics in Nāgārjuna', in B. Kellner & al., eds., 2007, pp. 757-93.

Schopen, Gregory (1987), 'The Inscription on the Kuṣān Image of Amitābha and the Character of the Early Mahāyāna in India', *JIABS* 10, pp. 99-134.

——— (1997), 'Burial "*Ad Sanctos*" and the Physical Presence of the Buddha in Early Indian Buddhism: A Study in the Archaeology of Religion', in id., *Bones, Stones, and Buddhist Monks: Collected Papers on the Archaeology, Epigraphy, and Texts of Monastic Buddhism in India*, pp. 4-47. University of Hawa'i Press, Honolulu.

——— (2004), 'Doing Business for the Lord: Lending on Interest and Written Loan Contracts in the *Mūlasarvāstivāda-vinaya*', in id., *Buddhist Monks and Business Matters. Still More Papers on Monastic Buddhism in India*, pp. 45-90. University of Hawa'i Press, Honolulu.

——— (2008), 'On Emptying Chamber Pots without Looking and the Urban Location of Buddhist Nunneries in Early India Again'. *JA* 296, pp. 229-56.

Schouten, Jan Peter (1991), *Revolution of the Mystics: On the Social Aspects of Vīraśaivism*. Kampen.

Sen, Amulyachandra (1956), *Asoka's Edicts*. Calcutta.

Sen, Dinesh Chandra (1911), *History of Bengali Language and Literature: A Series of Lectures Delivered as Reader to the Calcutta University*, 2 vols. Calcutta.

——— (1917), *Chaitanya and His Companions (Being Lectures Delivered at the University of Calcutta as Ramtanu Lahiri Research Fellow for 1913-14)*. Calcutta.

——— (1920), *The Folk-Literature of Bengal*. University of Calcutta.

Sen, Tansen (2003), '*Buddhism, Diplomacy and Trade: The Realignment of Sino-Indian Relations, 600-1400*. Association for Asian Studies and University of Hawai'i Press. Honolulu.

Seneviratna, Anuradha, ed. (1994), *King Aśoka and Buddhism: Historical and Literary Studies*. Kandy.

Settis, Salvatore, ed. (1996), *I Greci. Storia cultura arte società*, I. *Noi e i Greci*. Torino.

Shah, Kirit K. (1988), *Ancient Bundelkhand: Religious History in Socio-Economic Perspective*. Delhi.

Shah, U[makant] P[remanand] (1983), 'Rāmāyana in Jaina Tradition', in K.R. Srinivasa Iyengar, ed., *Asian Variations in Ramayana: Papers Presented at the International Seminar on 'Variations in Ramayana in Asia: Their Cultural, Social and Anthropological Significance', New Delhi, January 1981*, pp. 57-82. Sahitya Akademi, New Delhi.

Shakabpa, Tsepon Wangchuk Deden (2010), *One Hundred Thousand Moons: An Advanced Political History of Tibet*. Translated and Annotated by Derek F. Maher (Brill's Tibetan Studies Library 23). Leiden-Boston.

Sharma, P.S. (1980), *Anthology of Kumārilabhaṭṭa's Works*. Delhi.

Sharma, Ram Sharan (1965), *Indian Feudalism: c. 300-1200*. University of Calcutta.

——— (1980²), *Śūdras in Ancient India: A Social History of the Lower Order Down to circa AD 600*. Delhi.

——— (1987), *Urban Decay in India (c. 300–c. 1000)*. New Delhi.

——— (1988), 'Problems of Peasant Protest in Early Medieval India'. *SocSci* 16, pp. 3-16.

——— (1996), *The State and Varna Formation in the Mid-Ganga Plains: An Ethnoarchaeological View*. Delhi.

——— (2001), *Early Medieval Indian Society: A Study in Feudalisation*. Kolkata.

Shastri, Dharmendra Nath (1964), *An Outline of Critique of Indian Realism: A Study of the Conflict between the Nyāya-Vaiśeṣika & the Buddhist Dignāga School*. Agra University, Agra.

[Shastri, Haraprasad] Shāstrī, Haraprasād (1911), 'Introduction to Nagendra Nāth Vasu', *The Modern Buddhism and its Followers in Orissa* [= Second part of the Introduction of Vasu 1911, above, published as an independent book], pp. 1-28. Calcutta.

Shepherd Slusser, Mary (1982), *Nepal Mandala: A Cultural Study of the Kathmandu Valley*, 2 vols. Princeton.

Shizuka, Haruki (2007), *Ganacakra no kenkū. Indo kōki mikkyō ga hiraita chihei [A Study of* gaṇacakra. *The Frontier Explored by Late Indian Vajrayāna]*. Tōkyō.

——— (2008), 'An Interim Report on the Study of *Gaṇacakra*: Vajrayana's New Horizon in Indian Buddhism', in *Esoteric Buddhist Studies*, pp. 185-97.

Silk, Jonathan A. (2002), 'What, if Anything, is Mahāyāna Buddhism? Problems of Definitions and Classifications'. *Numen* 49, pp. 355-405.

——— (1993), *Kings, Brāhmaṇas and Temples in Orissa: An Epigraphic Study, AD 300-1147*. New Delhi.

Singh Deo, Jitamitra Prasad (1987), *Cultural Profile of South Kōśala [From Early period Till the Rise of the Nāgas and the Chauhans in 14th Century AD]*. Delhi.

Sinha, Binod Chandra (1977), *History of the Śuṅga Dynasty*. Varanasi.

Sinha, B[indeshwari] P[rasad] (1954), *The Decline of the Kingdom of Magadha (Cir. 455-1000 AD)*, with a Foreword by L.D. Barnett. Patna.

Sircar, D[inesh] C[handra] (1939*a*), 'Date of Patañjali's Mahābhāṣya'. *IHQ* 15, pp. 633-38.

——— (1939*b*), *The Successors of the Sātavāhanas in the Lower Deccan*. University of Calcutta.

——— (1948), *The Śākta Pīṭhas. JRASB* -Letters 14, pp. 1-108.

——— (1966), 'Landlordism Confused with Feudalism', in D.C. Sircar, ed., 1966, pp. 57-62.

——— (1967), *Cosmography and Geography in Early Indian Literature*. Sir William Meyer Endowment Lectures in History 1965-66, University of Madras. Calcutta.

——— (1968), *Studies in Indian Coins*. Delhi.

——— (1971[2]), *Studies in the Geography of Ancient and Medieval India*. Delhi.

——— (1983*a*), 'Migration of Southerners to East India', in id., *Problems of Early Indian Social History*, pp. 55-67. Calcutta Sanskrit College Research Series 122. Sanskrit College, Calcutta.

——— (1985), *The Kānyakubja-Gauḍa Struggle from the Sixth to the Twelfth Century AD* (Dr. Biman Bihari Majumdar Memorial Lecture for the Year 1982). The Asiatic Society, Calcutta.

Sircar, D[inesh] C[handra], ed. (1966), *Land System and Feudalism in Ancient India*. Centre of Advanced Study in Ancient Indian History and Culture, Lectures and Seminars1B. University of Calcutta.

Smith, David (1996), *The Dance of Śiva: Religion, Art and Poetry in South India*. Cambridge University Press, Cambridge.

Smith, Vincent A. (1920[3]), *Asoka, the Buddhist Emperor of India*. Oxford.

——— (1967[4]), *The Early History of India from 600 BC to the Muhammadan Conquest Including the Invasion of Alexander the Great*. Oxford.

Snellgrove, David L. (1987), *Indo-Tibetan Buddhism: Indian Buddhists and Their Tibetan Successors*. London.

Soifer, Deborah A. (1992), *The Myths of Narasiṁha and Vāmana: Two Avatars in Cosmological Perspective*, Delhi. (State University of New York 1991).

Song, Yong Kang (2003), *Die Debatte im alten Indien. Untersuchungen zum Sambhāṣāvidhi und verwandten Themen in der* Carakasaṃhitā Vimānasthāna *8.15-28*. Philosophia Indica, Einsichten–Ansichten 6. Reinbeck.

Srivastava, Kanhaiya Lall (1980), *The Position of Hindus under the Delhi Sultanate, 1206-1526*. New Delhi.

Stein, Burton (1969), 'Integration of the Agrarian System of South India', in R.E.

Frykenberg, ed., *Land Control and Social Structure in Indian History*. Madison.

——— (1980), *Peasant State and Society in Medieval South India*. Delhi.

von Stietencron, Heinrich (1977), 'Orthodox Attitudes towards Temple Service and Image Worship in Ancient India'. *Central Asiatic Journal* 21, pp. 126-38. Wiesbaden.

——— (2005), *Hindu Myth, Hindu History: Religion, Art, and Politics*. Delhi.

Strickmann, Michel, ed. (1981-85), *Tantric and Taoist Studies in Honour of R.A. Stein*, 3 vols. (1981, 1983, 1985). Mélanges chinoises et bouddhiques 22. Bruxelles.

Taubes, Jacob, ed. (1984), *Gnosis und Politik* (Religionstheorie und Politische Theologie 2). München.

Tambiah, S[tanley] J[eyaraja] (1976), *World Conqueror and World Renouncer: A Study on Buddhism and Polity in Thailand against a Historical Background*. Cambridge.

Telang, Kāshināth Trimbak (1876), 'The Śankaravijaya of Ānandagiri'. *IA* 5, pp. 287-93.

Thakur, Upendra (1956), 'A Brief Survey of Buddhism and Traces of Buddhist Remains in Mithilā'. *JBRS* (Buddha Jayanti Special Issue, 2 vols.), pp. 428-39.

——— (1964), *Studies in Jainism and Buddhism in Mithilā*. Chowkhamba Sanskrit Series 43. Varanasi.

——— (1988²), *History of Mithila from the Earliest Times to 1556 A.D.* Mithila Institute, Darbhanga. (1st edn. *History of Mithila (Circa 3000 BC-1556 A.D.), with a Foreword by J.N. Banerjea*. Darbhanga 1956).

Thapar, Romila (1978), *Ancient Indian Social History: Some Interpretations*. Hyderabad.

——— (1992*a*), 'Black Gold: South Asia and the Roman Maritime Trade'. *South Asia* 15, pp. 1-27. Armidale.

——— (1992*b*), *Interpreting Early India*. New Delhi.

——— (1994²), *Cultural Transaction and Early India: Tradition and Patronage*. Oxford University Press, New Delhi.

——— (1997²), *Aśoka and the Decline of the Mauryas*. Delhi. (Rev. edn with new afterword, bibliography and index; 1st edn, Oxford 1961).

——— (1999), *Historical Interpretations and the Secularising of Indian Society*. Kappen Memorial Lecture. Bangalore.

——— (2000), *Cultural Pasts: Essays in Early Indian History*. New Delhi.

——— (2002), *Early India from the Origins to AD 1300*. London.

[Bhikṣu] Thích Thiên Châu (1999) *The Literature of the Personalists of Early Buddhism*. Delhi.

Thomas, Terence (2000), 'Political Motivation in Study of Religions in Britain', in Armin W. Geertz, Scott S. Eliot & Russell T. Cutcheon, eds., *Perspectives on Method and Theory in the Study of Religion: Adjunct Proceedings of the*

XVIIth Congress of the International Association for the History of Religions, Mexico City, 1995, pp. 74-90. Leiden.

Toffin, Gérard (1984), *Société et religion chez les Néwars du Népal*. Ed. du CNRS, Paris. (English trs., *Newar Society: City, Village and Periphery*. Lalitpur [Kathmandu] 2007).

Trautmann, Thomas R. (1971), *Kauṭilya and the Arthaśāstra: A Statistical Investigation of the Authorship and Evolution of the Text*. Leiden.

Tripathi, Rama Shankar (1964), *History of Kanauj to the Moslem Conquest*. Delhi.

Tripathy, S[hyam] S[under] (1988), *Buddhism and Other Religious Cults of South-East India*. Delhi.

van Troy, J. (1990), 'The Radical Social Protest of the Pāśupatas'. *Indica* 27, pp. 1-10. Bombay.

Tucci, Giuseppe (1958), 'Preliminary Report on an Archaeological Survey in Swat'. *EW* 9, pp. 279-328.

——— (1971), *Opera minora* (Università di Roma, Studi orientali a cura della Scuola Orientale 6), 2 vols. Roma. Contains (1971*a*) *Linee di una storia del materialismo indiano*, pp. 49-155; (1971*b*) The Sea and Land Travels of a Buddhist Sādhu in the Sixteenth Century, pp. 305-19; (1971*c*) Some Glosses upon the Guhyasamāja, pp. 337-48.

——— (1977²), *Storia della filosofia indiana*, 2 vols. Bari. (1st edn. 1957).

Ungemach, Anton (1992), 'Introduction' to: *Śaṃkara-mandāra-saurabha. Eine Legende über das Leben des Philosophen Śaṃkara* (1992), pp. 1-28. Text, Übersetzung, Einleitung von—Beiträge zur Südasienforschung 153, Südasien Institut, Heidelberg. Stuttgart.

Upadhyay, Govind Prasad (1979), *Brāhmaṇas in Ancient India: A Study in the Role of the Brāhmaṇa Class from* c. *200* BC *to* c. AD *500*. New Delhi.

Vaidya, Karunakar (1986) *Buddhist Traditions and Culture of the Kathmandu Valley*. Kathmandu.

Vattanky, John (1978), 'Aspects of Early Nyāya Theism'. *JIP* 6, pp. 393-404.

Vedāntaśāstri, H. (1956), 'Buddhism in Bengal and Its Decline'. *JBRS*, Buddha Jayanti Special Issue, 2 vols., pp. 66-76.

Veluthat, Kesavan (1975), 'The Cattas and Bhattas: A New Interpretation'. *PIHC*, pp. 98-109. Aligarh.

——— (2006), 'History in the Construction of a Regional History', in Radhika Seshan, ed., *Medieval India, Problems and Possibilities: Essays in Honour of A.R. Kulkarni*, pp. 79-100. Jaipur.

——— (1996), 'Religion, Rituals, and the Heaviness of Indian History'. *AION* 56, pp. 215-53.

Vidyabhusana, Satis Candra (1920), *A History of Indian Logic: Ancient, Medieval and Modern Schools*. Calcutta.

Waddell, L[aurence] A[ustine] (1934²), *The Buddhism of Tibet or Lamaism with Its Mystic Cults, Symbolism and Mythology, and Its Relation to Indian Buddhism*. Cambridge. (1st edn London 1895).

Walser, Joseph (2008), *Nāgārjuna in Context: Mahāyāna Buddhism and Early Indian Culture*. Delhi (Columbia University Press, New York 2005).

Warmington, E[ric] H[erbert] (1974²), *The Commerce between the Roman Empire and India*. New Delhi (1st edn 1928).

Waterhouse, David M., ed. (2004), *The Origins of Himalayan Studies: Brian Houghton Hodgson in Nepal and Darjeeling 1820-1858*. Abingdon-New York.

Wayman, Alex (1977), *Yoga of the Guhyasamājatantra: The Arcane Lore of Forty Verses. A Buddhist Tantra Commentary*. Delhi.

Weber, Max (1958), *The Religion of India*. New York (*Aufsätze zur Religionssoziologie*, 3 vols., 2. *Hinduismus und Buddhismus*. Tübingen 1947⁴).

——— (1993), *Storia economica. Linee di una storia universale dell'economia e della società*. Roma. (*Wirtschaftsgeschichte. Abriss der universalen Sozial- und Wirtschafts-geschichte*, Berlin 1958³).

——— (1995²), *Economia e società*, 5 vols. Milano. (*Wirtschaft und Gesellschaft*, Tübingen 1956).

Wheeler, James Talboys (1869), *India from the Earliest Ages, 2: The Rāmāyana and the Brahmanic Period*. London.

——— (1874), *India from the Earliest Ages, 3. Hindū. Buddhist. Brahmanical Revival*. London.

Whittaker, Dick (2009), 'Conjunctures and Conjectures: Kerala and Roman Trade'. *Journal of Asian History* 43, pp. 1-18.

Widengren, Geo (1952), 'Die iranische Hintergrund der Gnosis'. *Zeitschrift für Religions-und Geistesgeschichte* 4, pp. 97-114. Leiden-Heidelberg.

——— (1964), *Il Manicheismo*. Milano. (*Mani und der Manichäismus*, Stuttgart 1961).

——— (1967), 'Les origines du Gnosticisme et l'histoire des religions', in Bianchi (1967), pp. 28-60.

Williams, Michael Allen (1996), *Rethinking Gnosticism: An Argument for Dismantling a Dubious Category*. Princeton.

Williams, Paul (2008²), *Mahāyāna Buddhism: The Doctrinal Foundations*. London-New York.

Willis, Michael (2001), Buddhist Saints in Ancient Vedisa. *JRAS* 11 (3rd series), pp. 219-28.

Wilson, Horace H. (1828), *The Mackenzie Collection: A Descriptive Catalogue of the Oriental Manuscripts, and Other Articles Illustrative of the Literature, History, Statistics and Antiquities of the South of India Collected by the Late [. . .] Colin Mackenzie*. Calcutta.

——— (1850), 'On the Rock Inscriptions of Kapur di Giri, Dhauli, and Girnar'. *JRAS* 12, pp. 153-251.

——— (1862*a*), 'Notice of Three Tracts Received from Nepal', in R. Rost, ed., vol. 2, pp. 1-39.

——— (1862*b*), 'On Buddha and Buddhism', in R. Rost, ed., vol. 2, pp. 310-78.

——— (1864), 'Analysis of the Puráńas', in R. Rost, ed., vol. 3 (= *Essays Analytical, Critical and Philological on Subjects Connected with Sanskrit Literature*, vol. 1), pp. 1-155.

——— (1865*a*), 'Preface to the Sanskrit Dictionary', in R. Rost, ed., vol. 5 (= *Essays Analytical, Critical and Philological on Subjects Connected with Sanskrit Literature*, vol. 3), pp. 158-252.

——— (1865*b*), 'Notice of European Grammar and Dictionaries of the Sanskrit Language', in R. Rost, ed., vol. 5 (= *Essays Analytical, Critical and Philological on Subjects Connected with Sanskrit Literature*, vol. 3), pp. 253-304.

Witzel, Michael (1994), 'The Brahmins of Kashmir', in *Nīlamata*, pp. 237-94.

Yadava, B.N.S. (1966), 'Secular Land Grants of the Post-Gupta Period and Some Aspects of the Growth of Feudal Complex in Northern India', in D.C. Sircar ed., 1966, pp. 72-94.

——— (1968), 'Some Aspects of the Changing Order in India during the Śaka-Kuṣāṇa Age', in G[ovardhan] R[aj] Sharma, ed., *Kuṣāṇa Studies: Papers Presented to the International Conference on the Archaeology, History and Art [. . .] in the Kuṣāṇa Period, Dushambe [. . .] September 25-October 4, 1968*, pp. 75-97. Allahabad.

Yamaguchi, Zuiho (1996), 'The Fiction of King Dar-ma's Persecution of Buddhism', in Jean-sPierre Drège, ed., *De Dunhuang au Japon. Etudes chinoises et bouddhiques offertes à Michel Soimyé*, pp. 231-58. Geneva.

Zimmermann, Michael (2002), 'Introduction' to: *A Buddha Within: The* Tathāgatagarbhasūtra. *The Earliest Exposition of the Buddha-Nature Teaching in India*, pp. 12-92. Bibliotheca Philologica et Philosophica Buddhica 6. The International Research Institute for Advanced Buddhology, Soka University. Tokyo.

Zürcher, Erik (2007[3]), *The Buddhist Conquest of China: The Spread and Adaptation of Buddhism in Early Medieval China*, with a Foreword by Stephen F. Teiser. Leiden.

Zvelebil, K[amil] V[eith] (1975), *Tamil Literature*. Handbuch der Orientalistik, 2 Abt., 2 Band, 1 Abschnitt. Leiden-Köln.

Zydenbos, Robert J. (1997), 'Vīraśaivism, Caste, Revolution, Etc'. *JAOS* 117, pp. 525-35 [review of Schouten 1991].

——— (1999), 'Jainism as the Religion of Non-Violence', in J.E.M. Houben & K.R. van Kooij, eds, 1999, pp. 185-210.

Index